MESSENGERS
OF THE
LOST BATTALION

The Heroic 551st and the

Turning of the Tide at the

Battle of the Bulge

GREGORY ORFALEA

THE FREE PRESS

New York   London   Toronto   Sydney   Singapore

THE FREE PRESS
A Division of Simon & Schuster Inc.
1230 Avenue of the Americas
New York, NY 10020

THE FREE PRESS and colophon are trademarks
of Simon & Schuster Inc.

Manufactured in the United States of America

10   9   8   7   6   5   4   3   2   1

Library of Congress Cataloging-in-Publication Data

Orfalea, Gregory, 1949–
    Messengers of the lost battalion: the heroic 551st and the
turning of the tide at the Battle of the Bulge / Gregory Orfalea.
        p.   cm.
    ISBN 0–684–82804–9
    1. Orfalea, Aref, d. 1985.   2. Ardennes, Battle of the, 1944–1945.
3. United States.   Army.   Parachute Infantry Battalion, 551st—
History.   4. World War, 1939–1945—Regimental histories—United
States.   5. United States.   Army—Biography.   6. Soldiers—United
States—Biography.   I. Title.
D756.5.A7074   1997
940.54'21431—dc20   96–43681
                                                                    CIP

Page 272: Wilfred Owen, *Collected poems of Wildred Owen.* Copyright © 1963 by
Chatto & Windus, Ltd. Reprinted by permission of New Directions Pub., Corp.

Page 325: "All the Things You Are." Written by Jerome Kern and Oscar Hammer-
stein II. Copyright © 1939 PolyGram International Publishing, Inc. Copyright
Renewed. Used by Permission. All Rights Reserved.

For my mother and father

Was it for this the clay grew tall?
—Wilfred Owen

CONTENTS

PREFACE

It is hard to say where this all began.

On August 2, 1985, my father died of a gunshot wound in his store in Woodland Hills, California. No one of the thousand people who came to the funeral could find the words to speak at the burial ground. After long minutes of listening to the wind at Holy Cross Cemetery in Los Angeles, an adopted son of our family, the philosophy professor Dr. Nicholas Habib, volunteered an eloquent farewell. It was filled with silences.

I had just become a father myself for the first time and feared the cord between generations recently and delicately brought forth had been abruptly cut. My wife and I observed our first anniversary two days after the violent tragedy. I remember a confusion of flowers.

The family was more or less exploded, and the vacuum created by the explosion pulled the oxygen out of my writing system. Years went by. Words withered inside me. It was all I could do just to get to work and back on time and to bring three boys from infancy to school age. I can honestly say I was not undergoing a writer's block for those years; I simply had no will to write, and in fact found the whole notion of writing empty. Understanding, and the will to understand, had deserted me.

Still, my father's past life twisted like a nettle inside me. A young and vibrant sixty when he died, my father was just turning the corner on personal failure. But we lived 3,000 miles apart for the hardest years of his life—a decade. Many times I contemplated the flag that had draped his coffin: How could someone who survived the Battle of the Bulge be felled one mile from home? And by friendly fire?

I would speak with his former friends, colleagues, and relatives late at night in bars, living rooms, backyards, or cars. I found out some things that disturbed or elevated, but they didn't cohere or give solace. Then I met the men with whom he had fought so long ago.

In the dark period when my father was out of work after he had closed his twenty-five-year-old garment manufacturing business, he gave in to the exhortations of a friend that he take his frustration to a shooting range. He was not a lover of guns. Unlike many in the San Fernando Valley who assure intruders of an "Armed Response," he did not own a firearm. I wouldn't say he was without fear, but he was without that kind of fear.

Nevertheless, from boredom or loneliness, he accompanied his friend—whose dress firm was still puttering along—to shoot. It was a fateful decision. It's possible, since my father hadn't fired a weapon since World War II, that, as he aimed a pistol at the target, the several explosions of an afternoon bent his eardrum. From that day forward he complained of a ringing in his ears—tinnitus it's called. No doctor or friend could help.

As he struggled to get his work bearings, he would put a hand up to his ear. His own voice and the voices of others began to echo; he was like some kind of Beethoven struggling to make music as the bustle of the world ebbed away. Seven years after the factory closing he lay dead on the floor of his new photocopy store, a smile on his face. The ringing had stopped; the symphony had begun.

On the many nights I have stayed awake thinking about him, I wondered whether he had heard that bullet coming at him for forty years without knowing it, and that the ringing from the shooting range was only the last warning. I mean forty years after a bad winter in Belgium in which he, like so many men, had dropped.

My father repeated only two things about his experience as a paratrooper in World War II: "I ate my K-rations on a silver platter at the Hotel Negresco in Nice," and, "All my friends were killed around me." The latter referred to the Ardennes in the winter of 1945. In retrospect, though I see him now as the freest man I've known, for him the war was too painful an event to dwell on. And at the knob-end of midlife he was dead, the secrets of the most jarring events in his life, it would seem, buried with him.

In 1988, on a lonely afternoon in a small bookstore that is now out of business, a certain book caught my eye. It was *Ridgway's Paratroopers* by Clay Blair. In it I was startled to discover something I had never found in a history of World War II, mention of my father's little unit: "Nowhere were casualties heavier than in Wood Joerg's 551st Battalion."[1] Nowhere? Blair was referring to the Battle of the Bulge.

Having spotted a footnote about a unit history by someone named Dan Morgan, I managed to reach Blair and to learn Morgan's phone number. More clicked in that first conversation than the receiver. Morgan suggested I come to Europe with the unit's veterans for their first sizable over-seas reunion the following summer.

My brother, captivated by the notion that we might find someone who knew Aref Orfalea and might discover how his war experience had shaped the unusual man he was, eagerly agreed to go along, as did my seventy-nine-year-old Aunt Jeannette who, at age five, had sung "Over There!" for a World War I war bond drive.

By summer 1989, we were hustling down the Promenade D'Anglais in Nice, halted momentarily by the vision of a man in a parachute being towed out to sea by a speedboat, "para-sailing." The carmine dome of the whitewashed grand old Negresco loomed. We ducked in over the plush red carpet and under a giant chandelier.

The floor manager's mouth pursed cynically at our story of traveling with American veterans who had run the Nazis out of Nice long ago, "Oh yes, we were captured by Italy, then Germany, and we were lib-er-a-ted by you Americans." It was like a *salad Niçoise*—sour and cold.

But when I wondered aloud if the Negresco still served K-rations warm on silver plates and mentioned that my dead father had liked them that way, the man's face visibly changed.

"Go into the bar please, and order whatever drink you would like—on the house."

Jean-Paul Marro later joined us, shaking his head at our gin-and-tonics, "What, no champagne?" He motioned for a mint drink himself and told us of his war experience in Algeria. When his wife and he had toured the United States for their twentieth anniversary, he had found himself most moved by Arlington National Cemetery. "I realized there how many lives had been given by America for us," he bowed his head.

Seeing us off at the front of the Negresco, Marro took a green package from behind his back: "This is for your mother. Tell her France appreciates what her husband did for our freedom." It was a bottle of French perfume.

That one gesture may very well have snapped the spell and begun this book. On return to the United States, I started to do research, casually at first, and then more intensely. It was not long, however, before I realized that the 551st Parachute Infantry Battalion was one of the most extraordinary units to fight in World War II, and almost nothing existed in archives about it. After its abrupt disbandment in February 1945, its men, not to mention its history, seemed to disappear into thin air. That it took the worst, or second-worst, rate of casualties at the Battle of the Bulge and yet was a blank on the official record mystified me.

One day I dug up from a box in a closet a little book my father had given me on my ninth birthday, a children's guide to the airborne in World War

II: *The Story of the Paratroops,* by George Weller (1958).[2] Perusing it for the first time in thirty years, I realized one reason why I had been remiss all those years in questioning him about his unit: There was nothing in the book about the 551st, in fact, nothing at all about its two combat zones—southern France and Belgium. I must have concluded then that my father's outfit was inconsequential.

I began interviewing the men around the country and at their annual reunions. Dan Morgan's unit history served as a cornerstone, though I knew I had to reach beyond it to tell the full story, if indeed the full story could be found at all. I traveled three times to Europe researching in archives and interviewing Belgian and French civilians, as well as German veterans from units that opposed the 551st. (Interestingly, its chief antagonist, the 62d Volksgrenadiers Division, appeared almost as lost to history as the 551st.) The men graced me with most of an extant thirteen wartime diaries and memoirs, a bumper crop for such a small outfit, inasmuch as soldier diaries were strongly frowned upon and in many cases forbidden by the U.S. Army during the war for security reasons. The intrepid GIs who had the nerve to keep one had to do so on the sly. The fact that so many of the 551st had risked a journal in combat told me that they were going through something that cried out for expression.[3]

My journeys took me to places I never expected to go—for one, Fort Benning, Georgia, where I stood in front of the 34-foot jump tower and appealed to a skeptical jumpmaster to give me a shot at it. I explained briefly that I was writing a book about my father's battalion in World War II, the 551st.

No change in expression.

"They were an independent unit," I said. "The only other one in the war like them was the 509th."

His furrowed brow suddenly loosened, and his lips crept upward. "Ah, the 509th. I was with them when they were reactivated for a while in the 'sixties."

"Great unit."

He nodded, looking left and right.

"You ever jumped before?"

"No, sir."

"Ever want to?"

"No, sir. I'm scared to death of heights. I look down in elevators. I stared at my wife's sweater all the way to the top of the Eiffel Tower."

"Uh huh."

"Please, sergeant. I will be deeply in your debt."

"It's against regulations, you know."

"The 551st and the 509th had to do a lot of things that were against regulations at the Battle of the Bulge."

He nodded, looked at my forlorn tie wafting in the breeze, my seersucker suit and polished dress shoes.

"Nice shoes," he smiled.

"I try."

"All right, hook 'im up!"

It was a fair hike up the metal stairs, the equivalent of four stories. At the top was a female corporal. Thank God for women. A yard to my left was an open ledge 34 feet off the ground. "I'm going to clamp your static line to the guide wire, and when I say 'Go' you don't hesitate," she said, "You go."

Thank God for tough, lovely women, and for orders. If she had said, "Go when you're ready," I'd still be up there.

"Go!"

I jumped out and felt my stomach fall out of my body. Nightmares of falling and that strange trick I have had in sleep of jerking myself awake before hitting the ground leapt with me. But this wasn't sleep. I could see the headline now: "Author Dies While Trying to Be a Man: Leaves Manuscript Undone." Then the guide wire caught and bounced me upward, up and down, until I was sailing free across a football-size field, like a touchdown pass, fast. Halfway across it, I remembered to bury my chin in my chest. "Lift your legs!" the soldiers on an embankment shouted as I flew toward them. Up they went in the nick of time, missing a hummock by 2 inches.

First Sergeant James Prince of the 507th Regiment came up to me and smiled, "Well, what was it like?"

"Thrilling."

"Looked sharp. You want to enlist?"

"You never know," I smiled.

Along that road of eight years, people were intrigued and helpful, like Sergeant Prince, but it would be an overstatement to say I received universal support. One veteran from another unit physically threatened me. A lieutenant colonel tasked with an official Pentagon study of the 551st for late awards spat out over the phone, "You're f—-ed up." Another said if I were to reveal what he had told me about the unit's ultimate demise, someone in the unit would commit suicide. (Needless to say, though I felt that highly unlikely, I revealed nothing of the theory.) One day a fellow appeared wanting to look at my father's uniform in the attic for what he said was a Smithsonian Institution exhibit of which he was the supposed curator. An instinct held me back. Before the year was out he had conned several 551st men out of their priceless war uniforms and memorabilia;

they had moved via the black market to collectors in Europe. The alleged confidence man from Bethesda, Maryland, is under FBI investigation.[4]

There is more than one reason that 551st memorabilia are so prized and so rare. (An original 551st patch will fetch a price of several thousand dollars.) But what cloud was this unit under?

Having garnered the unexpected will, was I able to write the story? And then, I asked myself, did I have the right to write it at all? I have never been to war. (I have been, for whatever it is worth, to war zones as a correspondent and visitor.) My only military commitment was to the U.S. Army for one year in the Reserved Officers Training Corps during the Vietnam years at Georgetown University in Washington, D.C. I learned in that year to shoulder and take apart an M-1 rifle, which I would never use in battle; I also learned, after several weeks of missing the target, that I had been squinting my down-barrel eye. The weary ROTC major who finally caught this error did not smile.

That was freshman year at the Hilltop—1968, a pivotal year for my generation, as was 1941 for my father's. Some years back my mother reminded me that I wrote home early that year expressing disgust at the unwashed bumpkins of the Students for a Democratic Society whose protest brays broke the calm of class registration. By year's end, Robert Kennedy and Martin Luther King, Jr., were assassinated. My generation was marked by those bullets. I had no knowledge then that a senior named Bill Clinton was taking blankets to those left homeless by a rioting city, and could not possibly guess that he would become the American president 25 years later and that his Administration would consider an extraordinary Presidential Unit Citation for my father's ill-fated, valiant battalion a half century after its demise.

I was against the war in Vietnam, and so, too, was my old GOYA (the unit motto: Get-Off-Your-Ass) father, though we were not without arguments on the matter (I think Nixon's invasion of Cambodia tipped him over the edge). By the time I encountered a girl on Healy Lawn who had seen the four students at Kent State shot to death by the National Guard, I had been the recipient of a 4-F draft registration status, the compliments of a doctor against the war who unexpectedly stretched my childhood asthma further than was probably warranted. I accepted the gift horse.

Those years are filled with regret for me, not for having opposed the war, but because I didn't take a greater stand against it, a stance worthy of the same sort of courage my father and his fellow GIs had shown two wars back. It should have been far better, in retrospect, to have lodged a conscientious objector's stand (which I toyed with but abandoned because at that time COs had to take a stand against all war, which I could not agree to, feeling, as I did, that my father's service in Europe had been right).

I came to understand President Clinton's sense of being "cheated" by history by being served up a war that should not have been fought. A sense of guilt, too, that others not as fortunate (or callow) as I did risk or give their lives with reasonably good motives in a lost cause.

Yet there are other ways to serve—so many pressing ones today—the battlefronts are right in front of us. And though my life has so far been spared a foreign war, it has not been spared a domestic one.

This all combined to lead me to the task at hand. I have always been attracted to buried histories. But my encounter with the men of the 551st, and the pathos and strangeness of their story, was more than attraction; it was revelation. The more I found out about them, the more I discovered I was plumbing the mysteries of my own father's life. Perhaps in coming to grips with their violent end—I told myself—I might do so with his.

But I made myself no promises. The dogged efforts on the brink of death by the old men to resurrect their past and to set the record straight spurred me and became a part of the narrative itself. If my first book, *Before the Flames*—about immigrants to the United States from the Arab world—was a tribute to my grandparents' generation, this story of my father's lost battalion might be a salutation to the generation of my parents, through the crucible of its signature event, World War II.

To those who follow military history, the "lost battalion" is associated with World War I; New Yorkers of the 1st Battalion, 308th Infantry Regiment, 77th Division, were surrounded by Germans for five days in October 1918 in the Argonne forest. Unlike the 551st, however, it was never really "lost" in position, in recognition, or to the better judgment of high command. Everyone knew just where it was, and it was celebrated—three men had the Medal of Honor pinned on them by General John Pershing. One of them, Lieutenant Colonel Charles Whittesley, went on extended lecture tours, though he cried out once in exasperation, "I want to forget the war!"[5] The brave battalion took 50 percent casualties—a dreadful sum, indeed— but the 551st took more in Belgium, at least 84 percent.

There are details about the life and death of the 551st that are controversial and still in dispute. (For one thing, this book confronts the myth of Bastogne as the centerpiece of the Bulge campaign, in a very concrete way, questioning the selectivity, if not blindness, that mythmaking entails.) Where the facts run out, I indicate that. In a few places, I have also taken some narrative liberties with dialog or inner thoughts (italicized), but I have taken pains to flag them for the reader as conjecture or probability and have grounded them in material culled from my research and interviews.

A mechanical note: Where dialog or quoted material is not footnoted, the reader should know its origin is either in my ninety interviews with the men or those of Dan Morgan.

Although I am not a professional military historian, what some (including the Pentagon) have let pass for history concerning the 551st is astonishing. My research has had several motives: to fill a gap, to let the true record speak as strongly and compellingly as possible, and to bring to a great story all the craft I could muster in order that it might endure. It seems the imagination has a legitimate role to play in history, not to distort, but to pull the gold from the dross and to give it life. And so I have tried to make this a history of human beings in strife, and not solely a record of which unit moved where and when with what weapons.

I have not written this book for military buffs, per se, nor am I particularly interested in fulfilling the needs of romantics or sensationalists. I have written the book primarily out of gratitude for the men themselves and to fulfill in some part the impossible debt of a son. The book is for ordinary people such as myself who have sons and fathers, with a special nod to those to whom something extraordinary, even incredible, has happened. It is obvious the 551st fits that description. I hasten to add that though the book certainly guarantees no recovery from any particular trauma, the writing of it has helped me. That is the most anyone should claim.

To state my final motive plainly: I wanted to try and keep my father from dying again. Neither he nor the unit should have ended at the precipices at which they found themselves. Neither's story—at least in my obsession—could be written about separately, one divorced from the other. I was to find that one might pull the slip-knot of the other, but only if they were cinched together in the first place.

Here is the story sewn of a lost battalion and a lost father. As my father would have said, jumping out the air door of his warplane or pulling away from bumper-to-bumper L.A. traffic for a few precious seconds of freedom: *Geronimo!*

ACKNOWLEDGMENTS

Over the eight years' work on this book, an atomized battalion of people helped me resurrect the story of the 551st Parachute Infantry Battalion. They deserve special thanks.

Because the unit's history was obscure and its extant official records scant, thoughtful and devoted archivists were invaluable, including David Keough and Dennis Vetock of the U.S. Military History Institute at Carlisle, Pennsylvania, and its archivist historian Dr. Richard Sommers; David Giordano, Maria Hanna, Ken Schlesinger, and John Butler at the National Archives and Records Administration in Suitland/College Park, Maryland; Robert Wolfe and Robin Cookson (Captured German Records) and John Taylor (U.S. military section) of the National Archives; Dr. Stephen Paczolt and Nancy Hunter of the Geography and Map Division, Library of Congress; Stephen Rogers of the Office of Special Investigations of the U.S. Department of Justice; the staff at the Air Force Historical Research Agency, Maxwell Air Force Base Library, Montgomery, Alabama; John L. Clark, Jr., and Louis Alley, Air Force Safety Agency, Kirtland Air Force Base, Albuquerque, New Mexico; Robert Anzouni, U.S. Airborne Museum, Fort Bragg, North Carolina; Captain Rich Donoghue, Judge Advocate General's Office, Fort Bragg; Mary Dennis, U.S. Army Judiciary, Falls Church, Virginia; Brad Castleberry (public affairs director), John Graber (technical adviser to the Airborne School), Private William Hall, and First Sergeant James Prince (507th PIR) at Fort Benning, Georgia; the U.S. Army Mortuary and Support and Casualties Office; Richard Anderson of the Dupuy Institute; and Bill Connelly and Patricia Haberer of the U.S. Holocaust Memorial Museum. I should also mention that some of the U.S. Army Command records on which I relied were declassified as late as 1994.

In Belgium, the assistance of several Ardennois officials associated with the Center for Research and Information of the Battle of the Ardennes (CRIBA) and the Comité D'Accueil des U.S. Airborne (CADUSA) was invaluable, including André Hubert, Ferdinand Albert, and the Belgian historian Serge Fontaine, whose monograph on the 551st, *L'Enfer a Trois Ponts*, is invaluable. The CRIBA vice president, Christian Kraft de la Saulx, who at times served as my translator, and his wife, Gaby, were great hosts at Beaufays. My indefatigable friends Claude and Martine Orban of Grand Halleux housed me for several days. Many thanks to the entire Cornelius family, in particular Marie Hollange. The 1995 death of Leo Carlier of Saint-Jacques, Belgium, leaves a void for all who knew him.

In Germany, Captain Lutz of the Bundesarchiv in Freiburg im Bresgau was patient and helpful, as were the staff at Freiburg's Militärgeschichtliches (most of whose World War II documents have by now moved to Berlin). The hospitality and assistance of Lieutenant Josef Bannert of Petersburg was much appreciated, as was the testimony of Colonel Arthur Juttner of Bramstedt and Helmut Hennig of Bad Orb. Many thanks to Carol Troiani, Adda Rikken, Michael Trost, and Ulrike Pohler for help with German translations. John Kline, editor of the 106th Infantry Division Association's CUB newsletter, was kind to include me in a rare reunion of survivors of that brave unit with German veterans in Auw.

In southern France, anyone associated with the 551st is greatly indebted to Aimé Leocard of Draguignan and John Willems of Nice. I should also like to thank the Bidegain family of Pau, whose patience with my French many years ago bore late fruit.

My old companion-of-the-road Robert Hedin granted me a detailed, penetrating, and valuable critique of half the manuscript. Neighbors William and Mary Lou Byler gave a full cup of insight virtually every morning throughout these years; I've never met the likes of them. John Hildebrand, Pablo Medina, and Max Holland provided the special kind of friendship it takes to trim a behemoth of wood pulp. Three exceptional teachers in craft and life were my luck: Sister Mary Mark, O.P. (St. Boniface), Fr. John Columba Fogarty, O. Cam. (Crespi Carmelite High School), and Dr. John Glavin (Georgetown University). I also wish to thank John Millsfield and Philip Pictaggi for understanding that stretches back to our childhoods and in particular for their unflagging support for this endeavor.

Robert Fogarty, editor of the *Antioch Review*, published my distillation of this story, "The Lost Battalion of the Ardennes," in *AR*, vol. 52, no. 2 (Spring 1994). Anne Gordon, editor of the *Cleveland Plain Dealer Sunday Magazine*, printed a version of part of chapter 2 as "Contact: The War, Sandlot Football, and My Father," March 1, 1996.

In one of those rare little miracles that occur in publishing, Karen Braziller, president of Persea Books, rescued the project from oblivion by printing virtually without a word changed a version of the first chapter of this book as "The Messenger of the Lost Battalion" in her 1993 anthology, *Visions of America,* edited by Amy Ling and Wesley Brown. In turn, she pointed me in the direction of The Free Press and a young editor whom she said was one of the few in New York whose taste in books ran like hers.

Adam Bellow, editorial director of The Free Press, saw something in this story that many others didn't or, if they did, did not have the support from above that Adam received from his predecessor, the late Erwin Glickes. To my indebtedness, both men took a chance, GOYAs at heart.

Joyce Hackett attacked the monster manuscript with great elan and drew blood (and not a little ire), but unquestionably improved the book. Stephen Morrow of The Free Press showed great sense and sensitivity.

There is no one who understood better and more intuitively what I was after—the unorthodox braiding of a hard-used battalion's story with that of one of its members, my father—than my agent, Tom Wallace. His confidence in the project and in me personally expressed itself at just the right moments, the dark ones. I treasure his friendship.

All of the men of the 551st—several of whom have died since this project began—have inspired me in ways that, finally, may be beyond explanation. The book itself is an attempt at explaining. The ninety men I interviewed are listed, with my gratitude, in the Appendix; many of these also supplied photographs. But those who bore the brunt of my questions with aplomb, devotion, and remarkable patience are Dan Morgan, Colonel Douglas Dillard (ret.), Fred Hilgardner, and Joe Cicchinelli. Their wives—Jo, Virginia, Shirley, and Jean—are just as remarkable. Charles Fairlamb did generous duty with photographs. Thanks, as well, to all the fine relatives who gave insight into their men, in particular Heidi Joerg.

The exceptional maps are the work of Lieutenant Colonel Albert "Durf" McJoynt (ret.). The tape transcriptions were ably produced by Deborah Gabor, Sheila Hawkins, and Jo Tingle.

The untoward ordeal of the Presidential Unit Citation would require a page of acknowledgment in itself, but one man needs to be singled out: Major Tom Risgbee of the World War II Commemoration Committee. He never gave up. Our dear friend and neighbor John Devaney gave generously of his time at his law firm of Perkins Coie. The witness of Colonel William Holm (ret.) and Major Richard Goins (ret.) was important. Lieutenant General John Norton (ret.) was this unit's treasured late-in-life spearhead and perceptive reader of the manuscript.

My father's four sisters and brother informed my efforts with great devotion—Jeannette Graham, Adele Scanlon (deceased), Vernice Jens, Bette Unrein, and Major George Orfalea (ret.).

My mother Rose opened not just an old trunk of letters but her bottomless heart, all the way, at all hours. My brother Mark traveled with me physically and emotionally throughout. A lifelong tip of the hat and a raise of the burrito.

The sheer stamina of my wife Eileen to carry on these years raising our three children while a husband who, when not working at his day job, seemed given over to ghosts, is certainly, for me, a wonder of the world. On one occasion, when said husband in despair wheeled out of a driveway heading to parts unknown, she hurled herself on the car hood. She is my windshield. Our love endures.

Finally, our boys—Matthew, Andrew, and Luke—gave up many hours of play with their father while he worked in his brick hut, give or take a few calls for catch. Their good cheer, love, patience, and understanding are the light of our lives. I pray they will never have to go to war, though I hope someday they will find here, through men who were like him, the grandfather they never knew.

I

THE OLD MEN RETURN

Europe, August 1989

But I know you set great store on what opens up a fresh field.

—Natasha to Pierre, *War and Peace*

1
Band of outsiders

"Can you imagine the enormous sound then, and how quiet it is now?"

Chuck Miller, who carried a bazooka then, for many years afterward a wrench, and now a heart condition, was walking the green hills and fields of the Ardennes. It was August 1989 in eastern Belgium, the site of the greatest battle the American Army ever fought, the Battle of the Bulge. He was one of a million men in uniform clashing in the snow amid deafening sound. And now it was green and silent, except for the lowing of a few cows, and the clanking of their iron bells.

Miller stood in a depression in the woods, filled with a half-century of pine needles, a good place to lie down, he thought, testing the thick natural cushion with his hand. Long ago, he had thrust a steel bayonet through the chest of a German soldier who had stood up in that very hole with no pine needles to catch him.

"I didn't want to live it," Miller said, feeling the old sap on a pine's bark. "I didn't have to relive it. Maybe it's better to keep it cloudy. But I seem strong-willed enough not to be torn up by the past. I've been called cold-hearted. I knew we had taken a horrible beating. But until my first

1

551st reunion last year in Chicago, I was under the impression we only had three people left."

A few more than that, but not too many more. Memory—the dread and strange allure of it—was beginning to seep into Chuck Miller of Rancho Cucamonga, California, late in his life. Like my father, Miller had managed for most of his life to blot out his experiences in World War II. The unusual, ill-fated Army unit in which they both served seemed to call the white-heat of their war back into a dark, still pool. And now it was being disturbed.

One of only two independent U.S. parachute battalions created during the war, the 551st was made up of a highly individualistic, cantankerous band of outsiders welded together in a national emergency. One of them was among the first U.S. soldiers to jump out of planes in 1940 at Fort Benning, Georgia, as part of the original paratrooper Test Platoon. The battalion was the first (and last) to hazard test jumps out of gliders. Two months after D-Day in Normandy, General Eisenhower overruled Churchill, who wanted an invasion of the Balkans, by opening up a second front in southern France. On August 15, 1944, the 551st executed a near perfect jump in the foothills behind Nice as part of Operation Dragoon—the first daylight combat drop in U.S. history.

The 551st was the first American unit to capture a German general in Europe (at Draguignan), the first U.S. force to reach Cannes and Nice. The 600-man battalion patrolled a 45-mile stretch of the France–Italy border in harsh winter conditions under Nazi shelling in the Maritime Alps—a job that normally called for at least a division (15,000 men). Finally, on December 27, 1944, Major General James Gavin gave the 551st the signal honor of spearheading the Allied counterattack against the terrifying German "Bulge" in Belgium, on its northern shoulder in the 82d Airborne Division's sector. The battalion's heroic push came at great cost—on January 7 only 110 of its 643 men walked out of the decisive battle at Rochelinval; many of those were "walking wounded." Other than the wipeout of the 509th, the other independent parachute battalion, at Anzio, Italy, and later in Belgium, the 551st probably sustained the worst casualty rate of any U.S. battalion on the European front.

Strangely, shortly after Rochelinval the 551st was disbanded, its records destroyed, its valor left undecorated, and its existence forgotten—a fate more easily associated with the Vietnam War than the so-called good war. The unit should have been one of the most decorated units in U.S. military history; instead it became almost completely erased from the historical record.

The National Archives hold 12 cubic feet of official records for the other independent parachute battalion, which was also disbanded—the heavily-decorated 509th. For the 551st, there is one folder less than an

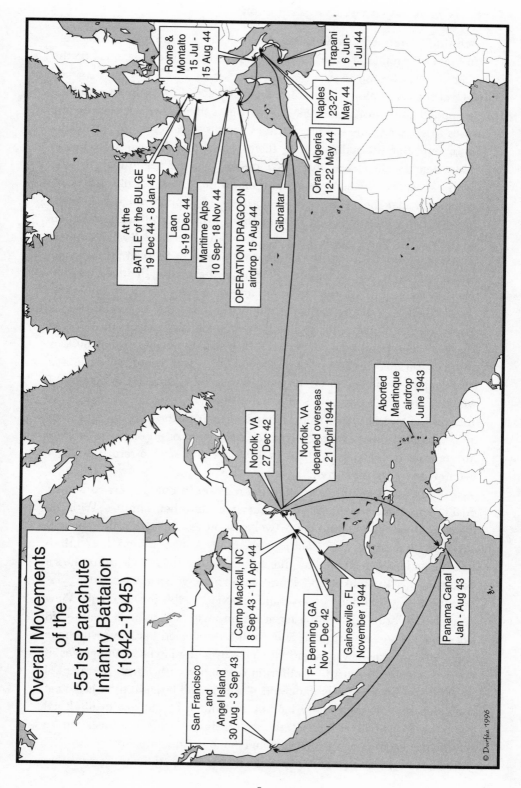

Overall Movements
of the
551st Parachute
Infantry Battalion
(1942-1945)

Rome & Montalto
15 Jul - 15 Aug 44

Trapani
6 Jun - 1 Jul 44

Naples
23-27 May 44

Oran, Algeria
12-22 May 44

At the
BATTLE of the BULGE
19 Dec 44 - 8 Jan 45

Laon
9-19 Dec 44

Maritime Alps
10 Sep - 18 Nov 44

OPERATION DRAGOON
airdrop 15 Aug 44

Gibraltar

Norfolk, VA
27 Dec 42

Norfolk, VA
departed overseas
21 April 1944

Aborted
Martinque
airdrop
June 1943

Camp Mackall, NC
8 Sep 43 - 11 Apr 44

San Francisco
and
Angel Island
30 Aug - 3 Sep 43

Ft. Benning, GA
Nov - Dec 42

Gainesville, FL
November 1944

Panama Canal
Jan - Aug 43

© Durfee 1996

3

inch thick. Even today at Fort Benning's McCarthy Hall, every parachute unit that ever fought for the U.S. Army has its insignia emblazoned on the walls—except for the 551st.

Over the years, alone or together, the men have chewed on several theories about their unit's fate: that Gavin was embarrassed enough by the losses to wipe out all records; that they were so heartbroken at their disbandment after Rochelinval, they themselves burned the records in the fields; that the 551st was just snake-bitten from the beginning; that the death of their commander deprived them of their most credible advocate for honors; that their "impossible" objective at Rochelinval was punishment for being a maverick unit. Some thought the unit's final humiliation lay with General Matthew Ridgway, in whose massive XVIII Airborne Corps they formed a small part; Ridgway apparently disliked the independent paratroop units and was on the verge of disbanding them anyway before the Bulge hit. At the age of ninety-two, however, Ridgway wrote Colonel Dillard that the extinguishing of the record of the 551st was "a grave error and injustice to as gallant a combat battalion as any in WW II in Europe."[1] The paratrooper icon wrote me shortly afterward that he was aware of "serious efforts" under way to bring the "full record" of the 551st's heroism and tragic fate to public light.[2] Little did I know at the time that I would devote eight years of my life to that effort.

After the few survivors were stripped of their history, thirty years went by before Phil Hand managed to track down a handful of old men for a first reunion in Atlanta in 1977. In 1989 the first sizable return of 551st veterans to Europe occurred.

It didn't take long to realize that the reunion in Europe carried a great deal of emotional weight for all the survivors and their families. With the twenty returning veterans were twelve spouses, thirteen children, and seven grandchildren. Phil Hand, for example, brought a son whose mind, he said, had been destroyed by glue sniffing in the 1960s. "He thinks he's a paratrooper," "Bubbles" Hand, a pink-faced man with sad Irish setter eyes, said to me one afternoon on a veranda in Nice. Ralph Burns of Lake View Terrace, California—no youngster at seventy with a Parkinson shake—did not leave behind his crippled wife Ruth but wheeled her everywhere we went, up and down war memorial steps, over the lawns of the graves at Henri Chapelle. A wealthy California developer with a taste for alcohol had brought his two feisty daughters—or they had brought him. Jack Leaf took sick in Nice and would be confined much of the trip to his hotel room. Leaf was no wet blanket, though. Early on in the trip I asked if he had married a French girl. "Every time I met one," he quipped.

Even Aunt Jeannette, to whom Dad had sent most of his war correspondence, would not let a black-and-blue knee bashed the week of our departure stop her. For our journey Aunt Jeannette became the older sister many of the men had written to during the war.

I never asked my mother to accompany us. I knew what her answer would be: silence. My father had promised her a trip to Europe someday, but the rigors of raising three children, the crazy fashion industry, and his subsequent financial decline prevented it. When she finally went to Europe it was with her brother and his wife on their invitation. Father stayed home and minded the store. It fell to me to reach her that dim August night; she was in London. I instructed my uncle neither to tell her her husband had been shot nor by whom. I had to get her home after all, so I concocted a lie. "Car accident, bad shape" was all I said.

For her I am sure as she flew home the whole continent of Europe sank to a bottomless Sargasso Sea.

2

"And there it is—my tree!"

The men seemed in a trance as they moved out—now in their sixties and seventies—across the vineyards of the Valbourges estate at LaMotte, France, trying to remember just which bush or plot of earth took their falling bodies forty-five years before. Their maroon berets, navy blue blazers, white shirts, and white hair flickered among the grapevines, raspberries, and apple and pear trees.

"There it is!" Will Marks of Pennsylvania pointed to a lone poplar in the distance fronting a pond. "All my life I dreamed of falling into a tree by itself. You guys have been telling me we fell in the woods. And there it is—my tree!"

Harry Renick, a retired machinist from Detroit who now makes wishing wells, commented drily, "I made a three-point landing here: feet, butt, and helmet." Others were seriously injured, impaled on stakes in the vineyard.

Approaching Valbourges to dedicate a plaque at the Stevens family chapel, Otto Schultz of West Virginia spied the tiled roof of a barn and remembered banging down on the tiles, riding his still-inflated chute to the ground. One of the Stevens family joked, "The broken tiles—they are still there. You may fix them!"

In the courtyard of the old, worn château sat an apparition in a wheelchair, ninety-one-year-old Mme. Henriette Stevens, who had bound up the first wounds of the 551st. The men spoke to her in low, hoarse English; she followed their eyes, hugged them. As I approached someone said, "But you are too young to be one of the paratroopers, no?" I looked at Mrs. Stevens—she resembled my father's irascible Lebanese immigrant mother, who had peddled on the streets of New York at the turn of the century. "I am here for my father, madame," I said in basic French, tipping my beret. "He is dead now, but I give you his thanks."

Colonel Dillard had given the maroon beret to me earlier in the day for a wreath-laying ceremony at the U.S. Rhône cemetery at Draguignan. It was cocked correctly for me by one of the *vieilles suspentes* ("old risers" literally, what the surviving French resistance paratroopers call themselves), who'd come all the way from Paris for the ceremony. When I heard "The Star Spangled Banner," "The Marseillaise," and taps, my hand instinctively moved from heart to forehead to join the men.

On our bus that night back to Nice I asked Harry Renick what the 551st motto—GOYA—meant. "Get Off Your Ass," Harry said mildly. That smacked of Dad's favorite, "Go get 'em!" cried out whenever he was happy, challenged, or off on his beloved motorcycle into the Mojave Desert. My brother's restaurant in Santa Barbara, in fact, commemorates both the motto and the motorcycle, where one hangs from the ceiling above the diners. Hearing that, Otto recalled: "You know, we requisitioned a motorcycle from the Germans at Cannes. One guy was fond as hell of that thing. It could have been your father."

Slowly the gray canvas of my father's life in the war gained an oval of color here and there; the anger and gaiety we knew as he was raising us began to dovetail with the verve in darkness that got him through the war or, indeed, was caused by it. My father was a life-messenger of sorts. He always seemed to want to urge life along; left alone, life could atrophy, self-destruct, or, worst of all, end up meaningless. GOYA! "Go get 'em!" "Rise and shine!" "Up and at 'em!" "We're off and running!" "Zing 'em!" For my father, reveille was a requirement in civilian life—and at all hours, I might add.

How many childhood car trips to the Sierras began with his lusty version of "Blood on the Risers" (sung to the tune of "The Battle Hymn of the Republic"):

"Is everybody happy?" cried the sergeant looking up/Our Hero feebly answered, "Yes," and then they stood him up,/He leaped right out into the blast, his static line unhooked,/AND HE AIN'T GONNA JUMP NO MORE! GORY, GORY, WHAT A HELLUVA WAY TO DIE![3]

I had one last question about the LaMotte drop. Dad once vaguely mentioned his most fearful moment in the service as a night jump. But the 551st had dropped in southern France on a late summer afternoon. Instead of fear of the night, there was fear of German guns which could sight them. So when had there been a night jump? The men figured it wasn't in Europe but in training at Camp Mackall, North Carolina, where they participated in dangerous, innovative airborne tests, such as the first live parachute jumps from gliders. There in the foggy night of February 16, 1944, eight GIs were misdropped in lakes; they parachuted with 100 pounds of equipment straight to the bottom and drowned. The disaster jolted the bereaved relatives of a drop victim to contact the columnist Drew Pearson, whose angry pieces prompted the Army to adopt the British "quick release" harness.

The only quick release the horrific event engendered in the men was of jets of anxiety. Restless by nature (their first mission to drop on Vichy-leaning Martinique was aborted), the 551st rebelled. At one point, two hundred of its men were in the guardhouse. I remember Dad once telling me, only half-jokingly, that he spent more time jumping in between two warring servicemen than in combat against the Nazis. When one is pumped up for war and the climax is withdrawn or, worse, one's own men are wasted in training, something in the muscles goes either limp or very taut. To blur training and combat, as Paul Fussell has noted, is "so wrong as to be unmentionable."[4]

Only the return of their charismatic, youthful commander, Lieutenant Colonel Wood Joerg, calmed them somewhat. Following a hearing, the older Colonel Rupert Graves, who had overseen the tragic Mackall night jump, was transferred after shouting at the 551st from his balcony, "You're not going to ruin my career! You're not soldiers! You're all rabble!"

In one of the ironies of war, Colonel Graves ended up commanding the 551st again when it was attached at the Battle of the Bulge to his 517st Parachute Regimental Combat Team. A day after its detachment from Graves, it was the 551st that got the nod to enter the meat grinder. Several of the men have wondered if they were the victims of a clash of personalities at the top, traceable back to their training days.

3

"Always the farthest one back"

Maybe rebellion was inherent.

What, in fact, makes a man want to jump out of a plane? And not just that, but to be one of the first to do it in battle? It's a bit like running away to the circus, but worse—no one shoots at the acrobat on the high wire.

I queried the men about being "airborne." Otto Schultz, retired from Union Carbide (he had worked on the Bhopal project and shook his head about it), thought back to childhood. "I'd run along a wall to leap into sand as a kid—always the farthest one back." Charles Fairlamb, at seventy-four retired from Boeing in Seattle, joined the 551st in Panama, where he was repairing lines for the phone company. "I figured I liked to keep climbing poles!" he grinned. The men seemed to possess an excess of energy, a critical mass of sorts, that had made them a chancy bunch. There was an almost cherished restlessness about them. "Most people who became paratroopers were dissatisfied where they were," Phil Hand said. "A bunch of malcontents," Ed Hartman put it bluntly.

Parachuting attracted the romantic. Dan Morgan of Washington joined the 551st after being disappointed to discover that there was no horse calvalry being mounted to fight the Chinese: "They had replaced horses with half-tracks." There was also the matter of status. "If you could see it lightning and hear it thunder you could get into the Army," said Charles Austin of Texas. "Not everyone could be a paratrooper." It wasn't so much a question of being fearless. "After jumping thirteen times, I had never landed in a plane in my life, so the first time I landed it was like a screw propeller going into the ground—I was scared as hell," a grizzled, trim Max Bryan from Yorktown, Virginia, admitted. "But you say to yourself, I was a man."

As for my father, I can only guess the motive. He was the last of six children, after four sisters and a brother who was already stationed in Burma. He'd certainly had plenty of babying and something to prove. Unlike his siblings, who had grown up in wealth, by the time Aref was coming of age in Cleveland, his millionaire linen merchant father had lost it all in the Depression. He watched his father move from being a gent with a gold fob at the cash register to operating a lathe, and he witnessed the ensuing rancor between my grandmother and grandfather. A life of grandeur and wealth slipping into penury—what else to do but jump? A good war is a good place to jump.

The men of the 551st seemed acutely distrustful of authority, not the best attitude for people involved in the U.S. Army. (The murderous blunder at Camp Mackall only reinforced their attitude.) Their very "551" was assigned out of sequence (battalions of its sort being numbered 501 to 517), so the Germans would think there were more U.S. paratroopers than actually existed. They savored their independent status, and relished it when their commanding officer, Lieutenant Colonel Wood Joerg, told them, "Each of you is worth five other men."

If one person appears to have epitomized the spirit of the 551st, it was Joerg himself. Ebullient, charming, an unreconstructed rebel "Jaw Jaw" (Georgia) boy at West Point, he was not a great student. The 1937 USMA yearbook lists him as 230 out of 298 in class ranking. But it also credits him as a "Rabble Rouser" who pumped up the stands during ball games, with "a heart a yard long and a smile a mile wide." By the time of the offensive at the Bulge, that smile and that heart would have to change places.

He liked to root, to work his deep Southern accent on the girls in a way that was both shy and confident, and to dance. He was not, according to one classmate, "a hive (bookworm)" but a "hopoid." Joerg was hop manager for the Point. He was not a "make" (cadet officer) but a "clean sleeve" (no chevrons to denote rank or authority). He was also "an area bird"—someone who spent many hours walking punishment tours around the Point with a rifle because of his horsing around.

A classmate who outlived him enough to become a brigadier general said Joerg was "full of the milk of human kindness." He had a weakness for plebes, who took a terrible beating, as he had, from upperclassmen, a sympathy he later exhibited—enough to be warned—for men under his command.

The line soldiers of the 551st loved him, it seems, and he returned the sentiment; some remember him on the phone in a frenzy to get the suicidal mission at Rochelinval canceled. It appears the man from "Jaw-Jaw" saw death at an early age, and it made him dance. Joerg's first roommate at West Point died as a cadet, sending him into great inner turmoil. The first American pilot killed in World War II was from Joerg's cadet company.

It fitted the dark irony surrounding the 551st like a hard chute that one Major General C. S. O'Malley would remember Wood Joerg's "heroic death at Bastogne." When the hot shrapnel pierced his helmet and killed him, Joerg and the men who fell around him in the snow were 25 miles north of where McAuliffe was to give his famous "Nuts!" reply to a German order to surrender. Brigadier General McAuliffe was rescued by Patton, but there would be no rescue at a snow-clamped, obscure knoll called Rochelinval.

4

A lonely hutch

My father was not a physical fitness nut. His generation as a whole saw nothing particularly worth worshiping about the body. Those who fought World War II worked like dogs to end up with a kidney-shaped pool and a circular drive, daily ate bacon and eggs, drank coffee not decaf, smoked Lucky Strikes or Marlboros, had affairs instead of relationships, and took up, if anything, bowling or the somnolent game of golf. Dad vehemently refused to be a golfer.

As a teenager in Cleveland his sports were football and ice hockey. A split end for a rather accomplished neighborhood football team, the Cleveland Olympics, just before he entered the war, he hit a peak when the Olympics copped a citywide championship.

His quarterback friend, Bud Lank, and he were the only ones who played on both first string and second string teams. They were never out of the Olympics lineup. Muscular in a lean way, at 5 feet, 10 inches, Aref was pound-for-pound the best tackler and blocker on the team, Lank thought. He recalled fondly, "Your father was a contact kind of guy."

That he was. He would hold your shoulder to make a point, touch finger to knee to underscore it, bear-hug with a grip that was not afraid to last. Lank said Aref was always slapping the players on the back in the huddle, spurring them on to a quicker stop-and-go, a blunter block. He was, in short, a Wood Joerg type.

Los Angeles was not the best place for an excellent ice skater to bring up a family. As much as he loved Mother, it was clearly a disappointment to him that she never learned to skate (and abhorred his motorcycle). I became his partner on ice as a boy, as did my sister, Leslie. But most of the time he skated alone with the slight crouch of a speed skater, crossing over smoothly on turns, weaving gently, swiftly, in and out of the fumbling Angelenos, an anonymous messenger of grace. He loved skating music; if he heard "Frenesi" or anything by Glenn Miller, he immediately took off. An evening at the small Valley rink would end with him unlacing our boots and wistfully blowing over his hot chocolate as he confided that that ultimate female skating partner had eluded him.

If he had found her, earlier, would any of us children have existed? Perhaps a son would not have been afraid of heights.

I tried. I skated pretty well for a native Angeleno—I had a good teacher. But I never learned to stop on a dime like my father, who barreled toward the wall, pivoted at the last second, bit his blades sideways into the ice with a shuusssh, ice shavings sprayed on my sister and me. I suppose if you know how to stop you're not so afraid of speed. If I speed-skate anywhere, it's on the page, or else I parachute to its bottom. It's not a bad substitute for innate, physical grace, which my father—unconscious of his own body—had in spades.

The jogging health mania that began with my generation and Jane Fonda-ed into a multibillion-dollar industry over the last decade seemed stupid and pointless to him even when he discovered, with everyone else, cholesterol. "I'm going puffing," he would announce to my mother's exhortations, exhaling smoke. And he smoked seriously—inhales and exhales were dramatic billowing caesuras, smoke signals of dilemma or pain. Strangely enough, smoke for him was a life-force. Toward the end he tried to quit for Mom, even adopted lower-tar cigarettes. But his heart wasn't in it.

I say all this to note the paradox of that generation of Americans that spent childhood in the Depression, fought in World War II as teenagers, and as adults built the country as we know it today, for better or worse, richer or polluted, in plutonium and in health. That paradox is one of excess and selflessness. It was a generation that acted first, thought later. Ours, on the other hand, thinks almost everything into oblivion. Ours projects all, yet seems at a loss to do anything that will substantially alter what we so brilliantly project, most of which is payment for fifty years of excess since the war—chemical water, dying forests, soaring deficits, clogged arteries, rockets and bombs like hardened foam from a million panting mouths.

I can't blame my father or his generation for the Age of Excess anymore than I blame my own for its Age of Informed Narcissism. History and time create us more than we fathom. I only note the ironies—Dad's excess was generous, selfless, and dealt the future some mortal blows. Our touted social consciousness seems drained to a pittance of the grand protest era that gave us "our" war crucible. We are late, curiously cranky parents. And we are not so hot with the future, either, sinking in the mire of the present, saving nothing but the bills from our credit cards. Our sin is presbyopia; his generation's—myopia. Even then by the day we escape from the immediate, from contact. We are all learning to draw our wagons in a circle quite well from the teeming hordes of the ghetto, crack wars, the homeless. We become kinder, gentler Republicans at a far remove from what needs our kindness and gentleness less than our ability to act. To act? That might entail uncertainty, even heartache.

Perfectly healthy as I was in my twenties—a bicycler, basketball player, swimmer—I once prodded Dad that he needed exercise. He snapped, "I got my exercise hauling fifty dresses at a clip over my shoulders up and down Ninth and Los Angeles Streets. I got my exercise lugging an 80-pound radio over the Maritime Alps." It was the closest he ever came to bravado. It was as out of character as it was for him to be out of work.

I used to dream about the Maritime Alps, unable to find them on the map. They held a lofty, Tibetan image in my mind. After the 551st came down from the Provence foothills of their parachute drop, taking Cannes, Nice, and other towns of the Côte D'Azur, it was ordered to go up into the high mountains separating France from Italy, where the retreating Germans fled. That was September 1944. Those were the Maritime Alps. (Three months after serving one of the longest uninterrupted combat stints in Europe, the 551st was relieved in the Alps by the heralded Japanese-American battalion, the 100th.)

On some bright August days in 1989 we veterans and family ascended the Maritimes. I had my eye out for old Army radios. His would have been an SCR-300 backpack version, good practice for hauling a garment bag stuffed with samples. German pillboxes still squatted in the crags of the mountain. Chuck Fairlamb remembered boulders the Germans had rolled into the dry riverbed of the Var River so that gliders couldn't land there. As the road narrowed and steepened, and as the clear green Var wandered in a lazy late summer fall past islets and cottonwoods, Harry Renick seemed dreamy.

"What a place to come at night with a girl!" he mused, his dull blue eyes brightening at the sight. "You lie down on a towel with the rocks and the water rushing by. And boy, the wind over you! After you're done, you go dip it in the cold water. Downstream, it gets warmer!"

I asked Harry, a tall man who looked as though he might hunt, if the 551st ever saw bears or other animals in the Alps.

"Animals?" he dropped. "We were too concerned with the two-legged animals."

At Saint-Martin-Vesubie a good-sized crowd swarmed us in the town square, where, *tilleuls* rippling in a mountain breeze, we had a wreathe-laying ceremony with the mayor and town council and *vin d'honneur*. One gap-toothed woman, eyes sparkling in a leathery face, insisted I translate for her that she had done the men's laundry during the war. Another with eyeglasses had given them gum, she nodded shyly. Everywhere we went were townspeople clutching forty-five-year-old photos, trying to compare the burnished boyish GI faces with the men whose skin had turned to many dry rivers, but whose eyes were searching for that one person who knew them then, who bound up a bullet wound or even sold them baguettes.

Swerving up the steep, narrow mountain road to the next village of their Alpine duty—tiny Isola—I imagined my father in his glory on the motorcycle bending to the precipice as he distributed messages to the battalion. A chapel from the Middle Ages thrust its steeple above the green valley.

"Helluva nice place to live—I wouldn't want to fight a war here," Max Bryan mused.

Phil Hand recalled that after the war his insomnia and bad nerves from the Bulge were relieved only by imagining the period the 551st had spent in the snow-covered Alps, "one of the most beautiful and peaceful things I'd ever known." It was arduous duty, as well. Many of the men had to learn cross-country skiing for their patrols. Some were picked off in the snow by German snipers. Some did the picking.

In November 1944 Dad wrote his sister Jeannette that he helped "serve Mass," avoiding in the V-mail tradition saying where he was. It was the Alps period. Attending Mass in Isola chapel, my brother and I lit a candle and thought of him pouring the cruets as a nineteen-year-old in fatigues. For all his passion, he had a deep well of humility and faith that began to ebb only with the onset of my sister's mental illness in the late 1970s. A rosary taken from a bombed shrine in 1944 by a scout, Joe Cicchinelli—miraculously unhurt—was worn by a statue of the Blessed Mother at Isola chapel. Outside the chapel, Bob Van Horssen of Grand Haven, Michigan—father of ten—gave his wings to a crippled girl.

Before having lunch at the Hôtel de France (which had been badly shelled during the war) we found ourselves made part of a procession for Saint Roch, the local patron, through whose intercession the Black Plague of the Middle Ages bypassed Isola. Down the cobblestones we walked behind a wooden statue of Saint Roch. Someone pointed up a building's high wall. Bullet holes from the war still peppered it. Saint Roch had not spared the village that. And some mute collective protest bone in Isola had kept that evidence from being repaired.

Higher we went, up to 7,000 feet and the last Alpine town patrolled by the 551st—Saint-Etienne de Tinée. We were mobbed. It seemed the entire population of one thousand turned out to greet us. There was another French Army band and a company of French troops for the ceremonies. A gaggle of French generals and an admiral stood pointing and nodding.

Chuck Miller remembered the long, arduous hikes up and down the mountain slope at Saint-Etienne, playing a kind of hide-and-seek with the Germans above: "We'd look up with our binoculars at them, and then they would go down and look up at us." As Melville said of the American Civil War: "All wars are boyish, and are fought by boys."

By midnight we were beautifully beat and traveling down the mountain. In the dark Glenn Miller tunes bathed us in memory, like a warm tide. Doug Dillard had put a tape on:

Hy-a Mister Jackson!" everything's O K-A-L-A-M-A-Z-O
Oh what a gal, a real pipperoo
I'll make my bid for that freckle-faced kid I'm hurrying to.
I'm going to Michigan to see the sweetest gal in Kalamazoo.

Wishing-well Harry, who really had taken to the willowy brunette waitress in Sainte-Etienne ("Tell her she's got class—tell her she's beautiful") in the dimness saw Aunt Jeannette drink some spring water from a bottle.

"Don't drink that water, it'll rust your pipes," Harry said, having a last beer.

"I'm not going to worry about that now!" squawked the near-octagenarian Aunt Jen.

Harry leaned over and flicked on my reading light as I was taking out my notebook. "You gotta put a little life in this life," he made us laugh, garbling "light" for "life." Considering the 551st, perhaps that was not a garble.

At LaTurbie, Joe Cicchinelli took me on a forced march up a hillside to a disturbing memory. In advance of the battalion and with the help of a French civilian, Charles Calori, Cicchinelli and six other GIs lobbed grenades into the machine gun nest in a shack, killing the gunner.

But it was at the shadowy hutch out back—where three more Germans were surprised with bullets—that Cicchinelli jumped back and forth in the underbrush, squeezing his jaw. "One of them didn't die," he shook his head. It was that one, Joe said lowering his voice, that he shot in the head and watched, agog, the youth's brains spill in a stream on the floor.

"What could I do?" Joe raised his head up to the sky. There was no answer—not from the bracken he was breaking as he paced, not from the bleached wood of the shack, not from us.

A shorter version of our father with his weathered tan, mustache, taut strength, and share of ghosts—Cicchinelli had spent years in psychotherapy working on that moment in LaTurbie, a bayonet attack at the Bulge, and months as a POW. Today he counsels Vietnam veterans. He still possesses the ID photos of the three young blond Germans, taken off their bodies fifty years ago.

That hutch. It was the first time Cicchinelli had faced it again since the war. And though he had returned three times to Europe and was staying with a Maquis veteran rather than at our hotel, he admitted, "The reason I come back—I hope by coming I can forget it."

On the dirt path back I came upon the incongruous rusted guts of a piano. My father had met Mother while playing his patented one piano tune at a party. Had he ever killed someone face-to-face in the war? My brother said he had asked him that question once, and that Dad had said, no, he hadn't.

He lied.

Some months after we returned from Europe, his old football pal Bud Lank sent me a revealing tape of his childhood memories of my father.

After the war, and after some months' stay at various Army hospitals for his frozen feet, my father came back to Cleveland. One night he, Lank, and two other ex-GIs (including Tommy Stampfl of the 551st) went out drinking. By midnight they were fairly well loosened up in a bar and began to tell what many GIs would never tell—their darkest moment in the war.

Danny Polamski's moment was his body, or what was left of it—he had lost both legs and an arm to a mine. Lank had broken his leg in a jeep accident. Dad's dark moment was not his injury, however.

He said about forty German soldiers had holed up in a bakery. The 551st opened up with machine guns and rifles. As two Germans tried to escape out the side window, my father shot them both. Later, as he was walking with a squad along a hedgerow, some Germans jumped up. At point blank range, he shot one of them.

At the Battle of the Bulge, the 551st fought through farmland, for the most part. The towns they went through were hardly more than clusters of stone houses—Dairomont, Odrimont. It's probable that the hedgerow incident was in Belgium. But the bakery?

One day I took a close look at an old photo of Joe Cicchinelli crouching with townspeople in Draguignan just after he had helped capture the Nazi general there and had torn down the Nazi flag from the mayor's office. I squinted at the store window behind him. The lettering there said: *Patisserie*.

My father had to kill two men whose faces he could see all too well only a day into battle, a day after the jump into France. It must have stunned him. After 1945 he told no one about it.

In childhood games of cowboys and Indians, Aref was the only kid who always played the Indian, Lank said. It must have jarred the young man who had always been the Indian suddenly to have the lethal upper hand, if only for a few seconds, the way Cicchinelli was shocked enough at LaTurbie to seize the photos of the boys he had killed, as if that would somehow resuscitate them.

Phil Hand spoke of "emptying into" a German soldier at LaMotte. "Fifty others emptied into him," Hand thought, the pure fear of the first day in battle. The idea of killing being an emptying of self—a draining of one, violently, into another—has something pathetically sexual about it, something utterly forlorn. You are emptying more than bullets. Your soul is switched in the kill. You become the dead one. In death he is full of you; in life you are a vacuum.

The day before we left Nice for Belgium, I sat with Cicchinelli on the roof of the Hotel Pullman. The sun glared off the mirror sunglasses of some topless women lounging by the rooftop pool. Around us the great bowl of Nice sparkled—its steeples, clay-tiled roofs, mottled, hazy hills. California by another name.

After a while we stopped talking. Joe fingered a napkin and looked up at me. "How did your father die?"

"He was shot." I startled myself. Few who ask get the truth, and no one else in the 551st asked.

"Who shot him?"

"My sister."

He clamped my hand. His grip was hard, as if he were squeezing the handle of an elevator cut loose in a shaft. His head bent, ticking slightly.

"Oh, ooh."

There was less oxygen in Nice that afternoon, and much less sun, and no topless women. That languid roof shrank into a lonely hutch in back of a photocopy store, a place where people are put out of their misery.

5
Peace in Nice

"I know him."

Phil Hand held up a black-and-white photo of my father, the dashing GI home from the war, Airborne patch on his shoulder, his thick black hair pleasantly awry at the widow's peak, ears lowered. A slight mustache. He looks like Richard Gere. There's a gal nuzzled alongside him, someone who didn't become my mother.

His feet are unfrozen, healed, and though they hurt in the cold, tonight is not cold. The liquor is flowing. He's at a club in Cleveland or at some family shindig. He's manly, confident, but not too confident. He isn't smiling. His eyes are tree-bark in snow.

"I know him."

Phil Hand didn't nod, looking at the photo as we sat on the veranda of our Nice hotel. He was staring steadily through thick glasses. I'd been showing the photo to the men of the 551st from the day we began the journey. Most wanted to recognize him, no doubt, for our sake. But recognition of buddies they knew then takes a while for the old vets, even with flesh-and-blood partners before them.

I began to realize that no one really remembered my father from the war. That would change over the next seven years, to my wonder; for one man, Chuck Bernard, it would take six years for recognition suddenly to hit him in the face. During that first journey the disappointment was real, but no surprise. A battalion is 600 to 800 men; a company is 150 men; a platoon, 40. Only four men from my father's Headquarters Company were on the trip.

In only one of hundreds of Hand's photos was there a face so darkened, so inscrutable, that I could pour my hope into it, one among fifteen faces of grease-smeared men waiting to take off from Italy for the drop into southern France.

"It's yours. Take it." Phil gave the shade-man to me. I had thought the trip might lessen, not lengthen, the shadows I had come to live with.

Our Nice farewell speaker that night at dinner was fifty-one-year-old Rear Admiral H. G. (Hank) Chiles, Jr., then commander of a submarine group with the U.S. Sixth Fleet.[5] "I and many of my generation stand in awe of you and the sacrifice of your generation during World War II," Chiles told the men. "You see, you are *legends*." The men, most of whom were privates during the war, looked stunned. To be praised by an admiral in such an intimate setting for feats long ago forgotten by the high brass was disorienting, to say the least.

Pointing to successful fleet exchange visits to Norfolk and Sebastopol under *perestroika* (the Soviet Union was to dissolve into fifteen states in two years with hardly a shot fired), Chiles told the vets, "There are signs of a more peaceful world, signs that perhaps future generations of Americans might know a world less disposed to violence than what you saw and fought for.

Who of us doesn't want to believe that? Yet I saw in my mind's eye the hot muzzle of my sister's gun—the wreckage it wreaked in a few seconds. That had nothing to do with Communism, *perestroika*, or external enemies of any kind. If all the wars in the world suddenly stopped, the impossible time bomb of our waste would have to be dismantled; 200 million guns, 60 million of them handguns, would remain marking time in their American drawers, closets, beds, hands. And 2 million people as sick as my sister was sick.

A poet of Russia's Silver Age, Valery Bryusov, noted that there are those who are freedom's "captives."

Admiral Chiles ended with a surprisingly pacifist reference to a soldier at Verdun, tipped his cap once again to the 551st for its "great contribution to freedom," and asked the men and their families to pray "for an America strong in peace so we don't have to be strong in war." I couldn't have agreed more. Two hundred million guns on our streets and in homes is not strength.

6
We are what we remember

The community of memory—the only community that lasts—quickened in the men when by train and bus following the route the 551st took in December 1944 as it rushed to the Ardennes to help stop Hitler's last onslaught, we arrived in Belgium. Few of the returning GOYA veterans approached the last killing field "with tranquil restoration," as Wordsworth would have it.

Memory. Drawn like moths to the flame of it, worried as to what it might contain, avid to share it with loved ones who might believe the otherwise unbelievable, or in Cicchinelli's case, to burn it so hot in the soul it would finally cool and come off like a scab. What else but memory makes us human? As if preparing for the original battle, however hard, the old men seemed to say: *We are what we remember.* Not the half of it we nurse or suppress, but the whole of it we find, usually, with others.

Five facts: Ardennes horses, more nervous and quicker than most, are exported to the United States. Belgians are the largest per capita drinkers of beer in the world. The towns of eastern Belgium in the Ardennes have been crushed three times this century by invading Germans. The world's largest mushroom industry based here uses the cool, damp old Nazi bunkers for growth. And lastly, according to our host, the former Belgian resistance leader Leo Carlier, Belgians are obstinately independent, each wanting "his house to be different." That sounded like 551st territory. It was also the scene of Hitler's last stand.

More than 600,000 Americans fought in the Ardennes in the six weeks after December 16, 1944, their fiercest clash of the war in Europe. They took most of the 81,000 Allied casualties in that battle. No one thought Hitler would attack in the dense Ardennes forest, or would intensify the attack in the midst of the worst European winter recorded in the century. He did both.

Pine shadows dappled the men on the bus while Carlier related, "You have been the 'unknown soldiers,' the 551st. I met Colonel Dillard in 1985 and heard for the first time about your story and your destruction. I promised him we would make a memorial and I vowed you would never be forgotten. Tomorrow, you will be invaded."

He wasn't kidding. Hundreds of people, some from as far as Brussels, showed up for the dedication. A poster inside the town hall at Lierneux still warned children not to touch live bullets and shells in the fields, destructive relics of two world wars.

Now in the village of Rochelinval a monument to the 551st exists. Not the Americans, not the U.S. Army, but the Belgians themselves built the stone memorial; it took them two years. A young construction equipment operator, Claude Orban, did much of the spade work. We watched in hushed silence as Heide and Bo Wilson, grandchildren of Lieutenant Colonel Joerg, who was killed in an artillery treeburst nearby, unveiled the memorial.

The next day, our last, the men roamed the fields and the woods. I stood with Chuck Fairlamb, who fired the first mortar in the December 27, 1944, raid on Noirefontaine ordered by General Gavin that commenced the Allied rollback on the northern tier of the Bulge. We stood together on the green turf where that mortar round was lobbed so long ago. Only the buzz of gnats disturbed our ears.

From January 3 to January 7, 1945, over a snow-filled, forested area south of Trois Ponts, the 551st pushed the Germans back 3 miles in five days to the Salm River—very slow, agonized fighting, often hand-to-hand combat. "It's always easier to defend, as at Bastogne, than to attack, as we did toward Rochelinval," Phil Hand explained. "We had to swing over the area like a gate."

"By God, did we take that many casualties in that small area?" wondered Doug Dillard, who feels closer to the 551st than to battalions he himself commanded in Korea and Vietnam. Dillard pointed out a creek where the men soaked their boots, the beginning of their battle with frostbitten feet and trenchfoot in the subzero weather. My father's feet froze up; he was evacuated to Liège. When I leapt over a barbed wire fence to photograph the creek, the men smiled.

It is not easy to picture in the green, silent farmland, but many froze to death, too. No overshoes were issued. The men were under a merciless order not to wear overcoats so that they would be distinguishable from Germans and could supposedly move faster. Cicchinelli remembered firing ("We were so pissed") at overcoat-clad 517th Regiment GIs. Hand recalled soldiers "circling a little sapling which they gripped," trying to stay both awake and warm. Sleep was death. After three days of little sleep or food some slept.

On January 4, 1945, one of the few fixed-bayonet attacks in the European theater occurred, carried out by Company A of the 551st. "I could very well have blocked it all out because of this day," Miller admitted. "And you know, I'm German. It's such a dirty shame that someone like Hitler could change people's psyches the way he did."

Finally we faced the 500-yard meadow sloping down from a hill then abruptly up to Rochelinval, now green, but covered on January 7, 1945, with a foot and a half of snow. Of the thousand rounds of artillery available to the 551st for its attack on Rochelinval, only four were shot off at dawn. Joerg tried to get the half-crazed unit relieved, to have the attack called off. All he got was an order to take the town, which was ringed by dug-in Germans and their machine guns.

Incredibly, their commander killed by an artillery treeburst, down to fewer than a hundred men and a dozen officers, the 551st crested the last hill and took Rochelinval, pushing the Germans back across the Salm River.

In late January 1945 General Gavin told the 551st that it had been disbanded by the Department of the Army. Survivors filtered elsewhere. As Harry Renick put it, "I was disintegrated into the 82d Airborne." How strange it is that these precious men could receive the French Croix de Guerre from General de Gaulle and many years later see a monument erected to their sacrifice in Belgium, but be completely ignored by their own country. For years the men talked about the Presidential Unit Citation somehow lost in the snow, but their hopes have dwindled.

7
Getting my orders down deep

One night in Liège, Fred Hilgardner of Missouri made me aware that my brother and I were not alone in our search.

"I'm retracing my father's steps, just like you," he said, taking a pull of his cigarette. The elder Hilgardner had lost a leg during World War I at the nearby Meuse-Argonne, and had died when his son was barely a year old. "Everybody loved him," Fred crushed his cigarette, and in the furl of smoke I saw emerge one last time in Belgium the phoenix-genie of our father.

Whether or not flag-burning should be unlawful, sentiments such as Fred Hilgardner's should never be taken lightly: "They'll play the national anthem at a ballgame—players will scratch their nuts, chew gum. Men in the stands sucking their beer, not taking off their caps. The flag means more to me than a piece of cloth. It represents men's lives." There is no blind patriotism in the 551st—quite the contrary. Becoming "a shadow battalion," as Dan Morgan calls it, ensured that. Medals are not what the 551st is after. "Setting the record straight" for a handful of children and grandchildren as to what their fathers did in history's near-suicide was really the purpose of going back, as Doug Dillard intimated one night.

Suddenly Hilgardner had a vision and tapped me on the shoulder. "You get around these guys and you don't seem so damn old. You know, there were two guys that last night in Nice who'd swing a gal around so well. They topped everybody. They danced jitterbug. Maybe your Dad was one of them."

It became clear to me. From the first day of the trip, when Joe Thibault, whose son died of a drug overdose at thirty-nine, came over with tears in his eyes, gripping me on the shoulder, to Otto's sequestered motorcycle, to Phil Hand's shadowy photo, to Hilgardner's last dancer, that the men of the 551st were looking for their messenger. He was unknown. That made him all the more sought-after.

I vowed then and there that I would find him, through them. My brother Mark caught it well in his toast at the farewell dinner in Liège: "It's been painful to realize that none of you knew Dad personally. But I must tell you extraordinary men that in these short days I found a piece of my father in every one of you."

It remained then to trace the pieces, to fit them in place, so that the shattered mosaic of a lost battalion could become fixed for time beyond each of their leavings.

II

HELLO, EARTH!

Training to Be Airborne

It is very lonely for a young man to be a seed in the wind.

—Norman Maclean

1
Contact

On November 29, 1942, my father's old sandlot football team, the Cleveland Olympics, defeated its crosstown rival, the Scarlet Hawks, 6–0, in a warmup game at Shaw Stadium before the professional Cleveland Rams took the field. That very month the 551st began to form up at Fort Benning, Georgia, exactly three months before Aref Orfalea himself would be drafted into the U.S. Army.

To what extent the Cleveland Olympics were kept together—raised to a fever pitch of devotion—by their coach, Ross Mudler, as an inducement to stay home from the war is hard to tell. But there was little doubt in my mind as I spoke with his old teammates at a reunion in East Cleveland in 1990 that Coach Mudler himself was angry about the way the war was chipping away at his starting lineup and his reserves. It appears Mudler—a lifelong bachelor who stored Olympics' gear and held chalkboard sessions in his mother's basement—had memories of World War I and was outraged that a second worldwide slaughter was on.

Mudler stood up that night, older than the old men around him. Even though he was well into his eighties, with a broken hip, the old Olympics coach had a clear, sharp look in his eyes, and his hair showed more steel-gray than what hair was left to his old players. It was immaculately slicked back with water from the brow, as had been common in the 1940s.

What issued forth from the little makeshift podium was a trumpet blast: "There were no playing fields then, and most equipment was too expensive for us. You should take pride in the fact that your football organization was housed in the basement of a home. Because of my age and impairment, I think of eight kids who went to war and never came back. It is unfortunate for a father to lose his sons to that ultimate obscenity called war."

In danger of losing control of his emotions, Mudler paused, cleared his throat, then recited from memory:

Sleep, my sons.
Sleep in the silent depths of the sea
Or in your bed of hallowed sod,
Until you hear at dawn
The low, clear reveille of God.[1]

Mudler pointed to the gentle giant Billy Vance (my father's favorite in anecdote), who had come in with a cane: "That was the greatest tackle in Cleveland." In fact, like most Olympics players, Vance was not beefy enough in high school (tackles needing 200 pounds) to earn his letter. That made no difference to Mudler: "There is something about a good tackle you can't duplicate."

From the times he would barrel into a rusher as a tight end or knock down a runner as a defensive back, to the days he was unemployed many years later and held my mother in the kitchen long, very long, as if giving up the clinch would be giving up the lifeline, my father's craving for contact was a constant in his life. Was that why he went to war?

Billy Vance moved his thick glasses and cane, and turned to me: "There was a game we played on sleet and slush. I'll take out the defense, you make the tackle, I told your Dad. And he did. Oh, I remember your grandmother calling him, 'Ah-Riff! Ah-Riff!' She once tried to put a blanket over his shoulders on the bench."

The one-woman cheering section, was Nazera Orfalea. The Orfalea household in Cleveland was like a collection of magnets with too similar a charge. Some, like my father and his oldest sister, Jeannette, were repelled outward. Though the Orfaleas were hardly of a military pedigree (many early Syrians, like Aref Senior, came to the United States at the turn of the century to avoid fighting in the Turkish Army), by the time of the Cleveland Olympics' victory in Shaw Stadium my father's brother, George, had already gone to war and was being promoted at his Army outpost in Burma.

George, in fact, stayed in the Army after the war, commanded the military guard at Los Alamos during the first hydrogen bomb tests, and rose to the rank of major before retiring early partly due to misgivings over the escalating Vietnam War. So by the winter of 1942 Aref Junior—restless by nature, contact-driven, a speed skater—was feeling left behind.

It is hard to understand today the excitement the sandlot football teams engendered in Midwestern cities in the 1930s and early 1940s.[2] The sandlot teams pretty much disappeared before the war was over, their ranks exhausted by the GI drain. Ross Mudler's Cleveland Olympics were the last of a proud, even loving tradition of that slop-in-the-mud sport. And for a time, for a boy, they held the war at bay.

I can see it now: my father running down the long column of steps from Mannering Road, his breath climbing the night air as he descends. At the streetcar stop on Euclid Avenue he meets Bud Lank, who promises him a breadbasket pass, and Billy Vance, who promises him a block as far as Lake Erie. The streetcar picks up passengers going to the game from the great old New York Central roundhouse, that iron cave which will stand half a century later mute and empty to Aref's son.

It's not hard to place myself among the 10,000 people at Shaw Stadium (there will be more for the game to follow with the pro Rams). I like being lost in the lights, lost in the cheers and whoops. Bud Lank has sent me the official program of that Sunday night—November 29, 1942—and it informs me that "Orf Orfalea" is playing right end next to Billy Vance at right tackle, and that he is wearing number 12. His nickname is the same as mine was all those school years. A kind of dog bark. The number is unlucky: boxcars. In college dorm football I, too, played end. We were both good with our hands.

While I am reading the program ads, Dad is placing his helmet—not unlike the first one he will use in jumping from an airplane—in front of him as he does situps to get loose. Soon the teams are airborne on the ground, as the crowd lifts with the first kickoff and everyone for one still moment is weightless, before the drop and the catch. Now the Scarlet Hawk blood spills into the black and white. Now there are young men sprawled on the ground. Bud Lank, who spent his life leading those who work with their hands (bricklayers) in unions, later tells me, "Aref and I were so tired we tripped over each other going into the locker room at halftime." No score yet.

At some point in the second half, with the two midget titans battling it out for citywide supremacy, Lank sends Orf long, no damn stop-and-go, because if you stop in this mud you'll never go again, just go as best as you can toward the goalpost. Lank chugs backward, tries to get a stable footing but can't, flips the ball to reserve fullback Bill Cerbin, who seems to be paddle-handing it away from frenzied tacklers. Finally, he grips it with everything he's got, throwing his shoulder out from a pass he's not used to attempting, and my father goes aloft, seeing the ball block out the moon. Just at that moment, halfback Johnny Hart smothers it just shy of Orf and slides his way to the goal line and over for the win. Not even an extra point. A bare-bones victory, 6–0.

My father falls on his chest in the young snow and the cold of it goes straight to his heart. He is happy, make no mistake: That someone who got it was his teammate. But he is empty, he is hugging not leather but a pile of young snow.

Billy Vance turned to me that night in East Cleveland, letting his cane drop to the floor. "About your sister and your father. Look. That is what the Lord was thinking of in the Garden of Gethsemane."

About the time my father caught nothing but snow in Cleveland, Major Wood Joerg at Fort Benning first ran his eyes down a list of names of some young men who were good with their hands, very athletic, and ready for the sky—the men of the 551st Parachute Infantry Battalion. And Georgia in November is warm as the Garden of Gethsemane.

2
A family steeped in war

Like his soon-to-be messenger, Wood Joerg had an older brother (Robert III) who beat him to war. But there the similarity between private and colonel ends. If my father's entry into the Army and paratrooping during World War II seem ordained by the patiotism of the time, an anxious home seized by unemployment, and his temperament, Wood Joerg's service in khaki at the head of a paratrooper battalion—one with almost no parallel—was set in stone long before his birth. Unlike my father's quaint immigrant family, the Joergs came from a proud Germanic military tradition, where leadership took its risks and stood out. (The Germans were the largest ethnic group in America.) In fact, General Douglas MacArthur once called Wood's father, Major Robert Joerg II, the finest regimental officer he had ever met.

The Joerg pedigree wasn't completely gung ho, however. In fact, Wood's grandfather, Robert I, had immigrated from Frankfurt, Germany, in 1884 to Columbus, Georgia, with the express purpose of avoiding service in the army of the "Iron Chancellor," Otto von Bismarck. He became a successful cotton broker. Still, devotion to the military came from both sides of Wood's family, and traveled far back on his mother Elizabeth Guice's side to the nation's beginnings. (They were descended from the royal French de Guice family.) Old Guice land deeds date from the pre–Revolutionary War period in Alabama. Juhan Guice had served on the staff of General George Washington. A great-uncle Ridenour, who fought in Stonewall Jackson's brigade during the Civil War, was wounded several times, finally getting his hand shot off at the Battle of Petersburg. He walked with bleeding wound all the way from Appomatox, Virginia, back to Eufala, Alabama, where he died in 1904.

Thus Wood Joerg was prepared for World War II before the cradle. He was born on December 14, 1914, in Eufala, Alabama, on a reservoir of the Chatahoochie River straddling the border across from Georgetown, Georgia. Barely an infant of two, he was taken by his parents to straddle the Mexican border of Texas and New Mexico, where his father was sent to chase the patriot-bandit Pancho Villa. Fatefully, a young officer with the senior Joerg for those forays into Mexico was Matthew Ridgway, under whom Wood would serve at the Battle of the Bulge.

In World War I Major Joerg was regimental adjutant of the 167th Infantry Regiment, composed of Alabama National Guardsmen, in the famed 42d "Rainbow" Division. It was there that he caught the eye of MacArthur, the division's chief of staff. The Alabamians had established themselves as a force to be reckoned with before going overseas. In training at Camp Mills, New York, they took "an instant dislike"[3] to one of the other regiments of the division—the local 165th—and the New Yorkers returned the compliment. Just before setting off for Europe there was a riotous fight between the two regiments in which one Alabama soldier was killed. The incident never made the newspapers and was transmogrified into a harmless spat in a 1940 movie with James Cagney and Pat O'Brien, *The Fighting 69th*.

In 1918, at the Vosges, Major Joerg "took a deep breath, and that deep breath did me in."[4] It was gas. While he recuperated in a hospital, he tried to contact family members in Frankfurt, Germany. They would not respond. Somehow word reached him that they were afraid to respond; "consorting with the enemy" was hazardous. Wood's father was bitter about that all his life. He uttered not an *umlaut* after the war.

It is uncanny how much of the World War II life of Wood Joerg tracked that of his father a world war earlier—from the tragedy in training, to volatile troops in Europe, even to trying unsuccessfully to contact German family members in the midst of war.

"Hard Robert" they called Wood's father. From an early age Wood Joerg seems to have craved an affection and warmth his hard, authoritarian father could not soberly display. He didn't drink a drop; his father drank gallons. He wasn't "hard." Born and raised straddling borders and the emotions of two headstrong parents who finally exploded apart, Wood Joerg was familiar with conflicting allegiances, for example, to his cantankerous, outrider men and to Army authority. As an Army brat schoolboy in Puerto Rico, he picked up Spanish and moved easily among the civilian population (and later used it for wicked comedy routines at West Point). He was a Southerner with a deep, slow accent in the Northern world of the Point, a man with an infectious sense of humor and of the ridiculous, someone who could charm a potential enemy or stranger, someone who had to work hard to fit, who developed a sense of story to overcome the strange or threatening.

What is certain, I think, is that the man who would be chosen to lead the 82d Airborne's counterattack at the Battle of the Bulge had an acute sense of the underdog, of mortality, and of the Other. You see the sensitivity in the eyes in photographs. To Heidi Joerg, "They were a deer's eyes—beautiful and large." Amber eyes, dark brown almost black short hair, full lips, and a head that bent to make himself appear shorter than he was. He grew to be 6 feet 1 inch, and shrank himself to get to the 6-foot limit for a paratrooper.

Just as his parents filed for divorce, Wood entered West Point in the summer of 1933 to undergo plebe hazing excessive even by Point standards. Several of his classmates remark on the singular punishment he took. Being boyish and winsome was one thing, of course. Another was that his brother Robert III had flunked out the year before. As it is the way of schoolmates to go for the weak spot, the younger Joerg was pushed to the brink. Somehow he hung on, not by the force of pure gray matter, but with masque. While hustling around for the seniors as an orderly, and walking "area" punishment tours for hours, the first of three close friends died. It was Roscoe Davis, his first roommate. That sent Joerg into paroxysms of inner anguish that changed his native lightheartedness into the more manic defense known as burlesque.

By junior year Joerg had developed a soft spot for plebes and for pie. The latter he received in the face as a climactic ad lib during the Point's variety revue, "The Hundredth Night Show." In senior year, sitting in the second to the last seat in the room (a reflection of low grades) of the Military and Civil Law class, he would often turn to the cadet with the worst grades in the class sitting behind him in the last seat—a Chinese exchange student—and announce when the fellow missed a question, "Mr. Yen, you have lost face." Needless to say, over several months that wore on Yen, but something of America rubbed off on him as he plotted and took his vengeance the day of the June Graduation Parade. At noon in the mess hall, with Cadet Joerg as Table Commandant, someone starting throwing food. It hit the officer in charge, who was standing right behind Joerg; he promptly sentenced Wood to three hours' punishment tour with rifle (borrowed, ignominiously, from an underclassman, as his own and those of all pending graduates had been checked with the Quartermaster). He canceled his afternoon date and some of his pride and ended his solitary area march, the laughter of his fellows ringing in his ears, at the Sallyport, where stood Mr. Yen, grinning from ear to ear, who shrieked, "Mr. Joerg, you have lost face!"

If he was not the most scholarly, or the most careful, cadet in the Class of 1937, he was probably the best loved of that West Point class, as attested by dozens of testimonials by classmates, many retired generals and colonels, at a 551st reunion in New Orleans in 1987. With the war brewing, there was a place for a rebel with a cause. "He was extremely outgoing and pleasant and developed a large group of friends in the Corps," William H. Lewis recalled. "I remember him as an unreconstructed rebel from Georgia. He retained his rich Southern accent and did not submit to regulation and discipline."

Rebels need anchors, and Wood Joerg's came within a year of his graduation, during his first assignment at Fort Sam Houston in San Antonio. Over Thanksgiving in 1937, at a "tea dance" Lieutenant Joerg met Ethel Holmgreen. Over half a century later, she recalled that first meeting: "He was so tall. And I went home and said, 'Mama, a big old boy from Georgia danced with me and he had a mouth full of white teeth.'"

Enticed himself, Joerg asked her out the next day, only to find that Ethel had returned to Baylor University. About a year later he escorted her to another tea dance, took her out the next day, and proposed marriage. It was February 6, 1939.

"When you know me better, do you think you will?"

"I think I will," Ethel said.

And that was it. Marriage proposal made and accepted on the second date, without even mentioning the word marriage. For such an extrovert, remarkably subtle, even shy. As for Ethel, she actually had the fraternity pin of another man (who would become a San Antonio judge) and was as good as engaged to him, but "he didn't send me so much." Ah yes, to be *sent*. To be crushed to a chest, stuffed in, licked, stamped, and airmailed.

The next day Ethel had a dozen red roses. In three weeks she had a West Point ring. Within a month she had a new first name. It appears that Wood Joerg had been dating two other Ethels when he was sent by Ethel Holmgreen. One day as they were out walking Ethel the Third, who had muscular legs from tennis, blurted, "I look like a Swiss Alps mountain climber in a bathing suit."

"Well, good, I'll call you Heidi of the Swiss Alps."

Ethel Holmgreen liked her new name, actually. The proliferation of Ethels in the 1930s and 1940s was not a boon for female nomenclature, and it is no surprise that there are almost no Ethels left on the planet. Wood Joerg was on to something. I am not sure the problem can be blamed on the fact that antiknock gas in the 1950s was called "ethyl."

The rush of the oncoming war could make two dates matter more. You could feel it after Hitler annexed Austria and then the Sudetenland, a mounting pressure on everyone around you to *mate*. But there were hurdles yet. Heidi's father, who owned the war matériel–producing Alamo Iron Works, thought Wood hadn't a serious bone in his body, was "fluff," as Heidi recalled. Wood's mother, a tough cookie who lived to be ninety-six, was living with him at the time in San Antonio. He was totally absorbed in his job, especially in coaching the 9th Infantry's boxing team to an Army boxing championship in the spring of 1939.

Nevertheless, one month after Hitler invaded Poland, on September 30, 1939, Wood Joerg and Ethel Holmgreen were married at the Fort Sam Houston chapel and drove straightoff to the Gulf of Texas for their honeymoon. Before Wood bought a newspaper or checked into a motel, he made a beeline for Western Union in Galveston and wired back to Parker Calvert, a Point classmate who had given the couple an encyclopedia of sex as a wedding present: "Do not understand page 299. What do I do next?"

One of the first things Wood Joerg did after his honeymoon was take out a life insurance policy. The reason was not the looming war, really, but the second loss of a childhood friend the year before.In the summer of 1938 back in San Antonio, cousin George Joerg, fifteen, had visited Wood from Georgia and while swimming in a pool on the base, adrenalin from glands in his neck popped open, shot to his brain and killed him. He was found floating face down. Shocked, Lieutenant Joerg, twenty-two, took the body home to Georgia and a year later took out the life insurance policy, naming his new wife as beneficiary. Two deaths of boyhood friends before he'd even gone overseas. Maybe there would be no overseas.

The third youthful death affecting Wood Joerg came two years into the couple's next assignment, at Fort Ord, California. There in picturesque Carmel-by-the-Sea they were visited by Wood's close friend and classmate Colin Kelly, by then a pilot with the Army Air Corps. Heidi was pregnant with their first child.

Looking to his own young son, Kelly announced, "If it's a boy, Corky will room with him; if it's a girl, he'll date her."

On December 7, 1941, while Heidi Joerg nursed her ten-month-old girl Charlotte, the Japanese attacked Pearl Harbor, losing sixty-five men but killing 2,330 Americans, many in their sleep, half of them on the battleship

Arizona. Churchill's first comment at a secret briefing by Roosevelt was, "What a holocaust!" Most history books say that 188 American planes were destroyed on the ground. But one that flew two days later into legend was the B-17 bomber of Colin Kelly, one of the first American pilots killed in the air in World War II. Kelly's exploits, for which he received a posthumous Distinguished Service Cross, were spun into a popular song during the war, though Paul Fussell deflates the myth somewhat. As the song goes, Kelly dropped a bomb right down the smokestack of the Japanese battleship *Haruna,* doing a kamikaze dive into its deck. What actually happened was that on December 9 Kelly bombed a "barely armed" Japanese troop transport in the Philippines and was set spinning to the sea in flame by a Japanese fighter. His crew bailed out, though Fussell wryly notes that Kelly may have tried to jump first but got his parachute caught on the escape door, and he was pinned to the falling plane.[5]

Be that as it may, Kelly's death expanded the dark cloud over Wood Joerg's prewar life. Three friends of youth gone. The idyllic Monterey Peninsula was no place to be now. It was time to go to war.

Like many ambitious officers, Joerg had wanted to be a pilot, but scar tissue on an eardrum kept him from passing the physical. Ironically, the same day he received orders to Benning, he received other orders to enter the Army Air Corps, the rush to war apparently overlooking that ear. But for him piloting had lost its luster; being airborne was newer. In 1940 Joerg had listened with wonder at Fort Ord to reports of American soldiers jumping out of planes for the first time back home at Benning. Through 1941 he made note of the quickly escalating program to match the Germans body-for-body in the air; by the time of the attack on Pearl Harbor, four parachute battalions had already been formed. The first—the 501st—had already been sent to Panama.

When Joerg arrived at Fort Benning and first saw the 250–foot jump towers, adrenalin laced his stomach. He had had a lot of emptiness to jump through. And there it was.

3

Geronimo!

Steadily during 1941 and 1942 the magnet of Fort Benning began to pull men from around the United States, where they would meet another magnet that would pull them to their deaths in ten seconds if their chutes didn't open or, if they did, ask them to stand up fifty seconds after jumping from the plane and face someone or something that wanted to kill them. That had never happened before to Americans. The sense of purpose, excitement, and fear was palpable from the jump towers to the latrines.

The parachute predated the plane in history. The whole world of para-chuting traces back to the era of hot-air balloons and the first attempts of man to fly. If the parachute, not to mention parachuting in combat, was still in the experimental stage for the Allies as the 551st formed up in 1942, it was an experiment that stretched back five hundred years to Leonardo da Vinci. (For that matter, the experiment continued to stretch ahead after the war to the hang gliders and mini-jet-propelled astronauts of today.)

The man who painted the most enigmatic smile in history on the Mona Lisa wrote in the *Codex Atlanticus* that a "tent of linen" with "stopped up" apertures 12 braccia across by 12 feet in depth would enable a man "to throw himself down from any great height without sustaining injury."[6] Thankfully there is no record of Leonardo's having attempted to prove his theory himself, else the world may have been short one quite enigmatic smile. But the theory, and the drawing of it, are remarkably close to what actually became the first parachute.

It was not until 1785, however, that someone actually got around to taking Leonardo up on his idea, and that someone was a dog. On a clear day several hundred feet above Paris, the balloonist Jean Pierre Blanchard threw his pet pooch out of the basket attached by harness to a crude cloth canopy. Amazingly, it made a perfect four-foot landing, but the dog then beat it out of sight, probably to join the Revolution.

The first recorded man to go from air to ground in a chute was an Eng-lishman named Robert Cocking. Cocking thought an inverted parachute might solve some problems he had observed in experiments with "turbu-lence" in the canopy. His chute was made of tin tubing, light wood, and Irish linen, and it resembled a giant upside-down umbrella. On July 24, 1837, the Englishman sailed downward to his death, the victim of wind and Irish linen. There may have been some legislators in the horrified crowd: For quite a while afterward parachuting was banned in England. (What affect this all had on the Irish troubles is not recorded.) No one seems to have questioned the weird notion of an upside-down umbrella.

The historic moment of success came in 1887, in America. Before a sellout crowd in Golden Gate Park in San Francisco, two American broth-ers—Samuel and Thomas Baldwin—took their skills as high-wire walkers into a large balloon basket, the *Eclipse*, with a special invention of theirs, a container housing an all-cloth parachute tied by rope to Tom Baldwin's body harness. Five thousand feet up, Tom, twenty-nine and looking like a man who was not going to reach thirty, stood on the edge of the giant wicker basket, greeted his Maker, and jumped. The weight of his body pulled the chute out of the container, and in just the time a paratrooper today counts before pulling an emergency chute—five seconds—the canopy whooped open and lowered him gently to earth. The crowd mobbed him, the ladies kissing him through the chute.

An era had begun. Soon people were jumping from balloons all over the planet, one method more death-defying than the other. A German couple engaged to be married thrilled crowds by using a risky "cutaway" method still used by some today—jumping together, each with two inflating chutes, the first cutting away and floating skyward when the second inflated.

Though the Wright Brothers made their epic flight over the sands of Kitty Hawk in 1903, for a while it seems not to have occurred to anyone that a parachute could pluck a pilot from a crashing dive. Two years shy of World War I, however, on February 28, 1912, a civilian named Albert Berry made the first successful parachute jump from an airplane, significantly at an Army post, Jefferson Barracks, Missouri. Berry missed the field and landed behind the mess hall, where the astonished soldiers—most of whom had never seen an airplane, much less a parachute—carried him to dinner.

The link between the parachute and the American military grew quickly, though not quickly enough for it to be used in combat in the Great War. Shortly before the outbreak of World War I, a carnival balloon designer named Charles Broadwick tested two inventions that would last in one form or another of parachuting—a static line and a backpacked parachute, called then a "parachute coat." In April 1914 Broadwick's adopted daughter, Tiny, twenty-two, demonstrated both jumping from a Curtis biplane and landing with precision and elegance at the U.S. Army Flying School in San Diego, to the amazement of the head of the Army Signal Corps, General Scriven.

The new parachute was put into immediate service by sausage-shaped balloon crews, which had been used in combat since the American Civil War as aerial observation posts and were now vulnerable to airplane gunfire. Many a Messerschmidt over Flanders exploded spy balloons, causing a rain of parachutists to fall with binoculars still in hand. The record for most parachute jumps by an American during World War I was made by Lieutenant Phelps of New York City, who bailed out of inflamed balloons five times. Possibly because of the cramped cockpit (or their early sense of invulnerability), pilots did not avail themselves of the last resort of a parachute until late in the war. Germany was the only country to issue its pilots parachutes, and then only in May 1918, when the war was almost over.

Through the interwar years, experiments continued. The 1922 requirement that all military aviators wear parachutes issued directly from the first successful jump with a "free fall" type of parachute—not one attached, as static line chutes were, by strap to steel cable in the airplane, but solely to the jumper's body. Without that key demonstration, the development of the concept of a reserve emergency chute would have been impossible. It must be credited to the design and the April 28, 1919, epic leap at McCook Field in Ohio of Leslie "Sky High" Irvin.

In the Roaring Twenties, the parachute saved the lives of the famed pilots Charles Lindbergh (three times), Amelia Earhart, and Jimmy Doolittle. But while Colonel Billy Mitchell's old plans for fighting paratroopers were mothballed, and most of the West saw the parachute as little more than a safety device, in 1927 the Italians began experimenting with dropping infantry by chute from planes. Then the 1931 Japanese invasion of Manchuria changed everything. The Soviet Union, reminded of its costly Russo-Japanese War in 1906, began to worry about a possible invasion, and by the fall of 1931 a test parachute unit was formed out of the 11th Rifle Division of the Russian Army, the first of its kind in history.

By 1936 Soviet paratroop regiments had conducted mass jumping exercises around Moscow and Kiev and in Belorussia. Though they had trained for defense, the first use of paratroop soldiers in foreign combat was on November 30, 1939, when a small detachment of Russian men were airdropped as part of a general attack on Finland. The drop—far north in Finland at Petsamo—was inconsequential. The attack bogged down, but intelligence wires were hot with the news that paratroopers had actually been used in war.

The purpose of air-landed troops was, in a word, chaos. The longstanding Magna Carta of paratroop tactics, the *Soviet Field Service Regulations* (1936), states paratroopers' chief purpose as "disorganizing the enemy's command and control." The element of confusion, the extra thresholds for surprise attack, the chance to outfox far greater or better-armed units—this was the air soldier's mission from the start.

Military parachute schools opened in Avignon, France (1935) and for the fascist army of Mussolini in Tripoli, Libya, and in Tarquinia (1938). But the first user of sizable airborne combat forces was actually Germany, when in 1933—the year Wood Joerg entered West Point—Hitler's new government dropped paratroopers not on foreigners but on his own people. For two weeks in February, a Berlin police parachute unit founded by Hermann Goering was airdropped over sections of the city where German Communists were in hiding. Thus did paratrooping in battle make its debut in an exhibition of terrorism, Germans landing on German roofs, in German gardens, pulling out fellow Germans to be summarily executed against an alley wall or right there in their living rooms.

Soon those airstorming police were forged into Goering's Luftwaffe, and the size and strength of Nazi airborne *(fallschirmjaeger)* troops burgeoned. By 1938 under Major General Kurt Student, a World War I pilot hero, German divisions of paratroopers were created. The occupation of the Rhineland in violation of the Versailles Treaty, the *Anschluss* with Austria, the taking of the Sudetenland of Czechoslovakia, and even the 1939 invasion of Poland were already accomplished before the Nazis unleashed Student's intensely loyal, skilled paratroopers. They were saved for the *blitzkrieg* of Belgium, Holland, and France.

On May 11, 1940, while Lieutenant Wood Joerg embraced his pregnant wife Heidi at Fort Sam Houston, a German parachute engineer unit landed by glider atop what was supposed to be the strongest military preserve in the world—a nine-fort complex known as Fort Eben-Emael just north of Liège, Belgium. Stunned by the demolition charges the German paratroopers exploded everywhere, the impregnable fort fell in hours. Simultaneously, Student's troopers in thirty gliders crashed across the Meuse River but managed to take three key bridges, while five hundred other German paratroopers fell upon Holland's bridges and airports, seizing them all. Those spearhead attacks opened the way for a panzer juggernaut such as the world had never seen. For the German Army, it was an exhilarating, glory-bound offensive that left them convinced they would be the masters of Europe as their leader had prophesied. After six weeks of the 1940 blitz, Hitler walked down the Champs Elysées and turned to regard a Paris dark and silent. He had won, for now, but the Parisians had turned the lights off.

After the rout of Poland had begun, in January 1940 General George Marshall gave orders to a World War I veteran commander, Major William Lee, to begin training paratroopers. But it wasn't until May, after Germany's extraordinary capture of Eben-Emael with airdropped soldiers, that a U.S. "Parachute Test Platoon" was given the green light. Lee would become known as "the father" of American paratroopers.

The pedigree of my own father's battalion traces directly to that original test platoon. On August 16, 1940, over Fort Benning, Georgia, forty-eight quivering bodies in airtight "Knute Rockne" football helmets followed the first scream "Geronimo!" out the door of a plane; their yells were quickly swallowed by a 110-mile-per-hour wind off the plane. Among the first American soldiers to do such a crazy thing was PFC Willie F. "Spotlight" Brown, who four years later jumped as part of the 551st over southern France.[7] So nicknamed because he was nearly bald at a young age, Brown would later perform in Panama with the GOYAs what one career officer said was the worst act of insubordination he saw in the military.

The original two hundred volunteers from the 29th Infantry Regiment at Fort Benning for the Test Platoon included Lieutenant William Yarborough, who later commanded the famed 509th Parachute Infantry Battalion, the first American paratroopers to be used in combat (over North Africa in Operation Torch). In France, the 509th fought near its brother separate unit, the 551st. A final Test Platoon selection, PFC Jules Corbin, was the brother of Sergeant Ernest Corbin, who served in the soon-to-emerge 551st.

How were the forty-eight men of the Test Platoon selected? They had to be "rugged, athletically inclined" and possessing "high leadership qualities."[8] They had to pass the stiff medical exam given for pilots-to-be, have two years' service logged, and weigh no more than 185 pounds (there were no height limits for that original group). The officers vying for two lieutenant slots had to take a two-hour exam (Lieutenant William Ryder, who had graduated one year ahead of Wood Joerg from West Point, aced it in forty-five minutes and received the TP command.). They also had to be unmarried. The first directive, read to the bleary-eyed men of the 29th Infantry before dawn on June 26, 1940, made it clear why: "It will require frequent jumps from airplanes in flight at various altitudes, which may result in serious injury or death."

The training the "lucky" forty-eight received formed the core regimen for the early paratroopers: an eight-week intensive course, which ranged from chalkboard sessions under a corrugated steel hangar at Benning to the daily 3-mile run before dawn because of heat. It was the summer of 1940 in Georgia; the cicadas chirred as the Test Platoon was ordered to jump off the backs of first stationary, then moving trucks in order to learn to absorb the shock over the whole body by rolling. If the wind was at your back, you were to somersault forward on hitting the ground; with wind pushing you backward, a backward somersault was appropriate. Pushups in the tall grass or dusty sod were meted out for the simplest mistakes. The Test Platoon was taught early on the simplest mistake meant death. Jumping from 1,000 feet, if after three seconds your backpacked static line chute did not open, you had all of two more seconds to open by ripcord pull an emergency chute carried on your chest. Otherwise it was, as Humphrey Bogart would have said, curtains.

True to parachuting's circus origins, the Test Platoon took its first practice jump aloft from two 150-foot parachute towers built by a company that had exhibited them at the 1939 World's Fair in New York City. The jump occurred in early August 1940 in Hightstown, New Jersey. (The four 250-foot Benning towers would not be built until year's end.)

Every man of the Test Platoon became intimate with his parachute, being taught to sew it, fold it, and pack it blindfolded. The final skill to be mastered, of course, was jumping. The week before the historic "first" jump on August 16, 1940 (almost four years before the GOYAs' jump into Southern France) fear had been injected in all when a dummy thrown out of a plane plunged straight into the ground, its chute unopened. It was the wide-eyed platoon's first experience of anything with a chute falling from a plane. Needless to say, it was not heartening.

Now, the first ten jumpers stood up, Spotlight Brown among them, and hooked their static lines to a steel cable that ran front to back like a garment rack along the roof of the C-33 plane. The lower end of the static line was connected only by a thin piece of string to the parachute, which the weight of the man falling would pull out, breaking the string. Tense with fear and excitement, the men felt the wind slap their faces and the propellor blasts ripple their thick cotton pants. The plane door open, the engines' roar blotted out all wisecracks, all speech. Lieutenant Ryder was first; the skin of his face felt as if it was being washed away by the door wind. He took the signal slap on the calf of his leg from the warrant officer, then hurled himself out the door into the white sky and disappeared, his parachute inflating nicely.

But the next man, who had gleefully won the lottery the night before to be the first enlisted man to go airborne, froze. He was looking down. The warrant officer slapped the man on the leg. "Go, jump!" he barked. But Number One was riveted in place. What could it have been? That dummy imbedded in the earth days before? A sprained ankle off the truck moving only a quarter as fast as now? The whiteness? The stomach like a steel cable entangled from which he could not throw himself?

The warrant officer tried to ease Number One's nerves, and ordered everyone to sit while the plane circled one more time and even flew lower, as if that would lessen his fear. It didn't work; he was still staring down, unmoved. Of the ten jumpers of that first "stick," only Number One was flown to the ground, where he was taken away by the Army ambulance and soon transferred from Benning. He was not punished; his only punishment was knowing that he had reacted like most normal human beings to 1,500 feet of emptiness asking for his body.

Dan Morgan's 551st memoir shows such scenes were ubiquitious: "We came to have a degree of compassion, of understanding for the poor guy who froze in the door. Every one of us saw it happen, and often as not, to the last guy you would expect."[9]

The man who did get the honors of being the first enlisted man to jump—Private William "Red" King—was appropriately nicknamed "the Spartan." But not everyone landed safe and sound. Private Tyerus F. Adams was knocked unconscious by a riser connector link, which shot at his head when his chute opened. (The early paratroop helmet, made of cloth, was of little use in such collisions; at times, earlobes were ripped off.) On the basis of those two mishaps, two jump rules still in effect today were quickly put into effect that August 1940: 1. Do not look below in the door of the plane, but stare straight ahead toward the horizon. 2. Tuck your chin to your chest when leaping out the door.

"Geronimo!"—the signature yell of a U.S. paratrooper—owes its origin to one Private Aubrey Eberhardt, who first uncorked it during the fifth and last test jump—the first mass jump—before a VIP crowd below, which included Secretary of War Henry Stimson and General Marshall.

Eberhardt, who at 6 feet, 8 inches was 8 inches over what would become the paratrooper limit, had been out the night before drinking with buddies. They had taken in a movie, a vintage Western in which the U.S. Cavalry vanquished the Apache chief Geronimo. One of Eberhardt's companions needled him, saying he was too chicken to jump the next morning. Eberhardt said he had a surprise in store; he was going to yell the Apache's name out the door. When he did, and everybody else did, following him in a slithering of chutes, a crescendo of "O's!" reached the ears of the Army brass below. Eberhardt's yell became a paratrooper tradition to this day, the ironic co-optation of an American Indian symbol of the fierce underdog.

As the canopies of light unfurled, they seemed too beautiful, even delicate, to be weapons. But things moved speedily from there. All throughout its training in 1940, the Test Platoon had read news of the lightning German capture of the Low Countries and France; before its first jump, Paris was in Hitler's hands. The formation of larger tactical parachute units was ordered. In September 1940, only a month after the Test Platoon's trial jumps had concluded, the Army created the 501st Parachute Infantry Battalion, commanded by the athletic director and star gymnast at Fort Benning, Major William M. Miley (who would become a general, as did many early paratrooper officers). The historic 501st would directly spawn my father's unit, as two years later the 551st would use as its core the seasoned paratroopers of C Company of the 501st.

Throughout 1941, four U.S. airborne battalions and one regiment would be formed; just after Pearl Harbor and the U.S. declaration of war, though parachutes themselves were scarce, four more battalions would be quickly ordered. It was during that feverish time that men who had enlisted in the Army were smitten by presentations given by officers from Benning about joining the new paratroop units. Benning was flooded with new volunteers eager to try their legs at jumping from planes.

There were also those eager to shed their irons, and the Army was only too willing to have them in the emergency. Those languishing in military stockades for various infractions could secure their release if they signed up to go airborne. In some cases civilians indicted or already in the slammer would be let off the hook if they enlisted to be paratroopers. The 551st was the legitimized "punishment" for several of those types, including Frank "Big Head" Powers, who had done time for armed robbery. The practice of allowing jailbirds to sprout jump wings continued through the Korean War.[10]

Unlike many Army units, which tended to draw from one state or region, the roughly six hundred men who would become the 551st in late 1942 came from diverse geographic, ethnic, economic, and social backgrounds. That was actually in keeping with the tradition of the original 82d Infantry Division from World War I, which drew from all over the country, hence its nickname, "the All-Americans." As the 82d went airborne on August 15, 1942, renamed the 82nd Airborne Division, the men who would become the independent 551st were still in boot camp or in parachute training.

Some GOYAs came from foreign countries to serve. Kenneth Hundley had actually been in the Hitler Youth before switching sides; he became a valuable mortar spotter against his former countrymen for the 551st. Several came from Canada. Dan Morgan, a Tyrone Power lookalike and avid horseman through forested areas of his native British Columbia and Washington, had figured he'd help head off the 50,000 horses the Japanese were reeling through China by joining Indian fighter Custer's old 7th Regiment at Fort Bliss in El Paso, Texas. When it dawned on him that horses weren't galloping over the Pacific and that Custer's 7th had been mechanized, Morgan read everything he could about these newfangled parachute jumpers down South. Soon he latched on to basic training at Camp Wolters, Texas, and by July 1942 had graduated from the thirty-ninth class in the jump school's history at Fort Benning.

Morgan's fellow Canadian Jim Welsh had actually "seen" more of the war than most of the original 551st. From his perch as a young teenager in St. John's, New Brunswick, he was a witness to Roosevelt's Lend-Lease program to arm the British at the war's beginning. Thick packs of U-boats prowled the waters around Nova Scotia and New Brunswick, and Welsh observed many a mangled ship limping into harbor.

From a maritime culture, Welsh defied his parents to join up with the U.S. Navy, whose standards he thought higher. But the American recruiting sergeant took one look at Welsh's dog-eared, sweaty induction papers, scratched out "Navy," and put in "Army." At boot camp in Fort Lee, Virginia, he tested high enough to put in for officer's training, but he spied the posters for paratroopers and something hit him. His friends laughed at his interest. "I was a sad-looking thing at 140 pounds," he confessed. "I stayed up half the nights roller-skating with my girlfriend." His friends chided him about paratrooping, "Why, you'll blow away! You'll be a second lieutenant with us and get killed as a private with them."

"I didn't buy it," Welsh said. "I was just being a rebel—same thing that got me in the Army in the first place." The extra $50 a month hazardous pay didn't hurt, either. Soon he was at Benning climbing the ropes like everyone, negotiating a huge set of monkey bars called "the plumber's nightmare."

Sometimes friends who met in basic training challenged each other as a kind of one-upmanship to go airborne. Such was the case of three GOYAs-to-be who met in basic training at Camp Wheeler near Macon, Georgia: the New Yorkers Roland Barhyte, Bill Amann, and Jim Demming. They took their lumps from an old Army private first class who didn't like "college fucks" such as themselves and would send them off to the latrine with a bark, "Go arinate!" Barhyte, always the last in school to follow the leader, saw paratrooping as a "good, clever type of warfare" and thought he'd take his habit of jumping off walls to overcome fear of heights to an extreme. When the three volunteered for the airborne, Barhyte cheated his way through an eye exam that would have disqualified him. At Benning he found the ropes for rope climbs thinner than those at basic training at Wheeler. Soon, Barhyte later laughed, "my mouth was so swollen and my arms so musclebound I couldn't get a toothbrush into it!"

In 1942 Doug Dillard was a sixteen-year-old Georgia boy with summer sky blue eyes and peach-rubbed cheeks, two years under the regulation age, an adopted Army brat son of a stepfather sent already to North Africa from his home base at Fort McPherson outside Atlanta. There the young Dillard had caddied for Colonel Jubal Early III, the base doctor and grandson of the famed Civil War general; he had also shined the brogans of officers for candy and Cokes. He loved listening to the radio and could mimic Fibber McGee and Eddie Cantor; it wasn't hard, after spying the poster of a paratrooper plunging with his chute not 100 miles away at Fort Benning, to want to mimic that. Dillard lied about his age on the airborne application, and later to the recruiting officer. He wanted to jump from a higher branch; they could make peach jam of him if they wanted to.

The kinetic opposite of Dillard, Joe Cicchinelli, like my father, was an Ohioan who went west after the war (to Arizona). Down the years, some considered Cicchinelli, with his captured Nazi flag and display cases of uniforms, bullets, memorabilia, a bit overboard. Calling reveillie on a bird whistle, however, he became the sparkplug of the old men, and, grudgingly or not, they knew it. He was, after all, living proof of the damage to that most precious thing that starts all wars: the mind.

The day Pearl Harbor was attacked in 1941, Joe Cicchinelli was stirring his mama's pot of spaghetti, reading the papers about Massillon High School's latest exploits on the football field. Like my father, only more so, Joe was too small to make Massillon's statewide champion team. After flunking the aptitude test for aviation mechanics, Cicchinelli enlisted in the paratroopers for the thrill and challenge of it, entering Fort Wolters in July 1942. He was pleasantly surprised at Benning to find that many paratroopers were short, muscular, and wiry like him. There he shocked the California state champion miler, Jack Carr, by beating him in a mile run of about five minutes. Both would end up in the 551st.

Like many of the 551st, in some way adept at tumbling as youth, some literal, some figurative, the man who became the 551st's graves register, Max Bryan, was born to a family on a slide. Descended from slaveowners in Lumberton, North Carolina, Max lost his father seven and a half months before he was born; Mr. Bryan, who owned a sawmill, was killed in 1924 by lightning while cutting trees. Over time the family lost interest in the 175 acres of land the father had garnered, including a millpond. Max grew up as one of six children working as tenant farmers on land they once owned. At one point the family lived near a funeral home, where Max would sleep when guests stayed over.

Bryan was the only athlete of the six children, having lettered in four sports. He liked being "the best" and being among them. He, like Doug Dillard, was also sixteen and lied about his age to get into the paratroopers. He went back home and saw his image in the millpond, blurred, iced-over from a freeze that December 1941. He took a stick and punctured the image, wondering "How the hell am I going to jump from a plane? I've never been on a plane."

4
The Frying Pan

About a hundred of the charter members of the 551st cut their paratrooper teeth with the first airborne U.S. battalion ever formed—the 501st.[11] Mearlen "Hedy" LaMar, who would lead a 551st squad in C Company as sergeant, arrived at Benning in November 1940. He was promptly assigned to tents above Lawson Field, which would become known, for its weather, as "the Frying Pan." He remembered there were at first only thirty-five parachutes for 412 men of the 501st and that the unit had to wait four months for its first battalionwide parachute shipment. By the time adequate parachutes arrived, half the members of the historic first battalion were so discouraged they simply left, "just dribbled away," as LaMar put it.

Six weeks was the typical "class" for paratrooper training. Carl Noble of the 501st and soon the 551st remarked: "If there was a way we could be made to quit, they were going to find it." If a trooper couldn't take the endless rope climbing, or vomited once too often after a run of several miles in 100-degree heat, or just lagged behind, he would be told to sit down; his barracks bag, tidied every morning at the foot of his bed with name facing out for the very purpose of being sent off with him, was fetched, handed to him, and the poor guy was (unwritten) history.

The Rubicon for most airborne trainees—then and now—were the six 34-foot "mock-up" jump towers. "If a man is afraid of height and falling in space then he will quit here," my father annotated in his *Parachute School*

U.S.A. souvenir booklet sent to his parents, alongside a photo of a man jumping out of the 34-foot tower to sail by guide wire across a stretch of grass the size of a football field. More than the imposing 250-foot towers, from which the jumper does not get a real sense of the ground, 34 feet is considered the psychological barrier, for the ground is all too visible. There the jumpmaster barked at the trainee to hold his riser straps away from his ears unless he'd like to lose them, to tuck his chin down, and to lift his legs at the other end of the field, where an embankment would break them if they didn't go up in time.

One of the first parachute instructors at Fort Benning, someone who actually had a hand in constructing the 250-foot jump towers still used today, was Lieutenant Dick Durkee, who would be the last officer still standing in doomed A Company at the 551st's destruction at the Bulge. ("They're exactly 258 feet, 7 inches," Durkee corrects.) William Ryder, commander of the Test Platoon, came by in those early days and asked for a volunteer to try something new: a 50-foot vertical free-fall drop from the top of the tower, face-and-belly down before the runner chord caught. Durkee shot his hand up. But on the platform, "Ryder had to call out three times before I did it. I was as scared as I have ever been in my life."

Then there was the matter of hitting the ground. A landing trainer taught a man how to roll on impact, because, as the smokejumper Norman Maclean once put it, "landing smoothly from the sky does not come naturally to man."[12] The key was to distribute the pain throughout the body. Chuck Bernard, who had been rejected by all services because of a kerosene burn on his arm and side and had somehow weaseled his way into the paratroopers, had "strawberry" burns all over his back persistently at Benning from tight buckles and snaps. He remembered a jumpmaster with 160 jumps on his record frozen in the door of the plane who had to be kicked out. As for Bernard himself, "I had to be kicked out, but if they asked me to jump today, I'd say yes."

How many lives were saved by disqualifying paratrooper wannabees through the training rigors is hard to say. Morgan notes that the 551st— begun primarily with the 42d, 43d, and 44th classes at Benning in 1942— averaged 8 percent disabling casualties on each training jump. The men watched some of their fellow adventurers die in training. The Army, even in those trial-and-error days, had a smug allegiance to method:

> They told us that if you burned in, it had to be your own fault—nothing could
> ever go wrong with a well-packed chute. I guess we believed them at first, but
> later, when we saw the old law of averages working out . . . Most of us called it
> "luck"—and if yours ran out, it didn't make much difference how you had
> packed your chute or what kind of swell body position you had when you

went out the door. You were going to wind up with a great big busted leg, or maybe a busted arm, or a handful of flowers.

During jump school Morgan himself saw three troopers fall to their deaths, including his best friend, who died on his second jump. "There was just a white streak," Morgan writes, "as he burned his way into the ground."

Why did Morgan hang on? "It was wild and free out there—those are the two words that wrapped it all up for me then, and they still do it for me now." In the sweating tents and later the wood barracks of the Frying Pan, under the glare of a drill sergeant, under all the chains of command, one was somehow freer than in civilian life.

Reviled by the townspeople around Benning, seen as strutting cocks by the regular infantry, the early paratroopers embodied a paradoxical mix of the wild and the intensely ordered. The men could find themselves emerging from a bar knocked unconscious by townspeople and dumped into the Chatahootchie River.[13] One night in August 1942 the Lone Star Tavern across the river in Phenix City was destroyed when a "townie" stabbed a paratrooper in the back and killed him (so the word went out), and the tavern owner let the murderer escape out the back door. About two hundred men rose out of the barracks and took a quick vengeance; they tore the Lone Star Tavern down to the ground. Only the side walls—attached to the adjacent buildings—survived. Otherwise the place looked like a bomb had hit it.

One night in late July 1942, well-oiled from a bar in Columbus, three troopers fell into a taxi, which had a shotgun on the front seat. The driver and his companion drove the men about one block toward Benning, stopped, and drawled, "That'll be ten bucks each." Jim Heffernan described the inevitable fight:

> We all got out [on] a dark sidestreet. Phil [Hammack] and I sat Emory [Albritton] against a tree—he was blotto, just completely out of it. . . . The driver got lucky and caught Phil square on the head with a coke bottle; it smashed the bottle, and you know how thick they were then. I was distracted at that moment by an old lady screaming.

The woman probably saved Heffernan's life; the shotgun rider had just emerged with his shotgun; hearing her scream, he jumped back into the cab and took off.

It wasn't just paratroopers against the world, those of the prized jump boots with special leather strap to secure the ankles, against the merely spit-shined. It was us against us: "There are only two things a paratrooper likes to do more than drink beer. One of them is brawling."[14] Sometimes students could overwhelm teachers, such as the day during jump school hand-to-hand combat training when a miner from Montana, Norman Novakovich, with "terrific hands," was asked by a tough drill instructor to demonstrate the headlock. Platoon sergeant Jim Stevens of Company A watched Novakovich tighten and tighten his grip, ignoring the instructor who was hitting him in the elbow as his eyeballs appeared to pop out and huffed from lack of breath. The Montanan finally let go of the beet-red sergeant, who eased up on the men thereafter.

In the Frying Pan, when a KP roster disappeared ("Maybe it blew away," Stevens speculated), the captain ordered everyone under guard and shut in the barracks, accusing them of mutiny. The troopers proceeded to open suitcases they had filled with bottles from Columbus that they had saved for the impending trip to Panama and drained them all. When the captain saw them all passed out and the whisky bottles rolling on the barracks floor, he yelled that they were guilty of mutiny in wartime. Someone then shouted, "You are chickenshit if you don't have us shot!" They were all confined to quarters with a rollcall every thirty minutes and a guard to go to the latrine. And they hadn't even gotten to the real war yet.

My father laconically spoke of jumping in between two warring GIs more often than confronting the Germans. It was a habit he, like many from the battalion, took into civilian life; I remember more than once his lurching the car into park at an LA intersection, running out, and jamming himself between two jawing motorists. Once at an LA Dodgers game, while he parted two heated fans, I was left holding his hot dog.

Pressure uncorked a lot of the intra-GOYA grappling, the pressure of unreliable chutes, omnipresent accidents and training deaths, and the pull of the war just ahead of them. Not to mention their own pugnacity. Being told each of them was worth five men, as Wood Joerg would tell them, made the men of the 551st occasionally try and prove it to each other.

That other favored outlet the paratrooper historian Gerard Devlin wrily fails to mention—sex—was well-exercised on leave, with a few paratroopers crying "Geronimo!" on a 2-foot leap into bed. "B girls," as they were called, hung out around bars in Phenix City, Columbus, and other leave towns such as Atlanta and New Orleans. But there were other townie girls whom the soldiers latched onto in their rather desperate lovemaking. The towns around Benning and the ports from which they embarked had an illegitimate baby "boomlet."

By June 1942, eighty-four men who had done their five jumps at Benning volunteered for Panama duty to fill slots of the original 501st battalion stationed there. First Major Jones and then Major Melvin Zais became their 501st commanders. Six months later, new trainees and assorted officers would join this "Panama bunch" in Panama, too, to form the 551st.

Volunteers continued to stream into Benning from other posts. Major Wood Joerg, twenty-seven, arrived from Fort Hood, Texas, in mid-1942, just in time to brush the khakis of Colonel James Gavin. Young for his rank (like the swiftly advancing Joerg), on July 6, 1942, Gavin, thirty-four, took over the newly activated 505th Parachute Infantry Battalion at Benning; it would soon be a regiment. By war's end Gavin would be the youngest major general in the U.S. Army, a hero of the 82d Airborne Division, America's best-known paratrooper, and the man who sent the 551st to its death.

Destined to be one of the best-loved men in the ornery bunch of GOYAs was Captain Jud Chalkley, the battalion surgeon and doctor. The day of the attack on Pearl Harbor he had been working as an intern at Kansas City General Hospital; all interns there went straight into the Armed Forces and were sent to Carlisle Barracks, Pennyslvania, the oldest fort in the United States, where German Hessians had once been incarcerated during the Revolutionary War. After studying map reading and other tasks, Chalkley was ordered to train young medics in making leg splints at Camp Barkley in Abilene, Texas. After several hundred mock leg splints and endless desert heat, he read a newly tacked-up sign with eagerness: "Join the paratroops and get immediate reassignment."

Chalkley drove to Benning in an old Pontiac with thin tires (the kind required by rubber rationing during the war years). His body was not as thin, and it took him extra weeks to get physically fit. He viewed the 250-foot jump tower with disbelief; the 34-foot tower resembled the watchtower of a prison. Soon he was an adrenalin-hot trainee ready to smash into the ground before two riser straps sewn into his shoulder and hooked to a cable wheel fully extended and halted his fall. "I remember hearing some poor guy screaming when he fell out of his bed late one night," Chalkley recalled. On his own first jump he was almost numb; when he later asked the tapping sergeant how his exit went, the man replied, "My God, I had to practically break your leg to get you out the door." On another jump Chalkley saw a lieutenant freeze at the sky door. Where would it end? Chalkley mused.

It would end in snow but would begin in jungle.

They had gotten their air wings—designed by William Yarborough— pinned on them, most by Colonel (later Brigadier General) George Howell. Following graduation tradition, many had gone to the tattoo artist in Columbus and gotten various eagles, flags, daggers, parachutes, and hearts cut by needle into their flesh. By November 1942 about 450 men passed through jump school were now mustered to the Frying Pan's "hutments," the crude barracks of poles and tarpaper in a wooded area beyond the training field at Benning. The streets were red clay and sand; each hut used a small smudge pot for heat as the weather cooled.

No one was being granted the customary ten-day furlough after jump school. Each day, wrote Don Garrigues in his unauthorized diary,[15] this became the main topic of every gripe session. On December 8, 1942, one month after the first American combat mission had dropped in North Africa, Joerg called the men out in formation in the midst of a steady downpour of rain. Their newly issued steel helmets gleamed in the rain; their new combat jump suits became soaked as Joerg spoke. There would be no furloughs; no one was to write home until further notice; all tattoos would be surgically removed or obliterated.

There were grumbles; some of the proud chins held up by straps moved with the slow grind of teeth. Anticipating their questions, Joerg said that they had been assigned a secret mission overseas where tattoes would give them away as paratroopers. The high command did not want spies tipped to this. The markings had to go.

Joerg spoke a little about the 509th. He must have been thinking of how the only other battalion in the whole Army like his own—independent— had gotten out in front of the 551st in Torch. He may even have suppressed a sly grin over the fact that the 509th had fallen so far off target as to miss the country it was to seize (the drop zone had been in Algeria, but the confused pilots had let the chutists go hundreds of miles west in Spanish Morocco.) Still, the 509th had fallen into history. Was the 551st destined to be Sancho Panza to the 509th's Quixote, Cain to its Abel? He knew that some convicted felons had found their way into the 551st.

From the very start, Joerg had a tough, independent group of men to corral, and he knew it. They were all Type A's—brash fellows filled to bursting with energy and initiative. And they were testy. As Morgan put it, only a little tongue-in-cheek: "One of our persistent problems was that we had maybe three hundred men in the battalion who were natural leaders, and maybe only 250 who would quietly follow where they were led." At any given time, Morgan estimated, seventy-five men could have taken over and led the 551st. To yoke together such an ungainly critical mass of individualism was no mean task.

The newly formed 551st was a volatile brew, a controlled fire, but these men showed promise that they could bear the toughest tests.

Martinique. Joerg had hardly heard of it before. Friends of Hitler had come to power on the small Caribbean island and were giving safe haven to U-boats attacking shipping to and from the Americas. As a Southerner, the idea of redeeming oneself by defending soil close to home must have appealed to Joerg. Martinique was close to Florida, so it was as good as home. The attack—the only one ever planned during World War II for the Americas—was to spring from Panama, and the 551st was to lead it.

III

PANAMA

The First (Secret) Mission

There is many a boy here today who looks on war as all glory, but, boys, it is all hell.

—William Tecumseh Sherman

1
Freaks of nature

A thousand nurses were heading south in their hospital ship. As Dan Morgan ran to his own troop transport boat's railing and waved, salt spray from the Atlantic hit his face. Throughout the night before he had been terrified by explosions of U-boat attacks. Two ships in their convoy had been sunk; the men in the hold had felt the torpedo blasts ring through the hull. Now they were topside, waving, and the women were waving wildly back. But the nurses were passing them south and west and would not tarry, taking their warmth and medicine through the Panama locks to the Pacific, while the men of the 551st were bound for Panama itself. They watched the women disappear, their waves indistinguishable from a flock of gulls.

Two of the GOYAs' eleven-ship troop convoy had gone down off Cuba in what was known as "Torpedo Junction"; six were destroyers, and if they had any luck with their depth charges, there wasn't much of a way to tell. The other ships carried precious cargo: 450 paratroopers with scraped skins. When the sailors, spotting the gauze wrappings over the removed tattoos, began to wonder why so many men seemed wounded before they'd even been to battle, the GOYAs would just tell them: There'd been a battle of sorts at Benning, and they were testing bandages.

For all their wounded pride, which would be a GOYA occupational hazard, they were alive and whole. Tattoos could be gotten in some other century. If they were delivered whole and fresh and eager to fight Nazis in the Caribbean, perhaps their newly pilfered mascot, a little dachshund named Furlough, could take the credit.

After the troop train from Benning arrived on December 13, 1942, at Fort Patrick Henry in Newport News, Virginia, some 551st men still smarting from having lost their traditional jump school furlough—at Christmas, no less—had taken their woes to a port bar. They had emerged sloshed, arms locked, wobbly on the port's backstreets, singing "GORY, GORY, WHAT A HELLUVA WAY TO DIE!" A dog picked her ears up at the ruckus and came running up to her picket fence. One of the men—no one knows who—reached down, picked her up, and drafted her. As the black-and-umber dachshund belonged to the port commander, it was a somewhat more serious larceny than it appeared.

The little pup, barely ten weeks old when stolen, was smuggled onto the USS *Dickman* in an empty gas mask container by Jim Heffernan. Heffernan, thinking quickly, had nudged Phil Hammack to hide his gas mask in his barracks bag, thus providing concealment for the dog. Heffernan and others crowded around her deep in the hold of the ship as she stood wobbly and excited on a bunk, barking. The theft aside, dogs were not allowed on military ships; Heffernan and everyone else involved, including Major Joerg, flirted with a court martial. But as Captain (later Major) Ray "Pappy" Herrmann, the battalion's S-3 operations officer, would later put it, naming the puppy "came about as naturally as had her acquisition." She would be the 551st's mascot till the end, where she would be last seen in a sling with a soldier running in the Belgian snow.

Except for the taking of Furlough, the two weeks at Patrick Henry were dreary and anxious. The men were injected with the new yellow fever vaccine the Army had created especially for tropics-bound troops, and eight came down with yellow jaundice. It was colder in port, and the men had already been doused by the first winter rains at Benning while hearing their war deployment order from Joerg. Many came down with severe chest colds and bronchitis. Doc Chalkley discovered that all the battalion had on hand was aspirin, so he went into Newport News and used $25 of his own money to buy terpinhydrate-codeine. "I still remember how miserable the guys were, and the terrible sound of their coughing," Chalkley recounted.

Although they were stripped of the signature tattoos, Don Garrigues thought a trained undercover agent might have become suspicious anyway, because they shouted cadence till they were hoarse and coughing while marching double-time, something regular infantry troops just didn't do. At the same time, a port town breaks down discipline; the GOYAs, never reverential toward authority and anxious to get on with their secret task, had brittle nerves in Newport News. Sergeant Bill Hatcher of B Company was in line for chow one cold, wet morning, when a jeep drove up honking for the men to move aside. Hatcher watched amazed as several of his fellows picked up the jeep and dropped it, with its startled lieutenant, into a nearby ditch. One morning Hatcher was awakened by the sound of troopers joy-riding on bulldozers they had found. "I am positive the post commander was happy to see us leave," Hatcher concluded.

On December 27, 1942, the 551st—with Furlough attached—left the United States for Panama. The rough bunch went in style. The USS *Dickman,* which had been a President Liner, amounted to a limo for the Dead End Kids. Security was tight. For the same reason they had obliterated their paratrooper tattoos, their cherished airborne boots were hidden away. Forbidden to sing paratrooper songs, lips sealed about who they were and what they were up to, their cover was temporarily blown by the movie that first night at sea: *Donald Duck Joins the Paratroops.* Pappy Herrmann remembered the botch: "Hitler himself must have heard the roar of laughter."[1]

Though they would be allowed to write home shortly in the censored V-mail tradition, almost none had gotten the chance to say goodbye to loved ones. The little sausage hound must have been overwhelmed with petting.

Later, the 551st adopted a vagrant German shepherd they named "Oscillation" (for a badly vibrating chute), but it was of Furlough about which my father fondly spoke to my mother when they were first married. Although at the time the GOYAs were sent to Panama he would have been salving his muscles from the climactic Cleveland sandlot football game, he was most definitely a dog person, preferring the dependable over the fickle. Unfortunately, his own small mutt, Pudgie, was killed by a larger dog that lived next door in Cleveland. I'm sure he would have considered it un-GOYA-like for the battalion to steal a Doberman as a mascot. Underplay it; underdog it; glory from the small unnoticed thing, or not at all.

The 551st headed to Panama to spell most of the troops of the first paratroop battalion, the 501st, which had been sent to Australia to fight the Japanese. The 551st men "fed the fish" as Don Garrigues put it, with seasickness. Garrigues and his friend Bill Hatcher discovered that fresh air was an antidote and thereafter snuck out from the hold at night to sleep in the lifeboats under the stars.

It is almost as difficult to pin down the 551st's exact birth as it is to muzzle its tragic end. Though Wood Joerg gathered the men at Benning in

November 1942, the official Army Lineage Book of 1953 states that the 551st was activated 26 November 1942 at Fort Kobbe, Canal Zone. Official Army records about the 551st are so scant, cryptic, and simply inaccurate, where they do exist, that it is no surprise to find that there are several anomalies about this first mention. First the 551st is called a "regiment," which by definition comprises at least three battalions. The GOYAs never grew past one battalion. They are noted as being activated in Panama— where they arrived in January 1943—in November 1942. The most important irregularity is the unit's number. The parachute numbering sequence had started with 501 and had gone up to 517. The 551st should have been the 518th. Why did the Army skip thirty-eight numbers?

Apparently, the 551st numeration (and that of the 550th glider battalion already in Panama) were ways of throwing German and Japanese intelligence off, to make it appear the U.S. Army had three times the number of paratroopers than it actually had. According to Major General Ridgely Gaither—then a major in the Office of the Chief of the Infantry— he personally decided "to muddy the waters a bit" jumping the unit number far ahead.[2] Calling the battalion a "regiment" may have been a similar attempt to frighten off U-Boats by an overstatement of strength. It's quite possible that the Army simply never got around to filling out the intended regiment. A bastard battalion could be lived with; a bastard regiment could be serious institutional trouble. Bait or not, the Germans swallowed it, for long past the 551st's tenure in Panama, and even into the Bulge, the unit was presumed by spies to be far larger than it was, which led to grave consequences in the end for an outmanned, outgunned 551st.

The first of several internal struggles flared to life at the unit's birth at Fort Kobbe, Canal Zone. The 501st's C Company—left behind by the rest of the battalion when it had taken off to Australia (to be formed into the 503d regiment)—took the numerical designation to mean that its officers would serve as cadre for those "fillers" due under Major Joerg in January. Friction developed when Major Joerg, getting off the ship in Balboa, shook the wary hand of Captain Bill Hickman of Company C, who thought he was taking over the new battalion.

The 501st remnant saw the 551st as a dark chute descending. It was a proud unit; they'd been in a movie, *Parachute Battalion*. They attempted by dint of seniority and experience to convert the men of the 551st to underlings. It didn't work. Hickman stood the new men from Benning up all night long while the Articles of War were read to them. But Joerg held fast against that bit of psychological warfare. He accepted some of the 501st officers as company commanders, including Marshall Dalton, Jim Evans, and Tims

Quinn, but Joerg let it be known that he had his own superstructure. Bruised, Hickman returned to Company C and only Company C, but not before yelling at Joerg for running the men ragged in the hot sun. Joerg was so ticked off he ordered Doc Chalkley to "Section 8" Hickman as a mental case to the hospital. Chalkley refused, and Joerg backed off but stayed sore at Chalkley a long while afterward. As for Hickman, he transferred out of the unit in the spring of 1943 to join the rival 517th Regiment.

Between the 125 men of the original 501st and the 450 Joerg brought from Benning, joined in unholy matrimony as the 551st, "some animosity built up and lingered on," according to the 551st's second-in-command, Major William Holm, but over time "it made us stronger" in the welding. "Between" became "among."

It would have to. The sense of being overtasked, of a unit's striving to be more than it was, infinite desire in an all-too-finite package, was embedded in the mystique of the 551st right at the start. The very breadth of its first assignment—spearheading protection for the entire Caribbean basin and supply ships to the United States—was a lot for not quite six hundred men.

The High Command seemed to decide that a green but game 551st could handle the Caribbean threat, which, for most of 1942, was real. With the U.S. entry into the war after Pearl Harbor, German Admiral Donitz shifted the focus of his "wolf pack" U-boat attacks from the North Atlantic to the American East Coast, the Gulf of Mexico, and the Caribbean Sea. The result was dramatic. Between January and March 1942, U-boats sank 1.25 million tons of shipping off the Americas, four times its rate of damage the previous year in the North Atlantic.[3]

Even before Pearl Harbor, with the U-boat threat far from home, U.S. intelligence had been worried about the susceptibility of Latin countries to Nazism, particularly the lifeline Panama Canal, which connected the Atlantic Ocean to the Pacific. Early German immigrants—those who came to pre-Revolutionary War America as well as those who had taken refuge from a Germany ravaged by Bismarck's and the Kaiser's European wars— had come to Latin America; Central American countries, in particular, had sizable German populations. The threat of unfriendly coups was the chief impetus in sending the 501st—secretly—to Panama in June 1941.

"We had seen the effect of the German fifth columns in Norway," recounted four-star General Melvin Zais, who was a platoon leader with the 501st in Panama. "We were concerned, in keeping with the Monroe Doctrine, that there be no German Nazi-supported coup in any of the Latin American countries." Ironically, though it was brought in to ward off Vichy-style regimes too close to America, when the Japanese attacked Pearl Harbor on December 7, 1941, the 501st sent platoons all over Panama—to Chorrera, Rio Hato, and Chamay, among others—as Zais put it, "preparing for a potential Japanese attack."

It was with this secret intelligence portfolio that Major Joerg began to train his troops in jungle warfare in January 1943 at Fort Kobbe, Panama. Their own sense of being a select group on an important mission intensified when Joerg told them they could write home but must avoid using any specific geographic names in their letters and must give their return address as APO New Orleans.

The rigorous training in Panama marked the third sizable training period for most GOYAs, following boot camp and paratroop school. It was the first time they had drilled together, and in spite of the internal crack at the unit's birth, their espirit de corps steadily mounted. Six-day weeks of endless setting up and displacing guns, eight-hour days of bayonet practice (which would serve them well in the fog of the Ardennes), and machetes hacking away at thick and poisonous black palms—all boiled a cauldron of hardihood for the GOYAs.

Away from Heidi and the baby, far from the college "hoplife" of West Point, and tensed by the task at hand, Major Joerg evolved into a strict disciplinarian. Still, he allowed a high degree of experimentation and initiative in training maneuvers—there was no standard operating procedure (SOP) but what worked.

On a team hike across the Panama isthmus, wear was checked on jungle boots, special hammocks, field packs, rations, and radios. Sergeant Lloyd Larkin had a notion that he could jump with a Browning 30-caliber machine gun attached to his parachute harness; he got permission to cut 6 inches off the barrel. Duke Spletzer made up a container for the "new" gun so that it would hold tight to Larkin's chest strap. When the 60mm mortar crews saw Larkin land successfully with his machine gun plastered to his body, they fashioned a way to jump with mortars as well. Bill Lumsden tested a "quick-release harness" that Spletzer and Captain "Jungle Jim" Evans jury-rigged, which would free a man who dropped in water from three bindings on the harness with one pull on a central cotter key.[4] All of this outdistanced what had been taught at Benning in parachute school.

The 551st refined other subtleties in Panama. For example, instead of a soldier hurling himself out the plane door into the void as had been taught at Benning, in Panama the GOYA worked on "sliding out the door" to avoid most of the propeller's blast. For a faster, smoother exit from the plane, the men practiced in eighteen-man sticks, each holding lightly onto the man in front with the right hand. The worst that would happen in this tight pattern was your boots would touch the chute below you, which happened to Don Garrigues after he'd experienced the dreaded delayed chute opening. "The guy in the chute below me hollered, but by that time I had slid on past him," Garrigues recounted.

Because planes were scarce in Panama, the 551st executed only six jumps in nine months. The drop zones were small and surrounded by hazardous jungle, which included, below those lovely green canopies that could cushion a fall, pythons that could squeeze your heart out, fire ants that went for the face, and, if you were lucky enough to fall into a tropical river, piranhas that could reduce your weight considerably in a matter of seconds.

Sometimes the tables were turned on the ground populace. On one jump Lieutenant Donald Booth, one of the larger men in the battalion, crashed right through the roof of a grass hut, scattering screaming, naked natives in all directions. On another occasion, training two Air Force colonels who wanted to be jump-qualified, the GOYAs dropped the two neophytes so close to an ambulance at the drop zone that the medics ran for cover.

One sergeant had been studying the Germans' roll out of a slowed-down plane about 10 feet off the ground onto the snow in Norway and thought something similar might be done into the jungle swamp grass in Panama. For some reason those 10 feet without chute seemed more forbidding than 1,000 feet with chute, and the plans to test the "Norway roll" were scrapped. Another intrepid rigger sergeant stuffed his chute in a barracks bag and jumped with it as an emergency, just to show it could be done.

The 551st developed a reputation not only as jumpers but as teachers of jumping. Fort Kobbe's chief engineer, Major Robert Alexander, anxious to earn jump wings, asked Major Joerg if the 551st would qualify him. They did so in five jumps, though he had to tape his eyeglasses to his face to do it. A grateful Alexander sent the men a jeep with a trailer full of iced drinks, extra cinderblock to help repair their barracks, and lumber to build an after-hours club.

All kinds of war games were conducted in which the men would make tactical jumps (no "Hollywood" jumps, according to Stevens) in full equipment and critique them afterward. The Army Air Corps staged mock attacks by the 551st to test their security. The GOYAs grew proficient in demolitions, learning how to destroy bridges, locomotives, electric power plants, roads, and industrial complexes. All the men were trained to drive bulldozers (enabling my father to get his first postwar job as a tractor driver); all had to be able to set up and fire artillery. They even had to learn to cut and sew their own parachutes, being issued 22-oz. duck and canvas and several darning needles (likewise, good training for the garment manufacturer that my father became). In short, each GOYA was a one-man army.

Joerg's love of innovation stoked the already independent spirit of the men, which caused him more than his share of command headaches. According to Doug Dillard, "During the entire life of the battalion it never had the constraints that a [normal] battalion or a regiment has." Joerg had a talent, though, for funneling—or exhausting—all the undifferentiated energy of the 551st. In addition to the tactical jumps, experimentations with equipment, calisthentics, and weapons training, Joerg had the men go on extensive jungle hikes of up to two weeks' duration. The short hike would go through a 4-mile "loop" with full combat load past the 18-inch guns, past a leper colony, to the beach, and then back to the Fort Kobbe barracks. On longer hikes—such as Captain Evans's 100-mile ordeal across the Panama isthmus—they would be required to march at night, wearing phosphorescent spots on their rifle muzzles and backs to keep from getting lost in the labyrinthine jungle crowded with the poisonous, cactuslike fronds of the black palm.

At some point in Panama, Joerg began to call the 551st troopers "GOYAs" or "GOYA birds." Joe Cicchinelli remembers, however, that an earlier slogan went around, "NJNSJK" (pronounced "Nensjack") for No Eat No Sleep Just Kill. That too-blunt phrase gave way to the anti-posterior-resting acronym, "GOYA," which the men to this day call themselves.[5]

Could GOYA have had anything to do with the brilliant Spanish painter? Joerg's wife, Heidi, loved art and became a painter. It is not hard to imagine the Spanish-speaking cadet Joerg on a pass to New York City taking in the New York Metropolitan Museum of Art and there encountering Francisco Goya, the first realistic painter of war's horrors. Joerg, without even knowing it, may have sensed in the soft roll of "Goya!" off his tongue that the 551st were unprecedented, deaf to stricture, pushers of the envelope.

Battling the Panamanian elements and wildlife became a daily routine. Some addressed the heat of the forced jungle marches humorously. Sergeant Jim Stevens, sweat pouring down his uniform, opened his fly and let his male equipment hang out and bounce down the trail with him. According to Sergeant Ralph Wenthold of the battalion's S-2 section, Stevens announced, "If they are going to work me like a mule, then I'm going to look like a mule." Others, like a meaty trooper named Herter, when told to pull his rolled sleeves down, was so incensed he reached up and tore the sleeves off, then stormed off into the jungle alone.

Fauna tended to slither. One day the medic Jack Affleck was sent out in what was called a "jungle problems" course for four men and a compass and told to come back to Fort Kobbe straight through the jungle—something of a contradiction in terms. They used their machetes liberally, paddled on a log underneath trees whose branches hung out over the water until someone shouted "Snake!" Hanging over their heads was a giant boa constrictor. No Nazi was ever shot at as quickly, but, Affleck concluded, "I don't think we hit it because we were so scared—I guess the snake was pretty scared, too." Snakes were great props for practical jokes. On one occasion, Lieutenant "Big Dog" Booth placed the unit's pet coral snake—its deadly venomous bite normally tucked away in a pickle jar—in the mail box of Lamar Tavoian. Reaching in to get the treasured letter from home, Tavoian touched something rather clammy, and seeing the bright yellow and red colors of death, was promptly airmailed.

Bugs buzzed everywhere in the tropical heat, like the earth itself come to crawling life. On a jump Lieutenant Buff Chisholm landed in tree covered trunk to fronds with fire ants, a type of quick-biting red ant. They covered Chisholm's body in no time, and he called in agony to Doc Chalkley to help cut him out of his chute. Dryly, Chalkley remarked, "We don't have any ladders, Buff. You have to get yourself down." Chisholm crowbarred himself out, shouting, and broke a rib hitting the ground.

Trying to ward off the outside bugs at night in the safety of the barracks proved futile. Although he "learned to love the jungle" and actually found it the only place in Panama with "cool air," native Angeleno Benny Goodman, a private in Company B, asserted, "Bedbugs would drag your shoes away from under your bunk." Bedbugs also loved to hide out in the gas masks each man had hanging from the foot of his bed. Don Garrigues described the bizarre confrontation:

> It was standard practice to have surprise alerts at night to keep us on our toes, and many times after being called out, we would have to put on our masks and run several miles to an assembly area. It was common to hear the men gasping and choking as the little varmints got into windpipes. It also took some will power to keep the mask on when you could see the pesky things crawling across your goggles—on the inside.

Only regular fumigation with DDT finally discouraged the bedbugs from wearing their goggles.

Even their commander took on nature at its most barbed. Lieutenant Paul Hoch set up a dark and spooky shack at the end of a battalion infiltration course, to which the soldier had to slither on his belly. Joerg himself was squirming up the path when Hoch quickly placed a giant iguana over a trap door in the shack's ceiling. When Joerg entered the iguana jumped down and grabbed what was left of his hair with its claws, scaring the daylights out of him. Joerg started blasting away with a .45 pistol. Doc Chalkley remarked, "It was one of the few times I ever saw [Joerg] really disconcerted."

A less amusing encounter thrust itself across the path of chief intelligence officer (S-2) Lieutenant Ed Hartman, a slender, soft-spoken career officer who had gone on active duty with the Citizens' Military Training Camp in 1934 and had escaped the deadend job of supervising PX and mess halls by volunteering for the airborne, a transfer no supervisor could deny. "I was never so happy as when I got into the 551st," Hartman's warm blue eyes twinkled at the age of seventy-nine, after a 100-mile drive alone from Knoxville, Tennessee, for an interview. In Panama, Joerg assigned Hartman to handle rescue duty around the isthmus which entailed not 551st jumpers but Army Air Corps pilots forced to bail out or crash-land.

An observation plane en route from France Field to Howard Field with pilot and copilot had crashed in the jungle. Hartman was alerted by one of the natives, who, while fishing, had spotted the burning plane in a swamp. The plane had evidently hit tall palms flying low at night. Hartman set out in a crash boat down the coast from France Field, hiked ashore for a while, then was led in little dugout canoes by San Blas Indian guides. They paddled endlessly down backwaters and sloughs until they found the burned plane and a pile of bones picked clean by vultures; the superstitious natives would not carry them.

Fighter pilots and paratroopers, elites of the U.S. Army, circled each other warily on the narrow isthmus. Doc Chalkley toured the half-dozen air fields in Panama, exhibiting jump equipment, and "tried to convince them they would survive if they would jump instead of riding their disabled aircraft to the ground." Mostly what he got were "snide remarks" about paratroop jump boots: "Hey, if I put on a pair of those boots, will I be a paratrooper, too?" Still, the Air Corps was grateful for 551st rescues, if not chutes. When William Dumas and Robert Dobart plucked an unconscious pilot from the sea, they both received a rare (for Wood Joerg) commendation—the Soldier's Medal.

Diseases flourished, a more common tropical enemy than flora or fauna. Many men came down with malaria, which was treated with quinine and atrabine. Everyone bore a case of jungle rot, a foot fungus that aped the severe frostbite so many men would suffer two years later at the Battle of the Bulge. Jungle rot was so bad in some cases they were sent back to the States; at any one time thirty to forty men could be found soaking their feet at the Kobbe dispensary in pans of gentian violet.

Athletics, antics, and alcohol—in these the GOYAs crushed their nervous energies, warding off a sense that the jungle itself was swallowing them while they waited to go to war. The 551st loved to defy nature's laws and to put every possible twist they could on the Army's. The unit bugler—a jitterbug instructor back home—played a swing version of reveille each morning. That had to appeal to Joerg himself, who had been the dance master at West Point. Not a few men literally danced out of bed.

Lieutenant Bud Schroeder, the battalion's keeper of the parachutes, twanged the ribs of fellow Lieutenant Jackie Haskell by filling his main chute pack with rags and his reserve chute with 6 pounds of sand. Both pranks were discovered with mock indignation by Schroeder and his partner in crime, Duke Spletzer, just before Haskell jumped, to his mortified relief. As for physical training, fifty pushups a day was the minimum, and most did them in a blur. Everyone knew George D'Agostino had been a lifeguard at Coney Island, had shown Air Corps pilots how to get in shape in Miami, and, most significantly, had taught Clark Gable himself calisthenics. He was adept at backflip somersaults, as was John Bishop, a notable hand-walker. Joe Chizar, a champion professional welterweight boxer, helped Joerg coach the new boxing team, which included the scout-to-be Joe Cicchinelli and all-service welterweight champion Virgil Dorr. Howard "Chief" Davis, a full-blooded Indian from Idaho, was an expert swimmer and had the men doing frenzied laps in the shark-lined lagoons. (Davis would die in 1966 trying to swim against a stiff current across the Clearwater River in Idaho.)

One day, Sergeant Jack Russell walked nearly a half a mile on his hands after ingrown toenail surgery. Russell had been one of the 501st group already in Panama when the 551st came down; he had joined the 501st in September 1942 after his ship, the *Ivan Capitz*, had survived a U-boat attack, laying up in Cuba for repairs. Born in Dubois, Idaho, and raised in Whittier, California, Russell, a red-haired, moon-faced man with an impish grin, did handstands as a child at age eleven; he soon progressed to handstands on a wire fence, on a moving truck, and on a balcony rail of the YMCA in Atlanta six stories up while on leave from jump school. Before he went to war he took his 28 inch waist and strong arms and chest into circus acrobatics. (His waist today is a libertine 29 inches.)

A jumpmaster in Panama who jump-trained fifteen officers as a sergeant, Russell developed ingrown toenails on each of his big toes. Surgery left him with an inability to walk. To take a shower in the hospital, Russell snapped a rubber prophylactic over each of his bandaged toes, did a handstand, and managed to turn the water on with his feet! Determined to get back to barracks on his own for a visit, he walked most of the half-mile trek from the hospital on his hands, as the post personnel marveled and gathered into a crowd, cheering him on. Even Joerg ran out of his office and gawked. *My dear freaks of nature! How could the Germans stand up against this?* His face bursting with blood, Russell finally tipped over in the road 100 yards shy of the barracks. The crowd caught his legs and carried him the rest of the way.

In 1983, at the age of sixty-two, Russell was asked at a 551st reunion in Miami if he still could stand on his hands. He promptly flipped his legs backward into the air and proceeded to walk the perimeter of the room, palms down. Everyone laughed, and Russell proceeded to tell, once again, a favorite 551st story, in which snow depth, blood quantity, and airdrop height varied according to quantity of liquor consumed. But one story he did not tell until he met me in a small hotel room a decade later in Reno, Nevada—and he was stone sober—was the story of how he saw his best friend decapitated in Belgium, and how he reached out with his arms to catch him but there was no grip in the hands or tension in the arms because the brain was gone to snow, and how that came to him one night a few years after the war when he was 102 feet up in the air, blood filling his head, on the trapeze as the catcher in a circus act with no safety nets or devices of any kind.

It was New Orleans, you know how soupy the air gets down there, as if someone were playing reveille in the fog, a damp, hot night really, and our tights were damp, I was on a ring, I could feel the sweat collect in back of my knees and I gripped harder with my thighs than normal and stared upside down at my partner on the ledge across the abyss and gave him a little warning signal with my hands rubbing the thumbs and he took this the looney as a signal to dry off on his tights but the tights I tell you were slimy, they were as wet as Panama when you walk halfway home on your hands, and he didn't hear my call across the crowd or my call was stifled by my own worry and when he flipped and grabbed my wrists my wrists and his hands were water as hot as the lagoons of Panama and as cold as Belgium and when I heard him die his head off on the floor in New Orleans and the crowd sucking all the oxygen out of the air I just lay there on the ring going back and forth not crying, not crying even when my Dad and Mom died, not crying until I left the circus and believed in gravity and am seventy-two now . . .

2
The Panama City riot

As for alcohol: "Drink up, boys! Jade Rodora's feathers are falling off!"

Major Joerg knew he had six hundred little volcanoes in tow in Panama, and with rumors of a drop on Martinique still cooking but not fully baked, he also knew it was best to give the 551st liberal passes. He had worked them to death in the heat; let the steam whistle out of them before they burst; if need be, let the steam fly at naked girls.

The closest respite was the Hook-Up Club on base, made with a gift of lumber from the base engineer, Major Alexander. There was also the weekly "laundry run" to Corozal on which the men would smuggle liquor underneath the sheets and coverall stacks on the returning laundry truck. Some men—like Lloyd Larkin and "Hedy" LaMar—had a secret hideout. After maneuvers they would take leave to tunnel through the fronds again to small shacks known only to them, deep in the jungle, which served cheap beer, chi chi (made from the fermented saliva of several old Indian women who would chew coconut meat and spit into a 10-gallon tub), and an occasional daughter or two. "I could hardly find it in the daytime, and they could find it in the dark," Sergeant Ralph Wenthold of Oklahoma mused. Others would take off, chi chi in hand, to various isolated coves, beaches, or the Venado River, strip naked, and drink and swim till the sharks came home. Farfan Beach was popular, about 8 miles from the base, and many cross-country runs were taken there around the leper colony. On at least one occasion a platoon returned from the Venado River naked en masse, carrying only their empty bottles, singing "He leaped right out into the blast, his static line unhooked!"

But most went to Panama City, to the Avenida Central and its nightclubs. The most classic show of all was at Kelley's Ritz: *Jade Rodora, the Beauty and the Beast.* Rodora was a slightly overcooked but not unshapely ex-actress from the States who dressed herself in feathers, and only feathers. She would rush onstage to the hoots of the drinking soldiers, chased by someone in a gorilla suit, followed by ten nude and carefree San Blas Indian handmaidens. They would run among the tables and through a gauntlet of desire, producing, in the view of the medic Jack Affleck, "a regular riot."

Partying was so prevalent in Panama during the 551st's off hours that Affleck himself was upbraided by Doc Chalkley for pulling him out of one particularly promising soirée to supervise the stitching of a GOYA's head wound earned in a bar fight. Chalkley blasted Affleck: "You sew this thing up yourself!" The poor GI got the benefit of Affleck's first needlework, without anesthetic.

That fight may have been the one at Kelley's Ritz, where it was the 551st against the world—the coastal artillery gunners and glider men from the 550th. Emory Albritton was thrown into the Balboa stockade and made to "turkey walk" by "some of the biggest MPs I ever saw in my life." On another occasion Jim Heffernan, who'd already begun to wonder if he was at war with America after the confrontation with the shotgun-toting cab rider in Columbus, Georgia, was told by an MP in Panama City it was time to get on his truck and get back to Kobbe. For looking down at his watch and looking up he got clubbed in the face by the MP. It broke his nose, and in the ensuing melée his friend Harold Lawler broke a hand. The two ended up in prison hospital, to be bailed out the next morning by a head-shaking Lieutenant Frank Serio.

Poetic (or pugilistic) justice occurred one night when, according to Jim Stevens, the 551st got word that "some sort of monster" had knocked out six MPs. The monster turned out to be the ordinarily "very unassuming" professional welterweight boxing contender Joe Chizar. Though Chizar weighed barely 140 pounds, his fists should have been insured (if not the chins of the MPs). He had beaten the man who later became welterweight champion of the world just before the unit had set off for Panama. Stevens retrieved him from the Kobbe stockade.

The 551st seemed to make the MPs stick-happy. Sergeant Bill Lumsden of Headquarters Company thought difficulty with MPs in Panama "seemed to be an ongoing thing . . . we felt they had taken us on as a project and anything could happen." Five MPs car-chased Lumsden and pals out of Panama City to the border town of Ancon, ran them off the road at a big billboard, and came at them with nightsticks. Two members of the GOYA boxing team were among the defenders, however. Lumsden said: "I can still remember with great pleasure—it was a marvelous thing to watch. [Carlo] Intinarelli [like Chizar, a pro boxer] was so fast, and so was Crooke [a Golden Gloves champ], that I sort of stood there and swung at the air and hit not much of anything. But every time those two would do something, somebody would drop. The only thing I got out of it was a hit on the head, a bump I still have. They never did get us, because Intinarelli and Toby Crooke were so efficient they put them all away."

The inevitable riot occurred on April 13, 1943, headlined in the Balboa newspaper the next day: "Panama City Cleared of Soldiers Following Riot." The news account mercifully does not name the ignition point, probably the one time the 551st was glad not to be recognized. Though T/5 Francis X. Leary points to one of his fellows leaning too heavily on a shop keeper's glass case and breaking it, it all appears to have begun when a GOYA bird shoplifted a bottle of whisky at a liquor store at the corner of J Street and Avenida Central. The proprietor screamed "Policia!" A Panamanian cop arrived and was promptly struck by a GOYA; the fight was on. For forty-five minutes soldiers and civilians rioted through the center of Panama City, smashing the windows of the National Bank. It took a combination of hundreds of MPs, the Panamanian police, and the Shore Patrol to clear the streets. Jim Stevens and friends were hustled out of a moviehouse by MPs with shotguns and submachine guns. For almost three hours the city was off limits to all U.S. soldiers.

Leo Urban of Colorado and Bob Johnson of North Carolina, both of Headquarters Company, ran up an alley to escape the mob. A Panamanian woman opened her door, letting them slip in to hide until things died down. Both men had witnessed the first altercation. Urban recalled that all the men of HQ Company chipped in and paid for a new set of false teeth for the proprietor. The thief had to face trial in Panama. It is not known if he served time, but Urban and his bunch were confined to the base for a month. Surprisingly few injuries resulted, and by 8:45 P.M. the curfew was lifted. Business was business, and fights were fights, and fights were business, sometimes.

The GOYAs had their angels. That anonymous Panamanian woman who rescued Urban and Johnson from the mob was one. Two others who protected Max Bryan from bar injury were the most unangelic fellows in the unit, two ex-convicts. Bryan, who for many years could not speak of his war experience, stuffing it inside himself as my father had done, cannot to this day remember their names, although they were his best friends. He does remember them as "Polacks." They were his bookends in Panama; they did not survive the war.

One of the 551st ex-convicts—Frank "Bighead" Powers, who had served time in San Quentin for armed robbery—"fitted right in" with the Headquarters Company light machine gun platoon and "performed his duties the same as anyone else," wrote the memoirist Don Garrigues. The two Poles, alma mater unknown, also seem to have been decent soldiers, or no more indecent than everyone else. They had been loggers in Washington State and perhaps that is why Max and they took to each other, as he had known the sweet whine of a sawmill from childhood.

They also took to him because he was young (along with Doug Dillard, the youngest in the 551st at sixteen) and they were older than the average unit member. The Polish loggers had once gone on a weekend spree in San Francisco, out for girls and booze. Drunk, they stole a fire truck from a local Army base, Fort Knight, and drove it into San Francisco Bay. They were put in federal prison, because it was a federal offense to steal a federal vehicle. The war was a lucky break for them, and the paratroopers, in particular, gave them a way to be sprung from jail.

Max Bryan remembered times when they helped him out of the blur of a Panama City bar. They guided him on night marches through the black palms and the beach apples. And at the Bulge, the day one of them was mortally wounded by a mortar shell, he looked up at Max from a stretcher at an aid station and wondered aloud if there were any bars nearby where Max might need protection. Before Max could answer, this person who will remain forever anonymous, forever out of jail and full of good pine smell, said to the graves registration man, "I am an atheist. Teach me how to pray."

3
Spotlight's rebellion

The "most flagrant public breach of discipline" that Dan Morgan ever saw in Army service or, for that matter, during the thirty-five years of his professional military career, took place in Panama.

It was a blistering Saturday afternoon when all 539 officers and men of the battalion stood on the parade grounds waiting for the final "retreat" order that would allow them to plunge into their Saturday night leave and Sunday holy hangover. The battalion scratched at fire ant and bedbug bites and poison ivy–like beach apples. Sweat poured down their faces. Major Joerg eyed his watch; when the minute hand hit the zenith and six o'clock, he shouted to the battalion's adjutant, Lieutenant Hugh "Soft Shoe" Robinson: "Call the battalion to attention!"

"BAAH—TAA—LEE—YAWN! TEN-SHUT!"

"My squad—AAT—EEZ!"

The members of the third squad, 2d platoon of Company C dropped their salutes and wilted. There was confusion and murmuring among the officers in front, but all Company C had heard the countercommand and knew whose it was: Sergeant Willie "Spotlight" Brown, third squad leader.

Spotlight was a rebel among rebels, the sole member of the original Test Platoon in the 551st. Doug Dillard, who knew him also as "Burr Head" Brown, once heard a .45 pistol go off in the barracks above his basement classroom and was sent by the lecturer to find out what the commotion was. Spotlight, fogged on marijuana, hadn't been able to get his room door open and had shot the lock off. He also had the bizarre habit of hiding under his chute at the drop zone after jumping.

Now, Captain Bill Smith, who commanded C Company at the time, identified the culprit and barked, "2d platoon, third squad: TENSION!"

Choking with bile, Brown uncorked a blood-curdling scream heard by the entire battalion and the 550th glider battalion 100 yards away: "I— SAID—MY SQUAAAD—AAT—EEZ!"

It was "a moment of absolute consternation," Morgan recalled. "We didn't know whether to laugh out loud or die from silent convulsions." Apparently, silence and sweat won out, pouring off everything. Major Joerg nodded to Robinson, stepped forward and roared, "Captain Smith, place that man under arrest!"

It took two large sergeants, under Smith's orders, to hold Brown down. He yelled and bit and clawed as he was upended and dragged toward the barracks: "Goddamnit, those men are mine! I ain't gonna let them die in the sun!"

Spotlight was an outstanding soldier in almost every regard, a born leader, tough as nails, and very resourceful. Perhaps it was that Sergeant Willie F. Brown—busted and rebusted to private—for one precious moment had something to tell Major Wood Joerg, wanted to let him know that enlisted men could pour sweat with the best of them but were all mortal, after all. (Brown was blasted on chi chi that day and probably had had a roll in the fronds with the San Blas Indian chief's daughter, his girlfriend.) I suspect Joerg understood all this, with his weakness for the line soldier. It was a tough test for him, as he had as active a funny bone as any man in the unit. But to allow Burrhead Brown to grandstand before the whole battalion in such a formal setting would have spelled the end of respect for the commander. And respect, among all these independent states gathered as one, was hard to come by.

In any case, God would call both Joerg and Spotlight to attention at the Battle of the Bulge, and God would put them both at ease.

The one element that identifies all paratrooper units—in fact, all U.S. Army units—the unit insignia, was denied to the 551st for many years. It was not officially approved by the Army until 1992. Though Joerg chose purple-and-gold as the official GOYA colors (because no one else had them) there appear to be no original sleeve patches using those colors; an original officer chest patch with a silver eagle embroidered on black appears to have been designed and made in small quantities during the Panama days, with a prominent palm tree on it. In any case, an original 551st patch with insignia fashioned in Panama is quite rare and will fetch a price on the collectors' market of around two thousand dollars, the equivalent in the baseball card world of a Hank Aaron rookie card.

In the mid-1980s the insignia authority Les Hughes was commissioned by the American Society of Military Insignia Collectors to identify the origins of the mysterious 551st patch, including its designer.[6] Hughes found himself in a maelstrom. At the time, he identified two possible artists, but it took another decade to narrow it to one: B Company's Private Vincent Artz, who broke his skull in a fall from a glider in 1943, leaving the GOYAs and the Army forever. Artz confirms that it was Joerg himself who spied him sketching one day and assigned him the insignia design and a little studio all his own for accomplishing it. Artz had the completed task secreted in his hip pocket in a matter of days, then "dog-robbed" six weeks for his own painting and sketching: "I milked it. It was better than going out and sweating my testicles off."[7] Hughes concluded that the patch was born and made in Panama, but hidden, like the 551st's clandestine life there, until 1943, when it was distributed at Camp Mackall.

On Artz's original design, the GOYA's insignia is one of the very few in the U.S. military that uses flora rather than fauna; the green palm tree at the center of a blue felt shield is leaning, not at attention. Is this the Spotlight Brown instinct? A white machete slices the tree base and almost meets the lean, as if it were dancing with the tree. "We were crazy over the tropics," Artz explains. A maroon lightning bolt slants across the scene (a paratrooper cliché for quick force). A scroll at the bottom announces in Spanish—this appears to be the only U.S. Armed Forces patch using a foreign language—*Aterrice y Ataque* (Alight and Fight). Encompassing all is an eagle of silver bullion thread in a phoenix pose, looking sideways. The claws, unlike many paratrooper patches, are hidden.

4
A shadow-box of lepers

Wood Joerg was shadow-boxing alone. Doc Chalkley saw him one night up late at Fort Kobbe, when most of the men were sleeping. It was May 1943. He saw him moving by the light of a bare bulb in his room, punching the air; Chalkley stopped to regard him from the street, lighting a cigarette.

The commander's shadow towered above him, filling the wall, punching the emptiness. The incongruity of the man: the boyish face, the toothy and winning smile, capped by an almost completely bald pate at twenty-nine. The enlisted men had elevated Joerg to folk hero status; he was always at the head of the forced marches through the jungle, always among the first to jump to the dime-size drop zones inside a wreath of palms. He boxed with them; they heard him speak Spanish with vendors, evidence of his learning and worldliness. He whistled swing songs of Glenn Miller when the bugler played reveille at dawn. The men idolized him, identified with his youth (he was one of the youngest paratroop battalion commanders in the army at the time), liked what they had heard of his rebelliousness at West Point. They were sure he'd outrace James Gavin to be the youngest general in the Army. They were going to pace him to it.

But with the officers he could be severe ("shorted in the sense of humor department"),[8] and some thought he was trying too hard to compensate for his youth, inexperience, and checkered performance at the Point. Some were turned off glimpsing him late one night practicing a quick draw in front of a mirror, wearing only a holster, helmet, and jockey shorts. Doc Chalkley was ambivalent about Joerg, who was a year his senior. He admired his inexhaustible energy but wasn't keen on Joerg's stiffness about deportment. Once when Chalkley rushed to the 5 P.M. retreat ceremony, late, with blood all over his class-A uniform from cutting a huge boil off the chest of a trooper, Joerg stopped him. "Where the hell you think you're going?" he eyed the doctor head to toe. "The review, sir." "The hell you are." "The hell I'm not," Doc snapped back. Joerg then drew a line on the ground with his finger and threatened Chalkley with a court martial if he crossed it. Apparently, decorum won out over punctuality.

The Doc operated at a pace too easygoing for the tense person Joerg was becoming. After one too many rules bent, Joerg confined the surgeon to quarters after dusk for a month. It was during that month that Doc spotted Joerg shadow boxing.

What was he punching that spring night? The top brass, perhaps, for mooring him here, far from Japan or Europe, while Lieutenant Colonel Edson Raff and Major Bill Yarborough were bursting with the 509th through the Casserine Pass to help throw Rommel back across Tunisia. A double blow to Raff and Yarborough! And Gavin himself? Two months hence he would jump into Sicily with the 505th (which would disappear from the GOYAs' right flank at the Bulge), leading the first Allied assault on Fortress Europe. Sicily had been secretly picked by Eisenhower and Churchill at Casablanca in January 1943 as the next stepping stone after North Africa to roll back the Axis powers. The airborne brass were abuzz with preparations, and it would not have been unusual for Joerg himself to know about it.

By January 31, 1943, as the 551st began its test jumps in Panama, the German Army suffered its first sizable defeat at Stalingrad. More than 160,000 Germans had been killed in action; 90,000 frostbitten POWs had been marched to Siberia. The incredible defense of Stalingrad by the Russian Army and its brave civilian inhabitants had shown the Nazis were not invincible.

Thus by the spring of 1943 the war was beginning to pass Joerg by. He and some other officers had arranged for a rendezvouz with Heidi and other wives in Mexico City to take the pressure off, but the Army disallowed it at the last moment for fear of spies. Joerg boxed that night as a man anxious but proud, ready to prove what his motley unit and, therefore, he himself, was made of.

Chalkley heard, against all the night's cicadas, Joerg's feet scratch-dancing. It's not difficult to imagine the commander pivoting on a punch as if throwing Heidi Joerg outward in a jitterbug move. He had sent her a V-mailed letter with a riddled news clipping about a parachute exhibition at a War Bond Carnival. In it, mention of the 551st is censored, as well as the name of the stadium near which they were dropping, the Field (probably Howard), and the carnival sponsor. The news report paints an ideal picture: "As the last man drifts lazily earthward, trucks will head directly to the Stadium, where each paratrooper will step up to the bond selling booths and buy a war bond." The Major's name is misspelled as "Jorge," pleasingly Spanish. At the bottom of the clipping is an exuberant hand-written inscription, "We dood it!"

Yes, they had done it. But only at a carnival; Joerg hungered for the real billow against fear. As Chalkley took a last pull of smoke into his lungs, Joerg's solitary boxing grew more intense, coming to a head. Perhaps with the memory of being bitten by that horse the men curried at the Hook Up Club, he punched the air hard, because he told them to get rid of it. Perhaps with a vision of Spotlight Brown's eyes bulging out of his head as he screams, "These men are mine! I'm not going to let them die in the sun!" whose sheer arrogant brotherhood sent a salty pang through Joerg's body to his eyes that he forced down by harder boxing.

Joerg dropped his arms and ran in place, waiting for the GOYAs to catch up. His eyes closed as if he had arrived at the leper colony, lepers emerging from the mirror, the naked bulb showing their emaciated faces, the holes, the carbuncles, the pus. And how thin they were like those he had heard about in camps in Europe. As if one leper with dark cloak over his head came directly up to the commander, touched him on the arm and removed the hood, Joerg's eyes flared open.

His roommate at the Point. His cousin George Joerg bloated in the pool at Fort Sam Houston. Colin Kelly's face unpeeled.

Jab jab jab. Joerg stopped, his chest heaving, his fists up on the wall. Chalkley's crushed his cigarette and turned away. *There is no such thing as fearless determination. There is only fear and these good men. I am thankful to lead them; for they lead me from my fear.*

It was midnight in Panama. Joerg joined his men in sleep. Shadows crowded on the road to Belgium.

5

Martinique

On May 13, 1943, the 551st Parachute Infantry Battalion, the 550th glider battalion, and the entire Sixth Air Force in Panama were alerted to prepare for an invasion of Martinique. The small Caribbean island was a French colony, and its armed forces were under the command of a Nazi sympathizer, Rear Admiral Georges Robert, who had been made High Commissioner of the French Antilles by Vichy's Marshal Petain. For close to a year it had been the one place in the Caribbean where Admiral Donitz's U-boats could surface, refuel, resupply, and be sent unbothered to their deadly attacks on shipping to and from the United States, particularly in "Torpedo Junction" between Cuba's Isle of Pines and Guantanamo Bay. Martinique was not the showcase Sicily was, but Joerg would take it.

A well-known oceanographer and geologist at Princeton, Dr. Harry Hess, had pinpointed Martinique as the problem. Hess, a German émigré, had reasoned that German U-boats would traverse "the proper way," that is, in great circles, and by plotting their various routes meticulously he found that they all intersected at Martinique.

By then the 551st had been in Panama more than six months. Its "secret" mission was becoming less so by the day, and both German and Japanese spies knew what they were up to. As they were drawing combat equipment for the jump on Martinique, Duke Spletzer discovered a supply chute riddled with holes. Sent to the Public Health Service in the Canal Zone, it was discovered to have been burned by acid. Though not an overwhelming act of sabotage, the wrecked chute aggravated the men's jittery nerves. Lieutenant Schroeder ordered all chutes locked up in the attic of the headquarters barracks, under guard.

The GOYAs drew battle gear. Several hundred concussion grenades were sent from the ordnance depot in Balboa, with fuses separate; men in each company were assigned to fit fuses to grenades. Doc Chalkley was contacted by the Surgeon General at Quarry Heights, who seemed to know more about the coming attack than he did—the size of the Navy and Army Air Corps support, for example. Chalkley received an issue of five thousand morphine syrettes. Maps of Martinique and its capital, Fort-de-France, were studied, and sand tables—sandboxes with the terrain of the drop zone shaped, grooved, and modeled in miniature—were prepared. The Company C commander, Captain Tims Quinn, indicated later that the 551st drop plan on Martinique may have been a "tester" for a far more ambitious project, the 1945 Allied jump across the Rhine River in which paratroopers would be banged right on German housetops.

Company A—with Cicchinelli and Dillard—was to fall on the airfield of the island. Company B—Morgan's group—was to drop right on Fort-de-France itself and take control of such key civilian functions as government offices, radio communications, water towers, and banks. Company C—Bryan's unit—was fingered to smack down on the military fort itself, where 3,500 well-armed and well-trained Senegalese soldiers, loyal to Vichy France, were waiting. The C Company drop would attempt to thread the needle right into the parade ground of the troops barracks. The 551st would finally test what Joerg had told them: Each would have to be worth five men of the enemy.

A captain from Trinidad, who presumably knew the contours of Martinique, was made temporary commander of Company A for the attack. He hadn't even jumped from planes and received the quickest jump training in the unit's history from Captain Quinn. Finally, just before the mini "D-Day," all pretense of a secret mission was dropped. In full paratroop battle dress the entire 551st PIB was trucked to downtown Balboa, the Panamanian capital, where the men stood at attention on both sides of the central boulevard for half a mile while the President of Columbia reviewed the troops.

The psychological weapon of unveiling the force had its effect. Behind the scenes the State Department and the Office of Strategic Services had been pressuring the pro-Hitler Admiral Robert's regime to step down, using the incipient invasion of the 551st as its stick. In the final moment, it worked. A quiet coup occurred. Robert was whisked off the island; his command was surrendered to U.S. Rear Admiral John Hoover; and the Nazi wolf pack of U-boats was denied access to its port.[9]

The effect was almost immediate. In June 1943 U-boat action took out the smallest tonnage of shipping since the war began in 1939: 30,000 tons, as against 200,000 tons the month before. Though some attacks still occurred off the central and northeastern coasts of South America, in summer 1943 U-boats had largely shifted back to the North Atlantic, where closer Anglo-American cooperation, faster transports, and strengthened escorts either eluded or sank them. In the heydey period of 1942, a German U-boat had an average lifespan of thirteen months; by the end of the war that had dropped to three months.

The 551st did not wear out its lungs shouting "Victory!" After all, Martinique had fallen without a popgun shot. It was no use telling the men that they had made a significant contribution to keeping the Nazis out of the Americas and the Allied resupply line alive. Perhaps, uncelebrated, they could sense what was beginning to happen: Later, virtually no history book would mention their Panama escapade or the small coup in psychological warfare they could claim. They took their pumped muscles and grenades out on the fish.

Thus the 551st's sojourn in Panama ended in the late summer of 1943 with a string of Friday night fish fries. "We did quite a bit of fishing with those grenades," Jack Carr said. Little by little the hundreds of concussion grenades packed in the storeroom began to disappear, as explosions were heard in the lagoons. Everything from mackerel to shark was blasted to the surface; the men swam out with gunny sacks, gathering the dead or deafened fish. Back at the barracks, two oil drums cut in half were filled, one with hot water and the other with hot oil. The only rule was: Clean your own fish. Soon the grenades were gone.

"Prop Blast Punch" is what the wry menu called liquor at one of those feasts, a July 26 Headquarters and Headquarters Company banquet. Soup was "Consommé à la Malfunction" and peas "Fresh Young Shot Bags." For dessert? Door Freeze, of course. And to wash it all down, Venado River Dew (water).

As for the morphine syrettes, some were turned back in and some taken back to the States. No one has told if any were used in Panama to remove the pain of not yet passing the war test. The men of the 551st in Panama had met every obstacle but their own fear. Their spirits had been raised to a fever pitch, and tested by fever itself in the jungle. (The malaria would rear its head sixteen months later in a frigid Belgium.) To large groups of men together for a long time, everything becomes a joke, or they become violent. The 551st's sense of humor was finely and wickedly honed in Panama. Its "war on MPs," as Bill Lumsden called it, was legendary. Lumsden had actually been accepted for officers' candidate school while in Panama but chose to stay with the 551st because of its extraordinary spirit. Joerg was proud of his GOYAs. He found them as battle-prepared as they could be, but he was uncertain what this aborted mission meant for them.

On August 20, 1943, the 551st boarded the U.S. Army Transport *Etolin* in Balboa and left Panama bound westward into the Pacific for what looked like combat against the Japanese. But it was not to be. For them preparation was becoming interminable. They still had a final reckoning back home with what would be their fourth, final, and most deadly training.

IV

FOREBODING

The Night Jump Drownings at Mackall

War hath no fury like a noncombatant.

—C. E. Montague

1
The pups' death

On the 551st's ship back from Panama, something happened that would haunt the battalion. It almost caused a mutiny, and Wood Joerg a court martial. A small wasting of life, the first killing, it would be a harbinger of tragedy to come in North Carolina and Belgium.

The Master of the transport ship, the *Etolin,* had discovered a few days out of port that the 551st had smuggled its mascot, the dachshund Furlough, on board the ship, with the quiet acquiescence of the recently promoted Lieutenant Colonel Joerg. Animals were not allowed back in the States with troops coming from combat or foreign duty of any kind. The Master ordered Furlough confiscated and put to sleep.

Several GOYAs, "very quiet, but very angry paratroopers," according to Captain Ed Hartman, surrounded the seaman who held the worried Furlough around her belly with two hands. She must have smelled fish on this fellow, whereas her own people smelled of earth or sky. The man could not move. On the point of attacking him, the men decided to wait for Joerg, who looked hard at Furlough and then at the seaman before banging the ship metal with his paratrooper boots. He went to confront the Master, who, realizing that he had a potential mutiny on his hands, backed down. He would report the matter in San Francisco to port authorities.

But the same day that the Master gave in, someone else took vengeance. Furlough was preserved, but her two pups were taken from their gas mask hiding places and thrown into the sea. Sergeant "Hedy" LaMar was convinced that two members of Company A, hearing that we wouldn't be allowed to dock in San Francisco with dogs on board or that they were be quarantined, had "volunteered" to kill the pups. "Our own men did it," LaMar said.

Others, like Joe Edgerly of Company B, who had come to be Furlough and the pups' chief protector and feeder, wouldn't or couldn't believe that. Edgerly, a homeless waif in Boston as a child, had empathy for the downtrodden. He had built himself up in school and in the Army as a formidable athlete, excelling as a boxer, weightlifter, and runner; among the 551st he was a one-armed pushup champ. When he broke down and wept inconsolably, insisting that it had to be the Merchant Marines, not any GOYA man, the GOYAs wanted to believe him.

"This incident added measurably to a feeling of disgruntlement that was gradually to erode our morale over the next several months," Morgan notes. Even for the modest, sensitive narrator that Morgan is, that is an understatement. The unit would soon register an alarming VD rate, become chronically AWOL, and find one-third of its members in the stockade.

LaMar may have blocked out the memory of the culprits' names on the *Etolin* for the same reason that Edgerly wept. It was too hard to believe. Protecting the guilty from vengeance, even a vengeance of memory. And protecting himself from meaninglessness. It is hard enough to know those you love have killed wantonly, easier to obliterate their identity into anonymity. A nameless obscenity is somehow more livable.

A direct witness to the incident, which "burned in my memory," recalled one culprit all too well and did not shy from naming him. Sergeant Forrest Reed saw Sergeant George Dickson of A Company toss one of the pups overboard (the name of another man escapes him). To Reed, Dickson, who later received a battlefield commission in the French Maritime Alps, was "ornery, an opportunist, and a sneak." It appears he went to strange lengths to curry favor. In Panama Dickson had recently beaten out Sergeant Steve Kicinski, who lacked a high school education, for the post of A Company's first sergeant. It was certainly an irony—that those who had so often slid over the edge of the rules, who had developed a reputation, in fact, for striking fear into enforcers themselves (MPs, among others), should strangely wilt, and in the wilting, kill. After all, Dickson and his confederate sent the puppies into the sea forever to obey rules. There was self-interest involved; bureaucracies sooner or later reward those who follow their rules, mindless or not, often the more mindless the greater the reward, a tacit acknowledgment of the difficulty of squelching one's humanity.

However, tossing the pups overboard was also a violation of plain smarts. Two Merchant Marine men immediately "laid into" Dickson, pointing out to him that any German submarines in the area that spotted the dead puppies in the water would know a ship was close by.

When they'd heard about the pups' killing, the men of the 551st "sat on our bunks down below and stared at one another speculatively," Morgan recounted. Morgan imagined them contemplating mutiny against the seamen, but word certainly would have gotten around that some Company A men may have done it, and that would have frozen their vengeance, directing their meditations inward.

Staring out a porthole at the sea, what could Wood Joerg have been thinking? *What manner of men is this? There's one thing about a band of outsiders—you've got to make sure there's no insiders among them. Who are these cruel insiders?* Joerg could have foreseen looking at a rusted sun drop in the sea that what made the men tick could easily explode. The pups' deaths—a slap from within—warned him there might be a cost for this elite fire he had fanned. The black lacquer spread over the waves could come calling for his men. And he could have, in that moment, doubted himself, his use to them, and theirs to him. And make the first seedling of a plan to unhook himself from the happy monsters, not so happy now on the way home with no glory, with nothing, really, but more training in sight, and not monstrous, but all-too-human in their disappointment. He said goodnight to the puppies sinking to the bottom.

Except for this incident and the presence of wounded men, the ten-day voyage to San Francisco was unremarkable. On board the *Etolin* with the 551st, lying out on cots or limping under the screaming gulls, were men going home from battle in the Pacific, specifically on New Guinea. Leo Urban wrote in his journal, "Some of them are in pretty bad shape from what I can see. They have bandaged hands, legs, feet, necks, faces—in fact, some have bandages all over them. Some of them sure don't look like they will ever get over it." The GOYAs saw where they were going and, with the salt spray off the Pacific coast of California, it sobered them.

If at first the 551st thought it was headed out to island-hop against the Japanese, three days out of port it was told that after San Francisco, it was going for training to North Carolina and a new base, Camp Mackall, named for the first paratrooper killed in the war overseas in North Africa during Operation Torch. Mackall would be their fourth training stint in what was beginning to look like an unending apprenticeship. *Maybe this time they'll ask us to drop on Bermuda in Bermuda shorts.*

Packed in "like fish" in stacks four bunks high, with only 2 feet between, the men would often come up on deck to smoke, write letters, or write in journals. Porpoises leaped out of the teal water—schools of them jumping in pairs—a sight many landlocked GIs had never seen. Inevitably, though the California coast was visible by day to starboard, many got seasick. It was like "riding in a car on a corrugated road."[1] There were some rifle inspections; showers in salt water wouldn't lather soap; there was no smoking on deck after sundown. With the red disk sinking into the sea, the ship seemed to be on fire, from smoke rising off the decks, as the men puffed their last.

Just before reaching San Francisco, the ship's Master tried to put the 551st to some use. He issued them chipping hammers to clean the deck. That had about as much effect as Hitler handing out breakfast. After one desultory chip—this was spread by word of mouth—everyone tossed their hammers into the sea: small retribution for Furlough's pups. In port the ship's commander complained about the dog to debarkation authorities. There was some delay, but Furlough was safely among the "disappeared," and the *Etolin* and its weary soldiers finally were allowed off.

Alighting with Furlough in a sack, the 551st had managed to keep something of itself intact. Its mascot embodied its sense of being, as Morgan explained it, "low man on the totem pole, but making no concessions." Furlough was no Great Dane, or Oscillation (who had run off in Panama). She had graduated from gas mask to tote bag, and when she stuck her nose out of it on the dock, smelling fresh crabs and San Francisco sourdough, not to mention civilians, she barked.

The wounded were taken to hospitals, and GOYAs were ferried to Angel Island in the middle of San Francisco Bay for a week of isolation, debriefing of the Panama experience, and checkups. Here they encountered a strange sight: Japanese prisoners-of-war jeering at them through fences topped with barbed wire. The 551st did double-time cadence runs each morning around the island. When they passed the POW pen, the Japanese made faces and mimicked the double-time shouting with falsetto shrieks. The GOYAs had already been slighted by fate when their drop on Martinique was canceled; they had been put down by the *Etolin*'s Master and by the killers of the pups. They did not need the enemy from the East rubbing it in. Wartime in those moments of strange language and all-too-comprehensible taunts, as if they, not the Japanese, were the captives, was surreal.

Maybe that is why they double-timed half-naked, cavalier, bronzed by Panama, hard-muscled, in nothing but boxer shorts and boots. The sight of them, and the sound of their shouts around Angel Island, aroused more than the Japanese POWs: Officers complained from the island's Fort McDowell. On at least one occasion Joerg himself was called to the Sixth Air Force to explain the GOYAs' irreverent behavior.

To the men's dismay, no one was allowed off Angel Island. But the GOYAs were an impossible bunch to hem in. It was like quarantining quicksilver. The ex-con "Big Head" Powers, who had a sister in San Francisco, cooked up a scheme for some members of the Headquarters Company light machine gun platoon: They would wear coveralls over their class-A uniforms and would pose as workmen going back to the mainland. Among the group were the boxer Joe Chizar and Jim Heffernan. The trick worked. For three days and nights they used Powers's sister's apartment as a base of operations for all sorts of forays into the strip joints of North Beach and the Tenderloin, as well as Chinatown. To get back, they had to pose as milkmen on a milk boat. Their journey, the first of hundreds of AWOLs the 551st would register in the months before its transfer to the front in Europe, merited a chewing out by First Sergeant William Dumas.

Joerg loosened up a little with passes to forestall the AWOLs. The first group allowed out stole a couple of orange crates the minute it got to shore, hijacked a cable car, and proceeded to pummel the populace with oranges flying wildly down a San Francisco hill. And they hadn't touched a drink yet. "I guess the people thought we were nuts," Sergeant Bob Van Horssen said. "The sailors just watched; they didn't mess with us." Even to their own they were unstable chemicals; the Germans would label them "devils in baggy pants."

What the men of the 551st really were—at least at this juncture in their checkered existence—was bored. Joerg quickly canceled passes after the orange-crate wars. On September 3, 1943, the GOYAs left Fort McDowell by ferry to Oakland, where they boarded three troop trains (along with the 550th glider men) on the Southern Pacific Railroad to travel east. Men slept in the aisles, even on top of each other. As they rumbled through a city, Tims Quinn spread the curtains and looked out at running lights. Someone said, "If you've never been to Amarillo, you're there now." Quinn shrugged and fell back to sleep.

2
The glider jumps

On arrival at Camp Mackall, North Carolina, the Colonel finally allowed the 551st to take the extended leave denied them a year before. It was probably a mistake. All but one of the men received twenty-one-day furloughs; upon their return the unit would be chastised by the Surgeon General himself for registering the second highest rate of venereal disease in the U.S. Army. They would also face a stark order to conduct the first experimental—and especially dangerous—mass paratroop jumps from gliders.

The only man to get less than twenty-one days free was Big Head Powers. He got only ten days, no doubt because of his escape from Angel Island. Powers's home turf was San Francisco; he'd already seen his sister, and in any case he couldn't make it back and forth across the country in time, so he went up to New York City. "Like most everybody else in the battalion," Jim Heffernan noted, "old Big Head was a drifter."

My father, hardly a drifter, affectionately dubbed the family "the traveling Orfaleas" when I was young. Growing up in Cleveland, Aref Junior loved summer trips to Chautauqua Lake, New York, where my grandmother would peddle linens from the family store to wealthy Eastern mandarins on vacation. One of my earliest boyhood memories is traveling in our three-nostril red Buick through what probably were the Sawtooth mountains while my father set up franchises of a women's dress shop chain in the Pacific Northwest. Also, and maybe this is more to Heffernan's point, Aref Orfalea had a GOYA-love for those left out. From the earliest times I remember strange people with sad stories being harbored at our home in Los Angeles (or should I say, homes; vagabond dad moved us five times when I was a child: downtown LA, Monterey Park, Highland Park, Anaheim, and finally Tarzana). Over time they would become less strange and not entirely sad. There was Father Jay Clines, his childhood friend, who would take a break from running Catholic cemeteries in Cleveland. There was Uncle Harry Orfalea, who lived in a single room downtown, a kindly man with a soft Homburg, who was said to have lost what little cash he had on horses. There was Hal Crasell, a fellow dress manufacturer fallen on tough times, who had endured a bitter divorce and who would jump up to our piano and pound out original, heart-rending tunes as my father, properly silent, mouth open, slowly felt his chin as if it had disappeared.

Big Head Powers typified the hard-luck characters come in from the cold my father originally grew to know in the 551st. The former thief would himself be taken for a ride by a New York pickup gal. She married him shortly after the first bourbon; she had married several others under assumed names and was receiving checks from her various spouses each month! Big Head's head wasn't so big after that one; he had the marriage annulled at Camp Mackall after two weeks, proclaiming to his buddy, Bob Lefils, "It was a helluva good two weeks." He then spotted a sixteen-year-old girl at a restaurant cash register near Mackall and courted her in record time, even for him: In twenty-four hours they were hitched in Fayetteville, with Lefils as a bewildered best man. Big Head got the clap in Nice after the invasion of southern France but returned to his happy second marriage, though children were not possible because of damage from Powers's childhood chicken pox. His bride died at twenty-nine; Big Head carried a sore heart around for years until, at forty-eight, he married his third teenager.

Staggered in time, the furloughs played out, and one by one the men reported back to Mackall. Joerg must have seen in their eyes the porchlights of all their homes. A sluggishness was noticeable in their response to reveille. He would have to act. Bad habits multipled in the absence of a concrete mission: The men drove other GIs out of the PX near their barracks, staking out their territory. Joerg moved them to another barracks; they did it again, causing rows (possibly with the new 517th Regiment men). When the men started auctioning off their own paratrooper jump knives to the regular infantrymen at Mackall, Joerg posted a notice. Volunteers for the first mass paratroop jumps from gliders were sought. "We badly needed something to do," Morgan admitted, and overnight the sign-up sheets were filled. (All other unit commanders at Mackall were queried about the glider test jumps, but only Joerg agreed to them, on condition that a majority of his men would assent. They did.)

By now the U.S. Airborne had not only caught up with the Germans, but was passing them. Throughout the summer and early fall of 1943, the Allies had logged three sizable airdrops into North Africa (Torch), Sicily (Husky), and Salerno, Italy (Avalanche). Though the operations were ultimately successful, paratrooper losses were so heavy, particularly in Sicily and Salerno, that the whole matter of using airborne assault groups was in question.

Airborne historian William Breuer called the Sicily drop of the 504th "a holocaust in the sky." German anti-aircraft had been ready on the southern Sicily coast near Gela, and many a C-47 transport plane burst into flame and fell before paratroopers could hook up. Some did so in a frenzy, without static lines, and fell directly to the ground, chutes unopened. As Breuer notes, "Jim Gavin and his [505th] troopers on Biazza Ridge heard sickening thuds as a few bodies hurtled into the ground."[2] Many others were mistaken for German paratroopers and shot in midair by their own troops. Friendly fire took down twenty-three transport planes and gliders carrying 229 airborne men. Even one as steely as General Patton, who had gone with General Matthew Ridgway to welcome the paratroopers at Farello airfield, was reduced to muttering "My God! My God!" as he watched the explosions and the falling men go rigid, then limp on their lines. The incident was totally blacked out from the news media for eight months. Neither the famed war correspondent Ernie Pyle, who witnessed Americans shooting their own troops in Sicily, nor the editors of the venerable Time–Life series on World War II ever included this disastrous blunder in their reportage.

The invasion force slowly webbed its way across Sicily. But General Dwight D. Eisenhower noted that the Sicily losses "were inexcusably high," laying the blame across the services, "with a large measure falling on me." He bluntly wrote the Chairman of the Joint Chiefs of Staff, General George C. Marshall: "I do not believe in the airborne division,"[3] a view he would alter later, though indeed he would have been more justified in withholding confidence from the "new and badly scared" gunners, as Fussell calls them, who mistook Americans for Germans. Gavin thought Ike too rash, too battle-removed: "I was puzzled by the fact that no senior officers from high headquarters came to Sicily during or after our operations. Certainly no high-ranking officer ever discussed our mission with me afterwards."[4]

Nevertheless, the slaughter of the Sicily skyjumpers—many by their own side on the ground—was part of the reason Ike precipitously called off the next two planned 82d Airborne mass jumps, code-named Giant I and Giant II. The first was to jump 40 miles north of Salerno, where the Allied sea invasion force into Italy—Operation Avalanche—was to land. Forty miles is a long way from friends. The second operation was to jump right on Rome itself. Both were canceled—the latter within hours of take-off—as likely to destroy the division.

On September 14, 1943, however, a three-unit emergency jump, arranged within hours, by the 504th, the 505th, and the 509th rescued the Sicily debacle by reinforcing the Allied beachhead at Salerno. The 509th battalion took severe punishment at nearby Avellino (20 percent casualties), with men in isolated pockets fighting bravely against far larger German forces. General Mark Clark, who commanded the Avalanche invasion of Italy beginning at the "shin" of Salerno, wrote in his memoir that "with victory or defeat hung in the balance" American paratrooper reinforcements "tilted the scales in our favor." Ike's wrath was quelled somewhat.

A month after the Salerno assault, the 551st's experiments with jumping from gliders began in late October at Mackall. The high command was looking to avoid the loss of expensive transport planes, not to mention troops (as in Sicily) as well as to increase the chance of a closely packed landing instead of a scattered one (as at Avellino). And though the Germans had taken severe losses in the 1941 airborne capture of Crete, U.S. planners had not forgotten the Germans' highly successful use of gliders at Fort Eben-Emael in Belgium at the war's beginning in 1940. With the 551st's tests, the Americans would up the ante, jumping from gliders on a double-tow of rope behind a plane.

For a GOYA force on the verge of full-scale rebellion, the glider tests went remarkably well. The honor of being the first enlisted American GI to throw his life out of a glider was given to the 551st's Jack Carr, the first officer Dick Mascuch (who at the age of seventy-six still makes exhibition jumps worldwide and was the only representative of the southern France invasion participating in the 50th anniversary jump at Normandy in June 1994). That first mass glider jump in U.S. history took place on October 18, 1943. Mascuch recorded a "soft landing." The next day's exercise one-upped the previous day's: The GOYAs jumped out both doors. Mascuch took a "hard landing."

There was something of the Hollywood sound stage to the October 21 exhibition. Some British and American top brass, including the British Air Marshal and Lieutenant General McNair—came down from Washington to rubberneck from the grandstands. Carr and about twenty others were lifted off the ground in a Waco CG-4A glider by a B-24 transport plane, with another twenty-man glider alongside, like a speedboat pulling two skiers on either side of a wake simultaneously. The gliders were engineless, ribbed by light wood. Bob Van Horssen checked a label on the slats of the vessel. They were made by a piano factory in his hometown, Grand Haven, Michigan. The "flying coffins," as they were called, vibrated severely in the prop wash of the transport; Van Horssen had heard better piano. Unlike a drop from a regular transport, the men bailed out of a glider from two doors, left and right, synchronizing themselves to keep the glider from tipping. They landed at the edge of the demonstration field, disappearing into the woods. Suddenly, forty-four fresh men came rushing out of the trees, stunning the brass. For some moments the sleight-of-hand worked, and the generals nodded their approval. The men who had jumped were still hopping in the woods on sore ankles! (One officer broke his leg down a gopher hole.)

Compactness was achieved, however. "You could walk over the drop zone on the parachutes without ever touching the ground," Ed Hartman noted. "We were that close together."

For the last two weeks of October and into November 1943, the 551st conducted five jumps from gliders, and from gliders and planes together. The November 23 exhibition was viewed by Secretary of War Harry Stimson and five generals. Some took place in Florida, as well as at Mackall. The workhorse C-47 transport and British Horsa gliders were added to the tests. At Alachua, Florida, Charles Fairlamb of the HQ Company mortar platoon found himself jumping out the wrong door, dangerously tipping the glider: "I knew I was supposed to go out the other one, but I was kind of hanging in the doorway. Why I didn't let go I don't know, but I gave one big push and hit the thin plywood flooring, skidded across, and went right out the other door like I was doing a swan dive. I was in a terrible position when I went out, so my chute malfunctioned." Fairlamb looked up to see his risers tangled and his chute bunched. He forgot to pull his ripcord for the reserve chute; in three desperate seconds he spun himself around like a top in the air, a textbook maneuver that probably saved his life, as the canopy loosened and whopped open. For Fairlamb, as for the 551st, combat at first would be a relief from training.

Structural problems shook the men. The anchor-line fasteners for the static lines would occasionally break loose in a glider. Contrary to official propaganda, much in the Allied arsenal, such as tanks, machine guns, and certain rifles, were inferior to the German variety. On October 31 the last man out the door of a "flying coffin" ripped the anchor cable and static lines right out of the walls; they fell with him. Don Garrigues, gripping the wooden struts on his bumpy glider before jumping, "had the feeling that the plywood floor [could] collapse at any time." Garrigues discovered another difference between a glider jump and a transport jump: lack of propeller blast made the fall almost vertical. Gravity seemed to pull quicker, harder. Garrigues hit his head on the ground, but the migraine that ensued was overcome by "the 'jump happy' sensation of completing a successful jump."

On a fateful late November jump at Mackall, the insignia designer Vincent Artz fell vertically into the canopy of Lieutenant Oliver Hord. Several chutes collapsed while Artz continued to the ground with a near streamer, fracturing his skull. He remained unconscious for forty-eight hours. The glider jumps stopped.

Body- and nerve-racking as they were, the glider test jumps elicited the only official U.S. Army commendation the 551st ever received. On October 21, 1943, Major General Eldridge G. Chapman lauded "the fine spirit existant in the 551st Parachute Battalion, which prompted many volunteers to hazard tests in parachute jumping of a type which had not been done before." Chapman said the tests "materially contributed to the progress of parachuting" and that the "unselfish cooperative attitude" of the men "insured success of tests in jumping from both doors of gliders in double tow." But perhaps because the technique was never used in the war, that praise appears in no commercially published history, including the two standard paratrooper texts by Devlin and Breuer.

Morgan ruefully comments, "The Airborne Command couldn't find anyone else crazy enough to try it." Their old friend, the engineer commander at Fort Kobbe, Panama, Major Alexander, had recommended them to boost their spirits.

Inexplicably, just as their spirits began to inflate again, their own leader left them.

3
Joerg departs

For Wood Joerg, the opportunity of a lifetime—the chance to command a real regiment, rather than a ruse of one—unfurled before him. He would first have to play second fiddle to a master. The newly formed 542d Parachute Infantry Regiment was led by Colonel William Ryder, the already legendary leader three years before of the parachute Test Platoon. The orders in late October 1943 were attractive in other ways: a chance to return to Fort Benning near his parents and where his wife and baby awaited him.

At Benning, Wood Joerg's presence lifted the spirits of Heidi and two-year-old Charlotte, who was on the verge of walking. Each night the Colonel briskly undid his tie and loosened his khaki shirt. He would let Charlotte thread her tiny fingers around his forefinger and squeeze, and would walk her, as a father does in those first upright moments of a child, as if the child were a doll on risers. During that time the Joergs conceived their second child, Susette.

Rumor had it that the newly formed 542d under Colonel Ryder was preparing for the first combat jump across the Rhine River into Germany following the D-Day spectacular at Normandy, preparations for which had been steadily gaining momentum as Operation Overlord. Ryder, in command of the 542d, would jump into history again, and Joerg would jump alongside him as a battalion commander or executive officer of the regiment. Joerg hoped to be one of the first Americans to make it into a liberated Berlin.

In addition, Joerg may very well have been happy to unhook his static line from the wobbly rack of the 551st. For a man who wanted to be a general—few colonels don't—the GOYAs were looking like a distinct liability. Joerg still had no fulfilling orders for them, and he knew their energies were pent up to critical mass. Renegade behavior that had endeared them to him in the past—the tearing down of the bar in Phenix City, the grenade fish fries in Panama, the risk of mutiny over the mascot Furlough, even Spotlight Brown's unbelievable insubordination—now may have seemed a self-destructive pattern ultimately impossible to harness. Sooner or later it would all come down on him. The furloughs he had granted hadn't helped; within a month at Mackall the battalion had seventy-six AWOL cases, about 15 percent of the group. And the number was climbing.

The man Joerg had appointed as officer of a special court to prosecute the AWOLs—C Company commander Tims Quinn—was hanged in effigy by some men of the 551st. Known to be merciless over a dusty rifle barrel or a poorly stitched chute, Quinn gave the AWOL stragglers two choices: the stockade and a court-martial trial, or the 104th Article of War, company punishment. The latter entailed standing at attention all day long without moving (with ten-minute breaks each hour), while Corporal James P. Houston lectured them on various Army behaviors, what Quinn called "The School of the Soldier." Quinn himself acknowledged later "some people criticized this" as the kind of senseless military punishment that Paul Fussell calls "chickenshit."[5] However, those who chose the stockade and risked court martial had an out Joerg himself devised; the Colonel allowed Lieutenant Donald Booth one challenge for each AWOL. And Booth, knowing Quinn would not be averse to throwing the whole lot out of the Army, saved most from Quinn's wrath with a challenge. When an exasperated Quinn told Joerg the whole thing was "ridiculous" and that his role was useless, Joerg responded cryptically, "Well, that's what they feel; they don't want you on there."

The whole GOYA experience was like a slow explosion. Joerg could see the first hot cinders descend, and brimstone yet to come. If the sergeants didn't get you, the officers would. There were some, like Quinn and Mascuch, it seemed he just couldn't win over. They looked on him with disdain, as if he were the chief ringleader rather than commander. Pappy Herrmann and Bill Holm, his executive officer, were in synch, but that whole bunch he had had to absorb from C Company of the 501st, who thought they were God's gift to jumping, would always be judging him, would always think he was too soft or too hard, a usurper come to Panama.

The omens gathered. At Mackall, Furlough bit somebody for the first time since her adoption, a plumber in civvies. Each black cloud had its madcap, if you could keep laughing. But how long? Someone blew up a toilet with a cherry bomb and had the gall to steal another unit's toilet to cover it all up. Why did they have to leave the shards of the wrecked toilet stacked up right outside the mess hall? Pure GOYA gall. It surged when Chizar beat up Joe Blaiszik in a brawl in a bar, leaving him nearly blind for weeks. At Rockingham, North Carolina, Duke Spletzer took on eight men from the 508th who tried to take his cab, breaking one man's leg, judo-chopping another in the neck, and knocking a third out. The 551st dentist, Lieutenant Roland Novak, took a bunch of medics for a basketball exhibition game against the varsity at Lenoir-Rhyne College in Hickory, North Carolina. Novak was drinking before the game started. The plays got sillier and sillier, and the purple-and-gold-clad GOYAs lost 60 to 20. A total wipeout. "If the Colonel had found out what we did there at Hickory he would have been furious," the medic Jack Affleck said.

What if he had, and instead of waxing furious or laughing it off, as he had had to so many times, he just decided to get serious and leave? With Overlord, the whole world was getting serious in a hurry. And that is why he broke down, cutting his farewell address short, and walked away to hide his tears. "He loved the battalion," Lieutenant Dick Mascuch was certain. With the glider tests, they were on the rise, but he did not believe they would sustain it.

He was right.

4
"You're all rabble!"

The man who replaced Lieutenant Colonel Joerg in late October 1943 could not have been a worse choice, at least for the unit he came to loathe as "rabble." He was Lieutenant Colonel Rupert Graves, and he was, by GOYA standards, an old man—forty-two, or thirteen years older than the departing commander, Wood Joerg. He was anything but swashbuckling, in appearance and manner the epitome of everything Joerg was not. His unfortunate possession of "a nose that never seemed to end and always appeared to be dripping"[6] led to the nickname "Old Hose Nose."

A Yankee from Massachusetts, Graves had graduated from West Point in 1924, when General John Pershing, the hero of World War I, was his commencement speaker. One of a number of interwar West Point graduates who ripened too soon for high advancement, Graves still had hopes of making a mark at the eleventh hour as World War II turned toward its 1944 climax. His career had been unexceptional. From 1935 to 1941 he was stationed in Hawaii, having the good or bad luck to have been ordered off the islands just before Pearl Harbor. The year before he was sent to put out the GOYA fire, Graves had commanded the 11th Armored Battalion at Fort Benning. His most recent experience had been with tankers and their hardware, not the infantry, and certainly not paratroopers. He was jump-trained in a special course shortly before taking over command of the chief daredevil parachute battalion in the U.S. Army.

It's possible that no matter who the new commander was, he was doomed to fail with the 551st; Joerg's shoes were fairly sizable ones to fill, at least for the enlisted men. Also, according to the battalion's executive officer, Major Bill Holm, Graves was more or less passing through. In Holm's view, the 551st was not much more than seasoning for Graves as he prepared to take over a new parachute regiment, the 517th. But for someone "who made you feel comfortable . . . like an old shoe,"[7] as Tom Cross of the 517th would later say of Graves, GOYA seasoning was extra hot.

What Graves had on hand when he took over command from Joerg was a full-scale military and social disintegration. A representative of the U.S. Army Surgeon General came down from Washington to tongue-lash the 551st in person about its rate of venereal disease, second only to a black battalion of stevedores who worked the docks in New Orleans. The medical officer showed the men a film on gonorrhea and syphilis. He probably would have done better with a Panamanian floor show.

In the first few weeks of Graves's command, the 551st AWOL rate nearly doubled from what it had been at Joerg's departure. At any one time, 135 men were absent without official leave, or 23 percent of the unit. For example, PFC John Eckhardt, a Headquarters Company clerk, took a furlough form and typed a fictitious colonel's name on it. He and Jim Heffernan even called a cab to pick them up at the door of the barracks. Heffernan headed for home in Indiana, where his policeman brother-in-law promised cover for him should Army MPs come investigating. But none did, and Heffernan had a "swell time" for eighteen days, when he headed back for Mackall. His money ran out in Washington, D.C., but he bumped into a sailor who had been at sea a long time and had a pretty good stash. The sailor paid for the hotel room and drinks for them both for three days. When Heffernan finally returned to Mackall, Lamar Tavoian slapped a thirty-day company punishment on him, digging up old wood stumps and sawing lumber. Heffernan was sore in more ways than one.

"Now, Heffernan, was it worth it?" Tavoian asked when it was over.

"You're damn right, Captain. I wouldn't have got to go home any other way," Heffernan barked in true Furlough tradition.

"I am canceling your company punishment and I am going to court-martial you," Tavoian said grimly.

Lieutenant Booth reviewed the case, questioned Heffernan for ten minutes, and threw him in the stockade for six months, with a deduction in pay. But true to the ways of the bureaucracy, the Army never found out about his forged furlough paper and got his AWOL time wrong—twenty-one days instead of the twenty-four he took. It was demeaning, but they wouldn't boot him out. This was 1944; the Army needed his body. And Heffernan knew it.

At the age of ninety-two the first memory Colonel Graves had of the 551st Parachute Infantry Battalion was that it was "a funny group [which] picked up bad habits in Panama."[8] A half-century earlier Graves had been determined to break the unit of its brazenness, with long marches in cold weather, a 5-mile "boot camp" run each morning before breakfast as collective punishment for AWOLs, and a mass reduction in rank for noncommissioned officers. Furloughs were abolished; the slightest infraction merited solitary confinement in the stockade. Graves even confiscated the men's cherished paratrooper boots, substituting regular infantry boots that lacked a steel insole and had a buckle that could tangle in a parachute's lines. The line soldiers hated him.

Morale went into a free-fall. The hard hand only fanned the the license it sought to repress. Cicchinelli wrote his sweetheart back home with some "awful news" about a promised three-day pass rescinded: "Damn it. I'm mad. I worked for those 3 days and I shot a darn high score for the Company now they take it away from us. Right now I feel like going A.W.O.L. I been so damn lonesome lately for you I sometimes think I'm going crazy."[9]

The 551st was locked in an unending spiral where "grudge" fights or AWOLs engendered "petty injustices."[10] Certainly the battalion's civil war left as deep an impression on my father—who was always jumping in to break up fights—as did combat.

But Graves was in a bind, too. He had little prestige on coming to the battalion, and he had to establish authority in a double vacuum: the poor personal behavior of the battalion on arrival at Mackall and the loss of its revered commander. Hardly the picture of physical prowess (or style—Garrigues remembered a telling detail of personal sloppiness in Graves, that is, one trouser leg was "dangling outside of his boot while the other was bloused as it should be"), Graves was quick to order respect rather than quietly command it.

It is interesting that the unit Graves would later lead and be identified with—the hard-fought 517th Parachute Regimental Combat Team—would be the subject of three full-scale histories, none of which mentions anything about Graves's short but cataclysmic association with the 551st. The two units rubbed up against each other early on, at Mackall, while Graves was still in the wobbly saddle of the 551st.

Inspite of the Graves's crackdown, three HQ Company sergeants—Martin Kangas, Harold Lawler, and Don Garrigues—had secured a weekend pass in early 1944 to Rockingham, where they sped to a carnival packed with paratroopers, some with their girlfriends but most on the prowl. Lawler and Kangas proceeded to get "pretty well fortified on some cheap wine." Lawler walked up to one 517th man who was trying to impress his girl at the penny pitch booth, and Lawler insulted him. Before the trooper could so much as ask what was on Lawler's mind, the GOYA knocked him unconscious. "As we walked away, I looked back and he was still stretched out on the railing like a teeter-totter with his frantic girlfriend in tears," Garrigues recounted.

Kangas duplicated that effort down the way with another 517th man, whom he accused of possessing "an unpleasant smell." Kangas had chosen to bait someone larger than himself, and he was large. "What did you say?" the trooper asked, and Kangas cold-cocked him on the jaw. He fell like a tree, out cold. The evening was shaping up as a classic "rumble," and soon a posse of the troopers' 517th friends was frothing for revenge. The three sergeants were the only 551st men at the carnival, and "it looked like the whole 517th Regiment was coming toward us." The GOYAs tore off. Garrigues successfully hid behind some farm wagons. Kangas and Lawler ran into the night, somehow eluding a thunder of boots, though Lawler returned to the barracks after midnight, cut up and bleeding. He'd run into a barbed wire fence in the dark.

Did Graves hear about this? Was he aware he would soon command the 517th? Such an incident might have been taken not just as the typical wild GOYA behavior but as a threat to his promotion. In any case, he wouldn't have forgotten such cocky affronts of "rabble." The rivalry between the two units, friendly at times, bloody at others, would have dire consequences in Belgium.

In mid-December 1943 the 551st got a preview of Belgian weather in North Carolina. On a day-long march, early morning rain turned to sleet and then by afternoon to heavy snow. Before dawn the next day the men had to dig their foxholes in snow and simulate an attack. Graves did not let up; it was at times hard to tell what was punitive and what was preparatory. At one point he injected live ammunition into drills and grew incensed when the results veered toward the deadly. In one such exercise, seeing that A Company was raining live ammo on B Company, he ordered the battalion's communications officer, Lieutenant Andy Titko, to alert them. But Titko's SCR-511 radio, designed for horse cavalry and perennially unreliable, was on the fritz. Graves, who, like General MacArthur, smoked corn cob pipes, blurted, "God damn!" and bit his pipestem in two. He boiled out of his foxhole and stalked off, sulking. Luckily, no one was shot.

But the unit was shot in another way. The daily 5-mile runs in the morning, meted on the disobedient and the faithful alike, intensified AWOLs. "As quick as ten or twenty came back, ten or twenty more took off," Morgan recalled. No one liked the idea of collective punishment, particularly with the type of regimen they'd all had in boot camp, three training missions back. Graves mortified the battalion by treating it like new recruits, or worse. It was a rare noncommissioned officer who was not downgraded at that time. That further frayed the delicate connection between the enlisted men and the officer ranks, several of whom enjoyed Graves's dry humor. The Battalion Special Orders at Mackall were rife with sergeants and corporals busted for "inefficiency," "without prejudice," and so on. Sergeant Benjamin "Beau" Preziotti of Company B was one.

According to Preziotti's sister, "Beau" actually wanted to be knocked down from sergeant to corporal.[11] Whether or not he rationalized this from a disciplinary action, she does not know. But Preziotti did write her about how difficult it was for him to "boss the men" and especially to tap the jumpers on the calf to go. "He felt it was like pushing them out of the plane," she said. He recalled only too well his own first day in the windy door to the sky when he froze and could not jump.

At Mackall, if the GOYAs were jumping anywhere it was out of the unit. According to Doug Dillard, in January 1944 a hundred men transferred out of the 551st. Others estimate that by March 1944 up to 175 men—or nearly one-third of its total—had willingly left the battalion. (Two of them, Privates Theodore Coley and John Ponder of B Company, would be killed in action on D-Day in Normandy.) The VD rate, AWOLs, collective punishments, and the general collapse of morale since the return from Panama sparked a brushfire of rumors that the 551st itself was going to be taken apart, if it wasn't intentionally being smacked apart by the hard hand of authority. In any event, the thought of dissolution became something of a self-fulfilling prophecy. That was only furthered by an outbreak of meningitis. Myron Splawn was rushed to the base hospital and his Headquarters Company barracks was given sulfa, with the entire battalion put on medical alert. It seemed that Job's afflictions were being visited on the 551st, with no end in sight.

Among the officers who left the battalion at that time were Captain Archibald McPheeters of Company B and Captain Don Pay of Company A, both well liked. Some men transferred into one of two new airborne divisions created at Mackall after its dedication in May 1943—the 17th "Thunder from Heaven" and the 11th Airborne, led by Major General William Miley and Major General Joseph Swing, respectively, both charismatic and already legendary in paratroop circles. Miley would take his division to the Bulge and drop across the Rhine in Germany; Swing's 11th performed admirably in the Pacific campaign. Other GOYAs had had enough of jump boots and their anarchic owners and joined the earthbound infantry. Sergeant Bernard Spidahl and Sergeant Charles Wilcynski of A Company both entered the 36th Division. Spidahl may have saved his life, as the 551st's Company A was nearly annihilated at the Battle of the Bulge, the worst hit of all GOYA companies. But his fate was hardly better: at the vicious Anzio beachhead and on up to Rome, Spidahl sustained four injuries, including a severe wound that left a plate in his cranium for life; he withdrew from the service on disability in 1950. Wilcynski, however, found the troubled unit irresistible; he rejoined the 551st just in time to drop into southern France. One GOYA ratcheted his risk up a notch and paid for it: Private Jake Brooks joined a bomber squadron, and his plane was shot down over Ploesti, Romania.

The GOYA course at Mackall would continue downward. Dan Morgan left the unit in January 1944 with a bitterness bordering on obsession. He wanted to enter Officer Candidate School and become a pilot with the Army Air Corps. The 551st had set an immovable heavy anchor in him; it would take a lifetime to lift it, and even then it would not be gone.

What pushed Morgan over the edge? Part of it had to do with something he could not bring himself to say in his own book—a choleric rage displayed by Rupert Graves:

> [Graves] stood there on this platform in the morning and shouted at us. And he said, "You're not soldiers. You're beneath contempt. You're all rabble! You're not gonna wreck my career!" We had 200 men in the stockade at one time, see; that's one-third of the battalion. And he said, "As long as one of you is over the hill, we will all take a 5-mile run every morning."[12]

Morgan admitted that at times Graves himself would join the run, but what threw him into a tailspin was a commander "livid with rage" chewing out people who had done no wrong, lumping the innocent in with the guilty. The twenty-three-year-old Morgan was greatly shaken; the commander appeared out of control. By that time Morgan was under no illusion as to the character of the 551st; the second paragraph of his book labels them "mavericks" and "oddballs." At Mackall, he writes, "because of our youthful irresponsibility, physical hardness, and a degree of bitterness then, we were impervious to Col. Graves' best efforts." But that "best efforts" is euphemistic. To Morgan, the 551st were welded inseparably and were not breakable by Graves, who he thought was trying to engender "hostility within the ranks against the malefactors." But up to 175 men did break, at least they left the unit, and Morgan was one.

Collective punishment is always demoralizing, but especially so for those who take pride in themselves as an elite. Its moral conundrum is obvious: If you are being punished for something you have not done, why should you continue to be correct? This rudimentary human psychology seems to have escaped Graves (though indeed Joerg's opposite tactic, a three-week furlough, did not exactly work either). Graves seems to have come down on the side of physical duress and fear. But both—fear especially—would prove a poor disincentive to rash behavior for the GOYAs. Fear and deprivation in Europe would only spur them onward.

There was a more immediate reason for Morgan's departure than the punishments: a direct confrontation. Morgan had put in his application for the Army Air Corps in September 1943; a month later he wrote to the investigations unit of Third Army Headquarters to ask why action was so slow. Another month went by before a full colonel with two armed sergeants pulled up to Graves's headquarters, walked right to the 551st's sergeant major and said, "Sergeant, stand clear of your desk." The inspecting colonel reached into the drawer and pulled out a stack of papers: several dozen requests, including Morgan's for transfer to OCS and other places. The GOYA command staff watched speechless as the visiting colonel went into Lieutenant Colonel Graves's office and closed the door. They heard shouts and twice the blare of "General court martial!"

An hour after that encounter T/5 Morgan was ordered "on the double" to Graves's office. Morgan arrived, walked with bewilderment right up to the commander's desk, and endured several moments of silence. Graves finally cleared his throat and looked directly at him: "Morgan, what have you done to this battalion?"

"Sir, I don't understand."

"By what right did you write Third Army Headquarters in Atlanta?"

Before Morgan could finish explaining himself, Graves ordered him to the barracks. "A jeep will come and pick you up and I hope I never see you again," Graves spat out. The Canadian–American was out of the unit.

If there was wholesale hemorrhaging of the 551st at Mackall, there were also those who were brought in to staunch the flow of blood. This may have been Graves's last realistic hope—fresh paratroop recruits with no stain of Panama or the GOYAs' frustrations about missing combat. One was Lieutenant Phil Hand, who had lamented to Graves that he "was about to go crazy doing nothing," which for him had been running troops through the woods with compasses five days and nights a week with another unit at Mackall. Another was Aref Orfalea.

My father was inducted into the U.S. Army one year shy of graduation from Cathedral Latin High School in Cleveland on February 17, 1943. My recollection is that he enlisted, but since his honorable discharge papers also list him as having "blue eyes" (they were dark brown), it is hard to give too much weight as to the official facts of his life in the Army. His basic training and first assignment as a clerk with the 324th Infantry Division were effected at Fort Lewis, Washington, where he got his first taste of the beauty of the Far West. He arrived at Fort Benning for paratrooper training about the time the 551st was testing gliders and Rupert Graves at Mackall, but he postponed jump school to cement himself with the 515th Parachute Infantry Regiment, for "I'd rather be trained with an outfit in combat than go overseas as a replacement for an outfit I don't know a thing about."[13] Still, he was excited: "I can't wait to be a qualified paratrooper. I've been lying awake at nights thinking about it. I guess it's just in me to be a paratrooper." It was also his way to leapfrog forward to catch his brother, who had just made second lieutenant and was on his way to Burma. A paratrooper made a standard sergeant's pay.

Aref completed four weeks of jump school at Benning by late December 1943; his best landing was on his sixth and last jump (with 44 pounds of TNT), though he splashed down in a half-foot of water and his chute was soaked to twice its weight. From December 20, 1943 to January 8,

1944, he successfully completed a course in "Parachute Demolition Training." He could not know that the unit to which he was about to be assigned in North Carolina as a dreaded replacement was undergoing its own self-demolition. A high fever put him into a hospital at Fort Meade, Maryland, before transfer to the strange new unit.

What could my father possibly have thought on arrival at Camp Mackall? No one likes to get to a party so late that everyone has either paired off or left. And what could he make of the fact that his new unit—of which he would write so proudly to his four sisters back home—had had three-quarters of its members either in the brig, AWOL, or fleeing to other units? It takes some of the wind out of your sails, as one of his fonder critiques of life went.

I can see him now with his barracks bag, mounting the wooden stairs of the barracks at Mackall, pausing for a second at the screen door of a life he will do so much to forget after his wound, a life that will creep unnoticed into his songs to his children as it has crept into my songs to my children, and I have never gone to war. Moths dance in the porchlight by the door. He opens it. The wire whine of the doorsprings draws a head or two toward him. The men inside are talking quietly or are absorbed in small things like polishing their jump boots or sewing a ripped chute. Some are resting on their bunks, reading, undershirts stretched by their muscles. Some see my father enter, and remove the pack of cigarettes from a fold of sleeve over their biceps. It is night time. It would have taken half a day to ride the train down from Fort Meade. He's another newcomer. Perhaps there's some suspicion in the glances or stares; perhaps some pity. They see he's dark, like Cicchinelli, but taller. He's handsome, a thick shock of black hair over his tall forehead, a tapered nose that follows the fine contours of his face, a slender mustache, a kind of darker Erroll Flynn. They figure he's probably Italian (they will be wrong). He probably loves women (they will be right). He's not shy with them (they will be wrong). They regard with a smirk, or perhaps a twinge of awe, his piano-luster jump boots, his finely pressed uniform, and the way he carefully smooths his soldier's cap with new jump patch and places it under his pillow. We were this way once, uncreased. And because one of the few things I know about his war is that he had friends who were killed around him, someone who is to become a friend approaches him, welcomes him with a handshake, and puts the first tentative crease of an ill-fated unit into his khaki arm.

By dawn he's been up half the night hearing GOYA stories of valor on leave, of stockade steak, grenade shark, and a horrific night jump. He's been jerked awake by a Glenn Miller reveille, seen Jack Russell walk across the floor on his hands to get his socks. Soon he has made the 5-mile run everyone has made and vows he will not go AWOL, because he has just arrived.

The run smells of wet tobacco leaves. He comes back winded and bewildered and takes a smoke before breakfast—Lucky Strikes, the cigarette that has turned his Syrian father's fingers caramel-colored. He briefly meets officers like Dick Mascuch and Jim Evans, commander of his newly assigned B Company, who will forget him and he them, because the ones he remembers are the ones who died nameless. Later, his assignment is to man the battalion's message center, which means that he will have met T/5 Chuck Bernhard, who will forget him, and Sergeant Paul Kjar, who will not. But he will traffic heavily in their notes to the battalion's company commanders and to others off base. He will put the message from the right man into the right hole for the right eyes. He does some wireless. He learns to connect people and orders. And he will see the name of Colonel Rupert Graves at the bottom of all these demotions, transfers, orders to the stockade, cancellations of furlough. He may even as a private catch sight of Old Hose Nose and want to offer him a handkerchief, as he did me just about every day of my life until I was eighteen, and some after. Since he is good with figures he can calculate that 75 percent of the 551st is in trouble, and he can see something is terribly wrong. He prays to God to keep the spit-shined image in his shoes each morning steady.

After the last cigarette is crushed at night, he thinks about the night jump he just missed, the one the men can't stop talking about. It drums his ribs from the inside. In February 1944, with the Allies struggling up the Anzio beachhead in Italy to crags that came too loose, and with the GOYAs stateside coming very loose indeed, old Rupert Graves thought the 551st was overdue for a trip to the ground in darkness.

5
"His legs were tangled in tree stumps"

I once asked my father what his most fearful moment in the war was. He replied, "the night jump." There was no elaboration; I was too timid to ask for any. I assumed for years that he was referring to the 551st's combat drop into southern France (and I published a poem with the erroneous title "The Night Jump over Draguignan"), only to learn after he died that that historic jump occurred in sunlight. His qualifying jumps at Fort Benning seemed to be a candidate, except for the fact that night jumps there almost never happened. All that was left was Mackall.

The only night jumps the unit ever took—two—were ordered by Colonel Graves at Camp Mackall, North Carolina, as a final test. The first took place on February 16, 1944. It was an extraordinary disaster: Eight men plummeted with 120 pounds of equipment to the bottom of a lake and drowned.[14]

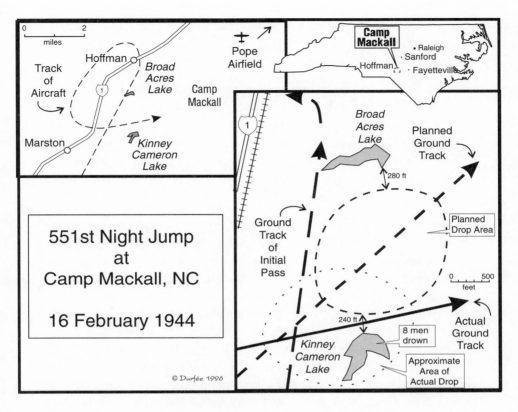

0
miles
2

Track of Aircraft
Hoffman
Broad Acres Lake
Camp Mackall
Marston
Kinney Cameron Lake

Pope Airfield

Camp Mackall
Raleigh
Sanford
Hoffman
Fayetteville

Broad Acres Lake
Planned Ground Track
280 ft

Ground Track of Initial Pass

Planned Drop Area

0   500
feet

240 ft
8 men drown
Kinney Cameron Lake

Actual Ground Track

Approximate Area of Actual Drop

551st Night Jump at Camp Mackall, NC

16 February 1944

© Durfée 1996

Although Graves cannot be faulted for arranging a night jump *per se*, most everything about the way the first one was planned and executed was wrong. The drop zone, so narrow as to cause two of seven aircraft to touch wingtips in midair, ran between two lakes, with a third lake not far away. Graves also assented to the first use of red and green jump signal lights instead of the verbal barkings of a jumpmaster. Some of them simply didn't work. The pilots had never flown paratroopers before, and the weather—a dark, misty rain that made for poor visibility—was terrible. Before takeoff the night, Garrigues confided to his diary, was "foreboding," and a "chilling drizzle of rain was falling."

The night jump on February 16, 1944, appeared to be the GOYAs' last hurdle at Camp Mackall. Though undocumented for almost half a century, it would also constitute one of the worst training blunders in the U.S. Army during World War II.

Graves's attempt to halt the 551st's disintegration, which had already elicited a threat of court martial over his withholding transfer requests to Officer Candidate School, was patently not working. He was at a loss as to what to do. A night jump, especially one into a risky drop zone, may have presented itself as a supreme test that could break the spell. Dan Morgan strongly believes Graves was making a last-ditch attempt to rescue the men's spirit, but in a very dangerous way. He likens the method to a custom of French Foreign Legion:

> When they had a disobedient unit, they would march them up to a cliff blindfolded and then at the last second, they would make them stop. And then they would take the blindfolds off. Or in combat, they would give them an impossible objective, and they would take terrible losses as punishment. Well, [Graves] had that concept, I think. And I think that he figured that when he jumped us between those two lakes ... it would be a successful jump. And it would mean that he had shown us the way.

Others, including Captain Ed Hartman, scoff at any notion that Graves was responsible for the loss of life that night. "No, no way," said Hartman. "He had nothing to do with it." Such men tend not to see an element of punishment or brinksmanship in the night jump itself.

In a postwar three-part magazine series called "Combat Team," Graves mentions nothing about the night jump at Mackall, never admits to his command of 551st, and says little about the GOYAs, except to note the death in Belgium of its commander "Col. Juareg." He does, however, talk about the efficacies of stiff training, with a faint note of regret: "Perhaps there was too much emphasis on physical conditioning, but it did serve to weed out any who were not determined to stick along with their buddies and with their outfit."[15] The shadow of the GOYAs may lie in those words. Graves goes on to speak—tongue-in-cheek, one has to believe—of the "headache of many a unit commander" that it was "almost an impossibility to wear them down." He is speaking of training the 517th, but this fits, as well, the 551st, perhaps too well, inasmuch as Graves really was trying to wear down the 551st.

The drop zone Graves chose, near the small town of Hoffman, North Carolina, threaded the needle between two bodies of water, Broad Acres Lake to the north and Lake Kinney Cameron to the south. The strip (1,600 feet wide by 2,000 feet long) was to fit thirty-one C-47 transport planes carrying 650 paratroopers, which were to be dropped simultanously on the strip, a plowed peanut and corn field between the waters.

It was too snug a fit, even for the most experienced pilots, which these weren't. The planes flew in "v of v's" clumps of seven each for Companies A, B, and C, with HQ Company jumping from a clump of ten planes. The drop zone indicated on the map on page 89 shows that A Company's seven-plane clump—even if it releases correctly—is dangerously close to Broad Acres Lake, less than a football field away (280 feet). Morgan calculated that a jump twelve seconds early by Company B would have landed its men no more than 240 feet from Lake Kinney Cameron. But again, that tight squeeze occurs if everything goes as planned. In fact, nothing did. The narrow longitudinal axis forced the aircaft into a pattern so close (300 feet between seven-plane elements) that there was little if any margin for pilot error. The brightest sunshine would still have made the drop zone a bad bet.

At least three of the 442d Troop Carrier Group's four squadrons, numbered 303d to 306th, were flown in from Alliance, Nebraska, in early February for the 551st's night jump, among other missions.[16] According to Captain Ed Hartman, their pilots "had no previous experience as trooper carriers." The 442d was green. It had been activated only five months earlier; for one month it had only one transport plane with which to practice. But on February 16 it dutifully loaded the GOYAs at Pope Air Field at Fort Bragg. Jim Stevens from A Company sensed something wrong that very afternoon as the men were trucked from Mackall to Bragg, getting lost on the way: "It was one of those days. Every paratrooper can tell you about those days. Seems as though just about everything went wrong. We finally got there and loaded up."

"I think everyone thought it was too slim between the lakes," said Emory Albritton, "Al" to the men, who in the early 1990s resolved to pull the Mackall tragedy up singlehanded from the brackish waters of the forgotten. The plan was for the planes to take off from Pope Air Field; fly about 20 miles south, where there was a checkpoint at Rockingham; swing over the border to South Carolina; then turn back and head between Rockingham and Hamlet to the drop zone near Hoffman. The azimuth was supposed to be flown at 40 degrees; instead it was flown at about 85 degrees on a second pass, at 10 degrees. A stick of pathfinders had dropped that afternoon, Ralph Wenthold and Andy Titko among them. They had planted red fusee flares at the base and had then held white signal lamps at the head of each of the four companies' intended drop sites on the "larger" zone itself, a snug oval indeed. It was as if Graves wanted the men to drop en masse at attention, elbows in.

Everything on the ground was prepared, at any rate. Wenthold recounts the approach of the thirty-one-plane armada in the dark: "When the planes came over, the whole formation was too far to the right of the planned flight path, so they went around. They were supposed to make a 320-degree turn, but they made about a 290-degree, so they were coming back at the wrong angle." That angle took most of the armada over Lake Kinney Cameron, which, surrounded by a misty pine forest, looked like open ground.

Ed Hartman remembers seeing the pathfinders "bounce their lights right off the front of the plane" he was in as jumpmaster, but then "somehow it all got screwed up." His plane was jarred into jumping. "As a matter of fact, I took my plane [troopers] out because they had a midair collision with another plane. Banged wings together. It was close enough to knock me down; I was standing in the door ready to go. As my chute opened I looked around and saw billows of parachutes coming down and planes flying below them. It was very dangerous. They were flying hit-or-miss everywhere. We must have scattered over 20 miles."

In the dark, sound told the story. Propellers buzz-sawed, then correctly feathered, as aircraft do just before a jump, by slowing down, turning the whine of the engines to a grumble. The sound of the chutes unfurling, a long whaaap or whooop, was everywhere. There was no sound of wind, because it was a misty night, except the billowing of the parachutes. Men called to each other as they landed. "Hey, Chick? You there?" But those yells were nearly drowned out by the propellers droning overhead. Paratroopers didn't hear the anxious curses of the pilots wanting nothing so much as to revoke this impossible seeding of the night with men. Mostly there was the sound of tree branches cracking, for that was what most people hit, the forest itself. But also, terribly, came the sound of splashing, signaling watery death.

It was a bizarre scene indeed, made all the more fearsome by the lack of light, even moonlight, which made any light seem meaningful and the darkness itself—such as Lake Kinney Cameron—inviting. Wenthold took hope at first when he saw bundles dropped from the planes, because each was tagged with a light or red reflector, so for a moment it was wondrous for him, a vision of lighted gifts. But the gifts were falling too far off, and this was way past Christmas or any Festival of Lights. It was the beginning of the Season of Suffering.

The strangest fact of that night in North Carolina remains that many of the forty-three paratroopers who dropped into water did so thinking it was land, actively urging their chutes toward it, as best they could in those days before the control of hang-gliders. Again, the flat black of it surrounded by the misted forest made it look like a clearing. Hartman describes it thus: "I was pulling all I could on the suspension lines because that was the only clearing I could see below me; I couldn't tell it was water. I'm sure nobody else could, either. So the jumpers, as they descended, tried to slip in that area. You pull on the risers on the side you want to slip in. That tilts your canopy and you slide to some degree, not a helleva lot, though. I came down about 75 feet from the shore of that lake. We tried our best to get the men out, and did pull a bunch of them out, but those who hit near the center of it, it was just too much."

Another who mistook the lake for saving ground was T/4 Albert "Pat" Garretty, who "spilled air from my canopy to drift in that direction" as it seemed "smoother."[17] Garretty had been out that day with Captain Quinn and Colonel Graves in separate Piper Cub planes scouting the drop zone, planning a risky four parallel single-file flight patterns. The planes ended up all over the place, their running lights flashing. Garretty caught what he thought was a streamer, falling between 500 and 800 feet before the chute stubbornly opened. Cries of "Help!" below made him realize he was above water; at the last second he jerked his risers in the opposite direction from what he first thought was safety, landing through pine branches along the shore in water up to his collar bone. The gutteral call of someone drowning was about 50 feet away. He swam out to get him but couldn't unbuckle his wet straps to disengage the water-logged chute: The straps, made of cotton, had severely tightened. Garretty pulled the soldier to shore and gave him artificial respiration. But it was too late.

Several planes got their signals literally mixed up. In the past the 551st had always jumped with a human being—usually a sergeant, whoever was designated as the jumpmaster—tapping the calf of the jumper's leg firmly when it was time to "go." That followed the human oral command, "Stand up and hook up." One might say that the home front tragedy at Camp Mackall, North Carolina, four months before the invasion of Normandy was at least partly the result of an experiment in mechanization. The system cannot be faulted for lack of simplicity: Ten minutes from the drop zone, the paratroopers were supposed to hear a bell; two minutes from the DZ, a red light flashed; right over the DZ, a green light flashed to jump. Executing that simplicity was something else.

The jumpmaster's Report written twelve days after the drownings by Captain Bill Smith, the 551st's then S-3, gives a picture, terse though it is, of the confusion with jump signals that night. Smith's plane in the 303d Squadron, no. 677, left Pope Air Field at 7:15 P.M.; the bell to hook up static lines occurred at 8:17 P.M. after a full hour of flying, which indicates some measure of delay for being lost. The red light snapped on at 8:28 P.M., three minutes late by the standard described above.

Four minutes later—at 8:32 P.M.—inexplicably the red light went off. A minute later it came on again—at 8:33 P.M. One can only imagine the confusion this sent into Smith, the jumpmaster, not to mention his riveted men. Seven minutes went by. Then, at 8:40 P.M., Smith saw the ghosts of several chutes "pass under the plane." Somebody else was releasing. At exactly that moment the green light flashed, fully twelve minutes later than it should have, going by the first red light that went on. Then Smith did something that probably saved his life and those of the eighteen men in plane no. 677. He paused ten seconds before jumping. He jinxed the jinx itself; it worked. Though his plane had gone directly over the water, Smith and his men

landed in the woods about 300 yards east of Lake Kinney Cameron. His official recounting, startling for its honest disclosure of ignorance, concludes:
"At no time after the first pass over Hoffman did I know where I was." He
also recounts his later knowledge that the men he saw passing under his
plane ten seconds before his own stick jumped landed in the water.

Irony of ironies, the one company—A—that suffered no deaths that
night was the one company outfitted with Mae Wests, or life jackets. The
original plan had A Company the only one dropping near water, Broad
Acres Lake, northwest of the intended drop zone. As it turned out, the
angle of the lost planes released A Company farthest from the water, southeast of the intended drop zone. In short, those who desperately needed life
preservers didn't have them; those who didn't, did.[18]

Cicchinelli and Dillard jumped with A Company, which was not ex-
empt from the signal lights fiasco. Jim Stevens got so tired of waiting for a
bell or a light that he ordered his assistant to stow the static line; just as
everyone had sat down and begun to relax the green light flashed. "We all
hooked up and went out the door as fast as we could go," Stevens said.
"We never got a red light at all."

Who was responsible for pushing the buttons for those erratic lights?
The pilots, apparently. That fact, more than the buttons themselves, had
the men nervous even before they took off from Bragg. Doc Chalkley says:
"I remember how upset we were when we switched from our own jump-
masters to the little green lights, operated by the aircraft pilots, to tell us
when to jump." In addition, signal lights on the field were used for the
first time; their power was strong, with a range of 3 miles. But even
though they flashed on the planes with such luminescence that Titko saw
the faces of jumpers, no one went onto the drop zone itself. Was radar at
fault? An electronics man had set a radar installation at the center of the
drop zone, which Titko described as "a rather crude device at the time." It
appears that the pilots themselves lost heart over the narrow drop zone,
misread and overflew the ground lights, and panicked with the red and
green signals to the men in the bowels of the planes.

The situation in the dark arms of the trees and the black water itself was
a mixture of dread and cold courage. Bill Hatcher of B Company landed 25
feet from the water and may have heard some of Benjamin Preziotti's last
words on earth, if they were words at all. Dick Fields of B Company, whose
stomach was so sickened by the syrupy coffee he'd drunk at Bragg before
taking off that he vomited while running down the belly of the plane before
jumping, alit close to the lake, and splashing and screaming. "'Help!' I
heard," Fields related. "And I'd just lost the noise of the plane. It was total
chaos." Bill Lumsden of C Company lost one of his platoon's favorites, PFC

Ishmael Petty, that night; Lumsden described the chaos: "It was absolutely pitch black, so that we were on the ground or in the water as the case may be, before anyone could even see what was going on, so they didn't have a chance to slip out of their chutes." This was a key to the tragedy, as well, a passive one, but without the darkness and without the bindings, the pilots' screwups and Graves's bad choice of drop zone may not have had their deathly effect. Once the men hit the water, they had almost no time, not only with 120 pounds of equipment, but a chute water-logged to 200 pounds of extra drag, to undo the three snaps that held them to their parachutes. They were entangled, as well, not only by their primary but also their reserve chutes, which in some cases came out of their packs. The men who landed in the deep water were dragged to their watery grave by the very things designed to save them: their chutes.

For the men in shallower water, where thirty-five touched bottom either to cut themselves out with knives or to drag their heavy loads like dinosaurs and slowly wade to shore, the sights and sounds were shocking. There on the deep water ghostly parachutes luffed like exhausted lungs. John Balogach, who jumped with the ill-fated C Company, saw the canopies as "mushrooms on the water," an apt nocturnal metaphor with its hint of poison. Balogach himself was especially heavy that night, jumping with two mines and two mortars on two bandoliers, in addition to the standard equipment. But luckily he landed in the trees, though spreadeagled, so that he thought he'd lost "the family jewels." What he actually lost was his voice, when a branch snapped up from between his legs, hit his throat, and collapsed his windpipe.

With the exception of a man who landed in water over his head and bounced up and down all the way to shore in an almost superhuman effort to breathe, Emory Albritton probably came as close as any survivor to drowning. He came to rest in a pine tree at first, but the tree had long branches out over the water. He flipped over, entangling himself in his lines to drop onto what he thought was ground but turned out to be water about 5 feet deep. It came up to his chin. In two or three steps, he thought, the water would be over his head. "I pulled the whole damn thing to shore," Albritton said of his load. "I went back several times. I pulled one guy out of the apex of his chute, a fellow named David Smith, who was later killed in southern France." Another he pulled out, though he was dead by then, was his good friend from B Company, Ben Preziotti.

Several makeshift rescue efforts were made, but most were in vain. The 551st did not have the necessary rescue equipment for such a situation, which would have included boats, long ropes, and wet suits. And of course, there was almost no time or illumination to find and reach those in the deep water. The signal lights would have helped, but they were at the wrong lake, which abutted the empty drop zone—Broad Acres Lake, a half a mile away. Lieutenant Phil Hand ordered trucks collected from the neighboring areas to point their headlights on the lake.

It must be said that a rescue effort was made that night by Colonel Graves himself, who landed 20 to 30 feet from the water: "I didn't have any trouble that night, but others did. There was no moon."[19] Graves apparently jumped with C Company, or somehow got mixed in with C Company's troopers on the ground. When John Balogach had fallen spreadeagled through the pine tree, he dusted himself off, stood up, and was staring at the battalion commander.

"Give me your riser lines," Graves ordered. "We'll try and reach the men with them." Graves and Balogach took out their knives and cut the risers, doubling and tripling them to make a kind of crude rope, which they tied to their waists. They waded out into the water. The idea was to throw the riser rope and pull a drowning man in. But the lake was too cold and too deep.

"Colonel, it won't work. My dick is so cold it's up to my larynx."

What struck Balogach was the silence. By the time they had waded into the water, all sound had already stopped. The lake had swallowed quickly.

One who broke that silence with anger was Captain Jim Evans, B Company's commander, who lost Preziotti. Having just completed a thirty-day punishment for a minor AWOL, Private John Bassaline was pulled from the muck of the lake's edge, only to see Evans "going beserk, smashing Tommy guns." Evans yelled for vengeance on the Air Corps before his own cries petered out.

By dawn a detail of 551st soldiers retrieved what bodies it could. One member was a stunned PFC Hank Warpechowski of Milwaukee, who had just joined the outfit the day before, too late to jump. Doc Chalkley describes the pathos of that scene well:

> It was daylight when we fished the first body out of the water. It was rigger John Hoffman who had been with us all the way from Panama, a beautiful physical specimen of a man. He was obviously dead, but his buddy was there with him. He kept saying, "Help him, Doc, he ain't dead." I tried to convince him—rigor mortis had already set it—but he was really beside himself.

Stevens, Albritton, and Bobbie MeHaffey were on the sad detail, listening to the jayhawks scream that it was morning, smelling the mixture of dew and pine needles and the awful odor of death. The bodies were bloated with lake water.

Writing his new wife something he ordered her not to tell his mother, Joe

Cicchinelli, who landed with "protected" A Company in a peach orchard, described the rescue scene: "The water was cold as the devil, almost cold enough to freeze. We dragged some of the men up from under the water and their bodies were blue, almost black. Their eyes were very big and open. Some of the positions they were in were terrible to see."[20] The night after the jump catastrophe, Cicchinelli attended his first church service in years.

Sergeant Jim Smith was a native North Carolinian who became the righthand man to Emory Albritton in securing a monument to the Mackall dead in 1992. Smith fell about 6 feet from the water that night. "I heard men hollering," he said. "Everyone felt pure misery. Men were so down-hearted afterwards; they didn't know what to do." Smith thought the whole experience was "nearly as bad as some of the nights at the Battle of the Bulge." Though Chuck Fairlamb of HQ Company kept a detailed diary throughout the war and fired the first designated mortar round in his sector of the Allied counterattack at the Battle of the Bulge, this was the night of the war he most vividly remembered.

Over the next twenty-four hours, seven of the eight lost men were recovered. One was Ishmael Petty, a country boy from West Virginia, who was "a very neat soldier, spotlessly clean, who spoke almost Elizabethan English."[21] To retrieve the body of John "Horsehead" Wafford of C Company, which sustained the most losses, Lieutenant Hand took a demolition team and blew the dam that held the lake and waited for it to drain. It took four days, but Wafford's body was found in the eerie muck canyon of the bottom. Lieutenant Dick Goins was present: "His legs were tangled in tree stumps."

The Army quickly cordoned off the tragedy from anyone not directly a witness to it. At Camp Mackall itself there was worry among the high command that direct contact with the rescue effort would only instill fear, hesitance, and distrust among the huge gathering of the airborne command. The airborne training and testing efforts for D-Day at Normandy, which was only four months away, could be poisoned at the eleventh hour. "At that time we were probably the oldest Airborne unit there at Mackall, and they didn't want the younger men to see those bodies, so we took care of everything ourselves," Jim Stevens recounted. "We got them out and buried them."

The men of the 515th Parachute Infantry Regiment at Mackall—of which GOYA-to-be Jim Welsh was then a part—were told to stand by for a rescue mission, but command backed off. "It was the first time in my life I heard those funny numbers 5-5-1," said Welsh. "I soon had it in mind that these were undisciplined, machete-wielding people who should be shipped back to Panama—an image of drunken renegades. I had never heard of them before and [after the night jump tragedy] never wanted to again."

The Army never explained the nature of the accident to the relatives of the dead. There was no financial compensation for their deaths. The Army official who delivered the telegram to Benjamin Preziotti's family barely managed to whisper why he was there before leaving; two soldiers detailed to guard the casket at the Brooklyn wake soon left because they could not bear it. The inquest that followed was secret. No one from the 551st command was disciplined; in fact, there is no record of anyone's being disciplined. Outside of the six hundred copies of Morgan's privately printed account, the incident has never appeared in any history book. Morgan himself did not list the men who died that night, nor did he acknowledge that sixty-one others were injured in the jump.[22]

Beau Preziotti had had a premonition; he had written his sister about an earlier jump when his chute hooked onto a tree: "Hope that's not telling me something." The popular son of Italian immigrants, whose father, an ironworker, fashioned wrought-iron borders for the booths at Coney Island, Beau was someone, his sister said, who "brought light into a room." He loved opera and sang around the family home; an Ink Spots favorite was "I'll Get By." Like most GOYAs, he was athletic—he had a rope climb hung from a tree in Brooklyn—and one of the best crapshooters in the 551st. Vincent Artz was so moved to see Preziotti kneel down by his footlocker to say a rosary at night that he converted to Catholicism after the war.

For years his sister remembered Beau's purpled, cut lip and supposed that he must have tried desperately to get out of his bindings. Her dreams were of him falling, calling her. The family wore black long past the ordinary time of grief. Four years after the night jump, his father died of a broken heart when he received—four years late—the first of his son's pension checks.

6

The spared

For various reasons, some men of the 551st were spared the trial by ordeal of the night jump. Some, like Bill Amann of HQ Company, were on legitimate leave. His friend from boot camp days, Roland Barhyte of A Company, would later refer to the child to which Amann's wife gave birth on that leave as "his little exemption."

Barhyte himself was not yet in the 551st, though he was at Camp Mackall with the 541st Parachute Infantry Regiment at the time of the night jump. "Word went around Camp Mackall of a night jump tragedy like wildfire," Barhyte reported. He was warned even before the night jump by Amann, "These guys are crazy—so many are in the guardhouse." But Barhyte would soon join his friends in the band of outsiders by a fluke. First, a penile discharge got him scratched from an overseas replacement assignment with the

82d Airborne as a gonorrhea case, though Barhyte protested years later, "I was a virgin! Probably they got someone else's results." The second time a lost pair of eyeglasses forestalled his shipping out. Barhyte was worried he would be thrown out of the paratroopers entirely, "I thought: Now they'll nail me for my bad right eye. But they didn't." What they did do was make him a replacement for one of the multitude transferring out of the 551st, as had happened to my father.

One officer probably saved his men's lives by using his head instead of following orders that night. Lieutenant Glenn Slucter of the HQ Company's light machine gun platoon arrived at the jump area late because of a mechanical problem that delayed his plane's takeoff. The night was still just as dark and the visibility just as poor as it had been for everyone ahead of him. When a crewman from the cockpit told him that the pilot thought they were over the drop zone, Slucter replied, "I'm not so concerned about what the pilot thinks as what he knows." The pilot circled once and repeated his guesstimate, and Slucter again rejected it as insufficient grounds to jump. On a third try, the pilot was still relying only on guesswork, and that still wasn't enough for Slucter, who ordered him to return to Bragg and Pope Air Field. Lloyd Willis, who was in Slucter's stick that night, saw others parachuting below his plane and had two good friends killed. A crack parachute test jumper who later discovered in test jumps in Florida that virtually no lifejacket would hold a man up with 120 pounds in the water, Willis was convinced that on the night jump "if we had been dropped on original orders, we would have been dead."

The day after the drownings, even before the lake was fully drained and Wafford's body recovered, Colonel Graves conducted a critique of the disaster with his officers. Slucter was apprehensive; he thought Graves would punish him for not jumping. As it turned out, "very early in the critique he mentioned me and said that I was to be commended for my action." To Slucter, Graves "seemed to be a pretty down-to-earth sort of guy."

Another man who felt his life was spared that night by a strange twist of fate was Don Garrigues. Originally due to jump last in his stick—the other half of the HQ Company light machine gun platoon—Garrigues was switched from last to first when the jumpmaster, Sergeant James McDuffie, approached him with the white nylon of his reserve chute sprung open in his arms.

"Sergeant Garrigues, my reserve chute accidentally came open, and of course I can't jump without it. Do you want to take my place and jump the plane, or do you want to go back and land?"

"Well, we're already up here—we might as well go ahead and jump," Garrigues replied.

"All right," McDuffie said. "I'll help you push out the bundles." The two sergeants proceeded to unload the bundles of disassembled machine guns and ammunition, with parachutes attached. As Garrigues moved from last man to first, he wondered about McDuffie: Was his reserve chute really opened by accident, or had he purposely tripped it so that he wouldn't have to jump? Anyway, it was the first incident of this type that Garrigues had encountered.

Like everyone else but Slucter, when Garrigues saw the green light flash in the panel next to the jump door, he yelled "Go!" though indeed, "I could see no lights on the ground anywhere." The first out the door after the bundles, he describes a curious kind of weightlessness: "After the opening shock of the parachute, there was no sensation of falling. It was completely black all around." Garrigues fell through a pine tree near the lake edge, his parachute canopy finally hooking on the top branches and leaving him rather pleasantly suspended a few feet off the ground. He unhooked himself by the triple-release snaps from his chute and, hearing calls of "Help! Help!" ran toward them along the shore of the lake, following a sharp turn to the left, until he came upon two men emerging from the water, the last two to jump from his plane. They were soggy but safe. After the yells died down, and the men from his platoon had found their equipment bundles and organized themselves, they realized one man was missing—PFC Kenneth McGrotty of Medford, Oregon.

The next day they learned that McGrotty had landed in deeper water and drowned.

Garrigues reflected more forgivingly on McDuffie's pass on jumping. His jumpmaster had a tendency to "hesitate a few seconds . . . before someone shoved him on out." That night, such hesitation by McDuffie would probably have been even more costly than what actually happened, as many more men would have been dropped in the middle of the lake.

But Garrigues was bedeviled by the fact that McGrotty was the only one of the stick to land in deep water. Private John Bellefontaine, who had jumped right in front of McGrotty, found himself in water up to his chest but was nowhere near the doomed man. How is that? "We never knew how he happened to [land] out in the lake unless he slipped his chute," Garrigues concludes with uncertainty. "Slipping your chute" means intermittently steering it by tugging on the risers. In that case, the way McGrotty wanted to go was not the way he should have gone.

7
The secret inquest

The press took virtually no notice of the Mackall tragedy, hence the public was shut out from it. Three days after the night jump—February 19, 1944—the *Fayetteville Observer* ran a two-sentence AP article on the society page, crowded by wedding announcements, a schedule of the week's church services, and the itinerary of the city library's Bookmobile. The headline read: "Eight Paratroopers Drowned Wednesday." The story in its entirety reads: "The public relations office announced today that eight paratroopers were drowned Wednesday night 'incident to a training flight and jump.' No details were released." The dead men's names and hometowns were listed. And that was it.[23]

It is not certain just who issued that terse statement, but it seems likely that it was the Army press or information office at Camp Mackall. Today, of course, it wouldn't take an overly enterprising managing editor of the local paper to assign a reporter to find out more, and within a few days such a story would land on the front page. In fact, such an extraordinary loss of life in training, not to mention the question of culpability, would today spread through the journalistic community like wildfire and would merit significant coverage far beyond the local paper. One need only think of the 1992 U.S. Navy accident at sea when an explosive was allegedly placed by a disturbed sailor in the breach of a heavy gun, or the collision of two planes at Pope Air Field itself in 1994, killing several paratroopers lined up on the tarmac.[24] Both incidents were front-page news nationally for days, and intensive investigations were held and covered by the media.

As it was, the *Fayetteville Observer* never probed further. It was wartime, and those were the lead-up months to D-Day, which would involve the largest single invasion force in the history of warfare. If the night jump tragedy was quickly hidden from soldiers at the camp itself, it is no surprise that bare dribbles reached the public at large. It would not do to rattle the nerves of either soldiers or American citizens at such a delicate time. The war effort relied on steel, resolve, and blind confidence. Training disasters, such as the massacre at Slapton Sands, England, when German U-boats slipped into a naval exercise off the English coast and sent 749 sailors to their graves, were kept from the public for decades. The myth of the good war died slowly indeed.

If the public was screened from the knowledge that its command had been mortally careless at Camp Mackall, one of those in command made an in-house attempt at patching morale together and eulogizing the drowned. One week after the night jump, a February 23, 1944, issue of *Hook-Up*, the newsletter of the 551st, contained a frontispiece list of the dead between two sketched candles under the heading, "In Memory of These Our Buddies Who Met Their Death in Line of Duty While Making a Parachute Jump on the Night of 16 February 1944." The crude, touching memorial is followed by an open letter to the battalion by Colonel Rupert Graves.

The address indicates that Graves was deeply disturbed by the tragedy, and his conscience was not altogether settled. Graves cloaks himself in that great muffler of individual responsibility, "we." He paints a picture of being trapped passively in the tragedy: "We all feel deeply the losses that have just been incurred by us in the recent night jump." Fair enough. But he moves quickly from sadness to the matter at hand, a unit which was already exploding with rebellion and was now heartstricken in its barracks: "We must resolve to make their sacrifice serve to bind the unit closer together." Even with its mawkish echo of Lincoln's Second Inaugural Address, Graves may have captured an honest emotion if he had ended there. Instead, pressing forward, stepping ahead of the bottomless, thrusting himself into the role of commander rather than eulogizer, he urged all "to show how to perfect ourselves in our training in order that future sacrifices will be avoided." With that sweeping exhortation, Graves spread the responsibility for the errors of the night jump throughout the unit.

Graves promised that "a board of officers" in the 551st would come up with a new technique so that "each and every one of us will be able to take care of himself in case of a water landing." That sounds quite reassuring, but no such "miracle drug" was ever synthesized during World War II for the 551st or any other parachute unit. The only technique, in fact, that fitted this bill was not a technique of jumping at all, but new equipment—chutes with the quick-release harness that the British had produced before the night jump ever occurred. The Americans knew full well of their existence then but did not make them standard issue until after the war.

Graves ended his message to the stricken battalion with a tribute to "the valiant efforts of many men in the battalion who worked for long periods of time in the ice-cold water in an attempt to assist men who were in trouble," listing ten men by name.[25] Many others helped that night, and Graves admits as much, but that owing "to the darkness and confusion, their identity could not be determined."

While Graves skirted the issue of the lack of a quick release with his "promise" of a tactical review of water drops, there was something else his open letter avoided: any specific acknowledgment of misjudgment. Mistakes, personal or battalionwide, are not admitted or described.

The place for that, to be sure, was an official inquest into the incident, which occurred some weeks after the night jump and was held in secret. Its findings were never released, and no one (myself included) has ever uncovered records of its proceedings or its final judgment. Oddly, two days after the tragedy (February 18, 1944), the 442d Troop Carrier Group history records a glider pilot of the 304th Squadron killed: "This was our first fatal accident and we record it herewith with deep regret." How that could possibly be a "first accident" when eight men were dropped to their deaths two days before by their pilots is explained by bureaucratic hairsplitting. For an accident to be logged as such in the Army Air Corps (later Air Force), the aircraft had to be damaged or an airman injured or killed. Dead paratroopers were considered a "ground mishap." Whatever its culpability, the Army Air Corps only received a casualty report, which was destroyed five years after the tragic event. Other authorities have told me papers from the inquest were probably shredded shortly after it was held.[26]

The sole surviving witness to the inquest—his testimony was taken—was the battalion's communications officer, Andy Titko. The secret inquiry was headed by Colonel Julian Broster Lindsay, commander of the 515th Parachute Infantry Regiment (which had at Benning been my father's home). According to Titko, the only person disciplined for the night jump disaster at Mackall was an Army Air Corps commander, but he did not recall who it was or the nature of the disciplinary action.[27] No official evidence survives that anyone else testified at the inquest. Rupert Graves himself was not disciplined, though he was hurriedly transferred (some might say kicked upstairs). A month later Graves was promoted to full colonel and sent to lead a group three times the size of the 551st—the 517th Parachute Regimental Combat Team, the unit with which history identifies him.

Dick Goins, a lieutenant with C Company, feels, as do most officers, that the drownings were tragic but essentially unavoidable, or rather that they were the result of human error, but not any error that could have been predicted. In short, the Goins interpretation of the night jump is that no one specifically was at fault. To use Jim Stevens's language, it was "one of those days," except that it was night.

Others are not so sure that the disaster was unavoidable or that no one specifically was culpable, beyond the Air Corps commander who has mysteriously disappeared from the historical record.

Before that sad night, Benjamin Preziotti had written his sister that he was convinced it was important to be good friends with the people who packed chutes. But no one told him that it would have been better to have been friends with those who designed them. It was unthinkable at the time to protest to the War Department, but his sister wrote to the columnist Drew Pearson about what had happened at Camp Mackall that night. Pearson was incensed. Without naming the victim unit, he published two columns in the spring of 1944 about the tragedy, railing against the Army for not adopting the British quick-release harness. He called it "a procurement scandal of the first degree . . . which may become a national scandal."[28] With the American harness, which had to be released at three points on the body, "if one hand happens to be injured, or if the flier fumbles a release, he cannot get free at all." A water drop, or being dragged by wind on the ground, was a death sentence for a U.S. paratrooper in this harness, one reason, Pearson wrote, why an American aviator in England "throws away his parachute and begs, borrows, or steals a parachute of the British type," with its chest release box operable with one hand. Otherwise he was the victim of 720 feet of tangled shroud lines that connected his chute to his harness. Pearson was not alone in his crusade. Brigadier General Newton Longfellow of the Eighth Air Force in England had reported the year before to Washington that "anything but a quick-release harness is murderous."

Ironically, the quick release was invented by "Sky High" Irvin in Buffalo, New York. It was in use all over the world at the time of World War II, but not in the United States. A rival manufacturer was the problem ("an insidious matter of patents and profits"), one who apparently was well connected at the War Department. The GOYAs' night jump disaster, however, made the Army "jump in at top speed"[29] after the second-in-command at Camp Mackall, Colonel C. B. DeGavre, flew to Washington to brief officials on the tragedy. Pearson reported 100,000 quick-release harnesses ordered. They must have been terribly hard to make, because they didn't arrive in time for general use in World War II by American forces.[30] Bickering between the Army and the Navy about the relative merits of the equipment did not help matters.

Beyond journalism, the night jump mystery triggered the imagination of a well-known novelist. In 1948 *Guard of Honor* was published to great critical acclaim. Its author, James Gould Cozzens, won the Pulitzer Prize that year, edging out two celebrated war novels that sold far more copies: *The Naked and the Dead* by Norman Mailer and *The Young Lions* by Irwin Shaw. An examination of tense relations between black and white airmen in the early days of the semi-integrated Army Air Corps, the novel's climactic incident is a September 1943 drop of black paratroopers over a Lake Lalage in the Florida panhandle near a fictitious Ocanara Air Force Base, a "monstrous snowfall,"[31] as Cozzens expressed it. In the novel, seven men drown. Like the 551st, the ill-fated paratrooper unit is testing new jump and attack tactics; like the GOYAs it is a separate group attached at a "satellite field" (as Mackall was to Fort Bragg during the war). The disaster is officially tagged to "a mechanical failure [which] caused one of the carrier planes to release part of its drop outside the designated drop zone." The novel discovers a stuck static line as an ostensible culprit, as opposed to the array of physical and emotional problems that was the reality at Mackall, such as nervous, green pilots, malfunctioning jump lights, darkness, rain, and the thin drop zone. The fictional jump is an exhibition at midday. Still, the resemblances are profound.

Cozzens was an aide to one of the top Army Air Corps generals during the war, and be toured most stateside air bases, including Pope Air Field. He must have caught wind of the tragedy of the 551st at Camp Mackall, if not inspected it himself. At least two sources have told me of the 551st linkage to *Guard of Honor*, including the editor of *American Heritage*. However, no direct evidence of that exists in the critical and biographical writing surrounding Cozzens's work.

Cozzens's own published wartime diary and memos mention nothing of the night jump tragedy, though they discuss at length insubordination of Negro troops at Freeman Field, which undoubtedly influenced *Guard of Honor*. In fact, three days after the Mackall drownings, other than working on a WAC film script, Cozzens noted, "There is nothing else to do."[32]

Intriguingly, Cozzens appears to have been obsessed with Drew Pearson, the columnist who blew a modest whistle on the Mackall incident, mentioning him three times. On September 28, 1944, Cozzens refers to Pearson's having material leaked to him on "the leak-proof tank matter" by "either or both Lt. Colonel [name withheld] formerly in the Troop Carrier Command office, and a girl." The "formerly" makes one wonder if this was the troop carrier leader disciplined or dismissed for the 551st tragedy at Mackall; even forty years later, when Cozzens's journals were published, someone deemed it necessary to protect this man by blacking his name out.[33]

The fact that as compulsively honest and high-placed an individual as James Gould Cozzens (he was chief aide to the general in charge of the Army Air Corps's Office of Information at the Pentagon) would allow nothing concrete about the drowning of eight paratroopers by green pilots into his diaries or memos is a testimony to how secure a lid the Army clamped on the Mackall incident and how powerfully such repression can reverberate in the mind of a novelist.

It would fit the pattern of the 551st's fate, in any case, that even the originating tracks of a heralded novel anonymously patterned on the GOYAs' experience would have been suppressed, perhaps self-suppressed under warning, for it is almost impossible to believe Cozzens knew nothing about the Mackall drownings or would have been unmoved by them. It would also fit that that novel would fade from readership as the battalion itself fell off the radar screen of history.

8

My father's hollow egg

Incredibly, just before Rupert Graves left the 551st, he ordered another night jump. He evidently hoped that this one would be under more favorable conditions and would shake the bugaboo from the men about jumping at night. The jump site lay in the opposite direction from the previous one, south toward Rockingham. Twenty-seven planes would fly in **V** formations from Laurinburg-Maxton Air Field. There were no lakes to worry about; it would begin in late afternoon and end in early evening with the moon out. A normal altitude for a parachute jump is somewhere between 800 and 1,000 feet. Graves, perhaps thinking a somewhat lower altitude would encourage the men, ordered a 600-foot drop. As it turned out, the men barely had time to breathe before they were banging onto the ground.

The problem was that the drop zone was 200 feet above sea level; the altimeter reading of 600 feet was misleading. Ralph Wenthold, a sergeant who later became a lieutenant in A Company, thought he jumped from less than 400 feet, the lowest of all his 170 jumps in the Army: "The red light was on as we came over Highway 1, but it didn't seem like we were at 600 feet. Captain Dalton said, 'God damn! If they don't get any higher, we aren't going to jump.' About then the green light came on, and when that happened we threw out the bundles and out he went and out I went, and my chute had no more than opened than I was standing on the ground." Wenthold was lucky; there next to him in a dead tree was a man whose chute seemed to have had no time to open, impaled on a high branch. He was seriously injured.

As if that dubious encore of the first night jump wasn't already sufficiently strained, Lieutenant Colonel Graves ordered the men to dig into the cold ground, powdered with snow, for maneuvers that evening. It was late when Doug Dillard, shivering in his foxhole, saw Graves drive up in a heated, covered jeep. No trucks were sent for the men. They were told to hike back to the base by the light of a frigid moon.

It would appear my father's most feared moment of the war was that second night jump. I remember his mentioning someone next to him being hurt badly in a tree, which fits in with Wenthold's account. But he never said it was in training. I think it quite possible not only that the shocking stories fed to him about the first night jump on his arrival at Mackall stoked his terror when he found himself directed to a similar jump, but that the two jumps became fused in his mind. The teeth-rattling landing from the dangerously low altitude may have strengthened the conflation.

This much is certain: He had never been on a night jump before. He was new, energetic, gung ho. But the anticipation of a disaster like the one he knew only by hearsay must have been unbearable. Unlike anyone else, he jumped with a hollow, painted eggshell that night, as he had throughout jump school, and it did not crack.

I see him coming down now. Just as he has lost the roar of the engine, he begins to hear human voices shooting up from the darkness below. All too quickly he is rolling in the pine needles with his own weight and that of his load—about 260 pounds. He snaps himself out and runs in the moonlight toward the voices, splashing into an icy pool of water that expands in his mind to Lake Kinney Cameron, just as he would wade in after me so many times when I was growing up. He once picked me up out of a pile of glass after I had, at age thirteen, run through a plate glass door and shattered it completely. The doctor said the speed with which I'd run and my lack of hesitation had saved me; that wasn't hard, since I hadn't seen the glass there at all. Blood covered both of us from where a wedge of glass had sunk 2 inches into my leg. Likewise, my father carried me, breathless with asthma, throughout the night until we both saw first light.

I believe he stepped into water, and for a few seconds before it registered as too cold and the voices had gone faint, the hollow egg painted with the paratrooper by his eldest sister Jeannette bobbed on the tide of his fear.

The last contact any GOYA soldier had with Rupert Graves before the final bloody days at the Battle of the Bulge was in late March 1944 at the train station at Hoffman, North Carolina. Graves had been swiftly reassigned after the night jump tragedy, and his driver, PFC Milo Huempfner, had taken him in a jeep to the train station.

It was to be a spectral goodbye. Huempfner, who would earn the only GOYA Distinguished Service Cross at the Battle of the Bulge, was not magnanimous. Graves had several suitcases. Stopped on the dusty drive in front of the station, Huempfner took the luggage out of the jeep and set them on the ground. The driver avoided Graves's eyes and jumped back behind the steering wheel, leaving Graves standing by his array of suitcases.

"Goodbye, Milo," the commander said plaintively.

Private Huempfner said nothing. He looked back while releasing the parking brake, and saw Graves's eyes welling before he drove off.

V

WAR AT LAST

Operation Dragoon into Southern France

Life is too short to be small.

—Disraeli

1
GOYA! GOYA! GOYA!

When the door to the stockade at Camp Mackall swung open at the end of March 1944, the men inside rubbed their eyes at the harsh knife of sunlight thrust at their feet. Particles of Carolina dust playing in the shaft of light seemed to taunt the men, reminding them that they were only dust, pure granulation at this point in their Army life, with no authority to carry any weapon other than a single razor blade. They could do that only under the watch of something called "a prison chaser," a usually morose guardian angel from the freer world of the battalion in the barracks, assigned for the day to watch over them while they swabbed the stockade floors, cleaned the latrines, or shaved.

It was Wood Joerg, the hopoid from West Point, who had left the battalion last fall for bigger and better things. Now he was back, standing in light particles that pointed, like a knife, to his old battalion. He was not smiling, but he left the door open.

The men slowly stood up, as if their former commander's unannounced, unexpected presence had imposed a cautious rhythm on their movements. Was this some sort of apparition? Were they dreaming? It had to be midmorning. Many had fallen back to sleep after the predawn chores.

Joerg's fiery eyes, half-concealed by the rim of his helmet, could barely be seen. One man nudged another: "Look. No eagle yet." Joerg was still wearing the "light colonel's" silver leaf on his shoulders rather than the full colonel's eagle.

Joerg surveyed them slowly, as if he were taking the measure of every man in the pit, ready to box with each in turn. The confrontation cut off words. On return to Camp Mackall, the stockade loomed large. He could not wait to do what he knew he had to do to rescue his old battalion from total disintegration. He searched the eyes—blank, cynical, but stirred by the dusty light. He smelled the bad breath of men kept from toothpaste, not to mention food, for long periods, as punishment. The listlessness of defeat could be sensed in this place; he had noticed it all over Mackall since returning the night before, in the heaviness of the beech trees and oaks, in the growth of moss as the sun coaxed it from spring rain and wood.

He looked up at the rafters as if something might be there to guide him. He saw a crossbeam. He looked down so that his face went entirely out of view. Then he took off the helmet, raised his young, exposed head, and spoke.

"You birds don't belong in this place."[1] His eyes watered. They listened transfixed; he sounded as if he were speaking to himself.

"You are soldiers. I trained you. And I know what you can do." He made the rounds of the prisoners again with his not entirely hard gaze. "We have been through a lot together. And apart. But we are a family and we belong together. I've come back."

He wiped some sweat from his rilled forehead, which, like a wintry battlefield, met a treeless plain at his crown. The men began to murmur. He stilled them by speaking more loudly, as if giving an order.

"I want to see the hands of every man who will promise me on his word of honor no more AWOLs or jumping each other if I put you back where you belong. Your hands . . ." He said the last emphatically, making it hard for them to refuse, but not ordering them, for then it would all be meaningless.

One by one, hands came out of pockets, up from the sides of lost men, from under jaws, from behind heads, a hand for each man, palm out and up as if seeing the flag in a man, as if being in school again at the beginning of the day. Soon the room was alive with hands, with which the light played.

Joerg smiled and put his helmet on.

"Men of the 551st Parachute Infantry Battalion, move out to Europe!"

They broke into a cheer: "GOYA! GOYA! GOYA!" Men drilling on the fields saw the crowd of inmates emerge behind Joerg in a surging column

and heard the chanting. They sensed that something unusual had happened. Some ran to see what it was. Some just stopped to watch their banished fellows push out the prison door and come into the knife-light,
following a helmeted commander to war.

Though Joerg's extraordinary speech to the men in the stockade indicated his personally felt kinship to the unit he had created in 1942 and
taken to Panama, no one seems to know for sure why he returned in the
spring of 1944 to the 551st from his lofty perch as second in command of
the 542d Parachute Infantry Regiment. On the face of it, it was something
of a demotion. A battalion is only one-third the size of a regiment, and the
542d was supposedly being groomed for a historic drop across the Rhine
once Operation Overlord—the crossing of the English Channel by Allied
forces—was accomplished.

There is no doubt of Joerg's favor with the 542d. As late as January 27,
1944, he assumed command of the regiment in the temporary absence of
Colonel William Ryder, the legendary leader of the Test Platoon and the
man who took its first leap into the air. But there was now doubt about the
Rhine jump. In fact, the tactical mission—to blow up Germany's electrical
power dams in the Ruhr by March—was canceled. For if the 551st had severe fissures in it, the 542d hadn't yet formed a whole to fracture. It was
still missing a third battalion to complete its strength—in fact, it would
never get a third battalion. Joerg had watched many of the 542d's officers
and enlisted men drain off as replacements for other parachute units
being hammered hard at Anzio and in the Pacific or to bolster the mam-
moth forces of Overlord staging in England. By March, the regiment had
shrunk to a single battalion. When Ryder himself was reassigned in February 1944 to the Pacific theater as General Douglas MacArthur's airborne
adviser, Joerg may have come to the conclusion that if the 551st was going
to hell, the 542d was going nowhere.

But all of that assumes Joerg had a choice, or at least expressed his restlessness to superiors. Issuing guard orders and other housekeeping measures for a regiment stateside made his 542d duty dreary, even though he
inspired his new men no less than he had the GOYAs.[2] As for Heidi Joerg,
duty at Fort Benning for the second time was not what she had hoped for.
Colonel Ryder, himself divorced, had "ordered" Heidi to be the official
"wife" of the regiment and to organize officer wives to play bridge, a game
she didn't know. She also detested the not-so-subtle jockeying for position
among the women: "There was one major's wife who always insisted on
sitting at the head of the table, you know, throwing her rank around." All
of that testified to a regiment made small and static.

Joerg wanted static lines and a shot at the war. He must have been informed of his old battalion's night jump tragedy and made to realize that only he could rescue the GOYAs from the depression and abject failure in which they were wallowing. His pride at stake, he confided to his mother that he sorely missed the men of his old command.

Though some officers grumbled, Joerg's return woke the GOYAs up. Shortly after the stockade release, the commander gathered the entire battalion to announce what the grapevine had circulated for weeks, that they were soon to ship out for battle in Europe. Their time had come, and everyone was needed, AWOLs included. As far as he was concerned, he reiterated, the AWOL chapter of the 551st was finished.

Through February and March 1944, the 551st had been going through tactical and physical endurance tests, and performance picked up almost magically on Joerg's return. The 558 men of the unit had actually had their orders to move overseas on March 15, 1944, shortly before Joerg arrived. By the end of March new combat equipment was issued to all the men. They began boxing, not each other but war matériel, in handmade pine crates. The packing went on for more than a month.

Parties broke out all over the sandhills of Camp Mackall and beyond, with the predictable licentious frenzy of those leaving for war. B Company took $1,500 it had left over from the Hook-Up Club in Panama and threw a bash in Cheraw, North Carolina, at a country club. At first, wives' attendance was forbidden, but the men relented. Dick Kelley, a bartender in civilian life, switched halfway through the party from giving out drinks to giving out fifths. Couples changed partners for dances, kisses, and who knows what else. Sergeant Bill Hatcher watched, with mock horror, Emmett Starkey elegantly ask his wife, Dorothy, for a "round dance." Where Emmett came from there were only two kinds of dances, square and round. By 2 A.M., Hatcher reported, "it looked like a battlefield with bodies everywhere from fights or just passed out."

At those celebrations Joerg introduced the new officers he had brought with him, including Lieutenants Charlie Buckenmeyer, Richard Hallock, and Dick Durkee from the 542d. Durkee, one of the most extraordinary combat soldiers in World War II, was a raw U.S. Army recruit from upstate New York, a professional middleweight boxer and baseball player with violence in his family lineage. His father had been clubbed to death in the 1920s by unionists who mistook him for a scab laborer.

Durkee would be the first Allied soldier to step into Nice and the last A Company officer left standing in Belgium in 1945. In earlier days Leonard Funk, a Medal of Honor winner, had been his platoon sergeant in the 508th, but Durkee's valor—like all of the 551st's—was hidden under a bushel basket of fate for half a century. A master paratrooper (which requires 60 jumps) who had jump-qualified some of the first airborne men at Fort Benning—including Colonel James Gavin—Durkee was one of the few men to study Wood Joerg in both the 551st and the 542d. The conclusion he drew differed from those junior officers who were "somewhat relieved" (Captain Hartman) when Joerg left the 551st, thinking him too stiff and tough (they bridled at Joerg's implementation of the "get off your ass" battalion slogan, which tended to lump officers with line soldiers). According to Durkee, "Joerg was very quiet and sincere, not especially gung ho, as some other officers. He never tried to take over conversation but listened to his officers arguing points of view. He was very patriotic, however, and would have taken any assignment." This more subdued impression of the man would gradually replace that of the barking tough guy, the West Pointer whose bravado bordered on the self-parody, of quick-drawing in his shorts in front of the mirror in Panama and the scoffing at seasickness on the way to Panama, when the commander seemed to spend the whole trip in his cabin vomiting.

As the round of farewells to college and high school joys went from party to party in North Carolina, the line soldiers toasted the return of their youthful original commander. The daring speech at the stockade had certainly boosted Joerg's stock. They would follow him to hell. Amid the drinking and swinging, jokes went around about who had the clap and where Rupert Graves had gone. Actually, after a short trip away—presumably to drown his memories of the 551st with family, friends, and tankards—Graves had come back to Mackall. Some men had seen Old Hose Nose, Sir Tombstone himself, marching other men over the sand hills. They turned out to be the 517th Parachute Infantry Regiment, which had also been relieved of its original commander, Colonel Lou Walsh, who had been demoted to a light colonel. Walsh's problem had been that an "intense focus on building a will to win, teaching his soldiers how to fight and survive, was not matched by an interest in administration."[3] Walsh had also, according to General Mel Zais who led a battalion of the 517th, "talked too much [and] got too big for his britches." The 551st had no trouble recognizing that Old Hose Nose's britches would always be sufficiently big.

Graves was welcomed as a mellow, witty gentleman by the 517th, but to the GOYAs he was an absurd tyrant. Ironically, he transferred out of the 551st to replace a tyrant, while Joerg, whom his junior officers saw also as a tyrant, would return, to the delight of the NCOs and enlisted men. The two units would rub alongside each other all the way to the Bulge. The 517th would sail for battle three weeks after the 551st.

The goodbye kisses were long, tongues were sore. Dick Durkee met a girl at the POE (port of embarkation), Norfolk. She and some of her friends insisted on touching the floorboards of the men's eros, for they stole onto the USS *Mulholland* with blankets. Joerg looked the other way as Durkee pulled a blanket over himself and his farewell partner.

For Joerg and Heidi it was mostly a time for keeping mum. The day of departure, April 11, was kept secret from wives. Wood Joerg said nothing to Heidi about Europe that whole month in Mackall. She sensed what was up the morning she saw her husband's packed duffel bag by the door and a certain look on his face. It was flushed strangely red, with splotches of faint green. His eyes glowed as if he had been staring directly at an eclipse without protection. Then he stared at the ground, hiding something. His eyes were watering. She stepped up to hold him, and he gripped her hard, then ran his hands along her flanks and torso and small waist. He kissed the two-year-old Charlotte on the wisp of her fontanelle. Then he drove away.

Swinging Charlotte that morning in the park, Heidi heard the train whistle blowing at Southern Pines. "I couldn't even go down and wave goodbye to him," she said. "It was supposed to be secret." Just before the 551st's train pulled out, two men were injured setting off demolition charges. One lost an eye, the other some fingers. That was not a heartening sendoff.

Wood called her that night from a pay phone at Newport News, Virginia, and Camp Patrick Henry. "We were all too choked up to talk much," she remembered. That hoarseness was the last sound her husband would ever make to her, inchoate and unsure.

After a week at Patrick Henry and two nights at the Hampton Roads docks in Norfolk, the 551st Parachute Infantry Battalion lifted anchor April 22, 1944, on three ships, really, for Europe: the *William Mulholland* carried Headquarters, A and B Companies, along with most of their sister outfit, the 550th glider battalion. Both battalions' C Companies traveled on the *Abraham Lincoln*. A third ship took the medics, including Doc Chalkley. All were Liberty ships in a convoy of about a hundred Liberties across the Atlantic.

As they plunged up and down in the stormy water, Heidi Joerg felt her new baby boxing in the hold.

2

"All of us are going to get it"

Maybe it was the Spam and chili—all they ate for three weeks across the sea—but the Panama duty hadn't steeled their stomachs. There were three holds in the USS *Mulholland*, each with an officer on watch at all times. Dick Durkee drew that odious assignment. The heave of the rough Atlantic would start one man throwing up, and the sour fumes from the vomit would create a domino effect; one by one by one, everyone got sick, including Durkee himself.

The battalion would fight more than the waves. With a chance to leave its stockade history behind, it was faced directly with reminders of its incarcerated past. As the men were boarding the *Abraham Lincoln* at Norfolk, a convoy of trucks with sirens and MPs had pulled up. Tims Quinn described it: "Lo and behold, these people get out and they had armed guards all around. Two hundred men, and they put them on our boat." They were not Germans, but men who had jumped ship to avoid battle, had been rounded up in port and taken to stockades. To Sergeant Pat Garretty, the 551st's transport looked like "a turn-of-the-century prison ship headed for Devil's Island."[4]

Predictably, the AWOLs and former AWOLs clashed. As the GOYAs did their calisthenics on the wobbly deck and trained in map reading, range finding, first aid, and weapons, the prisoners taunted them. "They laughed at the men who had to work," Quinn said. The prisoners began to steal food from the 551st's lockers. Quinn took matters into his own hands, and his "stalwarts . . . threw blankets over their heads and tied them up and just whipped the fool out of them with paddles." The ship's captain was oblivious. He and all the Merchant Marines could be seen at night chomping on their steaks and potatoes, to the gall of the Spam-oppressed 551st.

Don Garrigues wrote, "Fresh water was always a precious commodity on board a troopship." He noted that you could take only a saltwater shower on the *Mulholland*, which left one feeling worse than before. "Feeling every roll and toss" of the thin-plated Liberty ship, Garrigues didn't like being reminded there was only "about a half-inch separating me from the Atlantic." So he decided to do anything to get fresh water, which was being closely held in the steward's quarters on the upper deck aft.

Only officers were allowed to move from one hold to another. Everyone else was more or less stuck. Garrigues noticed that the officers wore coveralls like the enlisted men on ship and showed their rank only with an insignia on a wool cap. "It didn't take me long to promote myself to first lieutenant," he wrote, "by sticking a strip of white adhesive tape on the front of my wool cap." His fresh water shower that evening reminded him of the lakes of his native Missouri.

In the evenings, Garrigues's boyhood friend, Bill Hatcher, played clarinet in the hold, and the men would sing songs like "I've Got a Lovely Bunch of Coconuts," "Smoke Gets in Your Eyes," or "Sentimental Journey" to Hatcher's trill. Poker games sprang up and continued into the late hours, with more than a few unwanted deuces thrown out the portholes.

After threading the needle at Gibraltar on May 11—one day before it was to dock at Oran, Algeria—the convoy was attacked by several dozen German fighter-bombers, which strafed the decks at low levels. The troops dived flat on the decks, the rivets scraping their ribs. Several glider bombs were dropped in the water, and one hit the stern of a ship only a few positions from the *Abraham Lincoln*. The British frigates that were convoying the transports opened fire with 20mm guns. Their tracers shot through the ship riggings, scattering the men again. Several outgoing British torpedos got hung up in nets around the ship, exploding there. It was the 551st's baptism of both hostile and friendly fire.

American fighters got into the act, too. At least two of the Luftwaffe were hit; balls of fire spiraled into the sea. Luckily for the 551st, none hit their two main ships, and they took no significant casualties. But fourteen ships were lost in the attack.

Did Lieutenant Colonel Joerg know as he made the rounds one hour before midnight with the all-clear signal that his own brother may have shepherded him and his battalion through this attack? Commander Robert Joerg and his flotilla were based in the western Mediterranean at that time, and his mission was to protect transports coming through Gibraltar into *Mare Nostrum*, as the Romans had called the ancient sea. The depth charge explosions that resounded through the thin metal skin of the Liberties may have been dropped by Robert Joerg's destroyers to wreck U-boats below.

The Joerg brothers' putative reunion was matched by a real reunion just after the 551st's convoy docked in Oran on May 12. On pass to Oran from their pup tent camp 5 miles out in the desert at Merze el-Khebir, Corporal John "Mel" Clark met his brother for the first time in two years at a place called Al's Beer Joint. Not Ali's—Al's.

The ten days' stay at Merze el-Khebir was uneventful. Perimeter guards were set up around the camp to prevent Bedouins from stealing rifles, bedrolls, cigarettes. None did. The only real fight the GOYAs got into was not with the Arabs but with the French Foreign Legion at Sidi Bel Abbès, about 40 miles inland. While the 551st officers had gone to witness the French retreat ceremony, the enlisted men headed to a town bar. "Being Airborne, we got to wondering just how tough they were," Ralph Wenthold admitted, and Sergeant Lawler, broken hand in a cast, still managed to coldcock one of the Legionnaires, old men to the GOYAs, in their thirties and forties. The ensuing melée caused the Arab waiters to dive under the tables. The Foreign Legion MPs drove up, packed the drunken

GOYAs up in their trucks, and sent them back to the desert. *Zi rabble! Ali, anozair cognac!*

By the time the 551st arrived late in the spring of 1944, the fires of battle in North Africa had been snuffed. In the eighteen months since the first Allied assault on Vichy-controlled Morocco, the Germans, led by Field Marshal Rommel, had been beaten in Africa. Since the Allied conquest of Sicily the year before and the bitter landing at Anzio in January 1944, the battle against the Axis was now peaking in Italy. The final path to Rome was being cut by Allied forces. Italy was where Wood Joerg and his GOYAs thought they would meet their fate.

Aref Orfalea must have been glad not to meet his in North Africa that spring. It may have been confusing for him. To most, the Arabs would have presented a spectral, utterly foreign sight, particularly for GOYAs from the rural interior of America. A desert Arab around Merze el-Khebir with his kufiyah, long robes, leathery skin, and smug camel struck many as belonging in a circus. In Oran, Arabs rode donkeys between jeeps, whipping them with reeds; they begged in alleyways, nursing injuries from the late contest between Rommel and Montgomery. Though some were showed up in Western dress at a bank or café, looking not much different from Danny Thomas in bow tie—or, for that matter, Joe Cicchinelli on his wedding day, the quips about camel jockeys, sand niggers, and desert dagos soon emerged, particularly when one of them blocked a jeep in the narrow streets of Oran. Still, prejudices could be debunked. Garretty got his first lesson that "things are not what they seem to be" when a small Arab "wearing several layers of dirty robes" came up to him and spoke "seven languages fluently." Garretty admitted: "I have trouble with English."

Other than Nosreay Bayouth of Oklahoma City, my father was probably the only man in the 551st with Arab blood. That wouldn't have held him back from attacking the Germans in North Africa, any more than Joe Cicchinelli kept himself from firing on snipers in Sicily or Joerg from taking on the Germans of his own bloodline. The Arabs in Algeria were not especially fond of the Axis, though the Mufti in Jerusalem had spewed venom against the Allies, partly in the hopes of achieving postwar independence from the British for Palestine. The Arabs of North Africa had been pressed into war. And my father, born in Cleveland of immigrants from nineteenth-century Syria and Lebanon, would have felt sympathy for those dirty exotics of his first foreign port, who to him were not so foreign. He had seen old women in Cleveland smoke the *argilah.* He had been called what they were called, though he drove the family Packard and swing-danced with the best of them. These were people whose fates he felt his family had escaped.

Mutton and milky tea were served to the battalion in Algeria. Most had never had lamb before and were stricken with severe diarrhea, which lined the portholes on their way to Naples. Roland Barhyte recounted the 551st's arrival in Naples on May 23: "When we came off the ships at Naples, we were asked 'All present?' and we all yelled, 'Baaaa!' like sheep, from all that mutton!"

The third ship with GOYAs on it—the medics and Docs Chalkley and Battenfield—broke down just before Gibraltar and limped there for engine work. The only quarters available were in the Gibraltar jail, to which the medical GOYAs, lost after curfew, were dutifully deposited by a Scottish desk sergeant.

Unknown to them, the 551st was slowly being woven into complex cloth of an Allied invasion strategy that had begun in 1943. It took the form of a massive double sweep, two invasions of the European mainland, focusing on Nazi-held France: Operation Overlord at Normandy in the north and Operation Anvil between Marseilles and Nice in the south. But strands of the cloth were being pulled in opposite directions by General Dwight Eisenhower, the commander of all Allied Forces under the aegis of the Supreme Headquarters of the Allied Command Expeditionary Forces (SHAEF) and Winston Churchill himself, England's indefatigible Prime Minister.

The medical ship of the 551st did not go to Naples at first, but rather to Bari, Italy, on the Adriatic coast facing Yugoslavia. That was a small part of a larger feint, one of many Eisenhower had planned to throw the Germans off as to where the great blows were coming. He wanted them to believe that the Allies were staging on the east coast of Italy for a smash into Greece and the Balkans. The phony invasion force for Greece was code-named Operation Zeppelin, and the phony one for Rome, Operation Ferdinand. Churchill, however, didn't want those to be feints. He and most of the British military hierarchy had their eye on Stalin's advance from the east. More wary of the Soviet Union than the United States was, Churchill felt certain Stalin would beat the Americans and the British to Eastern Europe, which it would promptly swallow as booty for its role in the war. In short, Churchill wanted to heave Anvil out of France and into Italy, where it would bolster the sputtering Allied move northward in the peninsula and ultimately would cut off Stalin from the Balkans. Germany would be hit from its underbelly.

Despite the fact that Germany's underbelly had the highest mountains in Europe protecting it—the Alps—Churchill's argument appears, in hindsight, to have held merit. Some American generals sided quietly with Churchill, including Eisenhower's own chief of staff, General Walter Bedell Smith, who was no fan of the southern France invasion plan. But Ike, whose instinct was always for consolidation, held his ground. He aimed for a knockout punch to the head of Germany, and fewer body blows from around the periphery, which were what the British wanted. Eisenhower clearly felt the blow had to come from France and that all Allied forces had to concentrate there. Anvil, sweeping north from the Riviera, would link up with Overlord, sweeping east from Normandy. That column would become the mighty phalanx it would take to blow a hole in the Siegfried Line, beyond which lay the industrial heartland of Germany in the Ruhr Valley.

With the 551st's humble arrival on May 23 at Naples and later at Bari, all eyes were on Anzio, where the Americans had been sunk as if in bloody quicksand for four months. According to Pappy Herrmann, the GOYAs were quickly taken off their transport in Naples and herded onto another ship headed up the coast to Anzio. In the first concrete acknowledgment of their European mission, they were told that they were to reinforce the beleaguered American forces on that sandy slip not 30 miles from Rome. They had read about Anzio in *Stars and Stripes* at Camp Mackall; it was not a pretty story.

The January 22, 1944, landing of two American divisions 30 miles south of Rome at Anzio beach was to have been for Winston Churchill the great jump-start of the stalled Italian front. On December 19, 1943, Churchill had written his Chiefs of Staff that "the stagnation of the whole campaign on the Italian front is scandalous."[5] Part of the problem was the terrain, the mountainous spine of the Apennines running from Italy's head to its toes.

The Anzio plan was bold: a leapfrog amphibious landing 150 miles up the coast from Naples and the Salerno beachhead, 60 miles northwest of Cassino. It was code-named Operation Shingle, and bold as it was, the idea was sound—to draw off pressure from the Gustav Line at Cassino and confront the Germans with a two-front war in Italy. If all went well, the Allied forces would advance on Rome from two vectors, south and southwest. Field Marshal Sir Harold Alexander, who gave the orders for Shingle, was enthusiastic for the Anzio landing. He voiced the opinion that its incipient liberation of Rome would make Operation Overlord the massive cross-Channel landing in northwestern France, unnecessary. However, as John Keegan wrote, though "the logistical calculation was flawless, the operational practice was lamentable."[6]

Most lamentable were the two precious days after the January 22 landing that the U.S. invasion force, led by Major General John P. Lucas, was kept on the beach with no German resistance in front of it. All 227 German soldiers lightly guarding Anzio surrendered. The Allies had achieved complete surprise, and the road to Rome was open. But Lucas hesitated those two days—a costly pause.

Once having got wind of the landing, Field Marshal Kesselring threw a juggernaut force of three combat-hardened German divisions at Anzio, with reinforcements quickly on the way from southern France, Germany, and even Yugoslavia. Used as artillery, 88mm "flak" guns rained down from the Alban hills on the stunned Americans, and the bloodbath began. General Lucius Truscott soon relieved Lucas. From January 30, 1944, through late May, Allied troops were repulsed by the Germans four times as they tried to punch out of the killing dunes at Anzio.

What rescued the desperate Anzio situation—on which hung not only the capture of Rome but Operation Anvil, the jump into southern France, which required a launching pad from as far north as Rome to be success-ful—was not the 551st Parachute Infantry Battalion, not the British, and not the Americans, finally, but a band of irregular Berbers from Morocco fighting with French forces and the Polish II Corps. The hardy Moroccans, born and bred in the Atlas mountains, pressed through the passes to the base of Cassino, where on May 18 the Poles won the day in a suicidal frontal attack. More than eight thousand Allied soldiers, mostly Poles, were killed in that last assault on the sixth-century monastery, half of them listed as "missing" with "bodies so pounded by shell fire that they were never found."[7]

On May 23 the 551st was halted on the docks in Naples in mid-transfer to its ship heading to Anzio. That very day, 150,000 Allied soldiers broke out of the Anzio beachhead toward Rome. The capture of the German stronghold on Monte Cassino had forced the Germans to pull off their pressure at Anzio. Thus the GOYAs were spared the Italian cauldron and, perhaps, its glory.

Although there would seem to be little time for it, Bill Hatcher of B Com-pany remembers that one GOYA, itching to get into battle, fled Naples to the Fifth Army front at Cassino. Joe Edgerly went AWOL for four days—old habits die hard—but this irascible GOYA went in order to fight, which Hatcher called "derring-do of the highest order." Whether or not Edgerly ac-tually saw combat against the Germans at Cassino is unknown; he did return to the battalion and to his care of Furlough, its dachshund mascot, whom Wood Joerg had personally carried onto the ship to cross the Atlantic.

Within a few days the men were redirected south from Naples, toward Sicily, in 40-by-8-foot boxcars, the same rickety transports used in World War I. The train ride through southern Italy took about a week. Every few miles the train was stopped by someone's pull on the brake cord, bent rails, or blown bridges. Often everyone would have to get out, load up their gear, and make portage by boat across a river to the far bank, where another train would take them a few more miles. It was a tedious but not entirely uneventful trip. The men passed by the ancient ruins of Pompeii and smoking Mount Vesuvius. Twice the train stopped along the beach, and the men ran off to plunge in the sea and wash their clothes. They would trade their rations for wine or black bread with a hungry population. The blackened trees, burned-out buildings, and people with arms or legs missing stunned them. Sergeant Doug Dillard wrote home to his girl-friend: "The marks of war are everywhere." The great American gift seemed, at times, not military prowess but a good smoke. Wrote Dillard, "The people here really go for American cigarettes."[8] Benny Goodman of B Company remembered that it was common practice to swap a pack of Lucky Strikes "for a bottle of wine or a woman."

The civilian population's destitution south of Naples mirrored that of the great city, which the withdrawing Germans had wrecked, exploding its water, telephone, and electrical systems, as well as placing three time bombs in central markets that killed and wounded hundreds of civilians. All along their route, people begged. The GOYAs were loath to take their boots off, for the shoeless street urchins plucked them out of the boxcars, along with blankets and rations.

Somewhere in southern Italy Red Cross girls greeted the GOYAs with coffee and donuts. One of them introduced herself as the daughter of the greatest baseball hitter ever, Ty Cobb. That encounter inspired men raised on Cobb's vicious hitting and spike-thrust baserunning but it also served as a cathartic. The water used for the coffee was contaminated, as Tims Quinn reported, so "everyone got the trots."

Nourishment was uneven, at best. One man went into convulsions from bad wine, and they would not subside until Doc Chalkley pressed his thumbs to the upper edges of the man's eye sockets. He fell unconscious.

In the rural areas, the *paisan* would exchange tomatoes, onions, potatoes, and fresh eggs for cigarettes and candy. The GOYAs cooked some good meals along the rails while the Italian engineers argued over the latest stop. It was not easy to find firewood with trees already in ashes. Often the train would start moving before the meal was served, and the men would clamber aboard, spread sheet metal on the floor, and throw the burning faggots on it. "We would start cooking, the train would go into a tunnel, and we would all start choking from the smoke," said Sergeant Jim Stevens.

Stevens described the gradual dismemberment of the boxcars themselves. First holes were cut in the floorboards for crappers: "Then we started chopping up and burning the crossties; then pretty soon we started in on the sides of the boxcars. By the time we got down to where we were supposed to go, there would be mostly just the engine and the wheels of the train left. It was an ungodly sight." By the time the GOYAs reached the Straits of Messina, their rail convoy appeared to have been attacked by giant termites.

The 551st reached Reggio de Calabria and were ferried across the Straits of Messina to Sicily, leaving a glassy trail of empty wine bottles along the tracks and in tunnels. Drinking did not let up. In Sicily, while the unit was walking across a damaged trestle, Heffernan looked on in shock as one soldier who had been drinking wine since morning raised his drained bottle, tipped over on one leg, and fell to his death.

On June 4, 1944, as the GOYAs' train passed another along the northern coast of Sicily to Palermo, Rome was captured by the Allies. Two days later, on June 6, the 551st's communications officer, Lieutenant Andy Titko, picked up the BBC's announcement that the invasion of Normandy had been launched. The men gathered around the radio as the wobbly train clacked down the track. Lieutenant Colonel Joerg looked out the open boxcar door at the dry, hot Sicilian terrain moving by, its ancient olive trees looking sere and barren.

The 551st bivouacked in Sicily for the month of June. Its mission was to set up a parachute jump school for French and Polish partisans at Trapani at the extreme western tip of the island. The purpose was not revealed to them right away. Churchill was still arguing with Roosevelt and Eisenhower about the Balkans. Scuttlebutt had the GOYAs jumping anywhere from Yugoslavia to northern Italy to southern France. They may even be packed off back to Camp Mackall, for all they knew, where they could go AWOL forever.

In Palermo, while getting supplies, T/5 Chuck Bernard from my father's home town of Cleveland, Ohio, met an old crippled man by the side of the road. The man pointed with his cane to his leg, and Bernard could only imagine what was underneath his baggy blue peasant pants. Suddenly he was stunned to hear the man speak to him in broken English, "You are lucky." It dawned on Bernard that the 551st was billeted in a place of ghosts, and that, at least for now, it had been spared.

Doc Chalkley, Paul Hoch, and Harry Miller veered off the road one day in the battalion's commandeered ambulance, Miller insisting he wanted to buy some olive oil and see the locals up close. At one stop, Chalkley, ever the card, swapped his jump boots for clogs with some villagers, while Miller loaded up the olive oil. In another town, however, Miller made a pass at the mayor's wife and was thrown into the local jail. The ambulance was stolen, but somehow the oil and Miller were rescued by an angry Major Bill Holm. As it turned out, Miller stayed in Italy after the war, marrying an Italian contessa. "He made out pretty well with his olive oil," Chalkley concluded.

Others did not make out so well. Although the Germans were long gone from Sicily and the local Italians had been in the Allied camp for nine months, hard-core *fascisti* still took pot shots at the American paratroopers. On one of several mountain training forced marches across the island, PFC John Bassaline of B Company was hit in the knee by a wooden bullet. He spent months in a hospital in Palermo, missing the GOYAs drop into southern France, to catch up with them in Nice. A promising baseball player with a semipro team in Panama where he had joined the 551st, Bassaline could see that the injury would scrap any postwar sports ambitions. Though Italian himself, the wooden bullet in Sicily and a stern father made him something less than an ethnic cheerleader.

Spurred by a rain of diehard gunfire from the mountains that made Swiss cheese of an Army ambulance, Joerg ordered the battalion out on a raid into Trapani to confiscate firearms and war matériel. Newly arrived replacements joined in. Private Fred Hilgardner had just transferred into the 551st that day, and he was in for a shock. As the men boarded trucks for the raid, Sergeant Charles Cuddy—a coarse fellow who was about to enter the unit from the 515th via a Sicily replacement depot—forced himself onto a tightly packed bench, toppling a Greek–American soldier at the end off the truck. Hitting the ground, the fellow's rifle went off. The bullet ricocheted off a stone, pierced the shoulder of a soldier, and then hit Cuddy right between the eyes. "Jesus," Hilgardner said to himself. "I just arrived and here they are shooting each other." Ellery Sweat, not yet even enrolled in the 551st, was stunned too: "I saw Cuddy's brains spill out of his head." A friend of Cuddy, Sergeant Bernard Cheney of HQ Company, had the sad duty of informing the man's wife of his death. He lied, writing that Cuddy was shot by *fascisti* while on his way to church. The Greek–American was sent to Africa, and the matter was shelved. It was treated as an accident.

The partisan trainees had their share of accidents. One man who caught a streamer (an unopened chute) and didn't think to pull his reserve chute plunged 6 feet into the ground; Doc Chalkley had to dig the dead man out. Among the fifty French, Polish, and Italian paratroopers the GOYAs trained to jump to be translators once on the ground was one Italian orphan they adopted. They cut off fatigues to fit him, and he eagerly jumped with them into southern France, earning a Purple Heart.

On one of their forced marches near Trapani, evidence of *homo bello* met them: piles of excrement. They had been deposited by Italian, German, and American forces during the Sicily campaign and left uncovered. Joerg ordered the GOYAs to use their helmets and shovels to cover up the crap with dirt. "I never heard such complaining in my life," Emory Albritton recalled. "Whoever they were, those bastards never bothered to use slit trenches at all."

Along with testing their capacity for revulsion, the GOYAs were told to test benzedrine on their Sicily marches. They were made to get along with no water and little food. Charles Fairlamb was so dry he crawled on the ground and tried to lick the dew off the grass, only to discover there was no dew. Sicily was as dry as he was. His mouth had so little saliva, the gum he tried to chew stuck to his mouth. The bennies kept them awake for 20 miles of rugged hiking, but at night their affect suddenly wore off, and the men collapsed. "I guess they decided the stuff wasn't so great after all," Jack Affleck said. When they finally did make it back to Trapani, Joerg was there to greet them with coffee and donuts. He showered them with rare praise. Joerg clearly was pushing them to the limit, because he knew the limit was near.

One early morning Joerg roused his driver, PFC Milo Huempfner, and ordered him to saddle up his jeep, painted with the nickname of "The Rose of San Antone"! They drove out of Trapani as a brilliant orange band of sunlight burst over the mountains. Suddenly Joerg ordered Huempfner to stop and switch places with him. Although it was against regulations, Joerg loved to joy-ride in Sicily. "He would go down in the ditches and up on the hills and across the country like a madman," Huempfner recalled.

On this trip he jerked the jeep to a stop in an olive grove. Small bird twitters could be heard in the branches, but otherwise it was silent. Then Joerg turned to his driver-turned-passenger and said, "You know, Humpy, someday all of us officers are going to get it."

Huempfner shook his head and turned aside, embarrassed.

"Do you think you could take over the battalion?" Joerg asked.

Before Huempfner could consider whether that was a serious question or a joke, Joerg hit the gas and jerked them forward through the dry drainage ditch.

Dysentery swept through the unit, probably from bad water. At one point 75 percent of the men suffered from it. In the evenings a huge radio in the care of a Scottish unit nearby drowned their moans with news of the bogged-down invasion force at Normandy and the attempted breakout at the Falaise pocket. To distract themselves, Bill Hatcher, Joe Edgerly, Gene Cherry, Ted Bass, and a few others from the 551st decided to put on a floor show to entertain their Scottish counterparts. Hatcher played clarinet, and Charlie Giacomo played guitar. A lieutenant did a striptease of his combat arms, fatigues, parachute boots, even his underdrawers. The Scots brayed loudly.

The men rigged up their own place to unwind, a tent with five barrels filled with wine. Joerg approached it one evening, opened the flap, came out and asked Tims Quinn, "What's going on with those birds here?"

"It's a PX, Colonel," Quinn uttered innocently. "I'd rather the men get [shit-]faced here than go somewhere else and do it."

But Joerg would have none of it, and soon the barrels were drained. Predictably, the soldiers discovered a château in a beautiful town sitting on a mountain top called Erice, "the City in the Clouds," which had a bar and some prostitutes. One day a large American Indian boy named Corporal Ray Banks in a drunken stupor challenged Joerg. The commander was briefing his officers about a maneuver, holding a clipboard by a split-rail fence, when Banks wobbled up and yelled, "What are you bastards doing here? What the hell's going on here? Aw, you guys don't know anything."

Joerg, sensing an existential faceoff in the midst of Sicily and their held-up war, never even looked up and spoke to his clipboard, "Who's bird is that?"

Banks was from Tims Quinn's C Company.

"Get rid of him," Joerg growled to Quinn, who ushered Banks—a large man—into the HQ Company tent, intending to tie him to a pole to let him sober up. But the minute Quinn laid hands on the man, Banks went wild, pummeling Quinn, a husky man himself who took quips about his fat posterior. Banks tore up the tent and heaved Joerg's typewriter out on the ground. Here the story diverges. According to Quinn, though bloodied he finally pinned Banks to the ground, where the drunken corporal began to cry, "Oh, I killed an officer! I'm going to be court-martialed!" Lee Elledge and Charles Fairlamb of HQ Company swear it was not Quinn who emerged from the tent, but Banks, and that the C Company captain was the one found tied to the tent pole!

The next day a sobered and frightened Banks was absolved by Quinn, who gave him only light punishment. "I told him he was the kind of man I really wanted and that I didn't mind him hitting me," Quinn recounted. All hands were going to be needed in battle, and it was hardly the time for someone to remake the GOYAs into altar boys.

Private William Bustin would repay the same kind of indulgence at the Bulge. A replacement with the 551st just before shipment overseas, he got into trouble with Durkee's platoon in Sicily. A less than encouraging Sergeant Monice Ganz took one look at him and spat out, "A Company gets what no one else wants." Durkee didn't take it too lightly, either, when he inquired one day where Bustin's foxhole was, and the Rhode Islander drew a rectangle in the dirt with a stick simulating one. "There!" he proudly crowed.

As for my father, I can guess that his sheerest delight in Sicily would have been the mountains or the six motorized scooters that the higher command sent to the battalion at Trapani, on the theory that paratroopers needed more individualized and handy transportation. Each of the companies got one, and HQ Company got two. That is where father's role as

Joerg's motorcycle messenger began, as well as his lifelong love of the motorcycle, which he took postwar to the deserts of California. I see him barreling out into Sicily in the evenings, singing the Italian songs he sang to us, "*Cella luna menzi madi, mamma mia me ma de dadi!* (There's a half moon out, mother dear, I want to get married.) *Figha mia qu c'e dali? Mama mia pisacha du!* (My daughter, who shall I give you? Mother dear, please yourself!)." He also tagged on his own concoction, "If you marry the butcher boy he'sa come, he'sa go!"

Soon the 551st would a-go to the center of the ancient world.

3

Rome

In early July 1944 the 551st received an order to move with all speed—in World War I rickety boxcars—up to Rome. Stalled by the same kind of off-loading and on-loading they had experienced coming south, the trip took two weeks. The battalion's executive officer, Major William Holm, went ahead of the unit by jeep to scout out quarters and seek clarification of their mission. He was anxious to find out whether or not they would soon be jumping.

Joerg's second in command, Holm was a quiet Midwestern counterpart to the kinetic Southern leader who would gather his troops in France with a Confederate flag (though to Holm, Joerg was no crooked arrow—he "didn't smoke or drink or fool around"). Born in Chicago, Holm attended the University of Minnesota before graduating from West Point in the Class of 1940, three years after Joerg. He joined the paratroopers and the 551st at Benning after being bored with an assignment on an amphibious command that had no troops or even barracks, only classrooms. He was with the 551st from its beginnings in Panama.

At the 551st bivouac at Lido di Roma, a beach resort near the Pope's summer residence of Castel Gondolfo, Holm backed up to a balcony during an officers' party and fell backward off it, fracturing his skull and jaw. "This was by far the biggest regret of my war service," he admitted decades later. That fall hospitalized him through the GOYAs' classic jump into southern France. Holm did return to the unit, rubbing his jaw sheepishly, in the Maritime Alps.

Sixty miles south of Rome one night, those unlucky enough to be awake saw a vision of the underworld at Monte Cassino, which had been completely destroyed. Said Doc Chalkley: "We went through there about 0300 and there was a light mist and moonlight. The smell of death was everywhere. You would see a burned-out half-track, then a burned-out tank— everything wrecked—nothing but desolation everywhere, and the moonlight.

You could see the bombed-out monastery up on the hill. . . . I think there must have been bodies still in the area. I thought of Dante's *Inferno*."

For Andy Titko, the boxcar ride to Rome "conjures up bare bottoms greeting Benzino Gasolini's portraits on the sides of buildings, captioned with such inspirational sayings as 'Seven million bayonets will enforce the Fascist will!'" As for the bare bottoms, they were less an insolent "mooning" to Il Duce's memory than diarrhea resulting from a diet of eggs, cheese, and olive oil, a practice that "took its toll, as the starboard sides of the boxcars revealed at our destination."

Before arriving in Rome, Lieutenant Colonel Joerg ordered Titko to string a telephone line between boxcars so he could converse with the officers. Titko flatly told Joerg it wouldn't work with so many phones because of voltage drop.

"Don't tell me about voltage drop," Joerg snapped. "I went to commo school."

"Which one?"

"Infantry communications school in 1937."

"Well, sir," Titko razzed him, "that was in the horse and buggy days."

Joerg fumed and stuck his shaking head out the boxcar door.

By the end of July the 551st had moved from tents on a volcanic lake to the bombed out remains of the Collegio di 4 Novembre, a former maritime college, at Lido di Roma, 20 miles southwest of Rome, where Pope Pius XII was summering. If at first they thought they were being put into reserve to hold Rome, conquered by the Fifth and Eighth armies a month before, they were soon told their D-Day was to be August 15, 1944, as part of a 300,000-man Allied invasion of southern France called Operation Dragoon.

Operation Anvil, which was originally to have been an invasion of Normandy by a real, as opposed to imaginary, diversionary force prior to the massive Overlord, had become Dragoon, the last chapter of Churchill's summer-long feud with Eisenhower.

Eisenhower revived Anvil and the notion of a southern France invasion two weeks after Normandy. At SHAEF's London headquarters, Ike argued on two counts with the British General Henry "Jumbo" Wilson: The Allies were months away from taking Nazi-held Antwerp, the best port in Europe, and could shut off the second-best port, Marseilles, with a bold thrust in the south. Further, he pointed out, a French second front would pull pressure away from Normandy and confront and confound the Germans with a wide two-front war in France.

The British put up a grand fuss, insisting that Italian gains be consolidated, ever with an eye to Stalin and the Balkans. But Eisenhower had an important political ally for his plan: Franklin Roosevelt knew this was not the time to stiff-arm the Russians, who had sustained the worst losses by far in the Allied camp, facing the Nazis more or less singlehandedly in the East for four bitter years of ground fighting. If he did not respect the Communist system, he did respect the Russian people and footsoldiers, whose endurance probably saved England from invasion and prevented Hitler from spreading halfway around the globe to Japan. By war's end, the Soviet Union had lost 20 million people, half of all Allied fatalities. Roosevelt needed Stalin to keep driving west and not get caught up in a cat fight for spoils of a war that had yet to be won. He had read his Tolstoy, whose references in *War and Peace* to Balkan wars confirmed them as endless and tarlike.

Eisenhower, with Roosevelt's backing, carried the day. On July 2, 1944, as the 551st was on a boxcar trip toward Rome, General Wilson received orders to execute Anvil "as soon as possible." Still, even as the GOYAs were staging a week before the invasion of southern France, Churchill fulminated to Eisenhower to redirect Anvil to Italy, or even Brittany, where German forces were not yet defeated. It brought to a head one of the bitterest disagreements between the Allies in World War II. An Eisenhower naval aide, Commander Harry C. Butcher, wrote in his diary: "The boss told The Prime 'no' in every form in the English language."[9] A huffing Churchill left his protest stamp on the matter, saying he had been "dragooned" into it, and the invasion was renamed Operation Dragoon.

The man who orchestrated the final breakout at Anzio, Lieutenant General Lucius K. Truscott, was assigned to command the main amphibious attack at Dragoon. Two divisions hardened by the battle at Anzio—the 36th and the 45th—were assigned to its invasion force, as was another veteran of the Italian campaign, the 3d Division. A key element was a newly minted 10,000-man, division-size paratroop assault team, the 1st Airborne Task Force, led by Major General Robert T. Frederick, hurriedly activated on July 11 in Rome, where the GOYAs had just arrived. The 551st, along with its sister glider battalion the 550th and the fraternal separate unit the 509th, as well as Rupert Graves's 517th Regiment, were to be part of Frederick's flotilla in the sky.

The second 551st line fire death in a former combat zone (after the Cuddy incident in Sicily) was near Rome. It, too, was "friendly." During the intensified training with weapons that occurred in the days leading up to Dragoon, a practice mortar round that fell short of the target hit a forward observer, Sergeant Laurence C. Stankus of A Company. The accident "touched the whole battalion deeply," Don Garrigues wrote in his diary.

Mortars and the August heat were a deadly mix in other ways. During mortar fire practice in a wheat field, a hot wind fanned the smoldering salvos into a fire that quickly threatened the whole countryside. Italian peasants stumbled from their homes. For two hours the GOYAs were transformed into firemen before the flames went out.

One of the first things the 551st was required to do at Lido di Roma was to clear minefields still left by the Germans from the battle for Rome. Along with Stankus, another man is listed as buried in the Sicily–Rome Cemetery from the 551st, Sergeant Perry Ellis of Headquarters Company, who stepped on a mine.

Tragedy often preceded comedy. The 551st was never far away from deadly farce. Having secured permission to fire a German 76mm artillery gun at retreat in the evening, Sergeant Charles Fairlamb accidentally shot the chimney off a cottage, from which an Air Corps colonel emerged shouting. Fairlamb's hands trembled on the lanyard, and he forgot to salute.

By the first of August, Don Garrigues wrote, Lido di Roma was "a beehive of activity." Day and night tactical maneuvers simulated the ingathering of paratroopers once they had landed on the ground. To siphon off tension, the GOYAs received passes to Rome. There they toured the architectural masterpieces of the classical age, including the Colosseum, the Pantheon, the Circus Maximus, and Caesar Augustus' palace. They emerged from the gloom of St. Peter's to find orphans begging on the steps of the cathedral, sure that the American soldiers were angels, not the "devils in baggy pants" the Germans found them to be at Avellino, where the 509th slit throats to keep the noise down.

Maybe it was those contradictions—the beauty of art and the endless, bloody struggle the fallen angels represented—that sent some at night into Rome for less aesthetic release. Maybe it was the naked statues, maybe the half-naked begging women of the streets or the sense that one would soon die just a short hop over the water in France, that prompted those with experience of the flesh to crave it, and those with no experience to quest for it with fear and trembling. The chief magnet of carnality for those anxious men was a whorehouse and bar called Broadway Bill's, where they went down three flights of stairs to find a few precious seconds of pseudo-love. What they found there was usually young, always poor, waiting in a floursack garment (or sometimes with lingerie sewn from parachute silk).

My father was one. He told me that he had lost his virginity at twenty to an Italian prostitute. He did not elaborate, characteristically, as to whether it was satisfying or where in Rome it happened. My own research ties it to Broadway Bill's, probably a modern catacomb today. Embarrassed to tell of it, he inhaled and exhaled cigarette smoke, and changed the subject. He was a devout Catholic. At Mass on Sundays he would thump his chest at the elevation of the Host into the Body of Christ— thump it repeatedly, unlike anyone else in the congregation, as if he were unworthy. I almost heard his strong chest echo with his fist's striking. My father was haunted by the colder shadows of human nature and seemed to be trying to box them out. Mother would always lead everyone to the front of the Church for Mass and my father would hang back, growling, as if she were too confident, too close to the altar for him. "Rose!" he would whisper down the aisle, but it never halted her. He loved the parable of the Pharisee and Publican; the latter hung back in the last row of the synagogue, unlike the former, who beelined it to the front, certain of his salvation. My father definitely was of the "last shall be first, first shall be last" breed, a GOYA inclination.

What would it have been like that night for him at Broadway Bill's? I don't think he would have gone alone. He would have entered with others, gone down the clammy three flights of stairs to the bar. Not a drinker, he often proclaimed himself a "one-drink wonder," and he would have ordered that one drink. It would have made his conscience fuzzy.

I envision the girl who snared him as shy, olive-skinned in the yellow kerosene light. He tries to talk to her, sings to her his Italian song. Perhaps he breaks the men up with his patented version of "The Italian Base-a-Ball-a-Game," shtick he learned from Danny Thomas. "Out-a from the hole in the ground comma the fella they call-a tha Pitch." The girl smiles politely; she doesn't know what he is talking about. She doesn't know he is nervous. How can a paratrooper be nervous?

At a certain moment, she takes father by the hand, and the men crack their jokes. "Oh, here he goes! Check your reserve chute! You're going to catch a streamer with that one, pal!" She leads him up the stairs—three flights—past rooms where men are panting and women are huffing from the weight of them. In the room he wants to kiss her because he knows how to do that, but she turns away from him, pulls off her jumper, unbuttons her bra, and drops everything to the floor before getting on the flimsy bed, which creaks with springs worn from passion. He stares at her, the islands of her breasts round and spread on her chest in the moonlight coming through the little dirty window. She puts her arms up. He takes his uniform off, goes to her, runs his hands over her body. She is so disinterested, yet when she sees his shyness she speaks something softly in Italian that warms him.

Soon he drops the coin into a dish of other coins, and goes out into the night, his whole body throbbing with heat. He might have whispered to his pillow in his bunk at Lido di Roma: *I must marry as soon as I get home, if I get home.*

The GOYAs' high jinks became increasingly perilous the closer they got to battle. In some ancient ruins near Lido di Roma, Lloyd Larkin and Tims Quinn decided to take target practice on stones when all of a sudden Quinn found himself chased by a maniacal Larkin wielding a grenade. Quinn kept shouting at him to get rid of it, get rid of it, and Larkin threw it right at him. Quinn dived into a ditch, and the thing exploded. Quinn emerged, face full of dust, but unhurt. "You know, people talk about men fragging officers in Vietnam," he related many years later. "Well, that was nothing."

Anzio couldn't be kept off the GOYA map, somehow. Some men took their M-1s down to the smoldering beachhead when they learned the British Navy had shelled a zoo, and went hunting. On one occasion, according to Jack Carr, some GOYAs came reeling up to Lido di Roma with a tiger's carcass draped across their jeep. Carr prepared for battle in another way. As Headquarters Company's supply sergeant, he entered a deal with a master sergeant in ordnance, swapping HQ Company's two motorcycles (much to my father's chagrin, no doubt) for one hundred Thompson sub-machine guns. He also searched supply depots for jump suits for the men but couldn't find any. Instead, he procured five hundred tanker suits worn by tank operators, a heavy-duty garment that came in handy for some in the snows of Belgium.

About August 7, the 551st took part in a dress rehearsal for the final jump with Rupert Graves's 517th Parachute Regimental Combat Team and its attached 460th Parachute Field Artillery Battalion. A camouflage team set up near their quarters and proceeded to spray-paint all weapons and equipment in green and black. One by one, each platoon of men stood in line, a box placed over each head while two men with spray guns saturated their tanker outfits in camouflage colors. It was a scene reminiscent of a mass execution.

Hair cut like Mohawk Indians, faces smeared with green and black grease paint, thousands of paratroopers of the 1st Airborne Task Force moved in convoy through Rome, "creating quite a spectacle and no doubt a great deal of confusion for the Nazi spies who were trying their best to get a tip on when and where the invasion would take place," Don Garrigues wrote.

In fact, Operation Dragoon and the invasion of southern France was, one historian said, "the worst-kept military secret of the war. Maybe of any war."[10] Field Marshal Albert Kesselring, chased into the northern Italian mountains after being driven from Rome on June 4, surmised that the sudden disappearance from the battlefront of elite American paratrooper and commando units and three crack infantry divisions spelled an incipient invasion of magnitude. A shrewd card-shark with a sense of humor, Kesselring concluded that the Allies would strike in one of two places: Genoa (in order to bury the Germans for good in northern Italy), or southern France.

Soon Kesselring was getting information from everyone, from agents in Italy to Luftwaffe airmen flying over the warships docking in Corsica, Sardinia, Malta, and Naples, as well as from butchers and candlestick makers, that the site indeed was southern France. A shopkeeper in Puzzuoli had a run on maps of the French Riviera, which were stacked in his display windows. A GI from the 45th Infantry, slated to come ashore in the center of the line near St-Maxime, was startled to hear his favorite bar girl tell him as he lifted off her bed in Naples, "I guess you won't be visiting again if you're going into southern France."

That foreknowledge was made perfectly clear in a radio message from Mildred Gillars, also known as "Axis Sally," to whom Don Garrigues was tuned in one night. What he heard made him sit up in his barracks bed. "All right, you paratroopers, we know you are going to jump into southern France and we have a welcoming party waiting for you," Gillars cooed in her perfect, sultry English. "Oh, by the way, you don't need to bring your chutes. You will be able to just walk down from the sky on our flak."

That welcoming committee appeared to present immense problems to the Allies, and to General Frederick's airborne mission in particular. Compounding the difficulty was the extraordinary speed with which Operation Dragoon had to be put in motion. After all the postponements and intra-Allied arguments, when the "go" signal was finally given General Truscott and General Frederick had less than five weeks to pull it all together. When one considers the full year of planning and staging that preceded Operation Overlord at Normandy, Dragoon takes on the aspect of a stunning achievement, if not controlled frenzy. The stalled Overlord march to Paris only amplified the contrast.

Still, the coast of southern France was as wide as that across from the English channel, if not wider—there are 300 miles of Mediterranean coast between Spain and Italy—and the Germans were no more certain of the final landing points.

Two months after Normandy, with the southern France invasion bearing down, Hitler, shaken and bloodied by the bomb explosion on July 20 at his Wolf's Lair planning table in Rastenburg, pulled the reins of his maniacal will to power even tighter, even as he became more delusional and bizarrely listless. In May he had selected a new commander of the southern France sector, General Friedrich Wiese of the Nineteenth Army at Avignon, about 90 miles northwest of the Riviera. He had sent Wiese off to the seat of a rebel Papacy in the Middle Ages, with a harsh bark: "There will be no withdrawal. If anything happens along the Riviera you will fight to the last man and the last bullet! Do you understand, Herr General?" Rommel sped southward in his muddy Horch and raged at Wiese's superior, General Johannes Blaskowitz, in charge of Army Group G, that he was leaving the South Wall an open door: "Go all-out to strengthen the *Sudwall*—beginning immediately!"[11]

Feverish preparations were made round the clock by 14,000 impressed French workers and other prisoners of the Todt Organization. The 100 miles between Nice and Marseilles were laced with barbed wire, machine gun pods and bunkers, holes cut from rock for flamethrowers, and trenches in 578 positions, each with artillery or machine guns. Fearful of paratroopers, Wiese himself ordered *Rommelspargel*, "Rommel's asparagus"—the long poles that could impale descending soldiers and crack up gliders—planted in vineyards all over the Côte D'Azur. Bathers at the famed Riviera beaches were confronted with signs on barbed-wire fences warning of mines: *Achtung, meinen!*

The only German tank division in southern France, the 11th Panzers, was holed up in Bordeaux, in southwest France, about 400 miles from the Riviera. But no panzers could be moved without the personal order of der Fuhrer. On August 10 Blaskowitz's nerves began fraying at his headquarters near Toulouse, the famous "Pink City" of the south (so named because of the roseate color its Spanish-tiled roofs). Midway between Bordeaux and the Riviera, Toulouse was a good place for a German general to feel at wits' end over the impending invasion. For a week Blaskowitz had waited with growing impatience for Hitler to okay the swift movement of the 11th Panzers from Bordeaux on the Atlantic to the Riviera. It had not come. Blaskowitz complained to his staff how absurd the Wehrmacht's command structure was, an outburst that could easily have gotten him shot. In fact, Hitler had fallen prey to something called the XX Committee (better known as the Double-Cross Committee), a shadowy British intelligence outfit that had concocted several phony invasion spots in Europe and had filtered them out through spies to keep the Germans guessing throughout the spring and summer of 1944. Hitler had taken the bait known as "Operation Ironside," which floated a false second invasion of France in the southwestern region of Bordeaux. The Allies of Dragoon— the 551st with them—could thank the beauteous daughter of an Argentine diplomat in Vichy France and her seductions of Nazi officers over the past year. Code-named "Bronx," that women planted the Operation Ironside story. Hitler believed her. The 11th Panzers never made it in time across the Rhône to head off the Dragoon invasion.

Still, Wiese's Nineteenth Army contained virtually equal strength in footsoldiers—250,000—to that of the massing Dragoon forces. A rule of thumb for attack forces is that they need to have at least three times the numbers of a well-entrenched defense to overwhelm it, so Dragoon, for all its strength, was still operating at a tactical deficiency. The key, as at Normandy, would be the element of surprise, and the chief agent of that would be the paratroopers.

Wiese himself was flabbergasted when, on August 10—five days before the invasion—he received an intelligence report from Berlin that said, "No large-scale landings are contemplated by the Allies for the time being." A command mix-up of rare proportions was in the offing. Everyone from map-sellers to whores in Italy knew better, not to mention Axis Sally. Perhaps the Germans were not listening to their own radio.

On August 13, two days before the Dragoon drop, with Patton finally breaking out of the Falaise pocket east of Normandy and ramming toward Paris, Hitler's Wolf's Lair was anything but poised. Der Fuhrer's chief sycophant after the officers' bomb plot a month before, General Alfred Jodl, presented him with several contingency plans for France. Most of the other generals urged Jodl to press for a withdrawal, and even the Nazi chief of operations thought it was inevitable and opened that folder first. It was far after midnight. His will frozen, Hitler took one look at the withdrawal document and tossed it aside. The next document called for "resistance by all available means" in southern France.

"This is the one I will sign," Hitler looked at Jodl with the vacant blue eyes and the twitching face brought on by the desk explosion in July.[12]

The Germans prepared their flak. The Allies prepared to walk down it.

4

The last communion before the invasion

Wood Joerg was summoned with all commanders of the 1st Airborne Task Force to the headquarters of General Frederick in Rome.

"Here," Frederick pointed with a stick to a map of the Riviera. His pointer was placed on the little crossroads town of Le Muy, 15 miles inland from the coastal city of Frejus. All roads in the area led to Le Muy, a few miles southeast of Draguignan, the area's chief market city, where the German LXII Corps—in charge of defending the French Mediterranean coast—was headquartered, and it was there that the 10,000-man paratroop force was to concentrate its drop.

That in itself was a frenzied revision the night before of another drop plan that, according to one of Frederick's aides, had had the Dragoon paratroopers "dropping in small groups all over the South of France."[13] Frederick had rushed the ace airborne strategist Colonel William Yarborough up from Naples to remake the picture completely. Yarborough, now in command of the 509th, which had been the first American paratroop battalion to drop in combat in North Africa and had rescued the miserable situation at Salerno with its behind-the-lines spoiling raids at Avellino, knew concentration of forces was crucial.

The battle-seasoned Yarborough found the GOYA commander sober and keen: "I had been in combat a lot longer than Wood Joerg. I had come up from North Africa and all the way up the Italian 'boot.' You know, he listened."

Back at Lido di Roma, Joerg briefed his own officers. By the end of the first week of August, the GOYAs were restricted to their barracks at the old college. Weapons came off the racks. On August 9 a Headquarters Company platoon sergeant named Jim Vicars turned up missing. He was found in a basement near a 50-gallon barrel of wine lying on a cot with a cup in his hand, nearly dead from drink. He was placed in a hospital and missed the jump.

At 2 A.M. on August 12, the 826 men of the 551st were moved out in trucks to an airfield 90 miles north of Rome called Montalto. There Joerg gathered the battalion around a set of sand tables and for the first time showed them with small sticks in the sand exactly where they were to land in southern France. They studied maps and aerial photos. Towns code-named Milwaukee and Chicago had to be taken, as well as a hill where they would relieve the 2d Battalion of Rupert Graves's 517th Regiment.

For three days the GOYAs tried to sleep. They were distracted with movies and a swim or two. Archbishop Francis Spellman, appointed by President Roosevelt as apostolic vicar to U.S. armed forces, said Mass for the paratroopers under a stand of linden trees. Among those receiving Communion was PFC Pat Casanova of A Company, whose parents were among the hundreds Spellman wrote to after Dragoon about having blessed the troops. I am sure my father joined the communicants that day (after a doleful confession of his actions at Broadway Bill's), and he probably touched his silver medal of the Blessed Virgin, which he wore around his neck for most of his life. I say "most" because it mysteriously disappeared with the onset of my sister's psychiatric problems in the 1970s. (During that bleak time, he also would leave Mass early to smoke, waiting for my mother to emerge.)

Suddenly several GOYAs broke out with vicious cases of cerebral malaria, contracted in Sicily. Though Mussolini had drained the Pontine swamps, he'd done nothing of the kind in Sicily, and somehow the mosquitoes had taken their toll in the zero hour. It was not a new disease for the 551st; many had contracted it in Panama. Fifty years later, running a high fever in Bowie, Maryland, Doug Dillard suspected a remnant of malaria from Panama or Sicily. Doc Chalkley was stunned to find, as the clock ticked toward their takeoff from Montalto, the drug atrabine had no effect on the infected men. Most, like the weakened Leo Urban, defied Chalkley's orders and took their high fevers and their bodies racked with chills and sweats to the jump.

On the night of August 14, with Allied bombers roaring overhead to France, Corporal George Rickard went berserk. He was B Company's best mortar man, and Captain Jim Evans agonized over whether or not to scratch him from the drop. Evans got him to calm down, but just before boarding the planes he started shouting again and swinging at anyone who tried to hold him. Evans sent him to a hospital. It was a mournful decision, but, as Doc Chalkley put it, "One guy like that could really tear things up aboard a plane in flight."

Joerg handed Furlough, the GOYAs' mascot dachshund, to a messenger and told him to take the dog to one of the commanders of the naval invasion force. Furlough was to go ashore with that force and reunite with the GOYAs later.

On the morning of August 15, just after breakfast, the GOYAs took to counting planes returning from the 9,000-man middle-of-the-night drop of Dragoon, which included seventeen GOYA pathfinders. Chuck Fairlamb spotted one plane wobbling with its tail missing; most formations were incomplete, at best. While they were pointing and counting, a gunshot rang out. Someone had plugged himself in the foot. It was Sergeant James McDuffie, from Don Garrigues's HQ Company platoon. He was swiftly jeeped away from the jittery men and was later court-martialed.[14]

Throughout the day on August 15 the men of the 551st prepared to board their C-47 transports. The GOYAs got their last mail call and were told to destroy immediately all envelopes, anything with any kind of address that could identify them beyond their dogtags. They smeared on their last greasepaint, the blonds rubbing it through their scalps and hair. Chuck Fairlamb wrote in his journal, "We were a frightful looking bunch." A last-minute intelligence order came down: There was threat of German poison gas, and gas masks were issued to all men.

That day in Berlin, as the Dragoon invasion began, the Gestapo hanged the German capital's chief of police for his part in the July bomb plot at Rastenburg. Dragoon's D-Day was also the day the Paris chief of police ordered all his men to join the Resistance.

Somehow Wood Joerg found the presence of mind that last day to hide himself in the corner of his tent while the men filed out to the planes, take out a pad of paper and pencil, and write the following personal prayer: "Oh, God, Commander of all men, we stand before Thee asking Thy help in the execution of the many tasks which confront us. Give us the strength, courage, daring, intelligence and devotion to duty, so that we may perfect ourselves as fighting men . . ."

Joerg stopped. He inhaled the hot Italian summer air, caught the scent of thyme and the smell of greasepaint from his troopers. The elephant of combat was just over the horizon. He probably thought of Heidi, his daughter, and his child-to-be. The shouts of the man who went crazy the night before rang in his ears with the sound of the planes revving their engines. He wrote more: "And, oh God, if the price we must pay for eternal freedom of man be great, give us strength so that we will not hesitate to sacrifice ourselves for a cause so sacred. All of this we ask in Thy name. Amen."

5
"Jacques, there are three Americans by the pond"

In the wee hours of the morning of August 15, 1944, with no light but the moon, men rained down from the sky over southern France. Later, in the sunlight of early evening, men rained and rained. In those brief joinings of sun and rain, droplets can shine, and one was my father.

As was the battalion's wont from its 1942 inception in Panama clear through to the Battle of the Bulge, the separate 551st had a mission apart from the main airdrop of more than nine thousand fellow paratroopers who went down in cover of darkness. Nervous as they were, they were glad not to jump at night. The GOYA drop, code-named Operation Canary, occurred later in the day on August 15, at 6 P.M. precisely—the first daylight combat drop in U.S. history. They were to have the advantage of following the others, who could tell them where they were. But they would also forfeit the element of surprise and would carry the marked disadvantage of billowing down in broad daylight into the crosshairs of German guns.

The signature photograph of the U.S. airborne dropping from the sky into combat during World War II was taken of the 551st as it descended over LaMotte, a stone's throw up the road from Le Muy on the road to Draguignan. No doubt it owes its fame in part to the fact that it was taken, after all, in daylight, which is friendlier to the camera. However, most histories of the war identify the photograph as "U.S. paratroopers over Le Muy"—anonymous and inaccurate. As late as 1994 the first full-scale biography of General James Gavin featured the well-used picture with inaccuracies intact. The *Washington Post*'s review of the Gavin biography chose that photo as its graphic accompaniment and inadvertently repeated the error, all the more ironic because Gavin—the paratrooper's paratrooper—was to be the man who sent the battalion to its destruction and disbandment.

To Yarborough, whose 509th jumped at 4 A.M. on August 15, the 551st's leap was "the best drop of all." The retired three-star general called the GOYAs' role in the Southern France operation "a classic."

The first GOYAs to touch French soil, however, were among a hundred or so "pathfinder" paratroopers who went ahead of the 1st Airborne Task Force between 2 A.M. and 3 A.M. on August 15 to reconnoiter the area and set up the portable beacon signals on the drop zones to guide the main contigent coming one hour later.

At least seventeen known GOYAs were among those risky trailblazers, including four officers: Captain Tims Quinn, who had moved up to be the battalion's S-3 after Major Holm fell off the Rome balcony (Pappy Herrmann had taken Holm's executive officer slot), Lieutenant Russ Fuller,

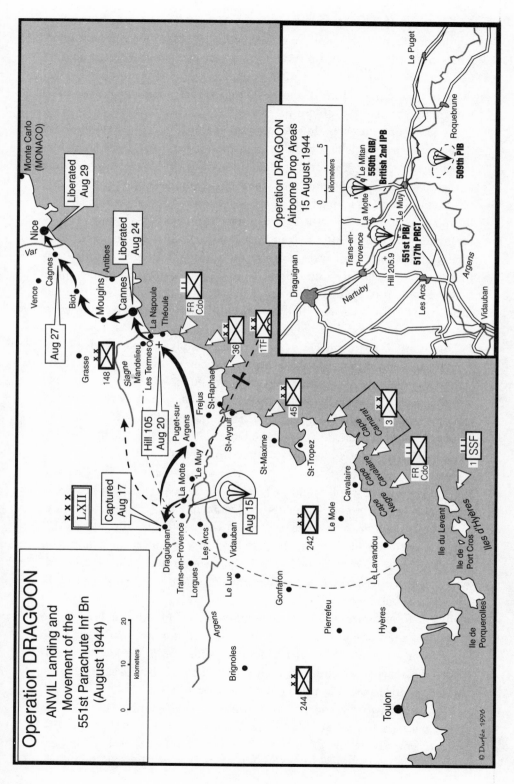

Operation DRAGOON
ANVIL Landing and
Movement of the
551st Parachute Inf Bn
(August 1944)

0   10   20
kilometers

Operation DRAGOON
Airborne Drop Areas
15 August 1944

0   5
kilometers

Le Puget

Roquebrune

Le Mitan
550th GIB/
British 2nd IPB

509th PIB

La Motte

Le Muy

Trans-en-Provence

551st PIB/
517th PRCT

Hill 205.9

Draguignan

Nartuby

Les Arcs

Argens

Vidauban

Monte Carlo
(MONACO)

Liberated
Aug 29

Nice

Var

Vence

Cagnes

Biot

Mougins   Antibes

Cannes

Liberated
Aug 24

La Napoule
Théoule

FR
Cdo

Aug 27

Grasse

148

Siagne

Mandelieu
Les Termes

Hill 105
Aug 20

Puget-sur-
Argens

Frejus

St-Raphael

36

1TF

45

Cape Camarat

3

St-Ayulf

St-Maxime

St-Tropez

Cape Cavalaire

FR
Cdo

1 SSF

Cavalaire

Cape Negre

Le Mole

242

Ile du Levant

Ile de
Port Cros

Iles d'Hyères

Le Lavandou

XXX
LXII

Captured
Aug 17

Draguignan

Trans-en-Provence

La Motte

Le Muy

Aug 15

Les Arcs

Lorgues

Vidauban

Le Luc

Gonfaron

Argens

Pierrefeu

Hyères

Brignoles

244

Ile de
Porquerolles

Toulon

© Durfee 1996

Lieutenant Frank Serio, and Lieutenant Milt Hill. Another officer named Hines from Indianapolis, an AWOL from his own unit, for some reason was chosen to hook up with the GOYAs for their historic jump. Oddly, there is no official record of the 551st's pathfinders, though there is for pathfinders from every other unit.[15]

As Dragoon's three pathfinder aircraft approached the French coast they saw below the island of Elba, their first checkpoint. The planes followed by air the exact route Napoleon took by sea in 1815 from his exile at Elba back to the mainland. But when they came near the coast, all the pilots could see was a long bank of fog. They circled back five times trying to find a hole, with only the first German fire from ack-ack guns to tell them land was below. After two and a half hours in the air, the pathfinders finally bailed out. Most were dropped 15 miles from the drop zone, and most from a perilously low height. None of the main paratrooper force had the benefit of beacon lights, as it turned out. The ghosts of the misdrops in North Africa and Sicily were with them. The paths they were supposed to find were lost in fog.

The first GOYA to hit French soil was probably the pathfinder Lieutenant Milt Hill, HQ Company's executive officer. Hill was supposed to set up firing positions for mortars and machine guns, but that mission was frustrated. Hill was stripped of a carbine and a .45 pistol by the shock of his exit out the plane door into the darkness. He didn't even oscillate falling, as paratroopers do at first, and banged down with his chute barely opened. He later figured he was dropped from less than 150 feet.

Feverishly, Hill pulled the pin of his grenade, pressing the handle as he got up, seeing the whole night as Nazi. It is recorded nowhere just what happened to that grenade, but its explosion must have wakened a few Germans. Together with some men from the 509th and the 517th, Hill came upon a hut of Frenchmen, delighted to see American patches on their uniforms. They were led by the Resistance through valleys to a point where they witnessed the 551st flying over. It took Hill two days to link up with the battalion.

Just before entering his plane at midnight, Tims Quinn lay on the ground of the airfield at Montalto near Frank Serio and read him some lines from a poem, *I Have a Rendezvous with Death*. Serio was unimpressed. He turned to Quinn and flatly said, "Look, let's be serious. If anything happens to me, I want you to contact my wife."

Quinn too was stripped of everything by the opening shock of his jump; perhaps the pilots, fearful, had accelerated upward too sharply. Seventy pounds lighter, all he had left on the ground were his compass and a trench knife lodged in his jump boot. He moved through the woods and soon heard someone's "psst ... psst." (Unlike paratroopers at Normandy, who had the famous metal crickets to clack recognition, the Dragoon droppers were told to say "Liberty," to an unknown voice, and the answer was to be "France." If you forgot that, you were supposed to answer, "Billy the Kid." Evidently, Quinn's interlocutor had forgotten that outlaw.) It was someone from the 509th.

Determined to find his own battalion, Quinn found that his first companions "resented it because I wouldn't get into a firefight along with part of the 509th." As he pushed on alone he ran into a clump of dead Germans; he stood frozen as the one man still alive, though badly wounded, motioned for a cigarette. Quinn gave him one and lit it for him. The first GOYA contact with a German turned out to be a moment of compassion.

Sergeant Pat Garretty had been struggling to undo some of his harness lines as he fell through a cloud bank; they were too tight. Landing in a vineyard, his first impulse was to get his pistol free, laying it on his chest as he unbuckled the straps. Then he ran around like a rabbit in the dark. He sardonically noted years later: "There are those individuals who think Roger Bannister ran the first sub-four-minute mile. Don't you believe it. It was run that night."

T/5 Hugh Roberts, a tall man with a dry wit, wrote in his diary about drinking "cocoa, as it was getting cool. I started to get that feeling, as always before a jump." The feeling is all the more poignant for not being described, except to say, "I was thinking of all the people I ever knew and wondering what they were doing." Just before jumping into the fog over France, noting "everyone getting that far-off look in their eyes," he threw up the cocoa. The last one out the door with "no one to push me," Roberts admitted, "I wanted to pray, but didn't know what to say."

He fell on a little hill, got out of his chute, and looked around at the gloom. Both he and Private Roger Carqueville had jumped in the same stick, but neither saw the other on the ground. Both, however, quickly realized they were far from the drop zone and proceeded to put some precious cargo out of commission for fear the Germans would use it to deceive the invasion forces. Carqueville buried his beacon light in the soil; Roberts, fearful that the self-destruct explosive on his radar would bring on the Germans, smashed it with a rock, hiding it under leaves and branches.

Soon Roberts spotted Duke Spletzer and another man with a broken leg; the two dragged him under a tree, where they left him. They lay down until daybreak, when they were roused by German anti-aircraft gunners shouting to each other not 50 feet away.

"Let's shoot the bastards!" Spletzer, whose family were German-speaking immigrants from Poland, whispered hoarsely.

Sensing they were outnumbered, Roberts spat out, "Jesus Christ! We're in enough trouble as it is. Don't shoot nobody!"

Slipping away, dodging brushfires from the naval bombardment, the two came to a vineyard. They chewed grapes to get moisture. Roberts heard the thrum of plane propellers and looked up at an uncanny sight: Lieutenant Colonel Joerg standing in the door of his plane not 500 feet above them. He was tempted to shout, "Colonel, here I am!" but stifled it. Even more amazing, the German anti-aircraft crews fired not one shell; the gunners just stood there staring in amazement. "We were watching them watching our airplanes," Roberts said.

As for Spletzer, he found himself pinned down by German sniper fire as he tried to reach the GOYAs' drop zone. In his family German, he cried out, "Help me, comrade, I am wounded!" The Wehrmacht were puzzled but feared they were firing on their own. When they came close to help him, Spelter raised his Tommy gun and "deliberately blew them out, laughing like a maniac," according to one of his companions in Headquarters Company, Phil Hand.

Young Carqueville was somewhat more placid than Roberts or Spletzer before jumping. Though he fell into a tree, it buoyed him so that the balls of his feet touched lightly on the ground. All the lost pathfinders suffered from the August heat. Carqueville was so dry his tongue began to swell. When he spotted a forester's dwelling, he moved toward it for water, only to find bullets kicking up the dry dust in front of him. In the exchange, he killed two Germans and wounded several others. He was joined by Lieutenant Hill, and the two ordered their prisoners into the basement of a farmhouse and escorted the French out of the area, which was under artillery fire. Then they began the trek south, where they would drop into their zone, exhausted, from no height at all.

The GOYAs dropped on all sorts of places that day—trees, farmhouse roofs, stakes, *Rommelspargel*—but the most electrifying jump of Operation Dragoon may well have been that of the pathfinder Sergeant William Lumsden of Idyllwild, California. Lumsden fell on the hot overhead wires of a railyard. The wires sparked and flashed, but luckily Lumsden was not electrocuted. His weight propelled him through to the ground, where he fell on his back on the train tracks, smashing his binoculars.

"The place became a complete maelstrom, with people shouting and running about shooting," he related. Before Lumsden could get out of his harness, a German with a Schmeisser submachine gun ran toward him and started shooting from 10 feet away, riddling him with bullets. The man turned to run. Somehow, Lumsden managed to get out his .45 and shot the German in the back.

Blood covered Lumsden's left arm. He staggered to nearby woods under tracer bullet fire and passed out. At dawn he woke, surprised to be alive. Then he found out why. The reserve chute on his chest had four holes in it, but miraculously the bullets had spun to a stop in its silken folds. Lumsden spent the rest of his life as a geologist studying the thicknesses of things.

Despite the fact that the directional lights of Dragoon pathfinders were rendered useless by the men's distance from the jump zone, when the main non-GOYA force of paratroopers in 396 transport planes came in at 4:30 A.M., the pilots dropped them in pinpoint perfect formation on the three specified areas around Le Mitan, Le Muy, and La Motte, all just south of Draguignan. According to the paratrooper historian Bruce Devlin, it was the most accurate night combat drop of the war; 85 percent of all paratroopers landed where they were supposed to. It would be surpassed only by the 551st's solitary unleashing in the air on August 15 in daylight.

At 3:15 P.M., the 551st Parachute Infantry Battalion (minus seventeen pathfinders)—42 officers and 784 enlisted men—put on their regular and reserve chutes and equipment at Montalto airfield north of Rome and began boarding at least forty-one C-47 transport planes. A few minutes before 6 P.M. orders were given to fasten seat belts, no mean trick with an average of 100 pounds of equipment strapped to each man. At 6 P.M. the planes carrying the GOYAs lifted off for France.

In the planes hip-to-hip with the GOYAs was an attached platoon of the 887th Engineer Company, brought along as sappers and earthmovers. One of them was PFC Charlie Speich, who later said he jumped-trained at Benning with my father: "Your Dad was a jolly type person—always laughing." No one was laughing over the Mediterranean.

A mortar platoon sergeant from Headquarters Company, Chuck Fairlamb, was carrying no less than 104 separate items on his body, 150 pounds of equipment—almost equal to his own weight. And his was not an unusual encumbrance. Included in that ungodly, potentially lifesaving and death-dealing bric-a-brac were the following items: an athletic supporter; a pair of suspenders; two dog tags; seven German rifle grenades; a medical kit containing salt tablets, atabrine, bug powder, sulfanilamide, sufladiazine, and fuel tablets; one nail file; a Bible; three notebooks; a fountain pen; two "D" candy bars; fifteen packs of cigarettes; sixteen packs of matches; four carbine magazines; one shelter (pup tent) half; a cleaning rod; a demolition kit; three "K" rations; four "D" rations; a first-aid packet with morphine, Carlisle bandage, and tourniquet strapped to the boot; mosquito repellent; a gas mask; one hundred rounds of carbine ammunition; a carbine; a 536 radio; one 5-gallon water bag; a burlap sack for sand; a Mae West life preserver; and two tubes of camouflage paint. Fairlamb was a living surplus store, with no quick-release harness.

The main 551st contingent's trip over was filled with silence, except for the engine drumming, the striking of matches, the long exhales of smoke, the soft clicking of rosaries, mumbled prayers, the heart poundings private to each man, and retching. In some planes the vomit was so thick it made the jumping slippery.

The planes headed due west then veered somewhat north at land's end at San Stefano. At Elba, the air fleet veered west again, just passing the northern tip of Corsica, following an armada of two thousand ships in the Mediterranean below. There were small accidents and alarms. Halfway across the sea, someone accidentally knocked a toggle switch that controlled equipment bundles in six bomb bays of the C-47, and Phil Hand's plane lost half its demolition gear, which tumbled into the water below. When the order was given to "Stand up and hook up!" a medic in Fairlamb's plane would not get up. "Had he been an infantryman," Fairlamb wrote, "he no doubt would have been shot."

Past Saint-Raphael on the French coast, the fog having been burned off by a day of steady sun, the green jump lights flashed, and the "Hook up!" order rang out. The GOYAs struggled with their loads to grasp their risers and clamped their static lines onto the horizontal cable running the length of the plane. They held the straps taut and away from their temples, as they had been taught, to avoid bloodying or even losing their ears with the force of the jump. Then, like 826 newborns tired of darkness and fluid and mother, they hurtled into the air. It was the second D-Day for the U.S. Army—August 15, 1944—but for the GOYAs it was the first and the Army's best. That "D" stood for "deliverance." From the no-go to Martinique, from their hell at night at Mackall, from their collective fears of not measuring up, the 551st took wing.

Actually, what they took flight on was less a wing than a slithering umbilical cord. That's what the men looked like to each other for the split second they were flying out the door. Each man was attached by a strap to the cable, until the force of his fall pulled the parachute out of his backpack and the small strip of adhesive tape unstuck from the top of the chute, leaving the static line loose. As each man heard his "Go!" and followed his fellows out, the naked umbilicals grew on the pole, flapping in the blast of wind like spaghetti on a garment rack. The owners were gone.

If the sight of the 551st's billowing chutes was breathtaking from the ground to the airborne hero William Yarborough, it was "awe-inspiring" to Pappy Herrmann, the battalion's second in command, who was in the plane behind that of Wood Joerg. It prompted him to a metaphor: "parachutes with little men . . . blossoming out." Below, Herrmann wrote in 1982, was the "smoking coast of France," largely from fires started by the naval and air bombardment. Despite Axis Sally's promises, the 551st received little flak. The bulk of the Dragoon drop sixteen hours before already had the Germans tied up in ground fighting. To the confused Wehrmacht, the GOYAs must have looked like an impossible lightning striking twice in the same place.

What may be the only known photo in World War II taken in descent of U.S. combat paratroopers by one falling with them was snapped by Milo Huempfner, Joerg's driver. Such things were forbidden by anyone but the Signal Corps. The photo is understandably blurred, and all the figures but one appear insectlike in size, sadly infinitesimal below their mushroom-chutes. The one figure that is larger has his head so blurred he seems headless. It took presence of mind to hold that camera with the risers in the wind.

Many fell onto the trees of lush Provence. Bill Dean fell into pine boughs, which touched him delicately onto the ground amid Germans covered with flies in their foxholes—dead from a Resistance rising up the day before. Dean himself took a sniper's bullet in the hip; he was evacuated to a hospital in Italy, where his kidneys and bowels stopped functioning. A chaplain asked him if he was ready to die. "Like the devil!" he snapped from his pillow. In a few weeks he rejoined his comrades in the Maritime Alps.

Doug Dillard of A Company, the youngest man in the battalion, tried desperately to angle his fall away from a tall poplar but was unsuccessful. Hanging in it 50 feet up, he watched men running around below trying to gather up. One of them shouted to him to pull his reserve chute and climb down it. Though a sharp pull in his groin felt like a hernia, he was able to slip down the reserve and head toward the shouts.

Company A commander Captain Marshall Dalton also climbed down a chute to escape—in midair! As he was floating down, an equipment bundle landed right on his canopy and collapsed his chute. At less than 500 feet from the ground, Dalton calculated he didn't have enough time to pull his reserve chute. He lunged at the equipment bundle, piggybacking it for dear life as it bore its human cargo to the ground.

If you are what you jump with, the 551st were a wacky lot. Jack Funk jumped with a guitar, but he would never play his favorite song "The Wreck on the Highway" by Roy Acuff, which went "I heard the crash on the highway/But I didn't hear nobody pray." Soon after landing he was killed by gunfire, the guitar playing nonsense music on the ground. He was the first GOYA killed in combat. Tims Quinn had *101 Best Poems* in his breast pocket; the Red Cross man for the First Airborne Task Force, Dave DeVarona (the father of Olympic gold medal swimmer Donna DeVarona), jumped with a duffel of donuts, but it was never found. Andy Titko carried a "Dear John" letter that arrived the day of his jump from his girl back home, saying she was breaking up with him. It got crushed, but he married her anyway. Benny Goodman carried a reminder of the GOYAs' earliest days, a machete from Panama. And my father fell with the hollow eggshell painted with a paratrooper into a sycamore tree, cutting himself out with his trench knife, his lucky eggshell whole.

"Miss Easter Egg is still in one piece," he had written his sister Jeannette on July 23, 1944. "She has gone on many a hike with me and always looks like a dream at the finish of each."

Many, like the pathfinders, had equipment stripped from them by the shock of the opening chutes, though more from high-altitude winds than the low drop of the pathfinders. Roland Barhyte jumped to his roughest opening shock ever and lost his grenade launcher; the rest of his squad from first platoon, A Company, lost all their rations in the fall and converged on Barhyte, who primly presented his tin from his pocket. He had landed, sitting like a Buddha, in a tree and was pulled out of harness by a man from the 517th. The cross-unit rivalries disappeared on the drop zone. Jim Heffernan was cut out of a tree by a 509th paratrooper.

Lieutenant Bud Schroeder and Doc Chalkley thought they were greenlighted at between 1,500 and 2,000 feet, twice the normal height for a parachute jump. To make matters worse, Chalkey's plane was hauling upward to avoid the slanting land below at about 120 miles per hour. "Everything you were carrying that weighed anything tore loose and went flying," he said. "Panels blew, men lost their equipment. It was a very hard opening shock." As he descended, the doctor smelled cordite, a propellant in naval guns. Schroeder's face was hit by what he thought was gasoline in the jump door until he saw men in the plane ahead throwing their water bags out.

Many, like Bill Dean, fell on or near the dead. Jim Stevens did his traditional roll on landing until his face rested inches from two big hobnailed boots: "I figured maybe I was dead, because if a German was that close to me he must have killed me, but then I saw he was dead." Shortly after landing, John Balogach came upon a German whose eye was hanging out. The man begged him in broken English to shoot him, to put a knife into him, anything to relieve his pain. "I didn't come into the war to kill an invalid," Balogach remarked. "I didn't touch him."

The excitement of the jump mixed with overwhelming anxiety on landing in enemy-held territory for the first time. Phil Hand was stunned to see the body of a German lying face up, staring at the sky and "just automatically, reflex or what have you, I emptied into him; but everybody did."

If the GOYAs were overwhelmed by anxiety, the Germans sent north from the beach—guarding 244th and 242d Divisions—were overwhelmed by the 10,000 men dropping from nowhere on top of them, a U.S.–Wehrmacht ratio in the LaMotte–Le Muy area of at least 5 to 1. Clumps of surrenders pocked the battlefield, but by no means consistently enough to keep the 551st off their triggers. Two Germans who turned out to be impressed Czechs actually helped cut Hedy LaMar out of his harness while they surrendered. When Lieutenant Dick Goins landed with C Company—the last GOYA group to jump—in a cornfield before he had even gotten out of his chute five Germans walked right up to him with hands reaching for the sky. "This scared me," Goins said. "I was petrified for a moment. Then I came up with my machine gun ready and took them prisoner. They tried to give me everything they had—cigarettes, watches, rings, everything."

For some, the struggle to remember the password devolved into a comic scene from an Ionesco play. Corporal Mel Clark landed in a vineyard, unhitched his chute, and began moving low among the grapevines, only to come to a rustling noise that sounded human. His finger stiffened on his rifle trigger. He called out hoarsely, "Liberty!" and awaited the necessary response, "France!" But nothing came. The rustling stopped; silence filled Clark's ears. He strained to hear anything. Suddenly a thick British accent spoke, "Jesse James, Tom Mix—oh, some bloody American cowboy!" It was a man from the British 2d Parachute Brigade, who had forgotten the emergency password, "Billy the Kid."

Fortunately, the Rommel's asparagus, the 12-foot poles stuck in the vineyards to impale gliders and men, hooked no more than two GOYAs, though one sustained a gruesome and nearly fatal injury. The pole went up the anus and into the back of Gene Schmid, who had caught a streamer and failed to keep his legs together. Many of the men mentioned seeing poor Schmid. Carl Noble found Schmid's back "telescoped" by the fiendish pole. Luckily, Doc Chalkley, though he didn't have any sutures, sewed him up with needle and thread as he howled in agony. Chalkley sewed quickly. Over his shoulder he saw the American gliders diving down. Schmid was hobbled for life.

Within minutes of the GOYA drop, Operation Dove carried 2,250 green but gutsy glidermen along with jeeps and artillery in 337 towed gliders near and onto the GOYAs' drop zone. Composed of the 550th Glider Infantry Battalion, Dove also included, in one jeep, three Japanese-Americans from an antitank platoon of the heralded 442d Regiment. Even before they cracked up on land, some of the armada of flimsy Waco gliders, lost in smoky haze from the fires below, found themselves heading right at other gliders and transport planes. It was a terrible spectacle. Frantic to avoid collison, scores of Wacos cut loose from their C-47s, weaving and darting to miss each other. In midair, thick cables swinging free sheared off wings and fuselages. Into the sky and to their deaths, men spilled out from the Wacos. Jeeps tumbled earthward bizarrely. Luckily the three men of the 442d emerged alive from the wreckage of their glider and jeep, though one had a cracked skull.

The sight of their sister 550th battalion helplessly careening was worse than anything else the GOYAs witnessed during Dragoon, with the exception of their own firefight near Cannes with the Germans. Ralph Wenthold watched in disbelief as one glider rammed through trees into a huge oak and disintegrated. No one survived. David Munoz, a C Company medic, had barely slid down his reserve chute from a tree when he saw gliders in chaos all around him. He ran about dodging them. "You were more scared of being hit by a glider than of enemy fire," he recalled. A GOYA chaplain later told Phil Hand that the closest he ever came to God in the war was when a nervous gliderman emerged from a cracked-up Waco and started shooting at him with his Tommy gun; the chaplain nearly lost his voice yelling that he was an American. As he was retrieving bundles, Doug Dillard saw a glider slide by and smash into some trees. Dillard and his fellows ran over to help, but there was no sign of life. Martin Kangas saw one glider pilot maneuver his tail smartly over treetops only to catch a wing on a *Rommelspargel,* flip in the air, and crash. Some who came in cleanly were wrecked by other gliders powerless to avoid them. "I'll stick to parachutes," Pappy Herrmann said to himself as he picked his way through shards of Wacos and dead glidermen.

Of 404 gliders in Operation Dove, only 45 were intact after the bitter landings in southern France. Of about 1,000 casualties sustained by the 1st Airborne Task Force on its D-Day, close to one-third were glidermen. The American airborne forces took 1,000 German prisoners on August 15, and hundreds of dead Germans littered the vineyards. As the GOYAs formed up in their planned assembly area around Joerg's rallying pole of a Confederate flag, the 551st commander was amazed to realize his own battalion's losses were minimal the first day of their crucible in combat: two dead, about five seriously wounded. But even those losses had already begun to unwind the tight mainspring inside him. That night junior officers who had thought Joerg too cocky, stiff, or aloof, thought they caught in his eyes as he rested in an eighteenth-century farmhouse the first droplets of sadness. He was changed.

The vineyards the GOYAs fell on that day turned out to be those of the Valbourges estate, owned by James Stevens, an Englishman, whose wife, Henriette, ministered to the wounded like a French Clara Barton. It was an extraordinary twenty-four hours for the winery. For three days bombardment from the coast had been severe, and after hearing three hours of aircraft droning in the dark morning hours, Mr. Stevens reinforced the door locks of his château. Before dawn, his sleepless son René's eyes widened at gunshots out in the Serbine woods around them, where the Germans had stacked gasoline. The gas stocks exploded, and fires broke out in the woods.

At 8:30 A.M. on August 15, a vineyard worker knocked at Valbourges and called out, "Jacques, there are three Americans by the pond." They were from the first large wave paratroopers of Dragoon; most of the first fifty Americans that came to the château were not injured seriously and gave the hosts their first chocolate and cheese in months. One conscripted Ukrainian with the German Army (possibly of the 661st *Ost* Battalion) was carried in with a bad thigh wound, his whole body soaked in blood. He murmured, "Mama," and crossed himself while a doctor gave him a massive injection. But the serum oozed from his bloodless veins, and he soon died, with his hand in that of Madita, a Stevens daughter.

At 6 P.M. the Stevenses were astonished at the sight of masses of white, blue, and green parachutes floating down. That was the 551st. James and Henriette ran from tree to tree to help extricate the stuck GOYAs. They marveled at the "fantastic and imposing" armada of gliders and cried out at those who crashed. Fifteen American dead and eighty injured were counted in the château's hallways and courtyard, mostly glidermen. One of the two French Maquis assigned to the GOYAs ran up to Mr. Stevens, pumping his hand, "I have been waiting for this day for three years. It is the most beautiful day of my life." He described to the proprietor how the whole of the Valbourges estate had been mapped out in sand tables in Rome before the invasion.

Stevens reviewed the considerable damage to his vineyards but remarked, "This will be our contribution to the liberation and we bless the Lord it is such a small one."[16]

Wood Joerg arrived, introduced himself graciously, informed the Stevens family that LaMotte had fallen with scarcely a fight, and requested a room on the second floor so that he could survey the fields. The family members retired to the cellar, where they slept on sawdust. Though it had been the Feast of the Assumption of Blessed Mother Mary, they had not had time or the presence of mind to hold Mass in the estate chapel. And so, just before sleep, a son retrieved the Host from the chapel, walking through the maze of injured soldiers in the courtyard, and placed it in the window of the cellar. A silent prayer ensued, with farmers from the area gathering by candlelight. There was no electricity. Bill Lumsden's fall on wires had taken care of that.

The 551st slept that night in the Valbourges barns, alongside its winepresses, or in shelter halves, combat no longer a dream.

6
The capture of Draguignan

The next morning Pvt. Marcel Charette, a French Canadian by birth, serving as the 551st's chief interpreter in France, chatted amicably with the Stevens family over potato soup. Roland Barhyte sipped it with pleasure; he had never had it before, nor would ever have it again. "It was delicious, extra delicious!" he remembered fifty years later. Charette offered one of his nylon chutes to a teenage girl, who, as usually happened, thought it perfect for underwear. When the GOYAs formed up to move north toward Draguignan and the headquarters of a German general who was military governor of the Var department, however, Sergeant Jim Stevens saw their chutes put to a more doleful use: wrapping the glidermen for burial.

Shortly after midnight on August 16, 1,000 miles away from the Riviera at his Wolf's Lair in East Prussia, Hitler called one of his endless emergency meetings. The news on all fronts was not encouraging. The Russians had blasted through on the eastern front and were streaming toward Warsaw; the Allies were on the verge of sealing the Falaise pocket inland from Normandy and were heading toward to Paris; and now, what to do about the south of France, where 150,000 Allied forces had dropped from the air and come ashore? Hitler's generals awaited for der Fuhrer to fly into one of his typical rages, demanding action. Instead, he remained oddly diffident. His only question concerned Field Marshal Guenther von Kluge, Commander-in-Chief of the Western front, who had mysteriously disappeared as Dragoon commenced the day before. Hitler had once called von Kluge "the savior of the Russian front," but for three weeks von Kluge had been a marked man. The Gestapo had presented Hitler with evidence that he had been involved in the July 20 bomb plot at Rastenburg.

"Any word yet on von Kluge?" Hitler asked listlessly, hunched in his chair.

"*Nein, mein Fuhrer,*" General Jodl said. Field Marshal Wilhelm Keitel also shook his head.

In fact, von Kluge had been driving all over France trying to surrender his forces. But he was out of luck. The Gestapo ran into him before he could find the Allies, and he was ordered to Berlin. He halted his car near Metz before the German border on August 18 and took his own life with poison.

Hearing one gloomy report after another from the generals on the southern France invasion, Hitler murmured, "This has been the worst day of my life."[17]

To the general staff's amazement, Hitler did not blare his previous order to hold at all costs but completely reversed himself, muttering that he was ready to consider a complete pullback of Wehrmacht forces in France to the Siegried Line behind the German border. Meanwhile, German newspapers the morning of August 16 continued their propaganda *shpiel:* Goebbels had fed them a line that American paratroopers had been wiped out trying to take Marseilles, and landing forces had been repulsed at La Ciotat. In fact, what fell on Marseilles were six hundred diversionary dummies; at nearby La Ciotat, a handful of speedboats raced around the bay carrying on their own ruse.

If the 551st could be proud that Hitler called August 15, 1944, his worst day ever, its own best day would be August 16. That morning Dwight Eisenhower smiled as he read a telegram from Winston Churchill: "I watched the [Riviera] landing yesterday from afar. All I have learnt there makes me admire the perfect precision with which the landing was arranged and the intimate collaboration of British–American forces. . . . It seems to me that the results [in France] might well eclipse all the Russian victories." The British Bulldog, who had earlier feared Dragoon would be "another bloody Anzio," had certainly changed his tune in a hurry. Naturally, Churchill had to declare victory over the Russians! But as for "British–American" cooperation, though it had been masterful at Normandy, in southern France the English contribution was one airborne brigade. If anything, Dragoon was a masterpiece of American–French teamwork, as the entire French II Corps of General Jean-Marie de Lattre de Tassigny had put ashore and moved on Marseilles and Toulon, primary objectives of the invasion. It was an emotional moment for those men who, for the first time in five years of exile, kissed their own soil.

Just before leaving Valbourges, Wood Joerg returned to Mr. Stevens the key to his cellar, where a new radio had been installed, with instructions that the key should be given to no one else. After the GOYAs moved out, Stevens checked his 5,000-liter storehouse of wine; only two liters were missing. "The occupants had been extremely sober," he concluded.

About 9 P.M. on August 16, with the GOYAs halfway between La Motte and Draguignan, 4 miles up the road from their drop zone, Captain Edward Hartman, the battalion's chief intelligence officer (S-2), rushed into the makeshift command post where Pappy Herrmann was flipping through casualty reports. Hartman bluntly asked where Lieutenant Colonel Joerg was; he had left an hour before to inspect forward positions with Tims Quinn.

"What's up?" Herrmann asked.

Hartman said a lovely French woman on bicycle—probably a Resistance member—had ridden up to him and told him that the Kraut garrison had abandoned Draguignan under Free French sniper fire after watching the paratroopers drop. The townspeople had unfurled their French flags and begun to celebrate prematurely. German forces had been ordered back into the town; already they were infiltrating back. The situation looked grim, as it seemed they would fight to the death.

Major Herrmann quickly radioed commander General Frederick of the 1st Airborne Task Force. Within fifteen minutes Joerg had returned and Herrmann handed him a compelling note just in from Frederick: "Hold present position with minimum force. Attack and seize Draguignan."

A patrol of the 517th had actually probed toward Draguignan but was ambushed and captured by 250 Germans. That German force was itself surrounded by a larger one of the French underground, demanding surrender. The haughty German commander, however, would not surrender to Frenchmen, and turned his men over to the "battling buzzards" of the 517th. The task of taking Draguignan, however, would belong to the 551st.

As darkness fell over the area, the GOYAs carefully made their way along the road and in a dry riverbed northwest toward Draguignan, population 20,000, the only city of size in the area. Headquarters Company ran into machine gun fire from a farmhouse, and an odd dance ensued. A Frenchman ran up to the advancing GOYAs and said that the Germans in the house wanted to surrender but had to hold onto their pride. They had orally provided the emissary with a script: We will fire a little, and the Americans will fire a little, and then we'll surrender. (Unlike their impressed Pole and Czech underlings, the hostiles most concerned about pride—and possible execution—were German officers.) The GOYAs maneuvered around the farmhouse in a 6-foot-deep irrigation ditch and set up a machine gun. Lieutenant Slucter asked if anyone spoke German, and Frank "Big Head" Powers volunteered his services. Slucter ordered him to holler to them to surrender.

"Hey, you *tediski* sons-of-bitches, *alles kaput!*" Powers jumped up and yelled.

Powers had exhausted his German in one sentence. The Germans kept to their script and opened fire, killing the GOYA machine gunner. A short, vicious firefight ensued and ended in a draw. The GOYAs let the farmhouse go, as the Germans did not honor the ending of their one-act play by giving up.

Leading the way, C Company came upon a site for sore eyes: a German mini-tank, radio-controlled and filled with high explosives, moving directly at them. Captain Quinn ordered it knocked out by a bazooka round, and the blast shook the men's ribs. It was the first time they had seen such a thing; they would see its very distant cousin down the road in Belgium, the 70-ton Royal Tiger tank. For now, the exhausted tankers of the 11th Panzer Division, which had been in Bordeaux two days before, clanked up on August 15 to the Rhône River at Avignon, 90 miles northeast of the Riviera beaches. The last bridge had been blown by sappers that morning. Frustrated, General

Wend von Wintersheim slowly loaded his tanks on barges, but a hornet's nest of Allied "Jabo" fighter-bombers rained hell on the barges and the loading and debarking tanks. It was four days before the remnant of the 11th Panzers formed up, too late to be of any use in warding off Dragoon.

The GOYAs were in for another surprise as they massed toward midnight outside Draguignan: The city contained two German generals. All during D-Day plus 1, General Ferdinand Neuling, commander of LXII Corps, and his subordinate Major General Ludwig Bieringer, the area's military governor, had been trying to contact each other. Telephone lines had been cut by the Resistance. Neuling's headquarters were just northwest of the city in a mountainside redoubt surrounded by barbed wire and mines. With communications similarly cut off from General Wiese at 19th Army Headquarters in Avignon, Neuling had no way of knowing Hitler had signed orders the day before for the Wehrmacht's evacuation from France. With no way to reach his two infantry divisions either (242d and 244th), Neuling had personally watched the spectacle of the Dragoon airdrop, and knew he was surrounded. But he had taken a blood oath of allegiance to der Fuhrer as an officer.

A couple of miles closer to town than Neuling's cave, the haughty and stiff General Bieringer, the very essence of the Prussian officer, listened to the Schmeisser fire outside and the hurrying clack of hobnailed boots running on cobblestones. On the afternoon of Dragoon's D-Day, Bieringer had reached by radio a top German regiment of the 148th Division stationed 20 miles east of town and ordered it to defend Draguignan, but with his radio now jammed by Allied ships he had heard nothing else from it, and it certainly hadn't arrived. Bieringer had no more than 750 men of questionable motivation to defend the city from the grease-faced paratroopers. He thrummed his fingers on his desk at his château headquarters.

Two bazooka shells hit his building, crashing windows. A voice called out amid Wehrmacht boots running down steps into a bomb shelter, "The Americans are here! Cease firing! Cease firing!" That damned Lieutenant Pfannkuche (trans.: Pancake), Bieringer muttered to himself, rushing back from the door to try General Neuling's telephone once more. It was still out.

At 11 P.M. on August 16 on the outskirts of town, Joerg gave the order to enter the narrow streets of Draguignan and take it. A and B Companies would lead, with C Company held in reserve. Now leading his A Company patrol down a dark alley, Cicchinelli thrust his hand up, motioning the men to stop. The men pressed themselves against a wall as Chick motioned toward a large building on the town square, which sported a huge Nazi flag.

"Let's take the bastards," Sergeant Donald Thompson whispered.

A four-man storm force of Thompson, Ed Schultz, and Bud Hook was led by Cicchinelli up to the high front door. Strangely, no one was guarding it. Grasping their Tommy guns and rifles, counting the longest three seconds of their lives, they rammed their shoulders into the door, breaking it down, and did the same to the first door on their right. General Ludwig Bieringer rose from his desk slowly, his hand clutching his monocle.

"He must be a colonel or general," one of the troopers said, pointing his Tommy gun at him.

"Naw. A general would have scrammed out of Draguignan long ago," another spat out.

Bieringer walked, head back, to Sergeant Thompson, pulled out his wallet, and handed him a mark note of sizable value. The bribe spared his life and later provided Company A with several bottles of wine. A German captain offered Cicchinelli his entire wallet, taking out his family photos. Chick was tempted to take out his, and they'd all have a reunion.

Now paratroopers had massed in the building. Bieringer was led away to A Company commander Marshall Dalton's command post, then jeeped to Wood Joerg, who was stunned at the catch. He radioed ahead to General Frederick that the GOYAs had captured a general alive, though not too well. While they escorted Bieringer in convoy to Frederick's headquarters at Le Mitan, Herr General climbed under a tarpaulin to avoid rotten vegetables thrown by the townspeople. At Le Mitan he officially surrendered the 750 men of his post.

Though they were not aware of it at the time, Joe Cicchinelli and his three comrades had registered the first Allied capture alive of a German general in Western Europe.[18] Later, Chick shinned up the flagpole outside Bieringer's headquarters and tore down the Nazi flag.

Each GOYA platoon had a different read on the taking of Draguignan; some encountered resistance in the labyrinthine streets, some did not. Captain "Jungle Jim" Evans of B Company led his men, including my father, into the city without his helmet, a parachute scrap wrapped around his head. In undershirt and suspenders, with his handlebar mustache, Evans resembled, to Lieutenant Dick Mascuch, "a goddamned pirate."

Three Maquis fighters led B Company down the streets in dress shoes, that clattered loudly on the stones; their white shirts were not taken as surrender, and soon B Company was fired on by machine guns and snipers, my father taking out two men escaping from the bakery. Bud Schroeder fell onto a patch of earth, crawling as the bullets drove dirt into his nose and mouth. One bullet entered his chest.

Schroeder sprawled by a stone wall in pain but remembered what he had learned two years before at Fort Benning: If you're pinned down, don't get up or go back, keep moving. He did, and he thought it saved his life, before he passed out. He was taken to a cottage and then a French hospital in Draguignan, where German doctors treated him with penicillin for the infected wound before he was evacuated to the beach and finally Naples, to rejoin the battalion later.

What follows has to be one of the more successful GI bluffs of the war. By 2 A.M. on August 17, three hours after the 551st began attacking the town, Lieutenant Colonel Wood Joerg set up his command post in Draguignan's center at the Hôtel Madeleine. Having secured the central hospital, Joerg, worried about mounting casualties, sent for Doc Chalkley. In turn, Chalkley sent for his colleague, Doc Battenfield, as the hospital was overflowing with German and American wounded. What Battenfield didn't know was that there were two hospitals in Draguignan, a small one the Americans had taken, and a large one still held by Germans. A Resistance man, evidently not briefed on the matter, promptly took Battenfield and his medic, Private Francis Perkins, to the hostile one.

The door of it was locked. Irritated by two days of sleeplessness, Battenfield banged on it shouting, "Let me in, damn it!"

When it swung open, Battenfield and his sidekick were face to face with a German officer; behind him were dozens of rifle-toting Wehrmacht soldiers, staring at the two visitors. Battenfield thought quickly; here they both were armed with little more than gauze, penicillin, and morphine. He figured his life was gone. He had nothing to lose, so he yelled, "We have your hospital surrounded! There's no way you can escape alive!" Only Battenfield knew this threat had all the force of attacking on a chessboard with a lowly pawn.

A German lieutenant colonel appeared and looked the two up and down. "We will surrender only to your senior commander," he declared.

"Like hell you will!" Battenfield screamed. "Either you surrender to me immediately or my paratroopers will storm this building and wipe you out!"

Battenfield felt the blood rushing to his head. Silent seconds dropped on the doormat between them.

Then the German commander said in perfect English, with a shrug, "All right, to save lives I hereby surrender the hospital to your force."

Perkins looked at Battenfield with astonishment. Battenfield remained cool and collected; he motioned Perkins to bring in the bulk of the force. With the luck (and stiff upper lip) of the English, Battenfield exhaled fifteen minutes later when a squad of GOYAs appeared on the scene and did the honors of taking everyone into custody.

Several men from A Company secured the German-held hospital, including PFC Lou Waters, who broke off from a search party for weapons and contraband in quest of a square meal. He ran into "a great big German nurse the size of Tannhauser's Brunhilde complete with long yellow braided hair sweeping into the kitchen like a mad water buffalo." Waters, trying out his "high school Dutch" on her, demanded, *Wo ist die Kuchen?*" Before the purple-faced bulldozer of a nurse could answer, Waters spied a half-loaf of bread and some jam and began to help himself.

"Raus! Raus! Americkanischen Schweindhund!" the woman screamed, grabbing him by the back of his collar with "hands the size of catcher's mitts" and propelling him out the door of the kitchen—a classic "bum's rush," Waters thought. The jam and bread, though, were still his.

The roundup of the Wehrmacht intensified. T/5 Otto Schultz of HQ Company, who knew German, marched a column of one hundred prisoners through the streets of Draguignan with an order to goosestep. One didn't comply, and Schultz cursed him up and down the vernacular, kicking his rear end until he obeyed. Another bunch shot up the white flag after Wood Joerg bullhorned, "If you don't surrender, we are going to call in the Air Corps and bomb the hell out of you." Lieutenant Andy Titko's repeated attempts to make good the threat came to nought: His radio was jammed, not the first time the GOYAs would find themselves uncovered. Somehow the Germans slipped away. A group of seventy Germans broke up an impromptu villa party where GIs were swigging cognac. Mercifully, the Germans threw up their hands instead of their Schmeissers. At 5:15 P.M. on August 17, Joerg radioed General Frederick at the 1st Airborne Task Force: "Draguignan secured."

But the other German general, Ferdinand Neuling, was still at large outside the town in his hideout. Two times the wily Neuling, a veteran of the Russian front, had rebuked GOYA demands that he surrender. Captain Jim Evans, in full "pirate" regalia, had gone in a squad car under a white flag to try to coax Neuling out of his bunker, only to be refused. The 551st's chief intelligence officer, Captain Edward Hartman, also made an unintended try when he set out in a car with an English-speaking prisoner to interrogate General Bieringer after his capture, only to find the French driver running them right out to Neuling's place. Hartman, with a carbine and several grenades on his lap in the back seat, suddenly found the car driving down a column of German armed guards "all eight feet tall."

"Sit very still," the captured German sitting shotgun said. Hartman slid his carbine to the floorboards. "I thought my war days were over," he smiled years later. The captive translator got out of the car at the end of the column and talked to a platoon leader of the Germans, who told him that the better part of valor would be for the American officer's car to drive to the end, turn around, and drive slowly back through and away.

As they crested the hill in retreat, a dazed Hartman told the prisoner, "That was the wrong general!"

Back in Draguignan's center, Hartman finally did meet General Bieringer, whose monocle was sweating profusely through an interrogation by Corporal Kenneth Hundley, an emigrant from Germany who had come to study in 1937 to Louisville, Kentucky. Once in the Hitler Youth himself, Hundley had a father—whom he was none too fond of—who was a major in the Gestapo; the son relished putting a German general on the hot seat.[19] Suddenly an irate G-3 operations colonel from 1st Airborne Task Force rolled up and immediately demanded the general.

"He's right there in the jeep," Hartman said.

The American colonel climbed into the back seat, took out his .45, cocked it, and aimed it at Bieringer's head. "I held my breath," Hartman said, fearing an execution. Then Bieringer, out of bribe money at that point but still with a flair for deflating peril, ordered an aide to draw some beer from a keg sitting on an ash pile along the road. The aide obeyed and handed the golden glass of beer to his general, who turned around in the front seat and handed it to the American colonel with the exhortation, *"Yah! Gut! Gut!"* No one seems to remember if the colonel drank it, but he sent Bieringer to Le Mitan and General Frederick.

As for General Neuling, his "liberation" was at hand. Up from the Dragoon beaches, at 6 A.M. on August 18 (D plus 3), Lieutenant Colonel Charles J. Hodge, commander of the 117th Cavalry Reconnaissance Squadron of the 36th Infantry Division, moved out of Le Muy and headed north through Draguignan. Two miles outside town his column received fire from a cave on a mountainside. Hodge ordered one of his tanks to invite the cave dwellers to breakfast with a few high explosive shells. Soon a German lieutenant emerged with a white flag. A deadly silence ensued. Then Generalleutnant Ferdinand Neuling emerged, his ramrod-straight figure covered with dust and cordite powder. He turned over his pistol to Hodge's aide, who presented it to Hodge. End of standoff. In four days the U.S. Army, thanks in large part to the 551st's capture of Draguignan, had bagged two commanders entrusted by Hitler with the defense of the entire French Riviera.

In an article published by the *Saturday Evening Post* in 1946 entitled "They'll Never Forget Mark Clark," the 36th Infantry Division erroneously received credit for the liberation of Draguignan.[20] That was typical of the 551st's ride into obscurity. To compound the error, the monument erected in Draguignan's town square pays homage to the 517th Parachute Regimental Combat Team for its liberation, though it never set foot in Draguignan. The long shadowy arm of Rupert Graves, the 517th commander, seemed again to extend over the 551st. The Dracenois cannot be blamed for the error; they probably got the wrong information from the 1st Airborne Task Force.

Even the Resistance member Aimé Leocard, who became a staunch friend of the 551st in later years, didn't know the GOYAs had liberated his hometown until 1984, when a few veterans revisited Draguignan for the first time. A portrait of Leocard and Draguignan in a June 10, 1968, article in *Life* magazine, "An Oasis of Love for America," is mute as to what unit was in the city during the war, though it does tour the U.S. Rhône Cemetery in Draguignan where 861 Americans from forty-seven states are buried, three from the 551st among them (about fifty GOYAs were wounded in the Draguignan campaign).

Draguignan, though a lovely city nestling in foothills with olive trees, fig groves, and vineyards, is somewhat off the beaten path, obscure to tourists doing the Paris–Côte d'Azur run. Its one claim to fame, in a country that loves butter, is the invention of margarine; its one well-known figure was the diva Lily Pons. In some respects the city the GOYAs liberated was as obscure as the GOYAs themselves.

After the German surrender, Joe Cicchinelli and two friends of A Company found, in a cave behind General Bieringer's château, five burlap sacks filled with French francs and German marks—the Wehrmacht's payroll, they figured—and some cases of cognac. They bounced through Draguignan's cobbled streets in a jeep as civilians poured from their homes that August 16, 1944, throwing the marks and francs in the air, a confetti the people ran around snatching. Along the route, paratroopers celebrated, were kissed roundly, and had their jump pants sewn up on the spot. Dick Mascuch and the acrobat Jack Russell held cups of brandy as they bent over for tailoring.

"Do you think they think we're Santa Claus or goddamned fools?" Cicchinelli was asked by a comrade.

"Probably a little of both," Chick called out, tossing the bills up.

7

First to Nice

The retreating German Army decided to make its last stand in the southeast corner of France on a hill just above Theoule, a few miles south of Cannes. The GOYAs would bear the brunt of the counterattack. The jewels of the Riviera, Cannes and Nice, did not fall into Allied hands until the 551st sustained at least twenty more dead and one hundred more wounded.

After being relieved by the 36th Division at Draguignan, the battalion took about a week to trudge through the mountainous terrain south to the Côte d'Azur beaches. Following the Argens River southeast toward Frejus on the coast, they marched in 100-degree heat.

Bearing 100 pounds of equipment in such heat up and down inclines dodging bullets and shells was only a part of the hardship the men battled. According to Lieutenant Dick Durkee, the GOYAs' chief enemy the first week in southern France was "starvation." Except for the odd bun or bowl of soup from a friendly French farmhouse, the men were surviving that first combat week entirely on one issue of K-rations on the tarmac outside Rome. By the time they approached Cannes, Durkee said, "we were digging up the gardens and doing just about anything to get something to eat." Nice would be another story, a veritable banquet. That pattern of feast or famine would dog the 551st all the way to the Bulge.

The night of August 18 an empty school sheltered the GOYAs in Puget sur-Argens. As they cleaned weapons in the moonlight outside, an air alert sounded. Don Garrigues heard a droning overhead and jumped into a slit trench, figuring the battalion was in for its first serious bombardment. He looked up. A lone German plane passed over. It looked lost; it dropped nothing but its sound. Garrigues looked down, his boots squishing. He had jumped into an abandoned German latrine.

In fact, the German forces in the south of France were under a crazy quilt of conflicting orders. General Johannes Blaskowitz had been told to gather as many forces from his southern France troops as possible and rush north to link up with the German Army retreating from Normandy toward the Fatherland. At the same time as the German 148th Division fought a spoiling action retreating eastward to the Maritime Alps, the 25,000 German soldiers in Toulon were ordered to dig in and resist the Dragoon invasion. Both Toulon and Marseilles were key ports to which Admiral Karl Donitz clung until the last moment. German resistance in those two southern ports lasted longer than it did in Paris.

Before Draguignan, according to David Munoz, medics were allowed to carry weapons, but afterward, as they moved toward larger concentrations of civilians (and the press, no doubt) in Cannes and Nice, Wood Joerg ordered all medical personnel to follow the Geneva Convention strictly and to turn in their weapons.

Moving out eastward in the arduous coastal foothills on August 20, Company A jumped to fill a dangerous gap between the 551st and the British 2d Independent Parachute Brigade. Increasingly, the GOYAs were coming under artillery and machine gun fire, and German forces of the 148th began to penetrate the gap, threatening to surround them. At night,

Captain Marshall Dalton sent out a party of eight men, led by scout Cicchinelli, to thread through the German positions and link up with the British to coax them closer. Amid the dark sage of the hills, some British vehicles spotted the GOYAs and at first took them for English-speaking Germans, almost arresting them. The British colonel was livid that the little American patrol had actually penetrated 200 yards into British lines without being discovered. He blamed the GOYAs for the presence of the gap; they were moving too fast (not the first time the battalion would be accused of outrunning those nearby).

The patrol withdrew carefully, catching machine gun fire and watching it rip the leaves. "Sarge, I'd rather be at Fort Benning doing pushups," PFC George Smith told Don Thompson as they moved methodically, stopping and starting, stopping and starting. When they finally made it back to the A Company command post, Marshall Dalton grabbed Thompson's shoulders.

"Did we lose any men?"

"We all made it back," Thompson assured him, stunned to see tears running down Dalton's ruddy cheeks.

The gap filled up, but so did the Germans' bore sights. The artillery rainstorm from Cannes increased as the 551st picked its way through wild sage, thyme, and its own growing apprehensions. On its right flank trudged its fraternal, well-decorated 509th, to which the 551st was attached at the time like a kid brother. Both units were about to be decorated by white phosphorus shells. When the men came 2 miles shy of Cannes on a hillock—now called Hill 105—they had entered the range of 280mm guns on retractable rails shooting inland from the coast near Nice, about 15 miles away. Far off, but not far off enough.

The fight on Hill 105 heaved on a bloody seesaw, with the Germans first surprising the GOYAs and the 509th by jumping out of foxholes and firing at point blank range. One aimed a rifle grenade right at Martin Kangas, who thought he was "going to get it right between the eyes." Instead, he got it between his feet; the explosion only kicked up a rock that split his finger. For his efforts, the *Feldgrau* (field gray, the designated uniform) was shot by five GOYAs at once.

One boy, identified by wearing "that little beanie hat" instead of his helmet, was not as lucky as Kangas. Was he Jewish and wearing the yarmulke? "We were always telling him to put his helmet on," Sergeant Joe Kosowski of B Company related. When a hailstorm of 88mm shells fell on his platoon, Kosowski and his fellows dived down below the bank of a dry creek. Looking up through the smoke, Kosowski saw the boy was headless.

All afternoon and deep into the night of August 21, the faroff rail guns boomed, the whistle of their shells filling the GOYAs' ears with something unearthly, like a woman wailing with grief, till they crashed. The shells ran in all sizes, from 88mm to 280mm. The men jumped around, stumbled, tried to crawl into the earth, nowhere finding a deep enough hole to take a live man for the night. Don Garrigues lay flat when through the sulfurous smoke he watched PFC Bill Lawson's legs sliced off at the thigh by shrapnel. Garrigues called for medics, who carried Lawson frantically down the hillside. But he was dead before daybreak from loss of blood.

Inevitably, friendly fire caught them. For days the U.S. Navy off the coast of the Riviera had no luck silencing the German behemoth guns retracting into concrete blockhouses. With the barrage on Hill 105 that night and the emergency call-ins for help from the 509th and 551st, the Navy guns boomed away. As he led his A Company platoon up Hill 105, the naval bombardment of Dragoon began to rain on Sergeant Roy McCraw and his group trying to take out German positions at the hill's base. B Company's George Kane, sipping cocoa in a draw, saw Private Louis Tenute killed by a round of GOYA mortar fire.

At one point Emory Albritton, still weakened from malaria that almost got him scratched from the Dragoon drop, was bending down to cup some water from a creek in B Company's area. Lieutenant Colonel Joerg came up and drank from the creek, too; Albritton's spirits lifted seeing Joerg there, obviously shaken himself by the beating B Company was taking. He watched the commander moving from man to man, patting them on the back, looking over the wounded, barking at a man here and there to fix his helmet on or to get his head down. Then, behind a tree, Albritton thought he saw something metallic protrude. It was a sniper rifle barrel aimed straight at Wood Joerg. Before Albritton could react, the colonel's bodyguard, Demosthenes Vakerlis, shot the sniper. Joerg looked up, smelling the sweet-sour powder that had saved his life. He stared at Vakerlis without saying anything and rocked his head slowly, confirming to himself as well as others that, indeed, he was still there. And he moved on.

Suddenly, the night sky burst white. A shell, a dud, slid near Albritton; he touched it and burned his hand. Another exploded alongside him, and the man in front of him, Everett DeBarr, was riddled by shrapnel from head to foot, gaping holes slashed in his back. Burning chemical flew in Lieutenant Charles Hecq's face. "They were using a lot of white phosphorus, and it was almost like daytime," Albritton said. "People groaned all around."

Though shot in the chest himself, Albritton managed to get DeBarr, a large man, over his shoulders. He carried the dead weight of the man as he moaned "Help me! Help me!" up to a ledge below which the Germans moved the next morning. Albritton gave DeBarr a shot of morphine to keep him quiet so the Germans wouldn't spot them. But he figured there was no way out for the two of them. So the soldier who had hauled out the last men from the deadly waters of the night jump at Camp Mackall, including his dead friend Benjamin Preziotti, now hoisted DeBarr over his shoulder again and staggered down the ledge toward the Germans. To his amazement, the enemy did not capture him or DeBarr; one *Feldgrau* even saluted him! Albritton nodded. He trudged with his delirious load, coming upon a field of dead Americans. He counted sixteen bodies, stepping over them. "My God, where is Company B?" Albritton murmured to himself. Much of it was sprawling in the dust.

Albritton finally fell with his load when someone called "Halt!"—F. M. "Field Manual" Reed of B Company, standing guard at an aid station, where men lay on stretchers everywhere. Old Field Manual (who did everything by the numbers) helped get DeBarr off Emory's back. Then Albritton blacked out; when he awoke, he was in a large tent surrounded by dead men. To his right was the mortally wounded Dave Smith from B Company, his arms blown off. Albritton heard someone outside shout, "All the guys in here are stiffs!"

"Up your ass—we aren't all stiffs!" Albritton called out.

Albritton was flown to a hospital in Naples with other wounded. There he developed a friendship with a fellow from the 34th Infantry ("Red Bull") Division named James Arness. The two played pinochle together, along with "Bucky" Nannis from B Company, who was paralyzed from the waist down and would remain so for life. Albritton almost fell off his chair years later watching the television show *Gunsmoke,* for Arness was its star. Only in 1983 did he discover, from an unexpected phone call, that Nannis had survived. Each had thought the other dead.

Many others carried their wounds from Hill 105 for life and found their lives redirected by them. PFC Milo Burke of C Company watched as if in slow motion a "potato masher" grenade come right at him. He turned his face—a fortuitous impulse, he said—and the thing exploded. He lost an eye; it kept him from his lifelong ambition—to become a policeman. Burke described his walk to an aide station: "You ever get your shoes wet? My shoes were squish-squishing from blood." He lay in a tent for three agonizing days, virtually unattended. In a Naples hospital, some slipshod doctor tried to force a "stock" eye into the ruined socket without any lubrication, and Burke passed out from the pain. Postwar, he had nightmares for years; by day he drove a grocery truck in Chicago.

Turning the tide against the Germans at Hill 105, the leader of HQ Company's mortar platoon, Lieutenant Robert E. Buscher, uncorked an on-the-spot innovation. With breakneck speed, Buscher's men fired their mortars and hurried them back and forth over the hills at such rapid fire and with such concentration that a captured German later asked, "What kind of new artillery are you using?" Buscher's artillery-like mortars finally wore the German resistance down. Dan Morgan likened that weaponry tour de force to the artilleryman John Pelham, who supported Civil War Confederate General Jeb Stuart's cavalry. Pelham organized a highly mobile horse artillery battery with eight guns, a critical factor at the Battles of Antietam and Fredericksburg. By the time of the Battle of the Bulge, Buscher had augmented his 81mm mortars to the point where he had the firepower of two battalions, able to fire more than eight hundred rounds of high explosives in ten minutes.

According to Sergeant Doug Dillard, who retired as a full colonel, Buscher had filled a chronic gap for the 551st: "This was a real innovation, another first to the battalion's credit. Thus, Buscher made up for the lack of 75mm and 105mm artillery support, which the battalion continually suffered."

As day dawned on August 22, the blue waters of the Mediterranean shimmering in the distance, the men of the 551st winced at the sight of their wounded and dead lying everywhere, some exposed to the sunlight and swarmed by flies, some under shelter-halves. The hill stood eerily silent. The Germans had apparently withdrawn in the wee hours out of Cannes, and before they reached the Var River the 280mm retractable "guns of Navarone" were still. Either the Navy had finally hit them, or they had run out of ammunition.

The surgeons Battenfield and Chalkley had their hands full. They had been up all night operating, rushing from body to body under a blood-splattered moon. On the road the day before the fierce battle, Chalkley almost got religion when a 509th surgeon's jeep hit a mine and blew up right behind him. Inspecting the scene on August 22, Chalkley found the man's remains hung on a tree. He realized just how close he himself had come to being the one on that tree when he saw in the dust the 509er's tire tracks following directly on his own jeep's, except for a slight deviation where the mine had been.

The battalion moved down from the mountains, collecting about forty old trucks, bicycles, and buses along the way, through Mandelieu and across the Siagne River. As their own motor transportation had not yet arrived over the sea from Italy, the GOYAs did what they did best—improvise—by "liberating" vehicles as well as men. The rickety motor convoy looked to Pappy Herrmann like "one of the funniest military columns the world has ever seen." Lieutenant Milt Hill, the Headquarters Company executive officer, said to himself, "If the Germans see us coming, they will figure we are the rag-tag end of everything." Taking Grasse with no opposition, the GOYAs rested; Charles Fairlamb took a bath in his helmet, as he put it, speaking for an entire generation schooled in the privation of the Depression and World War II in its typical understatement: "It was wonderful."

On August 24, 1944, the 551st and the 509th entered Cannes without a shot being fired. The two crack separate parachute battalions shared the honors of liberating that town on the glistening Mediterranean, already suggestive of the cinematic glamour for which it would later become famous. What a set greeted them: abandoned German pillboxes labeled "bain—douches" and made to resemble bathhouses. Fake street entrances painted on walls. This and a joyful crowd waylaid them. The townspeople ran out from their homes to embrace the foul-smelling men and perfumed them with a shower of flowers from the wrought-iron balconies. Soon the GIs were walking on a carpet of flowers. Champagne by the glass was handed out in all directions, and no one had to twist Pappy Herrmann's arm. "Yes, there were a few liberation kisses, too, and don't think there were any arms broken on that, either," he wrote.

The battalion's aid station was set up in the Dupont home in Cannes. Doc Chalkley counted twenty bodies lined up for Graves Registration there. Max Bryan of C Company walked by them and told himself what a terrible job it must be to tag the dead men, search through their private belongings (prophylatics and any love notes from other women were dutifully discarded), and begin to write the dreaded letters home. He was glad he didn't have that job, though in fact it would be his five months later at the Bulge.

North of Cannes at Grasse—the perfume capital of the world—Sergeant Bernard Cheney dipped himself in a perfumed bath to be scrubbed by some lovely young French women. But he was to be almost "scrubbed" in another way. As one of the fifty or so paratroopers hastily picked by the 1st Airborne Task Force Provost Marshal, Colonel Michael Isenberg, to be MPs, Cheney had taken a number of German POWs to the coast and into the custody of the Navy. On one occasion he noticed Isenberg "treating the POWs too well," gave him some lip, and then gave him a fat lip. Astonished, Isenberg sent the GOYA sergeant straight to General Frederick for a quick court martial. Frederick took one look at the strapping Cheney and decided he was needed more at the front.

After another day's rest at Mougins, between Grasse and Cannes, the battalion pushed east toward Nice, setting up defensive positions past the little village of Biot in the vicinity of Vence and Cagnes; Lieutenant Colonel Joerg placed his command post right in back of the vacated Gestapo headquarters in the area. There an English schoolteacher took Doc Chalkley by the shoulder and said she had something to show him. She led the surgeon to a large depression of freshly turned soil on a hill just west of the Var River overlooking Nice. The Germans had left the day before, taking with them all the able-bodied old men and boys in her neighborhood. On the hill between fifty and one hundred of those unfortunates were shot in cold blood and buried in a mass grave. The GOYAs had arrived in the area one day too late. Chalkley shivered in the August sun. "It was plain damn brutality," he later said.[21]

Over the next few days the GOYAs moved on foot or in their crazy column of commandeered vehicles, many of them coal burners abandoned by the Wehrmacht, toward Nice. Captain Ed Hartman dubbed them "Joerg's irregulars," a nickname the colonel did not appreciate. Passage was not entirely free. Bathing in a hilltop cistern used for irrigation, Roger Carqueville came under artillery fire. One unarmed machine gunner who'd gotten 20 yards ahead of his Headquarters Company platoon was captured by five Germans, including one officer. As he was being interrogated, a hole appeared in the officer's head, and a "wild-looking Frenchman" (Chuck Fairlamb reports) came running up and shot the rest of the Germans dead. It was not the first time, nor the last, that the French underground—now ebulliently out in the open—would come to the aid of the 551st.

By August 27 the GOYAs had reached the Var River, just before Nice, and more or less held up there, as several Free French and city dignitaries came out to arrange a triumphal entry. There is some confusion here as to just who was the first 551st man, or cluster of men, to enter the capital of the Riviera. Captain Hartman insists that in the early hours of August 29 he took a five-man patrol, including Ralph Wenthold, nimbly across a broken bridge on the Var into Nice, where they marched straight into the Place de Messina, up to City Hall and practically bumped into the city's mayor and archbishop, whose ring the non-Catholic Hartman kissed. Ushered up into the mayor's offices, Hartman watched crowds begin to emerge in the dawn, shouting in the town square. As the crowd grew and became more delirious, Hartman worried aloud to the mayor about how his little band would get through them to report back to Joerg. The mayor produced his own car and driver, who, when fired upon by Free French who mistook them for Germans, promptly rammed a lamppost on the Promenade d'Anglais, thrusting Ralph Wenthold's rifle gunsight into his forehead. He bled down the whole front of his uniform. The men emerged, shaken from that first fruit of peace, and walked back across the Var.

Asserting that he made it into Nice with a small patrol a day or two before the full battalion's entry, C Company's Captain Tims Quinn, who took refuge from the crossfire of the Maquis, Germans, and German collaborators ("Everyone was turning a good man now") at the grand Hotel Negresco. Quinn radioed Joerg to come on in but was ordered back across the Var, an order he disobeyed (and for which he was later "grounded" for half a day.) Quinn witnessed a lot of street fighting (some may have been between rival Maquis forces, some of whom were Communist). Riding in the Mayor's car, Quinn was shocked to see men beating up female collaborators in the street, shaving their heads, and stripping them naked. He jumped out of the car at one point and put a stop to one beating. The Mayor tongue-lashed him for that. Quinn retorted, "We've come to help you and not to watch you brutalize women." As Cicchinelli had done in Draguignan, Quinn tore down a swastika flag and shipped it home.

At 10 A.M. on August 29, 1944, Lieutenant Dick Durkee, the officer Dan Morgan names as the first to enter Nice, took a squad on orders from Major Pappy Herrmann to the rim of Nice to gauge the extent of German resistance. Though the streets were deserted and quiet, Durkee decided to continue. "Damned if I'm going back, we'll just go right in," he thought.

The first human being he saw was a five-year-old French girl, who ran out of her house yelling, *"Les Americains! Americains!"* People began pouring out of their homes and offices. A ghost town became a circus in seconds. Someone thrust a bouquet of flowers into Durkee's arms, and he threw his rifle over his shoulder. The handsome, hatless Joe Thibault was festooned with kisses. Durkee asked for directions to the best hotel in town and was promptly led to the grand old Negresco. That night a band played the American national anthem in the town square, cheering wildly as Durkee and the Mayor emerged from a balcony. That would be the first of two pinnacles for Durkee in the 551st where he would stand alone. The second would be deathly quiet, with the crowds face-down in the snow.

In a classic photo, a flower-bedecked Durkee, flanked by a Maquis member with a Navy hat and a gendarme with a bicycle, leads his men down the street. The crowd swells in the Place de Messina, whose columns seem to arch their excitement behind him. As there is no photo of Quinn or Hartman, that seems as good a reason as any to assign the liberation of Nice to Durkee and his buddies, give or take a few glasses of champagne.

The next day, August 30, the French officially celebrated Nice's freedom; it is the day the 551st marched en masse into the great city. (In most history books, the 509th is incorrectly credited with being the first to enter Nice.) Pandemonium reigned despite the best efforts of French officials for a proper and *propre* cortège. The only known GOYA rebuked for French kissing on the Boulevard d'Anglais was Roger Carqueville. Captain Bill Smith of Headquarters Company shouted at him, "I told you we were not going to take anything from the French!" Carqueville protested his innocence and went back to taking. Doc Chalkley was only too pleased to be hustled aside as he passed a corner bar by the drunken properietor, right down to his wine cellar to dig out a prized five-year-old cognac, which the owner had saved since the start of the war for just that day.

Trading was general, especially with privates. Parachute silk was especially prized, and nylon too; women traded a long kiss for a swatch of the chutes, and soon the cloth appeared in the markets as panties and bras. Jim Aikman had a tablecloth and napkins made of his nylon chute, prized possessions he would never be able to retrieve from Laon, France, from where the 551st was hurried five months later to the Bulge campaign. Most of the GOYAs' mementos were lost at Laon.

Celebrations for the GOYAs were as short-lived as their training had been interminable. The very next day after taking Nice, men were roused from warm French arms and hangovers from calvados and other spirits to move east to clean out pockets of resistance toward the Italian border. Lieutenant Paul Hoch, his head wrecked by a clear liquid from a bottle with three cherries on the bottom, which he compared to "raw gasoline," stared down on Monte Carlo, where it was rumored Maurice Chevalier had operated as a collaborator. Monaco had to be handled carefully, as it was a neutral country, but a company of GOYAs was invited in, searched around for Germans, and left without incident.

LaTurbie, a small town overlooking Monaco which boasts a large, crumbling 2,000-year-old monument to Augustus Caesar, appears to have been one of the last, if not the last, holdouts of German resistance. A machine gun nest in a shack on a hill was under the suicidal order to cover the elements of the 148th Division's retreat into Italy. And it was to that spot that a seven-man patrol led by Lieutenant George Luening and the A Company scout Joe Cicchinelli was escorted under cover of darkness by a French civilian, Charles Calori.

The machine gun nest had been raking the road out of Nice for days. The GOYAs crept up to the shack right to the muzzle of the machine gun, lobbing grenades. Rushing to enter, Sergeant Robert Anderson had to be pulled back by his web belt by Cicchinelli to avoid an explosion. After the dust settled, the Americans entered to find the dead German machine gunner torn up "like a bloody pile of old rags," according to PFC Lou Waters. In one sense, though, the GOYAs were lucky; a deep, long trench out back had just been vacated by two dozen Germans, who had gone to town for dinner. Only Lieutenant Luening was wounded during the raid. He took a bullet in the knee.

Behind that shack, though, Cicchinelli found his haunting. Waters, crashing through a window, landed on a man sliced with bullets by Sergeant Anderson, "his blood flowing out of him and running down a little rain ditch the Krauts had dug around the place." Another lay dead, but a third cowered in a hutch, badly wounded but breathing. His brains were spilling onto the dry grass. "One of them didn't die," Cicchinelli told me forty-five years later, rediscovering that very hutch for the first time, as if not dying were a terrible change in the script of war. The scout had witnessed a more amiable change in script at La Motte, where he had watched with wonder as Doc Chalkley treated a German soldier before the GOYAs' own because the soldier was hurt worse.

Joe Cicchinelli shot that last youth in what he thought was mercy. "Well, darling, I'm more cruel than I thought I was," he V-mailed home.[22] For years Cicchenilli kept the *soldebuch* pictures of the three teenagers killed in his wallet, reminding himself that he could have been born blonde, German, and pleading for mercy.

Absent from that scene, but not completely free of the unit to which he was destined to belong, was Dan Morgan. Some of the hundred or more men who fled the 551st at Mackall may have reconsidered their decision, having learned of the success of the GOYAs' southern France drop, but not many. One was Morgan. After his clash with Rupert Graves and his departure from the unit, Morgan pursued his goal of being a pilot. But on the eve of D-Day, he was told that new pilots weren't needed. Stung, Morgan was sent back to the infantry, the 106th Division at Camp Atterbury, Indiana. By August, observing more than a hundred men with eyes lost in battle in the Pacific as part of his unit's "new" replacements, Morgan thought, "This outfit isn't going anywhere" and transferred back into the paratroopers. At Benning he had to learn a newfangled way to tumble called the "PLF" (parachute landing fall), which had the jumper collapse on one side, from thigh to hip to shoulder. The conversion from the simple backward or forward roll caused many shoulder breaks, and Morgan took one. In a sling at Benning, he caught word of Dragoon and the 551st's liberation of Draguignan, Cannes, and Nice.

What was the significance of Operation Dragoon, and what were its costs? Overlord bogged down for two months at Normandy and Falaise, whereas within two weeks of its first landing on August 15 Dragoon had achieved its main objectives, the liberation of Nice, Toulon, and Marseilles. That occurred in less than half the time allotted for the mission. By September 9, 1944, the entire Côte d'Azur was in Allied hands. On September 12, near Dijon (about 140 miles southeast of Paris) the Dragoon and Overlord forces merged in a historic conjunction. General Eisenhower concluded that "there was no development of that period which added more decisively to our advantage or aided us more in accomplishing the final and complete defeat of German forces than did this attack coming up the Rhône Valley"[23] from the Riviera.

Little did Eisenhower know how critical his firmness about Anvil/Dragoon was. Beyond its effectiveness in France, six months later independent paratroop units formerly jumbled together in the 1st Airborne Task Force were to be crucial in stopping the unexpected German final counteroffensive known as the Battle of the Bulge.

Dragoon was not cost-free, however. At Toulon alone, 2,700 French soldiers were killed or wounded. The 1st Airborne Task Force itself suffered one-third casualties, dead, wounded, or missing—three thousand men. Comparisons with the Normandy invasion are inevitable, and probably they are to be blamed for the unfair characterization of Dragoon, whose initial 150,000-man invasion force was one-sixth the size of Overlord's, as the "Champagne campaign"[24] (though that force would double to 300,000 in the six weeks before the Riviera landing beaches were shut down). There was no Omaha Beach catastrophe on the Riviera, and that must be partly due to the very fact of Normandy, which absorbed so much of the Germans' attention that summer of 1944.

The relatively light casualties on Utah Beach at Normandy were partly due to tightly packed paratrooper action behind it; that lesson was not lost for Dragoon. There were, of course, mini-Omaha Beaches for the glidermen at La Motte and the 551st at Hill 105 at Cannes. As for the 551st, the battalion sustained 21 percent casualties in its baptism by fire in southern France: 30 dead and 150 wounded.

Among the dead was Roland Barhyte's old friend from the beginning, Jim Demming. Fulfilling his promise to Demming (a promise he, Demming, and Bill Amann had exchanged from training days at Mackall), he visited Demming's mother in Rochester, New York, in the spring of 1946. There he listened transfixed as Demming's mother played some of her son's original piano music for the grim messenger. Demming is buried at the U.S. Rhône Cemetery in Draguignan.

For a time that early September 1944, Wood Joerg set up shop in the Hotel Negresco in Nice. One of the world's great hotels overlooking the beach of azure water and smooth rocks, the Negresco was founded in 1913 by Henri Negresco of Romania. World War I broke out a year later, and the Negresco was turned into an army hospital. Hemingway and Fitzgerald drank at the Negresco's bar in the 1920s. Everyone from Churchill to actor Marlon Brando would spend a night there. But that fall the GOYAs were among its guests. Though lobster and filet mignon awaited them, several men insisted that their K-rations be served up warm to mark the first meal. And so, in tuxedos and bow ties waiters surrounded the tables with silver platters, plucking the covers up to reveal eggs and bacon, not to mention the pressed ham known as Spam, hot and delicately seasoned. Don Garrigues was not as lucky; his first big meal was "10-in-1" field rations outside La Turbie, eaten cold. (Also called "jungle rations," 10-in-1 rations contained a variety of mediocre food to last ten days for one man, or one day for ten men.) "We were hungry enough to eat the cold raw bacon, grease and all, but we had some choice comments about the supply services, who should have brought the K- or D-type rations," Garrigues wrote. (D or C rations were the "gourmet" of the lot, sometimes containing a reasonable stew.)

As they feasted, some sported what was known as a "K-ration Purple Heart," scars from former battles with the sharp-edged tins.

One of those high-class diners at the Negresco was my father. The K-ration feast at Europe's finest was one of the only two stories he offered about his war years. I'm sure he savored each forkful. He had been forged by the Depression, as had his generation, and he knew how to make a forkful last. Add in his case the lessons of a peddler mother orphaned on the streets of New York at the turn of the century. "Thank you, Father, for the food, bread, and roof over our head" was her mealtime prayer. My father liked creature comforts. He enjoyed his Harley Davidson, his leather jackets, and his Jaguar X-KE before he lost them. But when I think of him toasting with his canteen at the Negresco in 1944, I cannot help but conjure up another image of him many years later, in 1980—welcoming me in a closet-sized room at a run-down New York hotel, the only one he could afford as the years had turned lean. When I closed the door, the lid to a broken air-conditioner popped off. He laughed and gestured grandly out the grate-covered, sooty window to the grand view of a brick wall. It was not the Negresco.

VI

HOLDING THE CRAGS

Ski Patrol in the Maritime Alps

... the front, where other attitudes
Of death were waiting. He assumed them all,
One by one, in his imagination,
In order to prevent them.

—Louis Simpson, "The Runner"

1
Shellings on the border

On September 4, 1944, elements of the 551st moved 25 miles north from the Côte d'Azur to the foothill town of Puget-Theniers, hugging the Var River; three days later the battalion's rear assembly area was established in Villars, also along the Var, whose dry riverbed had been filled with boulders by the Germans to break up American gliders.

Wood Joerg finally relaxed enough to write Robert, his Navy commander brother, on September 6: "Dear Barnacle Bill: Greetings from Southern France. I leapt here on 'D'-Day August 15 via aeroplane. Didn't bust anything and am still in the pink." He assured Robert that he felt very kindly toward the Navy for silencing the German artillery, which had "really pounded us," probably referring to Hill 105 outside Cannes. He guessed that the war "ought to be over in a month, then we will get those yellow citizens," which seems to place American COs in the Joerg gunsights, if not the Japanese. Wood longed for a reunion at their childhood summer home in New Smyrna Beach, Florida. He signed off with typical wryness, "Your wonderful brother."

On September 8, Italy officially surrendered to the Allies; that same day Hitler ordered Operation Axis, the forcible seizure of an Italy once his partner in fascism. The 551st was rubbing close to the Italian border.

That September 8, Joe Cicchinelli lamented in a letter to his new wife, "Your ring darling is all broken up. I dug so damn many foxholes and the work I do is very hard on a girl's ring. All I have left to your ring is the face of it. . . . I haven't written in such a long time that I feel nervous and funny with a pen in my hands."

For a few days the GOYAs cleaned their guns of the Riviera's sand and heat, shaved, and tipped a little brandy into their canteens. Above them loomed the Maritime Alps, the abrupt climb of land that separates northern Italy from the beach umbrellas of southern France. It also separated the German forces retreating east from the Allies, a snowy, thick wall protecting the German underbelly of Bavaria. And the Nazis wanted their high southwestern border held.

As the GOYAs looked up, rubbing oil into their gun barrels at night, the peaks at the France–Italy border seemed to reach down with drafts and blow out their kerosene lamps. A clasp of cold air began to tug at this strange, separate battalion, and pull it into folds of ravines.

It was the fate of a battalion already apart from the mass of the Airborne as an independent unit, not to mention from the Army itself (which was racing northward), to be fissured for three months in the autumn of 1944. By September 10, the battalion's four companies had trucked 10,000 feet up into the Maritimes, and then each went its own way, spiraling upward to small alpine villages: B Company and the Battalion Command Post to Saint Martin-Vesubie; Headquarters Company to Saint-Martin and nearby Saint-Sauveur; A Company to the third village up the climb, tiny Isola (the very name meaning "isolated" in Italian); and C Company to the highest perch, Saint-Etienne-de-Tinée. The front stretched 35 miles, a bit more than the mile and a half a battalion is ordained to protect by the Army Manual, 35 miles of high alp, deep gorge, and knee-high snow. If only the GOYAs had been trained in Alaska instead of Panama.

The mission was to protect the right flank and rear of the Seventh Army as it churned northward from the Dragoon landing beaches of southern France to link up with the Normandy invasion forces now sweeping east through and around Paris. To prevent a counterattack from the Maritimes, the 551st had joined its brother and sister units, the 509th PIB and the 550th glidermen, to form the 509th Task Force. But the Seventh Army's progress north was so steady that the the separate parachute and glider units were left

Dispositions
in the French
Maritime Alps
Sept-Nov 1944

0 _____ 20
kilometers

© Durfée 1996

in a solitude that essentially changed their goal. For three months they played a nerve-racking game of cat-and-mouse with a crack Austrian ski battalion the Germans had left to guard the snowy wall. The mission had mutated from defense into a kind of perilous, almost fruitless, offense.

It turned out to be a bloody, exhausting stalemate. The Germans shelled the American positions from a high ridge nearly every day, and the GOYAs below returned their fire with mortars before scurrying into basements. The ritual began right at the start. Just as Charles Fairlamb was selecting the church steeple in Saint-Sauveur as the only reasonable spot for an observation command post, the steeple was knocked off by an artillery shell.

Daily patrols went out from the four GOYA-held villages up the precipices, probing, catching some Austrians off guard, rousing others to battle, causing still others to disappear. At night the Austrians would infiltrate into the valleys, lay mines, and steal supplies. Daylight was American time; the night was German.

One night that first month in the Alps Private Charlie Tatro of A Company made the mistake, coming back from a mountain patrol, of answering a GOYA outpost's halt order in German. It was a joke that cost him his life.

Through September the men watched the linden trees shed into the gorge of the Var River, their leaves falling on the rolled boulders, falling past the Wehrmacht's pillboxes in the rock of the mountain road, and laying a slippery carpet for the anxious, weaving motorcycle messengers of the 551st, who tried to keep the far-flung battalion together.

The French villagers in those Alpine enclaves did everything they could to express to the GOYAs their gratitude that finally, after five hard years of occupation, they were free. They harbored many men in their basements, welcomed them for meals in their kitchens, poured them liquor in the small bars, and shared that precious commodity in the wintry mountains, firewood. The Free French forces also participated in the combat as scouts and trench-digging, wire-cutting sappers, who hoisted rifles alongside the Americans where they could. Then there was the dicey matter of collaborators. One grim day in Saint Martin-Vesubie Ed Henriquez saw women who had helped the Germans shaved by the Resistance till they were bald.

Another day in September, Lieutenant Leroy Sano of C Company entered the town of Saint-Dalmas up the road from Saint-Etienne. He and his troops were met by a small deputation of the CDL, or French Liberation Committee. A little ceremony ensued, with a trumpet rushed into service and several clumps of roses clipped and wrapped. The CDL's special delegate, Louis Ferrier, minced no words in his stirring speech: "The barbarous Teuton, I repeat, launched a cowardly attack on us, gagged us, overpowered us, and reduced us to slavery."[1] Men found themselves taking off their helmets, even blushing in the brisk fall breeze, when Ferrier proclaimed, "We are so indebted to you, and so thankful! Mothers will praise you forever. . . . You make it difficult for us to tell an officer from a private."

C Company's Max Bryan rubbed his arched PFC chevron; he definitely knew the difference between his lowly rank and that of Lieutenant Sano! Finally, dry at the mouth, Ferrier presented a bouquet of Niçoise flowers to Sano and lifted a sapling to plant, "a tree of freedom and victory."

But victory was far from complete, of course, as the shelling from the high ridge at Saint-Etienne the next day proved. While trucking supplies up from Nice, Bryan spent much of his time on trips up the winding road in the Maritimes dodging fire from German pillboxes. Some trucks, chiefly those with the precious cargo of letters from home, never stopped to present a stationary target. "The trucks came through Isola as though it were a race track," Chuck Fairlamb wrote. "They threw the sacks off on the run. The only trucks to stop were the ration trucks and the pass [leave] trucks. After one trip on the pass truck, no one wanted a second. The shelling was too heavy and too accurate on the lower bridge."

No, the war was far from over. On September 26, Allied troops trapped at Arnhem in Holland surrendered to Germany, the result of the disastrous "bridge too far" airborne drop, Operation Market Garden, which failed to secure the northern levees and estuaries. The Nazis continued their genocidal policies unabated. On September 16 they even overruled Mussolini, who had not deported or killed Jews, by sending the first twenty-four Jews from the northern Italian town of Merano straight to Auschwitz, including a child of six. They were all gassed.

That same fateful day, a stoop-shouldered, jaundiced fifty-four-year-old Adolf Hitler, his right ear still ringing from its puncture during the July bomb attack, his right arm vibrating uncontrollably, gathered his general staff to his study at the *Wolfschanze,* or Wolf's Lair, in the East Prussian town of Rastenburg.[2] Though he had suffered what appeared to be a third minor heart attack in a week that morning, he had his own bomb to drop.

In his huge, steel-buttressed concrete bunker underground, in the heavy air with no view of the outside world, Hitler listened to the head of the operations staff of the *Oberkommando der Wehrmacht* (OKW, Armed Forces High Command), General Alfred Jodl, give a dreary status report on the crumbling Western Front. In the three months since the Normandy invasion, Germany had sustained a million casualties, half in the West. The withdrawal from southern France was continuing apace, and in northeastern France the Wehrmacht was attempting to form a new line of defense by using old forts of Franco-Prussian war vintage from the nineteenth century. In the north in Holland new lines of defense were being formed along canals and rivers, and troops were falling back to the eastern Belgian border, "the West Wall." Jodl was particularly worried about a heavily wooded section of east Belgium that was porous, the poorly guarded area known as the Ardennes forest.

Hearing "Ardennes," the Fuhrer sat bolt upright, his steel blue eyes widening as if alerted by some distant call. None of the generals had seen him so excited since the attempt on his life on July 20. "I have made a monumentous decision," he proclaimed, smacking his hand down on the map over the green area of the Ardennes. "I shall go over to the offensive, that is to say, here." He lifted his hand, revealing a forest devoid of anyone but lumbermen, small farmers, and a few American forces. "Out of the Ardennes, with the objective, Antwerp!"[3]

Jodl and the gathered generals of the High Command were stunned. It was an extraordinarily perilous idea, especially for November, Hitler's original choice of month to launch the attack, with the onset of winter. Tanks could barely move through the snakelike roads and labyrinthine forest, and Allied bombing runs over the Ruhr Valley and Romania were depleting gasoline supplies daily. Thus was the die cast for the Western European front's climactic clash—the Battle of the Bulge—while the 551st was breathing the rarified air of the Alps 500 miles south with hope that it just might be home for Christmas.

The first snow fell in the Maritimes in late September, slicking the steep roads with ice at night, with the morning sunlight melting freshets down the cliffs. In three days the thermometer dropped toward zero, and the freshets disappeared. Everything hardened but the blood of the men, so recently arrived from warmth on the Riviera. On September 23 Charles Fairlamb observed in his journal, "Every day patrols go up the valley and just about every day they are ambushed." To rid themselves of the menace above, Fairlamb's mortar platoon hiked 15 miles, taking out the Germans from the rim. By nightfall, all were relieved but Fairlamb and a few others, who stayed on as forward observers. A deep chill was his chief companion. He lay on the snow with no coverlet, overcoat, or fire. A cold rain punished his face and filled his boots. Nearby stone huts could offer no relief: They were booby-trapped.

Inching higher the next day, two men were injured by booby-traps. In early October Lieutenant Colonel Joerg received other ominous news. He sent his driver and "Rose of San Antone" jeep with two other men, including an officer, down the mountain toward Nice for supplies. Barreling around the chancey curves, the jeep hit a mine hidden in a woodpile, exploded, and careened off the road. The driver, Sergeant Arthur Beauchaine, was killed, and the two others were seriously injured. Joerg went down in another jeep to inspect the wreckage. The vehicle was on its side, its wheels riding the air and wheel wells blackened by gasoline fire, blood on the seat already dark and veiled with frost. The commander stood in the cold, shaken.

T/5 Otto Schultz of St. Albans, West Virginia, said his most fearful moments of the war came when he took over as Joerg's driver just after that incident. Approaching a favorite target of the Germans, a bridge just out of Saint-Martin-Vesubie, he'd feather the brakes or even stop in the shadows before barreling across. Coming back up the hill with Joerg one day, Schultz was really gunning it.

"You're sure gettin' hungry," Joerg shouted.

"Yes, sir, I am," Schultz returned.

Joerg's knuckles turned white gripping the window frame. "Can't you take a hint and slow this thing down?" he yelled again.

On October 5, 1944, a howling blizzard blanketed the entire area of the Alps on the France–Italy border. Snow fell on the helmets, muzzles, mustaches of the 551st from Saint-Martin-Vesubie to Saint-Etienne. It fell into the cross-country ski paths cut in the rocky slopes by the men, who were now called to 20-mile ski patrols, keeping soldiers of the Innsbruck-trained Austrian 4th High Mountain Assault (Höhesgebirgesjäger) Battalion (of the 5th Mountain Division) on its toes looking down from the

Italian rim. Snow fell on the dachshund Furlough, who had been reunited with the 551st after coming ashore with the landing craft on the Riviera. Combat tensed her brown coat.

On October 27 a team of men barreled out of Isola toward Saint-Etienne in a Special Services truck with a water-driven generator in tow to give the men a movie break. A cruel two-hour rain of artillery crippled the truck not 200 yards out of Isola, while the occupants bailed out to take cover in a nearby well. The truck and its tires were so shot full of holes it resembled Swiss cheese, and the radiator for the generator "looked like a sieve."[4] Fairlamb and others somehow got the truck towed back to town and even jury-rigged a water-cooling pipe for the generator with rainspouts they tore off a house and ran from a stream. But just as the movie started running around midnight, the shelling began again, and Fairlamb returned fire with mortars until 3 A.M. The only movie after that was the men's unquiet sleep.

In addition to the frequent rain of shells, drivers had to contend with increasingly cold, slick roads. No salt or cinders were spread on the ice-packed road in the Maritimes that late fall. Tires were not snow tires and didn't have studs. Having heard about a ski lift the Germans had kept running up in the village of Auron, just west of Saint-Etienne, Doc Jud Chalkley and Lieutenant Rushton Peabody jumped into the medical jeep one night and drove to the ski resort, where its owner plied them with *jambon de Bayonne* and cognac. Coming down the dark mountain road long after midnight toward Saint-Etienne, they had their headlights off so as not to draw German shelling. Peabody had to drive by what he could see in intermittent patches of moonlight. At a hairpin turn Peabody skidded and headed for a glistening that he took to be the moon on snow. Suddenly the jeep was flying over a 5-foot embankment. Moonlight had reflected off a mountain stream. The jeep plowed into a tree and crashed into the water. Peabody died instantly, his neck broken. Chalkley flew out of the passenger seat and tore his head open on a rock in the stream. "I thought I was going to die in six inches of water," he later said.

Chalkley ended up with a 105-degree temperature and septicemia in a Marseilles hospital, where a major who had known him from medical corps training injected him with penicillin before what was then a required blood analysis. That saved his life. His weight dropped 75 pounds to 125, and Chalkley was evacuated on a hospital ship to New York City. After a long recuperation, he emerged one day from Halloran General Hospital to amble the streets of New York with two other officers also on the mend. When the sound of a jackhammer startled them, they dropped to the pavement shaking—"hit the dirt" as he would later say, "to the amazement of the passers-by."

Carrying his messages on motorcycle, my father stopped to view the wrecked jeep and the dead Peabody. It disturbed him greatly, because he had liked Peabody, had found him to be a perfectionist in their daily workings at his newly assigned Headquarters Company, someone who, like my father, would explain something point by point to instruct an initiate. What really bothered him to speechless tears was the absurdity of it: a man dying in war because he was intoxicated.

My father and Sergeant Don Thompson of A Company leaned against a fir as the limp Peabody was hoisted onto a truck. Father wondered how you'd ever keep composure when telling a dead man's family what had happened. They spoke about why they were where they were. "So that Hitler won't set up shop in Cleveland," Thompson said, and Dad agreed.

"Country gentleman," my father said to the Minnesota-born Thompson, "you keep me in your prayers. I'll keep you in mine."

2
My father the messenger

I date my father's lifelong love affair with the motorcycle to the Alps period. He and Tony Isolli, HQ Company's other messenger, served as Wood Joerg's lifeline to isolated units. The message center chief, Sergeant Paul Kjar of Lexington, Nebraska, remembered my father and the zany runs: "I would send Tony or Orf up the highway with letters or combat and patrol orders, and the Germans had them zeroed in with artillery. We'd watch 'em go and the shells landing near them. It was hair-raising and dangerous. Neither got hit; they were too crazy to get hit."

Don Thompson, who had once been in the Army motorcycle corps before it was disbanded and who would jaw with my father about cycles, said, "He wore that motorcycle like a glove."

The only photograph of my father overseas during the war shows him in the saddle of the cycle, "551" painted on the gas tank, his dun wool Army cap with paratrooper patch cocked slightly to one side. His eyes and high cheekbones are without the basic training glee of a photo at Fort Lewis, Washington. Now he is intent, the hoods of his eyes darker than a year before. Above a chastened smile are the wings of a trim black mustache that he will carry into civilian life and never cut, will only let thicken to the brush of a landed animal. Now, hands clamped on the handlebars of his wartime motorcycle, pantleg creased in the saddle, he is poised to let the clutch out. *Sans* helmet, this may be a pose; the saddlebags look full. Behind him is a wall that sports the sign *"Les Cartes."* The best guess of his best buddy, the message center deputy Chuck Bernard, is that the scene is Saint-Martin-Vesubie in the Maritimes; he may have stopped to buy postcards.

During the war he was an incessant letter writer. One day in 1994 I discovered in the family home in Los Angeles an old foot locker in the garage that my mother had never opened. In it, protecting his uniform with its jump wings, was an incredible find—at least a hundred war letters he had written to various family members or had received. Incredible, because my father wrote very few letters in the forty years after the war. The war had leached more personal letters out of him in one traumatic year-and-a-half than he would write for the rest of his life. Clearly, it was a time of great loneliness and craving for connection. I cradled these browned envelopes from fifty years back with wonder. Some were V-Mail, cut in shreds to take out restricted information. Others were written on stationery or notepad. His first letter after the air drop over southern France in Dragoon appears to have been written on October 6, 1944, on American Red Cross stationery, with the address only "Somewhere in France." That would have been the Maritime Alps, and it would have been written in the howling snowstorm that had begun the day before. It was written to Nazera, his mother, and it begins: "Dearest Mother, I received six letters from home yesterday, one from you, two from Jen, two from Babe, and one from Vinny. Boy! Six letters at one time. It sure boosted my morale a great deal. I am in good health and high spirit. I was certainly relieved to hear that George arrived safely in India."

As I read this letter in a trance, a turquoise-and-purple bill fell out of it. It was *cinquante francs* with several signatures, many blurred, scrawled on both sides. Dad explains: "Enclosed you will find 50 F. We had to change our Italian lires for francs. This is one that I had the fellows sign before we took off. With all the equipment that I had on, I sweated quite a bit and the ink ran on the bill. This is what they call 'invasion money.' Please save it, Mother. It will always be something that I can remember my buddies by."

I held the turquoise-purple bill, half-soaked with my father's sweat from fifty years ago, and my own hands moistened. Here in a 2-by-6-inch piece of old paper was definite evidence of something that had eluded me to date: the people with whom my father jumped into combat during Operation Dragoon. He had carried this message of comradeship into the Maritime Alps and for some reason—was it the steep mountain roads and the pot shots from German pillboxes he dodged on the ice?—he felt it was time to send it home, to preserve it from danger.

Not once did my father pull the talisman bill out to show me or anyone, including my mother. I wonder if he ever saw it himself after the war, or wanted to. It may very well have sat untouched in the locker for half a century. Never did he hint at the existence, much less the content, of war letters, though he told my mother he wished they'd met before the war, as he missed having a sweetheart correspondent.

I slowly inspected the signatures scrawled on the front of the 50-franc note and on the back circling the red, white, and blue French flag, itself circled by the printed words *liberté, egalité, fraternité*. Many were too blurred by their messenger's sweat to read, but some were still legible: Tracy Sweat, A. Colaluca (nicknamed "Coca Cola"), Red Pyle, Willie Polson, Dan Hawley, Sergeant Charles Brubaker (later killed at the Bulge), Bill Dennis, Jack Sullivan, "Mike" Pierson (also killed at the Bulge), Edgar Harner, Robert West, J. W. Guffey, Sergeant Claude Farrar.

Only three names, however, did I recognize as survivors that I had come to know in the 551st veterans' association, all sergeants: Bill Hatcher, Frank Fiermonte, and Emory Albritton, the man who had fished the last dead men out of the water during the tragic night jump at Camp Mackall.

"Al" Albritton had once called out, in a gushing moment, when I mentioned my father's name, "What a swell guy!" And I had taken it, as I had a couple of other survivors' comments as well-intended but inauthentic. I figured they all had just wanted to make me comfortable with them and make themselves comfortable, too.[5]

Shortly after emerging from a hospital where he had had a lung and gall bladder removed for cancer, Emory confirmed, "That was invasion money, indeed." It was part of an "escape kit," which included French francs and a map made of silk like their parachutes, so that its ink would not run in the rain or wear off, and the map would not easily tear.

Emory confirmed something more: All the men on the bill were from Company B of the 551st, and on and off my father was detailed to HQ Company from Company B. For a while in the Maritimes, Aref was part of Albritton's own squad of a heavy weapons platoon. "Your dad manned a machine gun, Greg," Emory wheezed.

Though that later checked out in military records, at the time I was startled and skeptical. I asked him why he hadn't told me that before in the five years since I'd met him.

Emory was silent. I listened to him gather breath. "Didn't I?" he asked. "Well, I guess I always held back. Seeing you was too emotional for me, perhaps. But yes, he was a darn good soldier. He wore a crew cut, with black hair. We called him 'Orf.'"

Emory went on to say that the heavy weapons platoon may have been "the first and only one in the cotton-pickin' airborne." Captain Jim Evans had instructed Albritton to fashion one primarily with disciplinary cases, saying "You're the only guy I know who can handle all these damn guys." Most were sergeants who had been busted down to private. Al Albritton named some— Ted Bass, Gene Cherry, Scherzol Heater, Weiser Bates. So my father, a private from start to finish, was yanked into an outsider platoon in an outsider battalion, still more reason for a lifelong affinity with those on the edge.

A machine gunner. It fitted; uncomfortable though it may have been for him. He rode a machine to take messages. In civilian life he ran sizable machines at Cleveland Tractor and later used them in his garment factory, machines with blades like the electric cutter he used to cut cloth. He was not a big man, not the beefy type one might associate with such death-dealing weapons. Nevertheless, he was strong. Albritton had seen that, or he wouldn't have chosen him. Did he jump out of the plane with enough abandon to catch Al's eye? Or was it his willingness to be a target on the Alpine roads? In any case, a machine gun is more deadly than a rifle, and draws more hostile attention.

At the end of my father's October 6 letter he mentions, "I went to Holy Communion yesterday for the first time since the invasion. The reason that I didn't receive more often was due to the fact that we have no Catholic chaplain." Next came a switch to the secular: "I certainly am kept well-supplied with gum, thanks to all of you. I guess I chew more gum than anyone in the outfit."

Communion or gum. In another letter from about the same period, my father told his sister Jeannette he had served Mass as well, probably in St. Anne's chapel at Isola. If so, he would have looked up to pray before a statue of the Blessed Virgin ringed with a large rosary plucked by Joe Ci-cchinelli from a shrine blasted by shelling. The wooden rosary was still there on the Isola Madonna in 1989. There, in prayer in 1944, the scout of the 551st and its messenger fixed their hopes and fears in the dead language that they knew by heart, Latin. *Introibo ad altare Dei* [I will go to the altar of God], says the priest, and the altar boy responds, *Ad Deum qui laetificat juventutum meum* [to God the joy of my youth]. I am glad like my father I was an altar boy before the Latin Mass was abandoned. When my children are sick, I sing them to sleep with *Tantum Ergo* or *O Salutaris Hostia*, because my mother did to me, and it seems to work. Never short-change the rhythms of a dead language.

As for Chick and Orf, the candles they snuffed were fitted in shell casings.

If my father had chiefly to fear being picked off along the road by snipers, many of the 551st out on patrol in the mountains feared plain falling. Many, shot over a precipice, toppled and disappeared. The Maritimes were as fissured as the 551st itself. One who never came out of a crevasse was the well-loved, warmly rebellious keeper of their mascot Furlough, Joe Edgerly.

An orphan who had escaped the streets of Boston to move out west before he hit teen years, Edgerly was the point scout of a nineteen-man C Company patrol led by Lieutenant Richard Hallock, which left Saint-Etienne at 4 A.M. on November 4 in darkness to climb the cold mountain north of Molliers in search of Austrians. The group followed a steep frozen stream uphill all morning in two and a half feet of snow, resting when an exhausted PFC Ellery Sweat swapped his heavy Browning Automatic Rifle (BAR) for Private Joe Rowe's M-1. Leaving a radio team behind, they hiked on. Before a rock ridge, Private Dave Munoz had just gotten the words *Niente Tedeschi* ("Germans none," in Italian) out of his mouth when two machine guns opened fire ahead, and 20mm shells started screaming in. It was an ambush. Edgerly was hit and fell into a crevasse, where he was found frozen the next day, legend says, with Furlough at his side. The dog had stayed with his body until they were able to come back up there and pick it up the next day.[6]

Though most of the patrol managed to take cover behind a boulder and then, coming under more fire, escape below a rim by snow slide, their safe retreat was made possible in large part by the withering fire of Privates Carter, Chappell, and Rowe, who refused to get back and covered the men's withdrawal. Those who made it to safety listened to Rowe's BAR resound until he, along with Chappell, was silenced. Carter somehow managed to get out alive.

Rowe's and John Chappell's ultimate sacrifice went undecorated: Joerg's parsimony with medals. Their bodies, picked clean to the bone, were found ten months later, when the war was over. One of them was buried as X-160 until, years later, a laundry mark on exhumation gave Chappell away.

Edgerly had been considered an unstoppable stunt man;[7] his death was deeply mourned. Afterward his squad leader, Jim Guerrant, took extra protection, stringing a wire at night with grenades as a booby trap just beyond the patrol's observation posts. One night they exploded and the men woke up, thrashing for their weapons. When they ran to the wires, all that greeted them were two bloody cows. They turned into steaks. Another time the grenades tripped and Guerrant's men opened fire, only to find they had riddled a vagrant dog. The Alps were strung with the GOYAs' nerves.

For the three months that the 551st spent in the Maritimes, however, their casualties were remarkably light, given their exposure: eleven killed and ninety wounded, along with several missing in action. Trapped in the awkward position of fighting upward from a well in the mountains, they could not always protect the civilian population. Most of the injuries in Isola were to civilians, caused by the German mortaring and shelling. One French doctor astounded the GOYAs with his insistent running through town in the midst of shelling to help the wounded. "We used to warn him to wait until the shells quit landing, but he would never listen," the medic Jack Affleck said. The day came when the brave doctor ran into a flying shell, which blew him in two.

Compassion for the children who wore tatters through the Alpine streets and for the people whose lives had been "brutally upset" by the war was a quality Don Thompson recalled in my father. One day in Isola after handing over his messages, Dad caught sight of an old woman beating laundry on rocks in the mountain stream. She had a heavy wire basket she carried deeper into the stream, and soon she was struggling. My father apparently waded out in his paratrooper boots, took hold of her wire bundle under one arm, and gave the woman his other arm to balance on, slowly walking her over stones out of the cold stream. "I could hear the water sloshing in his boots and I was freezing!" Thompson marveled. "If I could paint one picture that represented the American paratrooper in the war, I would paint that scene."

On October 15 the 551st was detached from the 509th Task Force and was once again on its own. That time of jittery isolation was when men dressed in snow-whites for ski patrol, which made them hard to see—and hard to distinguish from the Germans—in the snow, especially from the air. On October 28 Jim Guerrant yelled at his men to take cover when four American P-39s flew over shooting at them. The planes strafed the highway between Saint-Etienne and Isola, hitting one French civilian truck, and strafed a column of French troops near Clans, killing a French soldier and wounding four. The wing also rained down on the ski village of Auron.

Daily life for the 551st in the Maritimes included encounters with one of the least noted casualties of war—animals. Though there were hawks and bear, the GOYAs were too concerned with, as Harry Renick put it, "the human animals." Nevertheless, the 551st put common animals through more than common hardships. There was plenty of simple foraging for food; John Bassaline liked to cook rabbits. Others were put to more innovative use. A pack of mules once shielded Dick Durkee and his men from gunfire. Durkee had brought them to link up northwest of Saint-Etienne high up the mountain with the 550th glidermen, one of the few times the GOYAs made contact with other American troops in the Maritimes. The goal was to haul back rifles for the Free French Forces (FFI). On the way Roland Barhyte shot a deer going up a depression, and all ate well that night. It tasted tough, but at least it tasted.

On that same patrol, Durkee had taken an FFI guide with him who bragged he knew all the trails, but as it turned out the man remained mum while Durkee exhausted the machine gun and mortar carriers going straight uphill off the trail. "I finally wised up and got on the trails," Durkee said. But just over the first ridge the scout turned around and left them, calling out as he exited "There are Germans up there." The GOYAs' experience with the Free French ranged from the heroic (such as Charles Calori's actions at La Turbie) to that shrinking violet in the Maritimes.

At Barcelonnette, as far north up the spine of the Alps as the 551st got, the GOYAs toasted their sister unit of glidermen. The next day they packed the mules heavy with rifles. Durkee gave the men a choice: Take the switchback trails or chance it on the road down the valley to Saint-Etienne. The men chose the latter. As Durkee had feared, they became targets. Durkee used the donkeys as a screen, wincing as they brayed from lacerations of "incoming mail" shrapnel. "We must have run a mile and a half with German artillery landing all around us," he recalled.

On other occasions, the GOYAs saw a gruesome reversal—animals eating men. On a patrol for firewood, HQ Company's Erwin Koerth and Sergeant Bill Dean had heard about a particularly strange-looking German corpse in the forest. After loading their truck with wood, they found it—not much more than a skull and hands. Said Dean, "While we were standing there looking at him, a German shepherd came out of the woods and I figured it was a German patrol coming. Buddy, I mean we really made tracks out of there. We hit that truck running." By the sound of it, the truck turned itself on. The dog (someone called her Gretchen) was later seen feasting on the ghoulish German, whose mouth was open wide forever.

Saving someone was back-breaking work in the mountains, and Captain Tims Quinn thought one man, Lieutenant Richard Higgins, should have earned a Silver Star for hoisting Joe Palmowski over his shoulder and carrying him to safety under fire after they'd all walked into an ambush on the sloping crags. Palmowski had been hit with a .50-caliber slug in the stomach, and that he survived that typically lethal wound at all is somewhat miraculous. According to Quinn, Palmowski wasn't the most exciting person to save. In a word, he was a "free-thinker," in those days tantamount to a Communist. "He would bellyache about everything and I would just let him talk," Quinn said. "I'd say, 'That's what you feel' and he'd say, 'That's exactly what I feel—everything is a waste of time!'" Everything but the body Higgins saved.

The GOYAs would take hundreds of German prisoners at the Bulge, but few were taken in the Maritimes (an October intelligence summary logs only three prisoners for the entire month). Jack Affleck was on a HQ Company patrol, a bone-breaking steep climb for five hours up around a particularly lethal German pillbox, from which the Germans emerged unsuspecting at dawn the next day, stretching and washing up, only to be completely riddled by GOYA bullets. None of them was pulled down into the village of Isola, to which Affleck and his fellows lowered themselves by rope. Though Joe Cicchinelli remembers repeated rumors of orders to take no prisoners, it appears more likely that the Germans who were hit were too high up to collect, or those that weren't were too much of a burden to haul down the mountain.

An almost gentlemanly custom evolved. Chuck Fairlamb wrote: "The Germans would take care of their own wounded, so when we pulled back we would leave them." This was a far cry from what would prevail with prisoners of both sides at the Battle of the Bulge.

The only press mention of the 551st during World War II combat dealt with the battalion's risky autumn mission in the Maritimes. In a November 20, 1944, article in the *Stars and Stripes* headed, "Only the Tall Mountains Know the Mystery of the Alps," George Dorsey waxed poetic about a battalion (unnamed for security reasons) "who know the machete better than the ski." He wrote about one GOYA who walked four hours over 6 miles to B Company "with a bullet in his liver."

Three outsize *Stars and Stripes* photos of the GOYAs on ski patrol portray a typically idealized portrait of the American infantryman. On the left a photo of soldiers in a truck shows no mines in the path or tires shot out. On the right a photo shows an "ever-present" medic, Private Frank Ryan, confidently shouldering his skis while flexing his biceps, the red cross on his helmet gleaming in the sunlight. (Ryan was later killed in combat.) The center photo is a perfect example of "flak" of another sort than anti-aircraft. A Company's clean-shaven Lieutenant Buff Chisholm and B Company's Sergeant George Reeves are outfitted like something out of Currier & Ives: white parkas with snow-flecked hood fringes, skis clasped with bare hands, gun holsters, binoculars hung from their necks, ammunition belts smartly buckled, and the two staring with determination into the sun.

In fact, the period of the Maritime Alps found most of the GOYAs' apparel, not to mention appearance, falling apart. Jim Stevens of A Company told the threadbare truth. After eighty-five days without a bath, "Our boots were all worn out and the seams of our pants were rotted." Stevens recalled the time an officer who had jeeped up from the Inspector General headquartered in Nice chewed Joerg out "because we looked so damn raggedy. He just couldn't understand why we weren't all fresh-shaved and so on." The men "kind of suffered because we just had our jump suits and they were thin." Even when the white jackets arrived, they were more like ponchos than actual lined parkas, and Stevens indicated that they were used only on patrols, though not ones when enemy fire was anticipated, because "you couldn't get shot in those because they had to be brought back undamaged for the next patrol." Currier & Ives it was not.

On patrols radios were the only lifeline, other than the messengers, to keep together the diaspora of the 551st. For all their weight, which my father once compared with several dozen sample dresses swung over two shoulders, the radio sets didn't work too well. According to the 551st's communications officer, Andy Titko: "The ruggedness of the terrain presented problems to our radio communications, especially to our SCR-300s, whose transmission capabilities were limited to 'line of sight.' This necessitated radio relays even though the patrols were only a mile away as the crow flies. Because of the great distances between companies, wire communications were limited, so the then-existing French telephone system was used whenever possible." Bobby MeHaffey was blown off a telephone pole by the concussion of a near miss. All that added to the existing isolation of the GOYAs, stuck like a colloidal suspension in the whiteness. Enduring the extreme hot presence of the living and the crawling in Panama, now they had to endure the absence of anything warm. Like some strange molten metal shaped by the South—Panama, Italy, southern France—the 551st was now finding its heart cooling, its form fixed in place by the North.

For the A Company radioman Sergeant Harry Renick, the Maritimes meant two things: a foot patrol of five men that never came back, and searing heat in cold that took his breath away. He was standing in the front office of a municipal building in Isola warming himself by the stove along with a companion, when several 4.2 mortar shells crashed into a stairwell just outside his window, blowing out the window and shutters and splattering the wall in back of Harry with shrapnel. "I felt the heat on my neck and boot tops," Renick recalled in his droll way, touching both entities. "I was in shock. I heard a voice on the radio and I thought it was St. Peter talking to me.

"There was a tin cup on the counter full of holes, and the stove was full of holes, and the back wall had holes in it three or four inches in diameter."

Harry hadn't suffered a pinprick.

"The guys out in the hall thought we were both dead. When I finally was able to make contact on the phone, I could hear them, but they couldn't hear me. And when I walked out of there after the dust had settled, the guys said we looked like two ghosts."

3
Cards and nerves

In Saint-Martin-Vesubie, a late night card game is in progress at the Command Post hotel, toward which Wood Joerg is headed down the cold cobbles. It is quiet; no shelling tonight. Suddenly he runs into Corporal Clell Whitener, lurching around a corner toward the hotel bar, the only one in town that hasn't been abandoned because of the shelling.

"You going in for a drink?

"Yessir."

"Well, that's rough stuff they serve in there. That cognac will eat the varnish off the table."

Whitener smiles and salutes his commander. He goes in, orders a co-gnac, and pours a drink, then a shell crashes and he spills it. Sure enough, when the nervous barkeep wipes it off an hour later, there's a white spot down to the raw wood.

Meanwhile Joerg has joined the card game. Lieutenant Ralph Wen-thold, newly promoted from sergeant (by General Frederick of the 1st Air-borne Task Force), his meaty face flush red with drink, is about to have the first and only conversation he will ever have with the 551st commander, who is slowly and tightly fanning his three draw cards for jacks-or-better. He zips them with his thumb—a quick, frustrated crack. His forehead rolls a carpet. Joerg does not have a poker face, but he bets two francs any-way, since he's the leader. Wenthold, on the other hand, scratches his red hair quizzically, disguising his luck.

"See your four bits and raise you a buck." He throws down a ten-franc note, holding his cards to his barrel chest.

Pappy Herrmann's wide lips stretch to one side in disbelief. "Wenthold, don't go getting sassy just because you're an officer now."

"Oh, big shot!" mumbles Ed Hartman, raising his thick black eyebrows.

Everyone stays in. What's there to fold for? And Wenthold uncorks his cards on the table, a fan of a full house—aces over sixes. He slowly sweeps up the pot with thick, pink, light-haired hands

"Lieutenant," Joerg drawls, staring at him in consternation. "There's one thing you have got to know—you don't win money from the colonel."[8]

Bad luck at cards or not, since combat Joerg had been making progress winning over recalcitrant officers (who may, after all, have been nothing so much as jealous of his charisma with the enlisted man, what Tims Quinn called "that very attractive smile").[9] A revealing letter from Colonel Joerg to his mother from the Alps in November 1944 shows the level of concern he had for the line soldier's welfare. It reports his personal break-through after a first battalionwide officers' party overseas:

> Well, I think that at last I am accepted as the Battalion Commander—a lot of my officers came up last night and told me that they wanted me to know that the officers and men were 100% behind me. They said they didn't like me in Panama but they saw the things I have been driving at were true and they appreciated my taking care of them and that I could fuss at them all I wanted to now.
>
> Boy, that was the sweetest music in my ear since I last heard you sing "Aunt Tabby." I sure did appreciate them telling me. I had a miserable time in Panama and am glad that is over now. I just hope that I can be worthy of their trust.

Joerg then mentions Operation Dragoon: "We were so fortunate, we had the lowest percentage of casualties in the entire group. It was just good luck but the boys think I was responsible for it. God was good to me on the campaign. . . . Pray for me on that. I do hope I will never let my lads down."

That card-shark night at Saint-Martin-Vesubie, Joerg rammed his chair back, took his coffee cup, and walked out into the night. He'd heard something far away getting closer. Something purring. Not a shell. A messenger on a motorcycle drumming closer.

Before I say what news that messenger brought in the dead of night that set Joerg's brain spinning, this is a fitting place to describe what the 551st did in those mountains to escape the shelling, the patrolling in magnetic crevasses, and pillboxes sniping on the road.

Besides the interminable games of cards, there were other indoor sports the GOYAs practiced while the shells fell. Mel Clark of Headquarters Company enjoyed regular chess matches with a Dr. Wuntz of Saint-Martin-Vesubie. On leave to Nice, Bill Hatcher spotted a soprano saxophone he craved but couldn't afford. Back in the Alps, he got B Company's men to donate packs of cigarettes, went back down the mountain dodging pillbox fire, sold his cigarettes on the black market, and bought the sax. From then on, Hatcher and a few other men who could wield a musical instrument (like Red Cross representative Dave De Varona) and those who could croak a tune constituted a regular 551st dance band, which played in the crammed room of an Isola schoolhouse or the Saint-Etienne municipal building as the GOYAs swing-danced with the local girls.

What movies were available were rerun until the dialog, terrible or not, was memorized. Dick Mascuch remembered "a stinkeroo" titled *What's Buzzin', Cousin?* Fairlamb and his friends risked getting shelled piping water to keep the water-cooled generator for a movie projector running. Then there was the madcap comedy of Angelo Pagliughi, whose specialty was dressing up in a Nazi uniform, hobnail boots and all, kicking in the door of a makeshift barracks, and yelling in perfect German accent, "Surrender! *Yawool!*" He tried it on Bill Dean and his fellows one late night, and everyone went wild. Unlike Charlie Tatro, Pagliughi didn't get shot.

Practical joking was a GOYA fine art; it took the edge off battle, but more often than not it ended up as a kind of ersatz battle, such as the fragging with grenades Tims Quinn experienced in Rome. One day at his châlet, Mouclay, in Saint-Martin-Vesubie, Roger Carqueville decided the way to clean a clogged chimney was to lower a chunk taken from a half-pound block of TNT with an electric cap and battery down the flue. Carqueville touched the hot wires and "Kabloom!" The whole fireplace in Captain Bill Smith's bedroom downstairs was blown out, including officer's "pinks and greens" that had been hung on a rack of deer antlers over the fireplace. But Carqueville counted the mission a success: The fire in the main living room hearth drew well after that.

One night while Joe Cicchinelli was writing home by gas lamp it exploded, singeing his hair and consuming his clothes in flame. Shaken but determined, Chick switched to candlelight.

Relations with the French grew closer in the Maritimes for the GOYAs than they had in the rush of the invasion of southern France. Many men were billeted in homes. Some befriended children, such as the nine-year-old Yvette, who took to Don Garrigues and called him "Oncle Wheez" after hearing his nickname, "Whiz." Chuck Bernard dated a teenage girl in Saint-Martin-Vesubie, though he had her mother as a chaperon. The girl was pretty, but her skin was blotched for lack of protein, because meat was scarce in the Alps during the war. After the war Bernard named his daughter after this wartime amour, Denise. Many years later he discovered that she had become a doctor, partly in response to the kindness he had shown her.

If soldiers got out of the mountains at all it was by way of the risky road 45 miles south to Nice, where there was plenty of wine, women, and the clap. Most officers came back from Nice broke, if not with a pleasure disease. Durkee had an amour there named Madame Leurogant, a member of the aristocracy who found Durkee irresistible and wrote him so many letters he finally responded to one, "KIA" (killed in action).

On a convoy of fifteen 2½-ton trucks with matériel and supplies back from Nice, Durkee found himself itching his crotch uncontrollably. Someone yelled out to a truck ahead, "Hey, we gotta stop! Durkee's got the crabs! We gotta dust him!" The whole convoy came to a screeching halt, men jumping out mimicking their stellar, hard-boiled lieutenant by pulling out their pockets on the road and itching.

If there was alluring danger in Nice and an ugly gauntlet of sniper fire to get to it, it didn't seem to stop anyone. Don Garrigues was puzzled one day when a sergeant asked for volunteers for Nice passes: "Volunteers for a pass? This sounded strange, but I didn't hesitate and in short order I was all set to take off." Snaking down the road without incident, Garrigues found Nice "bustling with activity" since the August liberation and headed straight for the USO Center. Though most nightclubs had little food and only watery soft drinks, there was plenty of dancing. One favorite spot was a club that featured an all-woman band. "They only knew one American song and they kept playing it over and over again, each time murdering it just a little more than the last," Garrigues recounted. After midnight he finally figured out what they were playing: "Flat Foot Floogie."

On the way back Garrigues turned pensive, "It was hard to imagine that this happy land we had just visited was only a few miles away from where men were still fighting and dying." Fewer miles than he knew. After he had crossed a bridge with the mountain jutting on his right and a river and valley on the left, German artillery opened up, shells exploding closer and closer ahead of his truck, hurling broken rock onto the path. Cold sweat popped out of Garrigues when one shell slid right alongside his truck. It was a merciful dud, though a very live one went off to the rear. "I don't recall I volunteered for many passes after that," Garrigues wryly noted.

When sex and friendship, dance and movies failed you, well, there was food. Always ready with his "legal tender" of cigarettes, Bill Hatcher of B Company bartered for potatoes, onions, and even chickens. With the help of a French chef, he cooked some feasts fit for a sergeant. On November 5 my father wrote home that he was taking turns with "my buddy" (Chuck Bernard? Emory Albritton?) as platoon cook in B Company and had fixed a meal that day of two chickens, cocoa, stuffing, peas, mashed potatoes, gravy, bread, butter and jam. "You know, Mom, I ought to make a swell wife for some woman," he joked. "What do you think?"

Distractions aside, after three months of being more or less pinned at the bottom of a 35-mile Alpine gorge, by November the GOYAs' nerves began seriously fraying. Intrabattalion fights flared, reminiscent of the dark days at Camp Mackall. One private who quarreled with everyone and constantly stole supplies from others was summarily discharged, thrown out of the battalion, and banished to Nice. Emory Albritton got into a fierce test of nerves with a lieutenant who accused him of cowardice for passing up a firefight on the mountain to remove his men to safety. "I told him off—I wasn't going to leave my men to die in the mountains," said Albritton. "Then he said something about taking me around back of the building and teaching me a few manners." Lieutenant Colonel Joerg got wind of the imbroglio, had Albritton sign a sheet setting forth his side of the story, and, to Emory's surprise, ordered him to drive the lieutenant into Nice and leave him there. The man had apparently been giving Joerg a pain in the neck, too.

"Grab my bag," the lieutenant ordered him in Nice.

"You grab the son-of-a-bitch yourself!" Albritton barked back. He threw the duffel out of the jeep onto the street and tore back up the mountain. "And I haven't seen him since," said Emory. The man never showed up at a GOYA reunion.

If the shelling was occasionally silent, it never stopped for long. During the first week of November Chuck Fairlamb wrote in his diary: "The shelling is beginning to tell on the men . . . if [it] keeps up much longer, I think some of the men will go crazy. There is no place to go and nothing to do but wait for them to shell us some more."

An average of twenty-five artillery rounds—mostly 150mm, many rockets with a double burst, one that penetrated a building and a second that exploded inside—fell on the GOYAs each day in October and November. On more than a few days a hundred or more rounds fell. The GOYAs fought back bravely with their mortars, jury-rigged by Buscher to mimic artillery, moving them so close to their cover that exploded casings hit their houses and the command post. To this day, the walls that line the slender streets of Isola are pockmarked with holes from fifty years ago, American and German.

And so when the messenger came to Wood Joerg that late night of his losing card game, he didn't come an hour too soon for men pressed to the breaking point. Joerg used the moon to read the unfolded piece of paper. On November 18, the 551st was to move from the Maritime Alps south to Saint-Jeannet near Antibes, from where they were to take a train to northeastern France through Rheims to Laon. At last!

Two days before the GOYAs left the high mountains, on November 16, 1944, 263 civilians—32 of them children in an orphanage—were killed by V-1 and V-2 rockets hitting Antwerp. The very next day a flying bomb hit an Antwerp convent, killing 32 nuns. While Joerg and even Eisenhower smelled a Christmas dinner stateside, Antwerp had captured Hitler's bloodshot eye.

4
To Laon

By November 18 the 551st Parachute Infantry Battalion had logged ninety-six straight days of combat duty, from their August 15 Dragoon drop at La Motte to the nerve-racking stalemate in the Maritimes. Along with the 509th, also relieved at that time, the 551st registered the longest consecutive stretch of combat by any U.S. Airborne unit of the war in Europe (the 509th had also suffered for seventy-three straight days at the Anzio beachhead).

The day before they moved south to Saint-Jeannet, the 551st conducted joint patrols with a heralded unit sent to relieve them in the Maritimes, the 100th Battalion of the most highly decorated outfit of the war, the Japanese-American 442nd Infantry Regiment (it won seven Distinguished Unit Citations). It seemed at times that the GOYAs were forever brushing up against gold with their silver, forever playing second fiddle, just shy of history, if not excised from it. In truth, what most felt was not honor but relief. "You can have it," more than one GOYA thought on turning their frustrating positions and their skis over to the Japanese-Americans.

Before coming down their mountain, the men of the 551st kissed the French girls goodbye. "Red lips are not so red/as the stained stones kissed by the English dead," wrote World War I poet and lieutenant Wilfred Owen, who would die at twenty-five leading his men over the Sambre Canal in Flanders. So, too, the GOYAs' brief romance chilled as they boarded trucks to go 30 miles south to Saint-Jeannet. The wind swirled into their open transports, closing their eyes for a last goodbye to their eleven dead left in the Maritimes.

For a little more than two weeks, the GOYAs took to pup tents in the hills above the autumnal sea at Antibes, on terraces west of the Var River. The training schedule was relaxed—some map reading, scouting, working small arms fire problems, the inevitable marches, inspections of gun barrels, triggers, and the men's very teeth. Most afternoons they would have off and stroll along the road with their buddies. Some went for a cold swim about 10 miles south in the Mediterranean.

Private Jack Leonard shared a pup tent with Tom Waller, who noticed him reading a biography of John Barrymore, *Good Night, Sweet Prince*, which took its title from Shakespeare—Horatio's farewell to the poisoned Hamlet, "Now cracks a noble heart. Good night, sweet prince, /And flights of angels sing thee to thy rest!" Perhaps Leonard himself was having trouble sleeping, wondering what angels were waiting for them all.

Mostly they drank. Bill Satterfield of Headquarters Company got a hold of a bottle of cognac, drained it, and, taking up an axe, bellowed like a bull chopping down the stakes from tent to tent before someone wrestled him to the ground and disarmed him. The next day he awoke with no memory of his rampage. The men were excited, in a slow way. Allied troops were regrouping throughout Europe, and word went around that they were indeed going to be part of the heroic drop across the Rhine that would topple Hitler. Excited, yes, but not an easy excitement. One that needed dulling.

Two days after the GOYAs arrived in Saint-Jeannet, with the Germans being rapidly driven from Alsace-Lorraine, on November 20 Hitler left his Wolf's Lair in East Prussia for the last time, to take up residence in his Berlin bunker. There he would live most of the remaining six months of his life, rarely coming up for light, and would begin to plot the final preparations for Operation *Wacht Am Rhein* (later called *Autumn Mist*). Five days later, Metz in northeastern France fell to General Patton's Third Army; that same day the Germans began dynamiting Auschwitz.

On December 6, 1944, my father wrote his mother ("my best girl") from Saint-Jeannet and enclosed a Care Package of postcards and booklets of the Vatican and Rome, as well as two photos of the jump into southern France with his initials on the back. Other than the photos, the package was his friend Chuck's, whose family lived in Strongsville, Ohio, not far from his own family in Cleveland. Both he and Chuck felt, he wrote, that it would be a swell idea if the Orfalea and Bernard families met at the latter's home on Pearal Road: "If you can't find the house, Mother, then go to the Strongsville Cafe, which is owned by Charlie's brother-in-law and sister and they will take you to his home. If you don't go and visit them, then please mail 'Chuck's' souvenirs home when you get the package. I'll be closing now." For the first time, he does not sign his traditional P.S.—"God bless my family"—but rather, "Write soon!" They must have felt something final brewing. One would trust the other to send precious mementos.

The first person I met of the 551st in Kennedy Airport in 1989 for the re-union in Europe was Chuck Bernard. He had no recall at the time of my fa-ther, though we took to each other. When I discovered this letter in the fall of 1994 and called him at his home near Cleveland, where he had just gotten over heart bypass surgery, he listened to the letter read over the phone and then wept, with a high, bitter whine. His memory was lost, but sadness was prying it back. A year later, at the GOYAs' reunion in Kansas City, he pre-sented me a photo of my father standing arm-in-arm with another GI. It is a young Chuck Bernard. Dad holds a cigarette in his free hand, Chuck loops a thumb in a pants pocket. They stand at ease alongside a pup tent, paratrooper boots shined like onyx. Behind them is a spring maple, and far back of them down a knoll is a road, and the hint of a telephone pole. It is Camp Mackall, North Carolina. They look like friends, message chief and messenger.[10]

On December 7 and 8, 1944, the 551st boarded 40-by-8-foot boxcars headed for northeast France and what they thought would be their staging area for the great drop. Stopping on the way, someone took out a football, and they threw stop-and-go passes in the light snow along the tracks, tackling each other, working off nervous energy.

Coming into a trainyard they spied a tank car loaded with barrels of wine. Someone took out his .45 pistol and laced the kegs. Men poured out of the boxcars and ran to the wine gushing from the casks, filling their hel-mets and canteens. After the bacchanal, the French train crew scurried about trying to plug the holes.

Emory Albritton's shove-off day from southern France was "the coldest night I ever spent, including the Bulge, North Carolina, and Alaska. They issued the first bedrolls the U.S. Army ever gave out and they were just a blanket with a zipper. Captain Evans, or the Colonel as the case may be, wouldn't let us build a damned fire."

But Jim Heffernan, Furlough's deliverer way back in Newport News, Virginia, would have none of that. In a boxcar filled with about thirty 5-gallon gasoline cans, Heffernan decided to start a little cooking fire with kindling he gathered along the tracks, just for a little hot coffee. Bleary-eyed, his mates gave it no thought, until someone noticed the gas can Hef-fernan had used to drench the faggots was leaking.

"Jim, don't!" someone yelled. But it was too late. The fire ignited and traveled up the leaking gas, whipping into larger flames. People ran over each other to jump out of the car as it moved—all except Ignacio Jiminez, who rolled on the floor with his blanket to snuff out the fire before the cans exploded. "I swear he saved all of our lives—some very quick think-ing," Heffernan concluded. Chuck Fairlamb, riding in the car behind, saw burning clothes flying past his boxcar door, and then a man clutching the embankment in his smoking bedroll.

As for Albritton, he was standing in the doorway of his boxcar, wondering how to get warm, when some of the twenty-five or so men in his car starting grab-assing him. Sure, he thought, that's one way to stay warm. Except he was shoved right out of the car. He stood up along the track, watched the GOYA train disappear around a bend, and threw his arms up. He slept that night in the bitter cold out in the open, hiding his sore head. After several days of walking north, dodging some Germans, he finally made it to an American supply depot and a friendly company commander, who hadn't the slightest idea where his battalion was, except that he'd heard all the airborne were concentrating in the Rheims area. Trucked to Nancy, he then hitchhiked to Rheims, bumping into a thicket of 101st Airborne troops, before finally hooking up with the 82d Airborne and his own GOYAs in Laon on his birthday, December 19. Captain Evans rasped, "Where in the hell have you been?" To this day, Emory asserts he doesn't know who booted him out of the boxcar, "but if I ever find out, even after all these years, I'm going to punch him in the nose at least once."

After the GOYA train passed through Lyon, Dijon, and Rheims, it slowed coming into the station at Laon, the end of a 400-mile trip north from the Riviera. The men crowded to the doors of their boxcars, trying to get the lay of the land. Up ahead, Don Garrigues caught sight of a figure standing "straight as a poker looking intently at each car that passed in front of him." What looked like two silver bars caromed sunlight off his uniform, and Garrigues nudged a buddy, saying the fellow looked awful young to be a captain.

"Imagine my surprise when I saw that they were actually stars," Garrigues said.

It was James Gavin, at thirty-seven the youngest major general in the U.S. Army, already a legend to airborne troops, the man who would shortly send the 551st to its doom.

Lieutenant Dick Durkee surged to the entry and saluted. He had actually been Gavin's jumpmaster at Fort Benning in 1941 and had once razzed him, "You're gonna give me some pushups for hands in the pockets, Colonel."

Gavin stood there, unmoving, eyes as blue as forever. The only thing about him that moved was his breath. Near him on the platform was Wood Joerg, seven years Gavin's junior, one of the youngest battalion commanders in the Army, fired by his nearness to Gavin; two hard, youthful flames, one with a great future, one with none.

Joerg had gone ahead of the battalion the week before with Pappy Herrmann, his S-3 operations officer, reporting into the XVIII Airborne Corps headquarters at Rheims, sparked with enthusiasm that, as Herrmann put it, "our battalion was about to become part of the 'big picture' of the U.S. Army." There, in the modest schoolhouse that was the nerve center of the

Allied command, where the Germans would sign their unconditonal surrender six months later, they were told that the 551st was to be attached to
the 82d Airborne at Laon, about 30 miles northwest, and there they
headed, putting an advance detachment to work with mops and brooms,
before reporting to Gavin.

Herrmann described their first impressions of the leader and their sense
that they had finally not only arrived in the big time, but transcended their
solitary status: "We were impressed by General Gavin's quiet manner and
sincere interest in our welfare. It was the first time we had ever had anybody of our own breed, with some rank, to help us with our problems. Back
in Panama, where we were getting jungle training and helping to defend the
Canal, we had been assigned to the Sixth Air Force, and those people had
been nice to us, but they weren't infantry, and they weren't parachute infantry by a lot."

In southern France, Herrmann said, the 1st Airborne Task Force had
been made up of separate units thrown together *ad hoc,* and it lacked espirit de corps. The Maritime Alps was isolation in the extreme. "But now
we were attached to a division that had already dropped in Normandy
and Holland," he said. "We looked forward to a busy training period that
winter and a probable airborne assault into Germany in the spring." My
own father's three-page handwritten account (called "Diary") at the Bulge
found in the old footlocker at the family home reveals that the 551st was
to begin training for a spring assault across the Rhine on December 27,
1944. They did not know they had one week.

But time seemed generous to them, with warm beds and good food in
the French West Point and cavalry garrison at Laon's Caserne Foch Nord de
Guerre. Furlough romped in and out of the barracks, sleeping around with
men from A, B, C, HQ, and Detached Service Companies, as well as the
medics. She sniffed around the hundred horse stalls laid out in a line in
back of the two multistory barracks. When some three-day passes to Paris
were raffled around December 10, Sergeants Don Garrigues, Vic Freitag,
and Roy McCraw were among the lucky winners. They set about spit-shin-
ing their shoes, shaving with new blades, and fantasizing about half-clad
women dancing in sequins that fell off.

Freitag, the HQ Company mortar platoon's supply sergeant, was one of
the first to hit the Champs Elysée. He had brought two sets of jump wings
from men in his platoon. He found a jeweler, who removed the parachute
from each set and recast them as custom-made collar insignia, instead of
the normal brass pins of crossed rifles. They were quite a novelty; when
Chuck Fairlamb wore his into Paris, groups of paratroopers gawked at
them and asked where in the hell they'd gotten them. "Oh, these are

issue," Fairlamb explained. "Haven't you got yours yet?" The commoners (i.e., anyone outside the 551st) set off to demand their own.

Most men didn't get to Paris; some made it to the hospital, and others did some makeshift parachute maneuvers. Private Joseph Viserta of C Company, at a hospital in nearby Sissonne nursing malaria caught on the onerous march across Sicily, hobbled to the window to see a bizarre sight: paratroopers of either the 517th or 551st dropping on top of the hospital. They had missed their drop zone by quite a bit, and eighteen men were injured by crashing on the hospital itself.

The afternoon of December 16, Dick Durkee took off to Rheims to fetch boxing gloves. He figured there was ample time to hold a full-scale boxing tournament, and the GOYAs didn't lack for champion pugilists. Their boxing team numbered twelve men. The 82d Airborne would be in awe.

About 10:30 P.M. that night, Private Roger Carqueville was sleeping in the Headquarters Company orderly room when Captain Jim Evans of B Company rushed inside and said, "Carque, alert the Company. We're moving out." Carqueville grabbed his pistol and cartridge belt, and the gun accidentally went off, piercing the ceiling to the second floor—a shocking reveille. No damage was done. In the morning word went around the mess hall like a brushfire about some sort of German breakthrough, no one knew just where. By evening, something started circulating about GI POWs shot in the snow.

At 7:30 P.M. on December 17, Lieutenant Dick Goins, who was Battalion Duty Officer at the time, received "a very important call from the 82nd Division Chief of Staff" to alert Lieutenant Colonel Joerg to come with all speed to Division headquarters at Sissonne. An hour later another call from Division ordered Goins to have the Battalion Supply Officer secure transportation in a hurry and a unit of fire—one load and one load only—for each weapon the battalion's men carried.

Goins hadn't a clue about what was going on. Just after midnight Joerg returned from his hurried meeting and told him to round up all company commanders at once and get them to the war room. Major Bill Holm, meanwhile, was to wake up everyone in the battalion and get them ready to move out by 10 A.M.

Don Garrigues was in a sound sleep, his arms around Marlene Dietrich, who, it was said, had just arrived to entertain the troops. She was Garrigues's own private entertainment in the smoky bar of his dream when he felt his arm slugged. He woke, rubbed his eyes, and heard a siren. He took a last look at the spotless dress uniform and polished jump boots he'd hoped to wear to Paris, tossed them in a barracks bag, put on all his combat gear—machine gun, rifle—grabbed extra ammunition boxes, and ran outside to assembly. "That was the last time I ever saw that barracks bag," he said. Garrigues would be severed from his personal belongings in the next twenty-four hours—souvenirs and photos from Africa, Sicily, Italy, and southern France, including many diary entries. He was not alone. Fewer than six men in the 551st would ever retrieve their personal belongings from Laon, and those who did would find them rifled. Garrigues would not see Paris for many years; only about a dozen GOYAs did before the alert. Tom Waller, who had pulled the first lucky ticket to Paris out of Joerg's box and had borrowed PFC Stan Kargol's OD (olive drab) trousers to impress the ladies, stuffed them back into his duffel bag. He would not retrieve them from Laon for several months and would not return them to Kargol for thirty-eight years, at which time he had to apologize: They'd shrunk 4 inches in the waist.

At 4 A.M. on December 18, Wood Joerg informed his company commanders that the battalion's destination was Bastogne, Belgium.

Belgium? Is that near the Rhine?

Suddenly, before dawn, the lights went out. Someone cracked that the Colonel forgot to pay the light bill, and the men laughed nervously. PFC Milo Huempfner, Joerg's favorite driver, walked outside and marveled that the whole of Laon was dark. A blackout.

That morning, guarding German POWs, Huempfner noticed that "they seemed real happy." While making the rounds, ordering them to swab trucks, change tires, and fill gas tanks, Huempfner noticed some of the POWs were singing. "I heard one of them say in plain English, 'Our spearhead is going to be in Antwerp, and we will retake France. You are all going to be killed.'"

Though the men were tingling, the order to Bastogne was later rescinded. "We would remain at our present location and would not be committed into action except in extreme emergency, since we had just returned from an extended period of front-line duty," Goins recounted the latest order. But confusion reigned. Just as the GOYAs began to settle back into their routine, their adrenlin subsiding, another order came in at 4 P.M., brief and to the point: Proceed to Stavelot, Belgium, and report to the Commander of the 30th Infantry Division. Goins concluded that the emergency must be extreme.

The next day, December 19, Wood Joerg wrote his wife Heidi ("Dear Miss Bootsie Dear"); though the battalion was about to move out to the Bulge, he gave no hint of it. He spoke of preparing to give the local French children two thousand candy bars. "There isn't much news," he says strangely. "I guess the lads up front are having a hard time stopping the German attack, but I am sure they will get the job done. War is so unfair—the best men suffer so that the 4Fs can survive." Of one thing he was sure, however: The war experience would make the men "lots better civilians." He even dreamily longed for civilian clothes: "What a caper I will cut—a 'zoot' suit for me, nothing else will do. What a sharpie I will be, you just wait and see. I do love thee."

At 2 P.M., after another delay when XVIII Airborne Corps commandeered all their trucks, the 551st Parachute Infantry Battalion were poured like human fuel into Quartermaster trucks known as deuce-and-a-halfs, or "GMCs," though many were Dodges. As the GOYAs moved out, the German Otto Skorzeny's thirty-two-man advance special force of *Operation Greif* had already taken positions at crossroads in the Ardennes forest, armed with English, drilled in American baseball and movie star names, and disguised in GI uniforms.

The GOYAs pressed together as the trucks flew out of Laon. They looked at the drivers, who were black, the first black soldiers most had ever seen. One driver leaped from his cab and nervously spoke to a HQ Company lieutenant just before taking off, "Sir, I just thought of something. I'm supposed to have this truck in the shop today to be worked on." The lieutenant looked at the truck and the man with the dark face and shook his head. "That truck stayed in the convoy," Sergeant Bill Dean remembers.

The blood of all those men in the trucks—black and white—was quickening toward the unknown. Charles MacDonald, the renowned Army military historian, would call it "the greatest battle ever fought by the United States Army." The Battle of the Bulge was on.

VII

SPEARTIP

At the Battle of the Bulge

It's the idea that we all have value, you and me,
we're worth something more than the dirt. . . .
What we're fighting for, in the end, is each other.

—Chamberlain, *The Killer Angels*

1
Huempfner's one-man war

Milo Huempfner lay in the snow, underneath a turning wheel. He wasn't sure if he was in France, Holland, or Belgium. He knew he was a long way from Green Bay, Wisconsin. Huempfner, at the tail end of the 551st's rushed convoy toward the Ardennes forest where the Germans had made a massive gouge in Allied lines, had skidded his truck around an icy bend, throwing stacks of 81mm mortar shell holders known as "cloverleaves" onto the road and himself into a ditch. It looked like the end of the war for Lieutenant Colonel Joerg's favorite driver. He waited to pass out and pass into heaven. But it didn't happen. The truck wheel kept turning, and he began to hear a telltale sign of life: gunfire.

Why hadn't the Colonel chosen Milo to chauffeur him into history? Joerg had left a day earlier than the battalion in a jeep whose driver floored it for 150 miles. To PFC Huempfner—at twenty-six one of the oldest enlisted men in the battalion—that had to be a driver without the finesse it takes to take a turn in winter. Someone who didn't know what water does to pavement when it freezes. Someone, in short, who wasn't from Wisconsin.

This was sure to be the biggest battle the 551st had ever gotten itself into, and here he'd been left to bring up the rear. Hadn't the Colonel remembered roaring off with his dear Milo in Sicily, kicking up the dust, bellowing to the withered olives that he was going to die—all the officers would be getting it, "so let's live and roar a little, Milo"? Joerg had paid Huempfner the supreme compliment by taking the wheel and being *Milo's* driver. The king had switched places with the serf.

But today, December 20, 1944, Huempfner wasn't feeling so exalted. He picked himself up and bumped his sore head on the turning wheel. That halted it, as if stopping a bad fate. He was lost somewhere on the way to the great battle. What else to do but start a little war of his own? Paratroopers were taught to do that, to cause mayhem for the enemy wherever they might land. So what if in this case his chute had not opened in a 3-foot drop from a truck?

Huempfner didn't know it at first, but his truck had plunged into a ditch in Leignon, Belgium, outside Ciney near the very tip of the German "bulge" into the Ardennes. The offensive had begun on December 16 with an artillery barrage that seemed to one sergeant in the hard-pressed 99th Division facing the Siegfried Line like "hell broke loose . . . the earth shook." Even the Germans themselves were stunned at the magnitude of the opening shelling: "The earth seemed to break open. A hurricane of iron and fire went down on the enemy positions with a deafening noise. We old soldiers had seen many a heavy barrage, but never before anything like this."[1]

In seven days, stopped here by small bands of American paratroopers trucked hurriedly into the Ardennes, there by clumps of American engineers who blew up bridges in their faces, the Germans had still managed by December 23 to thrust their forces 65 miles west of the Siegfried Line across three rivers and through a dense fir forest until they approached Ciney. In good times, the German Army could have driven in a few hours to the fourth river, their primary objective before Antwerp, the Meuse. They would spend a month trying, against a largely American defense outmanned at the start 3 to 1 in foot soldiers, and 7 to 1 in artillery. The German final juggernaut of the war would get within 3 miles of the Meuse on Christmas Eve, but no farther. They had not counted on other enemies: such as a bitter winter, Europe's worst in forty years; "those damned engineers,"[2] as the spearhead panzer leader would spit out in disgust; the thirsty gas tanks of their tanks, especially the King Tiger; and a little man here and there in the woods with inhuman courage, driven, as courage often is, by fear, like Milo Huempfner of Green Bay, Wisconsin.

Milo's wrecked truck was one of 180,000 vehicles of the First and Third Armies, many rushed to the Ardennes by General Eisenhower in the first

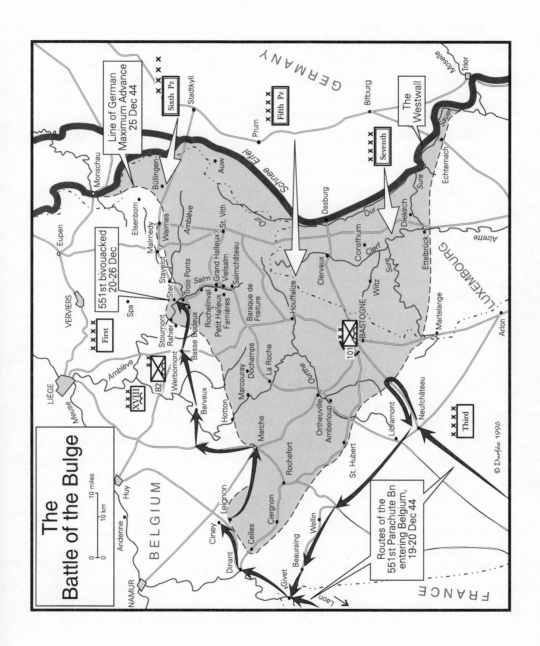

The
Battle of the Bulge

GERMANY

Trier

BELGIUM

LUXEMBOURG

FRANCE

© Durfee 1996

Line of German
Maximum Advance
25 Dec 44

XXXX Sixth Pz.

XXXX Fifth Pz.

XXXX Seventh

The Westwall

551st bivouacked
20-26 Dec

XXXX First

XVIII

82

XX 101

XXXX Third

Routes of the
551st Parachute Bn
entering Belgium,
19-20 Dec 44

0   10 miles
0   10 km

Moselle
Sûre
Sûre
Alzette
Sauer
Our
Our
Clerf
Ourthe
Amblève
Amblève
Salm
Meuse
Laon
Schnee Eifel

Stadtkyll
Prum
Bitburg
Dasburg
Echternach
Bullingen
Monschau
Auw
St. Vith
Consthum
Diekirch
Eupen
Elsenborn
Malmedy
Walmes
Grand Halleux
Vielsalm
Salmchâteau
Clervaux
Ettelbrück
Spa
VERVIERS
Stavelot
Trois Ponts
Baraque de
Fraiture
Houffalize
Wiltz
Martelange
Arlon
Stér
Rochelinval
Petit Halleux
Farnières
Stoumont
Rahier
Basse Bodeux
Werbomont
Marcouray
D'Ochamps
La Roche
Neufchâteau
LIÈGE
Barvaux
Hotton
Marche
Ortheuville
Amberloup
Libramont
Huy
Rochefort
St. Hubert
Andenne
Leignon
Ciney
Ciergnon
Wellin
NAMUR
Dinant
Celles
Beauraing
Givet
BASTOGNE

week of the Battle of the Bulge, a staggering logistical mobility that, as much as anything, saved the Allies in their moment of deepest peril in Europe. Or maybe not quite as much as the human cargo of those trucks, and Milo was only one of eventually 600,000 Americans who fought in the Ardennes. But what a one.

When Huempfner got up and dusted the snow off himself that day in Leignon, he feared that the 551st's supply sergeant, Clarence Nace, who was jerking to a stop in an empty 6-by-6 truck, would kill him for spilling all those cloverleaf holders for precious mortars and wrecking an equally precious truck. A crowd of townspeople had gathered, mostly women and old men, and Nace got them to help cart the cloverleaves into the good truck. Huempfner was spared execution but was ordered to sit tight with his vehicle until it could be towed.

"If the Jerries come, blow it up," Nace barked.

One historian would call Huempfner's last stand in Leignon a "particularly dramatic battle" of the Bulge campaign.[3] It would win Milo the highest—and one of very few—individual awards a man of the 551st would get in the war, the Distinguished Service Cross.

Over the course of five days after his slide into a ditch in Leignon, Huempfner would draw on Lieutenant Colonel Joerg's insistence that each GOYA train to survive in bad conditions alone and at the same time to inflict punishment on the enemy. He would do it with an M-1 rifle—the basic semiautomatic firearm of the U.S. Army—a .45 pistol, two borrowed hand grenades, and a stunning reserve of moxie and self-control that he would never match in civilian life.

He was tempted at first to let the cup pass, however. A lieutenant in a jeep with a driver told him German tanks from the 116th Panzers and 2d Panzers were headed down several of the five roads that intersected at Leignon, and that he'd better get in quick. Huempfner demurred, saying he had to keep watch over his dead truck as ordered. Another jeep with two officers in back of a driver gave him a delayed shiver. Speaking a cultured English, they asked him if any more paratroopers were in the area. Milo said he was the only one, that his unit was far off and had left him for lost. The nervous driver gunned the interrogators north toward Ciney, where Huempfner later learned they were executed as spies.

Without knowing it, Huempfner had run across three German commandos in disguise, sent by an officer British intelligence had labeled "the most dangerous man in Europe," SS Obersturmbannfuhrer Otto Skorzeny. In his great gamble in the Ardennes, Hitler had tagged three of his most daring special forces commanders to sow confusion and terror behind the lines in the blitz toward Antwerp: SS Colonel Jochen Peiper, spearhead of

No mustache yet, but game: Aref Orfalea during boot camp at Fort Lewis, WA, 1943 *(Bud Lank)*

(Above) On October 17, 1944, Pvt. Aref J. Orfalea of HQ Company saddles up his motorcycle (note "551" painted on the gas tank) to take Lt. Col. Joerg's messages to GOYAs in isolated villages in the Maritime Alps. The bags look full, so he's probably in Saint-Martin-Vesubie at the beginning of the run. *(Gregory Orfalea)*

(Right) A Company's Pvt. Chuck Miller in Nice, France, in August 1944. Miller, who took out a Panther tank with a bazooka shot during the Bulge campaign, was found almost frozen in the snow by the father of Nelly Sauvage, with whom he was reunited after forty-five years in 1989 in Belgium. *(Chuck Miller)*

Ohio farmer Urban Post (right) sits alongside disabled French resistance counterpart during a ceremony in Saint-Etiènne-de-Tinée high in the Maritime Alps, August 1989. *(Gregory Orfalea)*

GOYA! Meaning "Get Off Your Ass," the 551st's slogan flag is displayed by Dan Morgan *(left)* and Joe Cicchinelli at the dedication of the Rochelinval memorial, August 20, 1989. *(Gregory Orfalea)*

An expert marksman in the Maritime Alps, Sgt. Doug Dillard of A Company is pretty well part of the snow in November 1944, except for frostbitten nose, rifle with telescopic sight, and Austrian High Mountain patrol he targets. *(National Archives, Still Picture Branch)*

Before he became the 551st commander, cadet Wood Joerg is at West Point, Class of 1937, with his brother Robert and sister-in-law. *(Barbara Joerg Mitchell)*

Septuagenarian Ralph Burns salutes in La Turbie, France. In the distance toward Nice is a hilltop on which a large German artillery piece boomed in August 1944. This is forty-five years later. *(Gregory Orfalea)*

The unique helmet of the 551st Parachute Infantry Battalion with palm tree, which represented its origins in Panama.

A wartime opposite-hand salute from B Company's PFC Joe Edgerly—mascot Furlough's keeper—greatly loved by the battalion, here in Panama. He died in the snow in the Maritime Alps. *(Bill Hatcher)*

Sgt. John B. Reid (who will earn a battlefield commission after being wounded twice) of C Company tends to GOYA mascot Furlough in Panama, 1943. *(Joe Cicchinelli)*

The 34-foot "mock" tower, second stage of jump training, would reveal a true fear of heights because the ground was quite visible. Here a recruit at Fort Benning begins his sail across a 100-yard field on a guide wire. *(U.S. Signal Corps, 1942)*

With a veil not unlike a parachute, an exotic dancer entertains the 551st at the Atlantic Nite Club in Panama, 1943. The GOYAs were registering one of the highest rates of venereal disease in the Army. *(Robert Van Horssen)*

Looking comfy and confident before bailout in Panama, every 551st man here will be wounded in France or at the Battle of the Bulge, and the one with the greatest smile—PFC Frank Gould *(second from right)* will die of wounds, one of several men the official Army study on the unit lists only as "wounded." The other B Company men here, from left, are Sgt. Emory Albritton, "freethinker" PFC Al Palmowski, Pvt. Jim Gage, Sgt. Joe Blaizik, Gould, and PFC Vernon Bettancourt. *(Dick Mascuch)*

Training injuries on the drop zone averaged 8 percent each jump for the 551st. Here Lt. Buff Chisholm of A Company is carted off in Panama by medic Joe Lugo (right) and an unknown medic. *(Dick Mascuch)*

The 551st boxing team at Ft. Kobbe, Panama, led by Capt. Archie McPheeters of B Company, killed in action at the Battle of the Bulge *(center front)*. Back row, from left are Pvt. Nelson Dunkle (C Co.), Sgt. Lee Croft (C Co.), Pvt. Richard D. Kelley (B Co.), welterweight Pvt. Roland Emery (medic), and PFC Daniel Gudelunas; middle row, from left are lightweight PFC Benjamin Goodman (B Co.), Cpl. Ignacio Jimenez (HQ Co.), featherweight Pvt. Darrel Peterson (C Co.), All-Service Junior Welterweight Champion Sgt. Virgil Dorr (A Co.); front left is Cpl. Carlo Intinarelli (B Co., killed in action at Noirefontaine, Belgium); front right is pro middleweight contender Cpl. Joe Chizar (HQ Co.). *(Benny Goodman)*

Sand tabling the drop zone of Martinique just before the aborted invasion, June 1943. Pappy Herrmann, chief operations officer, is second from right, and Lt. Charles Hecq of B Company has one foot on the table. *(Lloyd Larkin)*

(*Above*) Anyone for shark? This 8-foot fellow was exploded up from his patrol in a Panama lagoon by GOYA Mark III concussion grenades after the invasion of Martinique was called off. Bringing "Jaws" in are HQ Company's Cpl. George Rickard and Cpl. Clell Whitener. *(Jack Leaf)*

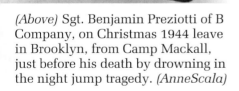

(*Above*) Sgt. Benjamin Preziotti of B Company, on Christmas 1944 leave in Brooklyn, from Camp Mackall, just before his death by drowning in the night jump tragedy. *(AnneScala)*

Lt. Dick Mascuch of B Company sizing up a glider door before the first jump of men from gliders. Mascuch, the first officer out the door of a glider, still makes exhibition parachute jumps around the world at age seventy-six. *(Dick Mascuch)*

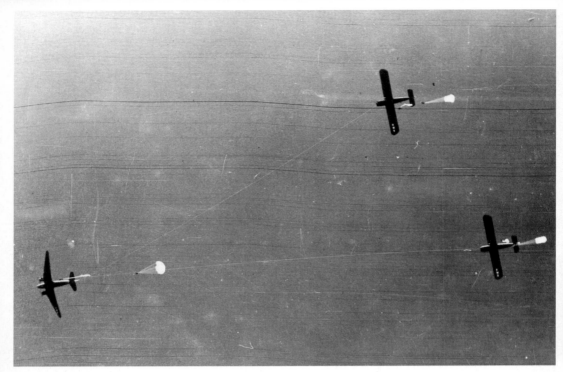

On a historic test jump, the first ever with men simultaneously going out of gliders and the C-47 tug plane, the initial six 551st paratroops are flung out over Camp Mackall, NC, in the autumn of 1943. *(Dick Mascuch)*

C Company's Capt. Tims Quinn surveys a German anti-aircraft gun in Sicily, June 1944. *(Marshall and Jean Dalton)*

(Right) The 551st S-2 (intelligence) section posing in Rome, July 1944. *Back row:* unknown, Sgt. Perry Ellis holding flowers (the second GOYA killed overseas—by a mine—in Rome); PFC Howard Scanlon; and Pvt. Bill Amann. *Center:* T/Sgt. Ralph Wenthold and Cpl. Wilbur Ponchot. *Front:* an Italian orphan; Pvt. Frank Mero *(interpreter)*, and Pvt. Vince Fiorino. *(Bill Amann)*

(Below) Sgt. Ed Schultz *(left)* leans on a liberated wine cask at the Villa Gladys in Draguignan shortly after the capture of Gen. Ludwig Bieringer, whose camera snapped the picture, at his headquarters, August 17, 1944. At right is Cpl. Joe Cicchinelli; at center is Pvt. Eli Gibson. All belong to A Company. *(Don Thompson)*

This must have been one of the few monuments to Benito Mussolini still standing south of the Arno River in July 1944. Keeping Il Duce company at Lido di Ostia near Rome are C Company's Pvt. John Fristick and Sgt. John West *(standing)*, Pvt. Billie Murray *(left front)*, and PFC Lee Shattuck. *(Richard Nichols)*

A signature airborne World War II drop photo shows the 551st on "D-Day" in southern France descending over La Motte, August 15, 1944, about 6 P.M. The photo is often misidentified as to place or unit in history books. One caption called it a shot of "supplies" falling. The long vineyard indicated by #1 is where C Company landed, and PFC Eugene Schmid was seriously injured by a stake of "Rommel's asparagus." At #2, PFC Dick Nichols tried to help a tall GOYA caught in a tree in a hedgerow but was ordered to the assembly area (#4), coming across several dead Germans at a thick hedgerow (#3) before finding his fellows. *(National Archives, Still Picture Branch)*

Sgt. Ed Schultz of A Company takes a water break in Cannes after the battle on Hill 105, August 1944. Pvt. James Dunn is at right. *(Joe Cicchinelli)*

Medics hustle to the wounded lying around the Valbourges vineyard estate at La Motte in the early evening of the 551st's drop into southern France, August 15, 1944. *(National Archives, Still Picture Branch)*

After being captured by the 551st at his Draguignan head-quarters, Gen. Ludwig Bieringer *(right)* gets the low-down by candlelight in St. Tropez on August 18, 1944, from Maj. Gen. Alexander Patch, commander of the U.S. Seventh Army. *(National Archives, Still Picture Branch)*

"Wait your turn, honey." Two Niçoises welcome Pvt. John Delmage of B Company as the first U.S. troops to enter Nice, August 29, 1944. *(Mel Clark)*

(Below) The first American to "liberate" Nice, the 551st's Lt. Dick Durkee, flowers and all, leads his A Company squad into Messina Square about 10 A.M. on August 29, 1944. *(Dick Durkee)*

Three young German soldiers of the 148th Division killed in an A Company assault on their machine gun nest at La Turbie, *ca.* August 30, 1944—one of the last direct combat exchanges on the French Riviera between German and Allied forces. Cpl. Joe Cicchinelli took the photos out of the soldiers' *soldebuchs.*

Near Malmedy, black quartermaster troops unload one of 72 American POWs shot to death at Baugnez Crossroads. The photo was taken on January 15, 1945, about a month after the Battle of the Bulge massacre by troops of *Kampfgruppe* Peiper of the 1st SS Panzers which faced, among others, the 551st. The men froze in the field and were covered by blizzards before they were dug out. *(National Archives, Still Picture Branch)*

Lt. Col. Wood Joerg with his signature beret and "Rose of San Antone" jeep on the road in the Maritime Alps, autumn 1944. His executive officer, Maj. Bill Holm, is with him. *(Heidi Joerg)*

A tense moment between generals at the Battle of the Bulge: A few days after the GOYAs were destroyed at Rochelinval, Lt. Gen. Matthew Ridgway, commander of the XVIII Airborne Corps *(left)*, and Maj. Gen. James Gavin, commander of the 82d Airborne Division, face each other. *(National Archives, Still Picture Branch)*

Col. Arthur Juttner, awarded the Iron Cross with Oak Leaves and Swords, for leading the 164th Volksgrenadier Regiment against the 551st and others at the Salm River in Belgium. Shortly after the Bulge campaign, Juttner's wife died of exhaustion fleeing the Russians in February 1945. *(Arthur Juttner)*

(Below) In November 1944 Field Marshal Ernst Busch *(right, walking)* leads the final review of the 62d Volksgrenadier Division in its training area in Silesia at Neuhammer, Germany (near Breslau). In one month it would be sent to the border of Belgium for the Ardennes surprise attack. At left with helmet is Col. Friedrich Kittel (recently wounded in the leg, thus wearing long trousers to cover his lack of boots), soon to be promoted to general and commander of the entire division; Reichsjugendfuhrer Artur Axmann, leader of the Hitler Youth; Maj. Gen. Hans von Hanstein; and Busch, who later commanded all German forces in northern Europe. *(Josef Bannert)*

Look closely: At a "Welcome Home" procession in Grand Halleux, Belgium, during the summer of 1945 for returning Belgian POWs from Germany, the little boy at the front of the column carrying the Belgian flag is wearing a helmet painted with a palm tree. That is a 551st helmet. It was probably found in the snow at Rochelinval, 1 mile north of Grand Halleux. *(Claude Orban)*

The only official Army photo that ever identified the 551st, captioned at the National Archives, "Men of the 551st Parachute Infantry Battalion moving up into the Bulge." T/4 Jim Smith of A Company leads the left column. Notice lack of overshoes or overcoats, as well as scarcity of snow, making the date early in the Bulge, *ca*, December 21, 1944. *(National Archives, Still Picture Branch)*

This is the only photo of the very few that exist of the 551st at the Bulge counteroffensive where the faces of the men are (barely) recognizable. These are the few soldiers left of the GOYA mortar platoon, either January 5 or 6, 1945, near Dairomont. The grainy portrait of the exhausted HQ Company men shows, from left, Pvt. Fred Hilgardner, PFC Eugene Burke (with a broken umbrella he carried for some reason throughout the Bulge), PFC Leo Baker, and Pvt. Red Patterson; squatting is Pvt. Vince Dalzell. *(Charles Fairlamb)*

the 1st SS Panzers westward; Oberst Frederich August von der Heydte, hero of the 1941 Crete drop and now head of the last German parachute attack, Operation *Stösser*; and Skorzeny.

Hitler personally prized Skorzeny, a 6-foot Austrian with a wicked dueling scar on his cheek who had plucked Mussolini from his captors in northern Italy in a 1943 commando raid and had recently kidnapped the son of Admiral Horthy to keep Hungary from defecting from the Axis. In late October 1944 Hitler had hardly finished welcoming his favorite back from the Hungary escapade when he gave Skorzeny less than five weeks to outfit a special panzer brigade for Operation *Greif*. Its primary goal, using tanks, jeeps, and trucks disguised with American markings and English-speaking Germans, was to make it to the Meuse River ahead of three panzer armies and seize at least two of three bridges between Liège and Namur.

But the Trojan Horse operation was compromised almost from the start. To Skorzeny's great consternation, three days after his conference with Hitler, printed orders for a "Secret Commando Operation" came to his in-box, signed by Field Marshal Keitel himself! Some secret. This was potentially one of the biggest "hard copy" botches of World War II. However, when Allied agents retrieved a sheet of the secret orders in November and later plucked another off a wounded prisoner of the 62d Volksgrenadier Division on the first day of the *Wacht am Rhein* attack, SHAEF discounted it as a ruse.

The first muster of English-speaking volunteers for Skorzeny's mayhem unit was quite disappointing. Only ten men could speak perfectly with a knowledge of slang (Kreigsmarine sailors, as it turned out); thirty-five others spoke passably, but with heavy German accents; three hundred others were limited to barely more than "yes" and "no." After the war, Skorzeny remarked acidly that most of his commandos "could never dupe an American—even a deaf one."[4]

Intensive language classes helped some. Those with particularly numb tongues if not skulls were taught profanities and slang. The proper response, for example, to a request for a password was, "Aw, go lay an egg." At final count, Skorzeny had 2,500 men, of which 150 were organized into nine special "jeep teams" outfitted in American uniforms who did everything from cutting telephone wires and creating fake minefield markings to switching roads signs and directing American troops the wrong way.

"Half a million GIs played cat and mouse with each other each time they met on the road," General Omar Bradley later said. Thus were spawned the now famous quiz shows at the crossroads that could wreak havoc for a man that did not know the name of Betty Grable's husband (Harry James), the name of President Roosevelt's dog (Fala), Babe Ruth's best season home run total (sixty), or the identity of "dem Bums" (Brooklyn Dodgers). Near Saint-Vith, General Bruce Clarke of the 7th Armored Division was arrested by his own troops on December 21, the day the 551st Parachute Infantry Battalion arrived at Werbomont 10 miles to the west. Clark did not help himself when he answered that the Chicago Cubs were in the American League. Omar Bradley barely escaped from one GI who insisted Springfield was not the capital of Illinois. On one occasion, two American soldiers were shot and killed at a crossroads by nervous U.S. sentries.

Indeed, Operation *Greif* lost eighteen commandos to execution (including the three Huempfner met). Only three of nine jeep teams returned intact to German lines. One team managed to reach the Meuse; in a desperate dash past a British roadblock, the four disguised Germans were blown up by a mine just before the bridge, several miles beyond any approach of their own panzers.

A few days before Christmas Huempfner awoke in his ditch to a sound "like a bunch of freight trains coming—just one hell of a roaring." It was a column of fourteen Panzer V Panther tanks of the 2d Panzers, along with a Mark VI Tiger, with sixty soldiers of *Kampfgruppe Cochenhausen* clinging to their armor. Huempfner soaked his truck with gasoline and set it afire. He ran to the Leignon train depot, where the stationmaster, Victor DeVille, against the protests of his wife, hid him, telling the panzer crew that accosted him that there were no Americans in town. Milo barely breathed in the toilet.

Escaping out a back window later, he ran north and came upon a jeep carrying an American captain heading a truck convoy, whom he warned about the German tank column and a 75mm gun it had emplaced to block the road into Leignon. The captain, filled with rumor fluid, quizzed him about his home state, sticking his carbine into Milo's belly.

"What is the capital of Wisconsin?"

"Madison," Humpfner retorted.

"What unit are you from?"

"The 551st Parachute Infantry Battalion."

The captain was not the first man in Milo's experience to wonder what in the hell that was.

"How do you spell your name?" the man grabbed Milo's ID bracelet.

Huempfner barely got that out when the roar of a German halftrack up ahead made the captain cut off the interrogation. As he took off north to Ciney, toward which the German "Bulge" was inflating, he shouted, "Good luck, trooper!" leaving Milo to deal with the tanks.

In a short time Huempfner spotted a Red Cross jeep pulling a trailer of Christmas presents barreling south; Milo ran across a field yelling for the driver to watch out, but it was too late. The medic was killed by machine gun fire from the German position. That shooting of a noncombatant, Huempfner later said, riled him enough to start him on his one-man war.

From a hill overlooking Leignon the next day Huempfner watched as four U.S. tank destroyers, with thinly armored turrets open on top, motored southward from Ciney and came under punishing fire from the German 75mm gun. He promptly shouldered his M-1, by luck found some armor-piercing rounds in his ammunition belt, and shot out the heavy gun. He then beat it to the head of the tank destroyers approaching Leignon, warned the commander about the heavy concentration of tanks in town, and volunteered to go back and scout them. He spotted two halftracks guarding the town's entry, came back, and asked the major for a handful of grenades.

Feverishly heading back to Leignon—all on foot—he climbed up on one halftrack, pulled the pin on a grenade, and laid it on top of the hatch. That blown off, Huempfner dropped a second grenade down the opening, exploding its interior and its occupants. He did the same with two grenades on the other halftrack, and the blast was louder (Milo thought a land mine must have detonated inside). A flock of Germans fled from a nearby barn.

Later Huempfner ambled straight up to a German sentry standing alongside a Mark-VI Tiger tank outside the Leignon church. One of only twenty that fought in the Ardennes (from the 9th Panzer Division), the Mark-VI Tiger I was a 60-ton behemoth with armor the thickness of brick; its 88mm anti-aircraft gun was a fearsome sight to Americans.

"Hi, Mac," the sentry said, thinking he had the GI cold, swinging his Schmeisser automatic pistol.

Milo quick-drew him and shot him dead. Luckily, the tank crew was absent. Shortly thereafter a Belgian man pointed down the street and whispered "Rat-a-tat-tat!" A German machine gun was firing at the approaching American tank destroyers from a barn window. Milo imagined the gun's configuration inside and pumped eight rounds of his M-1 through the barn door. The machine gun went silent. He later found it flattened by a tank along the side of the road, figuring the Germans had destroyed the gun while withdrawing and that he had killed some of its crew. By nightfall the giant tanks, chastened by what seemed a ruthless company of U.S. paratroopers, pulled out of town and billeted themselves in the woods, along with an 88mm self-propelled gun. The company had been one man.

Later, with Milo as forward observer, the 2d Armored Division lay a vicious "time-on-target" (TOT) artillery barrage on the woods where the Panthers and Tigers hid—a fifteen-second saturation salvo of many guns at once that smashed them where they sat.

Along with Milo Huempfner on his risky rounds was a fourteen-year-old

Belgian boy named Paul, who finally entreated the exhausted trooper in schoolboy English, "Meelo, it's dark and getting cold. Let's go to Grandma Gaspard's and get warm." There Huempfner met the astonished townspeople, who told him most of the men of the village had been hauled off to German labor camps years before.

On Christmas Eve the villagers of Leignon asked their protector to watch the church while they held a midnight Mass, which Milo graciously did. He remembered the evening with wonder years later:

> When we got to the church I went up and opened the door, and I had my cocked .45 in my hand, and there looking startled was the priest. He said, "*Entrez*, Meelo." They just had two little candles burning on the altar for light. I let them all go in past me and then I closed the door and stood guard outside. After Mass, the people all came to me and thanked me for standing guard. "*Merci beaucoup,*" they each said. Then they walked back through the town humming "Silent Night" very quietly, back to Grandma Gaspard's place. There were probably about fifteen people altogether. Inside on a table they had a little Christmas tree about 3 feet high with no decorations at all. But to me it was more beautiful than if it had been 40 feet high and decorated with a million shiny things.

On Christmas Day 1944, Huempfner heard the booming of an 88mm gun from the forest nearby; from a footbridge outside town he saw the four tank destroyers and many U.S. soldiers of the Combat Command B of 2d Armored, and soon realized that town was surrounded by friendly forces. On the way back to Leignon, on an impulse he went to a barn and discovered Germans hiding inside. He immediately took into custody eighteen German soldiers, marching them back to the 2d Armored, and informed a commander of the Panther Tiger hiding place.

A pair of German binoculars hanging from his neck, Huempfner was immediately under suspicion of his own troops. A 2d Armored sergeant challenged him: "What is your outfit?" He told them he was with the 551st.

"What division is it in?"

There Milo was stumped. "Well, we are a separate battalion and don't belong to any division."

The sergeant's eyes squinted to slits.

"Sure, pal. What is the password for this sector?"

Huempfner had no idea. He was immediately disarmed and told that a Belgian civilian had informed the 2d that a German straggler had been holed up in the town for days. Milo protested, but clearly they took him now for a spy. His German name didn't help any. Some MPs drove up in a jeep with a lieutenant, and Milo begged them to take him back to Leignon so he might plead his case. They did, warily, keeping him apart from his weapons and essentially under arrest. He directed them to his burnt-out truck and pointed to the "551st" painted on the bumper. He found Paul, who translated for him in a heated debate with Victor de Ville, the stationmaster who had hid him.

After a humiliating day, his guards began to relent. They took him to the 2d Armored's headquarters in a schoolhouse in Ciney, where a tall man emerged. He was Lieutenant Colonel Joseph Clema, the division's provost marshal, wearing a turtleneck sweater. He eyed the PFC head to toe.

"Well, how many did you get?" Clema dropped.

"I was too busy to count," Huempfner exhaled, cracking a smile for the first time in days.

Clema laughed: "A man could get himself killed doing all that by himself." Huempfner nodded, and was directed to get something to eat. Afterward he was taken to a cot adjoining the mess hall and slept for sixteen hours, wondering when he awoke why it had been so silent. Clema had ordered that no mess kits were to be washed while Humpfner slept. Once on the verge of execution, Huempfner was now seen as a hero.

After a week of resting with the 2d Armored, Huempfner longed to be with his old battalion, though Clema begged him to be his personal driver. Clema tried to convince Huempfner that the 551st didn't exist, or if it did, that it was nowhere in Belgium. All his battle maps revealed no 551st Parachute Infantry Battalion: "See? There's no 551st on here anywhere." Huempfner was now worried. Clema relented and sent him in a jeep to 82d Airborne headquarters at Werbomont, where a map revealed the GOYAs were, at least on January 3, at Basse Bodeux and had begun pushing toward the Salm River in the general counterattack at the Bulge. No one was sure quite where they were; in two weeks they had been attached to and detached from three different units. No vehicles were available to ferry him; he was told to start walking.

After walking eastward all day in the snow and sleeping in a barn that night, he hailed a jeep with a "551" marking on it and was driven to the battalion's aid station at Dairomont, where he promptly fell asleep, exhausted, in a tent. That was January 6, 1945. The next day he awoke to a horrid sight. Men covered with frost, shouting in cones of breath, were carrying into the medic tent on a stretcher a man covered toe to neck by a blood-soaked blanket. His head had a red hole in its crown. It was Wood Joerg. The commander's old driver buried his face in his hands.

Joerg's premonition of his own death and his officers' while driving on the dusty roads of Sicily was true. Before Huempfner could reach them, the scrappy separate battalion and most of its officers had been wiped out. Was that, subconsciously, why Huempfner had thrashed so lethally alone, 35 miles west of his GI family, at the tip of the Bulge, while they perished at its heart?

Joerg died before Lieutenant Colonel Clema's December 27, 1944, recommendation for the Distinguished Service Cross for Huempfner reached him. Huempfner had been officially listed as "missing in action." "He might easily have retired from this area without accomplishing these feats of daring and heroism," Clema wrote. "The bravery and resourcefulness of this soldier in vigorously harassing armed enemy forces singlehandedly, demonstrated extraordinary heroism and are a tribute to the Armed Forces of the United States."

When Milo had his DSC pinned on him in May, 1945, in Epinol, France, it wasn't by anyone from the 551st; the unit had been disbanded three months earlier. The citation oddly places him in the "2d Airborne Division," an inaccurate admixture of the 2d Armored and the 82d Airborne, an essentially fictitious nomenclature. Maybe that is why in the photograph of Milo receiving his award his face looks stunned. He seems to be staring far in the distance at something out of reach.

Though he would raise four children in civilian life back in Green Bay, Huempfner would never cross over that emptiness. It was as if he had received his award in a vacuum, on a strange plateau he would never crest again. His wife died of cancer at forty-three. He drank heavily and lived in a single room above a shop, making a meager income shoveling snow and sweeping floors in a bar. He wrote saucy ballads and bittersweet poems about the prevalence of war in this century, even one with a mild protest, when a son entered the paratroopers, that figured Vietnam "might just be the start of World War III." None were published, and he wrote bitterly to one veteran in 1971 about Green Bay that "no one lives here but football players." Out of work for nine years, he received a monthly pension of $21.60. Haunted by the eight drowned men at Camp Mackall, he deluded himself into thinking he was responsible for their deaths. He had led the column with Colonel Graves that fateful night and had gotten lost, and now he thought he should have gotten more lost and spared them all, or maybe the time lost in getting to Pope Air Field had let the deadly fog gather. He grieved, too, that in the final days at the Bulge, for all his heroism, he was lost from his men. "I blame myself for it," he spoke years later in a gravelly, broken voice, and cried out before weeping, "Sometimes I don't sleep!" He engaged in a long, pitiful attempt to gain the Congressional Medal of Honor. He was seen, at best, as a character around town, shunned by most.

Whenever a veteran died in Green Bay, Huempfner would show up at the funeral home and stand silently at attention all day. Sometimes he was the only mourner. When he died, a thousand people came to a pauper's funeral.

2
A bloody shirt

It was a cold, insane battle. Perhaps all battles are insane and evil at their root. Yet Hitler, after all, was human, as were Mussolini and Tojo of Japan. They had the spark that in itself is not bad—that great upstart of creation, man. But in them the spark became a fire, a firestorm, and pride-in-self somehow went out of control, or gave itself to fiendish control over others, deluding itself into thinking it was God on earth. Is it any surprise that when the good angels rally to defeat the evil ones they, too, become engulfed in the fires they must spread to defeat that hell? That war itself is hell for all? That it debases all? And that when the fires finally go out, mankind itself feels smaller?

But this battle was cold, bitterly so. Enough to scorch hands and feet black. Enough to hug a frozen mortar to your chest to transfer your last warmth to the weapon. Enough to die hugging a tree. And perfectly insane. Most of Hitler's generals knew Germany was either defeated or on the brink of defeat; most saw no ultimate likelihood of reversing the Allied march and therefore thought the Ardennes campaign foolishness in the extreme. Even SS Obergruppenfuhrer Josef "Sepp" Dietrich, Hitler's own chauffeur and bodyguard in the Fuhrer's early streetfighting days and his chief hit man in the murderous purge of the Brown Shirts in the 1934 "Night of the Long Knives," when told he was to head one of the three SS panzer armies in the Ardennes campaign, thought Hitler's plan was mad: "All he wants me to do is cross a river, capture Brussels, and then go and take Antwerp! And all this in the worst time of year through the Ardennes where the snow is waist deep and there isn't enough room to deploy four tanks abreast, let alone armored divisions! Where it doesn't get light until eight and it's dark again at four and with reformed divisions made up chiefly of kids and sick old men—and all this at Christmas!"[5] But they obeyed. They sent their men, young and old, the tatters of Germany, into *Autumn Mist,* the code name Hitler conceded to his generals as a replacement for *Wacht Am Rhein.* That fog killed and wounded almost 200,000 Americans and Germans. It was the death rattle of Germany, a very lethal rattle.

More Americans were killed or wounded at the Battle of the Bulge than at Gettysburg and Antietam combined; more in the blood-freezing six weeks in Belgium and Luxembourg than in the four years at the height of the Vietnam War, 1968–72. So overpowering was this climactic battle of World War II that those who fought in it were silenced by it for huge swaths of their lives. Gratitude that one had survived, or prevailed, could not help but run aground on the memory that one's soul was scorched by all the dead. Or made cold. And that cold, for the rest of one's life, too, had to be fought. We call that counterforce love. It is almost a pitiable thing, love, for it would seem if it were so powerful it would not have been smothered in men to begin with. But that is where war starts—in the barely perceptible self-smothering of affection for others, of failed recognition of the other in ourselves.

Most, like my father, would hardly ever speak of it. Yet many would feel, like one veteran of the Bulge, that "fifty years later, it is more vivid to me than what I lived and saw yesterday."[6] It put a dark brand on 600,000 Americans, many of whom are now dead or on the path to death, but at a threshold where they can finally speak.

I would speak with them, for them, and for my father, who did not speak of the war before he fell in Los Angeles, so many years from Belgium. I was approached by the man who had prepared his body holding his blood-spattered shirt and asked if I wanted it. Destroy it, I told him, not wanting to admit that he had fallen so abruptly, a victim of his own love.

They called the men who had been on the line too long, who suffered from too much cold and exposure and shelling, "rag men."

3
Hitler rolls the dice

The Bulge. Hitler called it *Wacht Am Rhein,* Watch on the Rhine, deceptively suggesting a defensive action. Hitler had taken a lesson from all the fake invasion plans of the Allies at Normandy. Though he enforced on pain of execution a complete radio and telephone blackout in the weeks approaching his second invasion of Belgium and Luxembourg of the war, he may have secretly hoped that Allied intelligence would discover but write off the massive troop movements to that innocuous title. Indeed, his own troops and most of their commanders were given no inkling until the last day or two as to what they were massing at the West wall for.

On a map, the "bulge" appears as an arrowhead on its side, coming to a western point at the town of Celles, 3 miles shy of the Meuse River. Nearly 90 miles at its base separating Germany from Belgium and Luxembourg, the westward bisector of the triangle travels about 65 miles. Thus the battle zone for 1.1 million men covered 2,925 square miles. But the subzero foxholes were hardly spacious to the men; at best, men fought in isolated pockets behind tree trunks. At the same time, the Ardennes is a patchwork of long fields and farms between the wooded areas, and soldiers were often utterly exposed.

Think of the head of a reptile in profile. The "bulge" westward into the Allied lines at its highwater mark on Christmas Eve, 1944, is smooth and bloated on its southern flank, like a toad's jaw. That is where Patton was.

The northern flank is a different story: It sports a wartlike knob about 25 miles out from the base, a small bulge on the larger bulge that seems to swell north toward Liège. When one squints, the big "bulge" looks like a dinosaur's head, with smooth throat, horned tip, and knobby ridge above the eyes. That knobby ridge, the small bulge, is where Sepp Dietrich's Sixth Panzer Army tried to force through the northern flank and where the U.S. First Army stood. Dietrich thrust his fiercest troops at that northern wall—the 1st SS Panzer Division—in order to reach the Meuse at its closest large city, Liège. This northern knob, battered by the Germans, is exactly where the 551st Parachute Infantry Battalion was ultimately sent.

If the GOYAs had reached Bastogne, where they were first told to go— near the southern flank, the "throat" of the reptile—this book would not have been warranted. They would have been part of history long ago, for the siege of Bastogne, the largest town in the Ardennes forest and a road hub, became a symbol of the whole Allied struggle to hold the line. In cinema newsreels flashed to Americans during the Battle of the Bulge, Bastogne is woefully outsized on a map, encircled by a wall, representing the wall-like 101st Airborne Division.

Sapped by the exhausting battle out of Normandy, in the first few days of the Bulge, Eisenhower's chief reinforcements for the green, overextended units on the "ghost front" of the Ardennes were two airborne divisions of the XVIII Airborne Corps, whose commander, Lieutenant General Matthew Ridgway, was in England. Before Ridgway rushed back, Major General James Gavin took up the Corps's reins in the emergency and ordered the 82d to move to Bastogne, followed by the 101st (whose leader, General Maxwell Taylor, was also absent, in the United States). On December 18, General Courtney Hodges decided to pull the 82d up to the northern shoulder, leaving the 101st at Bastogne.

In retrospect, Hodge's instinct seems sound. He helped tie up two of the three advancing panzer armies, rather than one, and Hitler became utterly obsessed with taking Bastogne, though he would have done better to pass it by altogether. Even General Bradley saw Bastogne strategically as little more than a sideshow. The Germans never planned their *schwerpunkt* (spearhead) through Bastogne. Their southern flank was protection, composed of General Erich Brandenburger's Seventh Army, for General Hasso von Manteuffel's Fifth Army (in the center). Manteuffel's force itself was a second layer shielding the critical mass with the most panzers, Dietrich's Sixth Army, sent to blow a hole in the line of the U.S. First Army northward. And into that cauldron, hardly spotlighted on the northern shoulder of the Bulge, was poured the little-known 551st.

In some ways Hitler's plan for a massive surprise attack in the winter of

1944 was a classic case of the cornered tiger. By September 1944 Germany's prospects were hardly encouraging: After the Allies' summer invasion at Normandy, the Reich was being pressed slowly and steadily on three fronts—the Soviet Union in the east, the Americans (including the 551st) through Operation Dragoon with French and Italian partisans from the south, and the Americans and British from the west. The only direction safe from incipient invasion was the Baltic Sea to the north, facing Scandinavia.

Hitler was cornered in other ways. The July bomb explosion at his map table had shaken him visibly. In addition to his blown eardrum and lacerated thighs, arm, and hands, the fall of 1944 was very much Hitler's own autumn, as well. His right arm developed a strange tremor that would not stop, his back stooped, and to many he began to seem an old, withered man, dazed half the time, in some private delirium.[7] His skin grew rilled, his thick eyebrows gray; some said that his famed black brush of a mustache by the time of the Bulge campaign was turning as white as the snow that fell on the Ardennes.

Germany had already sustained shocking losses. By the autumn of 1944 almost 4 million Germans had lost their lives in battle. For months now, the great German cities had been relentlessly pounded by Allied bombing raids freed by a steadily diminishing Luftwaffe. Paranoid by nature, not only about Jews and Russians, but about the professional Prussian officers in the German military who had kept him a corporal in World War I, after the bomb plot at Rastenburg Hitler purged some of the cream of the German officer ranks, including Rommel, his greatest commander.

Given the forces pressing against Hitler, the amazing thing about the Battle of the Bulge is not that it did not work for Germany, but that it very nearly did. In spite of its losses, the German Army in the fall of 1944 still had 10 million men under arms. When news of the breakthrough in the Ardennes of thirty German divisions hit Omar Bradley, his first reaction was, "Where in the hell did the son-of-a-bitch get all that?" In a word, the SOB got it underground. Throughout the autumn, in huge basement factories immune to Allied bombing or in small-scale plants deep in the countryside beyond the industrial Ruhr Valley, German war matériel production actually hit record levels: 1.3 million tons of ammunition, 750,000 rifles, 100,000 machine guns, 9,000 artillery pieces. Though tank production was down, a formidable total of 717 tanks was marshaled for the Ardennes onslaught, three times the initial American strength. Self-propelled assault guns, and the deadly 100mm *Panzerfaust*, carried on the shoulder like a bazooka—which would prove superior to the American bazooka for taking out tanks—were being manufactured in record numbers in Czechoslovakia, beyond the range of Allied bombers. The first jets, one of Hitler's vaunted secret weapons, which raced 20 percent faster than any Allied aircraft, were also coming off the production line. As MacDonald noted, "What Hitler needed was time."[8]

Pulled back as protection around Germany, this force might have held off the Allied offensives for another year. But defense and withdrawal were not words in Hitler's vocabulary. Imbued to the end with a sense of vengefulness for Germany's losses in World War I, conjuring the ghost of Frederick the Great in his various bunkers, Hitler was wedded forever to the notion of blitzkrieg, or lightning war, the idea that the best defense is offense. He had read his Clausewitz well: "When the disproportion of Power is so great that no limitation of our own object can ensure us safety from catastrophe . . . forces will, or should, be concentrated in one desperate blow."[9]

If nothing else, Hitler had an uncanny instinct for the jugular; unfurling the maps on September 16, he noted that though U.S. troops had inched across German soil on the Western front, while Stalin had yet to reach Warsaw, there was a weak link in the American line—very weak indeed—in the Ardennes, exactly where Germany had unleashed its juggernauts so successfully in both 1914 and 1940. If lightning could strike twice in the same place, why not a third? Especially if that place was so shoddily held. The Allies' supply lines also seemed grossly overextended. They hadn't yet managed to make Europe's greatest port, Antwerp, fully operational.

In addition to the failed "bridge too far," the September 17 airborne invasion of Holland known as Operation Market Garden, inconclusive battles in the fall at Aachen, Alsace-Lorraine, and the Huertgen Forest had sapped the U.S. First, Third, and Ninth armies of 134,182 men killed and wounded; twice that number were out of the fray because of disease, exposure, and fatigue. In the Huertgen, the 28th Division of the Pennsylvania National Guard, which had fought so relentlessly on the Normandy beaches, lost 6,000 men. Its red, keystone-shaped shoulder patch was dubbed "the Bloody Bucket." The 28th was sent to the Ardennes to lick its wounds and rest. The quiet sector had some of Europe's best natural hot springs (the word "Spa" derives from the town of that name, where First Army commander General Hodges was taking the baths).

Though Eisenhower's thirty-eight divisions facing Germany's forty-one divisions on Heeresgroupe B in the West were larger on paper, by November the supply of young men from America had dwindled to the point that infantry strength was barely 78 percent and falling. By early December, on the brink of the Bulge, Eisenhower warned General George Marshall and President Roosevelt that "our replacement situation is exceedingly dark."

"Night, fog, and snow"—these, Hitler proclaimed, would be his chief allies in the Ardennes. They would shield the skies from the dreaded Allied airpower; Hitler also arrogantly thought the German Army to be winter-toughened by the Russian campaigns in a way the Americans, in particular, couldn't match. He often derided the GI as on a par with Italians—the first of his Axis to jump ship—in staying power. In short, he hoped the Americans, thinned in supply lines and greatly undermanned in the Ardennes itself, would collapse there, if not run. The largest American surrender of the war in the West, of seven thousand men at Saint-Vith on December 19 (only the Bataan surrender to the Japanese was larger), would embolden him greatly.

In addition to the weather, Hitler counted on an amalgam of foot soldiers and tankers to carry the day: The spearhead Sixth Panzer Army would contain four divisions of the elite Waffen-Schutzstaffel (SS) panzers, the Praetorian Guard of the Nazis, who sported "death's head" insignia on their caps. (This was a slap to the regular army Wehrmacht generals Manteuffel and Brandenburger, whose mission was chiefly to support the SS thrust, though Manteuffel got further west than anyone.) Hitler also combed out various "rear-area swine" to form twenty-five new divisions from the Luftwaffe, the Navy, and bloated, desk-sitting elements of the Wehrmacht. The Fuhrer never let anyone forget he had been a foot soldier in the Great War.

Though their numbers have been exaggerated,[10] boys and old men—with draft limits expanded to include ages 16 to 60—were squeezed out to be the last rifle-bearers from villages and cities around Germany to form new divisions and restock old ones with the newly christened name of "Volksgrenadiers," fighters of the people. SS Reichsfuhrer Henrich Himmler, the mastermind of the concentration camps, forced the dark muster of those too young to know any better, and for whom Hitler was still an idol, and those too old to resist. Added to them were impressed soldiers from captured lands, such as Poland, Czechoslovakia, and Russia itself. Before September was over, forty-three of these new or reconstituted divisions were created; fifteen went to the Eastern Front, one to Norway, and the rest headed toward the Ardennes. Two of those last—the 18th and 62d Volksgrenadiers—would face (after they had helped overrun Saint-Vith) a force that included the 551st Parachute Infantry Battalion.

The plan had the mark of "divine intuition," as Hitler saw it. "The gods love and bless those who strive for the impossible,"[11] he wrote. The impossible looked good on paper; the three panzer armies would ramrod through the Allied lines, split them in two, and thread their way through the Ardennes forest in no more than three days to reach the Meuse River, after which they would speed on flat land to Antwerp. Thirty U.S., British, and Canadian divisions would be cut off from all supply. All, including the entire U.S. First Army, would be destroyed, and the great port would be shut off to the Allies in what Hitler called "a new Dunkirk!"

His generals, however, cringed. The German panzers had enough gasoline for 90 miles if all went smoothly, but Antwerp was 125 miles away. The generals knew, too, that although Germany had succeeded in using the Ardennes as its entrée to victory in the Low Countries in both world wars, those blitzkriegs had been staged in late spring. What would that great wild card—winter—do to roads and bridges, not to mention 70-ton tanks? Could the fog last long enough to keep off the Allied air raids that would surely eat up their supply lines? Would a sixty-year-old Czech fight like a true German?

Then there was the topography. The Ardennes is a thick forest riddled with a series of meandering streams, creeks, and rivers, many of which, though not wide, flow through deep gorges. Riverbanks are steep, and hills and hillocks abrupt and surprising. Typical are the Salm and Ourthe rivers in the center of the battlefield, which presented formidable problems to pontoon and bridging operations. In many places, artificial bridging was impossible because of the steep banks. Existing bridges had to be secured, but many of them were to be denied to the German onslaught by bands of dynamiting U.S. engineers.

Field Marshal Von Runstedt confessed he was "staggered." The generals tried everything to persuade Hitler to scale down his goals. They presented five separate plans; he threw out the three most pragmatic and combined the two most ambitious: a crossing of the Meuse on either side of Liège (over the few bridges the Belgians left on their great river after World War I), bypass Liège itself, and speed to Antwerp. The generals retrenched; they proffered what became known as "the Small Solution," a double pincer by the Sixth and Fifth Panzer Armies from above Aachen and through the Ardennes at the Schnee Eifel (Snow Tower) that would circle around and capture Liège, trapping the U.S. First Army and some of the U.S. Ninth Army—a 40-mile effort instead of 125. On October 27, Hitler dismissed it as "incapable of producing decisive results."

The only concessions Hitler made to his generals regarding the Ardennes offensive was to change the O-Tag (D-Day) from November 25 to December 16; he also let *Wacht Am Rhein* be renamed what Generalfeldmarschal Walter Model had originally dubbed the Small Solution: *Herbstnebel*, or Autumn Mist. Model, at fifty-three the youngest field marshal in the German Army, an energetic hero of the Russian front who had tried to carry out Hitler's order that Paris be burned to the ground, adjusted his monocle and sighed to his chief-of-staff: "If it succeeds, it will be a miracle."[12]

It was equally miraculous that the Allies caught no wind of what was up, though lower-echelon intelligence staff got signals that were hardly cryptic. Hitler put a lid on any direct reference to Autumn Mist in radio transmissions and required the few commanders who knew of the plan to sign a statement that a security breach would elicit the death penalty. Couriers for Autumn Mist were escorted by Gestapo agents.

One historian labeled the pre-Bulge intelligence of the Allies, which included the highly touted and previously fruitful ULTRA cryptography, "a total failure . . . among the worst in history," behind that of Pearl Harbor itself.[13] Overconfidence was part of the problem, no doubt.

On December 12, at his bunker in the west, the *Adlerhorst* (Eagle's Nest) near Bad Nauheim outside Frankfurt, a pale Hitler gathered his generals under security so extreme the Fuhrer placed an armed SS guard behind every general at the table. General lieutenant Fritz Bayerlein of the Panzer Lehr Division was so unnerved he confessed later of being afraid to take out his handkerchief.

"If we fail we face dark days," Hitler said, drilling his eyes—the only thing about him that still seemed alive—at his commanders, his voice crawling over inner boulders: "The battle must be fought with brutality and all resistance must be broken in a wave of terror."

German regimental commanders were told about Autumn Mist only three days before the attack, battalion commanders two days before, and company commanders the day before December 16. Some took the news with grim resignation; many a German line soldier had thought the war lost as early as Hitler's attack on Russia in 1941.[14] Others, like the logistics chief of the 62d Volksgrenadier Division, Major Fritz Blum, tried to keep up a good front: "I had to be an optimist, but personally in my heart I had strong doubts. Many officers did." Others simply gritted their teeth; a volksgrenadier sergeant already wounded five times on the Russian front, once by flamethrower, murmured to himself, "I hope all this dirt will soon be done and I will come out of this."[15] But thousands, too, were charged up, eager for a chance to avenge the ruination of German cities by years of Allied bombing, feeling there was nothing to lose. Even the bitter von Rundstedt was caught up in the emotion of the last moment, stifling every ounce of his better judgment with a zero-hour message to the troops: "Soldiers of the Western Front! Your great hour has arrived. Large attacking armies have started against the Anglo-Americans. . . . WE GAMBLE EVERYTHING! You carry . . . the holy obligation to give everything to achieve things beyond human possibilities for our Fatherland and our Fuhrer!"[16]

Before daylight on December 16, 2,623 artillery pieces erupted across the 90-mile front of forest on the German border of Belgium and Luxembourg. Behind them were 410,000 men and over a thousand tanks. Hitler's slowed veins pulsed to life. The vengeance hour was here: for the audacity of the Allies at Normandy; for the surrender at Stalingrad; for von Stauffenberg and his traitors at Rastenburg.

Three days after Autumn Mist seethed into the Ardennes, the little 551st Parachute Infantry Battalion began to take its place in front of the force of all that avenging.

4
The GOYAs face the 1st SS Panzers

Confusion was all. On December 19, moving ahead northeast of the discontinuous 551st column of trucks out of Laon into Belgium, Wood Joerg came to a crossroads where something was covered with blood. It was a horse in its death-shudder. Its head was a mass of peeled flesh; a pool of blood had gathered under its mouth.

"Which way to go, Pappy?" Joerg was staring at the horse, but he was speaking to his operations officer.

"Wherever that horse wasn't," said Pappy Herrmann.

"I think that horse has been everywhere," Joerg said.

Farther on, with the temperature at 15 degrees F., they were halted at another crossroads by a cluster of soldiers who Roger Carqueville thought were British. Joerg got out and asked which way was Bastogne. A lieutenant pointed. Well, which way was Werbomont? The lieutenant pointed the same way. For a time, Joerg argued with the lieutenant.

Joerg got back in the jeep and told Pappy he would swear that lieutenant had just the hint of a German accent. Besides, his map showed Werbomont north and Bastogne to the southeast. How could they be in the same direction? They went opposite the way the soldier pointed and were caught in a rush of civilians and soldiers fleeing Bastogne, who were shouting, "It's surrounded. Let me through! Get out of here!"

From early December 18 to early December 19, both the 82d and 101st Airborne had been rushed to the road hub of Bastogne in the Ardennes, until General Hodges quickly rerouted the 82d up to Werbomont. Some, if not all, of the 551st, attached but not joined to the 82d, made the long detour back west, then north from the outskirts of Bastogne, where many had gotten no further than a blown bridge and a barrage of German machine gun fire. Others' orders were switched as they prepared to move out from Laon. The long, cryptic combat notebook entry of Captain Marshall Dalton of A Company for December 19 begins: "Action—Red. 1200 move. Bastogne" and ends with "Trucks asked for. Werbomont, Belgium. First Army. Hodges***. Notify Colonel when ready. Ammo—all. H20. Stay closed up. 6 jeep. 1/2-ton. SKIDOO." Some men obviously moved out before the change of orders.

Frenetic preparations were made throughout December 19. Included in distribution with such winter clothes as raincoats, mufflers, sweaters, and wool undertrousers—most of which the men later would be ordered to shed—were gas masks. Dalton noted that the company had to be ready for bayonet fighting. Mail was suspended. Cigarettes were limited to "50 smokes per company." And there was no doubt they would be trucking straight into a firefight. Dalton wrote: "Attack at once . . . fire and movement, aggressive . . . keep moving . . . no pinning down . . . attack vigorously." In fact, like everybody else among the Allies, the 551st would be doing no attacking for eight days, but rather dire defense.

For two days—December 19 and 20—the GOYAs tried to get to Werbomont, a trip that, without gunfire, should have taken them four hours. They were constantly waylaid by the artillery and guns of the advancing panzers. One convoy was badly strafed by a Luftwaffe aircraft flying dangerously low under the fog. Word of that got back to Chuck Fairlamb's Headquarters Company mortar section as it threw its things together, causing "some of the men (to become) quite sick."

One man was sickened for a different reason when word of the Bulge hit. A few days before the order to move out came, Private Jim Welsh of Headquarters Company had been cleaning his .45 revolver in the barracks at Laon when he accidentally shot himself in the hand. He heard of the Bulge breakthrough, which he would miss, from a hospital bed in Rheims. "I travel on a tremendous guilt trip on this thing," he told me. "I missed the Bulge from a damn foolish thing." Clell Whitener, who witnessed the accident, would rib him about it years later, but "when talk gets too close to the Bulge," Welsh admitted, "I ease away. It's a burden on me."

Another man with a less debilitating injury—a dislocated rib from hitting the dirt at Isola during a shelling—Virgil Dorr, the class GOYA boxer, forged discharge papers for himself from his hospital in Nice and went AWOL to catch up with the 551st at the Bulge.

"It's a madhouse," Fairlamb noted. "Nearly 2300, very few lights, and we're drawing equipment and loading trucks and trailers as fast as we can." The only briefing his platoon received went as follows: "If anything happens, the convoy won't stop; if any trucks are disabled, get them off the road if possible and try to catch the last truck, which will be empty. If you can't do that, then proceed to Werbomont the best way you can. It's near Liège, Belgium." Werbomont is actually about 30 miles south of Liège, and for those who overturned a truck, as Milo Huempfner had, it was a long walk indeed. Only one truck and one jeep made it straight to Werbomont from Fairlamb's convoy—at 1:30 P.M. on December 21. The rest came in ten hours later.

Part of the reason so many GOYAs got lost was that they were told to drive without headlights—a convoy blackout. Roger Carqueville reported his group got so far off course that they ended up far north of the Bulge, in Holland. Bypassing Werbomont 10 miles north at Spa, Sergeant Jack Carr's eighteen-truck convoy, which originally included the hapless Huempfner, endlessly circled the town of General Hodges's First Army headquarters, without knowing it was even there, and ended up 50 miles south in Luxembourg! As they stopped to gas up, an old Luxembourger pounded on their truck, shouting, "*Kaput Boche!*"

"We didn't know whether he wanted us to kill Germans or whether he had some dead ones," Carr recalled.

The old man signaled for Carr and a friend to follow him to a barn. They cocked their pistols, kicked in the door, only to find a well-fatted pig. "*Kaput Boche!*" the man smiled, nodding quickly. Before Carr's buddy shot the pig in the ear, the farmer cried out, "No! No! Moment! Moment!" until his wife came running with two large basins. Then he gave the signal; the pig dropped from the shot, the farmer slit his throat, and the wife caught the gushing blood. "Blutwurst! Blutwurst!" the farmer sang. So went Carr's first contact with the German Boche. One can only wonder at the pragmatism of Luxembourgers.

The only official Army photograph from the entire war that specifically identifies the 551st is of that frenetic period. It shows a double column of paratroopers of the unit marching on either side of the road "moving up into the Bulge."[17] The GOYAs are not in trucks, as they were almost the entire time they were trying to get to Werbomont and Ster. A light powder of snow dusts the fields and ruts, and the road is wet but clear. Since a heavy snowfall blanketed the Ardennes late on December 21 and clung—the day most of the battalion reached Ster—it would appear that this photo was taken en route. The second man on the right is clearly smiling with embarrassment, his helmet tilted slightly downward. It may be that the picture was staged for the Signal Corps, and everyone had been ordered out of the trucks to look sharp and orderly in marching columns for history. The fact is, little of the headlong dash to the Bulge was orderly, and the worried face of T/4 Jim Smith of A Company on the left betrays that.

At Marche, facing the center protrusion of the "bulge," where the men of the 84th Division were digging trenches, the GOYAs stopped at a traffic jam to have early morning rations, a jittery meal at best with intermittent machine gun and mortar fire coming in. There Lieutenant Colonel Joerg hopped out of his jeep to try and clear the road, which was filled with fleeing civilians pushing carts piled high with their few portable possessions, baby carriages, riding mules and bicycles, in a stunned foot race from the battle at nearby Hotton. Even more bewildering was the sight of American tank columns and weary men of the front-line units through which the German juggernaut had finally burst, such as the 106th Division. Lieutenant Dick Goins described it: "We encountered several tank columns and artillery units moving to the rear. They were moving back quite rapidly, and we were moving forward. This was of concern to all of us. What were we getting into here? To the men of my platoon and also to me, it was most disheartening to see our forces on the defense—and especially withdrawing."

Goins was in earshot of one terrified Belgian who chattered in broken English: "The Germans are coming! They will kill everyone this time. They will stay because the Americans are beaten!" Suddenly an eight-year-old girl ran out of a stone house clutching a medal of Mary, the mother of Christ, and thrust it into the hands of Lieutenant Glenn Slucter, the battalion's supply officer, a Lutheran. She ran back in having said nothing. The medal became his most valued equipment. He would carry it throughout the Battle of the Bulge to the end of the war. He later converted to Catholicism.

According to Sergeant Roy McCraw of A Company, and recorded in my own father's journal as occurring at 6 P.M. on December 21, the 551st skirmished with troops that "should not have been there" between Marche and Hotton: German paratroopers. They were the remnants of Hitler's last parachute drop of the war, Operation *Stösser* (Auk).

With only a week to prepare itself, it was no surprise this Auk barely flew. Assigned to the unenviable task of cobbling together paratroopers from myriad airborne regiments on the western front for the special night jump to accompany Autumn Mist was Oberst Baron Fredrich-August von der Heydte, a hero of the German drop on Crete in 1941. Long disillusioned with the war, Von der Heydte had little latitude; as a cousin of Klaus von Stauffenberg, the man who tried to assassinate Hitler in July, his every movement was watched.

Dropped in high winds by green pilots, only one hundred of the 870 men hit the drop zone between Malmédy and Eupen at the northern edge of the Bulge. Most of the German paratroopers were scattered throughout the entire length and width of the Ardennes; one platoon fell just outside Bonn in Germany. Some of those forlorn paratroopers would fight alone or would try to trudge alone back to German lines; many, totally untrained, were crippled on impact and froze, only to be found in spring during thaw. A year later a German counterpart to the GI newspaper *Stars and Stripes* called the mission "Operation Mass Murder."

Still, as with Operation *Greif*, the *Stosser* fiasco tied up U.S. troops. More than three thousand men of the U.S. 18th Regiment near Eupen spent a week doing nothing but hunting down paratroopers of the ill-fated German drop. Other units, such as the 551st between Marche and Hotton, were waylaid in shootouts that took precious hours away from their journey to Werbomont. The day after my father and his fellows skirmished with some lost German paratroopers, on December 22, Baron von der Heydte, frostbitten and suffering from pneumonia, stumbled into Monschau and gave himself up to the Americans. Asked to confess, Von der Heydte thought he was to be shot; then he realized it was a Catholic chaplain preparing him for Christmas.

After their brush with the lost German paratroopers, in whose faces they may have seen something of their own fate at Camp Mackall, the GOYAs pressed on. At the Hotton bridge over the Ourthe River a few miles east of Marche, a GOYA HQ Company convoy came under artillery and small arms fire from the rapidly advancing 116th Panzer Division, under the aegis of General Manteuffel's Fifth Panzer Army. The battle in that sector of the Ourthe was especially chaotic, with the 116th surrounding with its trailing forces one battalion of the U.S. 3d Armored Division near Marcouray.

The GOYAs bailed out and took cover, while the 3d Armored and men of the 51st Combat Engineer Battalion stopped the 116th short of the bridge in "a hailstorm of fire." Lieutenant Andy Titko saw a figure dart in front of his truck; it was a German soldier. Quickly he tried to raise his carbine, but it caught in gear about as tangled as the convoy. After the long turning of their columns completely around to seek yet another road, the 551st men headed to Werbomont, still eighteen hours of zig-zagging away.

Fatigue set in for some of the black Quartermaster drivers of the 551st truck convoy during the eye-squinting, arm-tensing circuitous journey to and through Belgium. Lieutenant Ralph Wenthold spelled one who appeared to be about to pass out, though Wenthold had never driven a GMC. "I was grinding those gears pretty bad," Wenthold remembered. "And the men in the back were shouting, 'Hey, grind me a pound of those, will you?'"

The mixups caused by *Greif* were occasionally mirthful. Mel Zais, who was the 517th executive officer at the time, related that a black truck driver hustling toward Belgium was interrogated at a road crossing, and "asked about who pitched for the New York Yankees, plus a couple of other questions that he couldn't answer. Finally, in exasperation, he turned to the questioner and said, 'Boy, did you ever see a black German?'"[18]

At Hotton, Sergeant Doug Dillard, barely eighteen at the Bulge, peered out in the smoky dust of the battle and thought he saw SS men struggling to ford the icy Ourthe River on foot. The 3d Armored were "shooting them like ducks in the water and the SS were still coming. They looked like they were hopped up on dope." While his own convoy turned, Dillard watched, amazed, as a jeep of the 1st Army Engineers drove by with an SS man pinned to its hood. They seemed an inhuman, relentless force, and Dillard shuddered to think what was waiting for him and his fellow GOYAs up the road near Werbomont.[19]

The front, indeed, seemed to be everywhere, and the booming of guns was heard in all four directions. After finally reaching Werbomont, where both Ridgway's XVIII Airborne Corps and Gavin's 82d Airborne Division were headquartered, Lieutenant Dick Durkee—still wearing the "pinks and greens" dress uniform—ran into General Gavin.

"What the hell are you wearing that for? Where've you been?" Gavin blasted him.

"I went overnight to Rheims from Laon to get boxing equipment, and before I knew it we were moving out."

"Well, you're not going to be needing that boxing equipment up here, soldier," Gavin glared. Within a day, Durkee exchanged his dress outfit for the combat fatigues of a dead man.

At Werbomont the 551st's adjutant, Lieutenant Paul Hoch, and S-2 Captain Ed Hartman ran a gauntlet of colonels and majors down a long corridor, each frantic to get their sense of what lay on the roads coming north. A one-star general, then a two-star general plied them for information, then led them into a makeshift war room with a huge wall map on which flags and pins of various colors were being moved even as they talked. It was then that the 551st was unhooked from its two-week technical attachment to its natural mother, the 82d Airborne and ordered into defensive positions as part of the 30th Division, its one reserve.

Bivouacked 5 miles east of Werbomont in the little town of Ster at the winter solstice, it was a night "as cold as a witch's behind," said Emory Albritton. They were hit not just by snow but by a bombardment of German propaganda pamphlets urging them to give up, as all was lost.

The GOYAs had been placed in an especially grim spot: between Stavelot and Trois Ponts, in a flange of territory bounded by the Ambleve and Salm rivers, where the very spearhead of the entire German thrust in the Ardennes was thrashing forward in the forest. *Kampfgruppe* (battle group) Peiper of the 1st SS Panzer Division, known as "Hitler's Own," was probing everywhere for bridges.[20]

Peiper, leader of the battle group, blonde and Robert Redford–handsome, was originally christened Joachim but had long since changed his name from the Hebraic to the more Germanic Jochen. The Hollywood version in the movie *The Battle of the Bulge* renders Peiper through the dark-haired actor Robert Shaw and contains several other inaccuracies. It depicts the *Kampfgruppe* chief as gleeful to lead his column with thirteen of the 70-ton *Konigstigers;* in fact, Peiper was scornful of their sluggishness and infinite thirst (they got only one-half mile to the gallon of gas, half the rate of the U.S. Sherman tank), and sent his King Tigers to the rear early on. Also, though the movie shows Shaw racing toward a fuel dump that is set afire in front of him, in fact Peiper never did find a giant fuel dump, though he unwittingly came very close to one.

Overplayed, when it came to the massacres by Peiper's group, Hollywood actually underplayed their terror at the Bulge, focusing solely on the incident near Malmédy. In fact, the German spearhead which took Hitler's orders "to fight in a wave of terror" at face value, started its atrocities right out of the chute of the Losheim Gap, at their first objective, the town of Honsfeld. Known as the "Blowtorch Battalion" for its ruthlessness in completely destroying two towns and their inhabitants on the Russian front, *Kampfgruppe* Peiper made its presence felt in no uncertain terms in the Ardennes.

The day the German offense began, December 16, was the day Marlene Dietrich was to entertain GIs of the 394th Infantry at Honsfeld. Barely had the blonde actress slipped off her boots to put on black pumps when she was bundled into a jeep and spirited away from the nearing explosions. Peiper, frustrated by an early traffic jam caused by horse-drawn artillery, rolled into Honsfeld on December 17, slowly negotiating the narrow streets, spraying buildings with machine gun fire at the lead. Behind Peiper's lead vehicle with wheels in front and capterpillar tracks in back (a halftrack), some Americans gave frightened but heroic small arms resistance before they were routed. In five separate surrenderings, at least thirty-eight GIs, either carrying white flags or with their hands up as prisoners, were shot and killed. One American, wounded, was crushed by a tank as he cried for help. In one of those rare displays of conscience that ripple through the centuries amid the terror, a young German threw himself in front of a clump of horrified prisoners just as they were about to be executed. Not so lucky was sixteen-year-old Erna Collas, called the prettiest girl in Honsfeld, who was found after spring thaw in a shallow grave outside town with seven shots in her back.

Two miles up the road at Büllingen, Peiper seized 50,000 gallons of gasoline and ordered captured GIs to fill up his 90 tanks. Aided by a Belgian civilian wearing a swastika armband who saluted the German invaders with a Nazi salute, they rousted two hundred Americans from basement hideouts. One, the wounded Private Bernard Pappel, was shot in the head by a member of Peiper's unit.

Around noon, passing through the Baugnez Crossroads 2 miles south of Malmédy, Peiper, who spoke English, yelled out to captives from Battery B of the 285 Field Artillery Observation Battalion herded in a field, "It's a long way to Tipperary, boys!" The unit had been rushing south from Holland to help rescue the doomed 106th Division at Saint-Vith, when it had run smack into Peiper's tank column. Peiper pressed on south to Ligneuville, leaving rear guard troops and tanks to herd the prisoners near the Café Bodarwe at the crossroads.

What happened next injected into the Battle of the Bulge, and American troops in particular, a fierceness born of fear and revenge, the opposite of what Hitler's terror order had countenanced. Accounts from both sides at the Baugnez Crossroads vary, yet the official U.S. version of the horror that December 17 can be roughly summarized as follows:

While about one hundred prisoners, surrounded by SS, were stripped of everything from watches to buttons, one captain objected, "You're violating the Geneva Convention!" for which he was shot in the forehead by an SS trooper with a P-38 revolver. Around 2 P.M., a gunner from a Mark IV tank fired his pistol into the group and an SS man shouted, *"Macht alle kaputt!"* (Kill them all!) Machine guns from two tanks began spraying the defenseless GIs right to left and back again, several times. The moans of the wounded cracked through the silence when it was over, "almost like a lowing," according to one survivor who had lain under a dead man. There followed a *blutrausch*, or killing frenzy, in which those still groaning or caught breathing were executed by SS men walking through the piles of bodies. One followed an unsuspecting medic trying to bandage survivors, telling him *"Das ist sehr nett. Gut gemacht"* (That's very good. Good job.), before shooting the patients in the head.

Although badly wounded, about twenty Americans managed to feign death lying in the snow, squelching their shivers and breath in the 12-degree weather. Realizing they could not last that way for long, they rose up to hobble pathetically toward the woods or to the Bodarwe Café. The café was set a fire by the SS; some were shot when they emerged or before they reached the cover of forest.

Between 3:30 P.M. and midnight of December 17, seventeen survivors made it somehow—one had hidden in an icy stream for hours—to the friendly lines of the 291st Combat Engineer Battalion or to Malmédy itself, where elements of the 970th Counter Intelligence Corps were stationed. One special agent, holed up in the Belgian governor's mansion, was the American Gustav Berle. He was stunned by the screeching halt of a lightless jeep carrying three grime-covered GI, one with blood oozing from his chest. A .50-caliber machine gunner on a halftrack parked in front of the mansion mistook the jeep for German and foolishly pulled the trigger. Though the strange visitors were not hit, an errant bullet penetrated the palm of a soldier right next to Berle, and he cried out, an innocent victim facing innocent victims of the slaughter at Baugnez.

Forty-five years later, quite by accident, I found myself working with **Gus Berle** in his efforts with the Service Corps of Retired Executives. Berle was one of the first Americans to learn of what became known (somewhat inaccurately) as the Malmédy massacre when he brought those three forlorn men into an aid station.[21]

Word came to General Hodges at First Army headquarters about what happened near Malmédy by 4:30 P.M. on December 17; Eisenhower was briefed about the massacre the next day. Indeed, over the forty-eight hours after it occurred, few American troops in Europe, including those trucking into the Bulge like the 551st, did not know that a heinous war crime had been commited against U.S. troops. If any GI had had doubts about what he was fighting for, Malmédy effectively dismissed them.

A medic in the 551st, Private Ed Henriques, asserted: "At Malmédy we built up a horrible hatred." Henriques insists that he was part of a five-truck convoy that drove by the Baugnez Crossroads with an express purpose: "They took us there to see it." Five nights afterward, a heavy snow covered eighty-six bodies.

The massacre would haunt Jochen Peiper the rest of his life, though his sentence of death by hanging at Nuremburg was commuted to life imprisonment, of which he served only eleven years. (He was killed in 1976 when Frenchmen firebombed his home in Traves, France.) The typical German SS veteran explanation of what happened at the Baugnez Crossroads was that it was an "overreaction" to American POWs who were fleeing arrest. Untersharfuhrer Helmet Hennig of the 9th SS Panzers put it this way: "[Toland's book] on the Peiper massacre is a Wild West book— this is a novel! It was an error, a miscalculation. Someone might have become nervous there at Malmédy. The prisoners were not disarmed completely. There was not enough time for Peiper to do such things and not enough guards. Some Germans became nervous and overreacted. In war, anything is possible."[22]

En route to the Salm—including at Ligneuville, Parfondruy, Ster, Rehardmont, and Trois-Ponts—111 Belgians were killed by Peiper's band for no other reason than that they were bending in a certain way to drink water or turned a certain corner on a horse, or looked a certain way through a window. The *Kampfgruppe* murdered a total of 353 U.S. prisoners.

At Lienne Creek, Lieutenant Fred Chapin of the 291st Engineer Combat Battalion was all that stood between Peiper's tanks and Werbomont, a mile west, where sat Ridgway's and Gavin's hastily mounted XVIII Airborne Corps and 82d Airborne Division headquarters. Chapin ducked Peiper's lead tank's fire and for precious seconds lost sight of his signalman. Then he repositioned himself, caught the man's wildly flailing hands, and turned the detonator key. The bridge at Habiemont collapsed in "a streak of blue lights."

On the opposite bank, Peiper smashed his fist on one knee and exclaimed, "The damned engineers! The damned engineers!" It was the most portentous exclamation of the Battle of the Bulge. Though on December 19 he would double back through La Gleize for one last desperate try to cross the Amblève at Stoumont, Peiper would get no farther west.

Traveling through burning buildings in Stoumont on the way to Ster, the GOYAs got caught in crossfire between Peiper and the 504th Parachute Infantry Regiment of Reuben Tucker, a man whom General Gavin would later praise as the top regimental commander of the war in Europe. The worst casualty the GOYAs—who had a few more miles to go before they could sleep in frozen foxholes—took there was the lapel of one soldier crouching near Doug Dillard.

Pandemonium met Captain Tims Quinn of C Company on his arrival at Ster as he squeezed inside a ring of 155mm howitzers firing in all directions. Quinn's first thought was of Vicksburg and Shiloh. All around him lay Germans and Americans in the snow and wrecked tanks, as the smell of burning flesh and wood rose with smoke. "Everything was frozen— blood and ice," Quinn recounted. "This scene of wasted desolation stands out in my mind more than anything of that time."

Sergeant Harry Renick of A Company also found himself in the middle of the howitzer ring fired by the 117th Infantry Regiment of the 30th Division.

"Are we surrounded?" Renick queried innocently.

"No, we're not really surrounded," said one man who was cramming shells into a breach. "There's an opening you can get through." For the life of him Renick could not see that opening. He began to dig a 6-foot-square shelter with blankets and shelter halves folded on its floor roofed with pine boughs. "It was like sleeping in an icebox," Renick said. Later he tried sleeping on pine needles and shelter halves out in the snow. That wasn't so hot, either. At one point Renick just sat on his helmet and dozed for fifteen minutes. When he awoke, his posterior was frozen to the helmet. It took a half-hour in a farmhouse to thaw it off.

My father arrived in Ster at 10 P.M. on the night of December 21 and was consigned for a time, as were others, to a "hay loafted" (an interesting misspelling in his diary). He didn't rest long, but pulled guard duty that night. "I could hear the buzz bombs going over, but you couldn't see the flash because of the cloudy sky," he wrote. The threat overhead was opaque, but the sounds—what would Aref Orfalea have heard that night he stayed up while everyone else, exhausted from the drive to Belgium, slept? The thump in the chest of artillery resounding, the rattle of machine guns, here and there the popping of rifles that kept your lookout eyes ever wide peering through the snow that fell in huge flakes that night—the dire duet of the 117th Infantry, with two German units trying desperately to reinforce and connect a lifeline to Peiper: the 2nd SS Panzergrenadier Regiment of Lieutenant

Colonel Rudolf Sandig and the 1st SS Reconnaissance Battalion of Major Gustav Knittel. Did he know that the day before, Bastogne in the south had been surrounded by the Germans?

The GOYAs themselves were beginning to feel surrounded—by the cold. At Werbomont, they received an order to shed their overcoats and overshoes: "We were told we were going to be moving fast and could not afford to be bogged down with heavy gear."[23] Although some would get a vagrant pair of shoes or a mackinaw, the die was cast for the high rate of casualties they would sustain over the next two weeks from frostbite and trenchfoot. The heavy snow and the mercury drop near zero that very night as they dug in at Ster or pulled the hay around them only seemed to mock the order to disrobe. To make matters worse, when a few tried to start fires to keep warm, Joerg ordered them snuffed so that they would not give away their positions to German reconnaissance planes flying low throughout the night. Left thirsty because their canteen water had frozen, some men were allowed to light fires in stone houses, but only to "cook the snow" for water, according to Pvt. Joe Viserta. "That was a rap!" Viserta remembered, a rap that continued for two weeks until there were few men left to warm. Somehow, Tims Quinn managed to get away with digging holes in the wall of his foxhole and placing little candle stubs in them for heat. Andy Titko, on the other hand, was chewed out by Joerg personally for wearing a path with trips back and forth in the snow to fetch hay for his foxhole. He thought the path would also give them away. It seemed just about everything could give them away. On constant alert, the GOYAs listened, as General Gavin wrote about combat soldiers in his diary, "with every pore of their bodies."

In the three days before Christmas 1944, the German onslaught at the Bulge reached its high water mark. Units of Manteuffel's Fifth Panzer Army had poked the nose of the Bulge 3 miles shy of the Meuse River, while Peiper thrashed in his net trying to rip open the northern shoulder. On December 22 Eisenhower, sensing a climax, sent an unusual (for him) Order of the Day to all troops in the Ardennes: "By rushing from his fixed defense the enemy may give us the chance to turn his great gamble into his worst defeat. . . . Let everyone hold before him a single thought—to destroy the enemy on the ground, in the air, everywhere—destroy him!"[24]

The Germans must have thought they could one-up Eisenhower that day, for at noon emissaries from General Luttwitz's 47th Panzer Corps took a message under white flag to Brigadier General Tony McAuliffe, where he was surrounded with the 101st Airborne at Bastogne, threatening the Americans with "total annihilation" unless they gave up in two hours. McAuliffe groaned "Aw, nuts." His G-3, Lieutenant Colonel Harry Kinnard, thought that would suffice as a formal response, and when the German emissaries wondered if he were offering some Christmas package of fruit and *nusse,* another aide spelled it out—"In plain English it means, 'Go to hell.'"

Thus was the stage set for Patton's showy Third Army "relief" of Bastogne and the burgeoning of the myth of what one historian called that "consecrated town." In fact, a heavy assault on Bastogne did not occur until ten days later, when Hitler wheeled his forces in a mindless strike at the road hub after even he realized the *absoluter schwerpunkt* of the Sixth Panzer Army (and Peiper) had been stopped cold on the northern shoulder of the Bulge by the "steady, but unspectacular" forces of Hodges's First Army.

The GOYAs, perhaps the least heralded of the unheralded First Army, were about to make their contribution to that stoppage—in blood. The bastard battalion's first casualties of the Battle of the Bulge would be taken by the thinned forces of the Luftwaffe.

On December 23 the fog lifted like a lid from the Ardennes. For the first time in a week of battle, Hitler's weather luck ran out. Now the skies were an almost free ocean for Allied planes to sail in; more than 3,100 Allied bombers, fighters, and transport planes attacked every column of Germans they could sight in the white landscape, hitting hard on railheads to the rear to sever the German relief trains while dropping 144 tons of badly needed supplies for the resisting forces. Though the weakened Luftwaffe managed eight hundred sorties, many were headed off east of the battlefield. The German generals' nightmare was now here: a clear sky.

The 551st joined men of the 117th Infantry in crawling out of their foxholes to watch the mismatched show. The sky was laced with vapor trails, here long wavy signatures, there white helixes of death. Soon the clear sky grew murky with the artificial fog of the streakings. Pilots were bailing out all over the place. "It seemed as though there wasn't a time when you couldn't look up and see chutes in the air," said Charles Fairlamb. My father exclaimed in his diary about "mucho air activity," and recorded that "two of our boys were hit by a Me [Messerschmidt] 109 which strafed our positions," casualties confirmed by Fairlamb. My father also saw, for the first time, a V-1 rocket in flight, the weapon that had terrorized London in the war's early days. Now everyone was showing his cards.

The next day—Christmas Eve—the 551st got its card: to attack on Christmas down a bald hill south of Stavelot across the Amblève River into a wall of tanks. Along with the attack order came a reading of General Ridgway's Christmas Eve message to all the troops in his sector of the northern shoulder: "In my opinion this is the last dying gasp of the German Army. He is putting everything he has into this fight. We are going to smash that final drive here today in this Corps Zone. This command is the command that will smash the German offensive spirit for this war."

If Ridgway's iron-will order betrays a hint of anxiety, the prospect of reconnoitering barren hillsides that would afford no cover and facing tanks with no tanks of his own imparted to Lieutenant Colonel Wood Joerg more than a hint. That afternoon, after Joerg spoke some moments with his light machine gun platoon about the impending attack, Don Garrigues caught a cloud in the commander's eyes: "It was the first time I had seen him worried and not completely sure of himself. He was contacting as many of the small groups as possible and it seemed to me he wanted to tell us more than he could. . . . The news was not encouraging; in fact, we got the impression that what he wanted to tell us was that the mission bordered on the suicidal."

Though the Americans had retaken Stavelot, the Germans had not given up getting it back. Three days before, under cover of heavy fire from tanks and self-propelled tank destroyers, Sandig's 2d SS Panzergrenadiers waded into the icy Amblève in a daring attempt to cross over. The battle was bloody, and many of the SS, picked off in the water, were carried downstream with the reddened ice floes. Though some made it across, the attack as a whole was repelled.

Joerg took his company commanders, along with Captain Ed Hartman, Major Pappy Herrmann, Major Bill Holm, Lieutenant Dick Durkee and Lieutenant Andy Titko (who was hit by shrapnel in the leg during the reconnoiter), in the dark that night to see what lay in store for them. "We saw a dead American soldier lying there where he had fallen, his face turned toward the sky, and I couldn't help thinking what a hell of a Christmas eve it was for him," Pappy Herrmann recounted. In fact, dead American and German soldiers lay all over the hill covered with frost, their eyes vacant and glazed, eerily sparkling in the full moonlight.

Durkee thought some of the men were airborne, brought sadly and finally to earth—possibly of the 504th Regiment—because the blankets that covered them were too short and revealed their paratrooper boots.

The GOYA attack would require downward movement on open ground to confront Germans dug in on the near bank, and then, if successful that far, a dive into the freezing river just as Sandig's 2nd SS troops had attempted, to get to the far shore, where their bazookas, if not wet, would have an uneven chance at best against a line of panzers. The Germans were moving on both banks; it shaped up to be a disaster.

Infantry backup from the 30th Infantry Division was less than assured. Its 117th Regiment was already licking more than its share of wounds. On the telephone on Christmas Eve, Ridgway sounded uninformed about the situation in the GOYAs' sector and concerned that Leland Hobbs's 30th Division was weakening: "I don't know what's going on in the south of Leland's east flank. I'm going to put more stuff up behind Leland's area in the morning, if not before daylight. I want to get more infantry up to him. It's the only thing he lacks. He's got everything else in the world, a list of attachments as long as your arm. More stuff than any other division, and yet he's always crying for more. I'd have done that before. Just hope to God that he did destroy that final bit of resistance up there." Ridgway, who like Gavin was constantly moving all over the confused battlefield, his M-1 rifle slung over his shoulder, reveals with his own gasp the frenzy of the situation: "I'm trying to catch my breath here."

Where was that "resistance up there" Ridgway was praying Hobbs had rubbed out? If it was Peiper, he would soon be reassured: on Christmas eve, out of gas, bridges, and steam, Peiper ordered his men to abandon their vehicles (and thirty-four tanks) and walk out of the battle. But Sandig's SS panzergrenadiers and the 1,800 men of Knittel's 1st SS Reconnaissance Battalion were still in place along the Amblève facing Stavelot.[25]

Ridgway ordered that Christmas Eve day: "I want a river crossing site reconnoitered without delay. I want immediate measures taken to assemble bridge material to bridge streams." Among others—including the 82d Airborne in toto, which had been told to fall back from the Salm River—the GOYAs may have been assigned a bridge team for their attack across the Amblève below Stavelot.

The tension mounted for the 551st that night as the men drew ammunition. "I suppose that as infantrymen we dreaded a face-to-face meeting with tanks about as much as anything," Garrigues noted. But suddenly, around midnight, just as the Christmas began, even in the war-ravaged Ardennes, the GOYAs' baptism by fire at the Bulge was called off. It was an immense relief. "Quite a few of us breathed a little prayer before we went to sleep that night," Pappy Herrmann recalled. Garrigues says, "I had been given one of the best Christmas presents ever." My father, too, was back from the brink: "We were sweating out going into the attack or going back to the hay loafted. It turned out to be the hay loafted and you don't know how much I thanked God on that Xmas Eve that it was."

No one seems to know for sure why the attack was called off. What may have saved the GOYAs from a bloody Christmas was that most unlikely of things: a double retreat of German (of the 1st SS Panzers with Peiper et al.) and American forces (the 82d Airborne, to which the 551st was again attached on Christmas Day). The American pullback was ordered on December 24 by none other than General Bernard Montgomery, who was concerned that the eager 82d might just get outflanked by both the 1st SS Panzer and the 2d SS Panzer Divisons; he also was throwing in the towel on the doomed 106th Division at Saint-Vith. "Tidy the battlefield" was Monty's song for the smooth new battle line that ran southwest at a 45-degree angle from Trois-Ponts to Manhay. The move, at least at first, infuriated the American generals, particularly Omar Bradley, who had lost the northern half of his Bulge command on December 20 to Monty, but also Ridgway and Gavin, two men who did not understand the word "withdraw."

But as much as he groused, Gavin knew his right flank, in particular, was one more big assault by the 2d SS Panzers from collapsing. He had sped to Ridgway's headquarters on December 23 demanding tank support from Doc Eaton, XVIII Airborne Corps chief of staff, who said he had none. Eaton and Gavin got into an unrecorded war of words (Eaton later called Gavin "a goddamn Black Irishman, looking out for number one").

Ridgway's biographer, Clay Blair, thought the origins of the Eaton–Gavin faceoff lay further back in their professional association. Though Gavin later assessed his mentor Ridgway as "undoubtedly the best combat corps commander in the American Army in World War II," Ridgway and Gavin may have suffered from that most unfortunate of traits for close colleagues: They were too much alike. Of course, Gavin was younger and somewhat more impetuous. Gavin from the age of two was raised Catholic by adoptive parents in a poor Pennsylvania coal-mining town; Ridgway, on the other hand, grew up in New York in a well-to-do Episcopalian family, a mandarin who seemed Edwardian in his polish, rectitude, and tact. But they were both very aggressive, on-the-spot commanders, both charismatic, always walking the trenches among their troops, both in excellent physical condition.

Perhaps better than Gavin, Ridgway understood the political, as well as tactical, considerations pressing on Eisenhower to keep Montgomery happy, for most of the forces north of the Meuse were British. One outcome of the pullback, however, that ultimately determined the fate of the 551st Parachute Infantry Battalion, was that both the 9th SS Panzers Division and the 62d Volksgrenadier Division leaped across the Salm on the heels of the retreating 82d Airborne, attacking it before it even settled into new positions. Forces from those two German divisions would soon lock horns with the separate battalion and send it to the final inferno. Itching for a counterattack he felt too long postponed, Gavin would place the 551st at the tip of the spearhead in his new sector. Thus Bernard Montgomery's decision was the first of several that would seal the GOYAs' fate.

5

Christmas at Ster

Christmas Day 1944 dawned clear and cold. Those like my father in his hayloft slept like babes in a manger, soundly, knowing the Angel of Death had passed over them the night before. But the GOYAs awoke at Ster to bombardment and careening planes. The clear day meant more air battles. And they were now being hit by their own planes.

Emerging from their foxholes to watch the dogfights, Sergeant Bill Dean counted seven American B-17s being shot down. Then Dean spied a P-51 Mustang chasing a Messerschmidt right over the GOYAs' heads. Its .50-caliber machine guns ignited the German fighter but also sprayed the 551st. Two men cried out, wounded by the friendly fire. One was Private Strair Youngblood of HQ Company, whose Achilles heel hadn't made it into his foxhole in time. "Strair had a big smile on his face when they loaded him on the stretcher," Jim Heffernan recounted. "He said, 'Boy, there is a $10,000 wound. Ha, ha, ha."

Another treetop chase by an American P-38 of a Messerschmidt roused Sergeant Harold "Pappy" Sindler of A Company, who uncorked his pistol and fired wildly. The German plane burst into flames and crashed into a hill. Sindler, his buddy Jim Stevens reported, "got all excited that he had hit it . . . with all that fire that the P-38 was pouring in, poor old Pappy thought he had shot it down. Naturally, we razzed him." Nine days later, Sindler was killed.

Sergeant Roy McCraw dove into his foxhole to avoid shards of planes exploding in the air, as well as the machine gun fire of a Focke Wulf 190, which kicked up dirt into his mouth and eyes. McCraw peered out to see the Focke Wulf and a British Spitfire both crash together on the same spot, neither pilot getting out in time. Others from American planes bailed out, only to be carried by a stiff wind behind German lines or consumed in fire. Joe Cicchinelli looked on helplessly as seven Americans jumped from their fiery bomber, their chutes ignited like torches as they fell. They hit the ground as charred corpses. He took some measure of revenge on a German fighter pilot who looped close enough to the ground for the men to see him leering. When the pilot circled back for the kill, Don Thompson fired his Thompson submachine gun at the craft, while Cicchinelli unloaded with a .30 caliber machine gun; others shot their M-1s. The plane was hit, and the pilot lost his smile in a hurry.

Amid the aerial fury, German V-1 flying bombs and V-2 rockets could be seen once again slicing a seam in the sky, and one of them would meet up with a GOYA. Private Ralph Nichols of C Company was walking along a train track that Christmas morning when he slipped on an icy tie and smashed his back on the iron rail. Trucked to a hospital in Liège, before the day was over Nichols awoke to window glass crashing. The hospital was being rained on by V-1s; one made a direct hit on a wing where German prisoners were being held. More than fifty of them were killed by what the Fuhrer had once called "the decisive weapon of the war."

The night before, on Christmas Eve, England took its last sizable flying bomb attack of the war. Thirty-eight people were killed, including a six-month-old infant at Oldham. Those bombs contained a bizarre twist whose rationale could be found only in the sadistic mind of Hitler: British

POW letters home for Christmas were cached in the warheads. They littered English streets and farms like cruel confetti. From the autumn of 1944 to the spring of 1945, 2,500 Londoners died from nine thousand V-2 launchings. As their launching ramps were overrun by the Allies on March 29, 1945, a more advanced V-2 that could travel 2,800 miles was close to production, a quantum leap past the normal 160-mile range. Pegged to carry atomic weapons, as the eminent historian John Keegan put it, "It was the crowning mercy of the Second World War that it came to nothing."[26]

Somehow that Christmas Day, taking cover from the friendly and not-so-friendly fire above, the GOYAs celebrated the birth of the Prince of Peace. To each was issued a Hershey chocolate bar by Wood Joerg. Some took refuge in Ster villagers' stone bungalows where children marveled to find their shoes filled up with GI chocolate. The children wouldn't let the men go and often ran up to the firing lines to see those chocolate-mad soldiers. The Colonel was a special object of fascination: "The kids kept coming as close as they could to see Wood. They had to run them back all the time."[27]

In the Ster homes kettles of water were boiled for a few frozen turkeys. "The turkey was just like rubber," Tims Quinn reported. "That's not the way to cook frozen turkey." Most chipped away at frozen C rations.

As for my father, I can only surmise he ate the same as everyone else: poorly, and glad to be still alive to taste. He did love Christmas, a time when all the family would gather, and various GOYA-like stragglers either far from family or with none. It was always his task to string the Christmas tree with lights and top it with an angel while Mother stirred up hot chocolate and prepared the boxes of bulbs for us three children to hang. The ornaments included one small wooden paratrooper, which my father would hang. Sometimes after Christmas dinner, after he would say the prayer like Bob Cratchit unraveling a string of thanks, and fill people's drinks, the music would come on and my father would launch into something I have never seen the likes of since, something he called "The Poison Dance." One by the one, the records were spun and my father would begin dancing by himself in the gathering circle of the Christmas crowd in the amber den of our home in Tarzana, California. First the fare, selected by my brother, was rather tame—the Beatles, the Beach Boys. But by the time "China Grove" (the Doobie Brothers) came on with its back-scratching guitar opener and staccato piano, his clothes began to come off—first the shoes, then the socks, then his tie and shirt. When the climax was reached with his all-time favorite, "Who Are You?" by The Who, his undershirt was off, and my mother was hiding her eyes wondering what was next. "Oh I've got to get out the poison!" he would shout, socking the air, hopping rhythmically, dancing with his ghosts, yanking his fists back as if

cocking some rifle of joy, a Kirk Gibson motion when the crippled Los Angeles Dodger pinch hitter won a 1988 World Series game hitting one-
handed, egged on by the crowd, which would clap in rhythm for him.

Sweat would begin running off his gray-haired chest, and people would
laugh and cry out and clap as my brother bounced over the couches, bursting with poison of his own.

The GOYAs were beginning to do their own restless dance at Ster, and
it would continue till their feet turned black. The battle to keep feet from
freezing in thin leather paratrooper boots was unending. And the poison
had no egress. Phil Hand wrapped his feet in toilet paper, to little avail;
his feet turned purple and his toenails fell off. Easy Harry Renick developed a rotation method with his two pair of socks, warming one inside his
shirt along his chest, constantly exchanging it for the worn one of cold
sweat. It worked somewhat better than wax paper under the socks.

By late afternoon on December 25, 1944, the 551st received orders from
XVIII Airborne Corps to move out from Ster west to Rahier and hook up
once again with the 82d Airborne. It was the battalion's third reattachment
of the Bulge (they would have six before they would be taken apart), and the
GOYAs began to feel like firemen jerked here and there by a blowup fire,
which they were just barely escaping. They would not escape it for long.

Earlier in the day, about 10 A.M., General Ridgway, who would later erroneously state that he never had personal contact with the 551st and
would twice refuse me interviews, citing declining health, wrote in his
diary: "Called Gen. Hobbs and asked him when the 551st could be assem-
bled, where, and when ready to move; how it would be moved, either by
foot or by truck, would come later. A representative is to be sent to this
Headquarters without delay."

Ridgway was concerned about the 82d Airborne's punishment during
its withdrawal from the Salm River and wanted the GOYAs to be ready to
back the All-Americans up. But he revealed how strapped the northern
shoulder was getting for transport: "Gen. Hobbs informed me that it will
take very little time to assemble it, but he did not have the trucks to move
it. He also wished to bring to our attention that there was a considerable
build-up at Trois-Ponts, and they were bringing heavy concentrated artillery fire on it and he did not like to give up the battalion until that situation developed further." Clearly the 551st, an experienced unit but
unscathed yet at the Bulge, was a precious commodity the 30th Infantry
Division wanted to keep.

The next day at Rahier, about a dozen of the five hundred tank suits the
battalion's supply officer Harry "Candy" Miller had bartered for in Nice
caught up with them. "Very, very damn few," Emory Albritton snapped. A

few others got the precious gift of white camouflage snow suits, probably captured from Germans, since they were not standard Allied issue. What happened to the 488 other tank suits? No one knows. That was one in a line of mounting mishaps, Dan Morgan thought, in what would become a succession of smaller and larger tragedies, "each of which accelerated the destruction of our battalion."[28]

On December 27, with instincts telling him that the time was now right to move from defense to offense, General James Gavin came down in person to Rahier to inform the 551st that it was being chosen to make a night raid on the German command post at Noirefontaine. "He had, in effect, selected us to be his 'pidgeon' for the testing of German mettle," Captain Ed Hartman said. Thus the spearhead for the Airborne counteroffensive on the northern shoulder of the Bulge was being forged. Into its tip in the 82d Airborne sector were placed the Get-Off-Your-Ass boys.

By December 27 the second German rampage of the war into Belgium had ground to a halt, and "the initiative in the great Ardennes battle was slowly slipping into Allied hands."[29] After four straight days of punishing attacks by Allied aircraft in clear weather, their fuel gauge needles past empty, bereft of bridges to span the deep Ardennes river gorges, their supply lines reduced to blackened, twisted iron, Liège, not to mention Antwerp, seemed a long way off—to everyone but Hitler. On Christmas eve "one could see from Bastogne back to the West Wall a single torchlight procession of burning vehicles," said Generalmajor Ludwig Heilmann, commander of the 5th *Fallschirmjager* (Paratrooper) Division.[30]

To Hasso Von Manteuffel, Hitler's most adept and professional leader in the Ardennes campaign, the gutsy horseshoe American stand at Saint-Vith on the northern shoulder had been "brilliant and outstanding," even "decisive," despite the surrender on December 19 of seven thousand GIs. It had held up his Fifth Panzer Army advance in the crucial first five days of the battle, which combined with the monumental traffic jam past the Siegfried Line, had siphoned off all his momentum. On Christmas Eve Manteuffel recommended to Berlin that "the German Army give up the attack and return to the West Wall." On Christmas, reaching the same conclusion, Von Rundstedt appealed to Hitler that neither Antwerp nor the *Kleine Losung* (Small Solution) of circling Liège was possible, and it was time to head back to the Fatherland. Even Hitler's favorite toady, General Jodl, fanned it in spades: "*Mein Fuhrer,* we must face the facts squarely and openly. We cannot force the Meuse River."

Hitler would have none of it. "When all goes well people are on top of the world, but when everything starts to go wrong they just fold up and give in!" he yelled hoarsely, launching into one of his endless monologues on Frederick the Great, petting his dog Blondi, remarking, "The more I study men, the more I like dogs."[31]

As the tables turned, the Allies contemplated where and when to strike back. As early as December 20, Montgomery had approved a counterattack plan, but he hastily withdrew his approval as the Germans got a second wind attacking west. "Damn it, Bedell," Bradley rasped to Ike's aide Walter Bedell Smith on December 26, "can't you get Monty going in the north? As near as we can tell, the other fellow's reached the high water mark today." By noon on December 27, Ike learned, the ever careful Montgomery, who resembled no one so much as great procrastinator General George McClellan of the Union Army at Antietam, was finally scratching a battle map for counterattack.

The plan called for two slow but steady windshield wipers, sweeping all the German dark rain back to the base of the Bulge. Ridgway's XVIII Airborne Corps would lead the First Army from the north, while Patton's Third Army would press up from the south. Patton, who considered Montgomery the dawdler par excellence since the Normandy landings, and whose own far bolder plan had been to chop off the entire bulge at its base to trap the whole German advance, took what he could get. Informed by his intelligence of what was up, Von Rundstedt wrily termed the Allied counterattack plan a version of "the Small Solution."

Late the afternoon of December 27, crunching the crust of blue snow as he walked a field by himself, his rifle slung over his shoulder, Gavin looked like the quintessential lone warrior. He aimed himself at the Rahier command post of the 551st Parachute Infantry Battalion. Impatient with Montgomery's schedule, Gavin thought that the time was already ripe to punch the Germans back in Belgium. Certainly he could not order an offensive on his own timetable, but he could—and it seems he had Ridgway's blessing in this—launch a probing raid that might just fire everyone up for the giant push everyone knew was coming.

Thus it was that evening that General Gavin pulled back the flap of Lieutenant Colonel Wood Joerg's tent and called for "an attack in order to determine whether conditions were right for an Allied counteroffensive," as S-2 Captain Ed Hartman put it. "He said the Germans were not exerting a great deal of pressure on the front at that time and he thought it might be an opportunity to launch the first counterattack." The attack was to be a night raid that very evening on the German garrison at Noirefontaine, where a battalion-size formation of the 62d Volksgrenadiers Division was lodged, along with—to everyone's surprise—elements of the 9th SS Panzer Division.

The 551st became the initial spearhead in the XVIII Airborne Corps sector on the northern shoulder for the Allied counteroffensive at the Battle of the Bulge, but with the exception of Dan Morgan's *The Left Corner of My Heart*, that fact has been recorded nowhere. Like most of what the GOYAs would endure and accomplish in the next ten grueling days, it was lost, shredded like paper through time as they themselves would be disbanded and forgotten.

6
"He's fixing to sacrifice us"

Why was the 551st chosen? Gavin may not have known about other times the GOYAs had just missed a bloodbath, to a mixture of relief and chagrin: halted while the planes were drumming in Panama for their drop on Martinique eighteen months before, spared Anzio on the docks at Naples by a hair. But he might just have known about their seizure of Draguignan in southern France and their capture of the first Nazi general in Europe the past August. The city's monument would later say the 517th had done it, but Gavin surely would have known the truth.

Captain Hartman's view as to why the 551st was selected: "We were an attached unit and no sensible division commander is going to use anybody else." Gavin's chief integral units—the 504th, 505th, 508th, and 325th—had all taken punishment from the third day at the Bulge on and badly needed rest. The only other separate paratrooper battalion, the 509th, had been cut to ribbons in a heroic stand alongside the 1st Battalion of the 517th Regiment against the 2d SS Panzers between Soy and Hotton; what ribbons of the 509th were left had stiffened themselves in a bitter struggle that very day, December 27, at Sadzot. The GOYAs had been bloodied in southern France, but not in Belgium. Their commander, Wood Joerg, was known to be daring. They seemed to be the right choice.

One of the lieutenants who shook Gavin's hand that night was Phil Hand. He remembered Gavin's saying, "Hell, I wish I was going with ya." But Hand murmured, "Hey, this is going to be rough as hell." He later recounted, "You know, the general says he wishes he was going—this is a bunch of crap. He's fixing to sacrifice us."

What did the youngest division Commander in the Army see in the eyes of the one of its youngest battalion commanders (Joerg had just turned thirty, and Gavin was thirty-seven)? In a way, he was implicitly passing a torch to the youthful Joerg, as Ridgway had passed the torch to him. Joerg had those generals' trait of being an "out front" commander, jumping in the foxholes with his men.

Watching Gavin crackle the folds of the battle map on a table by the flicker of a kerosene lamp, Joerg felt honored, but he was not the same man he had been stateside since he lost his first GOYA-bird in southern

France. Something of his gung-ho toughness, his rough-and-ready approach to discipline, which had turned off several of his junior officers, had given way to something less sharp, even tender. Never loud, he was now quieter than ever; a squint had come into his eyes. He seemed to be enduring an inner wound that was slowly growing. One could call it maturity from combat; you could see it in the way he lingered in listening, in the way he gently held a man's shoulder. The tense capture of Draguignan, the ordeal at Hill 105 in Cannes, and the incessant shelling for those months in the Maritimes had worn on him, revealing something human, something grim. Always worshiped by the line soldier, Joerg had begun to win over the most recalcitrant of his officers. He saw mortality now, and they saw in his deer eyes his own.

Listening to Gavin, the senior GOYA officers "weren't too confident" at first, Pappy Herrmann recalls. Gavin, after all, was sending them at night with the command to be back behind their lines before dawn. He gave the GOYAs six hours to snare the unknown German forces at Noirefontaine. Most important, they were to capture prisoners for intelligence purposes. The whole thing would be a dive into the dark, and too much seemed to hang on it.

Yet here was Gavin, moving out into the cold, squatting, scarring the snow with a stick. The closeness to their top commander emboldened them, "make a general a General," Herrmann said, and made them feel greater than they were. The GOYAs had suffered long from feeling they were being left out, even ostracized, for being a bastard unit with a history of disciplinary problems. Things might be different now. "Realization that a two-star was interested in our raid made us all feel better," Herrmann stated. "We were eager to go."

Well, not everyone. No American patrols had combed Noirefontaine—it was an X factor. Major General Fritz Kraemer, chief of staff of the Germans' Sixth Panzer Army, said after the war that Americans were loath to attack at night ("Night attacks occurred very seldom."), that the system of command was too methodical and slow: "Successes were rarely or never exploited."[32] A large part of this was due to the bifurcated U.S.–British command, as well as Monty's natural caution. Gavin was determined to go against the grain with the 551st at Noirefontaine. He did keep an entire crack regiment in reserve—the 508th—through whose lines the GOYAs would move to the jumpoff point at Basse Bodeux. Otherwise, the stops were lifted. "To top it off," Sergeant Charles Fairlamb says, "General Gavin came to our area and informed us that it was suicide and probably we wouldn't make it back." Whether or not Gavin was joking to the enlisted men after his meeting with the officers is hard to tell, but it didn't seem like a mission for laughter. Fairlamb remembered Gavin's telling the medics that "they would have the toughest job of their careers, since the only means of transportation would be litters." The mission had to be completely silent until the mortars started firing. It was all to be movement through woods—no jeeps, trucks, no tanks, no heavy guns. Stealth. The kind of job paratroopers on land were made for, though Fairlamb was far from excited.

Ensconced at Noirefontaine, unaware of their own approaching peril, were parts of two very different German divisions thrust together in the close quarters for the night: the 62d Volksgrenadiers and the 9th SS Panzers.

The 62d Infantry Division had been refitted and rechristened as "Volks-grenadiers" by Hitler in the fall of 1944, after it had been virtually wiped out on the Russian front. The original 62d Division had been composed mostly of German-speaking peoples from the Silesian district of south-western Poland and the Sudetenland of Czechoslovakia, both taken by Germany in 1938–39. Three-quarters of the division were Silesian Ger-mans, and the rest Czech Germans. The Upper Silesians, in particular, were said to have Polish blood and to have fought hard against the Rus-sians. The 62d was dubbed the "Moonshine Division"; its insignia of cres-cent moon and Iron Cross derived from a Silesian crest.

Typical of the mindset of the officers of the division was a lieutenant in logistics with the original 62d. Born in 1909 under the Austro-Hungarian monarchy in Moravia, in 1931 Joseph Bannert became a reserve officer in the Czech Army, listing his nationality as "German—Czech German." He studied under a youthful Rommel at the school. "At first we were not pro-Hitler," Bannert recalled in 1994. "We wanted to keep the peace in Moravia. We were dependent on Czech industry."[33] In 1935–36 the Czech government began replacing German-speakers with those who knew only Czech, following a land reform of the 1920s, which turned over German-speaking owners' land to pure Czechs, the so-called Czechinization pro-cedures. When Hitler annexed the Sudentenland in 1938, Bannert admitted, "there was hope that conditions would be bettered with Hitler's rise. I was very happy and proud to be a member of the German Reich. We were no longer 'stateless.'"

Bannert, like other bilingual speakers, found himself out of a job. "I was dismissed with honor by the Czech Army; a Czech commander had tears in his eyes." Bannert did not become part of the 62d Division until October 1942, when it was deployed on the Don River campaign in Rus-sia. In the bitter fighting of the Russian counteroffensive that winter, the 62d was forced to withdraw, finding itself under a hail of Soviet leaflets stamped with the "Moonshine" crest that said, "The Crescent Moon shines no longer."

Bannert was among 20,000 Germans who surrendered to the Soviet forces in the Bessarabian town of Kishinev in August 1944, the site of the first large-scale killings of Jewish civilians—more than ten thousand—in 1940.[34]

Reconstituted in the autumn of 1944 under a new commander, Brigadier General Frederich Kittel, only about 10 percent of the 62d Volksgrenadiers remained from the original division rosters. About 12 percent of conscripts—now Czech and Polish native speakers—were over the age of thirty-five. Lack of replacements had also diminished the division's size from 12,000 to 10,000; regiments now contained two battalions rather than the standard three. It was a formidable task for Kittel, who was highly respected by his staff as a "wonderful, intelligent leader."[35]

Although General Gavin in *On to Berlin* later assessed the 62d VGD as a "poor division, not well trained [whose] patrols frequently wandered into the 505th area only to be destroyed,"[36] at the time of the Bulge General Ridgway gave a cooler assessment, perhaps informed by the knowledge of the division's savage fighting on the eastern front, not to mention Saint-Vith, and that its officer corps was fairly intact. On December 22, 1944, Ridgway, admitting that their training had not been especially rigorous, called the 62d "good—dangerous."

In the Ardennes offensive, the 62d VGD's three infantry regiments—the 190th, 183d, and 164th—were to be the chief antagonists of the 551st Parachute Infantry Battalion. But before they reached Noirefontaine on December 26; the 62d VGD—green or not—helped achieve the Germans' chief success at the Bulge, the capture of the beleaguered Americans at Saint-Vith, exacting the sizable surrender of two U.S. regiments. Though originally "shot to pieces" as the U.S. 424th Regiment held its ground in front of Saint-Vith on the first day of the battle, the 62d hardly wilted. "Our own losses, above all on battalion and company commanders, were serious, but the losses sustained by the enemy in the 183d sector were tremendous!" General Kittel later wrote.[37] The 183d Regiment was the first 62d VGD unit to reach Saint-Vith at 7 A.M. on December 22. For its first week at the Bulge, the 62d's stores were greatly enhanced by captured American matériel—guns, trucks, jeeps, and food.[38]

Before Christmas was over one of Kittel's regiments had attacked Bra and forced the U.S. forces a half-mile north of the town; the 62d was now about 2 miles from the 551st's bivouac at Rahier. The next day the 62d gained the Mount Fosse ridge. Its troops at that point, however, were exhausted, "subjected to too great a strain both in the fighting and owing to difficulties of terrain." One 62d sergeant who participated in that final German forward push at the Bulge told his company commander, "You're telling me to make a trip to heaven just like the Ascension of Jesus himself." But the coercion from behind overrode that. The commander retorted, "I prefer this over hanging."[39]

By December 27 the 62d VGD, now part of Corps Felber with the 18th VGD, in the Sixth Panzer Army, had been halted before Basse Bodeux by the 82d Airborne. At this point Gavin paid the 551st his visit, ordering the night raid at Noirefontaine to begin to reverse the tide.

Tending their wounds at the farmhouse at Noirefontaine, the volksgrenadiers were joined late the night of December 26 by troops from the 9th SS Panzers. Recently committed to the battle, to Gavin this armored division looked formidable, "of much better quality" than the volksgrenadiers. Its 19th SS Panzergrenadier Regiment had startled the 82d Airborne troops during their withdrawal with a rush at Vielsalm of "great spirit, whooping and shouting."[40] But that cold night they had their wounded, too.

If the 62d Volksgrenadiers sparked little more than contempt in General Gavin, the 9th SS Panzer "Hohenstaufen" Division craved blood wherever it went. Created three years after World War II started, in December 1942, on direct authorization by a Hitler inspired by the Russian campaign, by the time of the Bulge the *Hohenstaufen* had zigzagged across the continent trying to plug the increasing holes in the Fortress Europe. Named for the line of German nobility that began in the eleventh century, it was a tank division with a reputation for mobility, toughness, and fanatic devotion to the cause. On its first combat assignment in April 1944, the 9th SS Panzers rescued the trapped favorite of Hitler, the 1st SS Panzers (*Leibstandarte*), encircled by the Soviets at the Kamenets–Podolsk pocket. In two months it was rushed to Normandy, suffering heavy losses against the British at Caen and the Americans at Mortain, as well as giving and taking terrific punishment during the Allied breakout at Falaise. By August 21, the *Hohenstaufen* had only 460 men left of its 12,000, and about twenty tanks; amazingly, they would regenerate in a month and would help deal the British 1st Airborne Division a crushing defeat in Holland at Arnhem.

The *Hohenstaufen* was led through Normandy by Lieutenant General Willi Bittrich, described by one of his officers as "a Hitler enthusiast." At the Bulge, Bittrich headed the II SS Panzer Corps, which contained both his old unit, the *Hohenstaufen,* and the brutal 2d SS Panzers. The *Hohenstaufen's* new leader was SS Oberfuhrer Sylvester Stadler, at thirty-four perhaps the youngest division commander in the German Army. Even Gavin had three years on Stadler; the two faced off in the Ardennes woods, young pretenders to a dark throne.

There was something oddly endearing about the *Hohenstaufen,* if such terms can be applied to an SS unit. One officer admitted that many of its men were addicted to American jazz, though Hitler forbade it, calling it "nigger music." Still, the *Hohenstaufen* "copied and played American music wherever we could. We had German jazz players—one was nicknamed 'The Black Panther' *(Schwartzpender)*, and he played the *Tiger Rag,* but we had to rename it in order to play it at all."[41] Indeed, Bittrich had invited the surrounded British paratroopers at Arnhem to surrender after playing jazz over a loudspeaker. The response was jeers and pistol fire.

On December 27 an all-out 9th SS Panzer Division attack was flung against Gavin's men, though there was barely enough fuel left for one of the *Hohenstaufen's* panzergrenadier regiments. "The Panzers came in screaming and yelling in a mass attack," Gavin recounted,[42] from an axis of the Lierneux–Habiemont road. The 504th held fast at Bra and Villettes; a battalion of the 508th was smashed at Erria, though Colonel Louis G. Mendez retook the handful of stone structures that was Erria as the Germans bedded down that night. As things finally quieted down, Gavin visited the 551st to take the battle one step further, the mixed-unit German garrison at Noirefontaine, about as far west (excepting Bra miles farther) as the *Hohenstaufen* would get at the Bulge.

One NCO officer with the *Hohenstaufen's* 20th SS Panzer Regiment at Bra called the last lunge "a disaster—we took the edge of town, but had to withdraw for the Americans were too good there. They had better weapons—we were outnumbered by weapons."[43] A soldier in charge of radio equipment who fought at the fierce battles at Normandy, Untersharführer Helmut Hennig, felt at the outset of the Bulge that nothing could be gained; "motivation was high" in his division, though unlike SS units formed earlier in the war, the *Hohenstaufen* were 60–70 percent draftees. That aberration caused a little-known protest in Germany. With the flow of pure German volunteers for the Waffen-SS greatly thinned, in 1942 Heinrich Himmler resorted to conscription to fill out the 9th and 10th SS Panzers to "a storm of protest, not just from parents, but also from church leaders and other civilian dignitaries."[44] Inductees later were allowed to opt out of the SS after two months of training; few did, though just how much freedom they really had to do so is in question.

Wounded by Russian shrapnel when the *Hohenstaufen* finally surrendered to the Allies in Hungary, Hennig escaped to a British hospital and was arrested "because of being SS" and spent eleven years in forced labor at a coal mine in the Ruhr run by the British military government; there he developed black lung, a condition not aided by his chain smoking. Later, he started a family, worked as an engineer at a television and radio station and taught engineering until 1973 at a university, volunteering his time in retirement as a mediator to settle disputes between citizens and the local government. "You forgot the war," he said, but watching him push the plunger of an ashtray that caused the butts and ashes to disappear, I realized the war hadn't disappeared for him. He was still haunted by certain things: why the Americans came into the fray, why "professional" soldiering SS were not distinguished from those who ruled the horrors of the concentration camps: "Looking backward, it was good for business that Americans came into the war. It was good that the killing of the Jews was stopped. No one should claim there were no concentration camps." And of course, the Russians: "When I dream of the war they come and get me—the Russians. They did not abide at all by the Geneva Convention. We did not kill POWs; we didn't have enough food for them, so we let them go to their own lines. We killed in combat; but the Russians mutilated people. We had strict discipline. If there was any stealing or rape, we were punished. My wife was in Berlin when the Russians invaded." Only once in four hours of our interview did his wife briefly peer into the living room, before disappearing. No food or drink was brought, though Hennig offered cigarettes.

He quoted George Stein, who wrote that, of 900,000 Germans in the SS, 6,500 actually were stationed at the concentration camps: "The discrimination of the Waffen SS happened because our leaders did not resist Himmler. I asked [General] Hausser, Why did you not avoid this combination of the SS at camps with us, with our name? He said, 'Who could have raised a hand against Himmler? We also thought we would win the war.'"[45]

Hennig struggled, wheezing, during the entire interview. He seemed to want to set things straight, to redeem the unredeemable, even at this late hour; he was hardly sentimental, but stark about his past, and unregenerate with pride for what he felt was an elite unit tarred by things he wished hadn't happened but took no stand against. He picked up a book in German on the *Hohenstaufen*:[46] "It would have been better if this book on the 9th SS Panzers weren't lying here—the war shouldn't have happened. I disagree with Clausewitz. War is not policy by other means. We [former SS] have supported democracy. Eisenhower said we were a very good force; why should I say less? Yalta—unconditional surrender—it was not smart to do that. There was no chance for capitulation, or internal resistance. You could lose your life then if you said one thing against Hitler." He called today's neo-Nazis "idiots."

Had Hennig been there at Noirefontaine in darker times, the night my father and his 551st fellows struck into the dark themselves? He wasn't sure; only Abrefontaine, not nearby Noirefontaine, was on his battle maps.

The men of the 551st oiled their weapons after a quick C-ration dinner, rubbed the necks of their guns, said prayers, took a last look at photos of girlfriend or wife or mother, and gathered on the road from Rahier at 9 P.M. to walk the 2 miles to Basse Bodeux. By 11 P.M. they were at Basse Bodeux, where the 508th paratroopers were surprised to hear about the mission of the newcomers. They patted the GOYAs on the back, like prized cattle. Noirefontaine was another 2-mile walk southwest through the forest. The Cornelius family, which had lived in Noirefontaine from the early part of the nineteenth century as tenant farmers, did not know that its liberation—and the burning of its home—was imminent.

Noirefontaine ("black spring") was not much more than two large, centuries-old stone farmhouses with several outbuildings and barns now converted to a command post by the Germans, who had ordered most of the twenty Belgian inhabitants into basements.[47] The spring from which the place name derives feeds a dark pond. Near the property was a domicile for the mentally ill; over the years, three patients had boarded at Noirefontaine farmhouse. During the Battle of the Bulge one such patient was in residence.

Eleven days before, on December 16, 1944, the day the Germans began their Ardennes offensive, one of seven Cornelius children, Elodie, was getting married at a church at Basse Bodeux. No sooner did she emerge for embraces on the church steps than the faroff rumble of guns turned the wedding party's heads. No one believed the Germans would come back. They had been run out of the Ardennes in September; it must be Americans testing their guns. Everyone went back for a feast at Noirefontaine. They all ate and laughed in the golden bath of the oil lamps (the farm didn't get electricity until 1950). They disregarded the shadows. They put records on the phonograph and danced. The menfolk churned the cranks of their box cameras. But the photos and gifts of Elodie's wedding no longer exist. They were all burned the night the family was liberated by the 551st.

The Cornelius family, some of whom were members of the Belgian resistance, had known German occupation thrice in the twentieth century. The oldest sister, Marie, was born in 1914, the year the Germans first came through; she was twenty-six when they blitzed through the second time in 1940, on their way to capture the valuable mines and factories of Liège. They came a third time for her sister Elodie's wedding; they were always uninvited.

Logging is an important industry in the otherwise serene Ardennes, much of it used for planks to line mine passages. One of the most lasting marks of the three German invasions in the area can be felt whenever a logger gets out his saw. "It's difficult until now to cut wood in the Ardennes because many trees have cuts in them [from bullets and shells]," Marie Cornelius Hollange recounted when she was eighty. "The cuts hurt the blades."[48]

The demeanor of the hated Germans at Noirefontaine, Marie Hollange admitted, was quite proper during the invasion of 1940, unlike that of four years later during the Bulge. On the first day of the invasion at the war's beginning, they came on horseback in clean, starched uniforms, "*un armée impeccable*," Hollange recalled. A commanding officer was provided with lodgings for the night at Noirefontaine, and through the next four years a farmer in the area gave the Germans wheat, grains, and a half-pound of butter every two weeks to avoid trouble. It was all concealed in a barrel and placed in a hole in the ground on the property.

But there was a cost. A cousin in the Cornelius family, a teenage girl, who had been seen giving the Germans butter one day, was found at Hierlot the next day strangled, killed by the Belgian resistance.

At the same time the Corneliuses hid men who would otherwise be taken to the munitions factories or sworn into the army in Germany. Two men were alerted just before their arrest and lit out from the farmhouse, escaping the Gestapo to Coo across the Salm River. From the Belgian border town of Longfays, Joseph Servais (nicknamed Camille) had a similar close call. In the middle of a family dinner, German soldiers pounded on the farmhouse's front door. Camille barely had time to dive under a table in another room; he was forced to stand up and show his identity papers to the Germans. The Germans quickly ascertained that the documents were false—he had in fact obtained them from a dead man in French-speaking Liège—and Camille's face "turned white as a handkerchief." He was about to be shipped out for German Army duty as a German-speaking Belgian from the borderlands, when a motorcycle messenger drove up with urgent orders that made the German patrol pack up and fly, leaving the sweat-soaked Camille behind.

The food-in-the-hole trick did not always work. On at least three occasions during the occupation, German soldiers stormed into the farmhouse from all entrances with dogs in search of more food. Camille spoke German to them one time, saying no butter was left, then swiveled his head to Marie and whispered in Walloon, "I lied!" One time a German soldier spotted cream at the bottom of a locked and sealed butter churn, but Marie charmed him off with a finger to her lips, "Shhh!" The family restricted its movements. There was no plumbing at Noirefontaine at the time, and the outhouse was 100 meters from the main building. "All the time everyone was constipated!" Marie chuckled silently at the memory. But more than the Germans were working against them: The toilet in the outhouse consisted of a barrel with uneven slats. "The wind came through the wooden seat in winter and, ooh la la, it was cold!" Marie joked.

After fighting with the Belgian Army in the last battle against the Germans in 1940 at Ghent, Marie's husband, François, had been taken prisoner and sent to a labor camp in the rural Silesian town of Gorlitz. There he contracted an ear infection, which went untended to the point that he lost his hearing. He did not return home until after the war.

Just before the liberation, in August 1944, the Corneliuses looked out from their unshuttered windows and were startled to see planes dropping arms for the Resistance. Emile Cornelius, a brother, ran out into the fields to retrieve them and delivered them to the White Army.

Two days before the Allied liberation in the first week of September 1944, the White Army killed seven German soldiers at Gerardwez near Noirefontaine. Their bodies were discovered in the dark pond, so before retreating the Germans set fire to farmhouses near the pond, burning them to the ground. They also seized seven civilians from Reharmont and Fosse, told them to prepare trenches at Gerardwez, and shot them in the back, toppling them into the earth they had dug.[49] "The Germans said to us, 'In three months, we will be back,'" Marie said. But nobody believed them; everyone was caught up in liberation fever.

The Americans in September came bearing biscuits, chocolate, and chewing gum for the Cornelius family but passed through Noirefontaine quickly, pleased to pick up their favorite booty: cognac. When they heard the Germans had supplied Marie Cornelius with blankets to sew into trousers, the Americans promptly gave her American blankets for American trousers. According to Marie, a few German soldiers for some reason stayed in the woods after the September withdrawal. They may have been defectors, but the family was convinced they were spies. Lea Cornelius twice saw those furtive stragglers give light signals to each other. It was eerie, all the more so because the men stayed on and somehow were fed.

On Christmas Eve, 1944, Lea Cornelius heard the ducks quacking and went to the window. Although they had heard that the Germans had made a breakthrough and at least three V-1 rockets had hit Noirefontaine since December 16, the Corneliuses hadn't seen any Germans and figured the Americans were holding them off. The day before, while cutting a Christmas tree, Lea and Marie saw an American jeep in the woods firing a machine gun. They were tense but felt protected.

But the ducks weren't quacking for nothing. Lea listened closely. The ice was cracking from hobnail boots. American boots were leather or rubber. They didn't make that noise.

On Christmas Day, five tired, hungry American soldiers, probably of the 508th Regiment, came to Noirefontaine and were invited in for a feast of mutton and ratatouille. Playing it safer than safe, they asked the Corneliuses to eat the mutton first. They thought it might be poisoned. The family waved them off and tested it. It was delicious.

Halfway through the meal, Mother Cornelius looked out the window and cried out, "Oh my God, the Germans are here!"

One of the GIs jumped up and grabbed his rifle, nosing it out the window.

"Don't shoot!" Please! Not here!" the mother implored.

Showing "good manners" (Marie thought), the Americans took up their weapons and went outside to carry on the fight. When they returned, the Christmas dinner was cold, they were too nervous to order it reheated and took a few swift bites of their K-rations. After telling the family to take cover in the basement, the Americans disappeared.

The occupiers of Noirefontaine shifted back and forth at a dizzying pace. About midnight the family heard the metallic clinking of wheels and horses snorting, and concluded that the Germans were back. "We heard well, because the glass of the basement windows was all shattered from shelling," Marie said.

On the morning of December 26 the Cornelius family emerged from the cellars to find the K-rations left half-eaten by the Americans were now completely eaten—by the Germans. The Corneliuses began to feel as though they too were some sort of cheese straddling the line of warring mice. A column of the 62d Volksgrenadier Division's 164th Regiment was wearily marching under the stone archway into the farmhouse area. An officer came up to the first building and banged on the door. Mother Cornelius emerged with Marie at her side.

"What are you doing here?" the officer spoke in perfect French, surprised that any civilians remained after the shellings of the night before. He motioned them toward the oil lamp to see their faces.

"There are no Americans here," Madame Cornelius spat out.

"Raus! Raus!" the German soldiers called out to those in the basements.

"We have injured soldiers," the officer said softly to Marie, who began to tremble. "Please bring alcohol, gauze, hot water."

The German noticed Marie shaking. "Why are you trembling?" he asked with a surprising tenderness.

"It's cold here."

"Then stop everything and make a fire."

Suddenly shellfire hit the barnyard and the roofs. Now it was the American artillery coming in from the north, not the fire the officer had in mind. Just as the day before, the family was ordered into the basements, this time by the Germans. It was safe there—the old stone walls were 1 to 2 meters thick. Marie looked at the German officer, who looked at her, his knotted brows loosening momentarily, as she let the hatch of the basement down over her piled hair.

Toward evening the Wehrmacht's injured had to move aside for those of the 9th SS Panzers, who had happened on Noirefontaine. A *Hohenstaufen* officer came down the basement steps at Noirefontaine and ordered Marie, Elodie, and Pauline Cornelius to fetch gauze immediately for the wounded and make coffee. They wanted milk for it, too, and the sisters had to rush out and milk the cows at midnight. There they saw the SS soldiers rounding up the last of their three horses, which were sick, to take for artillery hauling.

The SS wounded overflowed into a small barn. Marie remembered one soldier whose bloody legs were amputated. "The soldier was crying," Marie recalled. "My God, it was horrible."

7
Night raid on Noirefontaine

The attack on Noirefontaine jumped off shortly before midnight on December 27, 1944. The GOYAs, shedding what few mackinaws and extra gear they had, moved quickly through the drained men of Colonel Mendez's battalion of the 508th Regiment, off the road at Basse Bodeaux into the forested areas of Avenaterres and Pré Massin. This was undoubtedly one of the "things cooking [that] have to be on a small scale for a time until you say the word" that General Ridgway had communicated on the phone to First Army headquarters the night before Gavin's scratch test for the big pushback. Although the reference is veiled, it appears the Noirefontaine raid was a version of the 551st attack on panzer tanks Ridgway had wanted on Christmas, which was called off, for Ridgway wrote in his diary in the late afternoon of December 26: "CG 82nd Div. reported by phone that he felt there was insufficient time for reconnaissance to justify execution of the mission I had given him tentatively. He stated he could, and would like to do it tomorrow night, which I approved."

B Company was to lead, followed by C and A Companies, but some of B Company held back until it was committed, fighting a rearguard action to cover the withdrawal. (It appears both A and C Companies "jumped the gun" and got out in front of B Company, as well.) Waiting at the farmhouse complex nursing their wounded were Companies 1 and 3 of I Battalion of the 164th Regiment of the 62d Volksgrenadiers, a company or less of the 9th SS Panzers, and the Cornelius family. The attacking GOYAs had somewhat less than a 2-to-1 advantage (about 500 men against 300), though the rule of thumb for an attack force was 3-to-1. But they also had night and surprise on their side. As they passed the line of demarkation, total radio silence was enforced.

Crossing a dry riverbed (possibly the Ruisseau de Boitrai), Roy McCraw at A Company's point ran head on into the muzzle of a large gun. "I was scared shitless," McCraw admitted. But it wasn't the Germans who gave him this first scare. "It was an American tank and General Gavin was sitting right up on top of it."

"Don't sweat it, buddy, we're friends," Gavin smiled wrily.

"I'm glad you're here, General," McCraw's face relaxed, and he kept on.

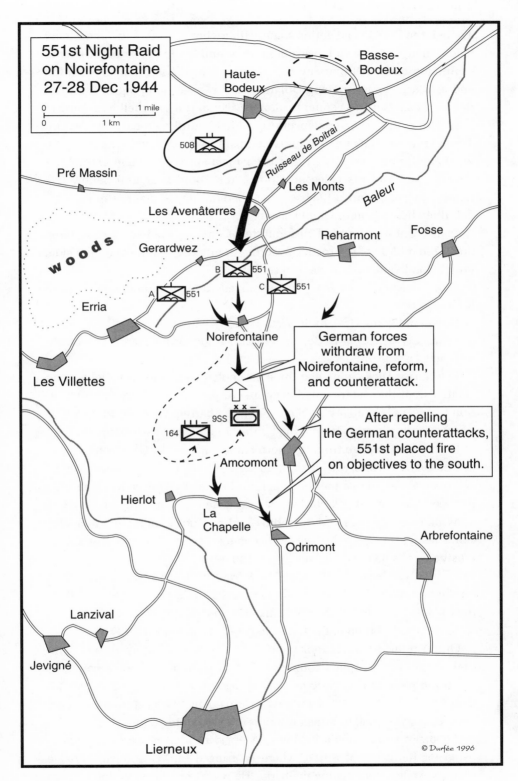

551st Night Raid on Noirefontaine 27-28 Dec 1944

0   1 mile
0   1 km

Basse-Bodeux

Haute-Bodeux

508

Pré Massin

Ruisseau de Boltrai

Les Monts

Baleur

Les Avenâterres

Reharmont

Fosse

w o o d s

Gerardwez

B   551

A   551

C   551

Erria

Noirefontaine

German forces withdraw from Noirefontaine, reform, and counterattack.

Les Villettes

x x —
9SS
164

After repelling the German counterattacks, 551st placed fire on objectives to the south.

Amcomont

Hierlot

La Chapelle

Odrimont

Arbrefontaine

Lanzival

Jevigné

Lierneux

© Durfée 1996

Though the GOYAs had gotten some artillery fire to "soften up" the enemy before their raid, the tank was not to be committed to the battalion's raid.

Spotted early, A Company came under a fusillade of small-arms fire and artillery. Sergeant Doug Dillard found himself hopping in the open field from one smoking crater to another, wondering if a shell was going to meet him at the next step. Uncorking a blood-curdling rebel yell, Captain Tims Quinn ran out ahead of his C Company, waving it on to the attack toward the farmhouse. Quinn had been nicknamed "Madame Quinn" for the high pitch of his voice in action. "You could hear him bellow five miles," Sergeant Martin Kangas remembered. The Germans, 1 mile away, definitely heard, and the fight was on.

Lieutenant Phil Hand of Headquarters Company spotted Joerg walking down the middle of the road toward the farmhouse. "Hey, get on the side, now!" Hand yelled. "You want to get hit?"

"Ah, come on," Joerg snapped back, fixed on the prey and unconcerned for his own safety.

"We're not going straight down the road like idiots."

"You ain't whistling Dixie," Joerg jumped forward, away from a crashing shell. "Come on!"

Lieutenant Dick Goins had three air-cooled machine guns, lighter and smaller than the water-cooled versions, in place and plenty of ammunition to cover C Company's charge. Soon the barrels were red-hot; so furiously had they been fired that the lightest touch would set them off.

Goins had a déjà vu from southern France, where the GOYAs had made up for lack of artillery with rapid-firing mortars. The initial division artillery cover stopped a half-hour before the attack. At least a five-minute barrage when the attack started was promised, but nothing came. "The guns had been preempted somehow and did not support us after all," Goins said. So began what was to become an artillery-starved counteroffensive for the 551st, their lot till the bitter end.

Suddenly at least one Panzer IV tank from the 9th SS Panzers appeared on the farmhouse road, facing the men charging in the field to the left of the road. Joerg yelled at Quinn, "Tims, get your unit back on the road."

"Goddamnit, Colonel, I'm trying to get my men moved out!"

Quinn hollered for bazookamen, who came running up to him with their long-tubed weapons bouncing on their shoulders: "I want you to go up to the road and don't come back unless you are dragging them goddamn tanks by the tail!" Lieutenant Goins sent two bazookas to face a tank; they were back in fifteen minutes after knocking it out.

Another tank, leading a halftrack, swerved in front of Joerg, who scampered for the cover of a tree, where he banged into C Company Private Thames Anderson clutching the bark. "He wasn't one to swear, but he sure did then," said Anderson. "He had a .45 and I had a carbine, and that was nothing against a tank." The tank crew, surprised by the onrushing men, may have had too cold a vehicle to fire and got away; though the halftrack was put out of commission.

As B Company moved into position, Lieutenant Lester Kurtz was blown apart when he stepped on a Bouncing Betty mine. The well-loved GOYA football coach, Kurtz had gotten a battlefield commission. His loss early on steeled the men but also made them look down a lot. Mines were planted all over Noirefontaine.

An air reconnaissance photo had shown what looked like a large haystack alongside the farmhouse. The GOYAs were told to ignite it as soon as possible to give some light to the mission. "Get that haystack burning!" Quinn yelled at Sergeant Carl Noble of C Company, who poured tracer fire into the big mound for ten minutes before he screeched, "She won't burn!" Frustrated, Noble turned his weapon over to Private Warren Arbogast and slithered up to the pile. It turned out to be damp manure!

The manure pile was good for something, however. Lieutenant Andy Titko, laying telephone line back to the jumpoff area from up front, came under fire from a 20mm ack-ack gun and jumped into the manure. From his singular redoubt, Titko saw Lieutenant Sano bark at someone standing against a tree, "Ok, get off your butt and get going!" The soldier turned out to be German, but he did get going.

Once off the bright canvas of a full moon on snow, there was the typical mixup in the dark forest over who was enemy and who wasn't. Lieutenant Ralph Wenthold plopped down in the snow and began firing his M-1, knocking off the helmet of a GOYA he couldn't see in front of him. It turned out to be a medic; the shot spun him around. He reached down, grabbed his helmet, put it on, then threw it off in confusion.

Many in Headquarters Company were so far back from the advance that some men of the 508th mistook a mortar platoon for Germans, and a small intra-American firefight ensued, with minor casualties, before things got straightened out.

Ordered across a firebreak to flank Germans hurrying out of the farmhouse on the road, a nervous Private Larry Lavine jumped the gun to the road instead, and some jackrabbit GOYAs followed, only to trigger a round of fire from B Company, who thought they were Germans. Thankfully, the only casualties were an ammo box shot out of one man's hands, and sheared shoelaces.

An illuminating bonfire was finally lit for the fight by PFC Jim Heffernan of HQ Company, who tossed a makeshift Molotov cocktail into a hayloft. Germans wakened by the fire rushed out, only to be hit by mortar shells and a stream of machine gun and rifle bullets. Heffernan's war came to an end farther along in the battle when the Germans began blanketing the GOYA withdrawal with artillery and machine gun fire, which hit him in the ankle. He and Jim Aikman, who had twisted his ankle on a dropped grenade, helped each other back to an aid station. Evacuated to Liège, the little dog Furlough's liberator back at Camp Patrick Henry in Virginia took twelve shots of penicillin a day to fight an infection. That meant a sore posterior.

Then there was Mr. Cold. Sighting a captured American halftrack painted over with a swastika, Lieutenant Wenthold clicked the trigger of his bazooka twenty times, and nothing happened. It was frozen. Chuck Fairlamb noted that the ground was so stiff from the cold that some German mines didn't detonate. Fairlamb saw men stuff bazooka shells under their shirts to keep the fuses from freezing.

The GOYAs were closing in on the farmhouse. The 81mm mortars Lieutenant Buscher had perfected in rapid fire in southern France were set up about 800 yards from the buildings. The battery received a radio order from Joerg to "open fire." Soon the whole place was ablaze, with Germans running everywhere. More than four hundred rounds were fired. "There was a hell of a racket; as soon as they started coming out we shot them like ducks," Fairlamb recounted. "It was almost like day with the fires burning."

As for the Cornelius family, trapped in their own home, they were bedding down against the stone wall of the basement when they heard a poof, poof, poof, which they mistook for rockets coming in on the farmhouse. It was probably the mortars. After the fray started, a German soldier ran down the stairs into a basement and shouted, "Do you know your farm is on fire?" Another followed: "Get out! Get out!" Terrified and confused, the family emerged to the crackling flames and the jumping shadows. They spotted SS men crammed against a wall, ducking and shooting.

The GOYAs, astonished to see civilians come out, for a short time held their fire as the people dashed to hide in haystacks and pigsties. But when the gunfire resumed, the family was afraid they'd be hit in hiding. "We were worried if we go in the direction of the Americans, whom we couldn't see, we will be shot," said Marie Hollange. So about 2 A.M. they fled south—Marie to Odrimont, others to La Chapelle and Lierneux.

Approaching the conflagration, Fairlamb saw Joerg standing under a tree; suddenly rifle fire snipped the leaves near the commander's head, and Joerg ordered Duke Spletzer: "Go get that apple." Within minutes the firing stopped, and Spletzer gingerly returned with the German's rifle.

Out of a hayloft near the farmhouse a German emerged firing a burp gun, surprising some C Company men, one of whom shot the man point blank with an Italian Beretta, then broke down and vomited.

Throwing away his useless bazooka, Ralph Wenthold marveled as a man next to him riddled the front end of the captured U.S. halftrack with Browning Automatic Rifle fire. "It sounded like a jackass in a tin barn," Wenthold said.

Steam and coolant poured out of the punctured radiator, and Germans poured out the hatch to escape. Wenthold jumped onto the vehicle and pulled so hard on the .50-caliber machine gun on top that the bolt handle came off. Getting it secured, he laced the retreating Germans. PFC Forrest ("Field Manual") Reed ran up to disable the machine further but found it covered with the blood of a B Company friend, Sergeant Jack Letcher, who lay nearby in a depression, severely wounded. Reed, so nicknamed because he followed the very letter of the Army field manual, pulled him to safety and called for the medics.

When Wenthold looked into the hatch of the captured halftrack, he saw it was piled high with Teller antitank mines. It was lucky his bazooka hadn't worked; the explosion might have killed his own men. Wenthold backed the vehicle out as the signal to withdraw came, piling on some wounded until they saw mines up the road. Not wanting to chance whether or not they were frozen, Wenthold got everyone off, fetched some gasoline, poured a trail back down the road, touched it off and all "ran like hell." The boom resounded and the makeshift swastika melted in a huge fireball.

The GOYAs had fought off two determined counterattacks, and by 2:30 A.M. the Germans were in disarray, the farmhouse complex routed. Gavin had wanted at least one prisoner for questioning; the GOYAs brought back at least twenty-five, a group of them from the exploded halftrack. Jim Guerrant of C Company recalled that he personally "backed into" the arrest of twenty Germans who were coughing heavily around the GOYAs in the woods. Standing with no rifle (which had been lost in the battle), Guerrant suddenly faced a German "who pointed his gun right at me. Hair stood up on the back of my neck." Guerrant lit out, plowing through the snow. He thought he was done for, as it seemed a platoon of Germans were following him every step of the way, coughing. Then he realized, "The coughing was a signal. They followed me all the way back to our lines. I guess they felt abandoned by their own troops and wanted to surrender, so I took them into custody, without my rifle. Colonel Joerg told me to fire at their feet to scatter them as we didn't want to be bogged down with prisoners, but I didn't. We kept them."

Other Germans managed to get away to Odrimont, a little over a mile south, where the 164th Volksgrenadier regimental command post was located. Oberstleutnant (Lieutenant Colonel) Arthur Juttner listened, appalled, to the report that two of his companies had been badly mangled at Noirefontaine. Then he himself took cover as his post was hit by machine gun fire. The GOYAs' secondary mission had been to lay small arms fire on the towns of LaChapelle, Amcomont, and Odrimont.

"Everything [at Noirefontaine] was blown up and a lot of our men killed or wounded, a big loss," Juttner wrote after the war. "The soldiers were cold and wet, so they had stayed in the houses there. Listening to the explosions outside, the alarm came too late and we were hurt badly. Noirefontaine and LaFosse were [also] important for the 1st and 9th SS [Panzers]."[50]

Though Holm reported "30 known German dead, including a company commander" at Noirefontaine, German records indicate close to twice that amount were killed. More than a hundred were wounded or missing.

It was a bad loss for Juttner, born in Katowice, Poland, in 1908, and an officer in the regular German Army since 1926—neither a Hitler Youth graduate nor a Nazi Party member. Hardly a fanatic, Juttner was a typical Prussian officer who swallowed his doubts about Hitler while he soldiered on. He was wounded four times on the Russian front, in the legs, throat, and back. (His adjutant in the 164th, Lieutenant Schwerdt, had lost both hands in Russia.) Juttner would fight against the American counteroffensive at the Bulge hampered by the bloodletting at Noirefontaine, but valiantly enough to earn an honor few German officers received in the war for his battles with the 551st and 508th along the Salm River.[51]

As for the GOYAs, their losses were surprisingly light. About fifteen men were wounded, and four killed (all from B Company).[52] It appears that B Company, first leading, then covering the withdrawal, took the worst hits. For a while Corporal Intinarelli was given up as missing in action, but in mid-January 1945, when the Cornelius family came back to the burned-out farmhouse, they discovered two American soldiers frozen in the snow. One had had his wrist caught in a booby trap. Another's hands held, as if in final prayer, a rosary. It was the GOYAs' cherished boxer Intinarelli—listed as missing in action—fighting his last round. Marie Hollange also found several American helmets in the snow in back of a shed, in the farmhouse, and in the barns, caked with dried blood. For years she would have nightmares in which that helmet blood would liquify.

In the dark early hours of December 28 another Belgian family in the area took in a GI—possibly a GOYA—at their home in Rochelinval. He had been shot in the forearm. Catherine Laverdeur hid him for almost two weeks in a hayloft, burning the ladder so no Germans could reach him. One night she warded them off, saying she had a very sick baby. The GI was eventually rescued on January 7 by the 551st at Rochelinval.

With orders from Gavin to return before dawn, the 551st walked back at 5 A.M. in the same footprints they made coming in to avoid mines. PFC George Kane of B Company hurried with a packboard of ammo on his back, jumping from depression to depression in the snow, when he came under rifle fire. He fell headlong into the snow, the bullets driving ice and rocks into his face.

"Rippling! Rippling!" Kane yelled out the password, hoping the return "Rhythm!" would come, as in Shep Fields's tune "Rippling Rhythm." The night-blind sniper, B Company's Private Lloyd McEllhenny, responded, and Kane was saved.

"That's the closest I came to death in the war," Kane laughed later. Dubbed the battalion's "Mr. Perseverance," Kane logged a mind-boggling array of injuries during the war, both before and after this incident. Initially rejected for the paratroopers because of severe hay fever, Kane was on the last day of engineer corps training when a bunsen burner exploded sixty-four small fragments of glass into his face. After he re-volunteered for the airborne, he promptly broke a leg during a "rooster fighting" exercise. In Sicily he dove into rather shallow water and dislocated a shoulder; as he hastened to the aid station, he stepped barefoot on sharp thistles, throwing his arms up and relocating the shoulder. He was hit by shrapnel twice in southern France, in the hip and in the leg. At the Bulge, his feet froze. A troop train he was riding to Hanover in the spring of 1945 was plowed into by a German train. Kane was thrown, and a nerve in his face was severed. Twenty-nine stitches later, unable to wear a helmet because of his bandages, he was riding in a truck that banged into an oak, one of whose boughs stabbed George in the head.

When asked to describe his war experience, Kane summed it up: "Traumatic!"

Back behind the 508th Regiment's lines at Basse Bodeaux, the exhausted men of the 551st were visited by General Gavin, who commended them for the raid, though few had enough energy for his handshake. Before they had time to wipe the camouflage greasepaint from their faces, the men were called to the only semblance of a Christmas service they would have in 1944—three days after Christmas. They stood out in an early morning snowfall, shivering, and marveled that they were still alive. "It was a funny feeling, standing there with a hymn book in one hand, a steel helmet on your head, and a rifle in the other," wrote Fairlamb. "But the service was still beautiful—the most impressive Christmas service I have ever attended."

Entwined with the Latin was coughing. Many, struck with laryngitis, could not sing at all. Their voices had been snuffed out by the cold and the excitement of the night raid. They looked up in the mists to see an eerie sparkling; the pine forest was covered not only with snow but with a metallic tinsel. It was the work of the Germans: shards of foil dropped from the sky to jam the Allies' radar. Quite a sight: tongues gathering a communion of snowflakes, tinsel from the enemy.

8
The counteroffensive hatched

I have not been able to determine what my father did at Noirefontaine. For the Bulge counteroffensive he served as a messenger, as he had in the Maritime Alps, shedding the motorcycle to trod in snow. As part of a Headquarters Company detachment ordered to guard Joerg's command post during the night raid, he may never have seen the flaming farmhouse. But he did later enter in his diary of the Bulge while recuperating in Liège that the attack on "Bellefontaine" was "very successful" and that "heavy casualties were inflicted on the enemy." Converting that "Noire" to "Belle" was a mistake of the heart: After the horrid counteroffensive of January 3–8, 1945, Noirefontaine looked like a last shining jewel of the war for the downward-plunging GOYAs.[53]

There were other Allied probing raids after Noirefontaine during the week that straddled the end of 1944 and the beginning of 1945 of varying degrees of success. Twice the 99th Infantry Division was repulsed by the 18th Volksgrenadiers at Malmédy. At the tip of the Bulge, the 83d Infantry Division pushed the 9th Panzers back to Jemeppe, and the Panzer Lehr Division was forced to abandon Rochefort.

After their night raid, a hard-edged week found the 551st busying itself with housekeeping, that is, digging foxholes in the icy ground around its bivouac at Rahier and on the hillside behind Basse Bodeux known as Haute Bodeux. The men tried to keep each other loose in the freezing cold with their great gift for practical jokes. Chuck Fairlamb and Tom Holland were victimized in their luxury hay-lined foxhole complete with little iron stove when "some joker" stuffed the stovepipe with rags, forcing them outside from backed-up smoke.

For others, as well, it was not a restful week. There were several casualties from artillery fire on U.S. positions. Sergeant Carl Noble thought he'd finally snatch some relaxation one night when, just as he laid his head on a feather pillow in an abandoned farmhouse, the place started doing "the Jersey Bounce," hit by a salvo of three 150mm shells, one out front, one out back, and one right over Noble's head, which he quickly dodged. That one penetrated the floorboards and came to rest in the basement—a dud. Noble brushed rocks and plaster off himself. He was all right, but a pal taking a bath was cut up from flying debris. Having had enough "R & R," Noble abandoned his hideout and went back to the battalion.

"Am in the pink and in Belgium," Wood Joerg began his last letter to Heidi on December 30. "Everything seems to be under control now. I think we ought to start kicking them around soon. My lads have done well. The weather is cold and snowy, but no one is suffering, so don't worry. We have been mighty lucky. The good Lord has been mighty good to us, all I need is a haircut and some clean clothes—We had a nice Christmas and I'm sure we will be together by the end of 1945." He signed it like a Quaker, "Love thee."

On New Year's Day Joerg was called to 82d Airborne headquarters to hear the news from Gavin: Montgomery had finally given the go-ahead for the counteroffensive, to start January 3. That same day the great German general of the Eastern Front, Heinz Guderian, cabled Hitler to call off the Ardennes attack and switch the forces to the East, where the Russians were expected to begin their big winter offensive. Hitler said no. Instead, he announced over radio waves that spanned Europe: "The world must know that this State will, therefore, never capitulate. . . . Germany will rise like a phoenix from its ruined cities and will go down in history as the miracle of the 20th century!"

Realizing now that Liège was too far, not to mention Antwerp, Hitler unleashed his frustrations in what seemed a personal vendetta on Bastogne. He knew it had become a symbol of the American defense, and he wanted to crush it. Luftwaffe attacks on the city increased on December 29 for three straight days of hellfire bombing. Patton's attempt to widen the corridor to Bastogne was repeatedly blunted. On December 31 the newly arrived 11th Armored Division took its worst one-day loss of the war near Chenogne, southwest of Bastogne: 661 men were killed, wounded, or missing, and 53 tanks were shot up. Showing nothing if not a flair for the unexpected, Hitler opened an entirely new front on New Year's Day with an attack in the Alsace area on Strasbourg, code-named Operation *Nordwind.* The Allies' already low reserves were severely sapped in the rush to cut it off.

New Year's Day 1945 also saw the last great Luftwaffe onslaught of the war: Operation *Bodenplatte,* in which a thousand German planes tried to cripple Allied airfields in Holland and Belgium. Though Goering's forces managed to destroy or wreck 460 Allied planes (280 on the ground), including Montgomery's personal plane at Brussels, the Luftwaffe lost one-third of its forces. The Allies could still count almost three thousand fighters and bombers unscathed, to Germany's seven hundred. *Bodenplatte* had been jarring, but for Germany, as one Luftwaffe officer reported, "in this total effort, we sacrificed our last substance."

In the northern sector of the Bulge—as the 82d Airborne drew ammunition for the great push of January 3—all was relatively quiet. That was not true of the punishment of Bastogne, where one of the war's great artillery battles continued unabated for eleven days until January 8, the Allies firing 53,054 rounds. The GOYAs would be bereft of artillery cover for their push and later envy the lot that was committed to the carnage at Bastogne.

By January 3 the 9th SS Panzers, most of which had been routed south to Bastogne, had only thirty tanks left and a thousand riflemen, having suffered a 26 percent casualty rate. Fed up with the bloodshed, General Manteuffel pleaded with Field Marshal Model to call off the Ardennes offensive. Model had given up trying to change Hitler's mind, however, and quietly refused. The newly arrived, green U.S. 17th Airborne Division jumped off in a whiteout snowstorm on January 4 and was so badly punished that several battalions suffered 60 percent casualties. Hammered by the all-out German siege of Bastogne, even Patton wrote in his journal that day, "We can still lose this war."

For Wood Joerg, looking up New Year's Day at Gavin's command post at the man to whom the 551st was to be attached for the counteroffensive, something else was lost. A heartbeat.

"Wood," said Gavin, "your men are hooked onto the 517th for this push." Across from Gavin at the map table was the last man Joerg wanted to be attached to, Colonel Rupert Graves.

The Gray Eagle. To his own men of the 517th Regimental Combat Team, a comfortable old shoe, a life-sparer. Someone who was not beyond putting his own men at risk to help other units. For example, in the general emergency to truck out to the Bulge from northeastern France, Colonel Roy Linquist's 508th Regiment was so sapped of important weaponry by its ordeal in Holland at Operation Market-Garden that he appealed to Colonel Graves to contribute some of its own matériel to restock the 508th. Graves generously responded, lessening his own regimental stores to protect the unit moving out first. But that graciousness did not necessarily apply to his peculiar, thorny relationship with the 551st.

The GOYAs knew Rupert Graves as the commander who dropped them into a lake during the night jump at Camp Mackall, drowning eight of them. He had tried to break them through collective punishment, the man from whom the GOYAs ran off almost en masse, hundreds ending up in the stockade. The man Milo Huempfner had left at the train station with his bags uncarried would now carry them into nonhistory.

Joerg gave Graves a nod and a forced smile, then looked out the window at the snow. What was he to say to his men? They would be excited to know they would now be part of the First Army–wide effort to close the lid on Hitler. And it wouldn't hurt to have Gavin's own famed 505th Regiment on the right flank, the men who stormed Sicily, who freed Saint-Mere-Eglise at Normandy, who took the Nijmegen bridge in Holland. There's class on the right. About the left flank, however, they might not be jumping for joy. He could tell them that the 517th performed beautifully at Soy-Hotton, and its 1st Battalion was up for a Distinguished Unit Citation for it.[54] But some things it was best to damper: *Do not mention Graves's name. Downplay the attachment. An arranged marriage, nothing permanent. Mention the 517th have artillery—ah, yes! We'd like that. Be pragmatic.*

Joerg had thought the GOYAs' stellar show at Noirefontaine would weld him directly to Gavin. He wanted to report straight to his charismatic paratrooper older brother, not his ancient Uncle Rupert. It did not soothe him to remember that the 551st had in fact rubbed shoulders with the 517th from

Rome onward. The two separate units had jumped into southern France in contiguous sectors (the 551st had done the work at Draguignan after some 517th artillery support). The 551st had passed the 517th at Sospel on the way for its autumn in the Maritime Alps. When both units were transported by rail up to northeastern France, they had set up shop within a few miles of each other, though the "Battling Buzzards" were pulled close to Gavin at Sissonne, and the GOYAs were farmed out to Laon. Had Graves grown close to Gavin? They didn't seem to have much in common, whereas Joerg was young and aggressive like Gavin. Maybe that was the problem.

The 551st had enjoyed free rein under General Frederick at Draguignan and Cannes and Nice. There was plenty of slack afforded the GOYAs in the Maritimes. They were out on their own under Gavin at Noirefontaine: He drew them on a tight bowstring and shot them like an arrow at that farmhouse. But it was all theirs, that tight night raid.

So Joerg loses something that day. A filament of confidence, a loss he must hide at all costs.

And what of Graves himself? Seeing Joerg, knowing he now had the bastard child on his lap again, could not have helped him digest his food that day. "Bad habits" in Panama was his first and chief memory of the 551st fifty years later. It was Joerg who released all the rabble from the stockade, making a mockery of his discipline. Graves had heard all about it; it would be a cold day in hell when he would lay eyes on that crowd again. And so it was. Cold and hell. Here they were reattached to him. The inquest after the night jump tragedy at Mackall and the dressing-down for not processing their transfer requests—why, his career had barely survived them stateside. Maybe Graves, too, loses a filament of confidence. Gavin, who may have known nothing of any of this, continued to shuffle his cards and maps.

Joerg briefed his senior officers on the counteroffensive. The whole 82d Airborne would swing like a 15-mile-wide gate southeast to the Salm River, eating up the territory it had relinquished in Montgomery's cautious withdrawal. The 517th was on the extreme left flank and was to recapture Trois-Ponts at the gate's hinge in the north, as well as Mont de Fosse and Saint-Jacques. Next was positioned the 551st. Its immediate goals would be to retake the ridge of Hèrispehe and the town of Dairomont in the direction of Rochelinval on the Salm. The 505th, which would flank the 551st on the right, was to retake Fosse, Reharmont and Noirefontaine. Essentially the little battalion would be a connecting tissue between regiments, an inherently perilous center unless the battalion could move quickly and boldly. To make matters worse, its route to the Salm River was the longest for any 517th component.

At 9:30 P.M. on January 2, after reconnoitering from a high hill the open terrain of Sol Me they had to cross, barely visible in a new blizzard, Joerg issued his attack orders. A Company would lead on the left with a four-machine-gun squad, C Company on the right with another four-machine-gun squad, with B Company and Headquarters Company in reserve. No one would be in reserve for long, not even the cooks.

The mile and a half of frontage given to the 551st to penetrate that first day was a daunting piece of geography. After crossing the "sitting duck" open field of Sol Me, it had to grapple with the high, long ridge of the Hèrispehe wood. This ridge had a natural "turret" outcropping offering a thick cover of fir trees. It was a dream defense for the Germans, who had been digging in for a week.

Though they had been positioned far apart in the Maritimes, the GOYA companies had waded together in the fray at Noirefontaine, and throughout the counteroffensive they would be rushed to help each other so that it was not uncommon that a private from B Company would come to know a lieutenant in A Company, and vice versa. That was unusual for an Army battalion, where companies kept to themselves. The GOYAs, in their last crucible, would become an extended family of loss.

The companies did take on the characters of their leaders, however: A Company had the understated strength of its commander, Marshall Dalton; B Company was physical and swashbuckling, like its leader, Jim Evans; C Company was tough and edgy, like the Southern banshee Tims Quinn; Headquarters Company bore a likeness to Bill Smith, reliable and straightforward.

The snow increased as the mercury dropped to zero. At 3 A.M., the GOYAs were served their last hot meal: "a good warm pan of stew washed down with some good hot coffee—I don't believe I ever tasted anything better in my whole life," said Quinn. It was all thanks to a cow hit by shrapnel. As for Headquarters Company, the men stood out in the snowstorm, hands out to be served pancakes. They held the steaming cakes up like sacrificial offerings, and the cooks walked by pouring syrup, which dripped off the men's hands and froze in the snow. Thus, says my mother, began your father's lifelong distaste for pancakes.

For canteens, it was icewater or ice. Some were blowtorched to keep them from being little more than ice grenades. Drinking water was to be a problem for the whole push. Three meals of rations were issued; the men ripped off the cellophane or paper to take their "favorites" and buried the rest in the snow. Gas masks were issued.

Though they were told to rest till dawn, no one rested. Men spoke to each other of loved ones, made impromptu wills, joked about the weather. Doug Dillard thought of his girlfriend, Virginia, wondered if she had been to a New Year's Eve party in Atlanta, tasted in his memory peach cobbler. Joe Cicchinelli took his place as A Company's scout at the front. He boxed his own breath, thinking that Massillon High's football season would be drawing to a close now, while he was about to make the toughest end run of his life on the left of the snowy field toward that hill of pine where the Germans were, a grim goal line. Max Bryan hung back in C Company with his Graves Registration tags, looking at the living men, pushing out of his mind thoughts of who would fall.

Nervous, Sergeant Paul "Cab" Callaway wrenched his copy of *The Grapes of Wrath* from Sergeant "Hedy" LaMar, to whom he had loaned it, cursing him up and down the road as if he were about to lose the Bible. Callaway would not survive to read Steinbeck again.

My father wrote his only letter home from the Bulge campaign ("Somewhere in Belgium") on December 29, thanking his parents, four sisters, and brother for various gifts of fruitcake, canned chicken, peaches, chewing gum, cigarettes, a styptic pencil, an inhaler that came in handy for a "slight cold," and a medal of the Sacred Heart sent by his mother. He was pleased that his mother was to buy a coat with the GI salary he had sent home earlier, adding, "I'd like to answer each letter individually but at the present it is impossible. I will try and write often, nevertheless there might be quite an interval between letters so please don't worry. . . . I am in good health and high spirits." Then his signature P.S.: "God bless my family."

Just where the merciless order originated, no one knew for sure, but the GOYAs were told, as at Werbomont, to shed all overcoats and overshoes so they could move quickly in the attack uphill. To S-3 Major Pappy Herrmann, it was a "command decision" for the overcoats, though he wasn't sure about the overshoes. Captain Ed Hartman insisted later that there were no overcoats and overshoes to shed. An entry by General Gavin in his diary of January 14, 1945, seems to indicate the practice originated at the top: "In all of my good paratroop units they attack in ordinary combat uniforms, hoping to bring up the overcoats and blankets later."

Though a few stray long coats and insulating shoes were scrounged, most of the winter clothing never caught up with the GOYAs, because the roads were mined. In any case they were too far from the roads, deep in the forest, most of the time. Radio signals could hardly reach them, much less shoes. That exposure might not have exacted the horrific toll of frostbite and trenchfoot it did if the men had been able to make the 3 miles to the Salm River in a day. But it took them five days of strenuous hand-to-hand combat; German resistance was fierce. Both sides fell prey to the greatest enemy at the Bulge: the cold.

At 6 A.M. the men began to walk down the road to Phase Line 1 at Basse Bodeux, slipping and sliding on the ice. "It was like walking on a sled run and I fell down several times and so did others, their weapons banging on their heads," said Dillard.

As he skated in paratrooper boots, Wood Joerg did not know that that very day his cousin Frank Joerg was captured west of Bastogne where he had been fighting with the 513rd Parachute Infantry Regiment of the 17th Airborne Division. His cousin's sizable threshold of pain Frank would think on while in captivity: how Wood as a boy had methodically dug out with a knife bee-bees accidentally shot into his palm. Frank's own battle was over, but Wood's had just begun.

As the 551st marched in the dawn light striking the snow into sequins, they began to hear support fire arching overhead; some rounds exploded near them. "We were annoyed by short rounds dropping in on us," said Tims Quinn, their first fire friendly once again.

They crossed the icy Baleur River, soaking their parachute boots before the battle had even started, a cold, portentous baptism. Some tried to jump the stream; just as Doug Dillard balanced on a rock to leap, a mortar round crashed in front of him and he landed in the river, the source of his severe trenchfoot three days later. Maybe the Baleur saved his life, and my father's as well.

Joerg was shoulder-to-shoulder with C Company's Quinn at the start. As the battalion emerged from the icy river, it faced a barbed wire fence, then a sunken road grilled with ice. Above the embankment on the far side of the road lay a field of snow so wide you could not see it end on either side. The field sloped gradually upward about a half-mile to a wooded ridge. There Joerg could see the Germans moving about at a crouch. They were dressed in white, as if the world had become a giant hospital. Then he looked at his gathering men in dark fatigues. They would be visible, too visible, in this snow.

What was a branch, and what was the barrel of a machine gun? To the left he could see two Panther tanks. They would have to seize the Germans' panzerfausts to nail them, for their own bazookas were virtually worthless against them. Other silent questions drifted up like breath: Why did the artillery stop? Why are there no U.S. tanks? Why no camouflage suits? There would be no air cover in the storm.

Squinting, shielding his eyes from the wind-blown snow, Joerg tried to spot mortar emplacements far off on the pine ridge. Then it came to him: *Is my German cousin there?* Wood Joerg would never know that his cousin Gunter Jörg was, of all places, in an American POW camp. He had gone into the German Army with great distaste, had served as a cook in Greece and Italy, then had driven a water truck in Africa under Rommel, until his surrender. Incarcerated in Florida, he was visited by Wood's Aunt Susette Joerg Flournoy from New Smyrna Beach, who came bearing peaches, while he was picking peaches in the fields. After V-E Day, photos of the German concentration camps were plastered on all bunkhouse walls.

The visits of the German Jörgs in the interwar years had been fond ones to him, but Wood would never know that a letter he sent early in the war to his great-uncle Adolf Jörg would bring the Gestapo to the man's home in Frankfurt. They accused him of consorting with the enemy and arrested him. Gunter's wife's father, Dr. Oscar Haller, lost his top chemist's job in Offenbach for words against Hitler and for refusing to pay the war tax.[55] Later, he gave travel money to Jews liberated from the concentration camps; some lifted their shirts to show him their wounds. Gunter's wife barely escaped death when an Allied raid on Frankfurt collapsed the opera house, and incinerated civilians who took refuge in the basement of the nearby metal factory in which she worked. "I went back to the factory and saw people piled up almost to the ceiling, dead, cooked, from spilled chemicals and coal," said Margaret Jörg.

"Is this my own family's Civil War?" Wood wondered, sensing that all wars are civil wars, finally. But that was the end of wonder. The German mortars were coming in now, incoming mail, faster than the snow and as ceaseless.

9

January 3, 1945

The mailsacks exploded.

The first fusillade of Screaming Meemie rockets (called "the Elephant Gun" for its six-barrel launcher) cut the GOYAs' lifeline from home. It hit a jeep at the GOYA command post stacked high with Christmas presents and incoming mail. Letters burned. Captain Hartman ran up and tried to rescue some pages, but they were already ashes flying over the snow. He looked up. There on the pine branches hung shards of fruitcake, burning socks, charred lockets.

The rocket attack prompted Lieutenant Andy Titko, in the midst of "taking a constitutional," to leap into a two-man foxhole dug by Sergeant Paul Kjar, the message center chief. Five men made it into that foxhole, Titko was pleased for the only time in his life to be on the bottom. Perhaps my father, one of Kjar's two runners, hopped in there too. It would not serve as hideout for long.

Up ahead of everyone, a 551st scout had discovered a German officer taking his dog out for a walk and shot and killed him. But if the GOYAs thought they might just have surprised the Germans, they themselves were in for a gruesome surprise. A Company on the left flank of the attack was hit by a rain of artillery and mortar fire before it could get across the sunken road. Crossfire from machine guns on Mont de Fosse to the north made it worse. A whole 60mm mortar squad attached to A Company was wiped out by the German artillery; there in front of a stable at Sol Me, the company's Lieutenant George Luening, a Montana schoolteacher and the best card player in the battalion, fell, mortally wounded. As his hurried replacement, Lieutenant Dick Durkee, put it, Luening "drew a dead hand."

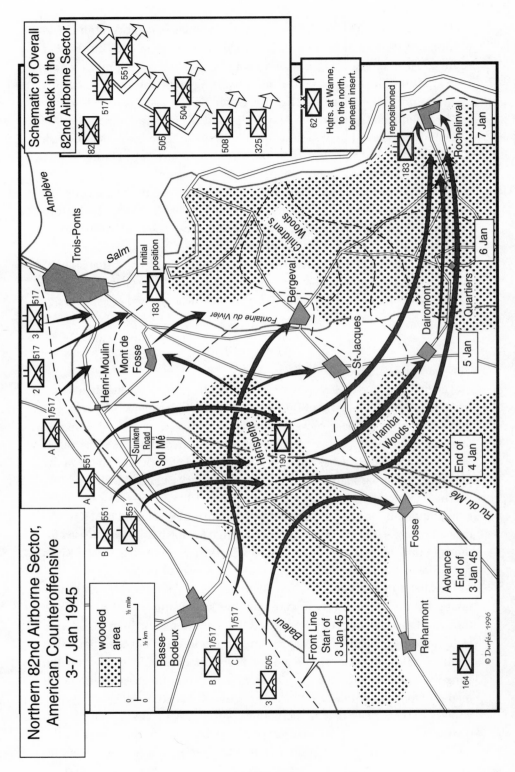

Northern 82nd Airborne Sector, American Counteroffensive 3-7 Jan 1945

Schematic of Overall Attack in the 82nd Airborne Sector

wooded area

½ mile

½ km

Amblève

Trois-Ponts

Salm

Initial position

183

Henri-Moulin

Mont de Fosse

Sunken Road

Sol Mé

Fontaine du Vivier

Bergeval

Children's Woods

St-Jacques

Hérispehe

Hamba Woods

Dairomont

Quartiers

reprositioned

Rochelinval

7 Jan

6 Jan

5 Jan

End of 4 Jan

Ru du Mé

Fosse

Reharmont

Basse-Bodeux

Bateur

Front Line Start of 3 Jan 45

Advance End of 3 Jan 45

Hqtrs. at Wanne, to the north, beneath insert.

© Durfee 1996

517

517 3

517 2

A 1/517

A 551

B 551

C 551

B 1/517

C 1/517

B 3/505

190

164

183

183

62

551

505

517

504

508

325

82

262

Though the 62d Volksgrenadier Division had suffered about 18 percent casualties to that point at the Bulge, some rifle companies were down to less than half strength (fifty men). Still, the 62d's stand was hardened by artillery batteries that were almost completely intact. Firing away were eighty-five light and medium German howitzers ranging from 75mm to 150mm in shell size. The evidence is, though they may not have known the results of their shooting,[56] that they fired away with impunity in the GOYA sector, wreaking great havoc from the minute the 551st attacked at 8:30 A.M.

"Here we go again," Captain Dalton feverishly wrote in his combat notebook as the battle commenced. "I wonder if I'll make it this time?" Dalton quickly jotted phrases with multiple question marks after them, ciphers of the dreadful chaos at the start: "Bn aid station? . . . First Phase Line??? . . . Tedeschi Reserves?????????" He was alert to the old *Greif* guises of the Germans: "Watch wearing American uniforms." Just before he was hit, Dalton wrote of essentials: "Keep men warm and watch for false surrender—KILL."

All along the sunken road bodies piled up. Others pinned themselves up against the embankment, but it afforded little cover. The scene began to resemble another sunken road in American history, that at Antietam, where Confederate and Union men were cut down like cane during the worst single-day battle of the Civil War.

Charlie Fairlamb, attached to A Company as a forward observer for mortars, witnessed the carnage at the sunken road at Basse Bodeaux: "As the men crossed the road, the casualties mounted very rapidly. It seemed as though we just couldn't get started. The Germans were holding the high ground with perfect visibility from dug-in positions, and we were out in the open."

Sensing A Company's ordeal, Joerg quickly ran from Tims Quinn's C Company to the left flank to bolster the spirits of Dalton's men. Sergeant Bill Dean, attached to A Company with his light machine gun platoon, witnessed Joerg's ministrations: "He was speaking to us and encouraging us. That was the last time I saw him alive. He was standing out there directing that attack. He wasn't lying down, trying to hide or take cover. It was an inspiration for his men to watch him."

Suddenly a most bizarre thing happened. A sniper came out from a stand of trees right into the open singing, "Pistol Packin' Momma" in plain English. Dean could see from the black-and-white lightning insignias on his left sleeve and collar that he was SS, probably from the 9th SS Panzers left behind to bolster the 62d Volksgrenadiers. "Lay that pistol down, boy, lay that pistol down," the man bellowed. He started shooting point blank at the GOYAs, killing and wounding several men before he himself was shot.

Finally, aroused by Joerg and Dalton, A Company pried itself off the snowy embankment and stormed into the open field. For about 200 yards they progressed through a strange silence and thought that perhaps the enemy had blown off its entire ammunition stores in the first barrage. Then, as Fairlamb recalled, "all hell broke loose." At least six machine guns began traversing over the charging GOYAs, along with 50mm mortar shells. "We were pinned down in an open field with nothing to get in, under, or behind," Fairlamb wrote.

As they hugged the snow, whispering "God" or "Mary," two tanks emerged, one near the Laurent farm, the other at the edge of the Hamba woods. At 150 yards away they started crossfiring their 17-foot, 75mm guns at the approaching men. It was a second slaughter, 75mm shells screamed in, and Dillard watched in horror as Dalton fell backward. Lieutenant Keith Harsh also fell, spilling blood from his shoulder onto the snow.

Private Roland Barhyte, who'd been made A Company's acting operations officer after his buddy, Jim Deming, had been killed in southern France, seeing Dalton fall, cried out "Medic!" The first medic to respond, however, Private John Stewart, another of Barhyte's friends, was killed.

Dillard ran up with two medics, Jack Affleck and Tommy Kane, to pull Dalton back to the tree line, where he was hoisted on a litter, but Harsh managed to get back up. Realizing he was one of the last A Company officers left, Harsh told Joerg on the radio he was shot but would keep command until replaced. "I will never forget that," Dillard said. He also didn't forget the sight of one of his best friends killed right near him by machine gun fire: Sergeant Wilbur Banks.

The Panthers' pummeling at point blank range was particularly gruesome. "It was just annihilation," Joe Cicchinelli said. "You could hear the cries and screams of the guys as they went down. The snow was red with their blood." Cicchinelli caught the moaning of his partner, Sergeant Don Thompson, whose left foot barely hung to his leg by sinew. Chick left the modest protection of some barbed wire and crawled 100 feet to Thompson, who seemed to have been crushed by a tank. Hit by shrapnel, his right eardrum shattered by a crashing 75mm shell, Cicchinelli pulled Thompson to safety.

So bad was the situation, medics themselves were being hit wholesale as they crawled to help the wounded. A particularly stunning sacifice was made by A Company Private Cloy Wilson, who left the cover of a foxhole and shimmied across the open snow to help several men who were hit, finally reaching a wounded medic whose head was bare. Though he wasn't a medic himself, Wilson had had medical aid training and put it to quick use. He placed his own helmet on the medic's head, bandaged him quickly, and draped the man over his shoulder to get him back to the aid station. But before he had gone six steps, Wilson himself was hit by shrapnel, which tore off a good part of his head. The medic was later rescued, but Wilson was dead. Like Cicchinelli's risky valor, and that of many others in the grim days ahead, Wilson's ultimate gift of a life for a life went unrecognized.

The German tanks had to be dealt with. The men had not been able to get far enough up the slope to seize a panzerfaust, the sole hand-held weapon that could pierce a Tiger or Panther tank's armor. The one chance their own bazookas had was for a close-in, broadside shot at the only place of vulnerability—between the metal track and the ironclad. Seeing Dalton fall, the bazookaman Private Chuck Miller resolved he would get one or die trying.

Miller plodded forward, then ran through the snow with his bazooka. He circled a Panther and got set from the side, squinting at the 2-inch slit of darkness above the clanking track, and fired. The machine exploded. Miller heard cheers go up among the moans. Bill Dean attested about Miller: "That was a brave man."

Dean cringed with some men from Headquarters Company along the barbed-wire fence before the slope uphill, hoping for minuscule protection from the wire and the posts. A young-looking kid, Dean thought about eighteen, was shot in the throat right next to him: "He looked at me with a desperate plea in his eyes; he was blowing red bubbles in that snow. I looked away; I never did look back at him."

Partly he couldn't look back. Wounded once in the hip in southern France, now Dean was hit in the arm by machine gun bullets. Hearing others crying for help—"lying there listening to them when no one could do anything"—Dean lay his head down in the snow, figuring it was his turn to face his Maker. Though he was not religious at the time, he murmured a prayer: "I promised Him if He'd let me live, I'd do anything He ever wanted me to do." Feigning death, motionless while other wounded were silenced by fire in the snow, by nightfall the warmth of his body had melted him clear through the snow to the ground. A few survivors on the slope rose, calling each other's names, and hobbled to an aid station, Dean helped by his best friend for the second time in the war.

Dean didn't forget his promise: He became a minister in Killeen, Texas (and later Bossier City, Louisiana), and four of his five sons became ministers, as well. During the Vietnam War, none of his GI parishioners were killed. But there was one whom Dean's fervent prayers could not ultimately save: the GOYA best friend who had saved him twice in World War II and had gone on to success as a builder. Haunted by the losses at the Sunken Road and Rochelinval in Belgium and two wounds, and later years of pain from a neck fractured in a car accident, Lieutenant Harold Lawler committed suicide at age forty-four.

The despair the GOYAs felt in that open field beyond Basse Bodeux in front of Sol Me that day gave way to sheer anger. Just after he saw his pal Banks killed, Doug Dillard ran into a small German POW just shy of the tree line, his uniform festooned with medals.

"What's this one for?" Dillard cried out, grabbing the man's shirt.

The man replied in German that it was for wounds, a "Purple Heart."

Half-crazed with grief, his fellows lying in the snow all around with no decorations but bullet wounds, Dillard ripped the medals off the man and pocketed them.

Lieutenant Dick Durkee, who, with Lieutenants Gerald Quinn and Charlie Buckenmeyer, was one of only three A Company officers left standing by nightfall, decided that the men had to get out of the line of fire. He jumped up and led them to the right flank, setting up machine guns, which finally drove off the remaining tanks and silenced the Germans' left flank. Following Durkee up to the tree line, Cicchinelli looked to the west and saw some American soldiers of the 517th wearing long overcoats, something "Dalton was so pissed off about" at the attack's start. Overcome with anger, Cicchinelli and others actually shot at the 517th men, who waved and called out, "Americans! Americans!" before the incensed GOYAs stopped.

Vengeance was taken also against the 190th Regiment, commanded by Oberstleutnant Herbert Franke of the 62d Volksgrenadiers, the GOYAs' chief antagonists on the ridge, along with the assorted SS men. C Company's Jim Guerrant recounted it: "Private Harold Magnuson and Private Denny Downes took about six or eight German prisoners over the hill and executed them. We'd seen what they'd done to us at Malmédy, and these Germans were wearing U.S. tanker coats on the ridge. I guess everyone was pure outraged." Neither lived with that for long. After spending time in a hospital in Atlantic City (Downes for a severed right arm, Magnuson for "nerves"), Downes was killed and Magnuson was "pretty well knocked to bits"[57] in a weekend auto accident in New York in June 1945.

About 9:30 A.M., while A Company was being shredded in the assault, C Company's Tims Quinn was alarmed to see that the 505th on his right flank had already become engaged in a firefight, probing up the hill. "This meant there was no coordinated attack but instead individual elements were fighting separate engagements," said Quinn, who had ordered a three-man patrol to keep in contact with the closest unit, 505th's I Company, commanded by a former GOYA, Captain Archie McPheeters, who had left the 551st during its troubles at Camp Mackall. The patrol quickly lost touch, however. Quinn saw four rounds of U.S. artillery hit the Germans on the ridge top and shouted to a 460th forward artillery observer, "That's perfect! Now give us the concentration."

Pulling his phone off his ear, the observer shouted back, "That *is* the concentration!" A shortage of ammo, the observer said, was limiting fire to definite targets, not that anything definite was to be seen in those shady woods ahead. In any case, no more artillery would shield the 551st after those four rounds.[58]

Another discouragement was the quick ruin of the four-man forward observer contingent itself. Crossing the snowy field, they were hit by 88mm shells. Three were wounded, the lieutenant in charge mortally. The big man, a radio on his back, hobbled up to Quinn and groaned, "Could I go to the rear?"

"Can I help you? What's wrong?"

Then Quinn saw the radio slide off the lieutenant's back, revealing nothing but torn flesh and blood. The observer trembled uncontrollably, in shock, and died shortly thereafter. The loss of the forward observers foreclosed any significant artillery cover in the days that followed for the GOYAs.

Quinn charged at the head of C Company into the open field with a characteristic rebel yell. The men echoed him. Committed behind them in B Company, Sergeant Bill Hatcher recalled the noise: "I couldn't believe my ears—there was actual shouting. I thought that went out with the Civil War, the rebel yell. But here was the 551st, this spirited outfit, going for the attack yelling . . . like something out of the nineteenth century."

According to one historian, "the bull-like charge seemed to unnerve the Germans."[59] Making good progress on the right flank (due partly to the Germans' zeroing in on A Company on the left), Quinn's C Company made it into the Hèrispehe woods before the road to Fosse—Phase Line 2—taking many volksgrenadier prisoners. Then Quinn received a rare radio message through the Germans' jamming and radio destruction from Joerg to wait for A Company to pull up alongside him. The halt was a mistake. It gave the Germans time to swing around their machine guns and 88s; in a fifteen-minute barrage, forty-five C Company men were killed or severely wounded. Quinn was hit by a shell in the embarrassing but well-padded zone of his posterior.

"I knew they would hit that big fanny of yours!" Pappy Herrmann exclaimed facetiously, ever ready with GOYA gallows humor.

Quinn scooted along in the snow, "kind of like a dog cleaning his rear end," and one mortified private tried to alleviate his embarrassment, if not suffering, calling out: "That's all right, Captain, that's all right."

"The hell it is! I've been shot!"

Quinn had had a bet with Sergeant Frank Nuck, whom he thought had the biggest nose in the battalion, that Nuck would get it someday in the nose, while Nuck was certain Quinn would get it in his own generous area. Fifteen minutes after Quinn was hit in the rear end, he came across

Nuck, who had a big hole where his nose had been, sheared from shrapnel in a tree burst. The two managed to laugh at each other in their mutual pain. They had both won the bet.

It didn't stop Quinn. "He was racing around bellowing orders like always, clipboard in one hand, a .45 in the other," Sergeant Martin Kangas remembered. "No helmet on, blood all over his rear. The medics tried to get him to stop, and he told them to go to hell."

Pressing the lead of the attack, C Company's PFC Dick Nichols and three other men came under mortar fire. The three, including PFC Andy Brookshire and Private Kimber Couch, had apparently picked potato masher grenades off some Germans and had hooked them to their belts; the mortars detonated the grenades and blasted the three men to pieces.

Up in the woods now, C Company fought fiercely man-to-man, but few Germans were subjected to the method of Magnuson and Downes. According to Lieutenant Dick Goins: "The Germans were well dug in, and it seemed impossible to disperse them." Many Germans were killed and more wounded; the wounded were evacuated back to the battalion aid station. Rage was still boiling for the killings in the field that day. Goins had to stay the hand of two troopers who wanted to kill a wounded German wailing on a stretcher. Instead, Goins ordered four shots of morphine for the man. Three days later, when Goins himself was taken off the line with frozen feet, he was startled at the aid station to see the same German alive. "You saved my life," the man said in perfect English; he had been a teacher at the university in Hamburg.

Not so forgiving, it appears, was Sergeant Bernard "Duke" Spletzer of Headquarters Company, who had been attached to C Company under Lieutenant Farren for the assault (he was moved to other units, too). Spletzer had been with the battalion's intelligence section because of his knowledge of German. His parents had immigrated to America in 1905 from a German community in Poland. Born in Minnesota, Spletzer joined the Army in Michigan before the war. Under Lieutenant Bud Schroeder, he served as the GOYAs' chief parachute rigger; Schroeder said of him, "There wasn't a finer soldier that ever hit the ground."[60]

Spletzer quickly displayed the unit's special taste for mayhem as a high art, and sometimes a low art. Under the influence of liquid spirits he was known as someone not to be tampered with. In training, he was busted half the time; when liquored up, he'd be found spouting German on the streets and was picked up a couple of times by the Counterintelligence Command (CIC), who wondered if he were a spy. At Mackall, he broke both legs of a taxi driver who'd tried to gouge him with a high fare. A pathfinder on the southern France jump, he'd use his German to bait the enemy into the open.

At Laon, while marching around a clump of POWs, he forced them to sing "Here comes the Wehrmacht!" until Joerg told him to "Tone that down, Ace."

Spletzer's brother, Lou, remembered his brother walking a wobbly line between daring and self-destruction. On one occasion, as the two brothers, on furlough, were taking a drive, Duke started climbing out of the moving car to demonstrate what it was like falling from a plane by jumping off the top of the car moving at 25 miles per hour. His brother had to restrain him.[61]

Making it to the ridge at the Bulge that first day, Spletzer quickly rounded up twenty to thirty prisoners with his tommy gun. Lieutenant Booth told him to take them to Captain Ed Hartman, the battalion's intelligence chief, for questioning. According to Lieutenant Phil Hand, this is what happened next: "So we get around out of sight from him, around the side of the mountain. I hear the tommy gun shattering, and I said, 'Oh, my God!' And I ran around, and he had already killed them all, pulled them apart like spokes of a wheel [beforehand]."

Hand was livid: "Spletzer, damn it! They told you to take them back."

"They ran, Lieutenant," was all Spletzer offered. The Germans had said the same about Malmédy.

Hand, unconvinced, later concluded: "Hell, they didn't run. He just deliberately killed them." But Spletzer's statement at the time was accepted.[62] Ironically, after the war and a stint with the Navy, Spletzer worked as a prison guard, and later as a mailman, near Jacksonville, Florida; he died at the age of fifty-eight.

Harry Renick, who had helped round up the prisoners, heard the tommy gun fire and the subsequent explanation (though he wasn't certain it was Spletzer). "You have to realize the pressures we were under. I didn't see the inside of a house the whole time at the Bulge. If I saw a house, I bypassed it, thinking it might be booby-trapped. I'd rather freeze to death than be exploded."

Renick also cited as incendiary to the GOYAs an incident that day when a POW pulled a grenade off the belt of his guard and threatened to pull the pin and blow everyone sky high, before he was wrestled to the ground and shot. Thus prisoners could be lethal, and the incident did nothing to instill charity.

There was plenty of bitterness and misery to go around. There on the forested hill, the GOYAs got a sense of the Germans' own difficulties. "Most of the Germans we took out of there that day were cold and miserable," Kangas said. "Hedy" LaMar jumped into a German slit trench to avoid fire and found his feet plunging through ice; he wound up hip-deep in icewater, working his rifle with bandaged hands.

Tom Waller and Earl Grinsted of A Company were part of a fifteen-man wounded contingent, including Marshall Dalton on a stretcher and one German prisoner, who were slogging to reach the aid station when they were ambushed by Germans firing automatic weapons. Dalton's stretcher was summarily dropped, and he let out a scream. The forlorn group were without weapons; they either dived into the snow or hobbled away. It was a pathetic example of how merciless the fighting was that day. Later, toward midnight, Waller and Grinsted came upon Dalton, with the prisoner oddly still attached to him. They hadn't found the aid station yet. The diminished group went forward in the snow. When Waller heard men mumbling in the forest, he was ready to call out "Dog" as the password response to "Fox," but instead he got a German challenge. The woeful group—not ready to be wounded for a third time trying to get medical help—surrendered. Stepping out from cover of trees, the Germans didn't make the arrest. They wanted to talk. In a mixture of English, French, and German, the GOYAs explained that they were all wounded, were unarmed, and were going to their aid station, where there was hot food and where all would be well-treated. "After much discussion of the pros and cons," said Waller, "they bought it."

After properly stacking their rifles in a corner at the aid station, as Waller poignantly described it, "That night all of us, Germans and GIs, the wounded and the able, slept on the floor together."

By this time, B Company had long been committed from its reserve, following behind C Company to bolster A Company, too. It took stubborn sniper fire up the slope of Sol Me, into Hèrispehe. A bullet zinged into a tree near Lieutenant Ralph Wenthold, and he shouted to a trooper leaning across from him to locate the sniper: "Where's that son-of-a-bitch?" But the man gave no reply; he was shot through the forehead. Moving up that night to the Hamba woods, Wenthold heard clanking so loud it sounded like a construction site. There A Company was trying to pierce the frozen soil for foxholes.

As the firing died down in the twilight that day, the commanders still standing walked the blood-spattered snow as if in a trance, bumping shoulders with the wounded moving to the rear. The Indian who, in a drunken rage, had thoroughly whipped Tims Quinn at Trapani in Sicily, before being tied to a pole, was now tied to another pole—a spruce tree— by shot. Corporal Ray Banks was found leaning with a small radio at his ear. Quinn thought he was dead standing. He wasn't quite; Durkee saw Banks being lugged in wheelbarrow (the litters had been used up) to an aid station, where he died.

Durkee turned to "a sight that will never leave me" looking back from the ridge at the battlefield. In an eloquent testimony written later that year, he described it:

The bodies of our comrades were strewn about where they had fallen and were partially covered with snow. I could see one man leaning against a fence-post. He apparently was going to climb over it, but just didn't make it. One of our machine guns was still there in position, and the gunner and assistant gunner were lying [dead] behind their gun. . . . Just before I rounded the bend in the road I looked back once more and bid the dead goodbye, as the snow completely covered them and hid them from the war-torn world.[63]

Medics Jack Affleck, Ed Henriquez, David Munoz, and others had the grim duty now of tagging and marking the dead by plunging their rifles muzzle-first into the snow and hanging their helmets on the stocks. Munoz was seen stringing the watches of the dead around his wrists; by nightfall, the watches had filled both arms up to his armpits.

Then the Graves Registration people rumbled in with their trucks, led by Lieutenant Ben Henry "Bee" Brown, who, according to his assistant, Corporal Max Bryan of C Company, "was afraid of dead people." So it was Bryan, who had grown up alongside a funeral home, and Private James Bywaters of A Company who directed the sad traffic that day and for five more dark days, till there were few left to die.

For Bryan, the day had started ominously. His jeep had hit a mine near the command post, and it tore up his right knee. But work was work; actually, most of the fetching of the bodies was done by German POWs, under guard:

> The unique thing about it was—all the people who were sitting there that got killed would freeze solid. And it sounds horrible, but the people in the battalion know what it was. You'd find two trees and you'd stack the bodies in there just like stacking cordwood, three or four deep. Then we used this three-quarter-ton truck and we'd stack about 12 people on it until the truck was full.

That truck made several deliveries before nightfall. It got so Bryan thought the whole world was pink human lumber. And then there was something that Bryan hadn't spoken of for half a century: He searched through the pocketbooks of the dead, not for money, but for condoms or photographs or names of "other women . . . anything that might be detrimental to their family."

Completely sapped, leading remnants of A Company that evening of January 3, Durkee decided not to try and take Phase Line 3—Dairomont— until the next day. Men groped in the dark, hand by hand. Finally, he ordered the weary effectives, about 50 of the 155 that started that day, to try and dig into the frozen ground of the Hamba woods for the night. Durkee took a few soldiers with him to link up with Lieutenant Gerald Quinn, who was in charge of the rest of A Company, on the way to Fosse. Before he reached the road, the moon sneaked through the trees and gleamed off the bucket helmets of some Germans. The GIs opened fire and took several prisoners up the road to Fosse, which they reached by 11 P.M.

The prisoners were turned over to the 505th Regiment. That great seasoned unit (hand-picked by Gavin and called by Ridgway "the best parachute regiment to come out of World War II") had been quick to tangle that morning with the 190th Volksgrenadiers, but it had run into fierce resistance at Fosse, with Company I losing two-thirds of its men. Despite its own ordeal, the 551st moved beyond the 505th on the right and the 517th on the left, though both caught up that night. Aided by tank support around noon that January 3, by 2 P.M. the 505th had exacted a German surrender in Fosse.

Whatever happened at Fosse (there were rumors), and earlier with the 551st's Magnuson, Downes, and Spletzer, no one—German or American— was immune to the terrors of the Battle of the Bulge, and the cold blood it boiled. It must be said, however, that nothing remotely similar to Hitler's personal terror-order to his generals existed on the Allied side, though a regiment of the 26th Division issued an order, later rescinded, which read: "No SS troops or paratroopers will be taken prisoner, but will be shot on sight."[64] The green 11th Armored Division, hammered by Hitler's fury at Bastogne, on New Year's Day shot twenty-one German POWs at nearby Chenogne. Danny Parker soberly explains, "These incidents must be understood in perspective. While execution of prisoners in the heat of battle is a seldom mentioned but undeniable aspect of war, the SS units were notorious in this respect."[65]

That night the men's extremities began to freeze. They wanted desperately to sleep. It wasn't just the wounds and the sheer exhaustion of the day's battle. The cold itself lulled you. Some had shoveled the snow off an area and tried to conk out on their cellophane gas capes, but Durkee ordered the noncombatants to wake anyone up who dropped off. The mercury was dropping below zero Farenheit, and a man could freeze to death in a couple of hours in such weather. A buddy of Cicchinelli, Private James Carroll of Hoboken, New Jersey, was found in the morning stiff in final sleep. No one had waked him. Or could. Up to two dozen other GOYAs also died of acute hypothermia. The poet Lieutenant Wilfred Owen speaks of it in "Asleep":

> Who knows? Who hopes? Who troubles? Let it pass!
> He sleeps. He sleeps less tremulous, less cold
> Than we who must awake, and waking, say "Alas!"[66]

Isolation invaded the 551st that night and hung on till the end for dear death. The cold itself, of course, was physically isolating—the body's blood retreats to the center, leaving everything outside with less and less feeling. Word of their Christmas presents' blasting spread, making them feel more cut off from home. Where was their parent group, the 517th? They were cut off from it. They were exposed on the flanks to extra fire, because the 517th and the 505th were nowhere near them. Where were their overcoats and shoes? Supply jeeps were cut off by mined roads and fields. Each man began to feel himself become a slow amputation.

To make matters worse, the radios had taken a beating. Of the thirty-eight SCR-300 radios in the battalion's care, by January 5 the GOYAs had only three or four left. What the extreme cold hadn't done to the batteries, or jamming, German marksmanship had done; any radioman could be spotted from that ridge, marked by a black antenna.

Harry Renick, who had one of the few GOYA radios left in the end, described the growing loneliness that seized the men and would not let them be: "There were times that there were so many people around you, and you got the feeling—I did, anyway—that you have buddies here but you might as well be all alone. You just got that lonely feeling that this was a lost cause, and where was it going to take you, and where would you wind up? You didn't get consolation from anybody because everybody was in the same mood—miserable, hungry, and frozen."

Those who could get away with starting a fire tried to melt snow before Joerg came around. The water leached out, however, was black with gunpowder. It was swallowed. You swallowed the war. It was called "gunpowder tea."

Men tried anything to stay warm: nuzzle in the snow against your fellow isolates, pile up sandwich-style, stamp your feet all night long in delerium, circle a sapling, as Phil Hand did, endlessly. Men welded themselves into the ground when the warmth of their bodies would temporily melt the snow and then refreeze, encasing them; Emory Albritton had to chip out several men before they froze in a natural sarcophagus.

A few, a very few, had coffee. Tims Quinn was treated to some in the dim light of a truck in which Joerg and Bill Holm had pulled up. Holm had found an overcoat; someone bitched about it and went off into the night. Quinn trudged up to Fosse, had his rear end sewed up by the 505th, as well as his pants, and learned the sad news that his fellow captain Archie McPheeters had been killed before he had taken six steps. It would seem the former member of the GOYAs had carried their hard luck with him to another unit. But the valiant 505th had enough hard luck of its own that day. In fact, for all its ordeals at Normandy, in Sicily, and in Holland, the 505th historian said of the first day of the counteroffensive at the Bulge: "This was the worst battle I saw in the entire war. The resistance was tough, very tough."[67]

Joerg got out of the truck, exhaling a bullhorn of vapor into the night. He tried to reassure the men, who barely acknowledged him. Then he found the tatters of Dalton's men. It was obvious that A Company was in a state of shock. From a cot at the aid station, where German POW doctors operated alongside Captain Battenfield, Dalton asked Joerg to put in his brave men for the Distinguished Unit Citation. A highly sensitive man who knew his men by their first names and, unique among the company commanders, insisted on writing all the letters of condolence himself, Dalton starting ticking off the names of the dead. Joerg stopped him. Never inclined to honors, Joerg patted him on the shoulder; it wasn't going to happen.

That night Joerg asked his battalion executive Bill Holm to call Melvin Zais of the 517th to have the GOYAs relieved. The 551st had sustained 189 casualties—nearly a third of the battalion's strength—in the first day of battle.[68] Nearly half of those were from A Company alone. Though neither the 517th nor any integral regiment of the 82d Airborne had suffered that loss rate on January 3, Zais refused. Joerg was stunned. He could see what was coming.

What happened to my father that day? His little diary records the losses that first day: A Company down to forty-five men, C Company about the same (this is off), his own B Company going into the attack the next day, then down to eighty-three men three days later on January 6, when he is taken out for frozen feet. But nothing else.

I write this just before midnight, January 3, 1995—exactly fifty years to the hour after my father must have delivered his last message that first day of the Allied counteroffensive at the Battle of the Bulge. *One thing is certain, Gregory: With those icy, mined, and snow-clogged roads, there was no more motorcycle.* With messages a half-century ago he was running in the snow, dodging fire, as I have dodged my own despair, with words—little orders—in his hands.

10
January 4: The bayonet attack

That first day of the big push back, and on into the next, General Gavin was upset. Not with the 551st *per se*—Gavin never mentioned the GOYAs in all his published postwar writings—but with Rupert Graves and his regimental combat team (to which the GOYAs were attached). In a word, the 517th was not moving fast enough. Rankled by Montgomery's insistence that the counteroffensive proceed by strict phase lines, holding up when those were attained, no matter what open ground lay ahead, Gavin wanted to leap forward. In addition, while Gavin was walking the trenches at the front in his singular, exposed style, three of his aides had been seriously hurt alongside him, two of them while he was barking at the 517th. Gavin himself was nearly hit twice. Colonel Graves's phlegmatic personality did nothing to calm him.[69]

It was also probably easier for Gavin to take his anxiety out on a unit that was not integral to the 82d Airborne, such as the 517th. In *On to Berlin,* he says flatly (and somewhat inaccurately) of the Buzzard unit: "It had had limited experience and was put into the attack abreast of the veteran regiments."[70] His Bulge combat diary is even less complimentary and more self-serving: "This business of making green outfits go is positively dangerous but it must be done." The 517th had been in combat in France, Italy, and Belgium since mid-August; part of it had received the Distinguished Unit Citation for valor at Soy-Hotton; it was hardly "green." Still, in *Berlin,* Gavin gives far more space to describing the supposed lassitude of the 517th than he does the activities of any other unit at the Bulge, four pages. It becomes a kind of lecture-on-the-move, a set piece to demonstrate the catalytic powers of a general.

Of his three encounters with the "hapless" 517th, the third appears actually to have been with the 551st. During the morning of January 5, Gavin came across "an 81mm mortar platoon that was in support of an infantry battalion in the attack," its mortars stacked neatly beside a Belgian farmhouse and the men inside enjoying a "cozy fireplace." Gavin wasted no time in rousting what he implies is a 517th group out into the cold and the war. But Private Fred Hilgardner of the GOYAs' Headquarters Company mortar section described the encounter quite differently.

The GOYAs were emplacing their eight mortars—the battalion's all, and twice what it normally had—ahead of the advancing foot soldiers. The mortar platoon was split; half were at the farmhouse, half out on the road, set up. In short, the men had a rather reasonable rotation going to spell each other from the cold. In Hilgardner's recollection, Gavin came up to the group on the road, which was also guarding eight German prisoners in a ditch.

"What the hell are you doing up here?" Gavin snapped. "Who's in charge here?" But before they could answer or salute, a heavy shower of shrapnel from artillery burst in trees overhead. Gavin's driver was hit in the stomach. "Oh, Christ!" the general cursed.

"What should we do with the prisoners?" Hilgardner called up to the general.

"I don't give a damn what you do with them!" Gavin shouted, pushing the injured driver over in the jeep and taking the wheel himself. He turned feverishly and headed out. (The damn-the-torpedos injunction about POWs dovetailed with what Gavin had said the day before: Prisoners were "not to be given food, water, or cigarettes.")[71]

That driver's bloody stomach, the harshness about POWs, and just who this unit really was are not part of General Gavin's written account.

What had held up the 517th on January 3? With a portion of 675 rounds of artillery they received throughout the day from their 460th Field Artillery Battalion, the Buzzards took their first objective of the day—Trois-Ponts at the hinge of the counteroffensive—rather easily, by 9 A.M. that morning. But the 2d Battalion was pinned down by a tough German stand on the ridge of Mont de Fosse on the GOYAs' left flank. From his command post on the Wanne Heights across the east bank of the Salm River, General Kittel of the 62d Volksgrenadiers watched with satisfaction as his 183d Regiment rained fire on the Americans from Mont de Fosse, a "murderous cul-de-sac."

Ticked off that the 517th hadn't, for all the severe punishment it was taking, stormed Mont de Fosse, Gavin himself stormed into Graves's command post at Basse Bodeux at dusk, stabbing a map at the towns of Saint-Jacques and Bergeval a mile south of the firefight: "I want those towns by tonight." Graves recalled, "With that, Gavin departed, leaving us to figure out how to get Seitz's 2d Battalion out of its trap."[72]

To appease Gavin's impatience, Graves deliberated sending his only reserve, the crack 1st Battalion, straight to Mont de Fosse. But the 1st's Major Bill Boyle hatched a counterplan: to traverse the area cleared at great cost by the 551st southeast to Saint-Jacques and Bergeval, and then to curl back north and hit the Germans on Mont de Fosse from the rear. "Feeling that [going to Mont de Fosse first] would only result in having two battalions chopped up, I eventually persuaded Graves to let me follow the 551st and strike from their area using the woods for cover."[73] As darkness fell, a guide from the 551st arrived to lead the 1st Battalion to the GOYAs. The one-and-a-half-mile stretch in cold and dark took five hours; the GOYAs could not be found.

The 551st's disappearance from physical or radio contact disturbed Boyle and Graves. An engineering party sent to clear mines saw Major Holm at the church in Saint-Jacques early in the morning, but the 517th S-3 reported at 5:20 A.M. that the GOYAs themselves could not be located. Around noon Graves received a map overlay with the 551st's positions, but it didn't help. The 517th's Russ Brami was injured when sent to find the GOYAs. The same would happen to Boyle himself. Twice he sent out scouts; twice they returned empty-handed, with no news of Joerg's men (pressing forward, they were to move throughout January 4 a mile southeast to Dairomont).

The rivalry between the 517th and its bastard attached battalion intensified in those moments. Years later, Boyle thought the GOYAs' progress was due to "concealment,"[74] unlike the 2d Battalion's out-in-the-open ordeal at Mont de Fosse, but he either didn't know or had forgotten how the 551st had been mowed down in the open snowy field in front of the ridges that day.

To the 1st Battalion's credit, by 4:30 A.M. on January 4 it had secured both Saint-Jacques and Bergeval in successful surprise night attacks of a half-hour's and an hour's duration, respectively, which cost only two casualties. According to the 517th unit historian, Clark Archer, the attack would not have been possible without the "hard fighting of the 551st and the 2/517th, which created the gap and held the enemy in place while Boyle's men hit from the flank."[75] The 1st's F Company crept behind Mont de Fosse and clamped the pincer; the German stand collapsed. Later Graves dryly noted, "At any rate, our night attacks prevented at least myself and perhaps General Gavin from having a nervous breakdown."[76]

Searching for the lost battalion that night, Boyle was hit three times by machine gun fire. He prayed in the snow, "Don't let me die" and managed to get up when brusquely challenged to do so by a sergeant. Limping into Bergeval, in severe shock, Boyle took four units of plasma. His prayer was answered, but not Wood Joerg's.

The GOYAs were crushing snow into a vast solitude. They were not the only ones. About 9 A.M. that morning, General Kittel reported that, with the American paratroopers pressing forward, backing the Germans ever more tightly toward the Salm River, his own contact with the 190th and 164th Volksgrenadier regiments was cut off. In addition, "a break occurred along the seam between the 183d and the 190th"—probably filled in by the 517th as it entered the Bois d'Enfants (Children's Woods) along the Salm. Thus the 62d Division was itself being fractured into many isolated parts in the snow.

Faces and noses began to turn black with frostbite. Aware that many of his men were beginning to lose touch with reality in the severe weather and shellfire, Joerg gave the company with the fewest casualties, B Company, the task of a frontal attack on Dairomont. Besides tiny Quartiers, it was the only village that lay between the unit and Rochelinval on the Salm River. C Company would circle around on the left flank. Blistered from the cold and wind and mauled by their assault of the previous day, A Company was placed in reserve, feeding chips of frozen K rations into their aching stomachs; they hadn't eaten for thirty hours.

About 4 P.M. on January 4, with B Company running into very heavy sniper fire, Joerg had little choice but to call on his remnant of A Company, which had some of his best sharpshooters. He told Lieutenant Booth, who by now had assumed command of what was left of A Company, to send in a platoon to settle the problem. The platoon was split into two squads, one led by Dick Durkee, the other by Gerry Quinn.

Spotting Durkee's squad first, the Germans opened up with rifle and well-entrenched machine guns. Quinn threaded his men in an encirclement through the woods. Now perceiving Quinn's men, the Germans sensed they were caught in a vise. They struggled to swing their weapons around to hit Quinn's squad. Durkee saw that if his GOYAs kept shooting into the nests, they could hit the others coming from behind in the misty forest. He gave a quick order, one they'd not heard yet in the war and wouldn't again: *Fix bayonets.*

Durkee led the charge through knee-deep snow. Doug Dillard was close behind with a tommy gun. The rest—Chuck Miller, Joe Cicchinelli, and Chuck Fairlamb among them—barely had a chance to see their metal points flashing before Durkee crested the first foxhole, whirled his M-1 around and smashed the head of the first German to rise up. The men leaped from foxhole to foxhole, over the machine guns, thrusting their bayonets into the startled Germans, some of whom tried to raise their hands up to surrender. Durkee said: "They never had a chance. The men, having seen so many of their buddies killed and wounded during the past twenty-four hours, were not in a forgiving mood." In all, sixty-four Germans lay dead.

"Suddenly it was over," Doug Dillard recounted. "The guys [were] lying there with the steam coming out of their mouths. It was a grotesque scene." A terror rush of adrenalin obliterated time. Durkee looked overhead and saw that the trees around the nests were decapitated. Fir limbs were strewn on the snow, as if a wild man with a chainsaw had been through. Evidently there had been a heavy artillery barrage, possibly German friendly, just before the bayonet charge. Durkee realized that half the Germans were dead before they'd arrived.

The men were yelling and cursing. He looked down and saw them repeatedly stabbing the corpses, sending the dead blood up in spurts, crushing the blue faces with their gun butts:

> It was terrible. To see these kids that, maybe two years before, had been going to church on Sunday, to see them now, running amok. Some of them broke the stocks of their rifles as they beat on the dead bodies.

The A Company platoon had, as Durkee described it, "gone berserk." He quickly ran back through the foxholes, pulling men off the bodies, yelling at them to stop. Then he "got the men back where they belonged."

Durkee said he restrained the men from their ferocity, "naturally," but probably what was most natural after so much pressure and horror would have been to join in. Clausewitz wrote his magnum opus *On War* to press the notion of a code of honor and restraining standards in war—"true war" as opposed to "real war." But on the modern battlefield, crisscrossed with flying hot lead, gas, napalm, and finally the force of the exploding atom itself, the line between "true" war and "real" war is blurred completely. As John Keegan has noted, "The facts of war are not cold. They burn with the heat of the fires of hell."[77] Clausewitz should have known that his theories for reasonable deployments and gentlemanly behavior and discipline went up in smoke in battle; he himself had lived through Napoleon's attack on

Russia in winter. But the capricious, cruel reality of war somehow didn't penetrate the brain that spun the theory that built the Prussian military might that, in turn, so enraptured a little black-mustached German corporal of World War I. That man was now being pushed toward the firing squad wall of Germany by the GOYAs and 599,000 other Allied soldiers in Belgium. What Durkee did halting the senseless mutilations was not natural, under the circumstances. His bayonet attack was.

Doug Dillard spotted Cicchinelli walking aimlessly and told him to pick up the ammunition belts of their own machine guns to prepare for a counterattack. The next moment, an artillery tree burst knocked the helmet off the head of Salvador Corillo, and he ran around crying, completely unglued. Dillard grabbed him hard and took him off to an aid station for a wound that couldn't be seen, that had finally burst inside him.

Something darker burst inside another man that day. Sergeant Stephen Kicinski of A Company was told by Durkee to take three cold, shivering Poles in German uniform after they'd given themselves up back to the S-2 Ed Hartman for interrogation. Out of sight, Durkee heard "the ack ack of a Thompson submachine gun. Sergeant Kicinski had shot them. I said to him, 'Sergeant, you committed murder. I'm going to court-martial you.'" Kicinski blurted, similar to Spletzer, that the prisoners had tried to escape. Brutality hadn't hurt the man who threw one of Furlough's pups overboard, Kicinski may have recalled; Sergeant Dickson had beaten him out for promotion and later got a battlefield commission. Durkee thought the execution may have occurred because Kicinski disparaged the prisoners for being from "a rival Polish area." Whatever the case, the court-martial never took place, because Kicinski was killed on the last day of the war in Europe, near the Elbe River.

Emerging from the woods, Durkee's men—sunk in their dark trance—beheld an apparition of an iron behemoth clanking in the snow, a 45-ton Panther tank. "It was big as a house," Durkee said. "It seemed as if the forest was moving." Its 75mm gun looked like a sewer pipe in the air. The men dove to the ground to evade light machine gun fire; oddly, the tank swerved to the left and took off. It slid a bit on the icy snow. Perhaps it was thankful; earlier in the day, guarding Dairomont, a Panther had taken a direct bazooka hit from a 551st man in the vulnerable slit above the track, but the round hadn't detonated. It had been frozen, though the shooter had been carrying the shell inside his jacket.

The GOYAs rejoiced when finally two of their own tanks were sent up to help the attack on Dairomont but were slightly chagrined when one tanker called out, "How many men will there be in support of our tanks?" He was assured there would be two companies. After the attack was finished, the tanker popped his lid and croaked at Corporal Clell Whitener: "Goddamn! I never saw more than ten or fifteen men."

Someone retorted, with not complete exaggeration: "Well, there are only about twenty men left in those companies."

"Goddamn," the tanker came back. "We would never have gone within a mile of that town if we had known you only had twenty men left to support us."

The few wrecked stone homes at the crossroads hamlet of Dairomont were taken at 9:50 A.M., along with thirty-three prisoners; but it appears B Company had to take the little place twice. Just as it was drying socks and chipping at rations in the stone hovels, a heavy shower of artillery forced the GOYAs to abandon Dairomont and maneuver out of range into the woods, before positioning itself under darkness for a counterattack. Tims Quinn thought the battalion would finally get an answering burst of artillery from the 505th, but that unit was now several miles south at Abrefontaine.

Punished by cold and shellfire, with their few radios left growing fuzzier in the thick, damp forest, the GOYAs found it very difficult to say on January 4 which path lay where and to what. It would be so until Rochelinval three days later. Even maps betrayed them. Quinn's C Company moved east of Fosse to search for enemy barracks. They could not be found. When B Company joined in, Ralph Wenthold spent hours trying to reach what his map told him were the telltale buildings: It was a fish hatchery.

The 551st's alienation from the 517th continued, though at dusk Graves sent Joerg a platoon of replacements. Such sorry men were filtered in through the next days; many would die or be lost in the snow before anyone learned their names. Twice late that night Joerg made "urgent requests" to Graves for mine-clearing outfits for the road south out of Dairomont toward the river. It appears they were not answered.

More and more men were being pulled out of the line because of trenchfoot, a condition similar to frozen feet except the deadening of blood vessels from lack of oxygen comes over time from immersion in freezing water. More and more fell out as they progressed, the whole battalion in single file to avoid total disassemblage in the early blue dusk. Jim Guerrant asked Harold Christiansen, leaning against a tree, "What's the matter?" The man pointed to the hole in front of his neck. "It's too late," he said, closing his eyes. Tims Quinn watched, appalled, as an artillery shell blew off Corporal Darrel Peterson's leg; the explosion was exacerbated by socks containing volatile Composition C, which Peterson had tucked into his belt, thinking they would help warm his feet. Another C Company man, "Hedy" LaMar, crawled out "from under a bunch of guys and parts of guys" dropped by shrapnel splintering in the trees to find both his legs masses of gore. With casualties like those, death may have begun to seem a blessing.

Bumping into a German medical detachment that night, the medic Tom Kane was asked by the officer in charge what the 551st's worst problem was. Kane said, "We are freezing to death."

"What do you stupid Americans carry in your medical kits?" the officer scoffed in perfect "British" English, and handed Kane two pills, one for him, one for Carl Noble, who was on a stretcher with legs he couldn't feel. The pill (probably benzedrine) warmed Noble's whole body; the German medics massaged the limbs of half a dozen GOYAs before the officer stood up and wondered who was whose prisoner. No one could tell. It was too much of a communion for anyone to be prisoner, so the medics went their separate ways, though two Germans later came back and threw in the towel.

Dave DeVarona, the Red Cross man who had jumped with the GOYAs into southern France, arrived with boxes of wool scarves. The men grabbed at them and squinted past them. No, DeVarona had brought no overshoes or overcoats.

His legs getting "stiffer and stiffer," Tims Quinn later lamented: "I'm not placing blame on anybody, but we didn't know where we were. If ever there was a lost battalion, it was us—single-file, walking along in snow better than knee-deep. Finally we were in a sparsely wooded area and we were all so cold that when somebody got on the ground it would take two men to get him up on his feet again, to keep him from freezing there." Before it was all over, about two hundred GOYAs had been afflicted with severe trenchfoot or frostbite.[78] Dr. Jack Affleck, the GOYA medic, called their frostbite casualties "horrendous." He saw "hands that could not longer hold a weapon from swelling and numbness; feet were like bowling balls, and blackened. It took months to recover from frostbite and trenchfoot, if you didn't lose your limbs. In some ways, frostbite is worse than a 'reasonable' gunshot wound." Many men suffered severe pain in their feet during winter for the rest of their days. A large portion of survivors today live in the Sunbelt.

His wound festering, his legs barely movable, when Tims Quinn heard Germans chattering in the night woods outside Saint-Jacques (to which the battalion aid station had been moved from Fosse), he went up to Lieutenant Colonel Joerg and begged to take a platoon to attack them for their greatcoats. Joerg refused. Quinn begged to build a fire; Joerg waved that one off, too—it would attract enemy fire.

"I'd rather get killed warm than freeze to death!" Quinn cried out. It was useless. Perhaps Joerg himself was drifting; his S-3, Major Pappy Herrmann, had been hit in the shoulder by a mortar fragment that evening and evacuated to Liège. Quinn spent the night of January 4 around Dairomont slapping men's faces to save them.

11
January 5: Russians in Belgium

On the morning of January 5 the men were blinded by a sun they hadn't seen for weeks; it created an oppressive brillance on the snow. Everyone had to look down—a direction that had become familiar in any event— until someone called out, "The fighter planes are here!" They risked blindness to see that sight: the first attack of the American and British air forces since Christmas. Sergeant Jack Carr of C Company watched, amazed, as a column of one hundred panzers on their way to a German fuel dump were hit from both ends by the diving fighter-bombers until the entire column was wrecked.[79] The GOYAs—and just about every other paratrooper in the area—were spared a terrible pasting.

The shellacking didn't last long, because the fog rolled in before noon. It lay so low—Carl Noble thought it was 2 feet off the ground—that men had to lie flat to see any enemy boots. Near Noble, one man remarked sardonically, "Well, if you see German boots and keep firing, you could cut off the feet, then the legs, then the body. Then you could tell if it really was a German or not."

Sometime during the period of January 5–6, much of which fuses in fog, the supply sergeant, Vic Freitag, reached the 517th command post and told the regiment's supply S-4, Captain Bill Hickman, that the 551st "had a drastic need for radios." Hickman hesitated. Hickman had once been a GOYA himself; he was, in fact, the commander of the 501st's C Company when he had to turn over command reluctantly to Wood Joerg in Panama, and was soon afterward drummed out of the unit entirely. Freitag had switched units in the opposite direction from him—517th to 551st—and had narrowly escaped conviction for "illegal supply activities" at Camp Mackall. Nevertheless, Hickman stifled his grudge and misgivings and turned Freitag loose in the 517th supply room. "He was like a kid in a candy store." Whether any of those radios got where they were supposed to, or whether, getting there, they made any difference at that late date, is unlikely. What is known is that Hickman was chastised by the 517th command for being too generous with its supply.[80]

By the afternoon of January 5 the GOYAs had progressed over two and a half days about 2 agonizing miles. B Company had retaken Dairomont at 8:30 A.M. and had moved through some soldiers of the 504th who were traversing southward, until the GOYA company managed to wade across the Salm River, running into hard German resistance, before hustling back. By the end of January 5 the 551st's original strength had been cut in half; it was down to about 325 men, including replacements.

The Germans facing the GOYAs sustained by then at least 160 killed and several hundred wounded; 75 Germans had been captured. Most of the casualties were from Oberstleutnant Herbert Franke's 190th Volksgrenadier Regiment. One of its battalions (II) was reported by a POW to be down to sixty riflemen on January 5, but it still possessed twelve heavy machine guns, a sizable repellent force some of which would come to bear against the 551st in the Germans' last stand at Rochelinval.

Kittel was extremely worried. In addition to the punishment taken and given by the diminished 190th, the 183d Regiment had had only six hundred men when the counteroffensive started (it had suffered badly during the first two days of the Bulge campaign toward Saint-Vith). On January 5 it had been completely expelled from the Bergeval area. But the worst-hit regiment of the 62d Volksgrenadiers appears to have been Arthur Juttner's 164th. As Kittel noted: "In the first three days of the defense all reserve troops had to be committed in the sector of the 164th Regiment," against which the 508th, the 505th, and later the 504th had moved briskly. The next day the only troops held back by the 62d VGD—some engineers and a Panzerjaeger antitank unit, whose guns had been damaged earlier—would also be thrown into the fray to staunch the bleeding of the 164th. The 164th's hemorrhaging had begun with the severe hit it took from the GOYAs' night raid on Noirefontaine. It was now being mauled by three American regiments, whereas one U.S. regiment (517th) faced the 183d, and one lone battalion (551st) and later a regiment (504th) stood against the 190th.

In spite of the dire situation of the volksgrenadiers, the Germans in the 551st's sector, far from giving up, were counterattacking. The GOYAs were stunned twice by counterattacks of the 190th on January 5; two times that day the 551st found itself in hand-to-hand combat, with no time to fix bayonets, as Durkee had done the day before. On a patrol approaching a treeline through a snow-laden meadow just northwest of Quartiers, the men of A Company, which seemed to draw the worst of everything like a magnet, looked up to the startling sight of what they thought were Germans leaping at them out of the woods and alder thickets. They were wearing white camouflage and looked like a stampede of mental patients on the loose. After a feverish hand-to-hand battle, twenty-five of the enemy and several Americans lay dead. Roy McGraw spotted SS among the enemy killed, but there was also a most unexpected force, members of the 669th Russian *Ost* (or "East") battalion, at least one company of which had been assigned to the 62d Volksgrenadiers, which had thrown them into a gap between two shredded battalions of the 190th Regiment.

The GOYAs took eight prisoners, whose babble of strange languages caused them to scratch their heads; among the 669th were Poles and Mongolians, as well as the Russians. One of its four companies had been completely destroyed by the American advance into Belgium in September 1944. The motley had been abruptly sent north from Petit Thiers to defend Quartiers, the last hamlet before Rochelinval on the Salm. They were a forlorn bunch, confused and hardly enthusiastic about their mission. Most confessed they hardly knew what regiment (190th) they had been attached to. Undoubtedly, the SS among them had provided a direct stimulus to fly out of the woods at the GOYAs: the point of a revolver.

Their presence at the Battle of the Bulge is almost completely absent in the standard literature, the *Ost* units were part of at least 800,000 Russians and others of the captured Eastern lands who were to have come under what one historian called "the farcical formation known as the Vlasov Army,[81] led by a Red Army hero of the defense of Moscow captured in 1942, Lieutenant General A. A. Vlasov. But it was never to be, though a few units were organized toward the end in 1945. Most came into the German Army after the early defeats on the Russian front in 1941–42: "Uppermost in the minds of most of them was to survive the war and not to starve. . . . They became auxiliaries or volunteers because fate had so decided, and because each of them had his own particular grudge aginst Stalin."[82]

Though the incidence of desertion of the *Osttruppen* was "more or less on a par with German units,"[83] they were never trusted, and were often treated like slaves. When in the autumn of 1943 Himmler (who called Vlasov a "swine" in a speech to the SS), declaring himself "absolutely indifferent to the condition of the Russians and Czechs,"[84] scapegoated the *Osttruppen* for German losses in the Crimea. Hitler, whose hatred of Slavs was legendary, in a rage ordered all of them sent to work in French coal mines. However, it was soon apparent that disarming the Russian irregulars would be immensely complicated, and Hitler's general staff persuaded him to filter them into the Wehrmacht in the West in fragmented fashion to militate against insurrection. His own motive strictly anti-Bolshevik and with nothing against the Americans or British, Vlasov was astounded ("What am I? What am I? What have you made of me?").[85] But he was completely trapped; his order signature was forged by General Jodl, and the *Ost* units were dispatched west. Vlasov remained in a tidy prison, while the *Ost* men appeared in the unlikeliest of places—three battalions (439th, 441st, and 642d) fought "with absolute bravery" at Normandy.[86] But results were mixed: A Georgian Guard collapsed during the liberation of Paris in August 1944; White Ruthenians fought savagely at Belfort; one-third of the North Caucausus Battalion deserted at Brest. By September 12, the *Ost* "volunteers" were all to be sent to fortifications work. Yet somehow, the *Ost* 669th met up at the Bulge with the lost American GOYAs, both units in different ways, and for very different reasons, what Vlasov himself called bitterly "cannon fodder."

A more traditional German lungeback against the 551st's C Company was preceded by an unearthly 150mm rocket attack, probably launched from six-barrel weapons east of the Salm River. Don Garrigues described it: "The well-placed German artillery fire was slowly chewing our battalion to pieces. The German *Nebelwerfer* could discharge six high explosive shells in a minute and a half and the rockets shredded the air with an eerie sound that made the hair on the back of your neck stand straight up. Wherever you were, each round sounded like it was headed straight for you."

Hobbled, using an improvised crutch, Jim Aikman had caught up with his light machine gun platoon attached to C Company when the Screaming Meemies rained in. "It seemed as if the whole German Army had discovered where we were," said Aikman, who was told to hold the ammunition belts. "Guys were screaming . . . there was a lot of confusion—we just lay there in our foxholes hoping the next one would go by." The Germans attacked on foot; a melée of thrusts and tackles and shootings ensued: The Germans "were in close and things got pretty wild. One of them got me on the chin with his rifle butt and knocked me out. I don't know why he didn't finish me off; maybe somebody shot him. We were fighting very hard then. It was kill or be killed."

Dazed by evening, C Company tried to regroup. "It was one of those times when it seems that nothing you do is right," Aikman said. "We tried to hold what we had taken and we managed in one way, but lost in another because so many of the guys died or were wounded or frozen."

Utterly exhausted after this encounter, Garrigues leaned his rifle against a tree, his thoughts "shifted into neutral," and he blacked out face-first on the snow. "I felt foolish as I got back on my feet and looked around to see if anyone had noticed," Garrigues recounted. But no one had. They too were standing in the snow with their eyes closed. Several froze to death that day, after collapsing. At least twenty-five GOYAs would freeze to death during the counteroffensive, not counting several dozen wounded who froze up before a litter bearer could get to them, or on the litter itself. The medics, however, were an extraordinary bunch; their sad loads were often carried well over a mile through thigh-deep snow before reaching an aid station.

Mounting single-file up the road toward Quartiers, Garrigues was startled by the vision of a King Tiger tank: "I started to move into the trees at the side of the road to set up the gun, but something made me take another look. The tank was still coming down the road, but something was missing—there was no sound. It was gliding past the men ahead of me and they didn't seem to notice it at all. Then, as I watched it, it gradually dissolved into the gray atmosphere. I blinked my eyes and shuddered." It may have been that the Tiger had cut its engines to preserve gas and was sliding down the ice-packed road. But Garrigues figured it was hallucination. Deprived almost completely of food, sleep, and warmth, nerves shot from the sheer physical terror of face-to-face battle with an enemy that couldn't be seen in the forest until the last minute, or against artillery for which they had no answer, the GOYAs by January 5 were in a collective state of shock.

After bolstering a dawn attack with mortar fire that lasted four hours, during which Germans wearing GI uniforms and carrying M-1 rifles were executed, Chuck Fairlamb took to eating snow to quench an unbearable thirst, the kind that makes winter not unlike desert conditions. He was too needy to melt it, thrusting it into his mouth like someone half crazed until "I thought I might turn into a snowball." At the command post at Dairomont, he was told to lift a case of newly arrived K-rations into a truck filled with the dead, but he couldn't do it. Fairlamb had been carrying the mortar loads of two men since the beginning. He was delighted, however, to find himself the heir to a rare pair of overshoes, a frozen overcoat, and a bedroll. By now his feet were so swollen, however, he could barely get the overshoes on.

At 6 P.M., slogging into an abandoned farmhouse, where he and two others got a pot of coffee going, Fairlamb was startled by a lieutenant from XVIII Airborne Corps (previously with the 551st) who stormed into the farmhouse and threatened everyone with a desertion charge if they didn't leave in fifteen minutes. The officer gave no hint of recognition of his former GOYA mates but rousted them out into the cold, saying Corps was taking it as headquarters, while two other officers from another unit moved inside.[87] Stung, Fairlamb and the mortar crew hobbled into the night, unable to find the aid station at the Gaspar farm for their throbbing feet, and ended up toppling into a hayloft.

What this rather cruel encounter portended for the final demise of the 551st is not hard to read. It bracketed another day of agony that had begun with an extraordinary tongue-lashing by Rupert Graves himself of C Company's Tims Quinn. At first light, Graves stamped up to the hurting company commander and squawked: "Quinn, I always thought you were a good officer. What the hell's going on?"

"Nothing," Quinn retorted.

"Well, why aren't you moving?"

"Because I was told to stay right here."

"Well, I'm telling you now—we've had a lot of casualties with our battalion. I want you to get this thing moving. Get going!"

In five minutes, C Company was up and running, flipping ammunition belts to each other as they ran. They knew how to follow orders, of course, though those weren't their own commander's, but Graves's.

Graves was bypassing, in fact, countermanding, the chain of command, dipping below Lieutenant Colonel Joerg to change Quinn's mission on the spot in order to help one of his integral units. The "battalion" Graves refers to as taking "a lot of casualties" would probably have been his 1st Battalion, headed by Boyle (now injured), and most specifically its C Company, headed by Charles LeChaussee (also wounded late the night of January 4). LeChaussee had taken his company south of Bergeval trying to get to the river under cover of darkness and had been bottled up in a vicious encirclement by volksgrenadiers guarding "the trail leading to the crossing of the Salm," as LeChaussee put it. That can only mean Rochelinval.

Graves was not only understandably worried about his own. He himself had been repeatedly chastised for slowness by General Gavin since the counteroffensive had started. If anything, the GOYAs had moved too quickly; Graves was livid that Boyle had been severely wounded looking for them. Now he had had enough and found a convenient scapegoat.

Graves was not alone in venting frustrations on the GOYAs. There was a gathering hardness going on, a concatenation of slights and threats. It is recorded that the Headquarters Company mortar men bivouacked that day in the stone farmhouse "undoubtedly saved many cases of evacuation for trenchfoot."[88] But apparently that didn't make any impression on the corps officers who expelled the GOYA mortar men, or on Gavin himself, who had run across the GOYAs that day—again the mortar platoon—though his narrative places them in the 517th, and vented his repugnance. Chances are that he knew who the "renegade" 551st was; several GOYAs mention seeing Gavin that day. One (Bill Amann) saw the general speaking to Joerg at his command post. Bobby MeHaffey, the 551st wire officer, recalled that the GOYAs were guarding some German POWs in their foxholes dug in the church graveyard at Saint-Jacques. While one German was leaning against a tree and cursing a guard, Gavin walked by and said, "Is he giving you a hard time, soldier?" "Yes, sir," was the reply. "Well, if he opens it again, blow his damned brains out," Gavin snapped, then marched off with his signature rifle slung over his shoulder.

About fifteen minutes after sundown on January 5, Joe Cicchinelli and Private Larry Poston were tending to several wounded and freezing A Company men, bolstering the efforts of a medic. Both men set to massaging their wards' feet to keep them from freezing, Poston taking off his coat to wrap Salvador Corrillo's feet and legs, when a suspicious telephone line was spotted. Poston was told by some sergeant to find out where it led. Going off by himself, within minutes he noticed about fifteen German helmets 25 yards ahead. Out of ammunition and rifleless, Poston had no time to think before the Germans forced him to surrender. Led back to his fellows, Poston called out to Cicchinelli, "Don't shoot, Joe. They have a gun in my back." Chick, too, was taken prisoner, and the two were marched away, the wounded left where they lay (only after the war would Poston find out they had survived).

The two forlorn GOYAs were the only prisoners the Germans took from the 551st back to their lines. They were marched all night—Poston thought about 30 miles—till they reached a German headquarters in an old stone house. En route, Poston felt something hard knocking against his leg and he suddenly remembered he had been carrying a grenade. He was tempted to pull the pin and toss it, except for the sobering fact that the Germans were no more than 8 feet behind him. At the farmhouse his captors used Italian, which Cicchinelli knew, and ordered, "Empty your pockets." Poston says: "I put that grenade right out there on the table and they didn't jump sky high, they jumped sky low!" Thus began a long, bizarre journey that would take them finally to Stalag 4B east of the Elbe River in Germany, where they would stay for five hard months.

Also that night, after weathering the Screaming Meemie attack and the hand-to-hand with SS and Russians, various snipings and machine gun-nings, Tims Quinn stumbled into the command post at Dairomont, plod-ding past Major Holm to the aid station in a tent. His wound now was so severely infected that he could barely walk. Told to lie on a cot face down by the chief surgeon, Captain Battenfield, Quinn started shivering uncon-trollably, then laughing and crying in bizarre crescendos.

"What the hell's wrong with me?" Quinn wept.

"You're going into shock," said Battenfield, who injected him with morphine.

Quinn went by truck out that night to Liège; he would never see the bat-talion again. In Liège he was put on a gurney as part of a long assembly line of wounded men the surgeons worked their way through. Quinn heard a running commentary over the sewing of the mangled hand of the man next to him: "Now, we are going to be able to save this one. And we will cut this one off—snip, snip, snip. And we will cut this—snip—and we will sew this one. Here, nurse, sew this thing up." Quinn looked over: There wasn't much left of that hand. Then the surgeon flipped him, opened up his wound, couldn't find the shrapnel, sewed him up, and pumped him with penicillin before packing him off for the next hospital stop in Brussels, where he was greeted by German buzz bombs. Soon his feet turned as black as if they had been painted.

With the battalion now a shadow of its former self, Joerg tried desper-ately to keep hold of himself, and it. That day he welcomed seven young glider pilots who had never carried a gun in combat before as replacements: "We are proud to have you on our team." Private Vince Fiorino of the intelligence section witnessed Joerg's welcoming of the well-starched glidermen and thought it showed remarkable character. "No matter what the Colonel did, how large or small the assignment, he always took care to indicate his regard for its importance."

Fiorino was directed to take the glidermen out on a two-hour "orientation" patrol. He pointed to some soldiers on a ridge wearing bucket-shaped helmets with overcoats: "Those are Germans." They walked hidden in the tree line in silence, which finally cracked open with artillery; everyone hit the snow. When they got up, Fiorino and his charges moved up to the shell craters. The German artillery, probably called in to hit Fiorino and the glidermen, had instead wiped out its own patrol down to its radios. The glidermen gaped at blood running in rivulets down the snow.

Late that night Lieutenant Dick Mascuch lifted the tent flap of a truck rimmed with light to find Joerg toiling over maps with Major Holm. Helmetless, his young bald head gleamed in the naked bulb, and for a second Mascuch felt such pity he wanted to grab Joerg. The veins of the Colonel's head were visible. The man's eyes looked out from dark culverts. He'd been out on his feet through most of the push and hadn't slept. Never one to favor Joerg, Mascuch admitted, "The Colonel changed after he went into the Bulge. He had been real gung ho, but when he got where the men were being hurt and killed he seemed to reverse his attitude."

On that map he saw Rochelinval, a little more than 1 mile east. The last place from which the Germans were escaping over the river. He knew the 517th were halted on his left and the 505th were long gone south on his right. Rochelinval was going to be theirs.

He did not want it. His love was in San Antonio, with two little girls, one a new babe. And for a second he watched Rochelinval blur on the map and become San Antonio and he an angel hovering above the San Antonio River, welcoming the Wise Men to view little Susette Joerg. He tried to alight. But his wings. They had frozen.

12
January 6: The fateful call

Before midnight, Oberstleutnant Franke, commander of the 190th Volksgrenadier Regiment, wandered into the woods from his command post, pointed a Luger pistol into his mouth, and killed himself.

Franke's body was found lying in the snow in the first hour of January 6, his identity papers strewn nearby. The body was taken to the newly positioned 551st aid station at Quartiers. In his combat diary, Gavin commented grimly, "He was guilty of advising his troops against taking prisoners so it is just as well that we did not get our hands on him." Besides Hitler's demand at the brink of the Bulge that his troops fight "in a wave of terror"—so gruesomely obeyed by *Kampfgruppe* Peiper—it is not certain just what led Gavin to his conclusion about Franke. An entry at 4 P.M. on January 6 in the 517th S-2 journal provides a clue, however. Two POWs taken from the 190th at that time said that a Captain Kugler, who commanded Franke's 1st Battalion, had murdered forty American POWs just before the Ardennes offensive at Habschmid, Germany, after U.S. artillery had made a direct hit on his command post. (The German prisoners also revealed the supply pressures the regiment was under from the outset; a Lieutenant Kaddler had given them a speech, saying the "food situation in Germany is serious. We don't want any useless eaters.")

If nothing else, Franke's suicide portrays the GOYAs' chief antagonist to that point in the counteroffensive—the 190th—as desperate as the GOYAs were. Rupert Graves, in a magazine memoir in 1948, is even more revealing: "In [Franke's] pocket was found a message to the division commander [General Kittel] stating the hopelessness of his position and asking for further instructions, apparently hoping for orders to withdraw. However, the answer from the division commander was to hold until the end, and this he had done."[89] His adjutant voluntarily surrendered the night of Franke's suicide. No doubt those untoward events played into Kittel's decision to move much of the 190th south from Rochelinval, leaving the 183d to defend the town and its crucial bridge. Those tattered regiments would hold, however, for two more days before the Germans were expelled east of the Salm River.

What is remarkable—though Graves gives no indication of this—was how closely Franke's despair tracks Wood Joerg's. On the night of January 6 the GOYA commander made an extraordinary, vehement appeal to his own Division or Corps command that the cup of the attack on Rochelinval be taken from him. The request was denied, by whom exactly is not entirely clear. Joerg felt the attack would be suicide and said so in no uncertain terms. As for Franke, it appears the Germans for half a century knew nothing of his self-destruction; Arthur Juttner, his fellow regimental commander, told me Franke was wounded and turned himself over to the Americans. General Kittel, however, may have known better but never told. Scrutinizing the general's report in the original German manuscript on the 62d Volksgrenadiers required of him as a POW by the Allies after the war, I caught something startling at the Bundesarchiv in Freiburg. In Kittel's own handwriting, just under the date "6.1.45," was the plaintive notation: "†O.Lt. Franke†" The 190th's commander's name is framed by crosses, a mute, strange memorial to a tortured man. Gavin himself would express less about Joerg, though Ridgway would indirectly speak to the matter forty-five years later.

The morning of that fateful January 6, two young, newly minted lieutenants arrived as replacements for the shattered A Company—Joe Kienly and Charles Dahl. They couldn't have come to a worse place at a worse time. The two new officers had arrived in Marseilles in late December 1944, had entrained to Liège, where they could get no regular transport to the front, and had hitchhiked to their assignment in the back of a truck carrying two corpses. Arriving at 517th headquarters on January 4, they were told that the 551st was badly in need of officers and were directed to Basse Bodeux. They armed themselves from a pile of weapons taken from the dead and wounded at the aid station and set off. After some rest and a change into combat fatigues, they reached the GOYAs in the woods near Quartiers, where Dahl was assigned to Durkee's withered platoon and Kienly to Lieutenant Charles Buckenmeyer. A patrol that afternoon under Durkee captured a heifer and butchered it, and the two green officers shared steaks that night.

The mail and Milo Huempfner also arrived on January 6. The Distinguished Service Cross candidate was fresh from his one-man war at the tip of the Bulge, but Huempfner had no time to talk about it. When he heard one of his friends, Private Don Harris, was trapped in a barn under fire with two others, he volunteered to hitch the only set of chains available to the front tires of a six-by-six truck and plowed off into the snow. Seeing Huempfner for the first time in three weeks appear with the truck, Harris thought he was witnessing an apparition: "How did you get here?" Huempfner smiled, picked him up, and headed back through the woods past a clump of Germans around a tank, who, Huempfner thought, were either "dumbfounded or out of ammunition." They didn't fire a shot.

It was zero Fahrenheit, with a light snow falling. The day was quieter than any so far—the lull before the avalanche. Still, casualties mounted. Some were running high fevers whose source was malaria caught in Panama two years before. But most could no longer walk. Among the many men taken out for frozen feet that last day before the unit's final destruction were Doug Dillard, Dick Goins, Aref Orfalea, and Roland Barhyte, who felt he was walking on "bowling balls." Dillard had advised the new lieutenants, Dahl and Kienly, to get a foxhole going, "because it was going to get hot pretty quick as soon as the Germans found out where we were." Their shovels on the hard ground "sounded like they were jackhammers pounding away on that damn ice." Sergeant McGraw had a look at Dillard inching along on his numb feet and told him it was time to go to the aid station. Goins could neither walk nor get his shoes on over his swollen feet. His evacuation would land him, like so many, in England, where the frostbite victims would don the typical "GI shoes" with toes cut out and blackened feet left to poke out from the sheets. That left C Company with only two officers and thirty-five enlisted men. Between the two of them, A and C Companies, which had started with 269 men, now had fewer than 90.

My father's feet were so ballooned with pain that he could no longer take

Joerg's messages another yard. His diary notes that Company B, from which he had been detailed to Headquarters, was now down to eighty-three men. He was sent to the 82d Evacuation Hospital with trenchfoot. Along with ten other men, he was trucked to Spa and the 97th Evacuation Hospital, then to the 28th General Hospital in Liège, where he heard the explosion of buzz bombs. On January 10 he arrived by hospital train in Paris at the 108th General Hospital, before crossing at Cherbourg on the *Duke of Lancaster* to dock at Southampton. By January 15 he was in the 116th General Hospital in England. It would be some months, and two more hospitals in America, before he was released at Camp Carson, Colorado, his delicate pocket companion, the hollow egg shell, intact and delivered to its decorator, his sister Jeannette.

Each winter, even in California, two of the toes on my father's left foot ached and turned blue—the stamp of the Bulge. Though it had taken so many lives, the winter in Belgium had spared his, and he knew it, for at one of the many hospitals he heard the GOYAs had had their worst battle on the last day. Besides seeing "all my friends killed around me" during the first four days of the counteroffensive, perhaps it was knowledge of the averted end that "clammed" him up, as he used to describe reticence. His luck was unspeakable.

That day Roger Carqueville ran into a German in the woods, ducked too late, and took a butt stroke in his eye socket. Bleary-eyed, he parried a bayonet coming right at his heart; it rammed into his thigh instead. Someone saved his life by shooting his assailant; Carqueville saved the bayonet till he died in 1986. B Company repelled a German counterattack at 9 A.M. Small skirmishes were fought with stragglers of the 190th Regiment and the 669th Russian Ost Battalion throughout the day.

But two fateful high command decisions on January 6—one American, one German—would have a direct, dolorous bearing on the very existence of the 551st Parachute Infantry Battalion, whose life clock was now ticking down its last forty-eight hours in the war.

At 3:12 P.M. the 551st was abruptly detached from its uneasy alliance with the 517th Regiment and placed into the 504th Regiment commanded by Colonel Reuben Tucker. Strangely, Rupert Graves's 517th (minus its 3d Battalion and 460th artillery, which were also given to Tucker) circled behind the 551st at Quartiers, bypassing Rochelinval altogether. The next day—the day the GOYAs were destroyed—the bulk of the 517th was pulled out of combat and went into the 82d Airborne's reserve near Abrefontaine, 8 miles southwest of Rochelinval.

Beleaguered German units had been retreating across the narrow bridge at Petit Halleux, 2 miles south of Rochelinval, into Grand Halleux on the east bank of the Salm; though on January 6 the cannon fodder Russian *Ost* battalion had two captured U.S. howitzers on the east bank, and thirty-five

Russians manned five captured U.S. light machine guns on the west bank, no infantry challenged them at Petit Halleux or Grand Halleux, and they made no real stand. The next day, inspired by a shower of artillery, the impressed Russians pulled back. The 517th's 3d Battalion crossed the bridge unopposed into Grand Halleux on January 10.

The one sizable stand the Germans would now make along the entire length of the Salm River from Trois-Ponts 10 miles south to Salmchâteau was at Rochelinval, through which the bulk of the 62d Volksgrenadiers were retreating east. To seize it was a task that fell to the GOYAs.

Why did the needle bounce off two regiments and point to a shredded battalion? It doesn't take much imagination to posit this scene: Graves, Gavin, and Tucker are bent over a battle map on January 6. Gavin is still upset that Graves has been moving too slowly. Graves protests mildly that his men are doing the best they can, but he feels the pressure and wonders how to displace some of it. Rochelinval is sitting there, the last German bridgehead on the Salm in the 82d Airborne's sector. Gavin says it has to be taken in a day. Graves points out that Joerg's intrepid souls (he would not say "renegades," "rabble," or "ingrates") are standing right in front of Rochelinval, and that they have moved so fast as to be often out of contact. Gavin takes note. He may know that the relationship between the 551st and the 517th is frayed, at best. He has great confidence in Tucker for the terrible assignments. Tucker likes Joerg and sees in him a kindred aggressive soul. Gavin unhooks the GOYAs for the last act from Graves to the 504th to get the perilous job done.

At first Joerg was buoyed by the attachment to the 504th. Tucker was highly respected, an intrepid, tougher-than-tough commander who had seen it all in Sicily, Anzio, and Holland. He had stared Peiper in the face at Cheneux and had not blinked; his men bodily leaped on Peiper's panzers. Gavin had later called him "perhaps the best regimental commander of the war." With Tucker in support, Rochelinval could be a romp. More to the point, the 504th was relatively fresh; it had not been committed by Gavin to the counteroffensive till the second day of the push, and then with only one battalion, which was brought in to help Graves's regiment at Fosse. Entering piece by piece, by January 6 it had taken Mont and Farnières with little trouble and was moving briskly to the Halleux area. Tucker would be raring to go, Joerg thought. But it was not to be. In fact, it appears the unhinging from the 517th to the 504th happened so fast, so late, that no communications line was ever laid from the 504th to the GOYAs' command post.

On January 6 Lieutenant Andy Titko, the 551st communications officer, ran into Tucker, who promptly ordered him to run a line of wire to the regimental headquarters, a reverse of the procedural norm.

Beside himself after four days of nightmarish combat in sub-zero weather, he blurted, "Colonel, I'm down to six men."

"Tell your troubles to Jesus," Tucker replied, before walking away.

Whether because of the quickly descending darkness or Titko's own sense of hopelessness, the hookup didn't occur.

As for Tucker's insensitivity, the man who suffered through Anzio and the agonizing friendly fire against his own descending paratroopers in Sicily was not exactly in a receptive mood. On January 4, the 504th's first day in the fray, one of Tucker's battalion commanders had reported that a man had been killed and two wounded by friendly mortars. The S-2 report is stark: "Believe to be a mix-up with the 551st."

To make matters worse, there is no reference in the 504th's daily record for January 6 of the attachment of the 551st. Beyond the chance encounter of Tucker and Titko, there is little indication of direct communication between the two commanders in the next twenty-four hours. That is confirmed by the 504th's S-2 intelligence officer, Captain Louis Hauptfleisch: "There was no contact between Tucker and Joerg the night before the attack on Rochelinval. None at all. In fact, the first knowledge I have had of Lieutenant Colonel Joerg was when I saw him on a stretcher the next day."[90]

However, a curious note here. The GOYAs' liaison officer, Lieutenant John Belcher, took Joerg by jeep the night of January 6 to the 504th command post in a small stone farmhouse. There Joerg received "frag" (fragmented) attack orders, possibly from a Tucker subordinate. Belcher, who was not present at the meeting but out in the hall or a side room, did not recall seeing Tucker that night. For all practical purposes, the GOYAs were cut loose in the moment of their greatest peril.

Wood Joerg saw it. He was dumbstruck. He now knew the withered 551st was holding the left flank of the entire 82d Airborne sector. Nothing was on his left. On his right was the 504th, and it wasn't long into the night before he realized that Tucker was not going to support him. It didn't take much of a reconnaissance of Rochelinval, either, for the Colonel to realize he was facing a massacre. Joerg would have an hour of daylight and few hours of night to try and understand. Or to do something to prevent it.

As for the Germans' portentous tactical decision that day, with Trois-Ponts lost and Petit Halleux holding only "a weak bridgehead" (General Kittel's phrase), Rochelinval was the only German chance in the area for a safe retreat over the Salm. Thinking his "last stand" on the Salm was threatened by a sizable mass of American paratroopers (instead of the withered vine of the 551st), and fearful that the Americans would jump the river and capture not only him but the command of the 18th Volksgrenadiers nearby, General Kittle made a feverish switch. He pushed south to Petit Halleux the riddled, and now headless, 190th and placed in its stead Major Werner Duve's 183d Regiment, a tougher, more intact unit, to hold the ridge at Rochelinval.

Though none of Kittel's regiments were formidable in size at that point, of the three the 183d was the strongest: about five hundred men. Not only was the ratio of Germans to the GOYAs for the last attack lopsided (almost 2-to-1 defenders over attackers), but Rochelinval sat on top of a ridge above a steep gulley. It was a fine redoubt, especially for the dozen or more machine guns Duve had at his disposal, supported by the division's eighty-five artillery pieces firing from across the Salm.

More important than strength or terrain, the 183d had the hottest fire in the belly of Kittel's forces. In front of Saint-Vith, though he admitted losses division-wide were serious, Kittel pointed out that "the losses sustained by the enemy in the 183d sector were tremendous!"[91] Its regimental commander, Major Duve, was a go-for-broke leader, considered "young, courageous, intelligent, and innovative."[92] Four days before the Allied counteroffensive began, a 183d battalion commander issued the ultimate stiff order to all his troops: "Fight to the last bullet regardless of the situation to the right or that on the left."[93]

The Germans prepared to face a far more formidable force than was there, and one of the reasons they did so was that, as the POWs Poston and Cicchinelli discovered during their interrogation, the Germans had fallen for the ruse devised by Major Ridgely Gaither in 1942, when he numbered and named the battalion. "Where is the rest of your regiment?" a general asked stabbing his finger on a report. Though it was in German, Cicchinelli saw that the Germans knew the 551st had been in Panama in 1942 and had listed it by its official name at birth: "1st Battalion, 551st Parachute Infantry Regiment (Reinf)."

Cicchinelli stifled his amazement; the Germans had tracked the GOYAs all over the world, though they seemed to lose them for a while in southern France.

"So you read German?" the general smirked.

"No, I can't."

"Then why are you looking at the paper?"

Cicchinelli blurted something about his thinking it described a panzer outfit.

"Where are the three battalions of the 551st regiment?" the general screamed.

Cornering him, the lieutenant slapped Cicchinelli, hit him with a rifle butt, threatened to shoot him as a spy because he was without his dogtags, and pointed out the window at a tree where they said they would tie him and throw ice water on him all night until he died. Still, Chick did not divulge that the 551st was far smaller than the Germans thought. Nor did Larry Poston, who was presented in his separate interrogation with a bulletin of the "551st Regiment" posted in Laon. "It was probably found by a French or German spy and picked out of the trash," Poston speculated.

The Germans may have thought the 551st was three times the size that it was, that it was a good-sized regiment and not a decimated battalion, but Wood Joerg knew better.

The telephone call came in late that night. The two surviving 551st witnesses, Bill Hatcher, B Company's radioman, who had happened into the command post, and Bobby MeHaffey, the battalion's wire chief in charge of all telephone communication, both say it came from General Gavin or his Command Post.[94] (Though it was not beyond General Ridgway to take a direct interest in manueuvering the independent 551st, Ridgway's G-3, General Alexander Day Surles, was certain the call was not made from Corps.)[95]

What the two GOYAs witnessed and heard has haunted them for half a century. Joerg and his senior staff were huddled in a trailer-like structure in back of a 3/4-ton truck that night when the call came in on the "talking box," as Joerg liked to call it. It was the final attack order for the 551st to seize Rochelinval.

At first Joerg, sensing disaster, would not speak to the man. "General Gavin wants you to move up," an officer who answered the phone relayed the message.

"You tell him I'm not moving another God-damned step until my men rest and we get something to eat!" Joerg stalked the floor. His voice went hoarse as he cursed; he began to break down.

MeHaffey remembered sadly, "Some may not agree to it. But anybody who says the Colonel never cried is lying. Because he definitely did that one night."

Overcome with emotion, Joerg then grabbed the phone himself. Hatcher overheard the Colonel pleading with someone to have the battalion withdrawn from the action. Nearly all the 551st's men had frostbite, Joerg argued; gunshot casualties had been extremely heavy. Hatcher assumed Joerg was talking not to General Gavin but probably to a colonel, because the language Joerg was using was "forceful, not four-letter words, but words you might use in speaking to an officer of your own rank."

Fifty years after that fateful call, retired Lieutenant General John Norton at first could not remember the 551st, not to mention the call.[96] But after several interviews and a checking of his own personal records, they came into focus. He realized that though Gavin "wouldn't cross regimental commanders like Tucker [504th] or Billingslea [325]," it appears that there were no regimental commanders in the electronic loop that night of January 6, 1945. Lieutenant General Norton compared the GOYAs to the independent 509th Parachute Infantry Battalion: "There's a pattern here with a similar fate to the orphan battalions. I remember terrible stories of both the 509th and 551st being chewed up, but since the 509th wasn't attached to us [but to Maurice Rose's 3d Armored Division], I put the 551st in the same category in my memory."

General Norton described the extremely strained atmosphere at 82d Air-

borne Headquarters at that point at the Bulge: "I was stretched beyond belief. Our G-3 group had only five officers to cover five regiments, or sixteen
battalions. We had only six snowmobiles for the entire division. I had no
more than two or three hours sleep a night. It went on and on." Conceding
that "maybe the 82d was the weak link," General Norton thought that, however unusual, the direct telephone hookup between Gavin and Joerg must
have occurred, given the empty air between the 551st and the 504th. Most
unusual was Joerg's last-minute plea to get the attack postponed, which
Norton said "had never happened before. But whoever he asked it of, it
wasn't in the cards. This was a typical case of wham, bam, thank you
ma'am. You're moving out at dawn."[97]

It was also a case of a separate battalion, one fluid on the organizational
charts, that seemed almost impervious to pain. Though the 551st had captured Draguignan and the first Nazi general in Europe for the Airborne and
had done an outstanding job at Noirefontaine, it also had a reputation for
defiance and rebelliousness that stretched all the way back to its training
days. It was one step shy of a renegade outfit. But maybe that was what was
needed at Rochelinval.

Though no battalion had asked to be relieved before, a regiment had. Before the July 3, 1944, attack on La Haye-du-Puits halfway down the Co-
tentin peninsula, the 508th's Colonel Roy Lindquist complained of a
"shortage of troops" from the vicious fighting since the Normandy invasion.
Lindquist wanted his men relieved; Gavin says he referred Lindquist to
Ridgway, who was commanding the 82d Airborne at the time. Ridgway
later intimated, disapprovingly, that Gavin had supported Lindquist. Ridgway cut the quavering off fast and gave Lindquist his marching orders.

In 1984 Gavin wrote Clay Blair: "Ridgway was of the World War I school
[that] never got over the experience of trench warfare." He quoted his own
training at West Point under General Charles Summerall in 1925, who said
to students soaked by a miserable rain, "Just remember, the infantryman can
always take one more step, fire one more shot." Gavin later told Blair in an
interview, "That isn't so, but [Ridgway] wanted to believe it."[98]

Was Gavin worried the night Joerg made his feverish plea to stop that if
such a request were granted, Ridgway would later catch not only shades of
Wood Joerg in him, but shades of Roy Lindquist? Gavin later thought Ridgway wrote off Lindquist as a combat infantry commander after the sharp exchange. More than Gavin's nerve was at stake the night before Rochelinval.

No doubt he was torn inside about such matters. Though Gavin writes in
On to Berlin that "Troops must be properly equipped . . . to succeed at what
they are going to do. [A general] must be sure that the missions given to
them are realistic in terms of their capabilities," he was fond of telling a
story that unmasked other go-for-broke feelings on missions impossible. He

told it to West Point graduates in 1982; he wrote it to Clay Blair in 1984. It concerns the 504th's imminent attack on Jochen Peiper's 1st SS Panzers at Cheneux and a supposed conversation between Reuben Tucker and one of his battalion commanders, Colonel Harrison. Tucker got Harrison on the radio and asked, "How are you doing?"

"Fine," replied Harrison.

"How many men do you have left?"

"Two in A Company, three in B Company, one in C Company" replied Harrison.

"What do you intend to do?" asked Tucker.

"Continue the attack," replied Harrison.

"That's it; you are right," said Tucker.

Gavin concluded the story to Blair, "That was the spirit of the 82d. They cleaned the Germans out to a man."

The story leaves little doubt why Gavin's own attitude toward Joerg and Rochelinval was *Go!*

Lieutenant Colonel Joerg's impassioned plea to get the 551st either relieved or reinforced, or the attack on Rochelinval postponed, was rejected. The telephone went into its holder with a light click.

"It was rough and cold and the troops were hungry, but I don't think many, if any, went without food for three or four days," said Major William Holm, Joerg's executive officer, who was not in the command truck when the call came from Gavin. "I don't think anyone considered it a suicide mission." However well-intentioned, Holm was wrong. Joerg and key company commanders considered it just that. At 9 P.M. on January 6, Lieutenant Booth informed his A Company officers about the attack order for the next morning on Rochelinval, and A Company—what was left of it— would be at the point. "We can't take that hill," Booth stated sharply. "You can hear the damn Germans digging in—clang, clang, clang. There's heavy machine guns. They're sandbagged. They could hit a fly 100 yards away."

Lieutenant Dick Durkee agreed in no uncertain terms, "I told Booth how I felt and said a few words that can't be printed. I had reconnoitered the area surrounding the town and it was suicide to attack with our small company, and I told him so. There were plenty of Krauts in that town."

Booth said he had told Joerg much the same, but the Colonel had said coldly and slowly "that these were the orders handed down from General Gavin." That was that, Durkee concluded.

VIII

TALL SNOW

Death at Rochelinval

... the soldier knew
Someone had blundered.
Theirs not to make reply,
Theirs but to do or die.

—Alfred, Lord Tennyson, *The Charge of the Light Brigade*

1
"A large spark flashed on his helmet"

It was the end of their road: a field of snow, a bluff of stone, a slate-blue river. About 4 A.M. on January 7, 1945, a Sunday morning, blessed only by each others' vaporous breath, the 551st began moving out from Quartiers in the dark over a forested hillock until they faced Rochelinval below. They did not have six hundred men, as the British had for their immortal cavalry charge, but rather 250 tired footsoldiers. What they did share in 1945 in Belgium with the British in 1854 in the Crimea was an open, targeted field, a tangle in high command that put them there, and a general sense of hopelessness.[1]

Rochelinval was a sleepy little village of a dozen homes on an overlook of the Salm River. It was a rocky place, hence the name (derived from the French *roche*, or rock). The people there were dairy and poultry farmers, supplying the larger towns in the area, such as Trois-Ponts, with milk, eggs, and chickens, and Germany with men for slave labor.

Two country lanes from Bergeval and Dairomont barely wide enough for a horse-drawn cart joined as one before entering Rochelinval. A line of its stone and brick structures ran atop a bluff, from which a thin road precipitously declined east to a bridge over the river, the last bridge on the Salm over which the Wehrmacht and the SS were withdrawing. The Salm River was one of three north-south rivers in the Bulge that the Germans had to cross to get home intact: the Ourthe, the Salm, and the Our. The Salm was dead center in the Bulge. If the Germans could be pushed completely behind it, the Ardennes offensive would be all but finished.

Below the Rochelinval bluff facing west (and the GOYAs) ran a steep gulley. That topography provided the Germans a veritable castle keep against assault, complete with a kind of moat of ice-coated snow. The terrain eerily resembled that in front of Sol Me-Herispehe on the first day of the counteroffensive, but with difficult differences. As on January 3, the 551st would have to cross an open pasture strung with barbed wire with virtually no artillery cover, but instead of moving steadily upward, as at Sol Me, they would be plunging downward into the gulley before having to crawl up to the bluff. Gravity would be on their side, then turn against them. At the top along a rock wall sat several machine guns, including at least two American guns the Germans had seized and were now pointing at their former owners.

From the west, the two Bergeval and Dairomont lanes cupped into one approach to Rochelinval, rounding through scrub on the battalion's right flank. To the road's left and up to the rock wall girding the town, the open meadow descended. The GOYAs could use the cover of trees and bushes for a while on their approach, but ultimately they would have to seize the town by coming out in the open ground. The Germans had all the forest—left, right, and straight ahead, where Wood Joerg placed his command foxhole on the forest lip—targeted with their howitzers and mortars. It would be a deadly shower in the needles. It would force many into the open.

Why Joerg chose to place his observation post at the edge of the forested hilltop looking down across the meadow directly at the German muzzles no one knew. There was only about 300 yards between the commander and those muzzles. The command post in the 3/4-ton truck was back in the woods toward Quartiers. His intelligence officer Ed Hartman felt Joerg was "probably too far to the front." Lieutenant Phil Hand thought it was ambition as well as guts: "He wanted to be a general. He really did. He was go, go, go." Though he had essentially bowed to the mission under protest, Joerg knew the only chance the GOYAs had was in their intestines and their minds. Never one to hang back anyway, he would now be their human guidon. He was going to stare fate right in the eye and hope, somehow, it would spark the men to do the impossible.

Just before dawn, Joerg made one last attempt to get artillery and tank sup-

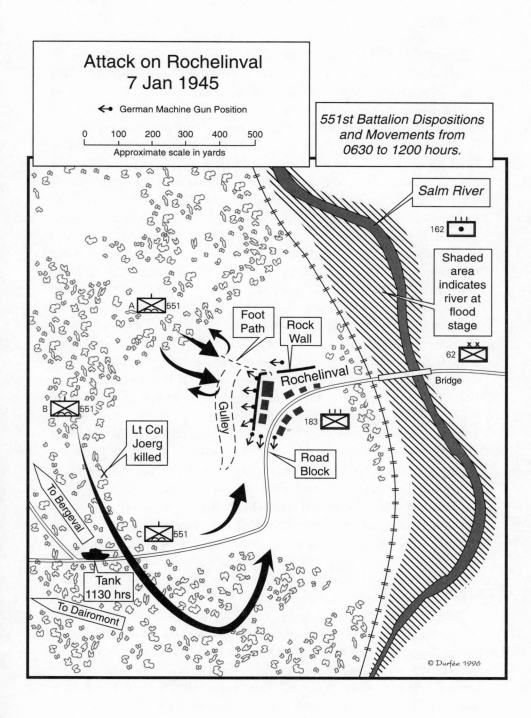

Attack on Rochelinval
7 Jan 1945

← German Machine Gun Position

0   100   200   300   400   500

Approximate scale in yards

551st Battalion Dispositions and Movements from 0630 to 1200 hours.

Salm River

162

Shaded area indicates river at flood stage

A   551

Foot Path

Rock Wall

62

Rochelinval

Bridge

B   551

Gulley

183

Lt Col Joerg killed

Road Block

To Bergeval

C   551

Tank 1130 hrs

To Dairomont

© Durfée 1996

port for the 551st's attack. He yelled at Lieutenant Belcher, grabbing him by the arm: "We're supposed to have three tanks. Where the hell are they? Go find them."[2] He had sent A Company to spearhead the assault from the left in two "mini-platoons," using every last hand, including a clerk and a supply sergeant. B Company would pincer around in the woods on the right; he held C Company—actually the weakest unit now—in his reserve in the hilltop woods. Just before the attack, Sergeant James Davis of C Company went into a nervous frenzy and had to be restrained; he would shortly be seriously wounded.

Something went wrong before any shots were fired on the left for the ill-fated A Company. Buckenmeyer's and Kienly's emaciated platoon was in front of Durkee's and Dahl's, but instead of turning toward a foot path road it went straight forward into the meadow. Thus Durkee was dismayed to find himself at the lead angling into town. "Shit, I knew we were all gonna die," Durkee later admitted, "but at that point I couldn't say it out loud." He sent up a yellow flare at the Line of Departure before the final move down the slope, where there was a little creek to cross. Setting up the light machine gun platoon from HQ Company, Lieutenant Booth told the forward observer with him, Lieutenant Chuck Minietta, to call the artillery unit on his staticky radio and tell it to lay down a concentration of artillery beyond the flare. Minietta relayed the request through Lieutenant William Nolan, who was a forward observer at the side of Wood Joerg.[3]

But what Nolan and Minietta got was an argument that, according to Durkee, "the target was out of their area." The unit on the radio should have been the 376th Field Artillery Battalion, which was supposed to cover the 504th and its attachments, but its recalcitrance may have meant that it was actually Rupert Graves's artillery battalion, the 460th, which on January 7 "fired no missions" from its spot in Corps reserve.[4] The 376th's Minietta conceded that perhaps he hadn't fed in the right coordinates, or that the staticky transmission was misread, if not outright blocked by the woods.[5] Whatever the case, when Joerg got into the radio exchange, he was livid. Considerable discussion ensued, until no more than four rounds were fired, which served only to warn the Germans that they were about to be attacked. Don Garrigues, shivering at his machine gun, was even less complimentary: "It just succeeded in waking the Germans up."

Fred Hilgardner, who that day was priming the mortars, situated behind the front lines in the woods, appears to have identified the goat. Spotting a 90mm long-nosed gun in a field off from the woods, Hilgardner ran up and yelled, "Where the hell is our artillery?" The gunners grumbled that they were it. "Well, do something!" Hilgardner spat out. Then the four rounds were shot off. "Is that it?" Hilgardner was dumbfounded. The gunners said that was all the ordnance they had.

But there was no shortage of American artillery to be had that day. On January 7 the 319th Glider Field Artillery Battalion fired 275 rounds to help the 508th; the 320 Glider FA Battalion fired 341 rounds to cover the 325th; the 456th Parachute FA Battalion shot 1,781 rounds for Gavin's own 505th; the 254th FA Battalion unloaded 740 rounds of 155mm howitzers in general support all over the 82d Airborne sector. As for the 504th—to which the GOYAs were now nominally attached—it received 1,052 rounds from the 376th Parachute FA Battalion, some of it a "very effective" saturation on Grand Halleux, on which no immediate attack was being made and which, in three days, would be entered to virtually no resistance. But the unit in the most dire attack position that day, with the most casualties in the 82d Airborne—the 551st—for three hours got four rounds.[6]

The secretary of the 517th veterans' association, Bill Lewis, indicated that the problem of the artillery-starved 551st was Joerg himself; in effect, he outran the artillery cover that was there for him: "Our artillery battalion was supporting the 551st for the last push at the Bulge. But Joerg wouldn't wait—he always went ahead. That sonofabitch wouldn't wait!" But of course, he was waiting that last day at Rochelinval, waiting unsuccessfully to get the attack postponed, if not actually called off. Lewis hinted at a lingering rivalry: "We didn't really know them [the 551st]. We were separate units fighting to outdo each other." But on January 7 the only separate unit fighting was the 551st.

All around the forest was awakening in silence, except for the chatter of the Germans, so close up on the ridge their breath could almost be touched. When the boxer Joe Chizar left his machine gun half-loaded to get more ammunition, his ammo man returned ahead of him and full-loaded it. Chizar returned to cram it full, but it was already full, and nerves or something or the dawn wind or the Germans' breath lit the thing and eight rounds shot out, aimed at nothing. Before Chizar could look up, the Germans commenced firing from on high. It was 6:30 A.M.; the battle had started.

The light machine gun platoon opened up in the frenzy. Durkee yelled for his men to follow him off the road up a little dirt path lined with linden trees to the extreme left of town. But the trees and the barbed wire fence on the right of the path gave little cover. At the top of the path was a German machine gun firing directly down into the draw; across on the ridge, two other machine guns behind a rock wall were aimed at A Company, one broadside at the end of the path and the other head-on at men coming forward in the meadow.

The mortars and artillery resounded overhead, toward Joerg. Every fifth machine gun bullet was a tracer; German and American tracer fire crisscrossed in a deadly streams of yellow and red light, so that the whole meadow looked like a calliope. Men yelled, screamed, fell. The man feeding Don Garrigues's ammunition belts, John Pascal, was quickly hit in the shoulder; just after Garrigues yelled for a medic he, too, was sliced by bullets in the shoulder and back. His gun fell away from him. He crawled to a ditch and received a shot of morphine from the medic David Munoz.

Everything was going too fast. A Company's out-front scout, Private Robert Mowery, was the first to be hit, in the stomach and straight through the head. Others fell from the intense torrent of bullets as if flicked by an invisible giant. Sergeant Robert Hill, a small, happy-go-lucky red-haired youth who had just finished whispering to Durkee that few were going to make it to the top, ran forward, picked up Mowery's Browning Automatic Rifle, and shot off two magazines before he was riddled fifteen times by machine gun lead, the snow kicking up all around. Hill got up twice before, as Lieutenant Kienly saw, "he finally threw himself on that horrible pile of killed and wounded men" on the footpath, now a bloody lane.

Admired for his clear-headedness and solidity, the man who had been assigned from Headquarters Company to take up the lead of the mangled A Company, Lieutenant Don Booth, had jumped out from cover of a tree on the footpath in an attempt to take out the machine gun firing mercilessly straight down the funnel. Just as he threw his hand up to wave everyone forward, he was cut virtually in half. "One of the best combat leaders" Durkee ever saw in the Army, Booth sank in a river of blood.

Seeing Booth fall, the artillery spotter, Lieutenant Minietta, frantically called for a cover of smoke to screen a withdrawal of A Company. Unfortunately, it came at 9:30 A.M., three hours too late.

Durkee scrambled up the sloping footpath, trying to marry a tree while firing. He took up a dead man's fallen bazooka and managed to fire directly into the most punishing machine gun nest at the top of the draw; it exploded. The Germans cried out and fell. Durkee dropped onto the snow and started to crawl uphill, pulling the pin of a grenade to take out a sniper by a building. But his throw fell short. He shouted at Lieutenant Dahl to keep him covered as he unhooked another grenade. But suddenly Dahl's fire stopped. Durkee looked out on the meadow, and there was Dahl—his first day of combat, only his second with the 551st—kneeling in the snow, dead. He had been shot through the neck. For that single day in battle, he would be buried in North Dakota.[7]

Durkee managed to get to the top of the ridge, just on the rim of Rochelinval, with one bazooka man. He turned around. About 5 feet behind him was his runner, Pat Casanova, but no one was behind him. Durkee yelled at Casanova to bring up the rest of A Company to continue the attack into town. Casanova shouted back, "I can't—They're all dead!"

Horrified, Durkee "figured we had had it. There wasn't any sense in attacking the town with three men." The bazooka man withdrew and started running; he was hit by a quarter of a box of machine gun ammunition. Somehow, Durkee and Casanova crawled out around the bend in the lane over the moat of bodies. Durkee spotted the brave redhead and dragged an expiring Sergeant Hill by his feet. Standing now, Durkee saw a sight worse, if possible, than the first day of the counteroffensive: "They were lying this way and that, some face-up staring at the sky with sightless eyes, others face down in the snow. The Krauts had been using them for target practice or something because they had been hit many times. How I ever came out of that alive, God only knows." A Company was now down to seven men, most of whom were walking wounded; Durkee was the only officer left standing.[8]

Alarmed at A Company's ordeal on the left flank, First Sergeant William Harper of C Company crossed the field alone, shimmered up the steep embankment, and lofted a grenade, taking out one of several machine gun nests and two Germans torturing A Company. For his trouble, Harper was laced by shrapnel, crawling to his lines.

The radioman Renick had stood right next to Lieutenant Booth when Booth was almost split in two by machine gun fire. Around Renick fell John McAtee, Norm Michaud, and John Pieniazek; the medic crawling to Booth had his helmet shot off. Renick could hardly move; he was weighted down by a rifle and rifle belt, two bandoliers of ammunition, a .45 pistol, a 30-pound radio, and an overcoat he had scrounged. General Gavin undoubtedly would have frowned on that overcoat and would have had a grim "I told you so" for the dryest wit in the 551st. Renick waited for the bullets: "The gun traversed right on up, chopping snow and pine needles all over me. If he had traversed another 2 inches he would have got me from head to butt." Somehow, Renick was spared. He called out over his radio back to Joerg: "Mayday! Mayday!" As if the 551st were a ship sinking into a lake of blood, or a bomber with its props shot off, diving into the sea.

It's possible that "Mayday!" was the last word Lieutenant Colonel Wood Joerg ever heard. About 8 A.M. on January 7, alarmed by the hellfire of machine guns on the left, Joerg stood forward out of the protection of his foxhole at the rim of the woods overlooking Rochelinval. Chuck Fairlamb, who had been among those manning the four mortars, firing them until they were white-hot, watched Joerg rise as if in a trance and stare frontward.

"Isn't the smell of mortars sweet, Chuck?"

Fairlamb was startled: "I think he knew he was doomed and we all were doomed. He just sort of stood up to take his fate."

Artillery and mortar fire started flying in on the hill. Joerg's radio operator, Corporal John "Mel" Clark, had just laid his SCR-300 on the snow when a shell severed its long antenna, cutting off Renick's "Mayday!" Clark ran off to find wire to patch it, thinking to scrounge some barbed wire if necessary, and he gave his assistant Frank Galope charge of the dead radio.

Meanwhile, Private Joe Thibault, whose French Canadian origins had made Joerg choose him as his French translator and sometime bodyguard in the war, was now closer to his commander than anyone. Joerg told him: "Go get the self-propelled [gun]!"

"He saved my life by giving me an order," Thibault recalled sadly. "I saw it in his eyes. He knew."

Thibault had barely taken two steps when another hailstorm of artillery crashed into the forest. Shrapnel from a 120mm gun burst in a tree directly over Joerg, piercing his helmet, the crown of his skull, and his brain. Lieutenant Richard Hallock and Lieutenant Leroy Sano were also near Joerg, who had just crouched with plans to commit their C Company to the battle. Hallock was looking directly at Joerg when "a large spark flashed from the top of his helmet and without a word he fell on his right shoulder from his sitting position."[9] The shrapnel sprayed bone of the commander's skull over Hallock and Galope, who himself was felled by shrapnel in the thigh and shoulder.

After a brush with a sniper, who finally surrendered to him, Clark returned with the wire, but it was too late: There lay his commander in the snow, his head gushing blood. "I almost went berserk," said Clark. "It was the only time in the war that I wanted to kill someone."

Bobby MeHaffey was not far from Joerg when he was hit. He rushed over with several men and heard someone call out bizarrely, "Get a helmet and put it under his head!" MeHaffey and others gripped the helmet in a pitiful effort, as if collecting the Colonel's blood could save him, as if his blood were holy. "We were actually in that much shock," MeHaffey said. Joerg's breath was visible in the cold, but he was unconscious. Litter-bearers ran up and carried him to a jeep, which took him to the aid station to the rear.

The mortal blow to the colonel rippled like a shock wave through the battalion. Fred Hilgardner, who was back in the woods with the mortars, heard of it five minutes after it happened. "You couldn't have had Western Union go faster." Men collapsed in the snow, praying. Others cried out. Some sank into a deep, speechless stupor. Lieutenant Phil Hand had come up from the left flank, where he had seen the last of A Company shot to pieces, when he discovered Joerg flat on the jeep. Lieutenant Milt Hill, Headquarters Company's executive officer, tried to comfort Hand: "He was so upset he could hardly speak."

Hand had had an abrasive relationship with Joerg from way back, and it all flashed before him as he regarded his prone commander, incredu-

lous that the blow had come to his head. He remembered the day before
the jump into southern France at Montalto airfield north of Rome, when
Joerg got on a little stump and addressed his officers: "Let me tell you people one thing. We're gonna put medals on your chest that the buzzards
will be picking off, one by one." Hand wrote his girlfriend back home that
night: "Hey, this crazy son of a bitch is trying to kill me. I don't know if I
want to stay in this outfit or not."

Joerg had always ridden Hand for not wearing his helmet, exposing his
red-curled head to fire. "Bubbles, put on that damn tin hat!" Joerg would ex-
claim. Hand would for a minute, then remove it when Joerg passed on. For
Hand, the helmet liner sufficed. In fact, Joerg himself, for all his chastising,
often stuck to the knit liner, too. "What good did the helmet do you, damn
it?" Hand sputtered, hyperventilating, as he watched Joerg expire.

For all their heartbreak, though some wandered, no one ran away. The
few left in B Company and C Company stumbled forward with the terrible
news in their chests. There was too much to do. Where they could, they
tended to those who were down. At 9:30 A.M. for about ten minutes the
men heard the popping sound of smoke shells going off—113 rounds of a
smoke screen for A Company to retreat by.[10] But it was too late.

After Roger Carqueville had helped carry Joerg's stretcher to the jeep,
he returned to the empty observation post where Joerg had stood, only to
be welcomed by another artillery treeburst. Shrapnel cut right through
the thigh of PFC Salvador Valdivia near him, tearing out his muscle,
which hung loose. Carqueville quickly gave him a shot of morphine and
fashioned a tourniquet with compresses, before throwing the man over
his shoulder to carry him back. "He was bleeding like a stuck pig," Carqueville said. Valdivia's savior was then knocked down himself by mortar
fire: "I was on my hands and knees, shaking my head." Already wounded
by a rifle butt-stroke in the eye and a bayonet stab in his thigh the day before, Carqueville hoisted Valdivia again until he reached a medic and laid
him on a litter. The medic asked him if he were hit; Carqueville didn't
think so. "Well, you're all covered with blood," the medic said.

"I looked down and the front of my tanker's jacket was covered with
blood, and I was bleeding from my eyes, ears, and mouth," Carqueville recalled, unable to tell which blood was his and which was Valdivia's. Some
was from the concussive effect of exploding artillery, which could make
blood pour out a soldier's facial orifices "The next thing I knew, I woke up
in England." Like many GOYAs that day and the days before, Carqueville's
courage and triple wounds received no decoration save a badge of sorrow.[11]

Knocked senseless by the blast that killed Joerg, Joe Thibault ran into
Major Bill Holm, who, with Joerg dead, had now taken command of the
551st. Holm led him to another farmhouse in Rochelinval and mournfully

explained that an American mortar shell had hit the place, severely wounding the mother of the family. Holm asked that Thibault try somehow to apologize in French. Joe walked upstairs and saw the woman on a bed, dying. He was utterly mortified, but before he could explain the inexplicable, the husband touched his shoulder and said, "Don't worry. It's no one's fault."

Dazed, Thibault wandered out of the skimpy cover of the forested hill, somehow ending up 3 miles north near Trois-Ponts. As he approached the board-frame home of the LeGrande family, built over an ancient stone base, two girls ran out the front door and whispered to him excitedly that there were two Germans hiding in the shed next to the house.

"*Retournez entre la maison!*" Thibault said, motioning them back into the house. Then he spied a sack of potatoes alongside a wall. Whether from his shell-shocked disorientation or from an intuition that he could blow himself up, along with the girls, Thibault reached down into the sack, pulled out a potato, and threw it instead of a grenade into the shed. Perhaps Thibault instinctively knew the Germans would see the connection of potato with "potato masher," which is what Americans called the long-handled German grenade. Whatever the case, it worked. He heard some commotion inside and pulled out his gun. The two Germans emerged with their hands up. It has to be the only instance in World War II of Germans surrendering under the threat of potato.

The next three weeks remain a blank to his memory, until January 27, when Thibault, now part of the 508th, was hit by artillery fire in a pine forest, together with a friend, Private Bob Murphy. His mind even more torn than his body, Thibault wandered out of the aid station, getting lost for two days until he was picked up.

With the early death of their commander and the rapid destruction of A Company, by 8:30 A.M. one might have expected the tattered battalion, not even the size of a company now, to withdraw. Instead they would fight nearly four more hours that morning to capture Rochelinval.

Where was the high command during all the carnage? After four hours of battle, at 10:15 A.M., Colonel Norton entered into his journal at 82d Airborne headquarters that he had sent a messenger to the 504th Regiment "to get sit. clarified." He sensed something badly amiss, however, and offered a rescue, "If 551 needs help, 3rd Bn 517 can be asked to bring fire down to assist 551." It didn't happen. The 504th was inexplicably blacked out from the 551st all morning, and by the time Norton's message came, it was probably too conditional and too late.[12]

In the meantime, Holm committed what was left of C Company, barely missing a step from the fallen Joerg's intentions, while B Company curved around on a forested ridge on the right. A platoon of C Company had been sent up at dawn to dislodge a German roadblock on the right flank and open the area for B Company. That it did with effective surprise, killing the entire German detachment of twelve riflemen along with a machine gun section, while suffering no casualties. The rest of C Company, now led in Tims Quinn's absence by Lieutenant Leroy Sano, had taken severe casualties in the artillery treebursts that killed Joerg. Still, its three light machine guns didn't move until they had fired 15,000 rounds. Now C Company, down to fewer than twenty-five men, would move out to try and take the town, mixing with B Company on the right.

A terrible accident typified the GOYAs' trauma that day. Attacking with B Company, Sergeant Bill Hatcher discovered that the telephone line he had laid the night before was chopped up. He left his radio with an assistant and went off to repair the line. Coming back, Hatcher found the man dead. In the interim he had taken a German prisoner and, infuriated by the bloodletting that day, smashed his own rifle stock against a tree, discharging it. The rifle went off accidentally and shot the assistant right through his radio and his back.

Pushing forward and punished by mortar fire, B Company seemed to ignite with rage. Suddenly, as they approached Rochelinval, a squad of Germans 35 yards away ran at them; a squad of B Company men rushed forward, too. It was rare double charge of opposing foot soldiers. Emory Albritton saw "Big Stoop" Sergeant Thomas Dixon perforate three Germans in the melée with his BAR before he was felled by a mortar round. Already suffering from pneumonia and frozen feet, Albritton was sliced by shrapnel that almost cost him a leg. Several others hit the snow, wounded in that charge: Lieutenant John Ryan (mortally), Sergeant Frank Fiermonte, Sergeant Joseph Kosowski, Lieutenant Dick Mascuch, and Sergeant Joseph Blaizik were among them.

The Germans, still holding the high ground and cutting the GOYAs into ever smaller and smaller bits, should have carried the day. But they too had been taking severe punishment from Buscher's rapid-firing mortars, the American machine gunners, and the never ending forward push of these ungodly paratroopers. They were on a high-tension wire, too, when something occurred that may have pushed them, at least psychologically, over the edge.

A tank appeared. It was probably a "light" Stuart M5, and it appeared to be lost on the road down from Dairomont before noon. It did not seem too eager to join the battle for at least one good reason: Its cannon—whether from an artillery hit or malfunction nobody knew—was frozen at an oblique angle, pointing out at the woods on the right. In short, it could not aim at Rochelinval. Lieutenant Sano of C Company came running back to it, ordering the driver to cover the GOYAs' final assault on the town. "The driver wasn't too happy," the medic Jack Affleck remembered thinking it the light M5 with its feeble 37mm gun useless; the man told Sano his turret was jammed.[13] But Sano, thinking quickly, saw an advantage in its mere presence and repeated his order before running back to the spearhead.

There is considerable disagreement as to what the tank did and its effect on the final scene. As Affleck recalled it, the tank continued down the road and broke the Germans' resolve: "Then, as we grimly started forward with the disabled tank and forty men, fortune suddenly smiled on the 551st; the Germans' morale collapsed and they came pouring out of the houses and buildings with their hands held high, yelling 'Kamerad!'" To Affleck, the mere sight of the tank—and the possibility that it was only one of many coming to get them—broke the volksgrenadiers' back.

The GOYAs' chief intelligence officer, S-2 Captain Ed Hartman, saw it quite differently: "The tank was way back. The Germans didn't even know a tank was there. And the tanker refused to move forward. It did no firing. If anything, it had a negative effect."

To complicate matters, Lieutenant Colonel George Rubel, commander of the 740th Tank Battalion, an *ad hoc* motley of armor hastily thrown together when the Bulge began, would write in a unit history after the war that he had committed the three tanks of his D Company's first platoon, led by 1st Lieutenant Lloyd Mick, to the 551st for the assault on Rochelinval, and chastises Wood Joerg for recklessly exposing his troops in a futile infantry attack without utilizing the tanks from the outset: "The 551st P.I.B. had suffered severely through the absence of a plan of attack."[14] Naturally, as Rubel scripts it, Rochelinval is taken after Joerg's death when the three tanks are finally committed, spearheading the attack that made Rochelinval fall in half an hour.

The 740th, which had tested in Arizona 2 million-watt candlepower lights to blind the enemy (top secret, rarely used)[15] was a sort of armored version of the orphan 551st. One officer quipped about it, "They're bastard tanks, but we're fighting fools!" The tin can battalion had seen some vicious combat in a short span of time, however. Attached to the 30th Infantry Division, it had helped stop Jochen Peiper's 1st SS Panzer *Kampfgruppe* at its most westerly lunge at Stoumont. Later, a 155mm self-propelled artillery piece Rubel had found reduced Peiper's last hideout in La Gleize, and much of the village, to rubble.

Whatever Rubel's armored battalion's ramshackle prowess, there is no evidence from any 551st enlisted man or officer—including Ed Hartman and the acting commander, Major Holm—that the GOYAs had three tanks at their disposal. Nor is there written or anecdotal evidence to that effect in any other unit's records, including the higher command's. Rubel's oddly accusatory recounting has no corroboration, save his own battalion S-3 report for the day. Why Rubel wrote what he wrote is a mystery. He may have sent the tanks up to the 551st, but only one arrived late in the assault. The others may have slid off ice sheets to stall in the forest. What does appear to have happened to the two "ghost tanks" is that they arrived long after the battle was over at about 3 P.M., out of ammunition. Graves register Corporal Max Bryan was told by acting Commander Mayor Holm to take three boxes of ammo to the latecomers: "There were two little ones that looked like push toys, really 7' x 12' at most, with only two men for each. The shells I carried were small. The two tanks had come down the right side road to the edge of Rochelinval. The Germans were on the other side of the river—they were watching my truck and mortar rounds kept following me. I jumped out of the truck and under one of the tanks. Three or four shells fell in there, and then they quit firing. Then we got the ammunition off to the tanks." But the battle was over at noon, three hours before.

One thing is certain: For a commander who was willing to risk court martial in pleading for the Rochelinval attack to be called off in order to spare his men what he saw as a suicidal mission, to have tanks and not use them to cover the men would be absurd. Rubel's view simply does not square with Joerg's situation at Rochelinval, his actions, or his frame of mind.[16]

The effect of the presence of the one known tank during the battle is probably less than Affleck's interpretation, but perhaps somewhat more than Hartman's, who said "C Company's attack really turned the tide. C Company simply overwhelmed them." Whether it moved or not, the tank not only could not fire its cannon but did not fire its coaxial gun. PFC Urban Post of C Company was of an opinion similar to Affleck's, however: "It may have saved our ass. We were lucky. We came in from the woods and here's this tank. He kept their heads down."

A last testimony splits the difference. Jim Guerrant of C Company swore that the notorious tank was neither ahead of nor behind the men, but rather alongside them. He marveled that Captain Rudy Hlavaty, whom he placed walking right in front of the tank, was not felled in the advance: "He must have been charmed." Guerrant clearly remembers four men to the left of the tank—himself, Private Urban Post, Lieutenant James Needham, and PFC Joseph Arbeiter. Miraculously, they were not hit by fire coming their way as they moved forward, but several men on the right of the tank were, the medic David Munoz and Corporal Gerald McCoy among them. Up ahead Private Victor Piccirilli dropped to the earth; he looked up at Guerrant and croaked, "Guess where?" He had been hit twice on either side of his privates.

Hardly unscathed, B Company took several explosions of shrapnel, one of which blinded PFC Marshall Clay, a Navajo Indian. He was carried back to the aid station by PFC Dick Field, who, removing his boots, found ice between his toes; they would burn for years whenever he was out hunting. By the time they got to town, Bill Hatcher realized he was the only noncommissioned officer left in the company, a buck sergeant suddenly the ranking man by attrition. Old Willie "Spotlight" Brown had been killed in the last moments before cresting the hill. The man who had once challenged Joerg himself on the parade ground in Panama had now joined his commander in death.

Led by Sano, C Company, with B Company men mixed in, did not relent. About noon, what was left of the GOYAs stormed the barricades at Rochelinval. They were partly aided, no doubt, by the sloping off of the gulley on the right, where it was not as steep.

The Germans did not simply fold on seeing GIs breach their line. There were several incidents of close-in, even house-to-house fighting. In one, Arbeiter took out a smirking machine gunner at the ridge with a gun-butt stroke in the face before the German gunner could aim his barrel. Though a German officer surrendered his pistol to the charging Guerrant—*Nicht schutzen!*—turning the corner of a building Guerrant was shot in the chest. "I spun around like a top," Guerrant said, and then laughingly recounted, "I had tried putting cows in front of me—it didn't work. I even tried putting Germans in front as a shield. And that didn't work either."

Nevertheless, the Germans did begin surrendering, first in patches, then in droves. Though "even on this day, artillery and antiaircraft troops from the [62d Volksgrenadier] Division were able to bring the enemy large-scale attack to a standstill,"[17] as General Kittel wrote, they did not do so at Rochelinval. The 183d Regiment was completely shattered that day; what was left of it staggered across the bridge from Rochelinval and was filtered (together with the remnants of the 190th Regiment) into the 18th Volksgrenadiers Division east of the Salm River, a disassembling that would soon be the GOYAs' fate. What had happened that day had bled both sides white. As one historian noted, "Like the Americans, the Germans at Rochelinval had nearly reached the limit of human endurance."[18]

If anything, both sides toppled over the edge. The medic Ed Henriquez saw a GOYA put a pistol in the mouth of a German POW in Rochelinval and hold it there for several tense seconds before removing it.

General Gavin in his war memoir wrote: "On the first day's fighting [of the counteroffensive], the 82nd completely overran the 62nd Volksgrenadier Division and the 9th SS Panzer Division."[19] That is simply untrue. As we have seen, for five hard days, January 3–7, most of the 82d Airborne's units encountered an enemy that fought with the ferocity of a cornered tiger. The Germans knew this was the last stand before the Allies would break into their homeland en masse.

If the 62d Volksgrenadiers were very much alive and resisting for five days of the counteroffensive, by the end of January 7, Kittel intimated, the division was practically destroyed. As Kittel recounted it: "The infantry regiments of the 62 VGD each had at most the strength of a rifle company, and heavy losses had been suffered among our heavy weapons in the previous few days; one could no longer speak of a real and genuine line." By midnight January 7, the 62d Volksgrenadiers had sustained about 33 percent casualties, three times those of the 82d Airborne.

Hitler, finally, took note. After resisting his generals' urging that the offensive be scaled down if not put off entirely for weeks before the invasion, and after three weeks of the Battle of the Bulge during which he repeatedly rebuffed his generals' pleadings to stop and withdraw, the next day—January 8—the Fuhrer personally ordered his first pullback of German forces from the Bulge, from its nose-tip. The fall of Rochelinval on the Salm River to the 551st and the 508th Regiment's capture of the high ground of Thier-du-Mont near Salmchâteau no doubt contributed to that decision.[20]

The rounding up of long columns of prisoners began. Estimates of the number of the prisoners the GOYAs took that day range from two hundred to five hundred Germans; Affleck's three hundred seems the closest to reality. In one photo taken by their guard, Chuck Fairlamb, they appear dwarfed by a stand of large snowy fir trees, lined up like stunted trees themselves, with less life than a stump. In addition to the Volksgrenadiers, some Russians of the 669th *Ost* Battalion came, only too gratefully, into custody. Big, brash Lieutenant Roy McKay, though wounded, one of C Company's last two standing officers, broke down the front door to a house; no one was there. But McKay spied a cutout in the floor used as a trap door and rattled off a burst of tommy gun fire. "We heard a chorus of frightened yells," Affleck said. "I watched as about fifteen white-faced and shaking Krauts climbed up a ladder from the cellar."

One officer—not the 183d Regiment commander, Major Duve, who was wounded that day but managed to escape—read C Company's other officer, Lieutenant Sano, the riot act because Sano was too junior an officer to whom to surrender; Sano snatched his pistol and brushed him aside.[21]

During the mopping up, the battalion's aid station was moved from the woods on the hill into the same house at Rochelinval used by the German wounded. The German medics were cooperative and helpful and shared splints and bandages. The horror of the battle had thrust the healers together, and several GI and German wounded exchanged smokes across gurneys.

Then Jack Affleck was taken by a German medic to a bleak site: four fresh graves in the snow of American soldiers, each with a rough-hewn cross hung with dog tags. Only one of the tags could Affleck recall: that of Lieutenant Joseph Farren of Headquarters Company. He had been shot in the head. (Some have speculated that "Cab" Callaway, who disappeared in the forest just before Rochelinval, may have also been one of the unfortunates.)

Though Affleck questions why the Germans would have led them to the telltale graves of those shot as POWs, not to mention marked them with crosses, there is strong evidence that at least Farren was executed. Roger Carqueville of Headquarters Company, on his way to Joerg's observation post, where he had been ordered to serve as a bodyguard, ran into Farren that morning of January 7. Farren said he was going the opposite direction, a twenty-minute hike to the command post in the truck. Farren never returned.

Rupert Graves himself noted that Farren had somehow joined his own 517th's Lieutenant John Neiler to reconnoiter the Salm bridge crossings when the two ran into a German wielding a rifle: "Farren, who was in front, didn't have much chance, as the German about 15 feet away had him covered, and he therefore threw up his hands; but Neiler, who was armed only with a pistol, started to fire and took off back up the trail." Another German fired at Neiler and knocked his helmet off, but he escaped. Colonel Graves reports that Farren's grave later was found behind German lines. He then ends with an odd, offhand remark: "This should have been a warning to the 551st, but when they started the attack the next day, one company got pretty badly shot up by approaching Petit Halleux along a road with steep banks on both sides."[22]

The sentence contains several inaccuracies. The attack occurred the day Farren was shot, not the day before; there was more than one company that got badly shot up; the steepness was not just at a road but cupped the entire ridge with a gulley, as we have seen; and finally, the attack was not at Petit Halleux but at Rochelinval. It seems Graves's own perhaps unconscious blotting out of the word "Rochelinval" and all it meant began two years after the war, persisting to my interview with him in 1994, when he had no memory of such a town.

But what is most disturbing about the passage, is the implication that, having been given a "warning," the 551st could have either been prepared for the attack or somehow avoided it. Graves's version has the same insidious effect as Lieutenant Colonel Rubel's—that Joerg, rather than the higher command, was irresponsible that day.

Graves describes the German positions at "Petit Halleux" (Rochelinval) as camouflaged "almost perfectly" by snow to the point that "there was no indication whatsoever that a German was within miles." In fact, the GOYAs had reconnoitered Rochelinval the day and night before and knew what they were facing.

For all that, Graves acknowledges that Joerg (misspelled as "Juareg") was "a courageous leader, and had worked tirelessly during the past several days under extremely adverse conditions to make the attack a success."[23] The compliment is jarring, and, in the context, left-handed. It has the same effect, in a way, of Gavin's own concluding nod to the 517th in *On to Berlin*. After lambasting the unit for four pages of text, Gavin says that the 517th "improved as the fighting went on and became one of our best regiments."[24] Those gentlemanly gestures, so abrupt and dissonant, seem nothing so much as an attempt to soften the blow.

As early as 4 A.M. that January 7, the Demolitions and Antitank platoons of Headquarters Company had been sent out to blow the bridge at Rochelinval. They had been repelled twice by troops holding the bridge "in overwhelming strength."[25] After the capture of Rochelinval, however, at 3 P.M. the bridge was successfully dynamited, and the platoon returned to town just after dark.

Now tending to the wounded and dog-tagging the dead began in earnest. It was not without harm. After A Company's demise, Dick Durkee had gathered his wounded in one place back on the hill. Out of stretchers, while they waited for more to come from the 517th, three men were killed by mortar fire as they lay on the snow. "Our tough luck hadn't quit us yet," Durkee noted. One man ran around with his arm cut off, delirious, the tendons hanging through his torn sleeve; Durkee slapped him back to reality: "Control yourself! You're not hurt as bad as others!"

After some were taken to the 517th aid station, his six "walking" survivors sat around a fire and ate what remained of the steaks that had been prepared by men who were now dead.

Not even the shred of A Company would get to sleep that night. Major Holm informed Durkee that the other two companies had also been severely hit, and his six men were needed to guard the entry to Rochelinval (though Lieutenant Hand and others had blown the bridge) in case of a counterattack. Forlorn, Durkee approached his few surviving fellows: "I saw the men leaning against the trees or lying in the snow, asleep, and it broke my heart to have to wake them up and ask them to once again undergo torture both mental and physical, but they all seemed to know just what I wanted. They sleepily nodded their heads when I asked them if they would volunteer to go back with me to the front lines."

Durkee thought it was sheer mental fortitude that made them go: "The spirit may be beaten down, but the mind controls the body." Durkee himself was a stunning example of that. Sergeant Jim Stevens placed the saving grace in the GOYAs' hankering sense of humor. He'd seen LeRoy Scott make light of "two new holes in my butt" after getting shot. No matter how desperate their situation was, somebody could wake them with a joke.

If any one man can be credited with the GOYAs' hopeless victory that day it must be Wood Joerg. Martin Kangas put it simply: "All the guys would

have gone to hell for him—that's why we fought so hard and lost so many."
Bobbie MeHaffey echoed that, with only some exaggeration: "Joerg was an
enlisted man's officer. If he had told any man to jump off a building without
a chute, they'd have done it."

The salubrious effect on the suffering of the many in the midst of the most
trying circumstances of the courageous fall of a leader has no better evocation
than Edgar's speech on the mental and physical torture of King Lear:

> When we our betters see bearing our woes,
> We scarcely think our miseries our foes.
> Who alone suffers suffers most i' th' mind,
> Leaving free things and happy shows behind;
> But then the mind much sufferance doth o'erskip
> When grief hath mates, and bearing fellowship.
> How light and portable my pain seems now,
> When that which makes me bend makes the King bow.[26]

2
The infant

Someone from the 504th finally arrived: its commander, Colonel Reuben
Tucker. He encountered Wood Joerg, still breathing unevenly, though unconscious, on a sawhorse-and-wooden-door pallet outside the regimental
aid station at the Dairomont schoolhouse, placed in the open air for lack of
room because he had been deemed mortally wounded. Tucker, as hard-
nosed a commander as existed in the U.S. Army during the war, began to
break down at the sight of Joerg lying there with a scarlet hole in his head.
His emotional unraveling totally surprised his S-1 aide, Captain Lou Hauptfleisch, who was even more startled when Tucker began to remove Joerg's
West Point ring. (Tucker had graduated two years before Joerg from the
Point, and knew him well.)

"I want to make damn sure this gets back to his home," Tucker said
hoarsely.

Realizing that "his impulsive action was probably not proper" and that
there were other standard procedures for the removal of the personal effects of a slain soldier, Hauptfleisch softly reminded him of them.

Tucker backed down, cursing in every direction, "Those goddamn Krauts!"

Field Marshal Montgomery called a press conference January 7 in Brussels; needless to say, there was nothing about the destruction of a small
battalion at the Salm River that day. Ostensibly held to counter the British
press's snipings at Eisenhower and to promote the notion that teamwork
between the Allies was carrying the day in the Bulge counteroffensive,

Monty committed something of a Freudian slip when he described the battle in the Ardennes as "one of the most interesting and tricky I have ever handled." Predictably, Omar Bradley called his own press conference two days later to set the record straight as to who was handling what. The great wonder is that the sparring egos didn't capsize the Allied ship, as Hitler had predicted when he began the Bulge offensive. Hitler probably came closer to winning that battle than the one on the ground.

As for General Gavin, he was nowhere near the GOYAs on January 7, but rather 10 miles south at Thier-du-Mont, where an oft-printed photograph of him was snapped sitting on a snowdrift half covered in snow himself using a field telephone. It is a classic photo. He was with the 508th Regiment, which had taken some punishment capturing the lookout. Their commander did not protest the attack; he was also alive.

There are no photos—official or unofficial—of the Battle of Rochelinval.[27]

After the medics came the Graves Registration men. The billowing smoke of the battle, like snow clouds going up—which General Kittel himself had noted—had now begun to disperse into the cold sky. Jack Affleck went around mechanically checking clumps of bodies in the snow for any signs of life. There was little: "Stiffened already, their faces had a sallow, waxlike hue and were contorted with open mouths and wide, staring, sightless eyes. This ageless stamp of the wartime dead made them all similar and hard to recognize as the individuals they once had been." On A Company's side, he found Booth and Dahl and a man he had known from jump school with half his face shot away. In his helmet, upturned to the coming moon, were unopened letters he had received the night before.

It is one of the tricks of life, one of its chief graces, that at the center of the worst carnage and cruelty of man, something beautiful may bloom. The true scope of this beauty can take time, a long time, to unfurl. It was so at Rochelinval.

That afternoon, as the battle subsided, the soldier who had been piling bodies like cordwood from his old lumber mill days—Max Bryan of Graves Registration—was working his way up the hill tagging bodies, upending rifles, thrusting them into the snow, and capping them with the dead's helmets, when some residual mortar or artillery fire came over from Wanne on the other side of the Salm River. Bryan, who had seen Joerg killed, and later been shelled resupplying the "ghost" tanks, took dangerous cover in the woods and then looked out on the snowy meadow. A woman was running across it, carrying something in her arms, which she dropped.

"I don't know what caused it, and it was probably the most foolish thing I ever did in my life," said Bryan. "But I just walked out of the woods and picked it up."

It was an infant boy. The mother, Alice Gabriel, had been through an ordeal for a week. On January 1, the Germans had ordered her and her husband and baby out of their home in Bergeval, along with the entire village. Her husband, René Gabriel, placed some baggage on a bicycle and the little child, Léon, in an attached basket, and they fled toward the woods near Rochelinval, where they spent the night with twenty others. The next day, because they were the only family with an infant, they stayed in the Drugoet barn in Rochelinval. Four days passed; the husband, determined to find out what had happened to their farm in Bergeval, went off. He found the place totally burned down—its furniture in cinders, the cows dead, and the food rotted, a victim of the 517th's attack on the town. Though his brother had been killed in the Belgian resistance the first day of the German invasion of Belgium in 1940, American soldiers, suspicious at René's German accent, took him into custody as a spy and sent him for interrogation halfway to Liège at Remouchamps.

On the day the GOYAs attacked Rochelinval, Alice Gabriel's hideout was set afire by mortars. At first the Germans would not let her out: "The Germans let out the cows from the stable, but not the humans. They could eat cows." But finally she sneaked with her child out of the basement, leaving their clothes to be consumed in the flame, and ran out. "The entire day was hell," she later said. She resolved, however, to make it back on foot to Bergeval. When the shells started falling as she crossed the meadow away from Rochelinval, she smothered her fallen baby with her body, cringing in the snow. That is when she spotted Max Bryan.

"I was at the edge of the woods when you motioned to me to stay there and I began to cry," she wrote Bryan in 1989. She said to herself that day, "He is my savior," marveling that he would expose himself in the snow to shellfire.

Bryan picked up her eighteen-month-old baby, who began crying from the knock of his metal gun and ammunition, and motioned her into the truck filled with frozen corpses. Bryan told his German POWs to move off the seat and sit on the corpses in order to give Alice and her child room. He drove them to the aid station in Dairomont, where two Germans doctors with Captain Battenfield "were doing a good job for us as far as I can remember." He fed the woman some hot soup. "The many soldiers who were there hadn't seen a woman in weeks, and their eyes widened," Alice later said. "They were very traumatized." A soldier later told her, "You better not stay here. They will think you are a call girl."

The next morning Bryan, who had had plenty of experience milking as a boy, went out into the pasture with a steel helmet and milked cows for the boy's breakfast. The cows were in shock: "I think I ended up with about a pint of milk out of forty cows."

Alice and her child stayed with Bryan for four days, while mines were cleared from the roads. Each morning Bryan would cook a little food on a small woodstove he found for them, spend all day out in the war, and come back at night to care for his adopted family. "When you returned, you had always lost buddies and your spirits were very low," Alice told him so many years later.

Then Bryan took the two back to their home in Bergeval; seeing it wrecked, they moved on to Mont-de-Fosse, where Alice's brother-in-law lived. Max and his boss, Bee Brown, were provided with cognac to warm their bellies before returning to the truck filled with more stiff bodies.

"We said goodbye, but did not think of exchanging addresses," Alice Gabriel Willem wrote. That was the last Max Bryan saw or spoke of the mother and child for forty-five years. As reticent about his war traumas as my father, Bryan, in stories to his own children, stuck to an expurgated, happy version of his milking cows at the Battle of the Bulge, leaving out the cordwood bodies or what he was milking for.

Alice and her child Léon were escorted that last day to some cousins in Brume, where her husband joined them eight days later, very fatigued. Then "we started again with nothing, never forgetting those difficult times," setting up a small farm in La Gleize, having a daughter, before her husband died of cancer of the leg in 1951. Whether it was his accent or the German leather coat he wore, he had been pistol-whipped by his American inter- rogators, put in a trench, and beaten on the leg, which later contributed to his early death.

Time passed, and Alice married a bachelor named Camille Willem, and they settled in the town of La Vaux.

On January 6, 1990, exactly forty-five years minus a day from the day he was taken up by the American soldier from the snow, Léon Gabriel Willem, now a grammar school teacher who had been told little about the war, after meeting Max in 1989, wrote in an extraordinary letter to Bryan:

In those days my dear father René was arrested by the Americans in the woods of Mont de Fosse, then released after having been beaten. (Much later, a cancer appeared at the spot where he was wounded!) Often the young man Léon wished that secretly to those American soldiers who (I thought) were the cause of my father's death. That's how I became an orphan at the age of nine years. . . . This soldier who wanted to see me, he was an engineer from NASA. What an honor for a grade school teacher! On that day, in my parents' dining room, I was sitting, neither beside a horrible soldier, nor beside a super engineer, but beside a happy father, who offered his arms and his heart to his boy, Léon, whom he had found and saved [near] Christmas Day. I have accepted this gift and this adoption with respect and tender feeling. I didn't understand too well what was happening to me. I wasn't asking much about it. As friendship is something rare, and precious, I don't talk much about it. Thank you, Father Max!

3
The disbandment

And what about Furlough? The fate of the GOYAs' indomitable dachshund mascot appears to have dissolved into one of the many snows of the counteroffensive. Or earlier. Pappy Herrmann remembered a command decision to leave her in Laon with the duffel bags when word of the Bulge hit. It was a protective act, he intimated: "There were just too many uncertainties."[28] After the GOYAs' disbandment, said Herrmann, word came that Furlough had lit out to parts unknown from Laon. But one person caught sight of her during their nightmare in Belgium—Jim Stevens. He thought he glimpsed the dog being carried in a sling by a man from Headquarters Company, along with the rest of his equipment, during the counteroffensive. Some figured that Furlough was wounded or killed alongside Lieutenant Colonel Joerg by the same treeburst that killed the commander, but no one really knows. It appears, like the 551st's own history, that Furlough was lost.

The day after Rochelinval, January 8, the 18th Volksgrenadier Division of Generalmajor Gunter Hoffman-Schönborn, which had stormed into Saint-Vith two weeks before and exacted the surrender of thousands of Americans, made a half-hearted counterattack against the GOYAs at Rochelinval; it was decisively repelled, though some casualties were taken. Dick Durkee's mini-squad remnant of A Company had used frozen bodies like sand bags around their foxholes to shield them from both the cold and the counterattack. About forty German machine guns were captured, along with some prisoners.

Two of the few GOYAs left standing to help turn back the counterattack were B Company's Private John Peltzer and PFC Benny Goodman. Both had severely frostbitten feet and may as well have been standing in hardened cement. Goodman begged Peltzer to go with him to the aid station, but Peltzer refused.

"One more attack, then I go in," he mumbled in his ice foxhole. "Just one more attack."

"But you can't get your boots on," Goodman persisted.

"I'll wear my galoshes."

The next day, January 9, three of the First Army's hardest-hit divisions— the 106th Infantry, the 28th Infantry, and the 82d Airborne—were finally relieved, including the remnant of the 551st. The green 75th Infantry Division took up where the 82d Airborne had been and entered Grand Halleux on the east bank of the Salm against no opposition. But the relief did not come before one last tragic turn of the screw. On a routine patrol three GOYAs were shot by an outpost of their own men; one was killed.

The hundred or so GOYAs not in hospitals across Europe, at aid stations, or buried in the frozen earth were motored on January 11 to Juslenville, a small village not far from Rochelinval, where they were filtered into Belgian family homes to recuperate, usually two GIs to a family. Though the families themselves were strapped for foodstuffs, fuel oil, and wood for cookstoves and heat, they were exceptionally kind to the shattered battalion.

Many a young GI found a second mother among the families of Juslenville. Although the Coronet family could have used the little cabbage they had for food, when the mother saw Chuck Fairlamb's swollen feet, she cooked a large pot of cabbage leaves every day, then placed his feet in the hot broth. At night, buzz bombs zinging overhead sounded "like Model-T Fords." The family would retire to a bomb shelter, but Fairlamb and his buddy stayed in the house. In two weeks, the cabbage water had cured his feet.

When a totaling was made, the casualty count of the 551st Parachute Infantry Battalion was astounding—one-third of the entire 82d Division's casualties for that grim week of the push. Of 643 officers and men who went into the counteroffensive on January 3, 110 (96 men and 14 officers) were left at the end of January 8. All the rest were killed, wounded, or missing; at least 60 were killed in action or died of wounds from the Ardennes counteroffensive, bringing the number of 551st dead to just over a hundred.[29] With losses from Noirefontaine and other earlier combat in Belgium, the 551st casualty rate for the Battle of the Bulge was 84 percent.[30] Only the 509th PIB sustained a worse casualty rate: 92 percent.

However, it seems certain that many, if not most, of the 110 GOYAs left were "walking wounded." Peltzer and Goodman are only two of many examples. The 94 percent casualty rate for the 551st in the *U.S. Airborne 50th Anniversary Book* (1990) takes into consideration those wounded who never reported in. On that basis, the 551st sustained the worst casualty rate of all Allied battalions to fight at the Battle of the Bulge.

In addition to Juslenville, a few GOYAs unwound in the nearby village of Thieux. B Company's PFC John "Bill" Loven and Corporal Vernon Bettencourt were treated like kings by the family of Marcel Dubois. The family had sustained its own hard loss during the Bulge. One of the Dubois grown children, a schoolteacher, had been killed when a buzz bomb hit his schoolhouse. The family showered the two GIs with affection born of grief.

"The 'general order' was to find a home and keep warm," said Mel Clark. He and four others did so at the home of Monsieur and Madame Urbain Rouchet. When they could walk, they hobbled to the town square at

Juslenville, where dances and movies were offered. Dick Durkee remembered seeing there for the first time *The Song of Bernadette,* and its beauteous rendering of the miraculous apparition of the Virgin Mary to a peasant girl in a grotto outside Lourdes, France, in 1848, made young men older than their years bleary-eyed. "It bolstered us," Durkee said.

Some returned the favors as soon as they could. When Fred Hilgardner, who was treated for frozen feet and shrapnel wounds in the arm, was coming back through Thieux after the fall of Berlin in May 1945, he brought his angel family everything he could snatch from his new unit's kitchen, including a 100-pound sack of coffee.

Some would return the favor a half-century later, like Chuck Miller, the man who had expertly put the Tiger tank out of commission that first day of the counteroffensive with a perfect bazooka shot between the track and the ironclad. Miller had been through the worst moments of the GOYAs' Bulge ordeal. He had been with Dick Durkee during the bayonet attack; he had also been one of the few to stagger back from A Company's ill-fated attack up the draw to Rochelinval on the left flank. His feet frozen, shell-shocked, Miller had drifted off the battlefield away from Durkee and the others and wandered for three days in the woods, stricken with amnesia. He somehow made it 10 miles to the southwest of Rochelinval before collapsing in the snow behind a building in Lierneux. There he was spotted by the father of twenty-one-year-old Nelly Sauvage, who had followed suspicious tracks in the snow to the body of an anonymous American soldier. Nelly's father hoisted Miller over his shoulders and took him to their home.

Nelly's family had been through their own ordeal at the Lierneux crossroads, where soldiers and quasi-soldiers of many stripes passed through. They were wary of demands made by strangers. Added to the German occupation were many varieties of Belgian paramilitary bands. "It was almost a civil war here," Nelly related. It was unsettling, because she found it hard to tell who was a worthy Resistance member looking for food and who was a cheap brigand, dressed half in fatigues, half in civvies, asking for butter. She was more frightened of the latter than of the Germans.

Whatever apprehensions they may have had, Nelly's family took in Chuck Miller. He could barely walk, but soon her mother's massages rubbed sparks back into his feet. He remembered the pain of feeling itself: "It felt better out in the snow." But that numbness had been incipient death; Nelly's family had saved his life. He remembered with fondness the way her father would clutch a loaf of bread to his chest at dinner and rip out portions for all, Chuck first. He laughed at the memory of a salad they relished with chicken feet and heads. "The old man liked them," he said. "He would eat the comb and the whole bit." Miller passed on that, politely.

Miller later was taken to Southhampton in England, where he stuck out as the only combat casualty in an air force base hospital. On release he was sent to the 333d Combat Engineers and helped dig wells for clean water at Rheims and St. Lô, ending up the war welding struts for a display of tanks and heavy armaments in Paris, where he shooed the curious away from the hazardous sparks of his arc welding. After meeting Nelly Sauvage for the first time since the war in 1989, Miller and his wife Millie sent her Christmas gifts from Rancho Cucamonga, California, each year in gratitude for her father's hauling him up from his painless death of sleep in the snow of 1945.

Similar to Miller's blank-out, the Bulge counteroffensive is to this day a complete hole in the memory of A Company's William Bustin; he woke up one day in a hospital, went AWOL (a typically noncompliant GOYA) trying to get back to the 551st, only to discover it was no more. He was placed in the 508th, with no weapon and little food. But he drew solace from an unlikely source, Sergeant Monice Ganz, who had insulted him in Sicily. "You guys always heard how fuckups make the best soldiers," Ganz said. "Well, Bustin was a fuckup, and he was the best combat soldier I had." Bustin's reaction: "It was better than a medal."

Losing more than memory was Wallace "Wassie" Bailey of A Company, whose wounds from both southern France and the Bulge took out a kidney and inflicted spinal injuries that left him a parapalegic for life. He kept in high spirits, however, in spite of his handicap, and referred to himself as "a wheelchair jockey." Wassie participated in the Special Olympics and was active in civil and social affairs of his hometown of Paintsville, Kentucky, before dying in 1989.

Some mobile shower units were trucked into Juslenville on January 12, 1945. Chuck Fairlamb remembered with relish his first body cleansing and shave in three weeks. A less satisfying shower occurred for roommates Dick Durkee and Captain Marshall Dalton. Durkee, who had chafed at Dalton's desire to court-martial A Company's first platoon leader, Lieutenant Russell Fuller, for not attacking as he had ordered back in southern France after the Dragoon invasion, regarded Dalton's body as he showered.[31] He saw no evidence of a shrapnel wound.

"How were you wounded?" he asked Dalton.

"I guess the shell must have just knocked me out," Dalton replied, staring down, continuing to soap himself.

"Well, if you file a court-martial against Fuller, I'm going to file one against you."

Neither happened.

Many, spread out in hospitals in France and England, would begin to write home and make friends with their fellow wounded. John Balogach, pulled out for frozen feet the last day at Rochelinval, was sent to Antwerp and the north of England, where his feet "were white white white." Years later, whenever he would take a cold shower, his hands and feet would turn white. In one hospital he saw "guys with pipes coming out of them. They would say, 'Let me back to the battle!' No respect for death!"

Otto Schultz, who had taken an armor-piercing bullet that had penetrated a tree before lodging in him during the A Company pasting at Rochelinval, regaled his fellow bedmates at St. Lô with the story of the day he wore a woman's panties to get warm. During the counteroffensive Schultz had happened upon a house and, while inspecting it, discovered a lovely young woman putting on her underclothes in her bedroom. Otto was hit as if by a vision of heaven. Seeing that she was being admired, the lady barely paused and signaled to Otto, then talked him into putting on two pairs of her underpants after sampling "how warm her hip was." She even bestowed a kiss on his cheek.

"When I was hit at Rochelinval I damn well didn't want anybody to find me wearing girdles, so I pulled the things off right there in the snow before the medic came," Schultz revealed. "They were tough to get off!"

Those who could write or dictate a letter home did so as never before. Those with wounds that could heal wrote with great relief; those who had lost an arm or leg, or two, or whose minds had been twisted by it all, wrote with great agony. And then there were the telegrams.

Heidi Joerg could see from afar the Western Union boy, one like Homer McCauley in William Saroyan's immortal *The Human Comedy*. She had seen him before, and he had always passed her by. She was living at the time on a little hill east of San Antonio, a pleasant, semi-farmland area, with her father and her two little girls, one an infant Wood Joerg had never seen. Twice before the boy had stopped at two neighbors' houses. At one, a son-in-law had crashed in a fiery plane and his ears had been burned off. Another across the road had a pilot son who was injured by shrapnel so that "he wasn't ever quite normal again." She watched the boy messenger and prayed; he wasn't going up any steps or hillocks. He walked straight toward her house, and she closed her eyes. Then the doorbell. The boy had a cloud over his peachblossom face. Wood was dead.

"I went crazy," she later said. "Wood's mother never got over it," Heidi said. "She had a cough, a hacking cough that she developed then, and it never went away until she died at ninety-six."

As for Heidi, weeks stretched to months and even years when she had difficulty staying home at night. Often ringing through her head was one of Wood's favorite songs, "All the Things You Are," which ends: "Some day my happy arms will hold you/And some day I'll know that moment divine/When all the things you are, are mine." "I was just really the most maladjusted individual," she declared. "I'm seventy-six. I would rather be seventy-six years old, living this life, than to live that other again. I was that miserable." She was just twenty-seven at the time.

The day his battalion was destroyed at Rochelinval, my father wrote his first letter from a hospital, probably in Liège, which strangely did not even mention that he was wounded or that he was in a hospital, only that he now had more time to write. On January 9, from Paris, using American Red Cross stationary, he finally told his mother that he was laid up with "frozen feet." "I will be able to write to you quite often now and this ought to keep your worrying to a minimum." Over the next month his letters betrayed a growing anxiety over not getting any mail from home; it had not caught up with him. In England he was treated by a doctor from near his hometown in Cleveland, a Dr. Ford. Soon he secured some yarn to crochet his father a scarf (others were fashioning wallets and watchbands to while away the time). He marveled that a fellow inmate got a pack of cigarettes from a nurse for his birthday. He inquired if his sisters were still going to the local skating rink. The day after Hodges's First and Patton's Third Armies, driving from the north and south, linked up finally at Houffalize (January 16), Aref was elated: "The news sure looks grand and looks as if the war will end soon." His Uncle Kay Orfalea wrote him from New York City on "Gloria Negligees" stationary (that must have been provocative) that he was "very much worried" about him and that his cousin Victor Orfalea was in England now and should be visiting him soon. On February 3 he worried about the family's well-being in the wake of a Republic Steel explosion and fire in Cleveland. Little by little, he was coming back to life in the States, in short, his own life.

What is most unusual (though it would become usual for many survivors of the Bulge) is that none of his hospital letters over several months contains any mention of his combat ordeal. The blotting of the horror would last the rest of his life.

On January 20, after writing his brother Wood a month's load of unanswered letters from his ship on the "Murmansk run," to resupply the Russians, Lieutenant Commander Robert Joerg was worried. "It must be hell over there now," he wrote again. "We gripe about the cold, heaving seas, etc., until we think of you all. Compared with you, we aren't doing nuthin'." Robert feared, too, that boxes he had sent Wood were lost to the black market, "that gang in Cherbourg." He announced Wood would soon receive a winter coat lined with sheepskin. His brother was already two weeks dead.

The blotting of the history and very existence of the 551st was ongoing that January while the few left were recuperating. On January 27, General Gavin gathered the survivors still in Belgium at a theater in Juslenville for what they thought would be honors or at least a thank you. It was a thank you of sorts, but no honors—rather, to their mind, just the opposite. Not only was this to be the last day the GOYAs would ever spend together, but many have told me that, after all the agonizing combat they had been through, it was their hardest of the war.

Gavin wasted no time informing the men that they were being deactivated as a battalion and would soon be disbanded. He said they would be absorbed, most of them, into integral units of the 82d Airborne for the duration of the war.

The Morning Report of Headquarters Company for the day evoked Gavin's muted praise for the unit's "good showing, a record that they could be proud of in the Belgium Campaign." Major Holm said the general was "calm, quiet, concerned and complimentary of the 551st." Lieutenant Phil Hand remembered Gavin saying, "Your loss is my gain. I've never seen more courageous people." On the other hand, some got the distinct impression Gavin was uncomfortable and intimated that life in the 82d Airborne instead of with some ragtag independent outfit would be a step up in class. Bobby MeHaffey said: "I don't recall him being too complimentary. Of course, he was, to a certain extent. But I think he was prouder of the 82d Airborne than he was of the unit attached to it." Harry Renick captured the feeling of the stricken men most succinctly: "I was disintegrated into the 82d Airborne."

Gavin handed out a roster of the 551st to everyone, and the GOYAs buried their faces in their hands, weeping. "The sadness of that day has never left me," Bill Hatcher said.

Ed Henriques, though he thought Gavin was "the gutsiest fellow I ever saw in my life," took the news hard. Unlike most GOYAs, Henriques had been in three of the hottest spots in the war even before the Bulge: Sicily, Salerno, and Anzio. To be taken apart so unceremoniously made something snap in him. He growled in anger and frustration: "I want out. Send me home! Chickenshit outfit!"

Whether part of it for the two years since Panama or two months since Laon, the little separate battalion had inspired in its members fierce loyalty and group identity. The disbandment was like breaking off part of the self and throwing it away. Each felt diminished, disoriented beyond the effects of battle itself. After what the unit had endured at the Bulge, the lack of honors and loss of records only intensified a sense of betrayal and a skepticism of authority taken into peacetime.

Those who survived the experience of the 551st would hold widely divergent points of view as to the ultimate cause of its demise, ranging from elaborate conspiracy theories at the highest level (even unto Eisenhower and De Gaulle, in one man's studied view) to a flat assessment of bad luck and "war is war," as Helmut Hennig of the 9th SS Panzers said to me, flipping his cigarette-stained fingers backward dismissively. But even the chaos of war in which so much happens that is, by its very nature, out of control, has chains of responsibility that require and even showcase judgment in the severest conditions. War is made, after all, of individuals, though indeed in the course of extreme, deleterious battle such as that at the Bulge, selfhood becomes increasingly blurred and scarred, straining judgment and morality to the maximum. If war is a blight upon the human race, a contagion that affects even the most scrupulous of commanders, we still cannot excuse all actions of personal morality. There are gradations of leadership; there are decisions that are more or less better than others; there are strategies that expose one's own troops to the least injurious of positions in order to vanquish the enemy, or at least the less injurious, since war by nature is extended injury. There is, in short, wisdom in battle, as well as recklessness.

It is unthinkable that there was a deliberate plan to destroy the 551st. But neither does "bad luck" adequately explain the ungodly series of SNAFUs to which the GOYAs were subjected. Neglect of the orphan comes closer to it. And the neglect derived from that all-too-fallible vortex known as human judgment. At the bottom of that vortex with the GOYAs was General James Gavin.

My father spoke of General Gavin with complete respect and admiration. He was every paratrooper's embodiment of the very word "airborne," a man who could defy gravity if he had to. In all my travels and interviews with the men of the 551st, not once did I hear a man denigrate James Gavin. Even the most critical assessments of the battalion's ruination tread softly when speaking of him. My father had other affinities with Gentleman Jim. As a garment manufacturer in peacetime, he was always one to dress to the nines. He loved to hum the old Gillette shaving commercial "To look sharp . . . feel sharp . . . be sharp," a motto that would have fitted the meticulous dress code of General Gavin himself. My father may have taken solace in the fact that, when he began to question the wisdom of the Vietnam War— as he did around the time of the 1970 invasion of Cambodia and the Kent State shootings—General Gavin had been the first senior military man to take issue with our involvement, as early as 1966. He followed his leader, even in protest.

I have found myself, too, admiring a great deal about General Gavin and have kicked myself and fate more than once that I missed by minutes meeting and interviewing him in his Baltimore rest home in 1990. He would die a week later to a raft of praiseful obituaries. He was a man not only of great style and energy, but of substance and learning. His unpublished memoir, "Beyond the Stars," takes its title from Frederich Schiller's poem set to music in Beethoven's Ninth Symphony, "Ode to Joy."

After the battle for Sicily, Gavin wrote his daughter Barbara with a sensitivity uncommon for a military man of his rank: "When this war ends, I think I would like to be a curate in an out-of-the-way pastorate with nothing to do but care for the flowers and meditate on the wickedness of the world. I have had more than enough excitement and danger to do for a lifetime."

One dreary winter day in 1994 at the U.S. Military History Institute in Carlisle, Pennsylvania, I came upon something like a key, though no skeleton key, to the mystery of the 551st's end in a small leather-bound, loose-leaf war diary kept by General Gavin, just released to public viewing. I was the first researcher to peruse it there. In it were only two entries on the heat of combat at the Battle of the Bulge, one before Rochelinval (December 31, 1944) and one after (January 14, 1945). This showed how much constant movement and exhaustion there was during those difficult days, even for division commanders.

My eyes were riveted on a phrase: "my 551." I read with utter surprise and excitement a three-sentence entry on January 14. It was terse and factual (though not completely accurate), and all the more heartbreaking for it: "One Bn my 551 did not wear its overshoes in an attack and sustained about 230 trench foots [sic] cases in three days. Gun shot wounds and shrapnel are about 190. That Bn is comparatively ineffective now."

Gavin mentions only three other units in his long Bulge entries: One is less than complimentary (517th), one is just there (325th) when his aide Olsen is hit; and one is cited for capturing Thier-du-Mont (the 508th), "thus denying the krauts observation." Each of the three units is accorded one sentence, but "my 551" has three. Given his postwar silence, I thought the find extraordinary. Of course, the GOYAs had attacked for six days, not three, and their high number of frostbite and trenchfoot casualties, Gavin had to know, originated in his orders. But the devotion in private to what he could not address in public is remarkable for what it lacks, as well: no mention of the sixty men killed, especially Wood Joerg, who was the only 82d Airborne battalion commander killed at the Battle of the Bulge,[32] and certainly no mention of Joerg's objections at Rochelinval.

Yet he held them to him, he possessed them, the orphan battalion, like no other of his natural sons. "My 551." How piteous that expression is in the circumstances.

Certainly the 504th's tough Reuben Tucker as the immediate superior to Joerg bears some responsibility for the lack of reinforcements, artillery, or armor for the 551st at Rochelinval. Zero electronic communication between Joerg and Tucker before such an important attack seems bizarre, unless we give Tucker the benefit of the doubt: The attachment was precipitious, it was soon dark, time was short, the radios were konked out, commo men got lost, German artillery chewed up the telephone lines, and so on. But the fact remains that Joerg found something wrong enough in the situation to take his protest above Tucker directly to General Gavin during the call from the 82d Division headquarters that night before Rochelinval. One could fault the intermediary (if there was one) for not taking Joerg, who was hardly a shrinking violet, seriously or reconfiguring the attack. But the buck has to stop somewhere. Based on two NCO witnesses to the crucial conversation the night of January 6, 1945 (MeHaffey and Hatcher), and the statements of two attack officers (Durkee and Booth)—intermediary or no intermediary, Joerg's protest was rejected.

Haunted by Ridgway and perhaps by Rupert Graves, with an exhausted, overextended staff and overbloodied soldiers covering a battlefield of "unbelievable" (Lieutenant General Norton's term) confusion, the worst Norton saw in three wars, the weight of the 551st's end, nevertheless, falls inexorably on General Gavin. Perhaps he sensed, correctly, that a unit of such exceptional perseverance would not disappoint him. It did not. But the real disappointment, which he tucked far inside himself all his life, was the cost of it. And the decisions he could have made to reduce that cost.

That is a hard conclusion to reach for one of the great military leaders in U.S. history. It is mitigated somewhat by the enormous weight all commanders had on their shoulders during World War II, particularly in the worst battle of that war, the one at the Bulge. A May 31, 1945, diary entry by Gavin speaks to this: "No one but one who has been through it can appreciate the mental strain and anxiety of a combat commander faced with independent decisions. There are two things that are outstanding in war for an officer—fear and anxiety. Of the two fear is the least bothersome and the easiest to overcome."

The day after Gavin's announcement of the 551st disbandment, on January 28, the Allies pushed the Germans behind the Siegfried Line and the German border, reaching the ground on which they had stood when the Ardennes offensive had begun six weeks before. The Battle of the Bulge was over. Outside of the Soviet Union, it had been the bloodiest single battle of the war. The Allies, mostly Americans, had 80,987 dead, wounded, and missing in action; the Germans had approximately 100,000 casualties. The Germans' loss of war matériel was equally devastating: One-quarter of their entire panzer forces was gone, and 10 percent of their remaining aircraft, including one-quarter of their pilots. The elite 1st SS Panzer Division limped home with only six tanks left. Though the Allies lost 733 tanks and tank destroyers and 647 planes, the seemingly inexhaustible war factory steadily replenished them.[33]

Though Germany could be said to have forestalled the Allied thrust into the homeland by six weeks, little more was accomplished. By mid-January, with all the distraction in Belgium, the Soviets had broken down the door in the east and were racing across Poland into East Prussia. As General Jodl sardonically quipped, the Allies in the Ardennes were "executing the artillery preparation for the Russians." What was most broken, however, was the German soldier's fighting mettle. As a man in the 18th Volksgrenadiers wrote in his diary January 16: "Now everything looks hopeless."

On January 18 Sir Winston Churchill rose in the House of Commons and declared, "This is undoubtedly the great American battle of the war and will, I believe, be regarded as an ever famous American victory."

As for the GOYAs, it was not as if they were under any illusions about their diminished state. "There wasn't enough left," Bobbie MeHaffey admitted. "It had to go, you know. It had to go. But by the same token, if it had to go, it didn't have to go unremembered." MeHaffey knew that its brother unit had also been disbanded with heavy casualties, the 509th, but not before it had received two Distinguished (now Presidential) Unit Citations. In fact, some years later, the 509th was reactivated.

Part of the reason was that the 509th's commander, Lieutenant Colonel (later Lieutenant General) William Yarborough, unlike Wood Joerg, was still alive to throw a fit. One of the fathers of the U.S. airborne, the man who designed the jump wings every paratrooper gets after jump school to this day, Yarborough was taking a nine-week course at Fort Leavenworth in the winter of 1944–45, after which he ran into General Gavin in Washington, D.C.

"Gavin told me that the 509th had been decimated and disbanded," said Yarborough. "This made me so angry, I can't tell you. Nobody had told me this had happened and ostensibly I was still in command. The thought that the outfit had been pulled apart and its guidons sent back to the Quartermaster Depot, and its personnel dispersed, was to me a crime of the first order.

"So I went in to the War Department and tried to find out who had done this. I was very, very hostile. Instead of being thrown out, as I might have been, they sympathized with me and said that this was by order of General Ridgway. It was one of those things that should never have happened."

Yarborough spoke of the "intangibles" that make up an elite unit and called the shredding of such a unit as replacements "deplorable." He went on, "I think that for men to become intensely loyal to an outfit—to be willing to give their lives in order to safeguard the honor of that designated unit, is a rare and truly remarkable thing, and for the Army as a whole to forget this, or to sublimate it to the degree that it is considered less important than bullets and bayonets, is to break faith with the meaning of what it portends to be a soldier.

"When you see these unit associations of veterans, composed of civilians who fought for their country, and they have more respect and more feeling for what their wartime organizations did than the U.S. Army officially does, then you realize that there is something missing."[34]

4
No records, no honors

On February 10, 1945, the 551st Parachute Infantry Battalion was officially disbanded. As Don Garrigues put it, "A piece of paper did something the Germans couldn't do—eliminate our gallant battalion." In a sense, though the GOYAs took up the rifle again in other units, the core of them, the muscle in the center, would be missing in action for the rest of the war.

Wood Joerg was not there to cry out for them. Medal-stingy, it was as if he had bestowed on them the first and final medal: silence.[35]

But Major Bill Holm, just before the disbandment, was determined to do something. He first talked to General Gavin and then approached General Ridgway "to see if we couldn't go to Laon, France, to get our records and belongings together and close out the Battalion in some order." General Ridgway, however, quietly refused. The men were needed at the front, he explained. Ridgway also revealed to Holm that he had had earlier orders "to break up the separate parachute and glider battalions from the War Department, but had held up on the action when the Ardennes offensive started." (This contradicts Yarborough's statement that Ridgway himself disbanded the independent units.)

Then Holm popped the big question: "I told both Generals Ridgway and Gavin that I thought the 551st should be considered for the Distinguished Unit Citation." Ridgway, preoccupied at his desk, looked up in a stony silence. He had been stung by Eisenhower's refusal to decorate the 82d Airborne with the same honor, as he had done—highly unusual in the entire history of the award, which is generally reserved for battalion-size units or smaller—for the entire 101st Airborne Division for weathering the siege of Bastogne. Ridgway had argued that the 82d, though beyond the headlines, had been where the real strategic action was and held against the battering ram on the northern shoulder of Kampfgruppe Peiper and the 1st SS Panzers, and then had been the crucial ramrod forward in the north for the counteroffensive. Eisenhower had turned him down.[36]

Ridgway told Holm to "get the facts together and submit it, which I did." The recommendation died on somebody's desk. No action was ever taken, pro, con, or indifferent, until the issue was resurrected fifty years later.

General Ridgway was a man of great personal courage (he would be seen up at the front with a signature grenade attached at his collarbone), aggressiveness, discipline, and learning. He was also filled with Yankee rectitude. His 1956 autobiography, *Soldier*, devotes a scant ten pages (of 362) to the greatest battle of his career, the Battle of the Bulge. And he is reticent in the extreme about it: "The story of those battles is history now, and I won't try to go into the details about them here. There was heavy fighting for six weeks."[37] That is just about the sum and substance of his treatment of the Ardennes crucible, and it is a glaring omission indeed. One cannot avoid concluding that the Bulge and all its bloodshed was not something Matthew Ridgway wished to dwell on, and in that he was not much different from hundreds of thousands of GIs who pushed the experience deep inside in peacetime. Perhaps the fate of the 551st contributed to his own withdrawal.

When it came to the little 551st Parachute Infantry Battalion, one of two bastard independent units in his massive XVIII Airborne Corps, the memory of a great general could glaze over. On February 8, 1990, declining an interview by reason of ill health, General Ridgway wrote me a fine letter in which he said, "I have an abiding admiration for the members of the 551st Parachute Battalion's record of gallantry in the Battle of the Bulge, but as far as I can remember, I had no personal contact with it." That is not accurate. On at least two occasions Ridgway had significant personal contact with the unit—with its acting commander, Major Bill Holm, after the battle at Rochelinval, and with whatever emissary he personally summoned to Corps headquarters from the 551st on Christmas Day, 1944. In addition, a Corps secret memo on December 27, 1944, shows a tie uncommonly close between the separate battalion and its highest ranking superior; the 551st was "not to be committed without consent of Corps Comdr."[38] It is also quite conceivable that Ridgway took a personal interest in the progress of Wood Joerg, for Ridgway himself had served with Joerg's father, "Hard" Robert, on the Mexican border before America's entry into World War I.

Ridgway's ten "Bulge" pages, devoted to his anger at five men (three of them higher commanders, including General Bill Hoge) who were either so uncertain and shook up by the Bulge he relieved or fired them on the spot, may indicate, by inference, an attitude toward the GOYAs. His assessment of an obviously shell-shocked sergeant ("an object of abject cowardice") who had become hysterical after a shell exploded near him is nothing short of cruel. Handing him over to an MP, he ordered the man shot if he should run.

His rationale is stringently stated: "In time of battle, when victory hangs in the balance, it is necessary to put down any sign of weakness, indecision, lack of aggressiveness, or panic, whether the man wears stars on his shoulders or chevrons on his sleeves, for one frightened soldier can infect his whole unit."[39] What such an attitude might have made of Wood Joerg's agony the night of January 6, 1945, is not hard to guess.

It is unlikely that the mystery of the 551st's fate will ever be completely solved. At the same time, though the 551st suffered from some combination of Graves' contempt, Gavin's aggressiveness (and later, embarrassment), and Ridgway's rectitude, it is undeniable that, like others, it suffered most grievously from a fierce, cornered foe and that terrible Belgian winter.

A last note on the matter, and not the easiest to ponder. If, as Heraclitus says, a man's character is his fate, the 551st's fate may have been sealed from the start—that of being a bastard unit, exceedingly individual, bursting with dangerous (and useful) energy, but separate, no fans of arbitrary authority. The 551st were not yes men, and the U.S. Army—indeed, any Army—cannot exist without the principle of unquestioned authority. The story of the GOYAs is a sad testimony to the darker side of that proposition.

Concerning the unit citation, Bill Holm later confessed, "I should have done more at the time, but I don't think it would have done much good." Before the papers for the award would find their pigeonhole, orders were cut for each man the very day of the disbandment to depart to the integral units of the 82d Airborne: the 504th, the 505th, the 508th, and the 325th (in which Holm would command a battalion). A few went to XVIII Airborne Corps and the 17th Airborne Division. The Rhine was still there to be crossed. In the grueling four months before Hitler killed himself in Berlin, the GOYAs would find all their questions dying on their tongues in the daily effort to stay alive.

For some reason the 82d Airborne never got around to including the 551st in the list submitted to the Belgian Government of all units that had fought to regain Belgian soil in the Battle of the Bulge. Thus not only did the Distinguished Unit Citation disappear into thin air, but so did the Belgian Croix de Guerre, given even to supply and mess units that hadn't fought. It was as if they had never even been in Belgium.[40]

The 551st Parachute Infantry Battalion died thrice: once at Rochelinval, once the day Gavin announced its disbandment, and finally on March 29, 1945, when the Adjutant General of the Army, M. E. Stuart, wrote General Ridgway about the GOYA records: "Unit Journals and supporting documents that are required to accompany this Unit History for the period covered are not available. Copies of Unit Staff Journals are not among the Staff files of the First Battalion, 551st Parachute Infantry, at the time this Unit was disbanded. All maps and overlays were burned during the process of inactivation."

No mention is made in the 82d Airborne's official Bulge campaign summary or in the XVIII Airborne Corps's "Operation Report Ardennes," written on March 1, 1945, and declassified in 1981, of either the 551st's would-be historic night raid on Noirefontaine, lauded so enthusiastically by Gavin as the spearhead of the counteroffensive in his sector, or the tragically costly seizure of Rochelinval, the Germans' last sector toehold on the Salm River. Needless to say, about the near-annihilation of the unit at the Bulge both high command groups were mute. The strange blackout continues to the present day. Significant parts of an official 1995 Pentagon study on the worthiness of the 551st for the Presidential Unit Citation remain classified.[41]

Lieutenant Colonel Dan Morgan (ret.), a career intelligence analyst with the CIA for more than two decades after the war, assessed the message traffic:

> Where the regiments are concerned, each objective taken, each successful attack or repulse is documented in the classified radio traffic of those days in such a way that some small glory or recognition would settle where it belonged. People at Division or Corps read that traffic carefully each day and formed their opinions of the battle situation and participating troops accordingly. Looking back from this very distant time I feel compelled to say that it seems likely that there were persons in the staff sections of regimental, division-level, or both, who systematically struck out or downgraded the activities of the 551st Battalion.[42]

Morgan speculates that everything from "incompetence to callousness to deliberate malice" may have been at work.

5
To the end of the line unknown

They marched on, cut off from each other. At birth they were ornery, game souls whom Wood Joerg took pity on and shaped into a separate unit. They had been alone down in Panama; they had been dispersed high up in the Maritime Alps; they had been lost at the Bulge. Now, as if in final punishment for being too individual, what bound them together was pulled out.

In addition to the hundred or so still standing after Rochelinval, about a hundred more who had been away to be patched up returned to ask where their unit was, only to elicit blank stares at the number "551." Harry Renick took a three-day pass to Paris, only to return to an outfit that suddenly was no more. Their treasured acrobat, Jack Russell, had been in a hospital in Paris since the night raid at Noirefontaine. There he had been through a battery of psychiatric inquiries. "Did you ever play with yourself?" they asked him. "No sir," Russell replied. "I meant business." Back at the front in February, he couldn't find the GOYAs and hiked from replacement depot to replacement depot, asking after them. He even wrote General Gavin a letter asking what had happened. An aide to Gavin sent a truck to pick him up and tell him the grim news: He was now part of the 505th.

Emory Albritton also ended up in Gavin's favored regiment, the 505th, after some days spent with the 509th. In February he was a staff sergeant in E Company, helping to take Schmidt and the Roer (Rur) River dams, which had eluded the Allies just before the Bulge hit. One day Albritton chanced upon General Gavin and screwed up his courage to ask about his lost unit.

"Sir, I come from the little 551st Battalion."

"I sure do remember them," Gavin said. "They were my point battalion at the Bulge."

"Sir, what happened to them? Why'd they break us up?"

Gavin looked sternly at Albritton and said, "I'll have it checked out." But nothing happened. He never had a chance to speak with the general again until the next year at Fort Bragg. By now a lieutenant, Albritton had stolen some coal for his barracks during the 1946 coal strike and was caught by MPs. Gavin came by that night, and when Albritton explained the cold in the barracks, Gavin had a whole supply trucked in. Spying Albritton's worn paratrooper boots, Gavin asked him, "How'd you get those holes in your boots?" Of course, it was at the Bulge, but before there was much of an answer Gavin personally ordered a new pair for Emory, who was too grateful to bring up the 551st again.[43]

The GOYAs contributed in their dispersed state to the final nailing of the lid on the Third Reich's coffin that late winter and spring of 1945. Now with Reuben Tucker's 504th Regiment, Fred Hilgardner watched a harsh replay of something he had witnessed in Sicily: tankers stuffing GI infantry bodies into ruts in the road to level the tanks' passage. On the very last day of the Battle of the Bulge, January 28, Mel Clark, having just arrived the night before with the 504th, was shoved into an early attack at 4 A.M. to take the Belgian border town of Heeresbach. Heavy snowdrifts made progress very slow, but in late afternoon Clark and other members of the 504th's 3d Battalion ambushed a column of Germans, killing every last one of them. The bitterness of the waist-deep snow on the road to Heeresbach, not to mention the previous six weeks of privation, snapped something inside the "punch drunk" old vets of the 504th; the raid on Heeresbach was savage. According to a corporal in Headquarters Company: "Some of our boys went wild, shooting everything that moved in the town. The Krauts used up all their ammo shooting at our guys, then came out yelling, 'Kamerad!' Our troopers would reply with 'Kamerad, hell!' and a burst from a tommy gun."[44]

When the smoke was gobbled up by the snow clouds, 138 German corpses lay on the streets of Heeresbach, and two hundred more of the enemy were captured. "Believe it or not," said Mel Clark, who certainly knew what it was like to find his fellows shredded around him, "there were no casualties on our side." It was an extraordinary contrast to what had happened to him with the 551st three weeks before. Clark himself would finally fall in the first week of

February, attacking across the Siegfried Line, when a grenade exploded near his numb feet. By December 1945 he was at Camp Top Hat in Antwerp, where he watched amazed as German POWs washed and pressed his clothes and spit-shined his shoes, though he wasn't too happy with the amount of spit.

Not all the GOYAs who could lift a rifle had been thrust back into the front lines. Just after the disbandment, about twenty-two men (including seven officers) were attached directly to Ridgway's XVIIIth Airborne Corps to set up a rest and relief center for GIs who had been sucked completely dry by battle or who were shell-shocked, but not severely enough to be sent to a mental ward. Among the officers setting up the Macadam Rest Center in Huy, France, were Lieutenants Mascuch, Hand, and Hill. It was appropriate for the unit that had suffered so terribly at Rochelinval to provide the tender shoulder for others.

Not all the the GOYAs ended up with either Ridgway or Gavin. At least eleven were sprinkled about the 17th Airborne Division, which had taken the last shellacking at Bastogne. Vic Freitag ran an enlisted men's club in a casino in Vittel, France, with the 17th; according to Stan Strong, Harry Wood was "picking up empty cans and having a good time." Strong himself, stuck in an administrative job, wrote Bill Hatcher back in the States: "So here we sit and wait and wonder how old and decrepit we will be before the Army gets us home."

Most of the GOYAs, however, were still on the fighting lines in one place or another. Soon, in support of Field Marshal Montgomery's long-planned thrust in the north, the 17th Airborne Division and Britain's 6th Airborne Division were staging for a drop across the Rhine. The 551st's Don Pay and Bob Lefils dropped in that massive across-the-Rhine jump with the 17th.

By spring foot soldiers and Patton's tanks had made a hammerhead thrust into Germany, and the Germans were surrendering everywhere. Among those were the remnants of the 62d and 18th Volksgrenadiers, surrounded at Wuppertal on April 17 near Cologne. After the "very correct" surrender, Major Fritz Blum of the 62d, whose brother had lost an ear in the final fight, called out to the Americans, "Men, I invite you to a breakfast!" At the same time, sending his own forces southeast to Bavaria seeking the chimerical "national redoubt" of escaped Nazis, Eisenhower had given a nod to the Russians to be the liberators of Berlin.

The chief concern of the Germans at that point was not to fall into the hands of avenging Russians. One of those surrendering at Wuppertal was Colonel Arthur Juttner, who had commanded the 62d's 164th Regiment against the GOYAs at the Noirefontaine farmhouse garrison in the Bulge. Juttner had actually been placed in complete command of what was left of the 62d Volksgrenadier Division by that point. He carried into the POW camp not only a broken division but a heavy heart. He had just discovered that on

February 25, 1945, while fleeing the Russians out of Silesia with their two children, his exhausted wife had died of a heart attack at Halle/Salle.

Meanwhile, his trenchfoot somewhat mended, Doug Dillard had made it back to Sissonne, where the 82d Airborne was gathered for a short rest, reorganization, and resupply at its original quarters in northeastern France. There he hooked up with several GOYAs now in the 508th Regiment making a short-lived preparation with the 82d to drop on Berlin in Operation Eclipse; the only thing eclipsed was the mission. Each day planes would come into Sissonne and roar off filled with jerry cans of gasoline for Patton rather than paratroopers. Many practice and exhibition parachute and glider jumps took place in mid-March. On March 14, 1945, one brought an agonized shudder of *déjà vu* to the former members of the 551st.

Marlene Dietrich watched from the stands at Sissonne as the parachutes began billowing. Earlier in the week she had thrilled the men of the 508th by standing on a table in a mess shall and pulling up her skirt to show the length of her stockinged legs. Surprised to be picked to carry the 508th's rippling colors in the prejump parade and decoration, Dillard glanced at her and decided Sonia Henie was prettier (and more subtle).

Then, about 1,000 feet to the rear of the stands and 1,000 feet up, one C-47 plane began to stall out. Dillard had just hurtled himself out the door when he looked up to see the plane buck and falter. The pilot gunned the engine in an attempt to regain momentum, but the plane flew into six paratroopers who were smashed in midair or had their chutes punctured so that they fell to their deaths. Some, pinned in the dive to the ground, were dragged down to their death. General Gavin thought that the plane had lost a propeller, but it may have just lost power in one or both engines. Gavin wrote rather stiffly about the incident that the plane "dropped into the pattern, took six jumpers along in its crash to the ground. Thought it a good idea to jump with the troops in the pm and so did uneventfully. Lost twelve men including four air corps." That meant two more GIs must have been crushed on the ground. Typically, Gavin did not write of this tragedy in any of the postwar books and articles. It stayed confined to his unpublished diary, like his mention of "my 551."

The ex-GOYA Chuck Bernard barely escaped death in the path of that U.S. airplane. When he got to the ground, heard Marlene Dietrich and others cry out in the stands, and saw the mangled bodies thud on the earth, he buried his face in his hands and had a vision of the eight men drowned in North Carolina the year before. Camp Mackall and Rupert Graves all over again. The war in Germany was close to finished, but the mishaps were more lasting than Hitler. They were never quite eclipsed by the victory parades.

Perhaps the luckiest of all GOYAs in the 508th was Lieutenant Dick Durkee, who thought he had no more luck to draw on after Rochelinval. One day that spring, serving as officer of the day for Ike's headquarters in Frankfurt, Durkee set himself the task of retrieving food Germans were stealing from the American mess halls. The stores he confiscated he took to an orphanage in Frankfurt, where the head nun was delighted to have the badly needed food. Standing beside the nun was a lovely ten-year-old German orphan named Sigrid. In a correspondence reminiscent of J. D. Salinger's classic short story, "For Esmé, With Love and Squalor," Durkee wrote the young girl every day that year, and every day for five years back home, until they were married in 1952, when she was seventeen. (To celebrate his good luck in the occupation of Germany, he captured two Capuchin monkeys wandering out of a zoo in Munich, trained them, delighted little Sigrid with them, and later donated them to the Washington Zoo. Unfortunately, they did not breed—"One monkey was a lesbian!" Durkee laughed.)

Though Patton snuck across the Rhine a day before Montgomery (as General Hodges's First Army had done weeks before, on March 7), Monty led a behemoth Allied force that eventually massed 1 million men north of the Ruhr on the night of March 23. The next morning he was supported by a stunning airdrop of the two Allied divisions, which Gavin himself, though somewhat miffed that his All-Americans were not, for once, part of the show, called "an awesome spectacle." Within a week Patton and Montgomery sealed the fate of 350,000 German forces encircled in the Ruhr pocket; over the next month most of those not killed, including twenty-five generals, surrendered. The day of the final surrender of the pocket, April 21, Field Marshall Model walked into the woods and shot himself. The war in the West was all but over.

The 82d wasn't kept out of the action for long. It was assigned to Cologne and surrounding areas. The old GOYA mortarman Fred Hilgardner, now with the 504th of Reuben Tucker, helped seize the town of Hittdorf north of Cologne.[45] After dynamiting a door, Hilgardner discovered a cache of German marks; on an impulse he took two fistfuls of the money and threw them off a bridge into the Rhine. Bombs had transformed Cologne into a sea of rubble and weeds, with pitiful wagon-drawn civilians creeping east. The only thing that still seemed proud, oddly untouched, was the Cologne cathedral.

With the 505th on probing patrols south of Cologne toward Bonn, Ed Henriques, the former GOYA medic who wanted nothing more than to go home after the 551st's disbandment, found himself exchanging aspirin and codeine with German farmers for a ration of eggs and sausage near the small village of Godorf. "All the Germans had suddenly become Catholics," Henriques noted wryly of the troubling phenomenon of German wholesale disavowal of Nazism so soon after the entry of the Allies onto German soil.[46] One blonde farm girl, however, would have none of that mild fraternization with the enemy: "She was a real Nazi, and spit on us everytime we came by."

Henriques told her to quit it, to no avail. Then "a big goose she had bit me in the ass. We came back with a machine gun and shot it and ate it."

Henriquez's fellow medic, Jack Affleck, who also wound up in the 505th, lamented his estrangement from the 551st: "It was like losing your home. When I looked around at my new platoon in the 505th Regiment, there wasn't a soul I had ever seen before. I thought, boy, this is the end of the world." Ironically, one of the few to have nothing but scratches from his sojourn with the lost battalion of the Ardennes, Affleck got his Purple Heart with the 505th, when he was hit by a *panzerfaust* while riding the back of a tank.

Gradually, in the spring of 1945, the Allied mission transformed mile by mile and day by day from one of assault to one of occupation. In Cologne and the Ruhr pocket, in addition to the hundreds of thousands of German prisoners, there were 10,000 Russian prisoners of the Germans whom Gavin had to restrain from their announced desire to pillage the city of Cologne.[47] They would be rationed back to the Russian homeland one by one in exchange for American prisoners the Russians freed east of the Elbe, among them Joe Cicchinelli and Larry Poston.

There was trouble coming for peacetime of another sort—racial—prefigured in Aachen. Arriving there on the day Model killed himself, April 21, after some months in hospitals, Don Garrigues found "hungry people that remained there [who] stared at us with empty eyes as though they didn't believe this was happening to their once great Fatherland." Aachen was almost totally destroyed by Allied shelling and bombardment. Moving through the desolation to a "ripple dipple" replacement depot, Garrigues ran into an old GOYA friend, Martin Kangas.

The two joined two other troopers to reconnoiter the deserted town. As they walked down the road, they heard an army truck bearing at full speed down on them from behind: "Two wild-eyed Negroes in American uniforms were in the vehicle, and it appeared that they were intent on trying to run us down."[48] The soldiers on foot bailed out left and right, barely escaping the nonstop truck. As it passed Kangas yelled out "an angry insult to their intelligence and heritage." The truck suddenly whined to a halt and backed up, and the two black men jumped out. Seeing the four white troopers approaching, however, they got back into the truck and took off down the cobblestone street.

Turning another street corner, the ambulatory men suddenly faced the two black soldiers, one who pointed a .45 pistol and the other a carbine directly at them. The thought flashed across Garrigues's mind that "this would be the height of irony, to go through everything I had so far and then be wiped out under these circumstances." The two men from the truck demanded to know who had shouted the racial slur. Everyone protected Kangas; one man suggested that everybody drop their weapons and settle things "in an American way," meaning a slugfest. Raging shouts ensued. Then Garrigues heard a safety lever click from a another direction. Across the street a paratrooper had emerged and was pointing his M1 rifle at the blacks.

Now Garrigues and his fellows grew bolder, barking questions to the two from the truck as to why they thought they owned the road and the town. The men said this was the bivouac area of a company of black quartermaster troops, and the white soldiers had no right to be there. The argument seesawed back and forth, and finally everyone marched to town "surrounded by a black swarm of soldiers." Garrigues and his fellows somehow made it through the crowd to the commander's office. He was white.

The commander conceded that his truck drivers had overdone it, but he appealed to the new men to back off, implying a full-scale race riot was in the offing and that his boys would get the short end of the stick: "Look, fellows, there's only a couple hundred men in my unit and there are over three thousand troops in your ripple dipple. We don't want any troubles." Feeling they had probably "pressed our luck to the limit," Garrigues and Company backed down and left. Bewildered by it all, he wondered if the racing truck had held "a couple of agitators, like some we had in our ranks," but he later knew he had gotten a glimpse of the tensions of inequalities that would later explode in American society.

What the Allies were fighting for in Europe was obvious; that they were fighting for the rights of minorities not just to vote and go to school but to live at all was not so obvious until that springtime in 1945, when the armies advancing through Germany and Poland encountered, with great horror, the lost souls and bodies of the concentration camps. Men from the disbanded 551st would help liberate two camps: Woebbelin, a small camp about which little has been known told, and Dachau.

Gavin had been hankering for another battle: "I want to get to the Pacific. As this thing approaches a wind-up I realize that I will have a frightful time adapting myself to the years of peace and ways of peace. Fighting and excitement have become my daily sustenance." Nevertheless, he would change his tune on reaching the Elbe at the end of April, where, on reconnaisance along the banks of the river near Hitacker, he heard a low, squalid grunting and came face-to-face with a wild boar eating a German cadaver. "Reached the depths," he wrote on April 29, much disturbed by the sight but more by the sound. "The noise that he made was more bothersome than the act. I could hear it at lunch. I have seen enough of war for a lifetime."

On April 30, having secured the bridgehead at Bleckede, the 82d crossed the Elbe. That same day at 3:30 P.M., having killed his bitch Blondi, heard the Russian shellings blocks from his Chancellery, written a last testament blaming the entire war on the Jews, consigning his art col-

lection to Linz, and handing the keys to the kingdom over to a totally astonished Admiral Karl Donitz (a final slap to the Army and Luftwaffe,
whom he thought had lost the war), Adolf Hitler sat on a couch in his
Berlin bunker and slid a pistol into his mouth. Near him, poisoned to
death, was his wife of twenty-four hours, Eva Braun.

It all flashed before him: President Von Hindenburg's disdain during
the Weimar Republic; his imprisonment in Munich; that fat turncoat Mussolini; Eva Braun's scowls; the many things a Great Man must endure, like
all those "Small Solutions" amounting to nothing; the laughter they
heaped on him in that sick film of the British Chaplin; the treachery of the
Jews; the disgusting Gypsies; the days in Vienna when he was forced to
sleep under bridges; those who did not buy his paintings; being only and
forever a corporal; being told by a thousand glances an Austrian cannot be
a German; that newspaper which called him a coward in 1932; those who
snickered when he said at a Chemnitz rally in 1928, "Whatever goal man
has reached is due to his originality plus brutality"; being kicked out of
school in Linz in 1904; those who thought him lazy for living off his
mother in Linz when they never knew the destiny of an artist; his hard father; his three siblings dead before they were six; being the son of an old
man's third marriage; those who tried to stick his father's real name on
him—Schickelgruber!; his father's illegitimacy; his grandfather who
might have been a Jew. Then he pulled the trigger.

Hitler was unrepentant till the last. The final paragraph of his "Political
Testament," written the day before his suicide, states, "Above all I charge the
leaders of the nation and those under them to scrupulous observance of the
laws of race and to merciless opposition to the universal poisoner of all peoples, international Jewry." A postscript sent to the Army via General Keitel
shows him still urging aggression, his version of vengeance for World War I:
"The aim must still be to win territory in the east for the German people." As
per his wish, Hitler's and his new wife's bodies were burned in a hole
quickly dug in the courtyard outside. Only in 1995, when parts of Hitler's
skull and his teeth in a charred jaw were discovered quite by chance in a
Moscow archive, was the fate of their remains made known.[49]

Four days later, after securing the surrender of 150,000 soldiers—an entire German Army—36 miles east of the Elbe at Ludwigslust, Gavin, already
stunned at the suicide of the town's mayor and his daughter, stared into the
diabolic core of Hitler's ideology: 4 miles outside Ludwigslust, overcome by
a horrid stench, he came to the entrance of the Woebbelin concentration
camp and there "met a sight the equal of which I have never even imagined
nor expect to see ever again."

It was a small camp by Nazi standards: 4,000 inmates, a quarter of which
had died of starvation and exposure. Unlike Buchenwald or Auschwitz, it

did not have gas chambers, though it did have crematoria. Hurriedly put together as a transfer camp in late 1944 after the collapse of the Eastern Front, it was filled with emaciated political prisoners from all over Europe, as well as those deemed guilty by reason of their race, the Jews. The inmates were being systematically starved to death when the 82d arrived.

"Even after three years of war it brought tears to my eyes," Gavin wrote later. "Living skeletons were scattered about, the dead distinguishable from the living only by the blue-black color of their skin compared to the somewhat greenish skin, taut over the bony frames of the living." The dead were stacked in tarpaper shacks and strewn about the compound, their eyes seeing too much of the sky, their lips pulled back in the maniacal smile of the hopeless. Others lowed or moaned in gutteral whispers; others stood staring, on the brink of death, not knowing if these were angels or devils at the gate.

Lieutenant Dick Goins, a GOYA in ill-begotten C Company whose frozen feet, like my father's, had spared him from the last day's destruction at Rochelinval, was with Gavin's 325th Regiment as it entered Woebbelin. "The people—they were skeletons, really—were dressed in black and white jackets and trousers," Goins recounted to me. "The only food I saw in the whole place were rotten turnips or rutabagas. I saw bodies stacked up four and five deep like cordwood. There was nothing but filth everywhere. No one spoke; I did not talk with any of them. But I noticed in one stack of bodies someone moving. Dr. Battenfield [of the old 551st] immediately went to him and we pulled him out and treated him. When they saw the gates opened, the people that were confined moved out as if in a trance looking for food right down into the town of Ludwigslust. The population there was terrified, and hid from them."

When Gavin had a wagon of black bread and meat brought immediately to the camp, it caused a stampede in which some inmates were trampled. One man, roused from his deathbed of straw, ran out toward the wagon and dropped dead of convulsions before he could eat a morsel. Solid food distribution was halted, and doctors brought in cots and intravenous feeding. Among the prisoners was Peter G. Martin, a sixty-seven-year-old Parisian public works manager, who had mildly questioned Nazi policies two years before; a Dutch teenager had met a similar fate over German occupation of Holland. There was a ten-year-old Jewish boy from Budapest named Paul who had four times been taken to gas chambers at other camps and four times been halted at the last moment.

One of the few GOYAs to make it all the way from the North Africa campaign to Berlin, Fred Hilgardner, had deftly negotiated a path through stacks of sea mines (he had seen a truck and a tank blown up by them) when he came through the woods to the back of Woebbelin. Hilgardner and his 504th company attacked the 8-foot-high chain link fence topped with barbed wire using wire cutters and soon entered the compound. His first thought was: Animals are being kept here. Then he discovered huge bunkers of piled earth over concrete tunnels with narrow-gauge tracks going into and out of them. Inside he found the piled-up sea mines, which inmates had been forced to assemble. "Then we made it into their kitchen," Hilgardner recalled. "They had these big, stainless steel vats. The whole place was immaculate. From there we found rows of garage-like structures and opened the doors. That's where the bodies were, Jesus, it was stinking. One by one, we pulled them out, and if any moved, we'd call for a medic. The sunlight startled the shit out of those who were alive. The medics worked overtime. Later we discovered the ovens—they were still warm. They most certainly had been cremating bodies there. Also we found stacks of bars of soap all over the camp. When we heard that human beings had been rendered into soap, we forced the German townspeople to bury that soap in graves."

The next day Gavin forced every adult citizen of Ludwigslust to dig the holes for the dead of Woebbelin in the lawn of the town square in front of the palace of the Mecklenburg princes. Each body was afforded a private grave; when Gavin saw the German General Kurt von Tippelskirch of the 21st Army Group staring smugly at the procession of burials, he slugged him sideways and ordered him to take off his hat. Gavin had a French film crew document the burial ceremony; one of his daughters recalled that years later, whenever Gavin would show the film to his family, he would break down.

Chaplain George Wood of the 82d Airborne, who had said the eulogy at Wood Joerg's burial in Belgium, addressed the people of Ludwigslust: "Though you claim no knowledge of these acts you are still individually and collectively responsible for these atrocities for they were committed by a government elected in 1933 and continued in office by your indifference to organized brutality. It should be the firm resolve of the German people that never again should any leader or party bring them to such moral degradation as is exhibited here."[50]

Hilgardner knew no GOYA in the 504th to unburden himself to at Woebbelin, one of sixteen concentration camps the U.S. army liberated. The only two men who'd gone forward with him into Germany after the 551st's destruction had dropped out—Jack Brinkley, whose malaria from Panama days finally caught up with him at the Siegfried Line town of Holtzheim, and Asa Griffin, who had accidentally shot a finger off fooling with a 9mm automatic pistol just after crossing the Elbe River. Hilgardner busied himself with rounding up all firearms from the citizenry of Ludwigslust. It was an enormous stockpile of mostly shotguns, one kind with an octagonal barrel that seemed too large for one person to shoot. But the sight of Woebbelin and the shades in those sheds never left him: "I've seen some pretty raw things in my life, but nothing that stuck with me like that. I've seen movies like *Schindler's List*, and they're all pretty realistic, except for one thing. The people aren't skinny enough. Because you can't find live people that skinny."

Half a century after the war, the GOYAs' chief antagonist at Noirefontaine and the most decorated soldier in the 62d Volksgrenadiers, Colonel Arthur Juttner, reflected on the Nazi "final solution" for the Jews. While he acknowledged the appeal of Hitler for many because of the devastated economy of post–World War I Germany, he said, "Hitler lied. All he brought to Germany was war and devastation." About *Krystallnacht*, the night in 1938 when stormtroopers ransacked Jewish homes and shops in cities throughout Germany, he emphasized: "Those were many Nazis that did the burning and killing, not the soldiers. The Jews hadn't done anything to us." Like many in the professional soldier class (he had entered long before Hitler in 1926 and was forbidden to join a party or vote), he denied knowledge of the genocide itself: "I didn't know of the concentration camps. We had little knowledge of what was happening in the back [at home]. We had enough to do on the front. It was a horrible crime. But the good German soldiers had nothing to do with it."

How much of this is memory-polishing the past, how much bald fact, and how much residue of revulsion at the time that would not or could not surface on pain of death will remain one of the great, hard mysteries concerning the German people in World War II.[51]

The one 551st man to help liberate Dachau was Dan Morgan. Morgan had left the battalion at Camp Mackall convinced he was riding a runaway train. After several frustrating attempts to be a pilot or to get back into the airborne, he had arrived in Europe in April 1945, alighting in the great trainyards of Lyon, France, as a replacement. Just as he got out of the car, he caught sight, incredibly, of some wounded men from his old 551st battalion and called out to them, "Hey, fellas!" running across the snow-laden tracks toward them.

"Dan!" they called back. "What the hell are you doing here?"

The moment is branded in Morgan's memory: "I have a photographic image of their faces—they were enlisted men, all bandaged one place or another. But they recognized me."

"All of us were killed," one man said to him after an embrace. "The Colonel, too. There's nothing left of us."

Morgan was soon assigned to the 6th Tank Destroyer Group, which was to provide security for the 13th Airborne Division. "The poor GIs were so cold they would come up to our tanks and put their hands on the warm engines," he recalled. He handled a large SCR-290 radio for a time as the unit moved out into Bavaria. On May 7, 1945, two Germans riding a motorcycle, one carrying a valise in the sidecar, ran into Morgan's column and proclaimed, "It's all over!" The next day, May 8, the war in Europe came to an official end. It was Victory in Europe (VE) Day.

Unbeknownst to Morgan or to any of the 551st for many years, one of the last (if not the last) Americans to be killed in the European Theater of Operations (ETO) was the former GOYA Sergeant Stephen Kicinski, who had executed the Polish prisoners a month before at the Bulge, to Dick Durkee's great consternation. He was shot on May 8 while patrolling with his "new" unit, the 508th. Perhaps it was a mercy; he would not be court-martialed, as Durkee had threatened, or be forced to live with the harsh memory of his vengeance.

A week after VE Day Morgan came to the entrance of Dachau. There was the horrid sign: *Arbeit Macht Frei* (Work Makes You Free). Dachau was first entered by American troops on April 29. Unlike Woebbelin, from which the German guards had fled before the 82d arrived, Dachau's German contingent were caught, unrepentant. A young lieutenant, Heinrich Skodzensky, clicked his hobnailed boots together and flipped up his arm to the first American major alighting from a tank, declaring, "Heil Hitler! I hereby turn over to you the concentration camp of Dachau, 30,000 residents, 2,340 sick, 27,000 outside, and 560 garrison troops."

The major, who had seen corpses piled up at the crematoria and around the railway station, spat in the man's face and yelled: *"Du Schweinhund!"*

All the pent-up anger at the bestiality of the war seemed to burst in the Americans, and a killing frenzy ensued. Within an hour almost all five hundred members of the German garrison were executed, most by the U.S. soldiers sickened at the sight of the ghostly inmates, but some by the inmates themselves. At least thirty guards, however, resisted from the watchtowers. They were killed after they opened fire. One American lieutenant lined up 346 of the surrendering SS guards against a wall and machine-gunned them all.[52]

Sam Goldsmith, Jewish journalist who had escaped the Bergen-Belsen camp to Britain earlier in the war, recorded his first sight of Dachau: "On a railway siding there is a train of fifty wagons—all full of terribly emaciated dead bodies, piled up like twisted branches of cut-down trees. Near the crematorium—for the disposal of the dead—another huge pile of dead bodies, like a heap of crooked logs ready for some infernal fire."[53]

Of the 33,000 survivors at Dachau, 2,539 were Jews; all but 73 of them would die in the next month and a half.

Morgan would stay in Dachau a month, maintaining security and trying, impossibly, to stave off the living dead from death. He said that five thousand dead bodies had piled up in the camp when he arrived. On his second day a hundred ambulances drove up. A force of corpsmen set up kitchens, gave shots, and dusted the inmates with DDT. As at Woebbelin, the U.S. Army forced the townspeople to walk the quarter-mile from the city into the streets of the camp: "We were disgusted with them. They thought they were going to be shot, but we gave them shelter-halves and told each two of them to get a body and help bury them in common graves 20 feet by 12 feet across."

At least eight hundred people died the first week under Morgan's watch; 1,600 more were to die, most in hospitals, before he left. "Many had lips that couldn't close over their teeth from malnutrition," he remembered. "We shrunk from them, sad to say. It was a horrible experience. And the stench was worse than a thousand dead horses. You could still cut that smell with a knife weeks later."

Apparently, German POWs from surrounding areas were gathered at Dachau, and while Morgan and his fellows provided security, Army Intelligence took to separating them into three groups: Class 1 were SS, who had blue tattoos under their armpits. "These guys were harder looking," Morgan said. "They regarded us with contempt and arrogance." Some of them had tried to obliterate the mark by mutilating the skin under their arms with knives. Class 2 were indefinite. Class 3 were the Wehrmacht line soldiers, who were shipped to France to clear minefields.

Morgan knew at Dachau that something unspeakable in its horror had finally come to an end, not the least because people like the 551st had given their lives pressing toward, but not reaching, as he did, the Dachaus of the war. Later Sgt. Roy Rose of the 551st's B Company would serve for thirty months as Provost Sergeant at the Landsberg War Crimes Prison.

Two GOYAs reached prisoner-of-war camps as prisoners. After the battle at Rochelinval, the 551st's Tom Waller had found the dog tags of both Joe Cicchinelli and Larry Poston in the snow around Quartiers, with their rifles planted at the barrel. The two GOYAs were reported as missing in action, but most of the men had given them up for dead.

On the way to Stalag 4B near Muhlberg, the truck convoy of prisoners that included Cicchinelli and Poston came under attack from a British night fighter, which strafed it with 20mm bullets. Several bullets pierced the motor and back slats of Cicchinelli's truck; one hit him in the neck, shattering his shoulder bones. He received no treatment. His injury list had piled up over the past two years: a wrecked neck from a cracked helmet on a test jump in Panama; severely sprained ankle from a machine gun falling on it on a Panama forced march; the blown right eardrum and shrapnel hit in the chin from 88s at the Bulge; frostbitten hands and feet; the rifle butt in the face during interrogation; the onset of malnutrition in the POW camps; and now the slicings of friendly fire from the sky.

Five hundred Russians were kept in a separate compound at Stalag 4B, where they were being starved to death. For pushing a cigarette through a wire fence to the Russians, Cicchinelli was boxed around by the guards and punished. The Russians, Poston said, received the worst treatment by far: "When lined up, if one inmate was even a quarter inch out of line, six-foot-four German guard would knock him to the ground." Cicchinelli would be haunted long after the war by a "death odor" visiting him during seizures that he later identified as the nauseating stench coming from the dead and dying Russians at the camp.

For Larry Poston, the experience of being moored far from one's own among strangers was not entirely new. He had lived from age three to thirteen in an orphanage in Tennessee.

The GOYAs were put in with the British, who developed a makeshift first aid station that shoved a spoonful of tannic acid someone had scrounged into the mouths of those who suffered dysentery, like Cicchinelli. It dried everything up but his ailment. The British also did their best to keep their men's minds from falling apart and to discipline them to preserve them from worse punishment. If someone was caught stealing, they would give him a "GI bath," that is, strip him and scrape him with scrub brushes and cold water. On one occasion Cicchinelli demonstrated the American way of discipline. Someone had stolen his three-day allotment of bread that he would toast black to try and cure his "GIs" (diarrhea), and he beat the man up.

The work details were dreary, but no one was forced to work. An incentive system was actually in place: If you worked, you got double rations. Poston, who enjoyed better health than Cicchinelli throughout their incarceration, would be led under guard outside the camp to haul firewood from a forest that had been partially razed by U.S. incendiary bombs. Small pieces could be hauled with one belt, larger pieces with two. In the barracks with 350 others, the GOYAs used the small group stove and boiled their daily ration—a few walnut-size potatoes and hot water flavored with tea leaves. Occasionally they would get a turnip and mash it with the potatoes.

Poston and Cicchinelli had early hatched a plan to escape, but it dissipated. "We were too weak," Joe said. "And we were never able to save up any food. It was so cold. And where would we go? The best time to escape is right after capture. If you don't make it in the first two days, then you have had it."

In April 1945 Hitler made an announcement on radio that was broadcast over the BBC to the effect that all POWs in German hands would be shot. Needless to say, word of this ran through the already drained prisoners at Stalag 4B like verbal strychnine. But on April 23 the camp was liberated by the Russians leading a caravan of displaced Russian civilian and military POWs with their families, a marauding force let loose on the German towns. Except for the banks, which the Russian soldiers guarded, everything was fair game. Food was, of course, the commodity the freed POWs went after first, but women were next for the Russian soldiers. "You would see German women scratching their faces and putting mud on themselves so they would be ugly," Cicchinelli said. The Russian soldiers pilfered bicycles, trucks, and motorcycles, joyriding drunk until they ran into a tree or building. The first link-up of Soviet and American forces occurred only a few miles from Stalag 4B, at Torgau and Stehla on April 25. In Moscow, 324 guns fired 24 salvos to mark the meeting, while in New York City crowds danced in Times Square.

Though Cicchinelli and Poston exchanged songs and watched the Russians do their squat dances after the liberation (as Gavin would farther north at Ludwigslust), their own final lunge to freedom took several weeks. Meanwhile, they had to watch what came to be the standard Soviet victors' response to German aggression: summary brutality toward the German captives. Cicchinelli came across the carcass of a German guard who had been rough to them at Stalag 4B: "They had him hanging from his heels, degutted and deballed."

Just as the crop of victory in Europe was harvested by the Allies, bitter seeds of a new conflict were being sown in the late spring of 1945. Nowhere was it more evident than in the joint American–Russian occupation of Berlin. Ed Henriques with the 505th, who on occupation duty sold contraband watches to the Russians near the Brandenburg Gate, said straying into the Russian sector was dangerous. Each day of his three months in the Berlin, Fred Hilgardner tangled with the pillaging Russians. The Russians would gun their trucks and jeeps into the American sector of the city, "shooting anything that moved," Hilgardner recounted. "You had to take cover. At times, we shot some of them just protecting ourselves."

Disposing of Russian bodies proved equally difficult. Hilgardner's motor pool had a casket company that was working around the clock hauling in lumber and building caskets for the many dead in Berlin. The German families would lay out a dead body on the curb to be picked up by the Americans, like some kind of recycling. But Russian bodies presented problems. "The Germans wouldn't bury the Russians, of course," Hilgardner said. "The Russians wouldn't bury their own soldiers, either, that had been killed in our sector. They called them deserters. We didn't want to fill out all the paperwork for these bodies, so we took them and dumped them into the canal pushing them downriver to the Russian sector. I'd come in from a day of doing that with blood all over my uniform." He later wrote his mother: "The war is over with the Germans, but it's just now starting with the Russians."

The war was indeed over for the Germans, and the cost of it was to jolt them repeatedly as they returned home. At Dresden, the 190th Volksgrenadier Regiment's Sergeant Gerhard Kiesewetter found that his wife and two children had been incinerated in the fire-bombing of that old city.

Unable to bear their double jeopardy at the Russian stockade any longer, Cicchinelli and Poston with two other GIs climbed over the walls of the camp one night in May and reached the Elbe River, where they took refuge in a barn with others—mostly Poles—trying to escape the Russians.

American forces were just on the other side of the river. The escapees commandeered a hay wagon, hid the Poles under the hay, and raced across a bridge, with the Russians firing at them, into the startled arms of the Americans, who promptly sent them all to interrogation before bestowing on them bread so fresh it tasted like cake.

Home in Massillon, Ohio, in July 1945, Cicchinelli walked into his house at night and sat on his wife's bed as she slept. She awoke, startled beyond belief to see him, and wondered if she were still dreaming. Her seven-month-old infant, Polly, was sound asleep near her. Cicchinelli wrapped the baby's hand around his worn finger and growled a whisper: "Is she mine?" Jean cried out, "Yes! Yes! Joe, thank God, you're here!"

She watched, amazed, as the child was taken up by her husband for the first time. "Polly was always one to scream and bawl at strangers, but with Joe she didn't make a peep. She knew, somehow, this was her father."

It wasn't long, however, till Jean Cicchinelli found her husband a changed man. Before the war she had fallen in love "with his emotions, his free spirit—he was full of life." While they were courting, he would take her on picnics to the park and entertain her by walking on his hands. "He was just very strong and I thought that was wonderful," she said. They would go up to Cleveland and dance with the big dance bands of the 1940s: Benny Goodman, Harry James.

But there was no dance in Joe Cicchinelli now and for some time into the future. "He was never the same again," Jean said to me a half-century later. "He would look at you in conversation as if wondering what you were really thinking. It was like a bottle stoppered by a cork."

Forty years after the war, having gone four times to psychiatric hospitals for post-traumatic stress syndrome (PTSD), unable to work at a steady job after the age of thirty-nine, Joe Cicchinelli began to get partial seizures that would start with the mysterious "death odor." He would grow disoriented and surly, unable to let anyone touch him. The seizures could come several times in one day, and then pass in minutes. Then weeks or months would go by when he would feel that he was finally free. Free of the infernal odor of those rotting Russians. The disemboweled German. The burntout timbers they hauled outside the stalag. The smell of cosmoline, used to preserve a rifle barrel.

In air clear enough to heal, in Sedona, Arizona, many years after the Battle of the Bulge, amid the proud stellae of sandstone to which he had come in the 1980s to try, finally, to cleanse himself in the high desert, Joe Cicchinelli could not listen as his wife told me: "I'm sorry, Joe, I have to say it. Joe never got over the war. He has been guilty all these years that he led his men into an area where they were all killed."

Cicchinelli stood up and walked into the living room.

IX

HOME

But I feel like the worst old broken
window the wind blows through. Nothing tastes
good to me but the sight of my child.

—Reynolds Price, "The Foreseeable Future"

1
Abyss of peace

With a violent seasickness that bounced through four thousand shipmate veterans returning from Le Havre in November 1945, Corporal Albert "Pat" Garretty of the 551st's B Company arrived in New York Harbor. There he beheld the Statue of Liberty, "a grand sight," and commented in an unpublished war memoir: "As we passed, [I] looked back and thought, the ASS end of that babe is all I ever care to see."

Like many World War II veterans, especially those of the 551st, Garretty only too willingly forgot what had happened to him. "Bitter about some of the officers who led them or dumped them the wrong way," as his widow recounted to me, Garretty spoke little of his war experience. It did mean enough to him, however, to insist that the postwar home he built in Redwood City, California, have this address: 551 Quartz Street.[1] After toiling in title insurance for forty years, he tried to stitch it all back together again in his memoir. A modest inquiry into government sources in the early 1980s turned up nothing. The medals he had earned, such as the Combat Infantryman's Badge, which he had been too shell-shocked and disoriented after the disbandment to request, came in the mail only in 1985. Sadly, he died in 1986—as my father had the year before—thinking he was the last survivor, with no inkling that his companions had just begun to find each other and to chart an extraordinary gray-haired assault on silence.

No known GOYA, Garretty included, participated in the climactic World War II victory march up Fifth Avenue in New York City on January 12, 1946, though the soldiers who constituted that parade were supposedly the GOYAs' own celebrated umbrella, the 82d Airborne Division, with General Gavin at its head, "disguising the pain from his broken vertebrae, as well as the pain he felt for the dead."[2] More than 60,000 men had passed through the 82d during the war; fewer than 8,000 were left after V-E Day. The 13,000 who marched under the New York confetti, however, were mostly from the 13th Airborne Division, which would shortly be merged into a newly constituted 82d. Thus most of those marching in Manhattan with Gavin had not fought at the Battle of the Bulge, and in fact had not seen combat at all. The 82d vets of Belgium had already staggered back to their hometowns in the United States. As Fred Hilgardner put it: "I got an invitation to march. But I was looking for a job."[3]

The GOYAs spread anonymously throughout the United States and threw themselves furiously into peace. The country in the two decades after the war became a colossus of industrial and military strength and financial prosperity. At war's end only two percent of Americans were unemployed; liquid savings were three times what they had been in 1932.[4] The percolating era of unmatched growth after World War II became almost a reverse image of what the veterans themselves had lived through in their youth, the Great Depression and the worst war in human history, which had killed 40 million people.

Sporting the eagle-in-circle discharge patch button (which came to be known as the "ruptured duck"), the vets fanned out. The first thing they did, of course, was have children by the carload. It was the most immediate slap in the face to Death the country could make, and the vets made it with great zest and hope. Dan and Jo Morgan had eight children, and about that propagation of faith Morgan himself was certain: "I thought of all those men of the 551st who never had a chance to have sons or daughters." That filling of an abyss launched what became known as the "Baby Boom generation"—my lot. It took us a while to return the favor, and typically we did so with less urgency, more trepidation, late enough in life to diaper our babies while complaining of back trouble, but with enough *mea culpas* to announce a "Baby Boomlet" to the world: our children.

It is no surprise that men who had been "cross-trained" over so many manual disciplines—from demolition to parachute rigging to working machine guns and trucks of all sorts—should tend to take up professions that would tap those skills: manufacturing and heavy-duty equipment maintenance and repair. In Kansas City, Fred Hilgardner became a structural mechanic involved with employee safety at TWA. Paul DeLillio was the electrician and general fix-it man at a bakery for thirty-seven years in Wilmington, Delaware.[5] My own father flirted with Cleveland Tractor right out of the war after vocational school in Dearborn, Michigan, ending up on the West Coast, where after a stint as a regional representative of a ladies' gar-

ment retail store chain, Mode O' Day, he opened his own garment manufacturing company in 1952, Le Greg of California, proudly displaying a framed
sleeveless California orange dickey as his first "make."

With the exception of one night in 1945 in a bar in Cleveland with Private
Tommy Stampfl of A Company, my father never got in touch with or even
ran across another GOYA, at least to his family's knowledge. In 1990, two
years into my book research, PFC Benny Goodman, who had not cried at his
own mother's funeral, looked at me at the GOYA reunion in Washington,
D.C., broke down, and sobbed uncontrollably, stunning his wife, Agnes. We
had hardly met. Like my mother, Goodman had left Brooklyn after the war
for Los Angeles, where my father had also migrated at the time. Three years
after our emotional encounter Goodman explained to me in his home in
Woodland Hills, California (not 1 mile from our family home), why he was
so struck. In 1946, when my father was living on Commonwealth Avenue, a
mile from the Ambassador Hotel, Goodman had gone to the hotel pool
where my father occasionally went with his sister Jeannette. There Goodman met an ex-GI he recognized as being in the 551st. "There were all these
fat people at the pool," Goodman recounted. "We were in good condition in
the service, you know. And I spotted him and we recognized each other.
What entered my mind was—the only guy who looked good was this guy
from the 551st . . . he looked like you. And like these pictures.

"When I saw you, I started to cry, and it never happened before. Somehow I knew that your father was. . . . I didn't talk to him much, but your
father is dead, yet I didn't even know then how he died. There are certain
mysteries that can't be explained. I don't know what it is, but it was very
. . . why? When I've never done that before?" He discovered later that my
father had been shot to death in Woodland Hills.

Once you're airborne and live to tell of it—but have little to tell but a fog
of pain—you don't stop moving; Goodman himself established a thriving
moving and storage business. You are seen as a force, impatient, hard to
please, perfectionist; you have a temper, but your embrace is wide, warm.
Your spirit is a controlled fire.

Maybe it was the Maritime Alps, but they loved the outdoors, as a whole,
though snow would never be merely recreation again. Their throbbing feet
from Belgium assured that. Some few would take their labors purely outdoors.
For forty years Charlie Buckenmeyer coached Ohio high school football;
Urban Post farmed 700 acres in Celina, Ohio; Lee Elledge ran a tree nursery in
South Carolina. But because they carried that flair for the odd, that feel for the
outcast, animal husbandry would find at least one of them herding buffalo.
Nearly extinct as the GOYAs' history when "Buffalo Don" Thompson began
breeding bison in the late 1940s, today there are seven thousand head on his
farm in Mishicot, Wisconsin. Thompson also developed a $40 million bottled

mineral water company, the largest in the state, on three principles: self-re-spect, quality in all things, and a custodial attitude toward the environment. He is also informed by chronic osteomyelitis, because his leg wound from Jan-uary 3, 1945, the first day of the Ardennes counteroffensive, never completely healed. "Each day after work I pour the blood out of my shoe," he says. Every month for the last fifty years he has visited the veterans' hospital.

Like Cicchinelli, who seemed to get the upper hand in a lifelong battle when he returned his war memorabilia to a trunk in 1995, Bill Bustin was haunted in civilian life by the memory of the war. "I used to like to walk in the woods, but if I came to a field after the war I'd have to go around it," he said. "I could do it, but I'd pay a price."

After an endless series of jobs, finding it hard to "stand for the bullshit with people," he spent his last six working years in a boiler room with the Rhode Island State Department of Public Buildings. It took forty-seven years before he finally walked into a clinic, where he was diagnosed with PTSD, once known as shell-shock. And there he confronted the source of all his inner turmoil: his father.

Bustin's British father came out of World War I severely shell-shocked; when the son was only seven, the father went into a mental hospital and never came out. For years Bustin was worried that he would fall prey to something hereditary. It even influenced his decision to go Airborne and into the 551st: "I wanted to go into the toughest outfit, afraid something was wrong in me." In fact, there was nothing wrong with Bustin or his father but war.

A sympathetic hometown reporter described the GOYA hero Milo Huempfner as "that guy in the American Legion uniform decked with rib-bons and medals like he's his own Memorial Day parade, walking every-where in militarily shined black shoes going low at the heels, appearing at military funerals to give a salute and play taps on his harmonica."[6] Just before he died, Huempfner was visited by Milo Burke, a fellow truck dri-ver, who had lost an eye, and his chance to be a policeman, in the war. They went to a bowling alley, where Burke overhead a clutch of teenagers ridiculing Huempfner as the town drunk.

"I went over to them and told them what this man had done for them during the war, singlehandedly, against the Germans," Burke recounted. "They all came up and apologized."

It may have been with an apology in mind that I traveled to Stuart, Florida, in 1992 to meet Colonel Rupert Graves, who had retired from the Army in 1956. But that was not to be, and perhaps it was somewhat unfair to expect of a man then ninety-two, bedridden, and battling a host of ill-nesses. In a discontinuous interview filled with silences in which he could not remember Rochelinval, spoke of the 551st's "bad habits in Panama," and remarked that they "didn't do too well in combat," at one point the old colonel looked up and blurted: "The commander of the 551st was hit by a ball of fire!" Just before I left I asked, "Colonel, if men of the 551st were in this room right now, what would you tell them?"

He looked down at his bedcovers and then at the snow falling quietly in a soundless television. "I wouldn't tell them anything," he said.

As if to fill the embarrassed air, his good daughter sang out, "You don't have to share when you're ninety-two, do you, Daddy?"

I thanked them both and said goodbye. Graves put his large, bony hands around one of mine and smiled up from the bed with a vulnerability and loneliness that made me wonder if I had interpreted his cryptic remark too harshly.

After a long, gray period, Heidi Joerg married Wood's first cousin, John Joerg. If Modest Mussorgsky's comment, "Show me who you love, and I will show you who you are," is true, then Heidi Joerg became a different person in her second Joerg marriage. John Joerg couldn't have been more different from Wood. Though John had served in the war in the Army Air Corps, the military was not his cup of tea; in civilian life he ran an insurance agency in Orlando, Florida, then retired with Heidi to New Smyrna Beach, where the Joerg cousins had summered growing up. While Heidi called Wood "the most idealistic person I've ever known," John saw the ironies of life and had the pungent humor of a born skeptic. Wood was a total romantic; John saw the aphid in the rose.

No one took Wood's death harder than Elizabeth Guice Joerg, "a fireball" to her nephew Frank. The raven-haired, cobalt-eyed beauty was a "tremendous horsewoman and markswoman, too," but her youngest son's death plunged her into a deep depression. Determined that he would be a general, she had followed Wood all over, especially during the long years of separation from her husband—to the Point, to Fort Sam Houston in San Antonio—just as the mother of "the American Caesar," MacArthur, had trailed him. "Aunt Guice probably would have compared her son to Julius Caesar, too, only thought Wood was ahead of him!" Frank Joerg said.

When Frank visited the German Joergs shortly after the war in Frankfurt, Aunt Guice was shocked. When he returned from occupation duty in 1946, she shook his shoulders and coughed: "Kill the Germans. Kill all of them."

After the war and his son Wood's death, "Hard Robert" Joerg moved with his second wife, Helen, out to a country town near Seale, Alabama, where they converted an old plantation into the Villula Tea Gardens. Hard Robert drank more than tea, dying at Seale of a heart attack in late 1947, three months after Wood's body was brought home.

The bitterness toward ancestral roots in Germany that suffused Hard Robert Joerg and "Guice" invaded their son, Robert III, Wood's only brother. As late as the 1980s, when Margaret Jörg visited America from Hofheim with her daughter, Beatrix, Robert Joerg refused to see them. He never learned of the anti-Hitler strain in the overseas family.

On May 29, 1983, Commander Robert Joerg and General William West-moreland were on hand in Eufala, Alabama, when the city became the first in the nation to dedicate a memorial to its Vietnam veterans. After temporary interment in Dairomont, Belgium, Wood Joerg had been reburied in the town of his birth, Eufala. It was fitting, in a way, that Wood's grave was not far from a monument to those who had fought in a lost cause.[7]

2
A GOYA in 'Nam

It is no great surprise that few of the 551st pursued the military as a profession. Of those who did, there were no generals, and only four (Pappy Herrmann, Bill Holm, Bill Smith, and Doug Dillard) rose to the rank of full colonel. By way of contrast, the 517th produced eight generals.

As early as Korea, Dillard began to discern that the ways in which America was fighting wars were at troubling variance with his experience in World War II. "Unlike World War II, where there was a definite objective—you were here for the duration; there was an application of effort to get it over—Korea and Vietnam were not that way," he said. Inevitably, soldier morale and behavior were drastically affected. "There was a succession of commanders and staffers and troops rotating and rotating and rotating," he recounted. "The unit integrity or the spirit of the unit was just not the same."

Dillard's own experience with a separate unit punished beyond belief at the Bulge, which still managed to walk through the gore to secure its goal, translated into increasingly difficult, isolated, and morally perilous assignments. In 1968, after a stint teaching airborne and amphibious "offensive" counterintelligence operations at Fort Holabird in Maryland, where he trained "practically every Army intelligence unit that went to Vietnam,"[8] Dillard himself was sent to the Mekong Delta south of Saigon. There he would be told to rein in the excesses of a rogue operation while dealing with an enemy far more elusive than Hitler.

That was the Phoenix Program, the attempt at "pacification" to "win the hearts and minds" of the South Vietnamese population, whose allegiance, at least at the start of our involvement under President Kennedy in the early 1960s, we didn't think we needed to win. When all the euphemisms were brushed away ("neutralizing with extreme prejudice" meant kill), Phoenix was a CIA-hatched attempt to root out opposition to the Thieu government by assassinating cadre in villages in the South, few of whom wore uniforms. Who was Viet Cong and who was a water buffalo herder and only a water buffalo herder was often very difficult to ascertain.

Although nothing like what the GOYAs had been through in southern France and the Maritime Alps in 1944, Vietnam did bear a crude resemblance in a hot climate to the desperate Battle of the Bulge in the cold. As the 551st's Dick Field once pointed out, "like Vietnam, there were no fixed enemy lines at the Bulge." In the Ardennes, the Germans paid no heed to what was civilian and what was not, and both sides committed POW atrocities. Of course, there was one big difference: Almost all Belgians were grateful to have Americans with them. That was not only untrue in Vietnam, but friend and foe often lived in the same town, on the same street, in the same hut. In short, it was hell on earth, a hell into which Doug Dillard descended and from which he barely emerged.

At his home many years later, in 1989, retired twelve years from the Army, Dillard confessed: "It was frustrating because in Europe, and even in Korea, except for guerrilla bands operating behind the front, you could pretty much count on the populace. You didn't have to worry about them. In Vietnam, you had to worry about everyone who was not wearing an Army uniform. That ranged from children to very old grandmas."

Considered "the best man they could get down in the Delta,"[9] Dillard had the virtually impossible task of setting things in order. "A bunch of bums getting drunk in their hooches were used at the beginning of Phoenix," he related. "There was a lot of abuse and some atrocities then. I would not allow it. When I came in I told every one of my twenty agents: There will be no murder, rape, or violations of civilized standards in this operation. I won't tolerate any abuse."

The very nature of Phoenix, however, made it hard to hold within the bounds of the Geneva Convention. "It's kind of a conflict to our culture and experience over the years," he explained, "to take a U.S. Army element—whatever it may be—and direct it not only toward military and paramilitary enemy forces, but toward the civilians that cooperate with them."[10]

Though he felt the war should not have been fought, Doug Dillard did not dissent, at least not publicly; almost no active duty field rank officers did in those years. After Wood Joerg, his two other great role models in the Army were the paratrooper icons General Matthew Ridgway and General James Gavin, and they did dissent. They were retired, of course, an advantage Dillard did not enjoy. But Dillard took note of their message, with no small inner turmoil.[11]

To Gavin, the Vietnam conflict sorely sapped resources we should have used stateside to put our own house in order. Gavin launched the first widely disseminated warning from the military fraternity that we were going astray in Vietnam when he testified (along with General Ridgway)[12] before the Senate Foreign Relations Committee on February 8, 1966. Could it have been that this exceptional man's conscience was informed, even in a small way, by the tragedy to which he contributed concerning "my 551" at Rochelinval so long before? That something piercing and unwieldy from the "good" war had come back to haunt and catalyze him about the misuse of power in "the bad"?

Roland Barhyte of the 551st's mauled A Company took comfort from Gavin's stance (as did my own father): "I knew Gavin was against the Vietnam War. I was glad we agreed, that it was, in a sense, part of the paratrooper fraternity."

With professorial white hair today flying up from his pate, a knowing smile, and a glint in his eye, the high school mathematics teacher Barhyte went back into some hospital of the past where he was treated for frozen feet: "I remember men in wards crying out 'I don't want to live!' If these are the glories of war, forget it. I wanted to impress upon my pupils not only the importance of math, but of other people's languages. We had no business being in Vietnam. It was built up as a result of the McCarthy hearings [in the 1950s]. You know, 'There's a Communist under every rock.' But my point of view is socialist, that there are certain responsibilities a community has to care for individuals. There were precious people killed in Vietnam. I have had very serious qualms about that. Do we learn? I'm not sure."

Fifty-eight thousand Americans died in Vietnam. One of them was the son of a 551st man, Emory Albritton, serving with the Big Red One at Khe Sanh. Ken Albritton was killed on the first day of the 1968 Tet Offensive, shot off a halftrack after covering for a lot of men who got away. They named a junior high school for him at Fort Bragg after he received a posthumous Silver Star. But the father regarded the Star with great melancholy for years. His son had written him shortly before his death, "We don't really know what our objective is."

A few months after the Kent State tragedy in 1970, Colonel Dillard was in class at the Army War College in Carlisle, Pennsylvania, during a guest lecture by the now retired General Ridgway, when Ridgway objected to another speaker who said the Army was for intervention in Indochina in the 1950s. "You did not include my assessment, sir," General Ridgway said, reminding him of his strong stance against it. Escorting Ridgway around campus, Dillard eagerly asked the general to elaborate on his notion that, without a force of a million men, intervention in Indochina could not work and was not worth it. Ridgway said, "I don't want to get into it."

As the war finally began to wind down, from 1973 to its end in 1975, Dillard was charged with tracking down American soldiers missing in action (MIAs). It was frustrating, sorrowful duty; two years later he let go the Army green. Why did he leave the military? In a word, diverticulitis, sometimes called "the soldier's disease," pitting the stomach due to bad food, inadequate fluids, and nerves. Strange: That was the only illness my father had in his body when he died.

The year Doug Dillard retired, 1977, was the year that Phil Hand sounded his telephone trumpet: Were any GOYAs left in the world? By the good graces of Jack Kennelly, an officer of the 17th Airborne Division Association and a friend of Hand from jump school days, the first 551st reunion of twenty-four men took place in Atlanta as an adjunct to the 17th Airborne's own gathering, which had donated a hospitality suite to the GOYAs.[13] The 17th Airborne had long taken a back seat in the history books to the 101st, though it had suffered worse losses at Bastogne during the counteroffensive than the Screaming Eagles and (excepting the 106th) had the worst daily casualty rate of any U.S. division at the Bulge. It had never been headlined. No one in the 17th had said "Nuts!" It harbored brotherly feelings for the lost 551st.

It was a small, spirited, unlikely beginning. It may very well be that the GOYAs had gathered the tardiest veteran reunion for any sizable World War II unit.[14] Most integral units to the 82d Airborne—as well as the division itself—had been meeting annually for thirty-two years. Even the GOYAs' sister independent 550th Parachute Glider Battalion had been gathering yearly since 1952. Their brother 509th Parachute Infantry Battalion had regrouped four years before the GOYAs. But none of those had the quadruple vacuum of disbandment, lost records, lack of honors, and dead commander that the GOYAs were up against.

If they were going to set the record straight, the GOYAs knew they would have to get moving. In 1983, Dan Morgan visited the Center for Military History in Washington, the official historical section of the Armed Services, and met with its director, a full colonel. The man drew a complete blank when Morgan mentioned what he was after. He had never heard or read of the 551st, and ventured that Morgan must have been thinking of the 550th glidermen. Morgan assured him that that was not the case.

If Dan Morgan's role was the foundation-stone documentation of *The Left Corner of My Heart*, Doug Dillard and Joe Cicchinelli set about the task of memorializing just where the 551st had been in Europe. Dillard felt the best way to start was to commemorate the night raid on Noirefontaine. On May 18, 1985, a small group consisting of six GOYAs (including Dillard, Cicchinelli, and Max Bryan) and their families, along with Wood Joerg's daughters, Charlotte and Susette, and two grandchildren he never met, Heidi and Bo Wilson, stood in solemn ceremony to unveil a plaque in the stone wall at La Chapelle. It is headed *"Mission Accomplie, 551ème Bataillon D'Infantérie Parachutiste"* and reads in French and English: "On 27 December, 1944, with ardor and courage the battalion conducted the initial attack against enemy forces during the Battle of the Bulge." That was a slight exaggeration. The GOYAs' attack was the first in the 82d Airborne sector on the northern shoulder of the Bulge, but after fifty years of nothing, the GOYAs would let it ride.

One by one, the GOYAs raised the new timbers of the home of their history. In 1987 in Draguignan, at the intersection with John F. Kennedy Boulevard near the U.S. Rhône Cemetery, an old street was newly titled with the sign: *Avenue du 551ème Bataillon de Parachutistes Americains.*

Finally, on August 20, 1989, with the initiative of a former Belgian resistance leader, Leo Carlier, and a young enthusiast for the 551st who was raised in Rochelinval, Claude Orban, the most meaningful monument of all was unveiled to a crowd of more than six hundred Belgians and Americans at Rochelinval—a triangular, rough-hewn slate rock with a bronze plaque to the 551st and an inlaid photo of Lieutenant Colonel Wood Joerg. The site was the ridge where the Germans had mowed down the unit forty-five years before. It stands today, surrounded by pasture in the small hamlet, a modest testimony to the rough-hewn men and their sacrifice. For the first time, Rochelinval was officially on the historical map of the Bulge.

Until meeting GOYA vets in 1984, Leo Carlier had never heard of them or known of their role in liberating his home area. A connoisseur of Belgian beer, with a mien both irascible and distinguished, Leo took to the GOYAs as his very own. There is no doubt they were cut from the same cloth. GOYA-like, Leo spoke little about himself in his ten-year association with the 551st. I caught up with him in 1994 (the year before he died) in a veterans' hospital near Bastogne, where he had been put up after falling off a table, it was said, toasting with one of those fine Belgian beers. Though he was in something of a body cast in bed, his puckish eyes gleamed through his glasses, his fine silver hair was combed, and he greeted me in an inimitable accented English, "You now, Greg [he always converted "know" to "now"], we have to be like Coronel Joerg—we must get off your ash."

And he did. He cranked himself out of bed into a chair nearby, whereupon a hospital barber gave him a haircut. I interviewed him while the silver hair fell like Belgian snow on the floor.

From the day the Germans invaded Belgium in 1940, Leo Carlier went underground with the Resistance, becoming one of its leaders, in charge of a 20-mile radius in the Ardennes. His Group Comité had 1,200 clandestine soldiers (which made Leo the equivalent of a regimental commander). His chief mission, besides rescuing downed Allied pilots, was sabotage. He would order rail and telephone lines cut, switching stations blown up, train brake pipes severed, sand and sugar poured into the gas tanks of German tanks and trucks. It was a dangerous business. By 1943 Carlier had lost 450 of his men to summary execution by the SS or capture and transportation to concentration or labor camps.

Many men were sent to Breendonck, an SS labor camp near Antwerp, notorious during the war for its sadistic tortures. At least 187 Belgian and French Resistance members and Russian POWs were executed at Breendonck. Leo remembered the grisly case of a Russian who was being systematically starved to death, who one day out in the fields was so hungry he ate the afterbirth of a farmer's newborn cow. The farmer—one of many Belgian collaborators who dogged Carlier's efforts—turned the man in. His SS captors made him dig a hole and get in it, then ordered a cow hitched to a plow. They plowed the man's head off.

On two occasions Carlier came within a hair of being "deep-sixed" at Breen-donck himself. In 1943, while traveling with TNT explosives to Dinant (which later would be at the westward tip of the German Bulge), Leo was pulled out of a bar at Bois de Villers by the Gestapo. In the midst of being stripped and slugged, Carlier pulled an extraordinary fast one on his would-be torturers.

"You damn people," Carlier fulminated. "I am working for you and you put me in jail!"

The general rifled through his papers, which showed Carlier to be a engineer working with the Germans on the Atlantic wall at Normandy. He gave Leo a stern look, then apologized, asking, "Could you please take the two sentinels back?"

"Certainly." He buttoned his shirt in a huff. Pure GOYA chutzpah had saved his life.

In July 1990, in conjunction with the 50th anniversary of the U.S. Airborne in Washington, D.C., the GOYAs dedicated the only multicolored, multilingual stone marker in Arlington National Cemetery to their battalion; fittingly, it is placed at the beginning of the path to the Tomb of the Unknown Soldier.

Still, the battle seemed to go endlessly against them. As late as 1994 Fred Hilgardner protested to the chaplain of the 82d Airborne Association that its annual candle-lighting ceremony for those "killed in action" did not include the 551st. That was confirmed by the Association's executive director, Manuel De Jesus, who apologized and added the requisite candles. To this day, McCarthy Hall at Fort Benning, which sports the emblems of every U.S. paratroop unit that has ever fought for the United States, does not display that of the 551st.

The errors cropped up everywhere. In 1992 William Bustin, so lost from his fellows he was listed as "killed in action" on the Association's master list, was determined to find the grave of an old comrade, Charlie Tatro, who had been killed in a terrible mishap when he was taken for a German in southern France. Getting an unexpected lead, Bustin traveled from Rhode Island to a cemetery in New Bedford, Massachusetts, where indeed he finally found Tatro's grave. But the marker was wrong. It had his outfit as the 460th Field Artillery Battalion, a double insult since that unit had given the GOYAs almost no artillery at all at the Bulge. Bustin shook his head and said, "Jesus, even down to the last detail they squashed everything about the 551st!"

On July 1, 1992, the old GOYAs and their families trekked by bus to Lake Kinney Cameron, North Carolina, at Camp Mackall, now largely a wildlife preserve. Typically, the men went down the wrong way getting to the remote, forested site, and Jack Leaf chirped, "You never see the country until you're lost." The next weekend there was bumper-to-bumper traffic out of Fayetteville to see the memorial to the drowned men placed at the end of several dirt roads.[15] One not visiting, no doubt, was the North Carolina parks commissioner, who had tried to stop the monument's construction, claiming it was a "hippie" memorial!

The 5,600-pound, 6-foot-long granite wall close to the lake's edge unfortunately translates GOYA as "Great Outstanding Young Americans." Other than Emory "Al" Albritton, almost no one else, including Heidi Joerg, accepts that redundant phrase, and for a time it had caused a ruckus in the Association. But the men finally let the issue go.

I stood that day listening to Al Albritton call off the names of the men killed on American soil. The survivors wiped sweat from their bald, wrinkled heads, and seemed to squint up into the pines. Was this North Carolina? The Maritime Alps? The Ardennes? Briefly, I withdrew into the woods to face a charred tree. As an old but ready man answered each of the drowned men's names with a hoarse "Here!" and planted a small flag in the wind, I whispered my father's name, and I, too, said, "Here!"

3
The unspeakable

"You don't know what we are dealing with here."

My father's voice was unlike anything I'd ever heard before in his or anyone else's voice. The sheer, pure rage of it, calling from California.

It could have been Wood Joerg's voice that last night before the attack on Rochelinval, speaking to General Gavin's aide. Or A Company's Marshall Dalton after the first brutal day of the Bulge counteroffensive, his lungs full of gravel, appealing to Joerg himself to call it off before it was too late. *You don't know, Wood, what's been done already in the snow, what's up ahead for us if we don't turn back.* But Wood would know. *You don't know, General Gavin. Come and know like we know the core of hell.*

Was it Benjamin Preziotti speaking to his God the moment he knew that that smooth slate onto which he was falling had depth? The maw of water that was Mackall?

No. It was my father five months before he was killed on August 2, 1985. I had written a tough letter to my sister, thinking she was well enough now (we often liked to think she was cresting some hill and never thought that the other side of the hill was sheer) to take some sober, brotherly advice to calm down, compose, as I am composing now, herself, a self. As if she had had a choice.

I sensed something horrid in my father's voice that I couldn't put my finger or my mind on. I had evidently stirred her up. What he did not tell me that he knew, and what I never learned until they were both dead, was that she had handed over to him a pistol the year before. Only he, my mother, and her psychologist knew she had procured one—they are not hard to get—and had sheepishly given it up to him. He was living with the knowledge—unspoken—that she could go that far.

The year Phil Hand brought the first handful of men together in 1977 was the year two fateful events in my father's life took place: He closed, after three decades, his once prosperous, now failing garment manufacturing business, and his only daughter's mind snapped. He was not there for the latter; he was away on business. My mother, my brother, and I were present. It was I who called the psychiatrist who came in his candy-apple-red Cadillac to admit her to the hospital. And then I left for Europe, and later my life in the East, and my father came back to his in the West, that sheer-cliff world that now was hardly the refuge it had been for him after the war.

During the ensuing years of unemployment or underemployment, my father developed some poignant interests to distract himself from the abyss. Always fascinated with the Native Americans, he intently studied their history. Never a reader of books in his rag business days, he took to reading like a man possessed. On nights when I was home I would see him sitting up late, books stacked from the floor up the back of his deep chair. Always a lover of nature and the outdoors, he developed an obsession with animals. I remember him visiting the Washington Zoo with me once and spending the better part of an hour staring at the vultures.

"That is a face only a mother could love," he said.

Joke with death: that was the GOYA spirit. But also, watch all public television National Geographic specials on the animal kingdom. I remember him once remarking after a program on a protective pride of lions, the nurturing mother and the shield of a father: "Men are not animals. Don't insult the animals." Sounded just like Harry Renick.

My mother told me more than once in the decade after his death that I idealized my father, that I fashioned an impossible cynosure of a man.

But he was not perfect—far from it. He had a temper that could come on as abruptly as a summer storm (though it would be gone as fast as it erupted). I felt the lash of it when, as a boy, I threw a dirt clod at my sister and it hit her face, temporarily blinding her (she was about five). The doctor had to pluck the grains from her corneas with a rubber tweezers. She wore thick eyeglasses for several years afterward. When my father ran out in the street and discovered the source of all the wailing, he made me airborne, threw me bodily into the air, and whacked me repeatedly when I landed. I spent the rest of the day buried in my pillow, stunned at the power of a dirt clod, heartshaken at the malignancy of play.

My father did not ask questions when there was danger. He was all instinct. Fetching me up from shattered glass, breaking up the jawing motorists. How often, too, I remember his impatience with things that were out of place, were done poorly or carelessly. How many times he corrected me with his spasms of anger when I had folded a blouse wrong, watered the lawn too lightly or too heavily, or made a bad seal of a box of dresses at his factory (originally LeGreg of California, then Mr. Aref, Ophelia, Home Grown—children, self, tragedy, community—the eternal cycle). He would wrest the chore from me before I had a chance to correct it, and more than once I thought: Why do you always have to do it yourself? Can no one else meet the Aref standard?

A'arif. The word means "the knowing one," in Arabic.

Not entirely. He escaped more than once to beauty and had a feel for those left out. I remember, for example, his dreamy nonsense expression when we had exhausted all paratrooper, Army, Navy, and Air Force songs on car vacations: "Giddy Pokie!" Only years after he died did his early friend Bud Lank confide: "Giddy Pokie" was the nonsense drawl of the slow boy on their block when they were children. Aref was sought after by family and friends as a counselor, an arbiter. But who would be his counselor? After losing touch with his best friend, a Marine colonel, no one was really a "best friend" save Mother and, in confessing moments of carnal woe, me. Perhaps it was that early on in Belgium he had seen what happens to friends.

Beauty and the lost, an irresistible combination for one carrying a deep-sunk well in his chest. A woman in Texas had contracted cancer when he met her and soon died of it. Another who sold garments for him went through a painful divorce, and he roared out into the desert with her on his Harley Davidson for hours of a blonde sun. No, Mother, not perfect. No more perfect than I who fell into folds of flesh as into an inky lake with 100 pounds of my sorrow and no quick-release harness. Pain can be an excuse for indulgence. It may be a good excuse for a while, but ultimately if the indulgence doesn't dull pleasure or increase the pain, it spreads pain to others—a hopeless round.

Still, it was his knack to fill a void in someone or some place. During his employment troubles, when I was single, he spent some days at my apartment in Washington, D.C. The evening after he left I returned from work to discover my bare windows fitted with colorful drapes. He had been sewing them on the sly and had put them up quickly, neatly parted, like an oyster depositing his pearl.

Tonight, I am alone in Harper's Ferry, West Virginia, where some say the American Civil War began. A midnight train is passing. The iron of the past. Into the tunnel it goes, and I am clambering after it. Above, a silver-minted moon. Below, the confluence of serene Shenendoah and wily Potomac rivers, spilled with silver. The place where that indulgent, righteous man John Brown ripped history open for the sake of freedom, that noble, volatile substance.

It could be said that this story has been about freedom. Most stories about World War II are. Except that it isn't. Or at least it isn't so much as it is about duty, that gray brother of freedom. About the hard duty of family, about duty to one's doomed comrades in war, to one's country, and the hardest duty of all: to truth. It is a story of what men do when they are faced with an impossible situation in which the alternatives are all bleak, like my father's when my sister, after twenty perfectly normal years, lost her mind; like Wood Joerg's when the higher command failed him; like the 551st's when it stood before Rochelinval alone; like my sister's when she faced alone the fact of her lostness.

Another train coming through Harper's Ferry. Lots of freight tonight. The moon is higher now. The gloss off the rivers, now dark. The sound of the rivers in the middle of the night, as if the earth itself were breathing, pouring out oxygen, as the earth does every night, though we do our best to stifle or forget that salutory fact.

It has also been a story of fear of the unspeakable I have carried for a decade since my father and sister were killed, a fear of facing and telling, until I met some men who had been through the unspeakable themselves.

In March 1985, my thirty-one-year-old sister—a diagnosed schizophrenic who had spent eight months in a psychiatric hospital—walked into National Gun Sales at 18518 Parthenia, Northridge, California, and, in the midst of what I later learned was a "psychotic event," hyperventilating, with eyes dilated, staccato speech, and bloody hand, secured a second pistol no one would discover, a .38-caliber Smith & Wesson revolver. (The store personnel denied observing this condition.) It was not a cheap Saturday night special; it cost $253.41. It was an expensive gun, the standard issue for police forces. She had a checkbook, and the store personnel may have sensed, correctly, that she would write any figure they told her to for any gun they wanted to sell her.[16]

She bought it within an hour of a rampage at the family store, after flinging the phone from the wall disconnecting my father and then shattering with her hand the mirror in the store's lavatory. She had reached the gun shop within minutes of getting her bloody hand bandaged at the emergency ward of a local hospital. Buying the gun even in her disturbed state was as easy and unquestioned as buying a hamburger.

A strange symbiosis obtains between the National Rifle Association (NRA) on the right and the American Civil Liberties Union (ACLU) on the left. Concerning gun sales to the unstable, the right to privacy has devolved to something on the order of the Golden Calf. The right to privacy is now the virtual right to be lethal. The words "freedom" and "privacy" have been distorted, bent, and ripped away from their original, duty-carrying meaning. Gun stores operate in wanton disregard for even the weak laws on the books, and judges tend to support them.[17] The result: whole sections of our city life cordoned off by fear. This is hardly freedom. As the playwright Eugene Ionesco put it in his *Antigone,* "One is always free at someone else's expense." That notion has been taken by our gun mania to its logical conclusion.

In the early evening on August 2, 1985, my wife took a call at my home in Washington, D.C., from my brother. I had just undone my tie from work and was playing with our firstborn son. I put him in his mother's joyous arms on the bed and took the receiver. He said, "Greg, I need you for the rest of my life." My brother does not say things like that; he is impatient with flip affection. Soon I was on the last plane to California.

What caused it? No one really knows, exactly. It was an argument at the store over an advance on salary that quickly escalated—even after my father proffered the advance—to something terrible spoken behind the closed door of his office, father to daughter. Perhaps he told her the truth with a GOYA-like frankness and exasperation, that she was mad, and hearing it, knowing it, and worse, knowing he knew it, she fell apart completely. It could have been a gesture, a throwing up of the hands. It could have been anything, really, or nothing. No one will ever know. All that is known is that she sped to her apartment in her car; the man with whom she lived did not accompany her as my father had asked. She retrieved the hidden pistol, came back, and fired four shots, probably for the first time in her life. One went into a partition right in front of her, another sprayed wildly left into a wall display of booklet spines, one killed my father in seconds, and one killed her. A customer and clerk crawled out of the store on their bellies and were spared.

A detective later told me that for someone unstable, in a rage, or simply not used to firearms, the gun virtually "fires itself." He also said he himself could not have dodged those shots in that position or drawn his own weapon in time. For five years after the killings, I wrote virtually nothing. My inner resources were hollowed out, my will to express and understand completely gone.

Then, quite by accident, I discovered the 551st. The pity of their story, their enormous thankless sacrifice on the snowy fields of Belgium, cracked something open in me, and light has a way of crawling into cracks. Meeting the men of my father's old unheralded unit struck an instinct right at the start, a sense that here was a way I might speak with my dead father, might listen and learn what he could never tell me about the war, or about the gathering storm of my sister. Plumbing the depths of the GOYAs' tragedy might help me come to grips with my own. Burying sorrow in a greater sorrow may be seen as one of the better forms of relief we humans know.

Except for Joe Cicchinelli, whose instinct for loss was acute, and later Doug Dillard and Dan Morgan, I told none of the men what had happened to my father. They seemed to understand implicitly what I was after. It was enough for them to know my father died prematurely and that he had been their messenger. I never asked the men about their politics, and they never asked about mine. It was irrelevant. When they learned of it, the fact that I had not served in Vietnam and had been against the war did not faze them.

I came to find the men as charming in their differences as they were in their shared tenacity, generosity, and wry self-effacement. They came from all ends of the country, in all sizes and shapes, all faiths, many ethnic groups. They had once been part of, after all, a citizen army called to a national emergency. Bobbie MeHaffey spoke to this eloquently:

> You know what amazes me more about the unit than anything? I'd never seen a Mexican before joining the Army. We had quite a few Indians, and some Puerto Ricans. We had a lot of people who were college-educated, and a lot of peons like me, a hillbilly, and we were all one, you know. We could communicate as one. Nowadays, it's getting worse every day. You look at somebody who's with an ethnic group and that's all you see. See? And in that unit, when you looked at him, you were looking at your brother. Now, you may fight your brother if you had a little bit too much to drink, but he was still your brother. We don't have that sense in the country any more. I don't mean to get religious, but I think the fundamentalists of all groups—whether it be Jewish, Muslim, or Christian—have contributed to the misunderstanding between people.

Could it be that they instinctly knew that the story of the men's sacrifice under extraordinary duress could speak to the future? We as a society have forgotten what the word "sacrifice" means. We all want rights and privileges without the attendant responsibilities any true rights entail. From a generation welded into common purpose by world war, they implicitly sensed—as such veterans do—the war of the present among us now, and perhaps wanted to say that they too were not so privileged. They too knew what it meant to be lost and thrown away.

But they never ran away. They kept going forward until there was almost nothing of them left and no one willing to record that their sacrifice had even happened. Not even they knew the significance of what they had accomplished until their lives were almost over. Unwieldy, fraught with wrong—that's the story of the 551st, but it is also one of terrible beauty and great love.

And this is where the story of the 551st dovetailed with that of my own family, and my father's plight in particular. I cannot say that I failed to discover meaning in the unit's fate, harrowing though both fate and meaning may be. I don't think I will ever know completely why my sister killed the father she loved so deeply, and herself, any more than I can understand why she became mentally ill in the first place. Nor can I fathom the terrors that illness delivered to her. Here, too, meaning becomes harrowing, almost beyond comprehension, but unavoidable as a hammered nail.

I finished a draft of this book in the fiftieth anniversary year of World War II, what one might call "the bottomless war." Though there will never be a war like it, it continues to cast its long shadow over subsequent generations, from the unfinished business of the Balkans and the Middle East to a Nazi-developed nerve gas let loose in a Japanese subway, and to the

5,000-pound U.S. bomb discovered in September 1995 by a work crew digging near a Liège bridge over the Meuse River. Is life, at least as we have come to live it this century, especially today, a war? Is it inevitable that even the best, especially the best, are trampled on by those they are sent to save to the poverty of any reason or meaning? I have been tempted to conclude so, both about my father and about the unit.

But the 551st will not let that be. *Act for others, though in acting you will risk all. Give, with no thought of reward. You will come someday to your Golgotha. You may yet be able to say as the Sorrowful One said, "It is consumated." Neither we nor your father could explain what we were asked to do. It seemed in the end even those who were ours became suddenly an enemy. Go forward; meet the task at hand. Draw from within for those without. Or just because it is within you most preciously to draw.*

From the troubled exuberance of Joe Cicchinelli to the stoic avoidance of Chuck Miller which spared others pain—they all had our father stamped on them. Each was the kind of man in whose care you would place your life. My sister placed her life in my father's hands. He did not drop it, though it cost him his own. During her sometimes frightening ten-year struggle with schizophrenia, my sister did plenty to scare off the most devoted person. By neither him nor my mother was she abandoned.

In his old factory my father gave employment to a black with a cleft palate, a French dress designer with a hunchback, and a Jewish bookkeeper who, at seventy, supported an invalid brother. At home he brought in for help with housekeeping a wonderful human being named Margarita Cruz, whose son was killed by death squads in El Salvador. He was the Indian. He dropped from planes for others.

That inkling he had during the war intensified toward the end in his ear's ringing—of a war closer to home. He didn't see a way out of it. For one of his disposition, there wasn't any. Maybe that is why he clung so to life, with such abandon, knowing what a lucky gift a moment of joy was, knowing its duration, how a landscape could be green with friends and suddenly snow-covered with their bodies.

A few months before he died, he sat in front of me and said softly, looking up, "Life is hell."

I suppose I will think about that statement till I die. How out of character it was.

But maybe not. Maybe, for a GOYA, it was a compliment. I have come to see my father's fate as very much the fate of the men with whom he served in battle so long ago. They became in their sacrifice what he became: lost in a bottomless war, but a messenger of life at all costs.

In Eugene O'Neill's *The Iceman Cometh*, Hickey speaks of his doomed wife: "I could see disgust having a battle in her eyes with love. Love always won." Staring down the barrel of the past I think the 551st saw the same thing my father saw that terrible day in Belgium and in Los Angeles: ultimate love.

4

A happy death

How grand the growl of rivers! How fine to see two things so opposed and different come together to form a wider trail. It is Harper's Ferry at dawn on the first day of spring.

The night rain over the mountains, a gray shawl over an old head. What beautiful color are those waters of the confluence? Not gray, not blue. Touched by light to the palest green. Here the Union and the Confederacy fought thirty-six times; the town changed hands so many times it had to keep looking at the rivers for any faith at all.

The light retreats over the joining, but the joining shines still, a light of slate. A road that could be a roof. What are you writing on that road, dear Father?

I went to Mass alone at Saint Peter's Church in Harper's Ferry, one of the few things in the town not destroyed in the Civil War because its pastor was British and flew the Union Jack, saying God was not taking sides in this bloodshed. That flag is called intelligence.

It was the Feast of Saint Joseph, the patron saint of a happy death. My father's middle name was Joseph. It was his favorite saint. Joseph: unheralded, dutiful, the foster father of Love Incarnate whom he could not claim as his own. We don't even know how Joseph died, or when. Was he given cover? Did anyone mark where he fell? Saint Francis de Sales said Saint Joseph died from sheer delight at his son's eyes, for in them in he saw the Creator.

I thanked the priest that day for fine words, and he called me "Pepino." I don't know why. A man outside greeted me, and I learned he had served in World War II. His smile was gentle and wide. His name was Arens. It half-rhymes with Aref.

Could it be possible that you died happy that terrible day? You were smiling, on your back, my dear GOYA. You were a bridge from the Ardennes to the Appalachians. I know you have stamped "551" over all the sidewalks of the Capital. The train is calling over the bridge they tore down so many times: The weight is coming.

I know now: You were smiling because it was over. You had done all you could. Your Creator had called you in a loud report. Report to me now. I have found your old lost friends. Report to them, report to me that we are not lost any more.

EPILOGUE

Toward the end of his life, on March 20, 1989, General Matthew Ridgway wrote Colonel Douglas Dillard concerning the fate of the 551st Parachute Infantry Battalion that it had sustained "a grave error and injustice to as gallant a combat battalion as any in WW II in Europe."

In the summer of 1994 the World War II Commemoration Committee took up the cause of the Presidential Unit Citation for the 551st. The Army still owed the men a decision, which, though the original Holm recommendation was made to higher command well within the two-year period of limitations, was never reached because of lost records, the heat of battle, and similar vagaries. Such an award had been granted to only one unit from World War II after the war: the all-black 761st Tank Battalion, given in 1978 by President Jimmy Carter. The 551st Association had hopes that President Clinton, with his sensitivity to the aged and veterans, would right the old wrong.[1]

The PUC requires that a unit "display such gallantry, determination, and esprit de corps in accomplishing its mission under extremely difficult and hazardous conditions as to set it apart and above other units participating in the same campaign."

On August 26, 1994, the Pentagon's Center for Military History made what amounted to a routine "nonconcurrence" in the matter of a PUC for the 551st. The report's author shouted over the telephone and later repeated to me twice in person, "The 82d Airborne did not play an important role at the Battle of the Bulge." Three SS panzer and two Volksgrenadier divisions knew otherwise.

The 551st's case began to be pressed by Vice President Albert Gore, as well as several U.S. Senators, such as Ted Kennedy (D-MA), Slade Gorton (R-WA) and Robert Byrd (D-WV). Leon Feurth, Gore's aide on the National

Security Council, wrote the Secretary of the Army that the 551st "richly deserves recognition." Fellow unit associations, such as the 509th and 504th, officially supported the award. At Bastogne for Battle of the Bulge fiftieth anniversary ceremonies in December 1994, Colonel Dillard met Secretary of the Army Togo West, who confessed he knew nothing of the matter until reading an article in the *Washington Post* a few days before[2] and promised Dillard a personal meeting stateside.

A second, more detailed, CMH study was released on February 3, 1995. Several passages were blacked out as classified; repeated FOIA requests that those passages be released have been denied.[3] Even that expurgated version was not released without a Freedom of Information Act request. The study's chief author, Lieutenant Colonel Roger Cirillo, admitted he relied solely on extant official records of the 551st, which he called "less than poor" in number and quality. The study stood the record as we know it on its head. Contradicting its own maps and gathered evidence, the study said the 551st got "its fair share" and "adequate" artillery cover during the counteroffensive; that there was "little indication that the Germans presented a spirited defense"; dismissed the unit's high rate of casualties as "sickness"; and said "it would be difficult to conclude that its [551st] combat stood out as exceptional." In short, the second study, rather than admit—as bureaucracies are loath to do—any prior misinterpretation or misstep, compounded the errors of the first. It also betrayed a bias against the Bulge counteroffensive with a dubious and unsupportable claim that "the commanding generals of the division, corps, and army rated the fighting during the December defense not only as the most critical but also that which merited the highest awards."[4] It was the Bastogne myth swallowed whole by in-house bureaucrats themselves. It also flew in the face of written statements by two key Bulge combat commanders concerning the 551st—Generals Ridgway and Norton.

Astounded by these findings, Lieutenant General John Norton, Gavin's G-3 at the Battle of the Bulge, wrote a six-page letter in support of the Citation for the 551st to Secretary West, calling the GOYAs' attack on Rochelinval "one of the most difficult, desperate, and courageous attacks in the W.W. II history of the 82nd Airborne Division."[5] His words were ratified by the 82d's G-2 at the Bulge, Brigadier General Walter Winton, who wrote West: "For us to praise the exemplary valor of the 551st Parachute Infantry Battalion is not to deal in hollow compliments."[6]

On May 29, 1995—Memorial Day—a rebuttal signed by Colonel Dillard on behalf of the 551st Association was sent to the Secretary of the Army. A month later, at a meeting with Sarah Lister, Assistant Secretary for Manpower and Reserve Affairs, General Norton said, "This is the most overwhelming evidence for a Presidential Unit Citation I have ever seen." Ms.

Lister, who was taking her lumps at the time for medals the Army had awarded to a Gulf War officer for actions in which soldiers were killed by friendly fire, admitted she had not read the 551st rebuttal to the official study. She spoke vaguely about setting up an independent panel and getting back to the Association.

She did neither. Secretary West never responded to Colonel Dillard's request to make good on his promise of a personal meeting. On August 29, 1995, with no explanation saying only that "the criteria of the award of the PUC had not been satisfied," Ms. Lister, on behalf of the Secretary of the Army, denied the Presidential Unit Citation to the 551st.

APPENDIX

Veterans of the
551st Parachute Infantry Battalion Interviewed

The author conducted these interviews in person, by mail, or over the phone in the period 1989–96. The names starred are now deceased.

Jack Affleck
Emory Albritton
Jim Aikman
Bill Amann
Thames Anderson
Vincent Artz
Charles Austin
John Balogach*
Roland Barhyte
John Bassaline
Nosreay Bayouth
John Bellefontaine
Chuck Bernard
Max Bryan
Charles Buckenmeyer
Milo Burke
Ralph Burns
William Bustin
Jack Carr
Pat Casanova
Judson Chalkley
Bernard Cheney
Joe Cicchinelli
John "Mel" Clark
Earl Curry
Bill Dean
Doug Dillard
Virgil Dorr
Dick Durkee
Charles Fairlamb

Frank Fiermonte
Dick Field
Don Garrigues*
Dick Goins
Benny Goodman
Rupert Graves*
Jim Guerrant
Jack Guffy
Phil Hand
Robert Hanson
Ed Hartman
Bill Hatcher
Jim Heffernan*
Ed Henriques
Ray "Pappy" Herrmann*
Fred Hilgardner
Bill Holm*
George Kane
Paul Kjar
Erwin Koerth
Mearlen "Hedy" LaMar
Jack Leaf
Francis Leary
Bob Lefils
Bill Lumsden
Dick Mascuch
Bobbie MeHaffey
Chuck Miller
Dan Morgan
Ralph Nichols

Bob O'Neill
Elmer Noll
Stanley Pakel
Albert Pate
John Pidgeon
Urban Post
Larry Poston
Forrest Reed
Harry Renick
Hugh Roberts*
Phil Robinson
Jack Russell
Bud Schroeder*
Otto Schultz
Frank Serio
Glenn Slucter
Jim Smith
Charlie Speich
Bernard Spidahl
Myron Splawn*
Stan Strong
Ellery Sweat
Joe Thibault
Don Thompson
Andy Titko*
Robert Van Horssen
Hank Warpechowski
Jim Welsh
Ralph Wenthold
Lloyd Willis

NOTES

Preface

1. Clay Blair, *Ridgway's Paratroopers* (New York: Dial Press, 1985), p. 420.

2. George Weller, *The Story of the Paratroops* (New York: Random House, 1958).

3. The thirteen GOYAs (including three officers) identified as writing combat diaries, journals, or memoirs are T/5 Jack Affleck, Cpl. John "Mel" Clark, Capt. Marshall Dalton, Lt. Dick Durkee, Sgt. Charles Fairlamb, Cpl. Albert "Pat" Garretty, Sgt. Don Garrigues, Sgt. William Hatcher, Lt. Dick Mascuch, Pvt. Aref J. Orfalea, Capt. Tims Quinn, Sgt. Hugh Roberts, and Staff Sgt. Leo Urban.

4. The agent in charge of this investigation is Sara Kaufman, 202/252-7229. See Les Hughes, "The U.S.A. Airborne Fiftieth Anniversary Display Debacle," *Chute and Dagger* #88, Arlington, VA, 1993; and Les Hughes, "Fear and Loathing in Bethesda," *Chute and Dagger* #89, Arlington, VA, 1993.

5. Irving Weinstein, *The Lost Battalion* (New York: Norton, 1966).

Chapter I. The Old Men Return

1. Gen. Matthew Ridgway, letter to Col. Douglas Dillard, July 29, 1989.

2. Gen. Ridgway, letter to author, February 8, 1990.

3. Gerard M. Devlin, *Paratrooper!* (New York: St. Martin's Press, 1979), p. 660.

4. Paul Fussell, *Wartime: Understanding and Behavior in the Second World War* (New York: Oxford University Press, 1989), p. 25.

5. Today four-star Admiral Chiles is commander-in-chief, Strategic Command, Offutt Air Force Base, Nebraska.

Chapter II. Hello, Earth!

1. These lines are engraved on the Pacific War Memorial on Corregidor. Mudler had found them in "Corregidor Revisited" by William Graves, *National Geographic*, July 1986.

2. The Olympics had a remarkable predecessor in their crosstown rival, the Cleveland News Skippies. From 1933 to 1939, the Skippies' win-loss record was an incredible 70–2, with one string of 46 wins in a row. In the first four years of the streak, Skippies' opponents

managed to score three touchdowns and one safety. Little wonder that the team was dubbed football's "world amateur bantamweight champions," playing in pregame warmups to Red Grange's Chicago Bears, the Cleveland Rams, and the Washington Redskins where it, according to one five-cent program, "nearly took the play away from the big fellows."

3. James J. Cooke, *The Rainbow Division in the Great War, 1917–1919* (Westport, CT: Praeger, 1994), p. 15.

4. Interview with Major Frank Joerg (ret.), Mechanicsburg, Pennsylvania, December 9, 1994.

5. Paul Fussell, *Wartime: Understanding and Behavior in the Second World War* (New York: Oxford University Press, 1989), pp. 35–36.

6. Gerard M. Devlin, *Paratrooper!* (New York: St. Martin's, 1979), p. 2.

7. Interview with Charles M. "Swifty" Wilson of Lilburn, GA, August 4, 1995. Wilson is one of fifteen surviving members of the Test Platoon and is secretary of its veterans' association.

8. Devlin, *Paratrooper!*, p. 51.

9. Dan Morgan, *The Left Corner of My Heart* (Wauconda, WA: Alder Enterprises, 1984), p. 18.

10. Interview with John Graber, technical adviser to the Airborne School, Fort Benning, GA, October 26, 1995.

11. Eleven GOYAs who served with the original 501st Parachute Infantry Battalion survive today.

12. Norman Maclean, *Young Men and Fire* (Chicago: University of Chicago Press, 1992), p. 54.

13. Jim Heffernan, quoted in Morgan, *Left Corner of My Heart*, p. 26.

14. Devlin, *Paratrooper!* p. 124.

15. War Department Training Circular no. 15, dated February 16, 1943, p. 6, states: "In general, the preparing of private diaries and memoranda will be discouraged and may be prohibited by the theatre commander . . . . The writers of such diaries frequently keep them in their pockets or in kits where they are liable to capture by the enemy, thus becoming a source of danger." Those prohibitions and warnings make the existence of at least thirteen wartime diaries by 551st men unusual. Though sending diaries through the mail back home was also forbidden, many GOYAs smuggled their impressions of the unit and the war home in just that fashion.

Chapter III. Panama

1. Ray Herrmann, "551st Parachute Infantry Battalion News," *The Static Line*, March 1978.

2. Dan Morgan, *The Left Corner of My Heart* (Wauconda, WA: Alder Enterprises, 1984), p. 482.

3. John Keegan, *The Second World War* (New York: Penguin Books, 1989), p. 112.

4. Bill Lumsden, "Fort Kobbe Memories," *The Static Line*, May 1995, p. 23.

5. In an April 27, 1943, letter home, Emory Albritton announced to his parents that he had received a three-day pass and $25 war bond from Lt. Col. Joerg for inventing the battle cry "GOYA," meaning "Great Outstanding Young Americans." Of the close to one hundred survivors I have talked to or corresponded with, none said the acronym meant anything but "Get Off Your Ass." That is corroborated by Joerg's widow, Heidi. Vincent Artz, a friend of Albritton who won the same pass and money for drawing the 551st insignia at that time, was of the opinion that Joerg meant the prize to Albritton "facetiously."

6. Lester Hughes, "551st Parachute Infantry Battalion: The Insignia," *Trading Post*, American Society of Military Insignia Collectors, January–March 1985, pp. 7–9.

7. Interview with Vincent Artz, Mechanicsburg, PA, November 1, 1995.

8. Letter from Lt. John Belcher, 551st chief liaison officer, to author, September 5, 1995.

9. Typical of the vacuum of records concerning the 551st, the chief Naval historian of the war relates only that "in May 1943 an amphibious force was trained at Guantanamo and Puerto Rico to occupy the French Antilles." Admiral Robert capitulated in June 1943. Samuel Eliot Morrison, *History of the United States Naval Operations in World War II: The Battle of the Atlantic, September 1939–May 1943* (New York: Little, Brown, 1947), p. 33.

Chapter IV. Foreboding

1. Leo Urban, cited in Dan Morgan, *The Left Corner of My Heart* (Wauconda, WA: Alder Enterprises, 1984), p. 87.

2. William Breuer, *Geronimo!* (New York: St. Martin's, 1989), p. 92.

3. Albert N. Garland and Howard McGaw Smyth, *U.S. Army in World War II, Mediterranean Theatre of Operations, Sicily and the Surrender of Italy* (Washington, DC: Office of the Chief of Military History, Department of the Army, 1965), p. 425.

4. James Gavin, *On to Berlin* (New York: Bantam, 1979), p. 62.

5. Fussell makes clear he is not talking about the pervasive boredom of barracks life or the depersonalization (butch haircuts come to mind) typical of the military regimen. "Chickenshit," he says, "refers rather to behavior that makes military life worse than it need be: petty harassment of the weak by the strong; open scrimmage for power and authority and prestige; sadism thinly disguised as necessary discipline; a constant 'paying off of old scores'; and insistence on the letter rather than the spirit of ordinances." Paul Fussell, *Wartime: Understanding and Behavior in the Second World War* (New York: Oxford, 1989), p. 80.

6. Don Garrigues, "From Delphus to Destiny," unpublished war memoir (Carthage, MO, 1980), Chapter 7, "The Sandhills."

7. Gerald Astor, *"Battling Buzzards": The Odyssey of the 517th Parachute Regimental Combat Team 1943–1945* (New York: Donald Fine, 1993), p. 84.

8. Interview with Col. Rupert Graves (ret.), Stuart, FL, October 29, 1993.

9. Joe Cicchinelli, letter, January 30, 1944, to Viola Jean Ickes, Massillon, OH.

10. Timothy Corsellis, a British pilot and poet wrote that "petty injustices" were the toughest part of military service. Cited in Fussell, *Wartime*, p. 80.

11. Interview with Mrs. Anne Scala, Montclair, VA, February 21, 1994.

12. Interview with Dan Morgan, Nice, France, August 17, 1989.

13. Letter from Aref J. Orfalea to his mother from Fort Benning, GA, November 5, 1943.

14. Morgan notes that a ninth man, unnamed, was killed on landing that night, but not in the lake. T/4 Albert Garretty of B Company mentions that nine men died on the first Mackall night jump. But the contemporanous diaires of Lt. Mascuch and Sgt. Garrigues, as well as the short newspaper account, list eight.

15. Col. Rupert Graves, "Combat Team," *Blue Book* magazine, December 1947, p. 53.

16. Until arrival at Pope Air Field from Nebraska, the 442d had only a handful of planes. Just before the night jump, each squadron was brought up to 80 percent of normal strength: ten to twelve planes. Thus it appears the February 16, 1944, night jump of the 551st was one of the first, if not *the* first, maneuver of any sort approaching its full strength of planes.

17. Albert Garretty, unpublished memoir, untitled (Redwood City, CA, ca. 1986), p. 67.

18. Supply was not the U.S. Army's forte, at least before Normandy. Two years after the Test Platoon did its successful jumps, there were not enough parachutes at Benning

for the 501st Battalion to train. Normandy itself sucked so much material from other theaters and from stateside that everyone else was short; the southern France drop in which the 551st participated in August 1944 was itself postponed several times for lack of supply from the Normandy drain. It is no real surprise, then, that 650 lifejackets could not be found for the GOYAs.

19. Interview with Col. Graves.

20. Letter from PFC Joe Cicchinelli to Viola Jean Ickes Cicchinelli, February 18, 1944.

21. Interview with Bill Lumsden of C Company and HQ Company, Idyllwild, CA, November 6, 1995.

22. The eight men who drowned at Camp Mackall were:

PFC Shelley C. Ferguson. Athens, AL (C Company)

Cpl. John F. Hoffman, Pierce, NE (Detachment Service Company)

PFC Kenneth D. McGrotty, Medford, OR (Headquarters Company)

PFC Ishmael H. Petty, Coalwood, WY (C Company)

Sgt. Benjamin Preziotti, Brooklyn, NY (B Company)

Pvt. Zollie Ramsey, Hilham, TN (C Company)

PFC Norvil L. Reed, Clarksburg, WV (C Company)

Pvt. John L. Wafford, St. Stephens, SC (C Company)

23. Virtually the same terse story was picked up by the *New York Times* and back-paged in the seventh column on page 7 on February 29, 1944, as "Brooklyn Paratrooper Drowns," mentioning only Ben Preziotti's death. The *Washington Post* printed no story at all.

24. See John F. Harris and John Lancaster, "16 Paratroopers Die, 82 Injured After Collision of Military Planes," *Washington Post*, February 24, 1994, p. 1.

25. The ten honored for their "deep loyalty, ability, self-sacrifice" were Capt. Tims A. Quinn, Lt. Marshall A. Dalton, Sgt. Marvin M. Butenhoff, Pvt. William B. Collins, PFC Edward F. Courtney, Sgt. Arthur M. Crook, Sgt. John B. Long, S/Sgt. James E. Stevens, PFC Clyde L. Stewart, and Dr. Judson Chalkley, the only one of them still surviving.

26. The difference between aircraft mishap and ground mishap was provided to me in a June 30, 1995, letter from John J. Clark, Jr., Chief, Reports Division, Headquarters Air Force Safety Agency, Kirtland Air Force Base, NM. He had no record of the Mackall tragedy or inquest. One of the "other authorities" concerning quick destruction of such records was John Graber, special adviser to airborne operations, Fort Benning, GA. Repeated Freedom of Information Act (FOIA) requests and personal inspections of records at the National Archives, the U.S. Army Office of the Inspector General, the Office of the U.S. Army Judge Advocate General, Kirtland Air Force Base, Maxwell Air Force Base (AL), the 82d Airborne Museum (Fort Bragg, NC), the Center for Military History, U.S. Military Academy at West Point, and the U.S. Army Military History Institute, Carlisle, PA, turned up nothing. One curiosity, however: At Maxwell AFB, records for the relevant carrier group and squadrons for March 1944—the likely time of the inquest—are the only monthly records missing that year.

27. The commander of the 442d Troop Carrier Group at the time was Lt. Col. Charles M. Smith. The 303d and 304th squadrons were commanded, respectively, by Capt. Robert Whittington and Capt. Kenneth Glassburn. In his memoir, T/4 Albert Garretty of the 551st's B Company asserts that "all aircraft commanders on that flight were court marshaled (sic)," but there is no corroborating evidence of that.

28. Drew Pearson, "Washington Merry-Go-Round," *Washington Post*, March 9, 1944, p. 10. A more restrained version ran in the March 8 New York *Daily Mirror*, with an editor's

disclaimer above the column: "The author of this column is given the widest latitude. His views do not necessarily reflect those of the *Mirror*.

29. Drew Pearson, "Washington Merry-Go-Round," *Washington Post*, April 17, 1944.

30. According to John Ward, an original Test Platoon member (and one of the very few original CW-4 assistant parachute maintenance officers still living), the quick-release harnesses were not available for U.S. paratroopers at Normandy, and by Operation Dragoon in southern France—August 1944—only a very few had been shipped and prepared for use. Most of the 551st men I interviewed did not drop into southern France with the quick release, though Sergeant Forrest "Field Manual" Reed insists he had one. A March 20, 1944, *New York Times* article (p. 19) cites Drew Pearson as saying only a "driblet" of 2,500 quick-release harnesses chutes had been manufactured by March 11. Reed's may have been one of them. According to Ward, after the tragic night jump in February 1944, the time it took to order, manufacture, retrofit, and retrain paratroopers to use the quick release was not there before the war was over. Ward also indicated that there was rivalry over the matter between the Army Air Corps, which had responsibility for development of the parachute until 1953, and the Army itself, as well as bickering with the Navy, which was most resistant. The U.S. Army did not take over full responsibility for parachute development until 1960. Ward said complete training of combat divisions with the quick release did not occur until 1947, and it wasn't used widely in combat by the United States until Korea. (Author's interview with John Ward, Fayetteville, NC, December 26, 1995.) At the same time, according to the 82d Airborne historian, Bob Anzuoni, photographs of Operation Varsity—the March 24, 1945, drop across the Rhine—indicate that at least some paratroopers of the XVIII Airborne Corps wore the quick-release harness.

31. James Gould Cozzens, *Guard of Honor* (New York: Harcourt Brace Jovanovich, 1948, 1976), p. 523.

32. James Gould Cozzens, *A Time of War: Air Force Diaries and Pentagon Memos* (Columbia, SC: Bruccoli Clark, 1984), p. 28 (February 19, 1944).

33. *Ibid.* "We occupied ourselves with some new announcements by Drew Pearson on quick release parachutes . . . ." (November 19, 1944, diary entry). Oddly, this is seven months after the original two columns on the subject by Pearson, unnoted in Cozzens's diary. Also, an April 24, 1945, memo cites a general's objections to the quick release, based on its supposed discomfort and a "minor defect" in the release box.

Chapter V. War at Last

1. Dan Morgan, *The Left Corner of My Heart* (Wauconda, WA: Alder Enterprises, 1984), p. 125.

2. According to John Grady, the 542d historian, Joerg expected not only a salute from the men at the beginning of the day but a "good morning" as well. He promised them that they would "look better, drill better, with better equipment than ever before." But soon he was gone—back to the 551st. Interview with John Grady, January 20, 1996.

3. Gerald Astor, *"Battling Buzzards": The Odyssey of the 517th Parachute Regimental Combat Team 1943–1945* (New York: Donald Fine, 1993), p. 82.

4. Albert Garretty, unpublished memoir, untitled (Redwood City, CA, ca. 1986), p. 70.

5. Gerard M. Devlin, *Paratrooper!* (New York: St. Martin's, 1979), p. 334.

6. John Keegan, *The Second World War* (New York: Penguin, 1989), p. 357.

7. Martin Gilbert, *The Second World War* (New York: Henry Holt, 1989), p. 526.

8. Douglas Dillard, letter to Virginia Hornsby, Atlanta, GA, June 5, 1944.

9. William Breuer, *Operation Dragoon* (Novato, CA: Presidio Press, 1987), p. 15.

10. *Ibid.*, p. 34.

11. *Ibid.*, p. 24.

12. *Ibid.*, p. 71.

13. Col. Bryant Evans, artillery commander of the First Airborne Task Force, quoted in Robert Adelman and Col. George Walton, *The Champagne Campaign* (New York: Little, Brown, 1969), p. 71.

14. Sgt. Jim Guerrant remembered that another fellow from C Company did something similar that day: "I saw Lieutenant Sano go up to him and say, 'So you figured out how to shoot yourself, eh?'"

15. Besides the officers, the other 551st pathfinders for Dragoon were Duke Spletzer, Paul Balcavage, Dan Donovan, Roger Carqueville, Hugh Roberts, Bill Lumsden, Gerna Sizemore, William Satterfield, William Crutsinger, Pat Garretty, Francis McManus, and two men named Brown and Carter.

16. James Stevens, unpublished, undated memoir of the Operation Dragoon drop on his Valbourges estate, La Motte, France.

17. Breuer, *Operation Dragoon*, p. 204.

18. At Normandy, the 508th had shot and killed Gen. Wilhelm Falley, commander of the 91st German Infantry Division, while he was riding pell-mell toward the beaches in his car from war games at Rennes. On May 9, 1943, the first surrender of a German general to U.S. forces had occurred at Sidi Nasr in North Africa—to General Omar N. Bradley.

19. See "Local Paratrooper Gives Vivid South France Invasion Account," *Nashville Banner*, September 1944; also Tom Waller, "551st Pcht. Inf. Assn. News," *The Static Line*, May 1983, p. 23.

20. Sid Feder, "They'll Never Forget Mark Clark," *Saturday Evening Post*, May 18, 1946, p. 137.

21. Though the U.S. Holocaust Museum could not confirm the specific incident or its location, likely corroboration exists in a map of reprisals against civilians on the Riviera which shows five executions in Vence and one in Biot. See Suzanne Maron, *Internes, departes, fusilles, morts au combat des Alpes-Maritimes*, Comité d'histoire de la 2ème guerre mondial, conseil général des Alpes-Maritime, 1976.

22. Joe Cicchinelli, letter to Viola Jean Ickes Cicchinelli, September 14, 1944.

23. Dwight D. Eisenhower, *Crusade in Europe* (New York: Doubleday, 1948), p. 294.

24. The primary text on Dragoon until forty years after the war, Walton's and Adelman's *The Champagne Campaign* (1969), contains only one quote (anonymous) from a 551st soldier. Ironically, it addresses how the media determine what are subsequently recorded by historians as "major engagements." Wrote the anonymous GOYA: "I would like to make one observation: when one guy starts shooting at another guy, it's a major engagement as far as the guy being shot at is concerned. As a matter of fact, one might say it's a helluva big battle!" (p. 151). That book's centerpiece unit, treated extensively, is Rupert Graves's 517th Regimental Combat Team. A more recent (1993) book—the last official volume of the Pentagon's Center for Military History (CMH) multivolume effort on World War II—hardly restores balance, devoting a total of two sentences to the 551st. Curiously, Jeffrey J. Clark, co-author of that text (*From the Riviera to the Rhine*), routinely disapproved a Presidential Unit Citation for the 551st in 1994 as CMH's acting director.

Chapter VI. Holding the Crags

1. The speech was translated from the French by Florence Phariss of Carmel, IN, in 1982, when it was discovered by Sano's widow, Ruth.

2. Charles B. MacDonald, *A Time for Trumpets: The Untold Story of the Battle of the Bulge* (New York: Morrow, 1985), p. 10.

3. For Hitler's quotes, see Huge Cole, *The Ardennes: Battle of the Bulge.* U.S. Army in World War II series (Washington, DC: Government Printing Office, 1965), p. 2.

4. Charles Fairlamb, "World War II Record of Charles Spruance Fairlamb," unpublished journal memoir, p. 10.

5. After eight years' work on the book, I could count five men who had reasonably solid memories of my father: Al Albritton, Chuck Bernard, Paul Kjar, Don Thompson, and Charlie Speich.

6. Sgt. Carl Noble, Company C, 2d Platoon, quoted in Morgan, *Left Corner,* p. 281.

7. Sgt. Bill Hatcher said of Edgerly, "He was one of those adventurous sorts that come along once in a great while and would have been outstanding in the movie *Raiders of the Lost Ark.*" Morgan, *Left Corner,* p. 294.

8. Incidents described by Ralph Wenthold and Clell Whitener in *ibid.,* pp. 295, 308.

9. Tims Quinn was never completely won over. A May 9, 1984, letter from Quinn to Bill Hatcher touches on some sensitive areas: "I really wasn't aware of the final three days, but this is the part that saddened me. The lack of recognition, decorations and the vast amount of talent in that whole group. I always had mixed emotions over the aggressiveness of Joerg. He was 'hell on wheels' as a garrison soldier, but his own worst enemy in combat."

10. Ethel Bernard, Chuck's wife, carried the photo in her wallet for fifty years, thinking it an especially good rendering of her blond, handsome husband in the war. She never knew who that dark man was at his side until 1995, when it hit her that he was my father.

Chapter VII. Speartip

1. Charles B. MacDonald, *A Time for Trumpets: The Untold Story of the Battle of the Bulge* (New York: Morrow, 1985), p. 163.

2. The irate panzer leader was Jochen Peiper; see *ibid.,* p. 244.

3. George M. Devlin, *Paratrooper!* (New York: St. Martin's, 1979), p. 538.

4. Danny Parker, *Battle of the Bulge: Hitler's Ardennes Offensive, 1944–1945* (Conshohocken, PA: Combined Books, 1991), p. 170.

5. *Ibid,* p. 37.

6. "The Battle of the Bulge," *The American Experience,* WGBH-TV, 1994.

7. According to Baron von Steengracht, "all [Hitler's] movements were those of a senile man; only his eyes retained their flickering gleam and penetrating look." Quoted in Parker, *Battle of the Bulge,* p. 206.

8. MacDonald, *A Time for Trumpets,* p. 19.

9. Parker, *Battle of the Bulge,* p. 17.

10. A January 6–7, 1945, First Army Intelligence survey of 268 representative prisoners captured from the 62d Volksgrenadiers, for example, reveals the Volksgrenadiers to be less constituted of boys and the aged, and more experienced and "gung ho" than has been generally noted by Bulge historians. Only 12 percent of the group was over thirty-five, and only 1 percent were seventeen (the rest were older). Three-fifths of those surveyed had logged two years in military service. Newcomers since D-Day numbered only 10 per-

cent. At the same time, a sizable 40 percent had not seen combat until the Ardennes offensive. When asked if they thought the war was lost, a "bare majority" agreed, though 28 percent said "perhaps," leading the survey to conclude that "a sizable number still indulges in wishful thinking." A man with a glass eye was classified "1-A," as were several with missing toes or fingers. *First Army Special Report: Facts and Figures About the 62 VG Div—A Statistical Survey.* Those findings are reinforced somewhat by Major Fritz Blum, the general staff officer of the 62d VGD in charge of logistics, who estimated that no more than 50 percent of the division was underage or overage by normal standards. Interview with Maj. Blum, Auw, Germany, September 21, 1995.

11. Quoted in Parker, *Battle of the Bulge*, p. 21.

12. *Ibid.*, p. 23, citing Liddell Hart, *The German Generals Talk* (New York, 1979).

13. Parker, *Battle of the Bulge*, p. 43.

14. A former lieutenant in the 62d Volksgrenadiers, Josef Bannert, who had spent twelve years in Soviet labor camps after the war, told me as much.

15. Interview with Gerhard Kieswetter of the 190th Regiment, 62d Volksgrenadier, Auw, Germany, September 21, 1995.

16. Royce Thompson, "American Intelligence on the German Counteroffensive," cited in MacDonald, *A Time for Trumpets*, p. 97.

17. In one of many appropriations by other units of the actions of the 551st in photographs, on monuments, and in histories, the 508th unit history has this exact photograph identifying the marching men as of the 508th. See William G. Lord III, *History of the 508th Parachute Infantry* (Washington, DC: Washington Infantry Journal Press, 1948), p. 81.

18. Interview with Gen. Melvin Zais, USA (ret.), by Col. William Golden and Col. Richard Rice, *Senior Officers Oral History Program*, Project 77-3, U.S. Military History Institute, 1977, p. 195.

19. If the German soldiers Dillard saw were actually SS at Hotton, they would have had to be advance reconnaissance units. Though in a week the 551st would clash with an SS unit at Noirefontaine—the 9th SS Panzers—on December 20–21, the closest such troops to them were the 2d SS Panzers, who were about fifteen miles away near Houffalize. Known as the "Das Reich" division, the 2d SS Panzers had a reputation for brutality on the Russian front and had also been engaged in heavy battles at Normandy and effected massacres at Oradour-Sur-Glan. Stunned by what he saw, Dillard may have transformed what may very well have been 116th Panzer Division men into SS troops. It was not unusual for GIs at the Bulge to see every German tank as a Tiger and every rampaging German as a stormtrooper of Hitler's hated private army.

20. The only Bulge historian so far to describe the GOYAs' role at the Bulge, Danny Parker, noted in 1991: "The 551st Parachute Infantry Battalion was moving up to assist in throwing the 1st SS Panzer Division out of the Ambleve River valley." Parker, *Battle of the Bulge*, p. 160.

21. Berle would later write: "Once the Malmédy massacre became common knowledge, few SS prisoners were taken alive or left alive very long, and the spirit of even the greenest GI became that of a desperate she-wolf." Gustav Berle, "Atrocities, Malmédy: Case 6–24," *VFW Magazine*, December 1987.

22. Interview with Helmut Hennig, Bad Orb, Germany, January 16, 1994. Hennig refers to John Toland's *Battle: The Story of the Bulge* (New York, 1959). For an interesting discussion surrounding mistreatment and torture of German suspects in prison, see "Malmed: Massacre and Trial" (Appendix G) in Trevor Dupuy, David Bongard, and Richard Anderson, *Hitler's Last Gamble* (New York: HarperCollins, 1994), pp. 487–97.

23. Interview with Colonel Douglas Dillard (ret.), Bowie, MD, September 11, 1989.

24. Dwight Eisenhower, *Crusade in Europe* (New York: Doubleday, 1948), pp. 354–55.

25. When it was all over, out of five thousand men making up the Peiper-Sandig-Knittel spearhead force, only eight hundred would make it back to German lines.

26. John Keegan, *The Second World War* (New York: Penguin, 1989), p. 582.

27. Letter from Robert Joerg III to his uncle, Juhan Guice, March 21, 1945, after meeting GOYA Tom Holland in a hospital at Chester, England.

28. Dan Morgan, *The Left Corner of My Heart* (Wauconda, WA: Alder Enterprises, 1984), p. 358.

29. Parker, *Battle of the Bulge*, p. 209.

30. *Ibid.*, p. 187.

31. *Ibid.*, p. 206.

32. Fritz Kraemer, I SS Panzers Corps in the West in 1944, ms# c-048, Historical Division Command, U.S. National Archives, pp. 20, 23.

33. Interview with Josef Bannert, Fulda, Germany, January 15, 1994.

34. Because he had had the misfortune of being in the town of Voroshilovgrad in 1943, where the Germans had massacred civilians in 1940, Bannert was sentenced without trial to eleven years' hard labor. "For the Russians to punish someone eleven years was nothing—they gave twenty years for minor thefts to their own people, so why not me?" said Bannert. In 1951 Bannert's mother, carrying his photograph from one Siberian camp to another, found her son. He was released in 1955.

35. Interview with Maj. Fritz Blum, logistics chief of the 62d VGD, September 21, 1995, Auw, Germany. Kittel was often affectionately called *Fadder* (father); he was forty-eight. At the same time, the hastily reassembled 62d VGD had many soldiers who never knew who was at the top of their regiment, let alone division. (From author's interviews on same day cited above with Privates Alfred Tworeck, 162d Artillery, and Gerhard Kiesewetter, 190th Regiment.)

36. Several American historians, and Gavin in his memoirs, appear to confuse the Volksgrenadiers with the "Volstrum," the combing out of young teenagers for the defense of Berlin and other cities late in the war during February and March 1945. The Volkstrum, indeed, were a poor match for the American armies; but that was not the case with the Volksgrenadiers.

37. Brig. Gen. Friedrich Kittel, *Report on the Ardennes Offensive, The 62nd VGD*, The National Archives, p. 6.

38. Maj. Fritz Blum interview.

39. Kiesewetter interview.

40. James Gavin, *On to Berlin* (New York: Bantam, 1979), p. 283.

41. Interview with Helmut Hennig.

42. Gavin, *On to Berlin*, p. 284.

43. Hennig interview.

44. Bruce Quarrie, *Hitler's Teutonic Knights: SS Panzers in Action* (London: Bruce Quarrie & Patrick Stephens Ltd., 1986), pp. 123–24.

45. Hennig was quoting figures from the classic study on the SS by George Stein, *The Waffen SS: Hitler's Elite Guard at War* (Ithaca, NY: Cornell University Press, 1966). The extent to which the vast and complex SS organization, and the armed soldier units in particular, were involved in the concentration camps and other atrocities has been the subject of fierce debate ever since the war. According to the historian Charles Sydnor, two contrasting camps emerged. One made up of American, British, and younger West Ger-

man historians and journalists believes that the "armed SS" (the soldier, or "Waffen" SS units, as opposed to camp commandants and guards) "was responsible for its share of SS criminality." Over the years, an apologist literature in Germany has cropped up, written by former Waffen SS generals and often right-wing academics. The gist of their argument is that the Waffen SS "was an organization separate, independent, and distinct from the SS; that Waffen SS officers held Himmler in contempt and frequently disobeyed his orders; and that the men of the armed SS, as front-line soldiers, were in no way associated with or responsible for the crimes committed by other SS agencies in the Reich and in occupied Europe." Charles Sydnor, *Soldiers of Destruction: The SS Death's Head Division, 1933–1945* (Princeton, NJ: Princeton University Press, 1977), pp. 318–19. Typical of their arguments, rather widely accepted by the man on the street in Germany, is that evoked by the title of Waffen SS General Paul Hausser's book, *Soldiers Like Any Others* (*Soldaten wie Andere Auch,* Osnabrück, Germany, 1966). It is certainly beyond the scope of this book even attempt to settle the question, but Sydnor's exhaustive research into perhaps the most brutal of all SS units, the infamous SS *Totenkopfdivision* (SS Death's Head Division), shows the 24,000-strong organization to have regularly moved personnel back and forth to other nonbattlefield SS units, as well as the concentration camps, both as guards and as leaders, to such an extent that the evidence "flatly and overwhelmingly contradicts the apologist thesis" (Sydnor, *Soldiers of Destruction,* p. 320.) In any case, stating only 6,500 of 900,000 SS were in the camps begs the question. Waffen SS officers were tried for war crimes on the battlefield itself, such as the massacres of noncombatants at Le Paradis, Tulle, and Oradour-sur-Glane (France), at Malmédy (Belgium), and on the Arno in Italy. Half a million Jews were gassed on the Russian front by the notorious mobile killing units of the *Einsatzgruppen,* at least one-third of whose men in 1941 were pulled from the Waffen SS. One of the more chilling examples of the genocidal policies of the Reich and their relation to certain Waffen SS units was the present made by Hans Frank, the Nazi governor general of Poland, in May 1943, of 1,500 watches taken off the dead at Auschwitz to three Waffen SS divisions (five hundred each): the *Totenkopf,* the 1st SS Panzers (*Leibstandarte* Adolf Hitler), and the 2d SS Panzers. (Frank had already collected 94,000 such watches.) Officers from all three divisions (the latter two of which fought at the Battle of the Bulge) were convicted of war crimes. The 9th SS Panzers of Hennig do not appear to have engaged in mass civilian war crimes, and so it is no surprise to discover Hennig as a devoted apologist for the "soldiers like any others" theory. However, POWs captured at the Bulge admitted two incidents of *Hohenstaufen* troops shooting POWs—a Lt. Schnittker of the 10th Co., 19 SS *Panzergrenadier* Regiment ordered his men to kill U.S. POWs because "Europe is not the business of the Americans." A Sgt. Wolther obliged on December 24, 1944. Another incident cited was at Arnhem when an *Obersherfuehrer* (T/Sgt.) Werner Ackerman blew up a cellar of British POWs. (See 82d Airborne G-2 Intelligence Report, January 4, 1945.)

46. See Herbert Furbringer, *9.SS Panzer Division, "Hohenstaufen"* (Solothurn, Switzerland: Editions Heimdal, 1984). This bilingual German–French book contains nothing about the *Hohenstaufen* presence at Noirefontaine on the night of the 551st raid.

47. The Noirefontaine farm complex was under the ownership of two families, the Humblets and the family of Massage de Coullomb.

48. Interview with Marie Cornelius Hollange, January 9, 1994, Lierneux, Belgium.

49. A little-known monument between Erria and Avenaterres commemorates the Gerardwez massacre.

50. January 31, 1994, letter from Arthur Juttner to author.

51. Juttner received the Knight's Iron Cross with oak leaves and swords; only 160 German officers earned that particular accolade during World War II.

52. The four men killed at Noirefontaine were Cpl. Carlo Intinarelli, Pvt. Roy Rover, and two lieutenants, Lester Kurtz and John Ryan.

53. Another reason my father mistook the name for Noirefontaine was that there was a Headquarters Company man named John Bellefontaine, who happened to be an interpreter for Col. Joerg in southern France. Bellefontaine had been born and raised in Montreal, Canada, immigrating with his family in 1943. Like my father, he was pulled out of the Bulge for frozen feet.

54. The 517th Buzzards bequeathed eight generals to the military in later years, among them the greatly loved Melvin Zais, who took the GOYAs under his wing late in life. The highest rank a GOYA achieved was colonel; only four men made it (Doug Dillard, Pappy Herrmann, Bill Holm, and Bill Smith). The Buzzards received "a multitude of medals" and 1,500 Purple Hearts (averaging one for every two men). In contrast to that honorific shower, the GOYAs' medals could be counted on one hand, along with a few dozen Purple Hearts which could have numbered six hundred. The 517th information is from Gerald Astor, *"Battling Buzzards": The Odyssey of the 517th Parachute Regimental Combat Team 1943–1945* (New York: Donald Fine, 1993), p. 2.

55. After the war Haller was the only German worker allowed by the Allies to stay at the Hoechst chemical plant in Frankfurt, where he made medicines for the rest of his working life. From an interview with Mrs. Margaret Jörg, Hofheim, Germany, January 17, 1994.

56. Pvt. Alfred Tworeck of the 62d's 162d Artillery Regiment noted, "I had no idea whether our artillery was accurate or not. I was only hungry, hungry, hungry." Interview with Tworeck, September 21, 1995, Auw, Germany.

57. From a letter written by C Company Sgt. Stan Strong to his fellow C Company Sgt. William Lumsden from Vittel, France, July 29, 1945. "Maggy" Magnuson apparently survived the crash, though it is uncertain for how long. About the POW affair, however, Strong (now of Sioux Falls, SD) related to me on August 24, 1995: "The incident doesn't ring a bell. I don't believe it at all. Neither one [Downes or Magnuson] would do it. They were too happy. They have to have been drunk. They might have pretended to do it to make a show, get a laugh." However, S/Sgt. Charles Austin, who had been attached to C Company from Headquarters Company as a supply officer, corroborated the incident: "I'm pretty sure it was C Company. I remember a couple of guys were supposed to take prisoners back [to the command post], but the prisoners never got there." Austin knew Downs and Magnuson, and knew of their subsequent fate in the car wreck, but wasn't sure just who had perpetrated the POW shootings. A third witness, C Company Sgt. Thames Anderson of Frankfort, MI, heard about the incident the day it happened and remembered the men involved and the reason: "They shot them as spies because they had our uniforms on. I was given a German pistol by our battalion's top gambler, Private Charles Gwinn, but I wouldn't carry it for the same reason."

58. On January 3, 1945, the 460th Field Artillery Battalion fired twenty missions (separate times) for a total of 675 rounds of large shot. Though it was supposed to cover both the 551st and the 517th, maps plotting the hits show nothing zeroed in on Sol Me or Hèrispehe, the two ridges toward which the GOYAs were attacking. The hits were either on or around Mont de Fosse (where the 517th was getting hung up) or beyond the ridges. See the Center for Military History February 3, 1995, study, "The 551st Parachute Infantry Battalion in the Ardennes," p. 13 and Annex E, Map 5.

59 William Breuer, *Geronimo!* (New York: St. Martin's, 1989), p. 435.

60. During the Bulge, Schroeder was recuperating stateside from his gunshot wound taken the day of their southern France drop. He met an injured man from the 3d Division who had won the Distinguished Service Cross, "and he said he had killed I don't know how many prisoners." Schroeder reflected on what he called "the ugliness of war" and admitted, "I'd have killed a POW myself—the one who threw his hands up right after he had hit me and shot Jack Funk to death [at La Motte]." Funk was the first 551st soldier killed in combat.

61. Interview with Lou Spletzer, January 2, 1995.

62. PFC Forrest Reed, who knew Spletzer from their days together in the original parachute battalion, the 501st, had a different version of the incident or described a related incident. On June 10, 1995, Reed told me, "Two fifteen- or sixteen-year-old German prisoners wearing SS uniforms were queried by Spletzer. One of them was sarcastic and Spletzer shot him. The second kid was okay."

63. Opening the door one day to the abandoned home of a German industrialist months later with the 508th at the Roer (Rur) River, Durkee saw a typewriter on a table with a stack of letterhead "F. Faudi" stationery neatly placed alongside it, as if it were waiting for him. He sat down and wrote an eloquent eleven-page account of what he had just lived through at the Bulge for all those "who hadn't had a chance to do it."

64. Parker, *Battle of the Bulge*, p. 123.

65. *Ibid.*

66. Wilfred Owen, *The Collected Poems of Wilfred Owen* (New York: New Directions, 1963), p. 57.

67. Allan Langdon (author of the 505th history, *Ready*), quoted in Clay Blair, *Ridgway's Paratroopers* (New York: Dial, 1985), p. 420.

68. The G-3 Report for January 3, 1945, of the 82d Airborne cites casualties for the 551st that day of 18 officers and 171 enlisted men, including 2 officers and 29 enlisted men killed; based on 643 men going into battle that morning, this equals a 29 percent casualty rate, reported as of 1800 hours, or 6 P.M. The integral 82d regiments suffered between 15 and 25 percent casualties that first day of the counteroffensive. Inexplicably, the CMH report on which the Army relied to deny the PUC to the 551st, cites a GOYA casualty figure one-third the size of the official record: 61 vs. 189.

69. Of Gavin's opinion of Graves, Lt. Gen. John Norton, Gavin's G-3 at the Bulge, has said: "He saw Graves as a very conservative, cautious guy, not in the Airborne way . . . solid, but lacking in daring." Interview with Lt. Gen. Norton, Arlington, VA, April 6, 1995.

70. Gavin, *On to Berlin*, p. 293.

71. Charles LeChaussee, "Northwest for France," unpublished draft of a personal memoir, Chapter Six, "The Children's Wood," p. 14 (possibly an earlier version of "Trial by Fire: The Odyssey of the 517th Parachute RCT," unpublished manuscript by the same author).

72. Breuer, *Geronimo!*, p. 432.

73. Astor, *"Battling Buzzards,"* p. 259.

74. *Ibid.*

75. Clark Archer, *Paratrooper's Odyssey* (Hudson, FL: C.T. Associates, 1985), p. 131.

76. Breuer, *Geronimo!*, p. 433.

77. John Keegan, *A History of Warfare* (New York: Knopf, 1993), p. 6.

78. As with all casualty figures for the 551st, sources are widely divergent. The Morning Reports show 165 in the "Absent/Sick" category, most of which were severe hypothermia cases. The XVIII Airborne Corps listed 273 "non-battle casulties," most of which

were frostbite or trenchfoot. General Gavin in his diary lists "230 trench foots [sic]" for the 551st. Dr. Robert Joy, the chairman of the medical center chiefly responsible for training Army doctors and a worldwide expert on cold injury, has said that frostbite is tied to four things in war in order of importance: "1) combat; 2) bad gear; 3) bad leadership; 4) failure of high command to enforce discipline." Incredulous that the Army would consider such injuries at the Bulge as "non-battle casualties," or "sickness," Dr. Joy underscored, "It's a command problem." He urged that the Army contact him for an opinion on the crucial relationship of cold injury to combat in the case of the 551st and the Presidential Unit Citation. He was never contacted.

79. Carr's estimate of a hundred tanks destroyed that day is probably at least twice the actual count; though some 1st SS Panzers may have happened into the area, the 9th SS Panzers were the only panzer unit operating west of the Salm in the vicinity at the time, and they were down to fewer than fifty tanks. As for the Panthers that the 551st had met, they were probably scrounged from the 2d SS Panzers to the west. The only "tanks" the 62d VGD had were actually antitank assault guns, the Panzerjager 38-T "Hetzers." Concerning the dreaded Tigers, the only division that had them in the area was the 1st SS Panzers, which had pulled out south to Bastogne just before New Year's Day.

80. Later, in February 1945, after the 517th's withdrawal from combat to come under the wing of the 13th Airborne Division at Joigny, France, Hickman received administrative punishment from the 13th's Gen. Gary Chapman for having scrounged enough matériel—from extra coils of wire to extra jeeps and ambulances—"to outfit two regiments," according to Tom Cross, the regiment's supply officer. Astor, *"Battling Buzzards,"* p. 296. Conscious of a constant supply drain since Dragoon, Hickman may have overcompensated. Cross recalls, "He made Sergeant Bilko of TV look like a Boy Scout."

81. Jürgen Thorwald, *The Illusion: Soviet Soldiers in Hitler's Army* (New York: Harcourt Brace Jovanovich, 1975), p. xv.

82. Wilfred Strik-Strikfeld, *Against Stalin and Hitler: Memoirs of the Russian Liberation Movement* (London: Macmillan, 1970), p. 175.

83. *Ibid.,* p. 174.

84. Thorwald, *The Illusion,* p. 170.

85. *Ibid.,* p. 175.

86. *Ibid.,* p. 221.

87. This incident bears a curious resemblance to the one Gavin so incompletely recounts in his war memoir, when he rousted what he took to be 517th mortarmen from their "cozy" stone house.

88. 551st Headquarters Company Morning Report for January 5, 1945. Yet warmth and sleep would remain elusive. That very day, the 505th rejoiced to receive a shipment of overcoats and sleeping bags which allowed the men "their first real sleep in over 60 hours." (See A. Langdon, *Ready,* p. 115.) Such relief never made it to the GOYAs.

89. Col. Rupert Graves, "Combat Team," *Blue Book Magazine,* February 1948, p. 68.

90. Interview with Capt. Louis Hauptfleisch, April 10, 1995.

91. Gen. Friedrich Kittel, *Report on the Ardennes Offensive, the 62d VGD,* MS no. B-028, June 1946, p. 6.

92. Maj. Blum interview. Note the computer simulation of the Bulge campaign done by the Dupuy Institute shows German combat effectiveness to be superior to the Allies, due largely to "more professional" leadership (see Dupuy, et al., *Hitler's Last Gamble,* pp. 498–500).

93. "Battle Instructions for the Defense Sector of the 1st BN, 183rd GR REGT," Secret

Annex no. 1 to G-2 Situation Summary No. 2, 12 January 1945, Headquarters 82d Airborne, Colonel Walter Winton, First U.S. Army Document Section.

94. Among the top aides, the likeliest candidate is Brigadier General Ira Swift to whom Gavin gave sway over the left flank of the sector. Other possibilities are G-2 intelligence chief Lt. Col. Walter Winton, chief of staff Col. Robert Wienecke, or Lt. Col. John Norton, G-3 operations officer, who was personally involved with 551st movements the next day, but had no memory of Joerg's protest the night before.

95. Interview with General Alexander Day Surles, November 21, 1994. Though Joerg had been a classmate of Surles ("a helluva good fellow"), the retired general remembered nothing about the 551st's high rate of casualties, or even that it had been disbanded.

96. Gen. Norton initially placed the 551st in memory everywhere from direct attachment to XVIIIth Airborne Corps or the 3d Armored Division to the 508th Regiment. Told they were linked first to the 517th Regiment, then the 504th for the counteroffensive, Gen. Norton surmised that the Rochelinval attack "was a division decision orchestrated through the regiment. Rarely did General Gavin speak directly to a battalion, unless he did so personally [face to face]." Interview with Lt. Gen. John Norton (ret.), January 11, 1995, Arlington, VA.

97. Interviews with Lt. Gen. John Norton, January 11 and April 6, 1995, Arlington, VA.

98. August 6, 1984, letter from Gen. Gavin to Clay Blair; interview quote is from Blair, *Ridgway's Paratroopers*, p. 292.

Chapter VIII. Tall Snow

1. During the Crimean War, on October 25, 1854, although British, French, and Turkish troops had easily captured Balaklava, a small brigade of British calvary was thrown against the Russians in a useless mission that failed. The ensuing carnage for both sides has often been laid at the feet of a personal rivalry between two British officers. It was immortalized in the poem *The Charge of the Light Brigade* by Alfred, Lord Tennyson, which ends, "Into the Valley of Death/Rode the six hundred." Rivalries, implied or not, between Col. Graves and Lt. Col. Joerg, and between Generals Ridgway and Gavin, appear to have affected the final fate of the 551st. But there's a key difference between the two charges; the GOYAs, miraculously, took Rochelinval.

2. Belcher did search for the tanks, but after several hours he turned up only one (which had a malfunctioning turret). By that time Joerg, and a good part of the battalion, had fallen.

3. Nolan had been assigned to the 551st as a forward observer after the first man sent to the GOYAs the day before from the 376th artillery, Lieutenant Whitney S. Russell, had been killed.

4. The G-3 Periodic Report of January 7, 1945, 82d Airborne. It's possible Joerg called the 460th, as that had been his artillery backup under the 517th Regimental umbrella for the entire counteroffensive. The 376th had stepped into place when the GOYAs were attached to the 504th, only the afternoon before; as noted, there was no direct intercommander communication between Joerg and Tucker of the 504th.

5. Interview with Lt. Chuck Minietta, June 6, 1995.

6. The 376th did shoot three recorded missions for the GOYAs on January 7, but only one hit Rochelinval. According to 376th's S-3 Firing Report for the day (corroborated by spotters Lt. Chuck Minietta of Renton, WA, and William Nolan of Charles City, VA), it hit the town at 9:30 A.M., was 113 rounds lasting three minutes, and was composed of noth-

ing but smoke. It was a smoke screen to cover the retreat of A Company, which had been almost completely destroyed three hours before. The other two missions (28 rounds at 10:00 A.M. and 44 rounds between 11:00 and 11:25) were shot off when the battle was all but over; they didn't hit Rochelinval, but rather far in back of it at retreating Germans and across the east bank of the Salm River to interdict German artillery long after it had done its damage. Furthermore, Lt. Nolan reported that he was denied artillery to cover the 551st again at mid-morning for the same reason given at dawn—the area was "outside the 376th's sector." Interview on September 16, 1995.

7. It was rumored by several men that Lt. Dahl of North Dakota was related, and possibly married to, the screen actress Arlene Dahl, who hailed from nearby Minnesota. Ms. Dahl's first of several marriages, however, was to Lex Barker in 1951. A letter from the author on the matter to Ms. Dahl went unanswered.

8. The six others were Casanova, John Pieniazek, Chuck Miller, Roy McCraw, Harry Renick, and one other man who has not been identified.

9. Letter from Capt. Richard Hallock to Mrs. Robert Joerg, mother of Lt. Col. Wood Joerg, October 6, 1946.

10. Col. Douglas Dillard interview with Capt. William Nolan, Virginia, June 6, 1995.

11. See Suzanne Haney, "Wartime Lifesaver Meets 'Buddy,'" *Alley* (Illinois) *Sun*, July 7, 1980.

12. What Norton's alarm may have instigated was forty-four rounds fired by the 376th Parachute Field Artillery Battalion at 11 A.M. in back of Rochelinval at Volksgrenadiers retreating. The battle at that point was just about over.

13. Bulge historian Danny Parker assessed the M-5's armor as so thin it could be taken out by a Browning Automatic Rifle: ". . . the M-5 could hardly be considered a tank as much as it was a light reconnaissance vehicle" (Danny Parker, *Battle of the Bulge: Hitler's Ardennes Offensive* [Conshohocken, PA: Combined Books, 1991]), p. 60.

14. Lt. Col. George Rubel, *Daredevil Tankers: The Story of the 740th Tank Battalion, United States Army* (Werk Gottingen, Germany: Muster–Schmidt, Ltd., 1945), p. 86.

15. Interview with Neil Thompson, December 5, 1996.

16. Rubel says the 551st commander (he never mentions him by name) "apparently decided to attack this town with the infantry, leaving the tanks in battalion reserve." This squares with no 551st testimony. Quite the contrary, when the attack started, Joerg blasted his liaison officer, Lt. Belcher, as to the whereabouts of the tanks he had been promised. Belcher went off to find them; late in the battle he found one. There may have been some mixup with the precipitous 551st reattachment; the 740th's battle maps show Rochelinval in the 517th's sector through January 10, an error. Rubel tends toward bombast. If at first he received a "very cool reception" when attached to the 82d Airborne for the counteroffensive (the paratrooper brass told him that "most of the time tanks had been a liability to them and not an asset"), within hours of the counterattack he's getting nothing but rave reviews. In North Africa, Rubel had lost a whole tank battalion. The 740th may have been a "last chance" command, according to tanker Neil Thompson, who called Rubel "not quite as bad as Patton—tall, elderly, a rough man."

17. Gen. Friedrich Kittel, *Report on the Ardennes Offensive, the 62d VGD*, MS no. B-028, June 1946, p. 25.

18. William Breuer, *Geronimo!* (New York: St. Martin's, 1989), p. 442.

19. James Gavin, *On to Berlin* (New York: Bantam, 1979), p. 292.

20. The gallant 508th, which won the Distinguished Unit Citation for actions at Normandy, like the 551st on January 7 attacked over open, snow-covered ground to Thierdu-Mont, formidably defended by three 88mm guns. It was a difficult battle. But there

the similarity ends. The 508th benefited from a preparatory barrage of artillery, used three battalions in the attack, and was reasonably fresh, having spent the previous four days of the counteroffensive in reserve. According to Lt. Col. Lou Mendez, commander of the lead 3d Battalion, there were two hundred Germans on Thier-du-Mont (half the number at Rochelinval), and according to Sgt. Joe Kissane, "very few were captured." The GOYAs took several hundred German prisoners. The 508th Bulge casualty rate was 46 percent; the 551st's was 84 percent. Nevertheless, the Center for Military History's 1995 negative study of the 551st's worthiness for the Presidential Unit Citation said that the 508th attack at Thier-du-Mont received the "heaviest resistance" in the 82d Airborne sector during the counteroffensive, thereby discounting the 551st accomplishment at Rochelinval.

21. Major Werner Duve was killed in action at Schneppenheim, Germany, on March 3, 1945, defending Cologne. His grave and the graves of twelve other soldiers from the 62d and 18th Volksgrenadiers lie in a small cemetery in Adendorf.

22. Col. Rupert Graves, "Combat Team," *Blue Book,* December 1947, p. 68.

23. *Ibid.*

24. Gavin, *On to Berlin,* p. 329.

25. 551st Headquarters Company Morning Report for January 7, 1945.

26. William Shakespeare, *King Lear* (New York: Penguin, 1958), Act II, Scene vi, p. 116.

27. I have been able in eight years to find only one photo of Rochelinval in the war. It shows men of the 505th prone on an embankment of the rail line running along the Salm River near town. The picture was taken during the first week of the Ardennes offensive, just before Montgomery ordered the First Army pullback to "straighten the battleline."

28. Pappy Herrmann, "Furlough," cited in the 551st PIB column by Jim Welsh, *The Static Line,* June 1994, p. 23.

29. At least a dozen 551st men were killed in action after being filtered into other units following the Battle of Rochelinval; three of them were killed just before the official GOYA disbandment (February 10, 1945) and were so lost in the snow and in records as to be buried initially with their unit "unknown." They were Cpl. Donald Baldwin, T/5 John Opitz, and T/5 Jack Rolland.

30. The 110 figure is from Dan Morgan's unit history, *The Left Corner of My Heart* (Wauconda, WA: Alder, 1984); it was culled from rosters of various 82d Airborne, XVIII Airborne Corps, and 17th Airborne Division units into which those GOYAs still able to move were filtered. This figure is very close to estimates of those surviving the battle in three contemporaneous combat diaries—by two HQ Company sergeants and Joerg's messenger: Charles Fairlamb (124), Don Garrigues (100), and Aref Orfalea (175 as of January 6, the day *before* the Battle of Rochelinval). Several other testimonies influenced Morgan's figure, including that of HQ Company's executive officer, Lt. Milt Hill, who estimated between 100 and 150 GOYAs were left in the end. The Center for Military History's 1995 study of the 551st, however, found the battalion's strength as it moved to the Bulge to be 689 men; for the counteroffensive, there were 643 men going in, it said, and 341 coming out. These figures are culled from the battalion's January 1945 Morning Reports, which, strangely, were lost to all previous researchers, including myself and Morgan, for half a century. The CMH was only half right. Though the Morning Reports are reliable for unit strength before battle, after the counteroffensive started they became notoriously incomplete and unreliable. And that is not so unnatural, given the extremely cold weather, constant attack movements, isolation, loss of radio and telephone communications, and other vicissitudes of one of the most arduous combat scenes in U.S. history. Lt. John Belcher, the 551st's chief liaison officer with higher command, was incredulous at the CMH's 341 figure: "How

could anybody keep accurate figures with what we were going through? Sure, we may have pulled some [numbers] off the limbs of the trees." Belcher's finding at the time was seventy-five men left. Dr. Jack Affleck, the chief 551st medic, who wrote up many of the initial casualty reports that should have fed into the Morning Reports, called the CMH finding "absolutely not true. I estimate there were between 100 and 110 men left." The battalion adjutant who actually collected the Morning Reports, Lt. Hugh Robinson, ratified Morgan's 110 figure and said 139 GOYAs were killed in action—three times the CHM figure (43). An archivist at the U.S. Military History Institute in Carlisle, PA, put the matter succinctly to me, not just for the Bulge, but for any combat: "Morning Reports are always very slippery." My own father, for example, is not on any Morning Report as a "battle" or "nonbattle" casualty. Though the author of the CMH study admitted that he used extant official 551st records *only*, which were "less than poor" (interview with Lt. Col. Roger Cirillo, June 1995), this did not prevent the study from concluding: "The battalion's combat losses were not high by Ardennes campaign standards." And that utterly inaccurate assessment was one of the chief reasons the Department of the Army denied the 551st the Presidential Unit Citation fifty years later. The absurdity is compounded by the fact that the 517th's 1st Battalion won the Citation for actions at Soy-Hotton that cost it 20 percent casualties, half of what the GOYAs sustained by CMH's own questionable lights.

31. Fuller, probably a replacement officer in Sicily, appears to have been wounded in the Maritime Alps. He did not return to the 551st.

32. The only other airborne battalion commander killed at the Bulge was the 101st Division's James LaPrade, who led the 506th Regiment's 1st Battalion.

33. Parker, *Battle of the Bulge*, pp. 292–96.

34. Morgan, *The Left Corner of My Heart*, p. 485.

35. Ironically, other than Milo Huempfner (the DSC), Wood Joerg won one of only two significant medals among the GOYAs, the Silver Star, awarded posthumously. (The other recipient of the Silver Star was T/Sergeant Robert Van Horssen.)

36. Ike "added further insult to the 82d's injury," as Ridgway's biographer, Clay Blair, put it, by bestowing a DUC on two paratroop units outside Ridgway's command: the 509th and the 1st Battalion of the 517th, when they were both attached to the 3d Armored Division. One other division besides the 101st received the DUC for the Bulge campaign: the 4th Armored. Regulations state that "only on rare occasions will a unit larger than a battalion qualify for award of this decoration." Armed Forces Regulations 220–105, Section 12(3)(b).

37. Matthew Ridgway, *Soldier: The Memoirs of Matthew Ridgway* (New York: Harper & Brothers, 1956), p. 116.

38. XVIII Airborne Corps G-3 Periodic Report, Lieutenant Colonel A. D. Surles, Jr., p. 2.

39. Ridgway, *Soldier*, p. 121.

40. The bureaucratic bungling knew no limits. Fifty years later the 551st's Lt. John Belcher finally received a Bronze Star in the mail for his troubles. It cited him for valor in the Pacific Theater!

41. See "Memorandum for the Secretary of the Army, Subject: The 551st Parachute Infantry Battalion (v)—Action Memorandum," February 3, 1995, by Brigadier General John W. Montcastle, Chief of Military History, Center of Military History. The attached study is entitled "The 551st Parachute Infantry Battalion in the Ardennes."

42. Morgan, *The Left Corner of My Heart*, pp. 439–40.

43. Albritton did bring up the 551st to Gavin long afterward, in 1961. Gavin again affirmed that the GOYAs had formed his point battalion during the counteroffensive, but Gavin expressed deep surprise to Albritton that the 551st had received no honors.

44. Breuer, *Geronimo!*, p. 463.

45. German forces, however, threw the 504th back for a time to the river's edge in a vicious counterattack, for which Gavin took a tongue-lashing from his Corps superior, Gen. Ernest Harmon, for overextending his troops. It was hard to keep the 82d and 101st Airborne tethered, as Eisenhower was trying to do, in order to minimize losses to these crack units so that they might be preserved for a mission Gavin could only learn of by rumor: an invasion of Japan.

46. See the excellent treatment of this phenomenon by the journalists Martha Gellhorn and Janet Flanner in Hans Magnus Enzensberger, *Civil Wars: L.A. to Bosnia* (New York: The New Press, 1993), pp. 80–82.

47. Alan Bullock, *Hitler: A Study in Tyranny* (New York: Bantam, 1961), p. 13.

48. Sergeant Don Garrigues, "From Delphus to Destiny: Some Memoirs of a Paratrooper of World War II," unpublished memoir, Carthage, MO, 1980.

49. See the fascinating study by Ada Petrova and Peter Watson, *The Death of Hitler* (New York: W. W. Norton, 1995). The fire put to Hitler's and Braun's bodies did not consume them, though in the West, since no evidence of the corpses was ever revealed, it was assumed they had been turned to ash (or that they hadn't died at all but were living in various South American countries). In fact, the Soviets discovered the bodies buried crudely in an artillery shell crater outside the bunker and conducted two secret investigations, though only one autopsy, in 1945–46. From then until 1970 the corpses of Adolf Hitler and Eva Braun lay under a concrete slab in the city of Magdeburg under the Soviets' Counter Intelligence headquarters in East Germany. In 1970, when the site was to be turned over to East Germans themselves, the KGB head, Yuri Andropov, ordered the corpses disinterred and completely burned. By then, the bodies were all a "jellied mass" in rotted wooden boxes anyway, the bones of the Hitlers, their two dogs, and the Goebbels family—including the six children they poisoned—mixed together, "a suitably demeaning end of the high priests of the Third Reich" (p. 89).

50. Annex no. 4 to 82d Airborne Division After-Action Report, May 1945, RG 407, Records of the Adjutant General's Office, 82d Airborne Division, Box 11245, National Archives, Washington, DC. See also *Liberation 1945*, U.S. Holocaust Museum, Washington, DC, 1995, p. 17.

51. Juttner himself retired to Bramstedt after the war. There he took over ownership of a small tourist hotel. Concerned about Bosnia (about which he presciently urged in 1994, "The West should stop sending troops into Bosnia, instead bomb it!") and skinheads in Germany ("a big threat"), he declared, "The politicians haven't learned anything from World War II. When there are jobs, people are happy. The most important thing is the peace between East and West!"

52. Martin Gilbert, *The Second World War* (New York: Holt, 1989), p. 678. I note here that Dan Morgan spoke with a sergeant at Dachau who had been in the first wave of soldiers to reach it who witnessed fifty German soldiers (not 346) machine-gunned by U.S. tankers; he also said most were Wehrmacht, not SS, most of whom, he said, had already fled. Interview with Dan Morgan, November 16, 1995.

53. *Ibid.*

Chapter IX. Home

1. In this vein, Francis X. Leary once used "GOYA" as his ATM bank card code.

2. T. Michael Booth and Duncan Spencer, *Paratrooper* (New York: Simon & Schuster, 1994), p. 312.

3. About a half dozen GOYAs who had reenlisted, including Doug Dillard, did march in a smaller parade with the 82d Airborne later in the year, in November, down Pennsylvania Avenue in Washington, DC.

4. Joseph Goulden, *The Best Years, 1945–1950* (New York: Atheneum, 1976), p. 6.

5. The priest who for years has led my own parish retreat in rural Maryland turned out to be Fr. Richard De Lillio, the HQ Company sergeant's nephew. We marveled at the coincidence, GOYA-bound in many ways.

6. Arlene Levinson, "There Is No Peace of Mind Here," *Green Bay News Chronicle*, August 31, 1977, pp. 6–7.

7. In 1985, after staying up nearly all night reading about his brother in Dan Morgan's *The Left Corner of My Heart*, Robert Joerg woke the next morning clutching his heart—he had had a massive coronary, though he survived until his death from colon cancer two years later.

8. Col. Douglas Dillard, quoted in Douglas Valentine, *The Phoenix Program* (New York: Morrow, 1990), p. 203.

9. *Ibid.*, p. 205.

10. *Ibid*, p. 204.

11. Other high-ranking (retired) dissenters included Gen. David Shoup, former commandant of the Marine Corps, hero of the Battle of Tarawa, and Congressional Medal of Honor winner; Brig. Gen. Samuel B. Griffith, a former Marine and China expert; Brig. Gen. Robert Hughes of General MacArthur's staff in the Pacific; Brig. Gen. William Ford, who fought in both World Wars; and Rear Adm. Arnold True. See James Deakin, "Big Brass Lambs," *Esquire*, December 1967, pp. 144–48.

12. See Gen. Matthew B. Ridgway, "Pull-Out All Out, or Stand Fast in Vietnam?" *Look* magazine, April 5, 1966. In this article version of his Congressional testimony, Ridgway said, "It is my firm belief that there is nothing in the present situation or in our code that requires us to bomb a small Asian nation 'back into the Stone Age.' There must be some moral limit to the means we use to achieve victory."

13. The twenty-four attendees were Jack Affleck, L. D. Aughtman, Cooper Blackney, Bee Brown, Robert C. Boruff, Joe Cicchinelli, Eugene Cooper, Doug Dillard, Virgil Dorr, Lee Elledge, Benny Goodman, Phil Hand, Ed Hartman, Ray "Pappy" Herrmann, Bill Holm, Roy McCraw, Will Marks, Dick Mascuch, John Peltzer, Tims Quinn, Harry Renick, Carlo Ronilo, Bud Schroeder, and Andy Titko (six of them have since died). The first slate of officers of the 551st Parachute Infantry Battalion Association were Tom Waller (president); Bill Holm (vice president); Phil Hand (secretary/treasurer); and Bee Brown (recording secretary). Wood Joerg's brother, Commander Robert Joerg III, who also attended the first reunion, manufactured a few dozen GOYA palm-and-machete patches of their insignia (not officially approved by the Army until 1992). Col. Rupert Graves, attending the nearby 17th Airborne reunion, briefly stopped by the 551st room, and left. He was never again seen at a GOYA reunion.

14. Before the GOYAs' first meeting in 1977, there were already 370 veterans and military-related associations, societies, and clubs in the United States.

15. See Amber Nimocks, "'Tragic,' WWII Veterans Memorialize Eight Drowned Paratroopers," *Fayetteville Observer-Times*, July 2, 1992, p. B1; and Jeff Holland, "Marker Near Hoffman Honors Paratroopers," *Richmond County Daily Record*, Rockingham, NC, July 12, 1992.

16. The store personnel denied observing my sister's condition, of course. But National Gun Sales had a recent history of indiscriminate sales. Two years before, it had sold a handgun to a young woman, Tara Ann Katona, against the agonized warnings of her mother. The day after the daughter was released from a mental hospital she shot herself

to death within hours of getting the gun. The family filed suit and settled out of court one month before going to trial. See Bob Baker, "Suicide Costs Gun Store $175,000," *Los Angeles Times*, March 14, 1986.

17. The Orfalea family lawsuit against National Gun Sales, a mind-boggling four-year ordeal, ended abruptly without settlement or trial on January 9, 1989, when Van Nuys Superior Court Judge Richard Adler afforded the gun store a "summary judgment" in their favor, a highly unusual ruling for a case of such gravity. The Adler ruling, barely a page long, is an incredible document; it has no subject, and is written in code. The gun dealer not only won; it suppressed the fact that there was ever anything in question.

Epilogue

1. Capt. Dick Durkee, a Republican, had lambasted the editor of the *Washington Times* for taking a swipe at the President: "I remember you writing that Bill Clinton looks effeminate when he greeted people with a 'hug.' I am a retired parachute combat officer and my military unit has reunions each year. I love and respect my combat buddies, and we greet each other with 'hugs.' Along that line, most of us combat soldiers now seem to admire and respect President Clinton and would follow his orders into Hades, if so directed." Durkee's March 15, 1994, letter to the editor was never published by *Times* editor Wesley Pruden.

2. Gregory Orfalea, "Lost Heroes of the Battle of the Bulge: The Battalion the Pentagon Forgot," *Washington Post*, December 4, 1994.

3. See letters to Colonel Douglas Dillard (ret.) from Lieutenant Colonel Dale Woodling, Office of the Judge Advocate General, Department of the Army (June 23, 1995); and Lawrence M. Bashir, Office of the General Counsel, Department of Defense (October 16, 1995).

4. In his letter to Army Secretary West, Lieutenant General Norton flatly equates the achievement of the 551st in the Bulge counteroffensive with that of the 504th's DUC-winning actions stopping Peiper's panzers at Cheneux during the early weeks of defense: "In my opinion, the action of the 551st P.I.B. at Rochelinval on 7 January 1945 clearly also met all 'DUC' criteria and should have been so recognized in early 1945." At the same time, the CHM report totally disregards its own evidence that 16 percent of all DUC awards given for the Ardennes campaign were for the counteroffensive. More hypocritical—CMH report chief Cirillo unfairly lambastes author Trevor Dupuy for downplaying the counteroffensive: "The crucial and equally bloody January battle, wrongly glossed over by the official histories and all writers since, gets short shrift." (Review of *Hitler's Last Gamble* in *Army Magazine*, July 1995, p. 61.) Actually, Dupuy and his co-authors devoted more space—seventy-five pages—to the counteroffensive than virtually any other Bulge historian, certainly more than Cirillo's former CMH colleague Charles MacDonald (fifteen pages). Cirillo's report on the 551st was the real "glossing over."

5. Lt. Gen. John Norton, letter to Secretary of the Army Togo West, April 10, 1995.

6. Brig. Gen. Walter Winton, letter to Secretary of the Army Togo West, June 16, 1995.

SELECTED BIBLIOGRAPHY

Adelman, Robert H., and Col. George Walton, *The Champagne Campaign*. New York: Little, Brown, 1969.

Archer, Clark (ed.). *Paratroopers' Odyssey*. Hudson, FL: C.T. Associates, 1985.

Arnold, James R. *Ardennes 1994: Hitler's Last Gamble in the West*. London: Osprey, 1990.

Astor, Gerald. *A Blood-Dimmed Tide: The Battle of the Bulge by the Men Who Fought It*. New York: Donald Fine, 1992.

_____. *"Battling Buzzards": The Odyssey of the 517th Parachute Regimental Combat Team, 1943–1945*. New York: Donald Fine, 1993.

Biggs, Bradley. *Gavin*. Hamden, CT: Archon Books, 1980.

Blair, Clay. *Ridgway's Paratroopers: The American Airborne in World War II*. New York: Dial Press, 1985.

Booth, T. Michael and Duncan Spencer. *Paratrooper*. New York: Simon & Schuster, 1994.

Breuer, William B. *Geronimo!: American Paratroopers in World War II*. New York: St. Martin's, 1989.

_____. *Operation Dragoon: The Allied Invasion of the South of France*. Novato, CA: Presidio, 1987.

_____. *They Jumped at Midnight*. New York: Berkeley Publishing, 1983.

Bruccoli, Matthew. *James Gould Cozzens: A Life Apart*. Orlando, FL: Harcourt Brace Jovanovich, 1993.

Bullock, Alan. *Hitler: A Study in Tyranny*. New York: Bantam, 1961.

Clarke, Jeffrey J., and Robert Ross Smith. *Riviera to the Rhine* (U.S. Army in World War II, European Theatre of Operation), Washington, DC: Center for Military History, 1993.

Clausewitz, Karl von. *On War*. New York: Modern Library, 1943.

Cole, Hugh, *The Ardennes: Battle of the Bulge* (U.S. Army in World War II) Washington, DC: Center for Military History, 1965.

Cooke, James J. *The Rainbow Division in the Great War, 1917–1919*, Westport, CT: Praeger, 1994.

Cozzens, James Gould. *Guard of Honor*. New York: Harcourt Brace Jovanovich, 1948.

Devlin, Gerard M. *Paratrooper!: The Saga of the U.S. Army and Marine Parachute and Glider Combat Troops During World War II*. New York: St. Martin's, 1979.

Dupuy, Colonel R. Ernest. *World War II: A Compact History*. New York: Hawthorne Books, 1969.

Dupuy, Trevor N., David L. Bongard, and Richard C. Anderson, Jr. *Hitler's Last Gamble: The Battle of the Bulge, December 1944–January 1945* New York: HarperCollins, 1994.

Eisenhower, Dwight D. *Crusade in Europe*. New York: Doubleday, 1948.

Eisenhower, John. *The Bitter Woods*. New York: Putnam, 1969.

Enzensberger, Hans Magnus. *Civil Wars: From L.A. to Bosnia*. New York: The New Press, 1993.

Fontaine, Serge. *L'Enfer de Trois Ponts du 551st Parachute Infantry Battalion*. Trois Ponts, Belgium, Comité D'Accueil des U.S. Airborne (CADUSA), 1988.

Fussell, Paul. *Wartime: Understanding and Behavior in the Second World War*. New York: Oxford University Press, 1989.

Gavin, Lt. Gen. James. *On to Berlin*. New York: Bantam, 1978/1985.

_____. *War and Peace in the Space Age*. New York: Harper and Brothers, 1958.

Gilbert, Martin. *The Second World War: A Complete History*. New York: Henry Holt, 1989.

Goulden, Joseph C. *The Best Years, 1945–1950*. New York: Atheneum, 1976.

Jamar, Walthere. *Chevron: A Belgian Village*. The Netherlands, Centre de Recherches et d'Information, Bataille des Ardennes, 1987.

Keegan, John. *A History of Warfare*. New York: Knopf, 1993.

_____. *The Battle for History: Refighting World War II*. New York: Vintage, 1995.

_____. *The Second World War*. New York: Penguin, 1989.

Kline, John (ed.)/106th Infantry Division Association. *The Cub of the Golden Lion*. St. Paul, MN: West Publishing Co., 1991.

Langdon, Allen. *Ready*. Indianapolis, Western Newspaper Publishers, 1986.

Larson, Erik. *Lethal Passage: The Story of a Gun*. New York: Vintage, 1995.

Liberation 1945. Washington, D.C.: U.S. Holocaust Museum, 1995.

Lord, William G., II. *History of the 508th Parachute Infantry*. Washington, DC: Washington Infantry Journal Press, 1948.

MacDonald, Charles B. *A Time for Trumpets: The Untold Story of the Battle of the Bulge*. New York: Morrow, 1985.

Maclean, Norman. *Young Men and Fire*. Chicago: University of Chicago Press, 1992.

Merriam, Robert. *The Battle of the Bulge*. New York: Ballantine, 1957.

Morgan, Dan. *The Left Corner of My Heart: The Saga of the 551st Parachute Infantry Battalion*. Wauconda, WA: Alder Enterprises, 1984.

Morrison, Samuel Eliot. *History of the United States Naval Operations in World War II: The Invasion of France and Germany, 1944–1945*. Boston: Little, Brown, 1957.

_____. *The Battle of the Atlantic, September 1939–May 1943*, Boston, Little, Brown, 1947.

Mulligan, Timothy P. *Lone Wolf: The Life and Death of U-Boat Ace Werner Henke*. Westport, CT: Praeger, 1993.

Owen, Wilfred. *The Collected Poems of Wilfred Owen*. New York: New Directions, 1963.

Pallud, Jean-Paul. *Battle of the Bulge, Then and Now*. London: Battle of Britain Prints Ltd., 1984.

Parker, Danny, *Battle of the Bulge: Hitler's Ardennes Offensive, 1944–1945*, Conshohocken, PA: Combined Books, 1991.

Petrova, Ada and Peter Watson. *The Death of Hitler*. New York: Norton, 1995.

Price, Reynolds: *The Foreseeable Future*. New York: Ballantine, 1991.

Quarrie, Bruce. *Hitler's Teutonic Knights: SS Panzers in Action*. London: Bruce Quarrie and Patrick Stephens Ltd., 1986.

Richler, Mordecai. *Writers on World War II*. New York: Vintage, 1991.

Ridgway, Matthew B. *Soldier: The Memoirs of Matthew B. Ridgway*. New York: Harper and Brothers, 1956.

Rubel, Lt. Col. George. *Daredevil Tankers: The Story of the 740th Tank Battalion, U.S. Army*. Werk Gottingen, West Germany: Muster-Schmidt, Ltd., 1945.

Shaara, Michael. *The Killer Angels*. New York: Ballantine, 1974.

Shaw, Irwin. *The Young Lions*. New York: Modern Library, 1948.

Simpson, Louis. *A Dream of Governors*. Middletown, CT, Wesleyan University Press, 1959.

Speer, Albert. *Inside the Third Reich*. New York: Macmillan, 1970.

Sulzberger, C. L. *World War II*. Boston: Houghton Mifflin, 1987.

Sydnor, Charles W., Jr. *Soldiers of Destruction: The SS Death's Head Division, 1933–1945*. Princeton, NJ: Princeton University Press, 1977.

Tennyson, Alfred, Lord. *Selected Poems*. New York: Modern Library, 1951.

Terkel, Studs. *"The Good War": An Oral History of World War II*. New York: Ballatine, 1984.

Tucker, William H. *Parachute Soldier*. Althol, MA: Haley's, 1994.

U.S. Airborne 50th Anniversary. Paducah, KY: Turner Publishing, 1990.

Valentine, Douglas. *The Phoenix Program*. New York: Morrow, 1990.

Weller, George. *The Story of the Paratroops*. New York: Random House, 1958.

Whiting, Charles. *Decision at St. Vith: The Story of the U.S. 106th*. New York: Ballatine, 1969.

INDEX